tak

IE

About the series

take the kids guides are written specifically for parents, grandparents and carers. In fact, they're the perfect companion for anyone who cares for or about children. Each guide not only draws on what is of particular interest to kids, but also takes into account the realities of childcare – from tired legs to low boredom thresholds – enabling both grown-ups and their charges to have a great day out or a fabulous holiday.

Cadogan Guides
Highlands House 165 The Broadway, Wimbledon
London SW19 1NE
info@cadoganguides.co.uk
www.cadoganguides.com

The Globe Pequot Press
PO Box 480, Guilford,
Connecticut 06437–0480

Art direction: Sarah Rianhard-Gardner
Original Photography: © Tim Mitchell

Managing Editor: Antonia Cunningham
Series Editor: Melanie Dakin
Series Consultant: Helen Truszkowski
Author: Amy Corzine

Proofreading: Dominique Shead
Indexing: Isobel McLean
Production: Navigator Guides
Printed and bound in Italy by Lego
A catalogue record for this book is available from the British Library
ISBN 1-86011-1106

The author and publishers have made every effort to ensure the accuracy of the information in this book at the time of going to press. However, they cannot accept any responsibility for any loss, injury or inconvenience resulting from the use of information contained in the guide.

Please help us to keep this guide up to date. We have done our best to ensure that information is correct at the time of printing, but places and facilities are constantly changing, and standards and prices fluctuate. We will be delighted to receive your comments concerning existing entries or omissions. Authors of the best letters will receive a copy of the Cadogan Guide of their choice.

About the author

Amy Corzine

Amy Corzine is a writer and editor who lives in London. Fascinated by fairy tales as a child, she sought their source upon reaching adulthood. Discovering that many came from Ireland, she ventured there, only to become enchanted by its invisible, otherworldly denizens and very worldly inhabitants.

For my late mother, who helped me follow my dream

Series consultant

Helen Truszkowski is series consultant of Cadogan's *take the kids* series, and author of *take the kids Travelling* and *take the kids Paris & Disneyland® Resort Paris*. Helen is an established travel writer and photographer. Over the past decade her journeys have taken her around the globe, including six months working in South Africa. Helen's seven-year-old son, George, has accompanied her on her travels since he was a few weeks old.

Series editor

Melanie Dakin is series editor of Cadogan's *take the kids* series, having previously acted as consultant editor on the Time Out *London for Children* guide and editor of Time Out's *Kids Out* magazine. As a mother of two, Melanie has spent a great deal of time navigating round different countries with children, pushchairs, toys and luggage. To date only a couple of baby bottles and a small coolbag have been left behind.

Contents

Snapshots of Ireland

Top towns

1

2

3

4

5

6

7

8

1 Victorian Glass House, Belfast p.202-6
2 Temple Bar Market, Dublin p.49
3 Writer's Museum, Dublin p.50
4 National Library p.54
5 Grand Opera House, Belfast p.206
6 Galway highstreet, Galway p.161
7 Fitzgerald Park, Cork p.121
8 Waterford Treasures Museum, Waterford p.148
9 Playground, Dublin Zoo p.58
10 WB Yeats, Sligo p.182
11 Spanish arch, Galway p.161
12 Children's shop, Cork p.121

9

10

11

12

Bricks and mortar

1 Doonagore Castle, Burren p.141
2 Rock of Cashel, Tipperary p.147
3 Staigue Fort, Kerry p.134
4 Lough Gur, Co.Limerick p.138
5 Charles Court, Summercove, Co. Cork p.124
6 Cat Stone, Westmeath p.106
7 Tintern Abbey, Wexford p.88
8 Pearses Cottage, Galway p.169
9 Dunguaire Castle, Galway p.166
10 Clonmacnoise, Co. Offlay p.93

11

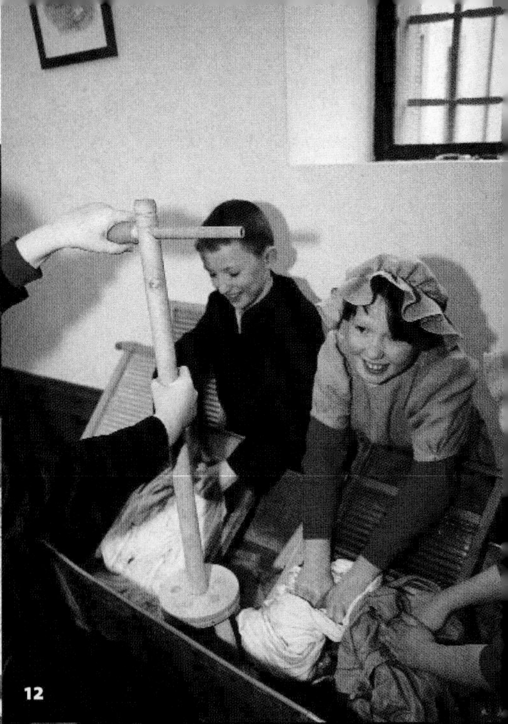

12

13

14

11 Bunratty Castle interior, Co. Clare p.141
12 Down County Museum, Co. Down p.212
13 Knappogue Castle Banquet Hall, Co. Clare p. 144
14 Trintiy Tree, Dingle, Co. Kerry p.132
15 Strokestown Nursery, Roscommon p.189
16 Mill at Ballydugn, Co. Down p.212
17 Cattle Raider's Feast, King House, Boyle p.188
18 Rosserk Abbey, Co. Mayo p.172
19 Bunratty Castle Folk Park, Co. Clare p.141

Buckets and spades

1

2

3

4

1 Rathacklan Bay, Co. Mayo **p. 180**
2 White Park Bay, Ballycastle, Co. Antrim **p.210**
3 Lone Surfer, Co. Cork **p.126**
4 Coast neat Ceide Fields, Co. Mayo **p.177**
5 Fishing boats, Donegal **p.235**
6 White Park Bay, Ballycastle, Co. Antrim **p.210**
7 Harbour sailing, Kinsale, Co. Cork **p.126**
8 Hook Head Lighthouse, Co. Wexford **p.88**

Animal magic

1

2

3

4

5

6

7

1 Lllama Farm, South Kerry **p.134**
2 Dublin zoo **p.58**
3 Duck Inn, Six Mile Bridge, Co. Clare **p.140**
4 Oceanworld, Dingle, Co. Kerry **p.132**
5 Belfast zoo **p.204**
6 Dublin zoo **p.58**
7 Wildfowl Reserve, Co. Wexford **p.87**
8 Horse, Co. Wexford **p.82**
9 Sheep, Co. Cork **p.120**

8

9

Nature lovers

1

2

3

4

5

6

1 Wicklow National Park, Co. Wicklow p.74
2 Lough Corrib, Co. Galway p.171
3 Polnabrone Dolmen, Co. Burren p.142
4 Giants Causeway Co. Antrim p.207
5 Slieve League Mountains, Co. Donegal p235
6 Killary harbour, Connemara p.159
7 Killarny National Park, Kerry p.129

7

8 Powerscourt Waterfall, Enniskerry, Co. Wicklow p.79
9 Bog, Wicklow Mountains p.74
10 Lauragh Bay, Co. Kerry p127
11 Cliffs of Moher, Co. Clare p.144
12 Glengash Pass, Southern Co. Donegal p.235

11

12

Trains, planes and automobiles

5

7

1 Flying Boat Museum, Foynes, Co. Limerick **p.139**
2 Bushmills Railway, Co. Antrim **p.208**
3 Radio room, Flying Boat Museum, Foynes, Co. Limerick **p.139**
4 National Transport Museum, Howth, Co. Dublin **p.69**
5 Donegal Railway Heritage Centre **p.236**
6 Ulster Folk and Transport Museum, Cultra, Co. Down **p.213**
7 National Transport Museum, Howth, Co. Dublin **p.69**
8 Model Railway, Westport House, Co. Mayo **p.176**

6

8

Eating Out

1

2

3

4

5

1 Juice, Dublin p.63
2 Hungry Elephant Restaurant, Cork p.151
3 Saturday Market, Temple Bar, Dublin p.292
4 Badass Cafe, Dublin p.62
5 Granny's Kitchen, Rock of Cashel, Tipperary p.154
6 Bewley's Restaurant, Dublin p.62

6

Chapter Index Map

Introduction

01

INTRODUCTION

The *Tuatha Dé Danaan*, or faeries, first came to Ireland on a magic cloud. That's how I first arrived there too.

I recall looking down beyond the blues of sea and sky to an emerald-green land ringed by a line of white nimbus as far as the eye could see, as if cloud soldiers were standing sentinel around Ireland, guarding it and welcoming foreign dignitaries to their great treasure...as if Ireland itself were saying *Failté agus beannacht Déi* ('Welcome and the blessings of God be upon you'). I felt embraced by a warm kind of presence, a feeling that even now I think of with awe.

I didn't know then that Ireland is shaped a bit like the Cauldron of Plenty, a giant bowl with mountains ridging a lower-level centre. Nor did I know that it is also encircled, and so kept temperate, by the Gulf Stream, the warm-water current that had flowed along with me all the way from my home near the Gulf of Mexico. And neither did I know that this island's ancient peoples once conceived the land itself as being a goddess with her own will – one that they named *Eiru*.

As I emerged from the plane, the air smelled sweet with the scent of burning turf and rain-washed fields – clean yet invigorating – with the softest mist I had ever felt upon my face. Lone trees sparkling with raindrops on small hills were pointed out to me as faery trees. The magical world of faery tales suddenly had substance here.

For children, this is a remarkable discovery – that an otherworldly dimension is taken seriously by adults who know more than they do, that there is history behind the stories they have heard. Despite the pall that adulthood casts on us, this small island enchants as no other can.

Geographically there are few boundaries but water in Ireland – whether lake, river or sea – but politically there are many, and not just between Northern and Southern Ireland, for people here have been warring for centuries. For all that, this feels like a markedly peaceful country. Its people will sometimes take you by surprise by being unremittingly generous – for absolutely no other reason than that they just feel like being so. These moments are like little solar flares that rise up from a sun that burns within them, reminding the fortunate recipient of the humanity we all hold within us. The Irish will tell you that there is nothing extraordinary about being kind – it is simply being human.

Statistically, the facts are that this 5,456-square mile island with 5.6 million inhabitants is run by two different governments. Northern Ireland's six counties are governed from Stormont, which is overseen by the British government from London. The rest of Ireland is an independent republic run from Dublin. Since 1973 both have been part of the European Union, although only the Republic uses the European single currency, the Euro.

The facts of history, however, can be altered slightly according to imaginings. For the Irish, history is a story. That is how they have told and retold what has happened to them over the centuries. And they love stories. One might say there are as many histories of Ireland as there are people in it, from the mythological past of the country's ancient oral tradition, the heroic legends of the ancient Celts and medieval times, and then the endlessly complicated political stories of more recent centuries, not to mention the influences from other cultures that the Irish have visited or been visited by. Added to this are the elaborations of the Christian monks, and of the all-important *shenachies* or traditional storytellers and tradition-bearers, who have been present in Ireland since the time of the druids, bards and Brehon Laws. Everyone, the Irish say, used to be a storyteller.

Have you heard the story in the Bible about the angel who goes from house to house asking for a little food and water? Well, some people gave, and some didn't. And those who didn't were visited later by another angel who was not so kind, so that a few people died in the houses where people had not been so generous. The Irish haven't forgotten these old stories completely. In the past, if there was some food in the press (Irish-English for larder), it was hard for a family not to offer it all to a stranger – as much as he'd have, until he said no thank you, I'm stuffed and replete with your generosity, your hospitality.

Ireland today

Foreigners often complain about how much Ireland has changed in recent years. In response, the Irish tend to say that visitors have always liked to imagine it as remaining the same, but the truth is that it is always changing, has always changed, and will continue to be changed by outside influences...which many Irish people welcome.

After all, its people have emigrated for the past couple of centuries to find work, and the notion of the homesick Irishman is famed in song and story. There are more people with Irish ancestry outside Ireland than in it. Today you will find Irish theme pubs, with Irish beer and sometimes even Irish people in them, all over the world, from Australia to Russia. Half of North America seems to have some Irish blood. For the Irish, America above all was once the land of gold, of milk and honey, of opportunity, as millions emigrated there, while even those who stayed in Ireland learnt to dream of one day going to the heaven-world of America. These days, however, the Irish no longer have to leave their own country to work, and have even become recipients of immigrants themselves from poorer countries. Nor do the modern Irish have to depend on other countries to provide their industries and businesses.

Nevertheless, for all the modernity that has exploded into Ireland with the birth of the now somewhat kittenish 'Celtic Tiger' and the influx of immigrants from countries that are as poor as Ireland used to be, the essentials of an older, more leisurely Irish way of life have not been lost. Irish people retain a charm and vibrancy that is all their own. Laughter and the arts – including the most traditional Irish art of all, that of conversation – are important to them, not to mention the lifeblood of happy children and families. You and your children will find a creative imagination and a buoyant sense of fun still alive in the Irish people you meet, together with a certain respect for things unknown and otherworldly, especially among those who live close to nature. Vestiges of this island's ancient traditions, whose roots are deeper than even the tree-centred beliefs of the druids, can be seen in the faery stories attached to many places. They hint of an earlier race who, sensibly, sought ways of protecting and regenerating their land, and whose deep respect for the unknown encouraged them to investigate what they could not see or experience ordinarily. The remnants of this attitude inspire the exhilarating kind of rebellious curiosity that is normal to Irish people beneath society's external veneers – controlled in the past by druids, Brehon Laws, Christianity, then the British government, and nowadays by the modern 'religion' of technology.

The best of Ireland unites the old with the new, improving upon the old by maintaining a high quality of architecture, food and natural surroundings inherited from the past while providing the comforts and variety of the modern world. When you find this, you may be forgiven for imagining you are in heaven, or in *Tír na n'Óg*, the Land of Eternal Youth so often mentioned in Irish mythology...the land of people who are young forever in their hearts.

Planning your trip

Long before you go to Ireland, think about the kind of holiday you want. Depending on what you and your family most want to do – explore Irish history or culture, try out new sports, fish, swim,

Acknowledgements

A hundred thousand thank you's are in order for all the Irish people I have ever met, who have always given something of themselves to me, as a stranger and sometimes as a friend. It would be impossible to list them all, but noteworthy ones are: Jim and Anne Henry; Jimmy Gilvarry; Paddy Tuffy; Eugene and Geraldine Kielt; Eugene O'Kelly; Christopher Sweetnam (with American wife Colleen and daughters Ainé and Niamh); Bernard Waldron (who stoked the fire of my interest in Ireland for years); folklorist Dáithí Ó'hOgain of University College Dublin; Basil Nulty; John Kelly; Vicky Sutton; Michael McCaughan; the employees of Bord Failté/Tourism Ireland, especially Orla Carey, Damian O'Brien, Joe Lynam, and Laura Duffy, and at the Northern Ireland Tourist Board, notably Maureen Durkan, Karen Houlahan, and Mike Moran; and the late Mrs. Katherine Lambert Ball, Kevin Danaher, and Liza Mitchell.

To my non-Irish supporters, thanks must go to my father, brother, ML, inspiration Mr. Radha, ex-Cadogan Editorial Director Vicki Ingle, editors Nick Rider and Mel Dakin, Virginia Ivey Sullivan, Lyn Carr Harris, and the North London Steiner School children in my classes from 1989 to 1993.

To Ireland, I apologise for my mistakes ('a man's mouth often broke his nose'). To the Otherworld beings, your stories are here because I hope others will respect you; I apologise for my impertinence, unconscious of it as I am, being nearly blind myself.

hike or otherwise enjoy the countryside – you may prefer to base yourself in just one place, or to spend a few nights in each of a series of centres before travelling on to the next. The longer you stay in any of Ireland's counties, the more treasures you will discover there – whether they are difficult-to-find tourist attractions, archaeological sites or fascinating spots recommended to you by local people. You need to have time to savour and enjoy the full variety of Irish arts, crafts, sports, music and other cultural activities in the places you visit.

The destinations, attractions and places to stay featured in this guide include locations in cities, towns and the countryside across Ireland. When planning a visit, choose your base carefully so that you are near the sites you especially want to see. Ireland may appear small on the map, but the traffic in its big cities (especially Dublin and its environs) can be heavy enough to occupy plenty of your time, and in the countryside, once you've left the main highways, you can easily find yourself rolling along seemingly never-ending, winding roads looking for tourist attractions that remain inexplicably well-hidden, particularly if a pooka or the faeries decide to play a trick on you. It's also not always simple navigating through Irish towns, where routes will not necessarily be clearly signposted. One thing that seems to work is to follow signs that indicate the direction of a highway to a main city like Dublin or Galway, and not to worry that you're driving in the wrong direction as you go through the town; once you reach the main highway, you will usually find a roundabout with signposts showing a road towards the place you are looking for. Be wary, however, as occasionally you will see a sign turned in the wrong direction, or placed where you are certain never to see it, particularly at night.

To make the most of a family holiday in Ireland, don't start by driving a car as fast as you can. Speeding down roads at 60 to 80mph is not conducive to relaxation or to meeting any faery people. To get to know Ireland, you must slow yourself down and talk to human beings, meet the animals in the fields, and listen to the whispers in the breeze and the stream trickling by. Otherwise, you may go mad just trying to get out of Dublin via the new housing developments that surround it, and the newly-built ring road that may not be on your map, or in rushing from tourist site to tourist site without a word from an Irishman except 'Pardon' or 'Excuse me' as they sidestep you on the street while you practically run into them in your efforts to see everything in too short a time.

Remember the old Irish saying, 'When God made time, He made plenty of it', or you may not notice the leprechaun sitting on the pavement, or in the tree you're rushing past. A word to the wise is: see everything in Ireland all at once and you'll see nothing. Especially with children in tow, you won't have much fun if you run yourself ragged dashing from place to place. In Ireland, everything takes time, so you may as well be prepared to take it easy and let the inevitable unexpected detours lead you where they will.

Travelling with kids

For children, these unexpected detours and discoveries can be exciting, so long as their adult companions don't convey tension to them by being too goal-oriented. Remember that the calmer and happier you are, the less anxious kids will be. Planning ahead helps take some of the anxiety out of a trip, and even if you do feel stressed, don't let on. Children will be better-tempered, too, if you pause for frequent breaks beside roadside ruins, and in the parks and green spaces you will come across while touring around. Always take along the basics of a picnic (snacks, drinks), in case you and your flock want to stop and eat wherever you are rather than carry on to the next town. And in between, be sure to stop for plenty of special treats at ice cream parlours, souvenir shops and so on.

When packing, it's best to keep it simple, especially if travelling with a baby or small child. There's no need to take along a whole nursery: just be sure you have enough nappies/diapers, wet wipes and so on to cover the first 48 hours, then buy replacements locally. Take only a few well-chosen, favourite toys – you'll almost certainly pick up a few more things to entertain the kids further into your trip. A favourite bear or other soft toy will help younger children settle at night, and a personal stereo is a great asset with older kids, especially if you're sharing a room with them. And as you pack, make sure to leave space for souvenirs.

Listed in this book are attractions and activities to amuse, engage and enchant children and their parents all around Ireland. All kids, though, get

Fun and games: Some traditional Irish children's games

Here's a choice of traditional games to learn from the Irish, and to try out as you travel around the country. And as well as these, don't forget to play 'I Spy' as you go along the country roads, to find faery hills, usually identifiable by having a solitary tree on top of them, or maybe a ring of three or seven red rowanberry trees; faery raths (raised rings of earth that show the sites of ancient settlements); oddly shaped hills or islands (like the pointed Croagh Patrick in County Mayo, and the Dead Man off the Dingle peninsula), or funny little sculptures of animals or faeries on the tops of walls or in specially cut trees or bushes.

Dogs and Hares

Play this with a group of kids. The children form two teams – of 'Hares' and 'Dogs' – then choose four 'safe corners'. The Dogs chase the Hares as they try to reach the safe corners. If the Hares get to the safe areas before the Dogs catch them, they stay there until the Dogs stand aside and chant 1-2-3, at which point the Hares get a chance to set off for another corner before the Dogs chase them again. If a Hare is caught, it must run with the Dogs. The last Hare to be caught wins the game.

Marbles

Marble games have long been very popular in Ireland, generally with boys. One simple common game of Marbles goes as follows.Each player needs at least one glass marble. One throws his marble into an enclosed circle or space. When it stops rolling, another boy shoots, trying to hit the first marble with one of his own. If he hits it, it becomes his. If he doesn't hit it, the first player gets a chance to shoot at his opponent's marble. Whoever gets the most marbles wins the game.

Soldier's Tig

Another game that was traditionally played by boys. One boy chased the others in a group and tried to hit one of them with his hand. The victim struck then had to hold one hand on the spot where he was touched, keeping it in that position while chasing the other boys and trying to hit them with his other hand, until all but the last boy are caught. For the next game, the last boy who evaded being struck becomes the one who chases the others.

Ring games

In Ireland, children used to hold hands and dance in a circle as they sang or recited different rhymes like these, especially under a new moon.

'I see the moon and the moon sees me,
God bless the moon and God bless me;
There's grace in the cottage and grace in the hall,
And the grace of God is over us all.'

A ring game popular in Co. Offaly involved singing the following rhyme:

'Sally go round the moon
Sally go round the stars
Sally go round in a gypsy van
Some day afternoon.'

After each verse, everyone falls down, and then gets up and starts again.

Skipping games and verses

Skipping, on the other hand, was thought of as a girl's game in Ireland – few boys learned to skip. In one popular Irish rope-skipping game, while two girls turned a rope for another who skipped, a group formed a circle around her and chanted:

'One, two, three, Mother caught a bee,
Bee died, Mother cried, out goes she...'

As the skipper recited 'out goes she', she would point to another girl, who then became 'it' and the skipper, and the game would carry on.

A variation on this, without a rope, was that one girl would skip in the middle of a circle of girls while singing the verse. When the skipper pointed to anyone in the circle, everyone would chase the 'it', who, if caught, had to go in the middle, skip and sing the verse to repeat the game.

Other verses for this game from Co. Limerick are:

'Abben a babben a baby's knee
Holsum polsom, wait and see
Potato rows, single toes
And out she goes!'

'Hide and seek all the week,
Sheeps' heads for Sunday.
Half a crown for Mister Brown
To pay the rent on Monday.'

(One child would point at 'Mister Brown', who would be 'it')

'Mary Mac, dressed in black,
Three gold buttons behind her back.
Hi ho, tipsy toe,
Turn the ship and away we go.'

(This time the chosen 'Mary Mac' would be 'it'.)

bored at least a few times while travelling, and especially on long car journeys. To keep these mood swings at bay, instead of just relying on familiar games, toys and audiobooks from home, a whole range of distinctively Irish pastimes and fun things may be discovered in Ireland that are linked to all the new things your children will see on the trip, and the people they will meet. Mythological story books or Irish songs and stories on CD or cassette will help introduce your children to Ireland's fascinating historical and fictional characters, some of whom are presented in the chapters of this guide. In the evenings, try telling an Irish story linked to a place you're going to visit the next day. After your visit, children (and you) could make something related to the places you've visited – like a *súgawn* (rope) or St Brigid's Cross braided from straw, or an animal or faery creature out of putty or plasticine, learn some Irish songs (from traditional to U2), colour your own postcards, or play a game – perhaps one of the Irish ones featured on p.25.

Storytellers and tours

Above all, Ireland offers one very special and unique means of entrancing children and adults – the telling of traditional stories, always best done by a traditional storyteller or *shenachie*. Rooted in two very Irish traits, a love of story and a love of language, and making use of only the simplest resources – the human voice – true storytelling can fascinate even kids apparently permanently hooked on electronic gadgetry, and brings alive the tales associated with historic sites in a way no conventional guide can. Any opportunity to see and hear a real storyteller is not to be missed.

There are many more storytellers around Ireland than the ones noted below, but those listed here are fairly well-known. Real *shenachies* are getting increasingly rare these days, and so are harder to find; however, you'll recognize the difference when you meet a real one. The first on the list below, Eddie Lenihan, is one of the modern storytellers closest to the *shenachie* tradition.

Eddie Lenihan, Co. Clare, **t** (065) 27191
Windhorse Productions, Sounds True, PO Box 8010/Dept. WH, Boulder, CO 80306-8010; or try **www**.soundstrue.com (**t** 1 800 333 9185 in the US).

This Irish folklorist, author and ex-teacher is based in Co. Clare, and tells stories of myth, magic and mystery masterfully to children and adults. Highly recommended for car listening is his *The Good People*, available on cassette in the *Storytelling from Ireland* collection, issued by Sounds True in their *Secrets of the World* series. He has also produced several books, and one of his most recent is *Meeting the Other Crowd, the Fairy Stories of Hidden Ireland*, co-authored and edited by Carolyn Eve Green (*see* **www**.carolynevegreen.com). Eddie Lenihan's story recordings are available from Windhorse/Sounds True in the USA, or via Amazon in the US and UK.

Martin Byrne, Sacred Island Tours, Co. Sligo, **t** (079) 66241, **www.gofree.indigo.ie**

Byrne trained as a painter and printmaker in Galway, then set off to visit the ancient places of Ireland and learn about the old stories that had always fascinated him. He now documents the alignments and artwork of chambered cairns.

Richard Marsh, Legendary Tours, **www.legendarytours.com**

Marsh conducts tours of countryside sites in Leinster, notably in Counties Wicklow and Meath. Wellington boots (waterproof boots) are provided as needed. Some of the stories told are legends and sagas that may be too long for children who don't already have a big interest in folklore or history, and certainly will not be appropriate for those below age 10. Walks may also go over rough terrain, and your children will need to be able to cope with being in the outdoors for eight hours or so, but it's a very rewarding trek.

Michael Roberts, Co. Sligo, **t** (071) 9168868

Mr Roberts arranges tours of the sacred sites of Sligo and has been a student of mythology and folklore for over 40 years. He can tell the stories and show the sights associated with the two battles of Moytura, Ben Bulben, Carrowmore, Knocknarae and Lough Gill for a day or a week, as there are multitudes of places to see and stories to hear around the county.

Pat Speight, Co. Cork, **t** (021) 455 1023, **www.patspeight.com**

Pat Speight also makes commercial tapes of his Irish stories, which you can obtain via his website.

History

02

IRELAND'S HISTORY

For more than one and a half million years, Ireland was covered in ice. A little irony of the universe is that Ireland was joined to both Britain and the rest of Europe at that time, during the Ice Age, about 20,000 years ago. Perhaps nature spirits, or even unicorns lived there, but there were definitely no people around. A fascinating example of the strange landscapes that were left behind in Ireland by its giant ice-shield is the great stone plateau of the Burren, in Co. Clare (*see* p.141).

Ireland was then part of a peninsula that pointed north from Europe. Around 12,000 years ago, warm ocean currents began to melt the ice, causing flooding that broke the peninsula off from the continent. Eventually Ireland separated from Great Britain too, but not before giant animals had moved there. Great elk, woolly mammoths, brown bears and arctic foxes fed on soft carpets of grass that stretched across the island. As the weather warmed, birds flew across to Ireland with the seeds of the great forests that began to fill the Irish hills. Hazel and pine trees appeared first, then elms and the great oaks that centuries later were so important to the druids. The giant animals that had depended on the grasslands for food began to die as trees became giants themselves and covered the island – trees like the huge ancient trunk at the prehistoric site of Ceidé Fields, Co. Mayo (*see* p.177).

Not until the Mesolithic era, or Middle Stone Age, (8000–4000 BC) did people finally move to Ireland, possibly from Scotland over the last land bridge. These hunter-gatherers roamed the forests hunting elk and bears, and along the coasts where they fished and dug for clams and oysters. Many of their tools have been found near lakes, like Lough Boora in Co. Offaly, and along the coasts of Waterford, Dublin, and Sligo. The first settlement we know about was at Mount Sandel in Co. Derry. Round huts were built there 6,000 years ago.

About 4000 BC, Neolithic or New Stone Age farmers moved to Ireland, bringing a new way of life based on stable settlements and growing crops instead of constant nomadic wandering. The remains of the largest Neolithic farming town in Europe are at Ceidé Fields, Co. Mayo, from around 3000 BC. Ireland's most dramatic prehistoric site is the round stone monument at Newgrange, Co. Meath, from about 2500 BC (*see* p.99).

By 2000 BC tribes had spread all over Ireland. Their chieftains often lived in the middle of lakes on manmade islands or *crannógs*, so that they could fight off attackers more easily. Examples can be seen at the Ulster History Park in Co. Tyrone, or at Craggaunowen (*see* p.143). Some *crannógs* were still used as homes until the 17th century.

Traders from countries with more advanced metal-working and mining skills soon discovered Ireland's metals, as the European Bronze Age developed. Beautiful Bronze Age gold metalwork can be seen in the National Museum in Dublin.

Did you know...?

The mythical battles between the Nemedians and the Fir Bolg (see p.29) and the Fomorians could be rooted in a folk memory based on fact. Some scholars think that a roaming Mesolithic hunter-gatherer tribe (the Fomorians) were living on the fringes of Ireland at the time that a farmer tribe (the Nemedians) arrived to compete for land. Others think maybe a sea-going race like the Phoenicians were the Fomorians, and that a farming tribe from Scotland called the Scythians were the Nemedians.

Mythical Ireland and the Early Celts

Ireland's mythology is another kind of gold that helps us trace early Irish history. The *Tuatha Dé Danaan* or faery people and old gods of the Irish myths, for example, are thought by some to be connected with the Beaker people, so-named because of the special pottery they made, who arrived in Ireland during the Bronze Age.

The Greek and Roman writers who left us the first written descriptions of most parts of Europe made only passing comments on Ireland, and never visited it – perhaps due to outlandish notions like those of the Greek historian Strabo, who wrote: '[the Irish] think it decent to eat up their dead parents'. A great many Irish place names, on the other hand, refer to mythological figures like Cúchulainn, Queen Maeve or Finn McCool, and stories attached to them are often the most concrete evidence we have of real events that may have occurred in these same places. Documents and records may be scarce, but the myths provide Ireland with a rare and richly elaborate 'parallel history'.

A story to tell: The Invasions of Ireland

Invasions occurred long before history was written down, and some are recalled in Irish myths. They carry the flavour of an earlier, forgotten history, and in them one senses something of Ireland's ancient people and a way of thinking that disappeared long ago.

Invasion 1 – Cessair

Ireland's first invasion is linked to the Bible story of Noah's Ark, when God was angry about the way people were behaving down on Earth, especially in Sodom and Gomorrah. People there only wanted to have fun, not caring what happened to anyone else. So God declared that He would get rid of all the living things he had created with a flood that would cover the entire world.

However, there was one good man that he refused to harm, Noah. God promised to save him and his family if he followed His instructions. Noah was to build a huge boat or ark, and fill it with a male and female of every animal he could find.

The Bible does not, though, mention the Irish legend about three other ships that set sail with the ark, nor Noah's granddaughter Cessair. Forty days before the Flood, Cessair took with her 50 women and three men – her father Bith ('Cosmos' in Irish), her sailor brother Ladra and her husband Fiontánn – to seek a place with no human inhabitants in the hope of avoiding the Great Flood.

One day Cessair spotted land that glittered like an emerald, and landed somewhere in Munster, perhaps at Waterford Harbour, or on the Dingle Peninsula in Co. Kerry. There were no other human beings around, so they felt safe enough.

But Cessair's father and her brother died, leaving Fiontánn to take care of all the women. This was too much for Fiontánn, so he ran away, leaving Cessair and the other women broken-hearted. Then the Great Flood came and drowned them all, except Fiontánn, who survived by magically changing himself into a fish. This trick saved him for the next 5,500 years. He changed his shape as it suited him, from a salmon to an eagle to a hawk.

This sly one observed many a subsequent invasion of Ireland, and told humans about them long after they happened until, one day, his luck changed. The Druid Finegas caught him on a hook in the form of the Salmon of Knowledge, the name by which Fiontánn was known (*see* p.143).

Invasion 2 – The Partholonians

Next to invade were the Partholonians – led, predictably, by Partholón. They came from central Europe (possibly Greece) to the plain of Elta Edar (now Howth, Co. Dublin), with Partholón's three sons. One enjoyed cooking and duelling; another spent his time making home-brew, while the last brought the art of hospitality to Ireland. Partholón created four lakes and cleared four plains with the four oxen he brought with him. Then he drove out of Ireland the demonic, cruel giant Fomorians. A mere 550 years later, Partholón's people were wiped out by plague – except for one man named Tuán mac Cairill, who, like Fiontánn before him, shape-shifted into various animal guises through the centuries to observe the doings in Ireland.

Invasion 3 – The Nemedians

The third invasion was by the Nemedians, led by Nemedh, his wife Macha and their four sons. He lit the first fire on Ireland's most central point, the Hill of Uisneach, and then on Ard Macha ('Macha's height') in Armagh. They also cleared 12 plains and created four lakes, pushing the Fomorians – who had returned – out to the coasts and islands.

Tory Island off Donegal is where the Fomorians are said to live today, although you'd be hard pressed to actually catch one. They are described as badly formed in body and mind, and can be one-legged and one-eyed as well, but mainly it's the spirit inside that makes a Fomorian.

Their leader Balor had only one eye, which would destroy whomever it looked upon. In battle, when he was tired, other Fomorians would prop his eye open with planks of wood. Thus they conquered the Nemedians, and every Samhain (Halloween), they demanded a tribute from the Nemedians of corn, wine and sometimes children. If they did not pay, their noses were cut off.

The Nemedians finally attacked the Fomorians again, but their response was so vicious that the Nemedians ran away, in two groups. One fled to Greece and the other to unnamed northern lands. The Nemedians who went to Greece returned to Ireland later, by which time they were called the Fir Bolg. Their leaders were five brothers, who won a battle against the Fomorians and divided Ireland into five provinces. The fifth, called Mide (Meath), had the Hill of Uisneach at its centre. They declared that 'order, justice and the fruits of the island's prosperity should be granted to everyone'.

Irish Mythology Facts and Figures

Aengus Óg Aengus the Young, the God of Love, son of the Daghda, whose palace was at Newgrange.
Balor Evil Fomorian leader with one eye that destroys everything upon which it gazes; his grandson Lugh killed him by casting a stone into his single eye in the Second Battle of Moytura (*see* p.183).
Banshee Faery woman who screams in the wind to foretell the deaths of descendants of Irish chieftain families; if you see her, you better not let her know you do or she may come after you too.
Beltaine 1 May or May Day: celebrated in pre-Christian times as a day when the door between the realms of the dead and living was open.
Brigid Goddess of healing, poetry and fertility: her festival on 1 February (Imbolg) became linked with a Christian saint, St Brigid.
Conchobhar Mac Nessa King of Ulster and lord of the Red Branch warriors; betrothed to marry Déirdre, he killed her lover Naoise out of jealousy.
Cormac MacArt High King AD 254–77 and patron of the Fianna, whose daughter Grainne eloped with Diarmuid after being betrothed to Finn McCool.
Cúchulainn 'The hound of Chulainn', a warrior-hero whose name was Sétanta until he killed the hound of Chulainn, a smith god from the Otherworld, to whom he pledged himself as the dog's replacement. Women always fell in love with him.
The Daghda Patron god of the Druids and 'father' of all the gods of ancient Ireland.
Déirdre 'of the Sorrows' Conchobar promised to marry her after being told by a Druid that she would be the most beautiful woman in Ireland, but that she would cause Ulster's ruin.
Diarmuid Foster-son of Aengus Óg, and a Fianna warrior who had a 'love spot' no woman could see without falling in love with him. He eloped with Grainne, pursued by Finn McCool.
The Fianna Warriors who guarded the High Kings of Ireland, whose greatest leader was Finn McCool.
Finn McCool or **Fiónn MacCumhaill** 'The Fair One', a legendary warrior made head of the Fianna by Cormac MacArt. He had a son, Oisín, with the goddess Sadh, suffered for love of Grainne (*see* p.184), and built the Giant's Causeway (*see* p.207).
Fionnbharr or **Fionnábar** God of the Tuatha and King of the Faeries (his wife Oonagh is Queen).
Fir Bolg 'Bog' or 'Belly Men':possibly descendants of the Nemedians (*see* p.29).
Fomorians Evil beings of Irish myth (*see* p.29).
Grainne Daughter of Cormac MacArt, who eloped with Diarmuid upon being betrothed to Finn.
Imbolg 1 February, feast of St Brigid and the pre-Christian festival of spring and the end of winter.
Leprechaun Shoemaker for the Sidhe who loves music, singing, dancing and riddles, and is fond of home brew (potcheen); also known for tricking mortals who try to take his pot of gold.
King Lir Ocean god of the Tuatha Dé Danaan, whose children were turned into swans (*see* p.177).
Lugh Half-Tuatha, half-Fomorian sun-god who slew his grandfather Balor and fathered Cúchulainn with a mortal woman.
Maeve or **Mebh** Mythical Queen of Connacht, and adversary of Cúchulainn.
Milesians The Sons of Míl or Milesius, the 'humans' who sailed perhaps from Spain or Turkey to Ireland and took the island from the Tuatha (*see* p.119).
Nemedians The first tribe to take over Ireland after defeating the Fomorians (*see* p.29).
Niall of the Nine Hostages High King of Ireland around AD 380–405: apparently a real figure, and the ancestor of the powerful O'Neill clan of Ulster.
Niamh of the Golden Hair Daughter of the sea god Manannan Mac Lir, she invited Oisín to live in Tír na n'Óg with her.
Oisín Champion warrior of the Fianna and the son of Finn and Sadh, who refused to help his father wreak vengeance on Diarmuid and Grainne and went with Niamh to the Land of Youth.
Partholón Leader of the second invasion (*see* p.29).
Pooka, Pouca Black dog or horse-like creature who brings bad luck to anyone rude to it and carries those who sit on its back on nightmare rides.
Red Branch Warrior guardians of Ulster during the reign of Conchobhar Mac Nessa, whose headquarters was at Emain Macha, Co. Armagh.
Samhain Celtic festival marking the time when the door opens between the worlds of the living and the dead, now called Halloween.
Sídh, Sidhe Faeries who live in the hills, waters or Otherworld of Ireland, a form of the Tuatha.
Tír na n'Óg The Land of Youth or Promise, a heaven inhabited by immortals who stay young forever.
Tuatha Dé Danaan The Sídh, Sidhe, Gentry, Good People or faeries, descendants of the goddess Danu who defeated the Fir Bolg (*see* p.163). Often thought of as the old gods of Ireland, but perhaps representing an advanced pre-Celtic people, once revered as gods and then sent to the Otherworld.

Back in the realm of more ordinary history, accounts vary about when the Celts first arrived in Ireland, but there seems to have been a steady stream of them coming from Spain, France and Germany from around 400 BC onwards. The Celts took control of Ireland by around 350 BC, and its eastern province of Leinster became a centre of Iron Age metal working. The Celts who came to Ireland decorated their swords and jewellery in what is known as the La Tène Celtic style, making spectacular use of whorls and spirals.

In the next few centuries most of the other Celtic regions of Europe fell under the rule of the Roman Empire, but in isolated Ireland Celtic culture was able to continue unhindered for over 1,000 years. It was during this time that Ireland was first described as divided into five provinces – Ulster, Connacht, Munster, Leinster and Mide (or Meath, later absorbed into Leinster). Irish legends tell of a society divided into many tribes (*túath*), each one ruled by its *rí* (king), helped by druids (philosopher-judges), and *cúire* (priests). The king of each tribe paid a tax to a stronger chieftain of their province, for his protection. At times there was also an honorary 'High King' or *Ard Rí* over all five provinces, who had his base initially at the Hill of Uisneach in Westmeath, and then at Tara (*see* p.106, p.103). However, no single king ever ruled effectively over the whole of Ireland, because tribal leaders were always fighting among themselves.

This was the world in which the Irish myths were first told and retold. Within Celtic society there were poet-musicians called bards, who kept alive the histories and traditions of each clan by telling stories and singing songs they had memorized, since they could not be written down. Some bards who showed special wisdom rose in society to become *vates* or seers, who also acted as advisors and teachers to the leaders of the tribe. At the top of the social ladder were the druids. A druid was a combination of wizard and wise man – one who had all the skills of the bards and *vates*, plus the authority to make laws and act as a judge.

The early Celts did not have writing as we know it, but used line markings known as *ogham* to mark directions or graves, or possibly to indicate 'magic' formulas. Carved on stones or tree bark, ogham had 20 characters, formed by drawing straight parallel marks on either side of, or across, a horizontal or vertical line. Each mark was named after a tree, so ogham is said to have a 'tree alphabet'.

> ***Did you know...?***
> ***Leprechauns could be linked to a Viking god, but in Irish folklore they're also associated with Lugh, the sun-god of the Tuatha Dé Danaan.***

The Isle of Saints and Scholars

Christianity came to Ireland in the 5th century AD, just as the Roman Empire was collapsing. Non-Christian Irish tribes had been raiding the west coast of Roman Britain for some time. A boy named Succat was kidnapped in one of these raids and brought to Ireland, where he worked as a slave and began to have visions. After a few years, Succat managed to go home, and became a monk. However, he dreamt that the Irish were calling him to come back to them, and in AD 432, now known as Patrick, he did return, and began the work of converting the locals to the new religion and, as the legend goes, driving all the 'snakes' out of Ireland (*see* p.178). Although he was not the first Christian to grace its shores, St Patrick is often given credit for bringing Christianity to Ireland. He and his followers focused on converting tribal or clan leaders, believing, correctly, that the people they ruled would follow after them. Patrick first won the support of King Dichu in Co. Down, and later King Laoghaire (or Leary) of Co. Dublin.

Helped in part by Laoghaire St Patrick rewrote Ireland's ancient Brehon Laws, to ensure they fitted in with Christianity. This book of laws was called the *Senchus Mór*. The Irish, though, mixed in many pagan ideas with their new religion to create what became Celtic Christianity. The pagan Irish had worshipped at spring wells and gone on pilgrimages to mountains like the pointed Croagh Patrick (*see* p.178) and islands like those in Lough Derg (*see* p.105). These became Christian shrines, and are still visited today. In the same way, a strong tradition of hermits, solitary pilgrims and like-minded spiritual groups seems to have always existed in Ireland. Part of the training that bards underwent included spells spent memorising poems alone in dark caves, through which, it was said, one could enter the many-coloured mystical land of *Tír na n'Óg*. This tradition was carried on by the early Irish Christian monks, who often became hermits and

A story to tell: Faery Origins

When Christians brought handwriting to Ireland, the old tradition-bearers, the poets and story-tellers, became less important to society, since history could be written down instead of told. People began to lose the habit of remembering long stories, and with them too the orally transmitted memories of the past.

Monks, for example, began telling everyone that the faeries were angels who had fallen from Heaven. Some of Heaven's angels, they said, led by the Archangel Lucifer, had gone against God. God grew mightily angry about this, and began sweeping his angels out of Heaven so that they fell to Hell. He was in such a fury that there was a great danger that soon there would be no angels at all left up there.

But luckily he stopped, and then all the angels froze on whatever level they had fallen to on their way down to Hell. Earth was midway between Heaven and Hell, and those angels who had fallen halfway to Earth became faeries, stuck in what the ancient Irish called the 'Otherworld'.

Humans could die and go to Heaven, but faeries, being immortal, could not, and so were jealous of humans. Because of this, the Monks said they were to be feared as well as avoided. Their magic could be countered and mischief combatted only by praying to God, and with the help of monks and Christian teachers like St. Patrick.

The priests began to say this sort of thing about the time that people started using up the earth for cities and stone towers to protect themselves from invaders like the Vikings, and from bad weather and the dangers of Nature. If Ireland's 'faery faith' does come from a pre-Christian nature religion, the monks' dislike of faeries makes sense.

chose the most uncomfortable and hostile places possible for their spiritual retreats – their disregard for cold and hunger was a sign of their faith. Remains of the lonely places where monks sought isolation can be found everywhere in Ireland, in places like Glendalough (*see* p.77) and, most spectacularly of all, on the wind-blasted Skellig Rocks off the coast of Co. Kerry (*see* p.133).

The centuries from 500 to 800 were Ireland's 'Golden Age'. While the rest of Europe suffered the many plagues and wars of the Dark Ages, the flame of learning was kept alight in Ireland. Monasteries grew up around many of its early hermitages, and grew rapidly in wealth and importance. Monasteries such as Clonmacnoise and Durrow were major centres of learning and art, like today's universities. It was during this time that Christian monks first wrote down Ireland's oral legends, such as the Ulster Cycle, including the great epic *Táin Bó Cúailgne*, and Irish monasteries produced magnificent illuminated manuscripts, the most famous of which is the *Book of Kells*, now in Trinity College Library, Dublin (*see* p.56).

Irish monks also travelled as missionaries to take Christian learning back to pagan, chaotic Europe. Irish scholars were respected advisers to many kings across the continent. Donegal produced its own homegrown saint in Columcille (521–597), better known in Britain as St Columba. In 561 he left Ireland to found a monastery on the inhospitable Scottish island of Iona, and returned to St Patrick's homeland what Patrick had brought to Ireland by converting much of Scotland and northern England to Christianity.

Troublesome Newcomers 1: The Vikings

Around 800, Vikings from Norway discovered Ireland's rich farming land and its monasteries, and began raiding and plundering all across the country. Used to fighting among themselves, the Irish had no united military force to fight them off, and the monks built tall round towers by their monasteries to shelter from Viking attacks. The Uí Néill high kings of Ulster had a try at throwing out the Vikings in the 860s, destroying their settlements north of Dublin. Despite this, still more Vikings arrived and began to settle in, marrying the native Irish and establishing trading ports which eventually became Dublin, Waterford, and Wexford (the Dublinia Museum has fine displays on Viking Dublin, *see* p.53). Battles between Irish tribes and Viking settlers lasted for 200 years.

During this struggle the only native Gaelic King ever to take over the whole of Ireland emerged from Munster: Brian Boru (942–1014). His name means 'Brian of the Tributes'. He was called this because the men of Leinster resented the heavy taxes he demanded after he became High King. They allied with the Vikings against him, but Brian defeated them both in the Battle of Clontarf. After this victory Brian Boru became High King over all Ireland – for a few hours. Then a Viking stole into his tent and murdered him. Still, this battle ended major Viking wars in Ireland. Viking settlers kept control of Dublin, while various Irish families continued to fight each other for the high kingship.

Troublesome Newcomers 2: The Normans and the English

At about the time that the Norman William the Conqueror was conquering England in 1066, in Ireland Archbishop Malachy of Armagh was building Mellifont Abbey and establishing four centres – at Armagh, Tuam, Cashel and Dublin – to control Ireland's churches. St Malachy was famous for his prophecies, and he brought the Irish church much more into line with the rest of the European Christian church based in Rome.

Disunity and battles between themselves among the Irish, though, continued. In 1169 the High King of Leinster Diarmait McMurrough was defeated by the High King of Connacht. Diarmait, however, has been remembered forever after in Irish history because he went to King Henry II of England for help, offering him loyalty if he would help him regain his kingdom. Henry II sent a band of Anglo-Norman warriors led by the Earl of Pembroke, known as Strongbow because he was so powerful in battle. The Normans were experienced in European war, and soon successful against the less organized Irish. Strongbow won the war for McMurrough in 1170, and in return demanded his daughter in marriage and the throne upon his death. A year later, McMurrough died and Strongbow became King of Leinster.

After that, other Norman adventurers tried their luck too. Henry II, though, got nervous about the growing power of some of his subjects and so in 1171 he set sail for Ireland with his own troops to impose his authority. With the support of the Pope he had himself declared 'Lord of Ireland', and made Dublin the capital of an English colony. This is how English rule began in Ireland.

Norman ways seemed quite strange to the Irish. The fact that a king became King simply because he was born to it – not chosen for his ability or physical qualities – seemed odd to Ireland's High Kings. However, the Anglo-Normans controlled only a few dozen square miles and, like the Vikings, many of the old Norman noble families – known as the 'Old English' – had begun marrying Irish people, adopting local customs and speaking Irish, so they didn't seem much of a threat. The Normans also built fortifications on the east coast like Carrickfergus Castle, north of Belfast (*see* p.206), but for centuries the only part of Ireland directly ruled by English governors was a small area around Dublin called 'The Pale'. Outside of it, Irish life often continued on pretty much unchanged. This is where the expression 'beyond the Pale' comes from, meaning an 'area beyond control'.

A New Division

In 1533 King Henry VIII of England divorced his Spanish first wife Catherine of Aragon because she could not give him a son, and so that he could marry Anne Boleyn. The Catholic Church did not allow divorce so the Pope denounced Henry, who then rejected the authority of Rome and gave England its own independent, Anglican, church. This soon joined the Protestant side in the Europe-wide split between Protestants and Catholics, the process known as the Reformation. In Ireland, however, the vast majority of people stayed loyal to the Roman Catholic church.

From this came centuries of trouble for Ireland. Henry and later English governments worried that their Catholic enemies – Spain, France – would use Ireland as a base for invading England. Determined to bring Irish leaders under his control, Henry VIII declared himself King of Ireland and took over the lands of Irish lords who wouldn't submit to him. Then he closed Ireland's monasteries, seizing their wealth for the Crown, and in 1534 crushed a revolt by the Catholic 'Old English' Fitzgeralds of Kildare. Henry's government also began the policy of trying to 'plant' communities of English Protestants in Ireland, to create a more loyal population. All these actions were deeply resented by the Irish. The terms Protestant and Catholic gained new importance in Ireland, where Protestantism now meant English rule.

Elizabeth I, queen from 1558–1603, continued her father's policies, only with still more determination to gain control over the whole of Ireland and not just the Dublin 'Pale'. She seized the lands of Catholic Irish lords who rebelled against her and gave them to English Protestants. She kept careful watch for invaders, especially those of her most powerful enemy, Spain, and by the time the survivors of the storm-wrecked Spanish Armada were washed up on Ireland's coasts in 1588 her henchmen and soldiers were able to ensure that they posed no threat to English power.

Ulster, however, was a big problem for Elizabeth. It was the part of Ireland where Gaelic culture and the Catholic lords still survived most freely. The Earl of Tyrone, Hugh O'Neill – who claimed descent from the old Uí Néill High Kings of Tara – and the Earl of Tyrconnell, Red Hugh O'Donnell, fought back bitterly against her governors in what became known as the Nine Years' War (1594–1603). At first, the Irish lords won a string of victories. In 1601, Spain sent an army to Kinsale, Co. Cork, to help. O'Neill marched south to join them, but, fighting in unfamiliar territory, they were badly defeated. The Spaniards withdrew, and O'Neill gave himself up to the English in 1603, not knowing that Elizabeth I would die the very next day. When the Earl heard the news, he wept with rage and grief.

O'Neill and O'Donnell were allowed to keep their lands, but the government in Dublin then harassed them and took away bits of their land on various excuses, and barred them from worshipping as Catholics. In 1607 O'Neill, O'Donnell and 90 other Ulster chieftains or 'earls' sailed away from Donegal, in the 'Flight of the Earls'. They hoped to get the help of one of Europe's Catholic kings and come back with a fresh army to fight on, but they never found enough support, and never returned. This left Gaelic Ulster without leaders, so that the door was wide open for Britain to take over completely, which it lost no time in doing.

Elizabeth I was succeeded on the throne by the Stuart King of Scotland, James, as James I of England and Ireland, which brought all three kingdoms under the same monarch for the first time. James I began the 'Ulster Plantation', which was on a far bigger scale than the earlier 'plantations' of Protestant settlers further south. All the best lands of the Ulster lords were given to English and Scottish Protestants, who were expected to be loyal to the Crown. The native Irish were pushed out to poorer quality land or wild, mountainous regions such as Donegal, which was practically left alone. British domination of Ulster was made complete.

The new 'Plantation' settlers formed much larger, more self-contained communities than earlier immigrants such as the Anglo-Normans, who had gradually blended in with the Gaelic Irish. The Ulster 'Planters' were a mixture of Anglicans and other more radical Protestant groups, such as the Scottish Presbyterians. They tended to remain separate and inward-looking, and live apart from the Catholic Irish communities around them. In Co. Tyrone's Ulster History Park there is a fascinating reconstruction of a Plantation-era house.

Britain's 17th-Century Wars Come to Ireland

King James I was succeeded by his son Charles I (1625–49), whose angry conflict with England's increasingly powerful Parliament and the more extreme Protestants or Puritans led to the outbreak of the English Civil War in 1642. In Ireland many Catholics, both Gaelic and Anglo-Norman, thought they could benefit from this situation. A rebellion broke out across the country, and Catholics, many of whom had only recently lost their land to Plantation settlers, launched vicious attacks on Protestants throughout Ireland, killing an estimated 12,000 people. These massacres have stayed in the memories of Ulster Protestants, and Plantation settlers believed that even larger numbers had died. Figures of over 100,000 dead were actually impossible, given the numbers of Protestants in Ulster at this time, but these stories helped draw a still worse enemy of the Catholics to Ireland's shores: Oliver Cromwell.

By 1649 Cromwell, the leader of England's Puritans, had won the Civil War and beheaded King Charles I. He then set sail for Ireland with his battle-hardened Roundhead soldiers – one of the best fighting forces in Europe – to settle scores in Ulster and flatten the Catholic rebellion. In Drogheda and Wexford, especially, thousands of Catholics were killed by Cromwell's soldiers. He also took still more land from Catholic landowners who opposed him, which he gave to his soldiers and supporters. Enemies who were not killed were forced out of the country or sent to rocky, barren Connacht (hence the saying 'To hell or Connacht', attributed to Cromwell). To this day, Cromwell is referred to as 'the butcher' by Catholics in Ireland.

After Cromwell died in 1658 the monarchy was restored in 1660 under King Charles II, whose reign was a time of relative peace in Ireland. Ironically, problems arose again in 1685 with the succession of a king who was a Catholic, Charles II's brother James II. He wanted to permit Catholicism to be practised openly again, and possibly to restore it as the main state religion. He appointed Catholics to powerful jobs in England and Ireland, arousing the suspicions and fears of Protestants, especially in Ulster. In 1688 England's Protestant ruling class rose against him and invited his son-in-law, the Dutch Protestant Prince William of Orange, to take over the throne as King William III. James II fled to Ireland, hoping to find supporters there and use it as a base to win back the British crown.

Irish Catholics flocked to support him, and James II soon took over the whole country except for the Protestant cities of Enniskillen and Londonderry, or Derry. When the citizens of Londonderry saw Catholic regiments marching towards them, 13 apprentice boys rushed to slam the city gates shut before the troops could enter, in an incident that has become an Ulster Protestant legend. For 105 days the city was besieged by James' followers, the Jacobites. A third of its population died, mainly from starvation. People ate rats, dogs, starch for laundering linen, and even candle wax. Eventually, though, British ships arrived with supplies, and James II's army was forced to withdraw.

The Jacobites retreated southwards, pursued by a Protestant army led by William III himself. They met at the Battle of the Boyne in Co. Meath on 12 July 1690, when William and his Protestant supporters decisively defeated James II and his Catholic followers. James lost heart and fled to France, leaving his army to fight on without him. The Irish were defeated by William at Aughrim, Co. Galway, and then besieged in Limerick, resisting as long and heroically as the Protestants had in Londonderry. The siege and the war only ended with the Treaty of Limerick in October 1691, when the Catholics made peace in return for religious tolerance. The treaty, though, was ignored by Ireland's Protestant parliament, and many of the Catholic 'Old English' nobility left Ireland to serve as soldiers for Catholic France and Spain. Their exit is known as the 'Flight of the Wild Geese'.

This is the most often-remembered of all Ireland's wars. For the Protestant community in Northern Ireland, the Battle of the Boyne took on mythological qualities (12 July is a holiday in Northern Ireland), and all over Ulster you'll see images of King William, or King Billy. The yearly marches held in memory of the Siege of Derry and the Boyne have led to violent clashes over the years. This is because these battles led to William's – and therefore the Protestants' – definitive takeover of Ireland.

The Protestant Ascendancy

In the 18th century, with Protestantism triumphant, many of Ireland's aristocracy grew extremely wealthy, and built elegant European-style mansions for themselves within beautiful landscaped gardens, like Powerscourt in Co. Wicklow (*see* p.79). Irish landowners had total control of vast estates, so their way of life was often even more resplendant than that of similar aristocrats in Britain or France (these mansions became symbols of Anglo-Irish control to Catholics, so many were burned down in the conflicts of the 1920s, often regardless of whether their owners were supporters of independence or not).

Literature and fine speech were very important among the ruling classes of the 'Ascendancy' (as the dominant regime after 1691 was known), and the arts, music and things of beauty were treasured. Dublin grew into an elegant Georgian city. The Ireland of this era produced many great writers, such as Jonathan Swift, author of *Gulliver's Travels* and many satires on British rule in Ireland, and the playwrights Congreve, Goldsmith and Sheridan. All were Anglo-Irish Protestants, since most Catholics were barred from education. Some Ascendancy Protestants were also interested in traditional Irish arts, and the early 18th century was also the time of the last and greatest of traditional Irish harpists, Turlough O'Carolan, from Co. Roscommon (*see* pp.186, 189).

Most Catholics, though, were humbled and treated as inferior people. By 1750, while 75 per cent of Ireland's population were Catholic, they owned just 5 per cent of the land. Most were poor tenant farmers, many of them living in harsh conditions. Their landlords were often absentees – descendants of Cromwell's soldiers, or followers of Elizabeth I – who never even visited their estates. Catholics were kept in check by a series of harsh measures introduced after 1691 to prevent them ever gaining power, known as the Penal Laws.

In response, Catholics in villages organized secret open-air Masses and 'hedge schools', where Catholic priests taught religion, the Irish language and history outdoors among bushes and hedges. Not all Catholics opposed those in power, however, for many were in awe of their wealth and fine manners. Some became Protestants themselves to protect their careers. The Penal Laws, too, did not only discriminate against Catholics but also

Some of Ireland's 18th-Century Penal Laws

1 Catholics were banned from joining the army or navy, or becoming Members of Parliament, and were forced to pay a tax to the Anglican (Protestant) church.
2 No Catholic could vote or buy land.
3 Catholic priests were expelled, and Catholic churches closed.
4 No Catholic schools were allowed.
5 A son of a Catholic who became a Protestant could take his parents' land for himself.
6 Speaking 'Irish' in public was banned.
7 Heavy taxes were placed on Irish products – like cloth, glass, wool, and cattle – so that Ireland could not compete with Britain economically.

against many non-Anglican Protestants, such as the Presbyterian 'Dissenters'. Middle-class Protestants were also excluded from power by the aristocracy. Many Dissenters left Ulster for Puritan New England, where, known as 'Scots-Irish', they played a major role in founding the United States (Co. Tyrone's Ulster American Folk Park gives some fascinating insights on this).

Secret societies formed in the countryside among Catholics, in rebellion against the laws that stopped them from getting jobs or owning land. Outbreaks of violence were frequent. Protestant gangs fought Catholic gangs, and in 1795 one clash led Ulster Protestants to found the 'Orange Order' to protect their interests (at 'The Diamond' in Co. Armagh). Named in honour of Prince William of Orange, it would become one of the most powerful groups in Protestant Ireland. Ireland still had its own Parliament, which, even though it was only made up of rich Protestants, tried to win more powers from the British government, and managed to relax the worst of the Penal Laws by the 1780s. Even so, dissatisfaction continued, among Catholics and many Protestants.

In the 1790s, inspired by the American and French Revolutions, some young middle-class Protestants formed a radical society, the United Irishmen. Its aim was Irish independence, and its most famous member, Dublin lawyer Wolfe Tone, urged people 'to substitute the common name of Irishman in place of... Protestant, Catholic and Dissenter'. Promised help by France, then at war with Britain, they launched an armed rebellion in 1798.

The revolt was strongest in Leinster and the Ulster counties of Antrim and Down, but spread to most of Ireland. However, the French troops sent to aid the rebels made little impact, and the rebellion was finally crushed in the Battle of Vinegar Hill, near Enniscorthy in Co. Wexford (*see* p.84), leaving nearly 30,000 people dead.

Following the 1798 Rebellion the British government shut down the Irish Parliament, and in 1801 instituted the Act of Union, putting Ireland and Britain together into a single United Kingdom with one Parliament at Westminster. This, though, solved nothing, as the Irish still demanded reform.

The United Irishmen had planted the seed of a new idea, that of total independence, but the bloody failure of their revolution caused a loss of heart among radical groups. In the years after the Act of Union, the balance swung back towards winning change through peaceful, political means. This campaign was led by one of Ireland's most inspiring leaders, the Kerryman Daniel O'Connell (1775–1847). He believed that 'no political change is worth the shedding of a single drop of human blood', and stood for election in 1828. As a Catholic, he was banned from taking his seat in the Westminster Parliament, yet he won by a landslide. Fearing another Irish revolt, the British government granted the Catholic Emancipation Act of 1829 so that 'the Liberator' – as O'Connell became known in Ireland – could sit in the House of Commons. Catholics were thus finally granted some basic political rights. However, Ireland was about to be plunged into a new disaster, as dramatic and devastating as any it had seen before.

The Great Famine and Exit

In the early 19th century Ireland's population shot up in size, doubling to around eight million between 1800 and 1840. The potato had become the staple food of the poor, and was often the only thing they could afford to grow and eat. Then, potato blight, a plant disease, destroyed almost the whole of Ireland's potato crop in 1845 and again in 1846. Left literally with nothing to eat, destitute families walked the roads seeking food, eating grass and berries just to stay alive, and building rough shelters when they could and dropping dead at the roadside when they couldn't. Many poor farmers were evicted from their homes as soon as they could no longer pay their rent, by landlords who refused to help them. Around 1.5 million people starved to death or died from disease, while over a million more left Ireland for other countries. The famine's effects were worst in the west, in Connacht and Munster, where poor farmers had been most dependent on potatoes for food.

Matters were made worse by the attitude of many British politicians, who thought the problems of the Irish poor were their own responsibility and saw no need to intervene. Although people were starving there was still plenty of food in Ireland during the famine, but the poor simply had no money to buy it. Cattle, sheep, oats and flour continued to be exported, and in Dublin life went on as normal. Ireland's unique situation, though, with so many absentee landlords, meant that many parts of the country were not well governed.

Some landowners were deeply disturbed by what was happening, and made themselves penniless trying to feed the wandering hordes of starving people. However, many absentee landlords, who lived in Britain or Dublin and scarcely ever visited their estates themselves, were largely unaware of and unconcerned about Ireland's poverty, especially since their own fortunes were still getting bigger. Others had already wanted to control more of their land themselves, for more profitable uses such as grazing sheep. The famine gave them a good excuse to clear their land of people, and so farmers and their families were evicted and thrown out of their homes as soon as they were too weak to work and too poor to pay rent. Sometimes landlords even paid their tenants to emigrate.

The famine years began the great flow of emigration out of Ireland. Thousands of people made their way to ports like Cobh, hoping to find a boat to their great hope, America. Conditions on the ships were so terrible they became known as 'coffin ships', because so many people died while crossing, but there were still plenty more ready to sail on them. By the end of the 19th century the population of Ireland halved, to just four million.

All over Ireland you'll find the famine mentioned, but one of the best places to take children to see its effects for themselves is Dan O'Hara's cottage in Connemara (*see* p.168). Here you can learn how the famine destroyed the lives of an ordinary family.

Thanks to emigration a strong Irish community formed in the USA, many of whom hated Britain for expelling them from their homeland. A new movement was founded among Irish-Americans called the Irish Republican Brotherhood (IRB). Its members called themselves Fenians, after the mythical Fianna warriors of ancient Ireland. Their aim was violent revolutionary action to win complete Irish independence from Britain. Back in Ireland, though, they did not have much impact.

In 1879 another potato crop failed in Ireland, and evictions were widespread. As usual, land ownership was a burning issue. A new movement of poor farmers appeared called the Land League, led by an ex-Fenian, Michael Davitt, who had been evicted from his Co. Mayo home as a child during the famine, emigrated to England to work in a cotton mill, and then returned to Ireland to start political action. The League sought fair rents and improvements in tenants' rights, and encouraged tenants to defy their landlords and refuse to pay rent, most famously when tenants refused to work for a Mayo landlord called Captain Boycott (a campaign that gave us the word 'boycott' for any similar action).

Davitt and the League worked in cooperation with the politician Charles Stewart Parnell, whose Irish Party had become an important group in the British House of Commons. Parnell's arguments and unrest over land problems finally persuaded Britain's Liberal Prime Minister Gladstone that Ireland needed major reform. His government introduced laws that at last gave Irish Catholics complete religious freedom, and the right to own land. The Irish, however, still wanted more, and relied on the sympathy of Gladstone to give them self-government, or 'Home Rule'. Their champion Parnell pushed the Home Rule issue to the top of the agenda in British politics. However, he was disastrously discredited by his affair with a married woman, Kitty O'Shea, in 1891, and Gladstone's Home Rule Bill collapsed in 1893, sadly bringing this attempt at peaceful change to an end.

The 20th Century: War, Partition and Independence

Ireland's drive for independence intensified in the 20th century. Winds of change were blowing in other fields as well as politics. More and more people across the country – apart from eastern Ulster – felt a new pride in a strong, separate cultural identity distinct from that of Britain. The time from the 1890s to 1914 were the peak years of the 'Irish Cultural Renaissance'. Writers and artists re-examined and began to value Ireland's historic culture, literature and traditions. Many were from Protestant, Anglo-Irish backgrounds, but were in love with Gaelic Irish culture, and hoped that by strengthening awareness of Ireland's cultural heritage they would encourage eventual Irish independence. Lady Gregory, an Anglo-Irish aristocrat, brought back to people's attention Ireland's Celtic myths, many of which had been virtually ignored for centuries. With her wealth she also helped nearly every Irish writer of the time (regardless of ethnic or religious background), and with the poet WB Yeats she founded the Abbey Theatre, the hub of Ireland's new theatre movement. Major initiatives to promote Irish culture were created, like the Gaelic Athletic Association, which popularized the uniquely Irish sports of hurling and Gaelic football, and the Gaelic League, founded to support the Irish language by the man who would be first President of the Irish Republic, Douglas Hyde. Even Dubliners began to study the Irish language, among them the writer-to-be James Joyce.

This growing Irish confidence was among the reasons why Britain's Liberal Party introduced a new Home Rule Bill for Ireland in 1912. It won huge support in most of Ireland, but alarmed the Protestant majority in eastern Ulster, who feared it would lead to Catholic supremacy – or 'Rome Rule' – and that a parliament in Dublin would favour the rural south against the industrialized north. This threat revived the Orange Order, and big demonstrations were held at which Protestant leaders such as Sir Edward Carson openly stated their willingness to defy the British government by force, by creating their own paramilitary army, the Ulster Volunteer Force or UVF. In response, former Fenians set up their own smaller paramilitary force, the Irish Volunteers, while a new group called Sinn Féin (Irish for 'Ourselves Alone') suggested that Irish MPs should withdraw from Westminster and set up their own parliament in Dublin. Trades unions had also been set up among the workers of Dublin's slums, many led by James Connolly, who was both a nationalist and a believer in socialist revolution. After a strike in 1913 Connolly formed his own paramilitary force, the Irish Citizen's Army.

Things had reached a stalemate, when the outbreak of the First World War in August 1914 put everything on hold, at least as far as the British government was concerned. Having other things to do, Parliament suspended the Home Rule Bill. Ulster Protestants, including the UVF, volunteered in thousands to fight in the British Army. Many Catholics – although this is often forgotten – volunteered as well, hoping their loyalty would be rewarded by a grateful Britain with Home Rule after the war. Irish regiments were among the most prominent in the British Army's front line, and over 5,000 Ulstermen alone were killed on the first day of the Battle of the Somme in July 1916.

Many Irish nationalists, though, were intensely frustrated by the end of the Home Rule debate. Feeling that Britain's battles had nothing to do with them, they began to see the war as an opportunity. On Easter Sunday 1916 the Irish Volunteers and Connolly's Irish Citizen Army launched the 'Easter Rising', seizing control of Dublin's General Post Office and other buildings around the city and proclaiming an independent Irish Republic. Fewer than 2,000 nationalists took part in the Rising, and the British Army had no trouble in putting it down in a few days. At first the rebels were treated with scorn by the Dublin crowds, until the British committed the huge mistake of executing their leaders. Fifteen rebel leaders, including popular figures such as Pádraic Pearse and James Connolly, were shot, and the only ones spared were Constance Markievicz, because she was a woman, and Eamon de Valera, because he was an American citizen. Making them martyrs, this had an enormous effect in outraging Irish public opinion and turning it against British rule, and created huge sympathy for the Irish revolutionaries in America.

By the time a new General Election was held at the end of the World War in 1918 Irish politics had changed entirely. Sinn Féin won a majority of Irish seats, but refused to attend the Westminster parliament and instead formed their own parliament in Dublin, the *Dáil Éireann* or Assembly of Ireland, as representatives of an independent Ireland. Eamon de Valera was made *Taoiseach* or Prime Minister, with Michael Collins as his deputy.

This amounted to a declaration of war – a bitter, bloody guerrilla war. Although Collins was officially Minister of Finance, he was also the foremost leader of the highly effective campaign of violence carried out against the British by the new Irish Republican Army (IRA). Against them were the Protestant Unionists, British soldiers, the police or Royal Irish Constabulary and a newly-formed paramilitary force, the notorious Black and Tans. Their undisciplined, uncontrolled violence became a focus for anti-British feeling in Ireland.

Did you know...?
The Irish flag was designed in the 1840s. The green symbolizes Catholics and the orange Protestants, while the white stands for peace between them.

British power over Ireland became impossible to maintain. In 1921, this war came to an end with the signing of an Anglo-Irish Treaty. This divided Ireland into half. The six Protestant-majority counties of Ulster were given the chance to opt out of the Irish state, which they duly took up. They remained part of what was now called the United Kingdom of Great Britain and Northern Ireland, but had their own regional government and Parliament at Stormont. The remaining 26 counties, or most of Ireland, became a self-governing dominion within the British Commonwealth, and was called the Irish Free State. Michael Collins and Arthur Griffith, the Dáil Vice President, agreed this compromise with Britain's Prime Minister Lloyd George, believing it essential to bring the fighting to an end. All of them, though, believed that the new province of Northern Ireland would not take root and would eventually be absorbed into the Irish Free State.

The ink was scarcely dry on this treaty when civil war broke out among Irish Nationalists, between 'Free Staters' and 'Republicans'. Hardline Republicans, led by De Valera, refused to take the oath of allegiance to the British Crown that members of the Dáil were expected to swear, as the Free State was still part of the Commonwealth. They also refused to accept partition and continued British rule in the North. They walked out of the Dáil when the majority ratified the treaty, and fighting began between former comrades. De Valera resigned as President and was imprisoned, while his supporters ambushed and murdered their former hero Michael Collins. This civil war finally ended in 1923 when De Valera called for a ceasefire, leaving much bitterness. Some IRA members still believed in fighting on for the goal of a united Ireland.

In 1926, De Valera set up a new party called Fianna Fáil, which gained power in 1932 and has been the Irish Republic's foremost political party ever since. He cut political and economic ties with Britain with a new constitution in 1937, which got rid of the oath of allegiance to the British crown, declared Ireland a sovereign state with its own President and established the use of the Irish word for Ireland, Eire, on government documents. Irish was made the national language, so that every teacher and child in state-funded schools was obliged by law to study it. Crucially, this Constitution claimed sovereignty over all of Ireland, including the six counties of the north. Eire remained neutral In the Second World War (1939–45), even though Winston Churchill tried to bring it into the war by promising immediate reunification. De Valera rejected the offer, and pulled Ireland out of the Commonwealth in 1949.

Emigration continued in the 1950s, and the Republic was a poor place. Few cars or telephones troubled it, and fewer than half its households had indoor toilets or running water. The Catholic Church played a central role in education and social policies, and kept a close eye on many other things: birth control and divorce were illegal and many books published freely elsewhere were banned, including those by Irish authors Samuel Beckett, James Joyce and Edna O'Brien. Catholics and Protestants often regarded each other with suspicion. One of the best descriptions of this time is Frank McCourt's book *Angela's Ashes*, a vivid description of his experiences in Limerick as a poor Catholic.

In the North, meanwhile, after the partition of 1921, Unionists – the usual term for Protestant supporters of the Union with Britain – moved fast to ensure that only property-owners were allowed to vote in local elections. This meant that most Catholics, who were usually poor and lived in rented houses, could not vote. In this way, Unionist councils could favour Protestants seeking employment and housing. For years, until the 1960s, this situation was ignored by Britain's governing parties, even though they held supreme authority over the six Northern Ireland counties.

Troubles in the North

In 1967, encouraged by the success of the Civil Rights movement in America, John Hume and other Catholic politicians in Northern Ireland formed the Civil Rights Association (CRA). They organized non-violent street protests about housing, jobs, exclusion from voting, policing and the other more blatant ways in which Catholics were discriminated against in Northern Ireland. The Unionist Northern Irish government at

Stormont had promised reform for years, but so far had done little, and was afraid to confront its own hardliners. These promises and the civil rights agitation, though, were enough to alarm big sections of the Protestant community, who were encouraged to believe that any concession to Catholic nationalists would threaten their whole way of life. Protestant organizations like the Orange Order revived and put pressure on the Stormont government to resist the civil rights campaign, and paramilitary groups like the Ulster Volunteer Force were secretly re-formed. The British government did nothing, missing the chance, perhaps, to avoid decades of violence.

This violence flared up during civil rights marches in 1968 and 1969. Most Northern Catholics had long had little trust in the almost completely Protestant Royal Ulster Constabulary (RUC, or Northern Irish police), and their confidence shrank more each time the RUC obstructed marchers, did nothing to protect them, or even joined in attacking them with Protestant mobs. This undermined confidence in the whole Ulster state. Wholescale violence erupted in August 1969 after the Protestant Apprentice Boys' parade to commemorate the siege of Londonderry in 1689 (*see* p.35), when barricades went up around the Catholic Bogside area of the city in an attempt to prevent the hated parade from going through the district. Rioting and street battles also spread to Belfast. The Northern Irish government was forced to admit it had lost control, and had to ask London to send in troops to restore order.

At first, the Catholic community welcomed British troops as their protectors against local Protestants and the police, but things changed as their presence and occasional heavy-handed tactics grew more obvious on their streets, and links between the British Army and the old Northern Irish state reasserted themselves. This led to the re-emergence of the IRA. It had been relatively inactive for many years and was at first split about how to respond to the civil rights campaign, but not long after the 1969 riots, a new faction gained the upper hand, the Provisional IRA or Provos, who believed violence was the best way of achieving their goal of a united Ireland. So clashes with the army and other violence escalated, and more British troops were sent in, moving events in a downward spiral. In August 1971, the British government gave the IRA another recruiting card when it accepted Unionist demands to introduce internment, or imprisonment without trial. It was claimed this would make it easier to stamp out terrorism on all sides, but nearly all the 1,600 people arrested were Catholics, and civil rights lawyers accused the British government of mistreating and torturing internees.

On 30 January 1972, a march demanding the end of internment was held in the Bogside area of Londonderry. When the crowd reached army barricades, stones were thrown, to which the soldiers responded with rubber bullets and water-cannon. Then firing began, and 13 civilians were killed. This event, known as Bloody Sunday, hugely boosted recruitment to the IRA and pushed the conflict to new depths. The British Army have said they were fired on first, but the marchers have denied this. In 2003, an official inquiry was still investigating the incident.

After Bloody Sunday, the Northern Irish parliament was closed and Northern Ireland was placed under direct rule from Westminster, but violence continued. At around the same time, the IRA began a bombing campaign, in Britain and Ulster. Hardline Protestants, meanwhile – who, despite being known as 'Loyalists', never trusted the British government to protect them – expanded their own paramilitary squads like the UVF and UDA (Ulster Defence Association), occassionally launching savage violence from their side against the IRA.

For years the conflict went on, with no visible end but occasional dramatic events, such as in 1981, when IRA prisoners in the Maze prison went on hunger strike to demand to be treated as political prisoners. The British government of Margaret Thatcher did not give way, and when the hunger strikers' leader, Bobby Sands, died, 50,000 people attended his funeral. Although Sands was unable to take his seat when elected to parliament thereafter, it played a part in causing Provisional IRA leaders to think they could succeed politically rather than through continued violence.

And, despite the violence, politicians in Dublin, London and Northern Ireland continued to search for a peaceful solution. In 1985, the governments of Britain and the Irish Republic signed the Anglo-Irish Agreement, which gave Dublin a consulting role in Northern Irish affairs. Northern Irish Protestants expressed outrage and there was an upsurge of violence and paramilitary activity on the Loyalist side, but nevertheless tentative moves towards a real peace process had begun.

In the 1993 Downing Street Declaration the British government stated that it had 'no selfish, strategic or economic interest in Northern Ireland', but assured Unionists that their consent would be required for any constitutional change. In August 1994 the IRA announced a ceasefire, and Loyalist groups announced their own shortly afterwards. The big breakthrough only came, though, after May 1997, when the landslide election victory that brought Tony Blair to power in Britain freed the British government to push peace negotiations in Northern Ireland to the top of the agenda.

The talks that followed produced the Good Friday Agreement in 1998. A major breakthrough on the road to a peaceful settlement, it provided for no change in the status of the North except by majority consent; the devolution of a variety of powers to a Northern Ireland Assembly; a North-South Ministerial Council between Northern Ireland and the Republic; and a British-Irish Council that would include representatives from other parts of the British Isles. The Constitution of the the Irish Republic would also be amended to renounce its territorial claim to Northern Ireland. A referendum held in both parts of Ireland endorsed this agreement on 22 May 1998. Since then, Irish politics have been dominated by the difficulties of implementing the Good Friday Agreement. Northern Ireland remains a deeply divided society, and there have been many hurdles and crises along the way. But 2003 was the most peaceful year in Northern Ireland since the 1960s, and the outlines of a non-violent future can at last be seen.

A Modern Place

While the North was entangled in its problems, society in the rest of Ireland had finally begun to change in the 1960s. TV, radio and cinema brought images of a wider world into Irish society, and began to change its long-held customs and habits, including its storytelling and music-making traditions. In 1972 the Irish Republic, like Britain, became a member of the European Community (later renamed the European Union). In 1973 Eamon de Valera, a symbol of an old-fashioned Ireland, finally left office as President, and he died two years later.

Ireland began to take on a new persona. While previously – despite its apparent independence – it had remained dependent on Britain, EU membership opened it up to an international economy. Grants of all kinds from the EU flooded in, and were added to tax incentives offered to foreign investors by the Irish government. The aim was to industrialize an economy still dominated by agriculture. And in the 1990s Ireland exploded, with the years of its so-called 'Celtic Tiger' economy. A media-based, international style of work and living, fuelled by new technology, from TV to computers and mobile phones, was energetically encouraged by business and government. Irish expatriates returned from countries like the United States with new ideas, 'blow-ins' arrived from other parts of the world to work in hotels and on farms, and Ireland even began to attract immigrants itself, often refugees from eastern Europe or Africa.

With all these changes came a new openness in Irish society. In 1990 a woman, the lawyer and champion of liberal causes Mary Robinson, was elected President. The political problems in the North had repercussions in the South, where people began to reassess their history, religion, and society. Joint British and Irish membership of the European Union, prosperity and secularization have done much to change sectarian attitudes, and smoothed the way in the south for the acceptance of the Good Friday Agreement. The Catholic Church was rocked by scandals, and its hold over society weakened. Although birth control and abortion are still hotly debated, divorce was legalized in 1995.

In January 2002 the Republic adopted the Euro, cementing its involvement with Europe and separateness from Britain. With modernization, industrialization, car-based transport and the intensification of influences from alien cultures have come new dangers that the Republic must address. It is now part of Europe, and looking outward at a more expansive universe. Although this new status exposes Ireland to many good things, it shouldn't be forgotten that the door is also open to the bad. Not only are Ireland's old religious and political ideas wavering, but at times it can seem too that some of the most valuable things in its special character are under threat – its beautiful countryside, its children, its old people, the uniqueness of its traditions and of Irish people.

However, the complex history of this small island might just have given its inhabitants a special perspective that could lead them to avoid the mistakes of others. The Republic's new status in the world is likely to draw Northern Ireland into a different future, if nothing else does. What kind of future that will be, it is time for the Irish to decide.

Some Names in Irish History

Gerry Adams (born 1948). Leader of Sinn Féin and a key figure in the Northern Ireland peace process.

Black Pig's Dyke A long earthwork wall that is thought to have been a series of massive defences guarding routes into Ulster. Folktales say an enchanted boar ploughed it up with his tusks.

Brian Boru (942–1014). The only High King of all Ireland, murdered on the day he won the crown, after winning the Battle of Clontarf. His castle was at Kincora on the Clare-Tipperary border.

Sir Edward Carson (1854–1935). Unionist leader and Protestant lawyer from Dublin who led the Ulster opposition to Home Rule in 1912–14.

Michael Collins (1889–1922). Organized and led the IRA in a guerrilla war against the British, 1918–22, and then signed the treaty that partitioned Ireland, which led to Ireland's Civil War, during which he was killed in an ambush in Co. Cork.

St Columcille, or **Colum Cille**, **Colmcille** or **Columba** (521–97). The 'Dove of the Church', a prince of the O'Neills of Donegal who became Ireland's greatest native saint, and founded the famous monastery on the Scottish island of Iona.

James Connolly (1868–1916). Key leader of the 1916 Easter Rising; born to Irish immigrants in Scotland, he returned to organize Ireland's trade unions.

Oliver Cromwell (1599–1658). English general and leader of the Parliamentarians who crushed the Irish rebellion in 1649 with notorious brutality.

Michael Davitt (1846–1906). Founder of the Land League, to fight for the rights of tenant farmers.

Eamon De Valera (1882–1975). The dominant figure in Irish politics for 50 years, he was born in America to a Spanish father and an Irish mother. He was Prime Minister of the Republic 1932–48 and 1951–4, and President 1959–1973.

Eóghan Mór Semi-mythical High King of Munster's Eóghanachta dynasty, who died in the late second century of the Christian era.

Eóghanacht or **Eóghanachta** Kings of Munster with a seat at Cashel, descended from King Conall Corc. They eventually lost power to Brian Boru.

William Ewart Gladstone (1809–98). British Liberal statesman and many-times Prime Minister who gave strong support to Home Rule for Ireland.

Lady Augusta Gregory (1852–1932). Benefactress of the Irish Literary Renaissance, who founded Dublin's Abbey Theatre in Dublin with WB Yeats and wrote many books on Irish myths and folklore.

John Hume (born 1937). Northern Irish Catholic leader from Derry who led the non-violent nationalist Social Democratic and Labour Party (SDLP).

Constance Markievicz (1868–1927). Born into the Anglo-Irish Gore-Booth family, she married a Polish Count, and became an Irish Nationalist and socialist. She took part in the Easter Rising and was the first woman elected to the British Parliament, although she did not take her seat.

Daniel O'Connell (1775–1847). Lawyer from Co. Kerry known as 'the Liberator' after his successful campaign for voting and other rights for Catholics.

Hugh O'Neill (16–17th c.). Earl of Tyrone and the last of Ireland's powerful Gaelic lords, who led resitance to Elizabeth I in the 1590s, until he left for Europe in the 'Flight of the Earls' in 1607.

Pádraic Pearse (1879–1916). Poet, teacher and promoter of the Irish language who led the 1916 Easter Rising.

Rev. Ian Paisley (b. 1927). Presbyterian minister who has been an outspoken leader of hardline Unionism in Northern Ireland and founder and leader of the Democratic Unionist Party (DUP).

Charles Stewart Parnell (1846–91). Anglo-Irish Protestant landowner who led the 1880s campaign for Irish Home Rule.

St Patrick (5th c.). Patron saint of Ireland, who is credited with converting the Irish to Christianity.

Strongbow (12th c.). Earl of Pembroke, a Norman warrior who was the first Anglo-Norman to gain power in Ireland in 1169–71.

Jonathan Swift (1667–1745). Dublin Protestant cleric and writer, and author of *Gulliver's Travels*.

David Trimble (b. 1944). Leader of the Ulster Unionist Party and head of Northern Ireland's regional government.

Wolfe Tone (1763–98). Protestant lawyer who sought support from Revolutionary France for Irish independence, and led the 1798 Rebellion.

Oscar Wilde (1854–1900). Notorious, extravagant Anglo-Irish dramatist, novelist, poet and wit.

William of Orange (1650–1702). Dutch Protestant prince who threw out Britain's Catholic king James II in 1688 and replaced him as King William III. He became a hero for Ulster Protestants after defeating James II at the Battle of the Boyne.

William Butler (WB) Yeats (1865–1939). Great Anglo-Irish poet and Nobel prizewinner, and a champion of Irish folklore. most associated with Counties Sligo and Galway.

Dublin

03

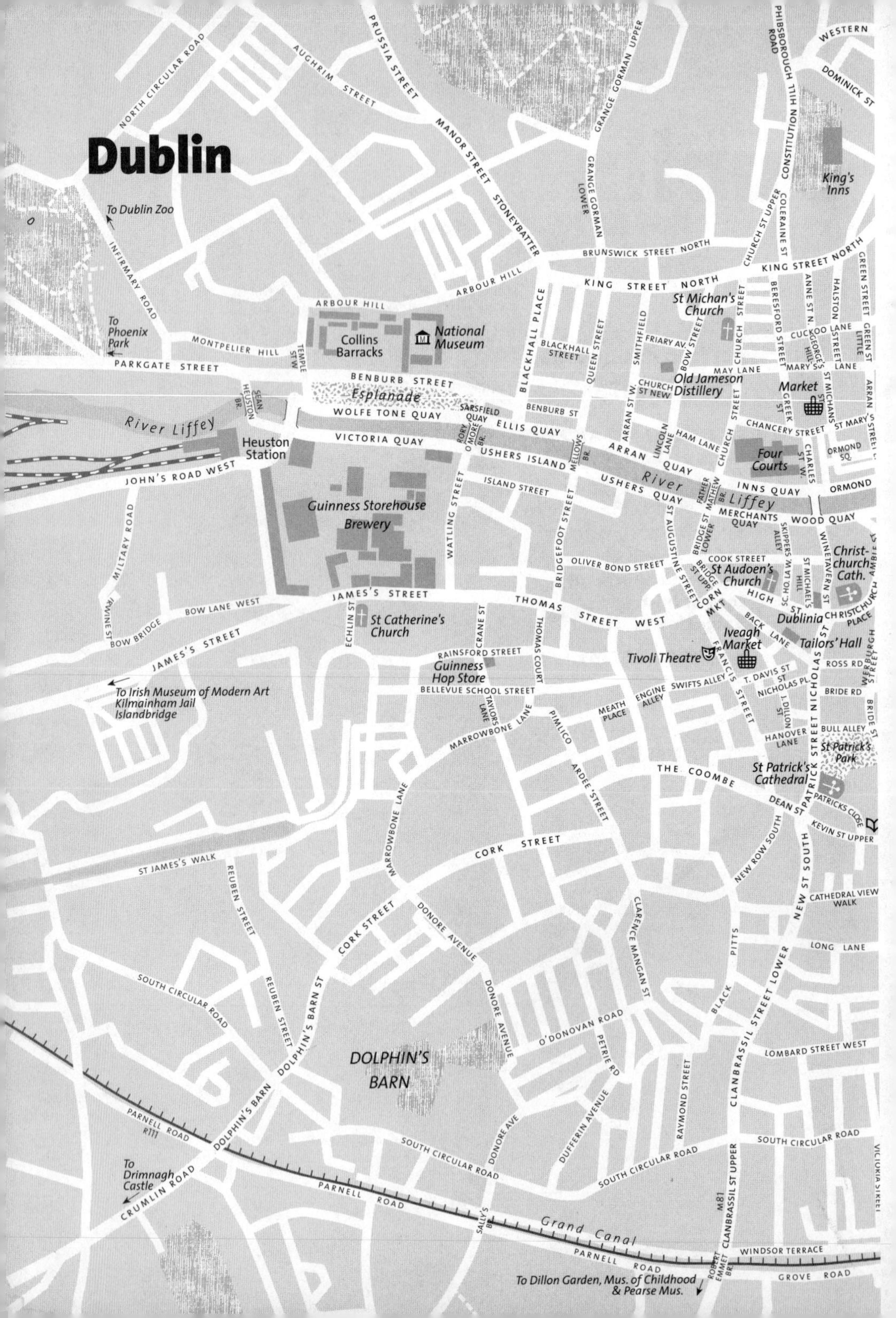
Dublin
To Dublin Zoo
To Phoenix Park
To Irish Museum of Modern Art
Kilmainham Jail
Islandbridge
To Drimnagh Castle
To Dillon Garden, Mus. of Childhood & Pearse Mus.
Collins Barracks
National Museum
Esplanade
River Liffey
Heuston Station
Guinness Storehouse Brewery
St Catherine's Church
Guinness Hop Store
St Michan's Church
Old Jameson Distillery
Market
King's Inns
Four Courts
St Audoen's Church
Christchurch Cath.
Dublinia
Tailors' Hall
Iveagh Market
Tivoli Theatre
St Patrick's Park
St Patrick's Cathedral
DOLPHIN'S BARN
Grand Canal
NORTH CIRCULAR ROAD
INFIRMARY ROAD
AUGHRIM STREET
PRUSSIA STREET
MANOR STREET
STONEYBATTER
GRANGE GORMAN UPPER
GRANGE GORMAN LOWER
PHIBSBOROUGH ROAD
CONSTITUTION HILL
WESTERN
DOMINICK ST
CHURCH ST UPPER
COLERAINE ST
BRUNSWICK STREET NORTH
KING STREET NORTH
ARBOUR HILL
MONTPELIER HILL
TEMPLE STW
PARKGATE STREET
BENBURB STREET
SEAN HEUSTON BR.
WOLFE TONE QUAY
SARSFIELD QUAY
ELLIS QUAY
BENBURB ST
BLACKHALL PLACE
BLACKHALL STREET
QUEEN STREET
SMITHFIELD
FRIARY AV.
BOW STREET
CHURCH STREET
CHURCH ST NEW
ARRAN ST W.
MAY LANE
MARY'S LANE
CUCKOO LANE
LITTLE GREEN STREET
HALSTON STREET
ANNE ST N.
GEORGE'S HILL
BERESFORD STREET
GREEK ST
ST MICHANS ST
ARRAN ST
CHANCERY STREET
ST MARY'S ABBEY
ORMOND SQ.
VICTORIA QUAY
RORY O'MORE BR.
USHERS ISLAND
MELLOWS BR.
ARRAN QUAY
LINCOLN LANE
HAM LANE
CHURCH ST
CHARLES ST W.
INNS QUAY
ORMOND
FATHER MATHEW BR.
USHERS QUAY
MERCHANTS QUAY
WOOD QUAY
JOHN'S ROAD WEST
ISLAND STREET
WATLING STREET
BRIDGEFOOT STREET
ST AUGUSTINE STREET
BRIDGE ST LOWER
SKIPPERS ALLEY
WINETAVERN ST
OLIVER BOND STREET
COOK STREET
BRIDGE ST UPR
FISHAMBLE ST
ST MICHAEL'S HILL
CHRISTCHURCH PLACE
MILITARY ROAD
IRWINE ST
BOW LANE WEST
BOW BRIDGE
JAMES'S STREET
THOMAS STREET WEST
ECHLIN ST
CRANE ST
THOMAS COURT
CORN MKT
HIGH ST
BACK LANE
WERBURGH ST
RAINSFORD STREET
FRANCIS STREET
T. DAVIS ST
ST NICHOLAS PL.
ROSS RD
BRIDE RD
BELLEVUE SCHOOL STREET
TAYLORS LANE
MEATH PLACE
ENGINE ALLEY
SWIFTS ALLEY
J. DILLON ST
BRIDE ST
NICHOLAS ST
BULL ALLEY
HANOVER LANE
PATRICK STREET
MARROWBONE LANE
PIMLICO
ARDEE STREET
THE COOMBE
DEAN ST
PATRICKS CLOSE
KEVIN ST UPPER
NEW ROW SOUTH
NEW ST SOUTH
CORK STREET
ST JAMES'S WALK
REUBEN STREET
DONORE AVENUE
CLARENCE MANGAN ST
CATHEDRAL VIEW WALK
LONG LANE
BLACK PITTS
CLANBRASSIL STREET LOWER
SOUTH CIRCULAR ROAD
DOLPHIN'S BARN ST
O'DONOVAN ROAD
PETRIE RD
LOMBARD STREET WEST
RAYMOND STREET
DUFFERIN AVENUE
DONORE AVE
PARNELL ROAD
R111
DOLPHIN'S BARN
CRUMLIN ROAD
SALLY'S BR.
M81
CLANBRASSIL ST UPPER
VICTORIA STREET
WINDSOR TERRACE
GROVE ROAD
ROBERT EMMET BR.

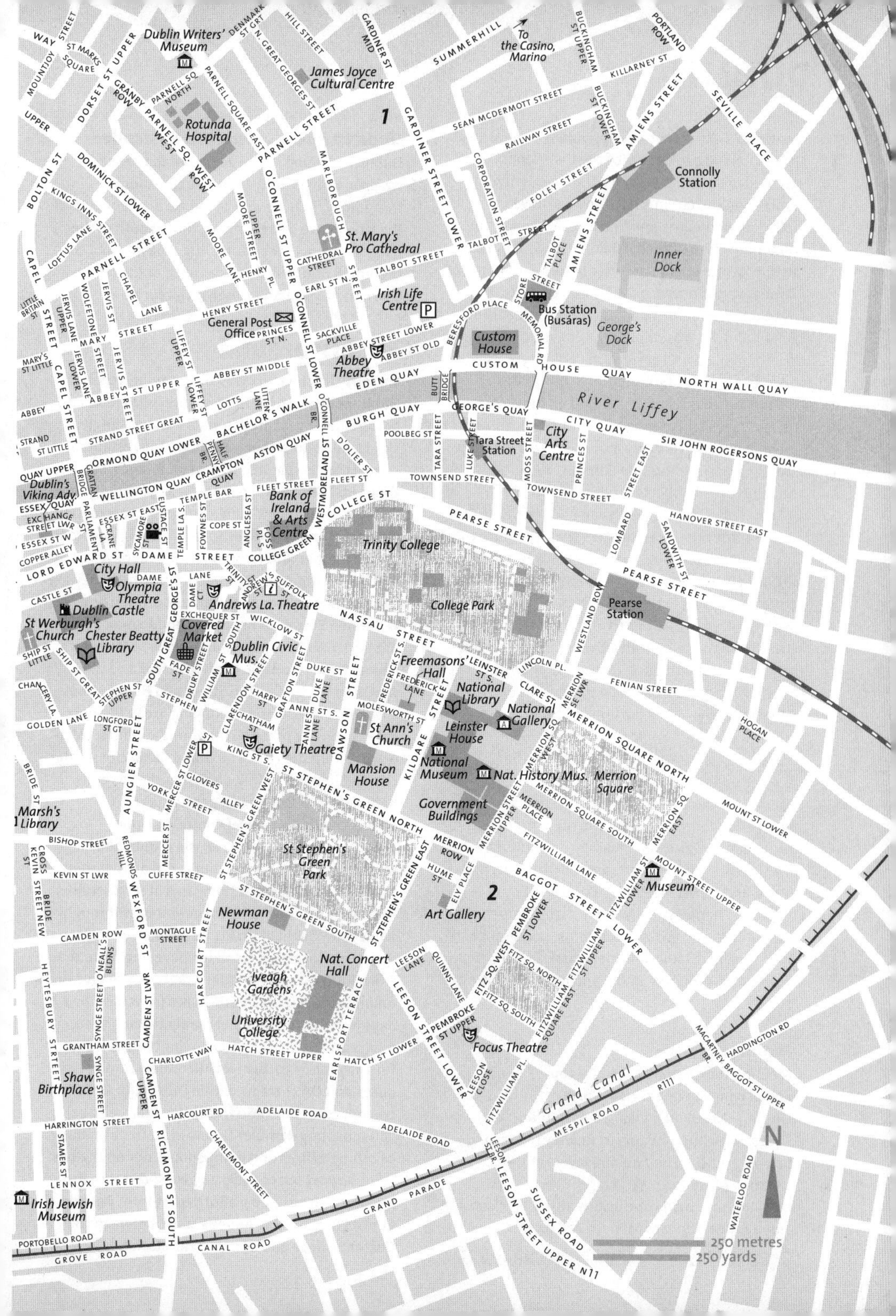
Dublin Writers' Museum
James Joyce Cultural Centre
To the Casino, Marino
1
Rotunda Hospital
Connolly Station
St. Mary's Pro Cathedral
Inner Dock
Irish Life Centre
Bus Station (Busáras)
General Post Office
Custom House
George's Dock
Abbey Theatre
River Liffey
Tara Street Station
City Arts Centre
Dublin's Viking Adv.
Bank of Ireland & Arts Centre
Trinity College
City Hall
Olympia Theatre
Andrews La. Theatre
College Park
Pearse Station
Dublin Castle
St Werburgh's Church
Chester Beatty Library
Covered Market
Dublin Civic Mus.
Freemasons' Hall
National Library
National Gallery
Leinster House
St Ann's Church
Gaiety Theatre
National Museum
Nat. History Mus.
Merrion Square
Mansion House
Government Buildings
Marsh's Library
St Stephen's Green Park
Museum
2
Art Gallery
Newman House
Nat. Concert Hall
Iveagh Gardens
University College
Focus Theatre
Shaw Birthplace
Grand Canal
Irish Jewish Museum
N
250 metres
250 yards
SUMMERHILL
PARNELL STREET
O'CONNELL ST UPPER
O'CONNELL ST LOWER
GARDINER STREET LOWER
AMIENS STREET
SEVILLE PLACE
TALBOT STREET
HENRY STREET
MARY STREET
ABBEY STREET LOWER
ABBEY ST MIDDLE
CAPEL STREET
EDEN QUAY
CUSTOM HOUSE QUAY
NORTH WALL QUAY
BACHELOR'S WALK
BURGH QUAY
GEORGE'S QUAY
CITY QUAY
SIR JOHN ROGERSONS QUAY
ORMOND QUAY LOWER
WELLINGTON QUAY
ASTON QUAY
D'OLIER ST
WESTMORELAND ST
COLLEGE ST
PEARSE STREET
TOWNSEND STREET
FLEET STREET
TEMPLE BAR
DAME STREET
LORD EDWARD ST
NASSAU STREET
GRAFTON STREET
DAWSON STREET
KILDARE STREET
MOLESWORTH ST
CLARE ST
MERRION SQUARE NORTH
MERRION SQUARE SOUTH
MOUNT ST LOWER
SOUTH GREAT GEORGE'S ST
AUNGIER STREET
WEXFORD ST
CAMDEN ST LWR
RICHMOND ST SOUTH
HARCOURT STREET
ST STEPHEN'S GREEN NORTH
ST STEPHEN'S GREEN SOUTH
ST STEPHEN'S GREEN EAST
ST STEPHEN'S GREEN WEST
BAGGOT STREET LOWER
MERRION ROW
FITZWILLIAM LANE
LEESON STREET LOWER
EARLSFORT TERRACE
HATCH STREET UPPER
ADELAIDE ROAD
HARCOURT RD
CHARLEMONT STREET
GRAND PARADE
MESPIL ROAD
LEESON STREET UPPER N11
SUSSEX ROAD
WATERLOO ROAD
BAGGOT ST UPPER
HADDINGTON RD
CANAL ROAD
GROVE ROAD
PORTOBELLO ROAD
LENNOX STREET
HARRINGTON STREET
HEYTESBURY STREET
SYNGE STREET
CAMDEN ROW
KEVIN ST LWR
BISHOP STREET
CUFFE STREET
YORK STREET
GOLDEN LANE
WICKLOW ST
DUKE ST
SUFFOLK ST
PARLIAMENT ST
ESSEX QUAY
WESTLAND ROW
LOMBARD STREET EAST
HANOVER STREET EAST
FENIAN STREET
FITZWILLIAM ST UPPER
PEMBROKE ST LOWER
MOUNT STREET UPPER
R111

Always a city for the young, Dublin is the largest city in Ireland and capital of the Irish Republic. Located in its busiest county, Dublin is where the ambitious and curious have always moved to follow their dreams and find jobs. No longer the dreaming town of Molly Malone, today it bursts with youthful energy as never before. This home of James Joyce is now that of U2 and Westlife.

A short ferry journey across the Irish Sea from Britain, Dublin was originally a convenient trading port on the island's eastern coast. Today it still absorbs all sorts of international influences.

Dublin's suburbs have gobbled up most of the little villages and green spaces north, south, and west of the city. This area, now defined as County Dublin, was once the sole domain of Anglo-Irish and British control in Ireland, called 'the Pale'.

Dublin divides into northside and southside, either side of the River Liffey. In the city centre the northern and southern halves are linked by O'Connell Bridge across the river. You can walk through the whole of central Dublin easily, even with children in tow. North of the Liffey, running away from the bridge with the same name, is the city's broadest and busiest street, O'Connell Street. Further out are the old, congested areas of Marino, Clontarf, Dollymount, Sutton and Howth.

South of the Liffey are some of old Dublin's most attractive areas, with pub-filled Temple Bar, Trinity College and the lovely St Stephen's Green. Beyond them, past the wealthy Ballsbridge neighbourhood, the suburbs south of the river through Dun Laoghaire to Dalkey and Killiney – all linked by the DART local train, *see* p.47 – are full of writers and pop stars like Maeve Binchy, Bono and Enya. Whatever happens to Ireland usually happens to Dublin first, and years of economic boom since the 1990s have certainly left their mark. Children will find Dublin's mixture of old and new fascinating.

Highlights

Meeting the animals at Dublin zoo and playing in Phoenix Park, p.58
Getting soaked on a Viking Splash Tour, p.48
Cakes and a bit of history at Bewley's Café, p.62
Pressing buttons and pulling levers at the Dublinia Museum, p.53
Drawing your own conclusions at the Hugh Lane Gallery of Modern Art, p.51

Good to know... Dublin's Postcodes

Dublin is divided into several postcode zones, which are given with all the Dublin addresses in this guide (as D1, D2 and so on). Postcodes north of the Liffey have **odd** numbers; those south of the river are **even**. In the centre, the area north of the O'Connell Bridge is Dublin 1; south of the river down to St Stephen's Green is Dublin 2.

Getting around

On foot The cheapest way to get around central Dublin is by walking. The 2 square miles (6 sq km) around the River Liffey contain most of the city's sights, museums, theatres, shops and restaurants.

The Liffey is spanned by several bridges, but **O'Connell Bridge** is the main focus of activity (and bus routes). Dublin's most engaging river crossing is the **Halfpenny Bridge**, a graceful iron pedestrian bridge built in 1816 (and you no longer have to pay a halfpenny to cross it). Streets lining the Liffey are called quays, and change names between bridges. **O'Connell Street, Henry Street** and **Parnell Square** are north of O'Connell Bridge, while **St Stephen's Green, Trinity College, Grafton Street** and the **Castle** lie south. Grafton Street and **Henry Street** are popular pedestrian shopping areas. **Phoenix Park** is about 2 miles (3km) from the centre, westwards along the river. The **Grand Canal** crosses the city and joins the Liffey, enclosing the southern half of central Dublin in a gentle curve.

By bus Dublin Bus Travel Centre, 59 Upper O'Connell St, **t** (01) 873 4222, **www**.dublinbus.ie Most of Dublin Bus's 150 routes run daily 7am–12 midnight, and at night there are Nitelink services. Fares vary by how many zones you pass through; adult fares begin at €0.80, but under-16s travel up to 7 zones for €0.50. Good for travelling more than a few journeys are **Rambler** tickets, which give unlimited travel on Dublin buses from 1 (€5) to 7 days (€17.50); the Rambler **family ticket** gives 2 adults and up to 4 children unlimited bus travel for 1 day for €7.50. **Bus+Rail Ramblers** combine city buses and DART trains within Dublin, for €7.70 (1 person, 1 day) or €11.60 (1-day family ticket, 2+4). You must buy Rambler tickets in advance (in bus or tourist offices and many shops), not on the bus.

For **Airport** buses, *see* p.283. Long-distance **Bus Eireann** coaches (*see* p.286) depart from **Busáras** Central Bus Station, Amiens St, D1, between the Custom House and Connolly rail station.

By train DART, Iarnród Éireann, **t** 1 850 366 222, **www**.irishrail.ie/dart

DART (Dublin Area Rapid Transit) local trains run around Dublin Bay through 25 stations from Greystones and Bray, just inside Co. Wicklow in the south, through the city and north to Howth, with 4 trains an hour in each direction, daily about 6am–11pm. A single fare from Dublin to Dalkey, for example, is €2; for under-15s it's €1, and under-3s travel free. One-day unlimited-travel DART tickets cost €6.50 (per person) or €11 (family, 2+4), but Bus+Rail tickets (*see* left, **By bus**) are more useful.

Dublin's mainline stations are **Heuston**, at the west end of the river quays, for trains to the west and south, and **Connolly**, northeast of the centre, for the east coast and Northern Ireland (*see* p.288).

By taxi Ranks are found outside hotels and railway stations, in special taxi parks in central Dublin, and on St Stephen's Green and O'Connell Street; they are often hard to flag down in the street. They charge extra per piece of luggage and at night.

Blue Cabs, **t** (01) 676 1111
Metro Cabs, **t** (01) 668 3333/478 1111/677 2222

By car Parking is difficult in the city centre. Main car parks are in Frederick Street and the St Stephen's Green Shopping Centre, and there is metered parking around St Stephen's Green and Merrion Square. North of the river there's additional parking in the Irish Life Shopping Centre (Lower Abbey Street). Driving in Dublin is disordered, so be on your guard. Using your horn is the worst insult, so keep it as a last resort. Car theft and burglaries are increasing, so check whether a hotel has secure parking when booking.

Car hire at the airport
AVIS, Dublin Airport, **t** (01) 605 7500
Budget Rent A Car, Dublin Airport **t** (01) 844 5150
Murrays Europcar, Baggot Street Bridge, **t** (01) 614 2800; Dublin Airport, **t** (01) 812 0410

Bike Hire
The Bike Store Ltd, 58 Gardiner Street, D1, **t** (01) 872 5399
Dublin Bike Hire, 27 North Great George's Street, D2, **t** (01) 878 8473
Harding for Bicycles
30 Bachelors Walk, D1, **t** (01) 873 2455

Special Events and Festivals

Feb–March

Six Nations Rugby Lansdowne Road Stadium, Lansdowne Road, Ballsbridge, D4, **t** (01) 668 4601

Held over several Saturdays at Lansdowne Road.

March

St Patrick's Day Festival
Information **t** (01) 676 3205, **www**.stpatricksday.ie

Celebrations, music and parades start on O'Connell Street, on and around 17 March.

April

Convergence Festival, **t** (01) 677 2255

Green, healthy and ethical living is celebrated in Temple Bar.

May

Heineken Green Energy International Music Festival, **t** (01) 456 9569

Past headliners include the Cranberries.

June

Bloomsday Festival, Information: James Joyce Centre, **t** (01) 878 8547, **www**.jamesjoyce.ie

Dublin's peculiar holiday on 16 June, anniversary of the day (in 1904) when all the action in James Joyce's *Ulysses* takes place. Various events are held in places visited by the fictional Leopold Bloom.

AIB Music in Great Irish Houses, 1st Floor, Blackrock Post Office, Blackrock, Co. Dublin, **t** (01) 278 1528

A 10-day festival of chamber music performed in mansions in Cos. Dublin, Wicklow and Kildare.

July

Dublin Jazz Festival, **t** (01) 670 3885

Week-long music at a number of Dublin venues.

August

Kerrygold Horse Show, RDS, D4, **t** (01) 668 0866

International equestrian event in Ballsbridge that's an annual date for horse-lovers.

September

All-Ireland Hurling and Gaelic Football Finals, Croke Park, **t** (01) 836 3222

Check out the local sports in action.

Dublin Fringe Theatre Festival, **t** (01) 872 9433, **www**.fringefest.com

A vibrant event for theatre fans.

International Puppetry Festival, **t** (01) 280 0974

Children who like puppets will love this.

October

Dublin Theatre Festival, **t** (01) 877 8434
Dublin City Marathon, **t** (01) 670 7918
Samhain Halloween Festival, **t** (01) 855 7154

All kinds of events take place around 31 October.

On tour: Dublin Tours

Bus tours

Dublin Bus 59 Upper O'Connell St, D1, **t** (01) 873 4222, **www**.dublinbus.ie

City tours depart daily, every 10 mins 9.30–5, every 30 mins 5–6.30pm. **Tickets** Adult €12.50; under-14s €6; students, over-65s €11

The city bus company offers handy 'hop-on, hop-off' daily tours, beginning at its O'Connell St office and going on a circular route around all Dublin's main sites. The full tour lasts 1hr 15 mins, but each ticket is valid for 24 hrs, so you can get on and get off the bus as many times as you like the same day. Ticket-holders also get discounts on admission to a range of attractions. Tickets can be bought on the bus or at Dublin Bus offices or Dublin Tourism, Suffolk Street. A good introduction to Dublin.

Dublin Bus also offers nightly **Ghost Bus Tours** around haunted houses and other places to do with the city's more ghoulish history (Mon–Fri 8pm, Sat, Sun 7.30, 9.30pm; €22). Fun for teenagers, but they're not intended for younger children. For tours to places outside Dublin city, *see* below.

Irish City Tours 33-34 Bachelor's Walk, D1, **t** (01) 872 9010, **www**.irishcitytours.com

Dublin City Tours depart from 12 Upper O'Connell St, D1, daily every 15 mins April–14 July and Oct 9.30–5; 15 July–Sept 9.30–5.30; Nov–Mar 9.30–4. **Tickets** Adult €14; under-12s €5; students, over-65s €12; family ticket (2 adults, up to 3 children) €35

Similar 'hop-on, hop-off' tours, passing all the main sights and lasting (the full tour) 90 mins. Again, tickets are valid 24 hrs, and ticket-holders get discounts on admission to many attractions.

The Viking Splash Tour 64–65 Patrick St, D8, **t** (01) 855 3000, **www**.vikingsplashtours.com

Tours run mid-Feb–Nov; check for current times. **Tickets** Mar–Jun (Mon–Fri) and Sept–Nov daily, adult €13.95, under-13s €7.95, family (2+3) €47; Mar–Jun (Sat, Sun) and Jul–Aug daily adult €15.95, under-13s €8.85, family (2+3) €50

This tour starts from Bull Alley, by St. Patrick's Cathedral, but tickets can be bought from tourist offices. Witty, costumed tour captains, aka 'Viking chieftains', settle you on board a reconditioned vintage-World War II amphibious vehicle (a 'Duck') to teach you about how Dublin natives behave. You are instructed in Viking customs (goats make a good tip for your Viking host) and behaviour – like roaring at passers-by as loud as you can, while throwing your arms in the air. Then your Viking chieftain drives you through the streets, pointing out all sorts of historical facts about the city. At the Grand Canal Basin docks you don lifejackets, before the 'Duck' drives into the water and proves its other function as a boat. Children under age 2 must leave the bus for this part of the tour, which takes 20mins. Afterwards you return to Bull Alley. Advance booking is very advisable in summer.

Guided walking tours

Signposts have been put up around the city to guide you to historical sites. The 'trails' include: Georgian, Cultural, Old City and 'Rock 'n' Stroll'. Dublin Tourism in Suffolk St has details. Several guided walking tours are also on offer, such as:

Historical Walking Tour of Dublin 64 Mary St, D1, **t** (01) 878 0227, **www**.historicalinsights.ie

Tours Oct–Apr, Fri, Sat, Sun 12 noon; May–Sept daily 11, 12 noon, 3pm. **Tickets** €10

Assemble at the front gate of Trinity College to be met by a knowledgeable guide.

Tours from Dublin City

Dublin Bus 59 Upper O'Connell St, D1, **t** (01) 873 4222, **www**.dublinbus.ie

As well as its city tours (*see* above) Dublin Bus offers 3 daily bus tours, of 3–5 hrs each, to areas nearby: the 'Coast and Castle' tour (north Co. Dublin, Malahide, Howth), the 'South Coast' tour (Dun Laoghaire down the coast to Bray, and back through the Wicklow Mountains), and 'City and Ballykissangel' tour, combining the City tour and a train trip to the Wicklow Mountains.

Irish City Tours 33-34 Bachelor's Walk, D1, **t** (01) 872 9010, **www**.irishcitytours.com

Also has one-day tours: Powerscourt, Malahide, Wicklow, Newgrange, Kilkenny.

Legendary Tours, www.legendarytours.com

Storyteller Richard Marsh takes tours of countryside sites in Leinster, departing from Dublin at 8–9am, and returning 4–5pm. Wellies are provided as needed. Not recommended for under 10s.

Over the Top Tours, www.overthetoptours.com

A small operation with 1-day small-group tours (maximum 14 people), departing daily at around 9am from outside the Dublin Tourism office in Suffolk St, on two main routes: the 'Celtic Experience' (Boyne Valley, Tara) and the Wicklow Mountains. Also longer trips to Connemara, Cork and Kerry. Not suitable for small children.

Tourist information

Dublin Tourism Centre, St Andrew's Church, Suffolk Street, D2, **t** (01) 605 7700, information line **t** 1 850 230 330, **www**.visitdublin.com
Open Sept–June Mon–Sat 9–5.30, Sun (Sept only) 10.30–3; July–Aug Mon–Sat 9–7, Sun 10.30–3.
Dublin's excellent main tourist office occupies a restored former church near Trinity College, by the top of Grafton Street. Its many facilities include information desks for the whole of Ireland as well as Dublin city, accommodation information and bookings of all sorts (hotels, B&Bs, hostels), bus and DART ticket sales, car hire, bus tour and theatre bookings, currency exchange, a café and a souvenir and gift shop. Dublin Tourism also has five more information offices:
Dublin Airport Arrivals Hall, **Open** daily 8–10
Dun Laoghaire Ferry Terminal,
Open Mon–Sat 10–1, 2–6
14 Upper O'Connell St, D1, **Open** Mon–Sat 9–5
Baggot Street Bridge (south of the centre, by the Grand Canal), D2, **Open** Mon–Sat 9.30–12, 12.30–5
The Square, Tallaght, D24, **Open** Mon–Sat 9.30–12, 12.30–5

Shopping

The old song 'In Dublin's Fair City', with the line 'cockles and mussels alive alive o', is about a 19th-century fish-seller called Molly Malone, who used to sell her wares on Moore Street. Today you'll still find street-sellers in this area, near Henry Street and the landmark department store of Clery's on O'Connell Street. This is Dublin's most traditional shopping area for basics, where things tend to be a bit cheaper; modern Dublin's prettiest, most varied and most fashionable shopping zone, though, is south of the Liffey around Grafton Street.

Fancy a souvenir?

For something in Irish tweed and for high-quality craft design, head for Nassau Street, on the south side of Trinity College, where you will also find souvenir shops, or explore the area west of Grafton Street and discover Avoca with its wholefood café. Among these winding streets is the **Powerscourt Townhouse Shopping Centre** (South William Street, D2), in a beautiful Georgian building, with inviting cafés and **Fresh** vegetarian restaurant (*see* p.63).

On Grafton Street itself there are branches of British chains like Jigsaw or Monsoon, along with the Harrod's of Ireland, Brown Thomas. If you are in Dublin at Christmas time don't miss its window display. At the bottom end of Grafton Street is the huge St. Stephen's Green Shopping Centre, with a branch of Mothercare, if you're in need of nursery accessories.

Avoca Handweavers

11–13 Suffolk St, D2, **t** (01) 677 4215

A showcase for the lovely handwoven woollens and tweeds – for kids and adults – made at Avoca in Co. Wicklow (*see* p.74). Also craft-made Irish cosmetics, foods and other things, and a great café.

Claddagh Records

2 Cecilia St, D2, **t** (01) 677 0262, **www**.claddaghrecords.com

All kinds of traditional Irish and folk music.

Cleo

18 Kildare St, D2, **t** (01) 676 1421, **www**.cleo-ltd.com

A small company with original Irish handmade woollens, including great things for kids.

Down to Earth

73 South Great Georges St, D2, **t** (01) 671 9702

Health foods of all kinds.

Eason's

40–42 Lower O'Connell St, D1, **t** (01) 858 3800, **www**.easons.ie

The flagship store of Ireland's largest bookshop chain has all kinds of books for adults and children, and massive magazine and stationery sections.

Hughes and Hughes

St Stephen's Green Shopping Centre, D2, **t** (01) 478 3060, **www**.hughesbooks.com

An attractive modern bookstore with an especially ample children's section, which hosts regular special events.

Magill's

14 Clarendon St, D2, **t** (01) 671 3830

A wonderful old-fashioned food store smelling of charcuterie and sourdough breads.

Can you spot... The Halfpenny Bridge?
It's across the River Liffey, just west of O'Connell Bridge – the next (arched) bridge down the river. It was first built by an Englishman in 1816, when you had to pay a halfpenny to walk across it.

THINGS TO SEE AND DO

North of the Liffey

Dublin Writers' Museum

18 Parnell Square North, D1, **t** (01) 872 2077
Getting there 5 mins walk from the north end of O'Connell Street and 15 mins. walk from Connolly DART Station, or on buses 10, 11, 13, 16 or 19
Open Mon–Sat 10–5, Sun and bank holidays 11–5, late opening Jun–Aug til 6pm
Adm Adult €6, child €3.50, family €16.50 (combined tickets available for James Joyce Museum and Shaw Birthplace)
Volumes Bookshop, ***t*** *(01) 872 2218; restaurant* ***t*** *(01) 873 2266, café, audio guides*

There's a special room dedicated to children's literature here, among the books and personal items of just about all the Irish literary giants of the last 300 years. Housed in an 18th-century Georgian mansion with sumptuous plasterwork and stained glass, the exhibits highlight Ireland's literary tradition, one of the most illustrious in the world thanks to its early oral storytelling and bardic beginnings. Ireland has produced four Nobel Prize winners and many writers of international renown, including Beckett, Joyce, Shaw, Sheridan, Swift, Wilde and Yeats.

A story to tell:
The Death of Cúchulainn

The most dramatic monument in the General Post Office is Oliver Shepherd's sculpture the *Death of Cúchulainn*. Although it commemorates the 1916 Rising, it portrays the legend that the great Irish mythical hero Cúchulainn, after he was mortally wounded in battle, insisted that his comrades tie him to a tree with his sword in his hand so that he would look like he was still standing. None of his enemies dared approach him, for fear it was a trick and that Cúchulainn would kill them if they went near, until a raven landed upon his shoulder, so that everyone realized that he was dead. For more on who Cúchulainn was, *see* p.31.

Dublin songs to sing...
In Dublin's Fair City (Molly Malone), Raglan Road, The Little Beggar Man, The Rocky Road to Dublin, The Spanish Lady, Lanigan's Ball, The Town She Used to Call Home

GAA Museum

New Stand, Croke Park, Dublin 3, **t** (01) 855 8176
Getting there 15 mins walk north from Connolly Station, or on buses 3, 11, 11A, 16, 16A, 51A
Open May–Sept daily 9.30–5, Oct–April Tues–Sat 10–5, Sun noon–5
Adm Adult €5 (*€8.50), child €3 (*€5), student €3.50 (*€6), family €13 (*€21); * with stadium tour

For children who love sport and want to learn about Ireland's most traditional games – hurling and Gaelic football – this is the place to go. Croke Park is headquarters to the Gaelic Athletic Association (GAA), which runs and promotes Irish games throughout Ireland. It's also Ireland's best sports stadium, although only Gaelic games are played here (as well as the odd pop concert). Gaelic games are closely bound up with Irish nationalism, and the museum's film *National Awakening* tells of Irish sport's cultural and political history. There are also interactive exhibits in which kids can try (if not master) the art of hurling, and the tour's closing film (*A Day in September*) leaves you with a sense of the thrill of All-Ireland Finals Day.

General Post Office

O'Connell Street, D1, **t** (01) 705 7000, **www**.anpost.ie
Open Mon–Sat 8–8 (some services close at 7), Sun and bank holidays for stamps and bureau de change only 10–6.30

The main post office (or GPO) for Dublin and the Republic, this imposing neoclassical building was built in 1818 halfway down Dublin's O'Connell Street. It is most famous for being the site of the 1916 rebellion by the Irish Volunteers and Irish Citizen Army, otherwise known as the Easter Rising (*see* p.37). Its repercussions resulted in a majority of Irish people demanding independence from Britain. Padráic Pearse read out his 'Proclamation of the Irish Republic' from the Post Office steps, but after defending the building in fierce fighting for nearly a week he and the other rebels gave themselves up to the British troops. Subsequently, 14 of the rebels were executed by the British in Kilmainham Gaol, which turned Dublin public opinion in favour of the rebels. Bulletholes from 1916 can still be seen in the steps and columns beside the main entrance, and inside there are several monuments to the Rising and the rebels.

Hugh Lane Gallery of Modern Art

Parnell Square North, D1, **t** (01) 874 1903;
Bookshop and workshop bookings **t** (01) 874 9294
Getting there Beside Dublin Writers' Museum
Open Tues–Fri 9.30–6, Sat 9.30–5, Sun 11–5, closed Mon. **Adm** Free

The Hugh Lane Municipal Gallery of Modern Art was the first public gallery of modern art in these islands. Hugh Lane was the nephew of Lady Gregory, who helped Yeats and other Irish artists and fuelled the Irish Literary Renaissance of the early 20th century. Lane bought and sold paintings in London and decided to set up a gallery for Irish and international artists in Dublin, which he did in 1908. Works by Monet, Renoir, Degas and Jack B. Yeats are on show, and it now houses Francis Bacon's unbelievably messy studio as well. It may not be such a great idea to take children to it as, forever after, they may claim you are stifling their creativity by making them clean up their rooms.

On weekends children can ask at the front desk for paper and crayons (the latter must be returned as you leave). Monthly art workshops are held for children, usually on Saturday afternoons; they're very popular, but numbers are limited so booking is essential (via the bookshop).

National Museum of Ireland at Collins Barracks

Benburb Street, D7, **t** (01) 677 7444
Getting there Just over a mile (2km) from Dublin centre, at the western end of the river quays. By bus: 39 from Middle Abbey Street, 79 from Aston Quay, 90 raillink from Connolly Station to Heuston Station or the Museumlink bus (172, *see* below)
Open Tues–Sat 10–5, Sun 2–5, closed Mon, Christmas Day, Good Friday. **Adm** free
Shop, café, supervised parking

An Irish proverb –
Do not mistake a goat's beard for a fine stallion's tail.

Good to know... Museumlink

If you want to visit more than one of the three locations of the National Museum of Ireland (Kildare St, Collins Barracks and the Natural History Museum at Merrion Street) hop on the **Museumlink** bus (route 172), which stops just outside the main entrances of all three (Mon–Sat 8.30–5.30, Sun 12.30–4.30).

Housed in an impressive former army barracks dating from the 1700s, this section of the National Museum is Ireland's new showcase for the decorative arts and the economic, social, political and military history of Ireland. The collections are enormously varied, and arranged to chronicle the development of a vast range of craft skills and arts, including silverware, glassware and ceramics. For younger kids, seek out the Dolls' House and the sections on folk life, costumes and period furniture. Older children may more be intrigued by the exhibits on weaponry and glassware. Many rooms have interactive screens that give comprehensive information on the displays.

National Wax Museum

Granby Row, D1, **t** (01) 872 6340
Getting there 5 mins walk from O'Connell St or on buses 10, 11, 13, 16, or 19
Open Mon–Sat 10–5.30, Sun 12–5.30
Adm Adult €6, child €4, student €5, family €18 (2+2)

After being greeted by a wax model beside the door and a poem by 20th-century Irish poet Patrick Kavanagh, you enter the faerytale dimension of very young children, with models of fantasy characters from the Frog Prince (who changes from Prince to Frog constantly) to more modern storybook and cinema creations. Horror characters are next – there's even a 'victim' on a stretcher in a dungeon. A video of a Disney film runs in another room and then you move on to the historical section, where there are wax models of Ireland's past revolutionaries and presidents, Pope John Paul II with the Popemobile that he used when he visited Ireland, various sports and entertainment personalities and Irish intellectual, political and literary figures, all in appropriately decorated rooms. The historical exhibits have recorded explanations, and sometimes even the voices, of the people they depict. After that, it's on to models of Ireland's pop stars and their noisy outpourings and out into modern Dublin again.

A story to tell: The Black Pool

On the east coast of Leinster, there was a very rough river that flowed down to the sea. It was called *Ruirtheach* ('the impetuous one') because of its flash floods. Around the 6th century, someone built a raft over it, of interwoven wood, which was called an *áth cliath* (hurdle). At low tide, people could walk over it, and some set up their mud huts nearby, in a place they called *Átha Cliath* ('the ford or shallow place of hurdles'). Later this became *Baile Átha Cliath* ('the town of the ford'), which is the name Dublin is usually known by in Irish.

A pool of water lay by this ford. Nearby lived a sorceress named Dubh ('black'), with her chieftain husband Enna, who had another wife whom he preferred. Dubh grew so jealous of her that she whipped up some magic and whisked her rival into the Otherworld. King Enna found out and was so angry that he threw Dubh into that pool of water – where she stayed. Thereafter, it was called *Dubhlinn* (or Dubh's Pool, i.e. 'black pool'), which is where Dublin's other name comes from.

Another sad tale about this place comes from a medieval poem. A great warrior's wife died while having a baby beside the Ruirtheach. Her name was Liphe, which means life, so gossips began to call the river 'Liffey'. People felt unhappy about these terrible things, so they started to pray there, and built a monastery nearby. Some say, too, that the Liffey was named after Livia, the wife of the Roman emperor Augustus... but then, the Romans never lived in Ireland.

St Michan's Church

Church St, D7, **t** (01) 872 4154
Getting there By the Four Courts and the Inns Quay, on the west side of central Dublin; bus 79 from Aston Quay
Open Mar–Oct Mon–Fri 10–12.30, 2–4.30, Sat 10–12.45; Nov–Mar Mon–Fri 12.30–3.30, Sat 10–12.45; closed Sun, Christmas, bank holidays, some days of Holy Week
Adm By guided tour: Adult €3.50, child €2.50

The current St Michan's was built in 1685–86 on the site of a much older one, built by Christian former Vikings in the 11th century and the only church north of the Liffey for some 500 years. The church is most famous, though, for the mummified bodies stored in its vaults. St Michan's has a peculiar ability to preserve bodies, some think due to the magnesian limestone in its walls or to its position, closer to the bed of the Liffey than any other Dublin church. Bodies tend to harden, while hair and skin remain rather than deteriorate.

Here you can find the death mask of Wolfe Tone and the corpses of many of the leaders of Ireland's 1798 rebellion. Some children, especially little ones, might find the dead bodies disturbing. You might prefer to take them into the church, to look at the organ and the exquisite carvings of musical instruments above the choir, while their older siblings get their gruesome thrills.

South of the Liffey

Chester Beatty Library

Clock Tower Building, Dublin Castle, D2, **t** (01) 407 0750
Getting there In Dublin Castle gardens, *see* right
Open Tues–Fri 10–5, Sat 2–5, closed Sun, Mon.
Adm Free
Free guided tours Wed 1pm and Sun 3 and 4pm or by request, gift/bookshop, café and restaurant, baby-changing facilities, wheelchair access, roof garden

This collection of approximately 22,000 rare books, miniature paintings, artistic works and objects from Early Christian, Islamic and East Asian cultures was bequeathed to Ireland by the late Sir Alfred Chester Beatty upon his death in 1968. Highlights include Chinese dragon robes, Japanese wood block prints and Buddhist paintings.

Christchurch Cathedral

Christchurch Place, D8, **t** (01) 677 8099
Getting there Buses 50, 51B, 54A, 77, 77A, 78A
Open Cathedral: Mon–Fri 9.45–5, Sat–Sun 10–5; Treasures: Mon–Fri 9.45–5, Sat 10–4.45, Sun 12.30–3.15
Adm Cathedral: free but donations of Adult €3, child €1.50 requested; Treasures crypt: €3 each

This is Dublin's oldest building and Ireland's oldest cathedral. Built on the site of a wooden

Can you spot...
The 8ft tall Crusader in St Michan's Church crypt? It is said to be good luck to touch his leathery hand upon leaving.

Viking church (founded in 1030), the current Norman design of Christchurch dates from 1172, when it was commissioned by Strongbow, the Anglo-Norman conqueror of Dublin, and Archbishop Laurence O'Toole. There are family monuments and treasures in the fascinating crypt where the 19th Earl of Kildare is buried. Like Dublin's other historic cathedral nearby, St Patrick's (*see* below), it is Church of Ireland (Anglican).

Dublin Castle

Dame St, D2, t (01) 677 7129
Getting there **5 mins walk from Trinity College along Dame St; buses 50, 51B, 54A, 56A, 77, 77A, 78A**
Open **Mon–Fri 10–5, Sat, Sun and bank holidays 2–5 (times vary due to state functions); closed bank holiday Mon, Good Friday, 24–26 Dec, 1 Jan**
Adm **Adult €4.50, under-12s €1.50**
Restaurant, craft shop

The heart of historic Dublin, standing at the junction of the River Liffey and its tributary the Poddle. A ring fort probably stood here first, and later a Viking fortress, the remains of which may be seen in the Undercroft. The oldest surviving part of the medieval castle, though, is the 13th-century Record Tower; most of the current castle was rebuilt in the 18th century, after several disastrous fires. Visitors tour the elegant Georgian interiors, where excellent classical music concerts are also held (for information contact tourist office or the Music Network, **t** (01) 671 9429, **www**.musicnetwork.ie.

Dublin Civic Museum

58 South William St, D2, t (01) 679 4260
Getting there **Buses 10, 11, 13 and others**
Open **Tues–Sat 10–6, Sun 11–2. Adm Free**

A small collection of artefacts mainly from the 18th–19th centuries in a fine building redolent of Georgian Dublin. Other material covers the city's history from the Vikings to the present, notably the head of a statue of Nelson blown off his column on O'Connell Street by an IRA bomb in 1966.

Dublinia

Synod Hall, St Michael's Hill, Christchurch, D8, t (01) 679 4611
Getting there **Buses 50, 51B, 54A, 77, 77A, 78A**
Open **Apr–Sept daily 10–5, Oct–Mar Mon–Sat 11–4, Sun and bank holidays 10–4.30, closed 24–26 Dec**
Adm **Adult €5.75, child €4.25**
Guided (pre-book) and headset tours available, tea room (Jun–Aug), wheelchair accessible

> ***Tell me an Irish riddle...***
> ***Question – What's 'Long and lanky, deaf and dumb, has no legs and still can run'?***
> ***Answer – A river.***

In the Middle Ages the name given to Dublin by Latin-speakers and scholars was *Dublinia*. Today this is also the name of a notably child-friendly, interactive museum. It occupies the old Synod Hall of Christchurch Cathedral, and overlooks the Wood Quay, where modern government buildings stand beside the Liffey. The story of how they came to be there is one topic of the exhibition: historians and archaeologists fought to keep Wood Quay undeveloped so they could study it further, as it may be the most important Viking settlement in Europe. Magnificent artefacts found there are on display in the museum, which focuses on the years 1170–1540. At that time Anglo-Normans lived within the city walls; the native Irish built their own Cathedral (St Patrick's) outside.

The first thing you notice when you walk into Dublinia is the noise of some strange-tongued city, while your eyes make out the timeline on the wall. Eventually you discover that the languages you are hearing were those spoken in Dublinia around 1170; the Irish, English and Vikings had been intermarrying for years and developed a way of speaking to each other. This became mixed with a form of French spoken by the most recent invaders, the Anglo-Normans led by Richard de Clare, better known as Strongbow. Meanwhile, Latin was spoken by the clergy, and Gaelic by the Irish people allowed to trade or work in the city.

As your eyes get more used to the darkness, you'll notice you're in a recreation of a fair in 13th-century Dublin. People bought hot swan pies from vendors, or had their blood let by healers using leeches, the most popular method of curing the sick at the time. You can try on clothes made by a tailor, and a knight's chain-mail and helmet. Look for a cure for what ails you at the apothecary's shop, where medicines were mixed from herbs, spices and insects. Copy a will, grant or a pardon at the scribe's booth, and play with the counters at the 'bank' and find out what 'debtors' sticks' were.

Later rooms tell you how the plague of the Black Death swept from England to Ireland, and how medieval dockyards worked. Look for the figure of Silken Thomas Fitzgerald, who led a rebellion against Henry VIII in 1534 which was duly crushed when Henry hanged Thomas and his five uncles. A scale model shows how Dublin would have looked during the 1500s: in the middle of the old town walls stands Christchurch Cathedral, and beside the southeastern wall is Dublin Castle. Particularly noticeable is how wide the River Liffey was in comparison to today, and how much open space stretched between Dublin's city walls and the pasture land that was then held in common for the townspeople's animals, an area that's still known today as St Stephen's Green.

At the end of the exhibit, you can walk to the top of St Michael's Tower to view modern Dublin and the tower's lovely stained-glass, and cross a bridge into Christchurch Cathedral itself.

Marsh's Library

St Patrick's Close, D8, **t** (01) 454 3511
Getting there Buses 49, 50, 54A, 77, 77A, 150
Open Mon 10–1, Wed–Fri 10–1 and 2–5, Sat 10.30–1 (closed Tues and Sun). **Adm** Adult €2.50, child free

Parents who want to inspire a love of learning in their children might want to bring them here, to Ireland's oldest public library, founded in 1701 and virtually unchangedsince then in its lovely Queen Anne house in a quiet lane beside St Patrick's Cathedral. It's almost like a time capsule: dark oak bookcases and elegant wired alcoves or 'cages' house rare leather-bound books that are kept exactly the same as they were 300 years ago.

National Gallery of Ireland

Merrion Square West, D2, **t** (01) 661 5133
Getting there Buses 7, 7A, 8, 10, 11, 13A or Museumlink (172); by train, DART to Pearse Station
Open Mon–Wed, Fri, Sat 9.30–5.30, Thurs 9.30–8.30, Sun 12–5. **Adm** Free
Guided tours, restaurants, shop, disabled access

This art museum is lovely and spacious, so it's easy to visit with toddlers and pushchairs. Kids who know the west of Ireland will like the modern landscape paintings, which have a simple mystical quality, as much as the more famous artworks.

National Museum of Ireland

Kildare Street, D2, **t** (01) 677 7444
Getting there Buses 7, 7A, 8, 10, 11, 13A or Museumlink (172); by train, DART to Pearse Station
Open Tues–Sat 10–5, Sun 2–5, closed Mon, Christmas Day, Good Friday. **Adm** Free
Guided tours, restaurant, shop, lecture theatre

Just visiting this impressive 1890 building is an adventure. Move through mausoleum-quiet to the Neolithic exhibition on the ground floor, and then forward in time through the Egyptian, Viking and Medieval Ireland 1150–1550 exhibits. The National Museum's artefacts cover a time span from 7000 BC to the 20th century, including the world's finest collection of Celtic art and ornaments. The fantastic examples of medieval and Celtic art on display include the famous jewelled Ardagh Chalice, the Tara Brooch and Derrynaflan Hoard, and the most important collection of prehistoric gold artefacts in Europe.

A story to tell: The Vikings are coming

The Viking invaders who sailed from Norway and Denmark to Dublin were mostly pirates and thieves. They weren't nice people. If you happened to own a good house, with a well-thatched roof, or live in a monastery with any kind of gold or money stored away, these red-haired fellows in their hats with the horns would break down your door and one way or another would bump you off as soon as they got their hands on your gold. Around the year 800, some Vikings discovered the rich monastery at Dubhlinn and plundered it. They settled nearby for a few years, but then the Irish High Kings got together and drove them away. By the 900s, they were back again, destroying the best of the Uì Néill warriors. With their eye on settling in for good this time, the Norsemen gave up their marauding and built a town to the east of Átha Cliath, which they called *Dyflinn*. They began to be more sociable, marrying the locals, and some even becoming Christians. Putting their energies to good use this time, they built the town and the first bridge over the River Liffey (Dubhghall's Bridge).

By the 11th century, Dyflinn was an organized place, with wooden houses made of thatch, mud and dung (which doesn't stink when it dries, by the way), and with streets, paths and plots, all behind an earth and timber wall. Dyflinn grew together with Átha Cliath. They say that the area now called Wood Quay, near Christchurch Cathedral, covers the oldest part of Dublin.

Did you know... What a torc is?
It was a metal plate worn at the neck by the ancient Celts, usually made of gold. There are wonderful gold torcs on show in the National Museum on Kildare Street.

National Museum of Natural History

Merrion Square West, D2, **t** (01) 677 7444
Getting there Buses 7, 7A, 8, 10, 11, 13A or Museumlink (172); by train, DART to Pearse Station
Open Tues–Sat 10–5, Sun 2–5, closed Mon, Christmas Day, Good Friday. **Adm** Free

This wonderful, unchanged Victorian museum is part of the National Museum of Ireland. Called Dublin's 'Dead Zoo' because it is full of stuffed animals and has a musty old atmosphere, it is famous for its Victorian cabinets and decorated panels depicting mythological characters. Its ground floor contains Irish insects, strange-looking earth and sea creatures in jars, and mammals, including skeletons of the extinct giant deer known as the Irish Elk and the skeleton of a basking shark. In the upper floor galleries there are remains of creatures from around the world, the centrepiece being the skeleton of a 60ft whale suspended from the roof. Buffalo and deer trophies are also on show, as are the pygmy hippopotamus and giant panda, and the Blaschka Collection of reproductions of marine life.

Number Twenty-Nine: Georgian Townhouse

29 Lower Fitzwilliam Street, D2, **t** (01) 702 6165
Getting there Buses (from city centre) 6, 7, 8, 10 or 45; by train, DART to Pearse Station
Open Tues–Sat 10–5, Sun 2–5, closed Mon and 2 weeks before Christmas
Adm Adult €3.15, under-16s free
Tearoom, gift shop, arrange groups in advance

This 18th-century house just off Merrion Square, in the heart of Georgian Dublin, belonged to a merchant and his wife. An explanatory video about middle-class Dublin life from 1790–1820 greets you as you enter, to give the historical background to goings-on inside the house, where you'll see life-sized mannequins of its original inhabitants. Then a tour guide will lead you through the rooms on its five floors, tailoring his talk to suit visitors' ages.

The tour first takes you to the basement, with the kitchen. Baking was done here in the morning, meat being cooked last because the coal-fuelled oven would grow warmer as the day progressed. Ironing was done in the evenings, often by candlelight, by the head servant in her own bedroom, with irons heated in fires. Household servants were summoned from here by a set of bells. Each bell denoted a different room in the house, which the servants had to remember.

Food from the basement had to be carried to the dining room on the floor above for the family's meals. The times for these and going to bed varied according to the season, since people lived by candlelight, so that the evening meal might be served as early as 2.30pm during the winter.

Visitors were received on the first floor in the front drawing room. Behind it is the drawing room, where friends and family would read and play card games, or play music on clavichords, lyres and other instruments of the era.

On the second floor, beside the mistress of the house's bedroom, is her boudoir or private sitting room. This was where she would entertain close female friends, who might sew together as well as gossip. Alongside it is her toilet and bathroom, with its very advanced system of piped hot water.

The family's children and their governess occupied the whole of the third floor of the house. Here, the children slept together in one room, where they could play with its most impressive dolls' house, and received their lessons from the governess, whose bedroom was just next to them. She would create elaborate embroidery and samplers in order to prove her fitness as a wife to any suitable gentlemen who might appear. Educated women without dowries generally became governesses; if they grew old without marrying, their lives often ended in poverty, in the harsh conditions of the public workhouse.

Back downstairs visitors can also enjoy some fine barm brack (*see* p. 103) in the coffee shop.

Did you know...?
The Dublin-born writer Bram Stoker, who created Dracula in 1897, was inspired by his own insomnia to invent the vampire's fear of daylight.

Oscar Wilde House

1 Merrion Square, **t** (01) 662 0281
Getting there Buses (from city centre) 6, 7, 8, 10 or 45; by train, DART to Pearse Station
Open Mon, Wed, Thurs for tours 10.15 and 11.15am
Adm €2.54 per person

The ground and first floors of this house where Oscar Wilde lived from 1855–76 have been restored by its owners, the American College Dublin.

St Patrick's Cathedral

St Patrick's Close, D8, **t** (01) 475 4817
Getting there Buses 49, 50, 54A, 77, 77A, 150
Open Mar–Oct Mon–Fri 9–6, Sun 9–3; Nov–Feb Mon–Fri 9–5, Sun 9–3
Adm Donations requested: adult €4, child €2, family €9 (2+2)

Don't miss this famous cathedral – which is Church of Ireland (Anglican), like Christchurch – known for its association with writer and satirist Jonathan Swift, who was Dean here, and with Handel's *Messiah*, which was first performed here in 1742. The Cathedral was begun in 1190, but it is said that St Patrick himself preached on this spot centuries earlier. An exhibition illustrates the role of St Patrick and the Cathedral in Dublin's history.

Shaw Birthplace

33 Synge Street, D8, **t** (01) 475 0854
Getting there 10 mins walk south of St Stephen's Green; buses 16, 16A, 19, 19A, 22, 22A
Open May–Sept Mon–Sat 10–1, 2–6, Sun, bank holidays 11.30–1, 2-6; Nov–Apr by arrangement (call **t** (01) 872 2077)
Adm Adult €6, child €3.50, family€16.50

The fount of George Bernard Shaw's genius lies hidden somewhere in this neat terraced house, where he was born on 26 July 1856, feet first – a portent of his tendency to go against the ordinary way of things. A peaceful feel is conveyed by the contents of this simple Victorian house's master bedroom, the drawing room where Shaw's mother held musical evenings and his own box room, along with the little walled garden – all restored to look as they did in the 19th century. The house has a fascinating feel of a real, modest mid-Victorian home, almost as if the Shaws had just left.

After working in an estate office, at age 20 Shaw followed his pianist mother to London. She had left her tippling husband four years earlier to follow her music teacher there, a man who had lived in the Shaw family home for years. Thereafter, Shaw earned around 50 pence a year for nine years, in which he wrote five unsuccessful novels. Then a friend helped him get a job as a book reviewer and music critic, while he wrote six unsuccessful plays. Then in 1896, his seventh play, *The Devil's Disciple*, struck gold in America. From 1898 on, he produced nearly a play per year. His plays' political and social themes did not always make him popular (he was an avowed socialist and anti-war vegetarian), but he lived amid great fame until his death in 1950.

Did you know...?
Which building houses the Republic of Ireland's Parliament?
...Leinster House, beside the National Museum of Ireland on Kildare Street.

Trinity College Library

College Street D2, **t** (01) 608 2320
Getting there 2 mins walk from O'Connell Bridge
Open Mon–Sat 9.30–5; Oct–May also Sun 12 noon–4.30; Jun–Sept also Sun 9.30–4.30
Adm Adult €7, students, over-65s €6, family €14; Dublin Experience, adult €4.20, students, over-65s €3.50

The grand Georgian quadrangles of Dublin's esteemed seat of learning contain one of Ireland's greatest treasures, the astonishing illuminated manuscript the *Book of Kells*, made by monks in around 800. Almost as impressive is the *Book of Durrow*, from about 670. An interesting background exhibit helps bring the manuscripts alive, and there's also the 'Dublin Experience', an optional audiovisual exhibit on the city's past. The College Library itself is magnificent, with a superb barrel-roofed Long Hall.

Other Ideas?

Cinema

Sheridan Imax

Parnell Street, Parnell Centre, D1, **t** (01) 817 4222
Getting there north end of O'Connell St

See eye-popping films on a screen four times the height of a double-decker bus; ask too about showings of 3-D movies.

Theatre and music

Abbey Theatre

Lower Abbey Street, D1, **t** (01) 878 7222
Getting there 2 mins walk from O'Connell St
Box office open Mon–Sat 10.30–7

The theatre imagined into being by the poet WB Yeats and Lady Gregory. Today there are matinée performances of international and national plays here, and occasional performances for children.

The Ark

11A Eustace Street, D2, **t** (01) 670 7788, **www**.ark.ie
Getting there off Dame St, west of Trinity College
Open All year Mon–Sat at different hours

A cultural centre for children aged 4–14, with theatre, gallery and workshops; call to find out about arts workshops, short sessions, one-off events, music and theatre festivals, and the regular drawing, printmaking and performance classes.

Gaiety Theatre

South King Street, D2, **t** (01) 677 1717
Getting there Off St Stephen's Green

At Christmas time the Gaiety hosts audience-grabbing traditional pantomimes.

National Concert Hall

Earlsfort Terrace, by St Stephen's Green, D2, **t** (01) 417 0000, **www**.nch.ie
Getting there Buses 6, 7, 8, 10 or 45
Box office open Mon–Sat 10–7

Occasional concerts and plays for children.

Lambert Puppet Theatre

Clifton Lane, Monkstown, **t** (01) 280 0974, **www**.lambertpuppettheatre.com
Getting there Bus: 7, 7A, 8 or DART to Salthill.

In the southern suburb of Monkstown – on the DART line between Dublin and Dun Laoghaire – this long-running theatre has a puppet museum and offers puppetry workshops as well as staging over 30 productions each year, from shows for the very young to productions for older children.

Parks and gardens

Iveagh Gardens

Clonmel Street, D2, **t** (01) 475 7816
Getting there Buses 6, 7, 8, 10 or 45
Open Summer Mon–Sat 8–6, Sun and bank holidays 10–6; winter same but closes at dusk
Adm Free

A hidden garden with a grotto, fountains, maze, archery grounds and woodlands in one of the busiest parts of south Dublin, behind Newman House, one of Dublin's finest Georgian houses.

Merrion Square

D2. **Getting there** Buses (from city centre) 6, 7, 8, 10 or 45; by train, DART to Pearse Station

These gardens are in the centre of one of the best Georgian squares in Dublin, where you can have a picnic while your children use the playground. A modern statue of Oscar Wilde stands across the street from the house where he grew up (*see* left).

St Patrick's Park

Patrick's Street, D8
Getting there Beside St Patrick's Cathedral

St. Patrick is said to have baptized the first Irish Christians here with water from the River Poddle, which now flows underground beneath the park.

St Stephen's Green

D2. **Getting there** Bottom of Grafton Street, D2
Open Mon–Sat 8–dusk, Sun and bank holidays 10–dusk. **Adm** Free

This lovely 19th-century park contains a lake, fountains, playground, scented garden for the blind and an engaging mix of statues. One of Dublin's most historic open spaces, today it's also full of peaceful ducks.

Sports

Croke Park

Croke Park, D3, **t** (01) 836 3222
Getting there 15 mins walk north from Connolly Station, or on buses 3, 11, 11A, 16, 16A, 51A

The lavish venue for Gaelic games – hurling and Gaelic football. Hurling is mostly played in summer, football in winter; for upcoming fixtures, check the GAA website, **www**.gaa.ie, and you can also visit the GAA Museum (*see* p.50).

Lansdowne Road Stadium

Lansdowne Road, D4, **t** (01) 668 4601

Dublin's main Rugby stadium, 1m (1.6km) south of the city centre, hosts the annual Six Nations tournament, and also international soccer games.

An Irish proverb –
There is no need like the lack of a friend...

AROUND AND ABOUT

Animal magic

Dublin Zoo

Phoenix Park, **t** (01) 677 1425 or freephone **t** 1800 924 848, **www.dublinzoo.ie**
Getting there 2 miles (3km) from central Dublin in Phoenix Park. By bus: 10 (from O'Connell Street); 25, 26 (from Middle Abbey Street)
Open Mar–Sept Mon–Sat 9.30–6, Sun 10.30–6; Nov–Feb Mon–Sat 9.30–dusk, Sun 10.30–dusk; last entry one hour before closing
Adm Adult €10.10, child €6.30, under-3s free, family €29.40 (2+2)
Gift shop, restaurant and snack kiosks, children's play areas, train, discovery centre, picnic area

You can easily spend a whole day in this award-winning zoo, so it's a good idea to bring a picnic (on-site restaurants sell mainly fast food). Dublin Zoo tries to educate people about endangered species it seeks to protect, such as its lemurs from Madagascar. At certain times, mainly in summer, zookeepers answer questions while feeding the animals (call **t** 01 474 8900 for feeding times).

Large enclosed grassy spaces and water holes serve as homes for once-wild animals from all over the world. The 'World of Cats' section shows off the big cats like the Jaguar, Tiger, Lion and Snow Leopard. On an island isolated from visitors, you'll see Colobus and Celebes Macaque monkeys, and the solitary 'old man of the forest', the Orangutan – with his long beard and feet that look like hands. Baby monkey breeds are housed in warm sheds near wooden slides, climbing frames and a mirror, where children can see themselves making monkey faces and mimicking their acrobatics.

Pink flamingos congregate not far from the 'Fringes of the Arctic' enclosure, where polar bears, arctic foxes, snowy owls and grey wolves live (the last wild wolves were seen in Ireland in the 18th century) . Nearby are water pools where seals and Humboldt penguins lounge about, as if on holiday.

Buggies must take the long path to the 'African Plains' sector, where larger animals live in more spacious domains, but the stairway is shorter. A replica African village, with several children's play areas, it discreetly houses toilets, a first aid and lost children hut, and the restaurant. Unless you take the African Plains Train, you may walk a while before you see zebras, oryx antelopes, giraffes, elephants and one family each of rhinoceroses and hippopotamuses. Lesser-known breeds include the Red River Hog, Bongo, the miniature Reeve's Muntjac deer and the mongoose-like meerkat.

Near the zoo's exit are the hothouse homes of reptiles, including a few snakes (otherwise banished from Ireland by St Patrick). Within the specially heated buildings lurk Bell's Hinged tortoises, mud turtles, Nile crocodiles and iguanas.

Did you know...?
The word 'reptile' comes from a Latin word meaning 'to crawl'. Reptiles never get beyond the crawling stage, and their body temperature goes up and down according to that of their surroundings, so they would literally freeze to death in very cold weather. They can't survive outdoors in Ireland, but you can see some at Dublin Zoo.

Bricks and mortar

Drimnagh Castle

Long Mile Road, Drimnagh, D12, **t** (01) 450 2530
Getting there Located 3 miles (5km) southwest of central Dublin; buses 22, 22A, 50, 56A, 77, 77A
Open Apr–Sept Wed, Sat and Sun 12–5; Oct–Mar Wed 12 noon–5, Sun 2–5, last tour 4.15, other times by arrangement.
Adm Adult €4, child €2

Inhabited until 1954, this is the only castle in Ireland that's still surrounded by a flooded moat. The tour includes its Great Hall, Norman keep with battlements, coach-house, dairy and folly tower. Around it there's a pretty 17th-century garden.

Rathfarnham Castle

Rathfarnham bypass, near Rathfarnham Village, D14, **t** (01) 493 9462, **www.heritageireland.ie**
Getting there Located 4 miles (6km) south of central Dublin; buses 16, 16A, 47, 47A, 47B (from Hawkins Street), 75 (Dun Laoghaire–Tallaght)

Open May–Oct daily 9.30–5.30; ring **t** (01) 647 2466 for Nov–Easter opening hours
Adm Adult €2, child €1, family €5.50
Car/coach park, restaurant/tearoom (accessible for visitors with disabilities)

Built around 1583 by Yorkshireman Adam Loftus, this semi-fortified castle has 18th-century interiors designed by Sir William Chambers and James Athenian Stuart. Layers of its earlier existence are now being uncovered by research at this ongoing conservation site, which interests budding archaeologists and conservationists.

Look at this!

Irish Jewish Museum

3–4 Walworth Road (off Victoria St), South Circular Road, D8, **t** (01) 490 1857/453 1797
Getting there 15 mins walk south of St Stephen's Green; buses 16, 16A, 19, 19A, 22, 22A
Open May–Sept Sun, Tues, Thurs 11–3.30, Oct–Apr Sun only 10.30–2.30, other times by arrangement
Adm Donations

The museum is in the restored Walworth Road Synagogue (two adjoining terraced houses) in the once-Jewish area of Portobello. Its exhibits include memorabilia from Ireland's Jewish communities, in Belfast, Cork, Derry, Dublin, Limerick and Waterford, over the last 150 years. The synagogue fell into disuse in the mid-1970s when the area's Jewish population declined, and was made into a museum in 1984. Old photographs and paintings dominate the entrance area; on the ground floor there is a wide-ranging background display on the social and business life of Jews in Ireland. Upstairs are the rooms of the original synagogue. Jews have lived in Ireland since the 11th century, but never in great numbers. Their population peaked in the 1940s at around 5,500, but today there are only about 1,400 in the Republic and 400 in Northern Ireland.

James Joyce Museum

Martello Tower, Sandycove, **t** (01) 280 9265
Getting there 8 miles (13km) south of central Dublin along the coast; by train, DART to Sandycove
Open Apr–Oct Mon–Sat 10–1, 2–5, Sun and bank holidays 2–6, Nov–Mar open by arrangement, call **t** (01) 872 2077

Tell me an Irish riddle...
Question – Why is a dog like a tree?
Answer – They both have a bark.

Adm Adult €6, child €3.50, family €16.50 (combined tickets with Dublin Writers' Museum and Shaw's birthplace are available)
Guided tours by arrangement, parking

This is one of a series of 'Martello Towers' – battlemented brick watchtowers – that were built around Dublin in 1804 to guard against the possibility of an invasion by Napoleon. The one in Sandycove is most famous, though, because James Joyce, the writer most closely associated with his native Dublin, lived here briefly in 1904 and used it for the opening scene of his classic *Ulysses*, one of the most influential novels of the 20th century. Since 1962 the tower has been open as a museum devoted to the life and works of Joyce. The tower itself, and the views over the sea beside it, will enchant children, while their parents try to take in the literary displays.

Kilmainham Gaol

Inchicore Road, D8, **t** (01) 453 5984
Getting there 2 miles (3.5km) southwest of central Dublin; buses 51, 51B, 78A, 79 to Inchicore Road
Open Apr–Sept daily 9.30–5 (last adm 4.45), Oct–Mar Mon–Sat 9.30–4, Sun 10–5, last tour one hour before closing
Adm Adult €5, child €2, family €11
Guided tours only; toilets (also for disabled), café, access with special needs by prior arrangement

Some of Irish history's most famous events occurred in this, Europe's largest currently-unoccupied jail, between 1795 and 1920. Charles Stewart Parnell, the 19th-century nationalist leader, was imprisoned here in 1881 for his part in the so-called Land War, and other inmates included the leader of the 1803 Irish revolt Robert Emmet. Kilmainham's most famous prisoners, though, were the leaders of the 1916 Easter Rising, including a woman, Constance Markievicz. Pearse, Connolly and others were all executed here, while Eamon de Valera only escaped the firing squad because he was an American citizen. The guided tours and displays don't pull any punches in describing 19th-century prisons and punishment, and younger children may find them all a bit gruesome.

Museum of Childhood

20 Palmerston Park, Rathmines, D6,
t (01) 497 3223/497 8696
Getting there Located 2 miles (3km) south of central Dublin; bus 13
Open All year Sun 2–5.30
Adm Adult €1, under-12s €0.75

Many children will find the original Hornby train sets on show here interesting, as well as the toy soldiers, prams and dolls' houses of centuries ago, including the wonderful travelling doll's house of Sissi, Empress of Austria. The oldest doll in Ireland is also here in this charming, privately-owned collection of nursery memorabilia from all over the world, as well as a strange three-faced doll.

National Print Museum

Garrison Chapel, Beggars Bush Barracks, Haddington Road, D4, **t** (01) 660 3770
Getting there Bus 5, 7, 7A, 8, 45; by train, DART to Lansdowne Road
Open May–Sept Mon–Fri 10–12.30, 2.30–5, Sat, Sun and bank holidays noon–5, Oct–Apr Tues, Thurs, Sat and Sun 2–5. **Adm** Adult €3, under-12s €1.50
Audio-visual show, café

A collection of machines and other artefacts (many in full working order) from every part of Ireland's printing industry, housed in a building that was created in the 1860s as a soldier's chapel. It was the first military barracks to be handed over by the British to the new Irish State in February 1922, and also the place where Irish revolutionary Erskine Childers was executed in 1922 during Ireland's Civil War. The exhibits on every aspect of printing have plenty of interest: children who are just learning to read may be intrigued to find out how books were first printed, while older children find the printing presses and processes amazingly archaic. An exhibit shows how the first printed book, the Gutenberg Bible, was produced in 1455, and how the invention of hot metal casting in the 19th century transformed the printing industry. Impressive ornate printing presses stand beside a Wharfedale press on which the 1916 Proclamation declaring Ireland's independence was printed. Next on show is a pen-ruling machine, used to make lines in the writing books that children used at school. Old newspaper headlines of world events are framed on the upstairs gallery wall, and children can be pleasantly surprised to discover that they enjoy the educational audio-visual show.

Pearse Museum

St Enda's Park, Grange Rd, Rathfarnham, D16,
t (01) 493 4208
Getting there Located 2 miles (3km) south of central Dublin; bus 16 (from city centre). Turn off Grange Road into car park at bus terminus
Open daily Nov–Jan 10–4, Feb–Apr, Sept–Oct 10–5, May–Aug 10–5.30. **Adm** Free
*Restaurant, **t** (01) 493 3053, open May–Sept daily, Feb–Apr and Oct weekends; guided tours on request, disabled access to ground floor and nature study room, nature trail; parking, concerts*

Set in one of Dublin's most charming and atmospheric parks, in the pleasant suburb of Rathfarnham, with riverside walks, a waterfall and walled garden, the Pearse Museum is a nature study centre that was once a school run by Padráic Pearse, the Irish writer executed for his role as leader of the Easter Rising of 1916. His executioner said, 'there must be something terribly wrong in the world for a man of his calibre to be executed'. A strong proponent of the Irish language, Pearse briefly taught it to James Joyce before starting this school, which was bilingual in Irish and English and run on experimental, progressive principles. His mother and sister kept the school open until 1935. There's an audiovisual exhibit on Pearse and his life, but for many visitors the most attractive feature is the combination of the school building and its lovely , peaceful setting.

Waterways Visitor Centre

Grand Canal Quay, Ringsend, D4 (entrance off Ringsend end of Pearse Street),
t (01) 677 7510/661 3111
Getting there Bus 3; by train, DART to Pearse Station
Open June–Sept daily 9.30–5.30, Oct–May Wed–Sun 12.30–5
Adm Adult €2.50, child €1.20, family €6.35

Called 'the box in the docks' by locals, this striking modern building houses an engaging exhibition about all the inland waterways (both canals and navigable rivers) of Dublin and Ireland. From inside the airy glass-walled building you get a real impression of being in 'a world of water'.

Tell me an Irish riddle...
Question – 'The more you take out of it, the bigger it gets.' – What is it?
Answer – A hole.

Nature lovers

Marlay Park and Demesne

Grange Road, Rathfarnham, D14, **t** (01) 493 7372
Getting there Located 2–3 miles (3–5km) south of central Dublin; bus 16 (from city centre), turn off Grange Road into car park at bus terminus. By car, an alternative route is to turn off the Southern Cross motorway at Kingston interchange.
Open House: tours by arrangement; Gardens: Apr–Sept Tues–Fri 12 noon–5, Sat, Sun 12 noon–6
Adm Adult €3, child €2, family €6.50
Sports pitches, model railway, nature trails, lakeside walks, craft yard with retail units, coffee shop

About 200 acres of parkland, a 4.5-acre walled garden and an ornamental garden surround Marlay House, built in 1794 for the Governor of the Bank of Ireland, David La Touche. There's a miniature train ride here for children on Saturday afternoons, along with a playground, golf course, woodland walks and two lakes. Teenagers know it as a music venue for acts like David Gray, Sting, Van Morrison, Westlife and Samantha Mumba.

National Botanic Gardens

Finglas Rd, Glasnevin, D9, **t** (01) 857 0909
Getting there 1 mile/0.6km north of central Dublin, along Dorset St; buses 13, 19, 19A
Open Summer Mon–Sat 9–6, Sun 11–6; winter Mon–Sat 10–4.30, Sun 11–4.30; closed Christmas Day
Adm free, guided tour €2, charge for parking
Toilets, gift shop, wheelchair accessible except Palm House, dogs on lead, parking outside gates on road

Ireland's premier botanical garden was established in 1795 on the 27-acre estate of minor poet Thomas Tickell, and acquired its magnificent Victorian glasshouses in the 1840s. The gardens contain over 20,000 different plant species, amid trees, shrubs and perennials. Botanically-planned plots contain roses, poisonous plants, native plants, herbs and vegetables, along with a large rockery, bog garden, wild garden and curving herbaceous borders that bloom beautifully in summer. Must-see exhibits include the tropical tree house, with orchids and flowering plants, and the gigantic Amazon water lily introduced in 1854 (the Victoria or Aquatic House was specially built to protect it). The cactus plant and fern glasshouses and the striking early Victorian chain tent draped with wisteria are equally special. Don't forget to look for the 'Last Rose of Summer' – an 'Old Blush' China rose raised from a cutting taken from a rose bush at Jenkinstown House in County Kilkenny, which inspired the poet Thomas Moore to write a famous sentimental Irish ballad with the same name.

Phoenix Park and Visitor Centre

Phoenix Park, D8, **t** (01) 677 0095
Getting there Phoenix Park is 2 1/2 miles (4km) from the centre of Dublin; 20 mins' walk from the gate at Ashtown Cross. or 30 mins' walk from the gate at North Circular Road. Buses from central Dublin include 37, 38 (from Lower Abbey Street), 39 (from Middle Abbey Street) and 10 (from O'Connell Street).
Open Park open at all times; Visitor Centre open Jan–mid-Mar and Nov–Dec, Sat–Sun 10–5, mid–end-Mar daily 10–5.30, Apr–Sept daily 10–6, Oct daily 10–5
Adm Park free; Visitor Centre, adult €2.75, child €1.25, family €7
Toilets (also for disabled), restaurant, café, car park

Enlightened Victorians created this magnificent 1,760-acre green space for Dublin's city-dwellers. Inside the park, among many other things to enjoy, are Dublin Zoo (*see* p.58), children's play areas and sports grounds. Located above water – which now flows underground – that was thought to have healing properties, the area was one called 'Clear Water', which is *fhionn uisce* in Irish, and this was later corrupted into 'Phoenix'). Around the park are several monuments, such as a giant column to commemorate the Duke of Wellington. From the No. 10 bus stop, you can walk for miles and miles through Phoenix Park, so depending on what the weather looks like go prepared, with decent walking shoes and rainwear.

The wildlife and history of Phoenix Park from 3500 BC to the present are entertainingly displayed in the visitor centre. A restored medieval tower house called Ashtown Castle, which was probably built in the 17th century, adjoins the centre and may be seen Saturdays on a guided tour.

WHERE TO EAT

Dublin has become a city of restaurants, bars and cafés as well as the ever-present pub. Many are in the centre, especially in tourist areas like Temple Bar, but excellent ones can also be found in the suburbs and out-of-the-way places. There's been a 21st-century renaissance in food in Ireland, so there are many more good restaurants than can be listed here. Below is a selection of old- and new-style restaurants and cafés, chosen for comfort and value, as well as an accommodating attitude to children. Most offer a few vegetarian options.

It is a good idea to book Dublin restaurants in advance, particularly in the evenings and on week-ends in Dublin – this applies particularly to upmarket, smarter restaurants, although we haven't listed them here.

Avoca Café

Inside Avoca Handweavers, Suffolk Street, D2, t (01) 677 4215 (*inexpensive*)

Open Mon–Sat 9.30–5.30

Excellent designer café decked out in wood and with organic produce used where possible, and tempting baked desserts.

Aya Restaurant

Clarendon Street, D2, t (01) 677 1544 (*moderate*)

Open Mon–Fri 8am–11pm, Sat 10am–11pm, Sun 11am–10pm

Japanese restaurant with Dublin's first conveyor belt sushi bar, which often offers special prices at lunchtime and weekends. The delicatessen next door offers freshly made takeaways, and children's platters, colouring sheets and crayons are offered to little ones.

Bad Ass Cafe

Crown Alley, Temple Bar, D2, t (01) 671 2596 (*moderate*)

Open daily 11.30am–12 midnight

Diner-style spot for pizza, chops and burgers, made famous because pop star Sinead O'Connor used to waitress here. You'll have to explain to your children that the restaurant's name refers to a donkey. Its casual surroundings are great for children and families who want to relax with American-style pizzas, burgers and salads. Children's menu, baby changing and high chairs are all available.

Beshoff

14 Westmoreland Street, D2, t (01) 677 8026 (*inexpensive*)

Open Mon–Sat 11–11 and Sun 12 noon–11

Good quality fish and chips in a self-service restaurant. Takeaway available.

Bewley's Oriental Café

78 Grafton Street, D2, t (01) 677 6761 (*inexpensive*)

Open daily 7.30am–11pm

After its renovation the Grafton Street branch of Bewley's has lost some of its charm but has returned to offering self-service. Bewley's was founded as a chain of coffee houses in 1840, and the smell of Bewley's roast coffee and sticky buns is nostalgic for Dubliners and visitors alike. Despite the redecoration, most of the branch's dark-panelled Art Deco and Art Nouveau architecture has been retained and it is a central place to have a cup of tea and try some traditional barm brack. The first floor once housed Bewley's chocolate factory, and has become a small museum – with family portraits, old equipment, teapots made in the 1920s and an old penny lavatory lock – that gives you some sense of Bewley's place in Dublin's social history.

Bewley's

11–12 Westmoreland Street, D2, t (01) 677 6761 (*inexpensive*)

Open daily 7.30am–7.30pm, Thurs to 9pm

This branch restaurant has also been renovated but has retained its old style. You can sit here for as long as you like and relax over tea, and one of their famous cakes or a traditional Irish breakfast.

Captain America's Cookhouse

Grafton Court, Grafton Street, D2, t (01) 671 5266 (*inexpensive*)

Open daily 11am–12 midnight

Something of a rock'n'roll institution in Dublin since it first opened in 1971, as the first 'Hard Rock'-style restaurant in Ireland. Children will love this noisy, casual restaurant, although it might be better to visit at midday rather than in the early evenings, as it'll be a bit less frenetic, although the music will still be loud. Activity sheets with crayons, children's menu and high chairs are all available for kids. As alternatives to burgers and all the classic American specialities, there are soups and salads also on the menu.

Casa Pasta

Clontarf Road, D3, **t** (01) 833 1402 (*inexpensive*)
Open Mon–Sat 6pm–12 midnight, Sun 1–11pm

This North Dublin Italian restaurant has a friendly, fun atmosphere and offers a children's menu, which includes small portions of pasta dishes or fast food. Highchairs available.

Caviston's Seafood Restaurant

59 Glasthule Road, Sandycove, **t** (01) 280 9245 (*moderate*)
Open Tues–Sun 12 noon–4pm only

An excellent delicatessen on the southside of Dublin bay with a small restaurant with extremely good, gourmet-standard seafood attached. Note: it opens for lunch only.

Cornucopia

19 Wicklow Street, D2, **t** (01) 677 7583 (*inexpensive*)
Open Mon–Sat 9–8; Thurs only 9–9

Queue for your vegetarian and vegan choices at midday, or there's table service in the evenings. Good value, imaginative and wholesome food is served in a casual place that was Dublin's first vegetarian restaurant.

Debenham's Restaurant

Jervis Shopping Centre, Mary Street, D1, **t** (01) 878 1222 (*moderate*)
Open Mon–Sat 10–6

VIP baby service here includes free jars of baby food (some organic) when you purchase an adult meal; bottle warmers; free bibs and baby wipes; and also kids' snack boxes where they can select five healthy food items. There's also a small play area for children inside this department store restaurant.

Dome Restaurant

St Stephen's Green Shopping Centre, D2, **t** (01) 478 1287 (*inexpensive–moderate*)
Open Mon–Sat 10–6.30

This large restaurant at the top of the shopping centre has views of St Stephen's Green and a varied menu, including children's portions if requested, and high chairs and a baby-changing facility.

Elephant and Castle

18 Temple Bar, D2, **t** (01) 679 3121 (*inexpensive*)
Open Mon–Fri 8am–11.30pm, Sat 10.30am–11.30pm, Sun 12 noon–11.30

Here you'll find a relaxed atmosphere that kids enjoy for brunch, snacks or early dinners.

Fresh Vegetarian Restaurant

Second Floor, Powerscourt Townhouse Centre, South William Street, D2, **t** (01) 671 9669 (*inexpensive*)
Open Mon–Sat 10–5.30, Thurs 10–8

This restaurant has good vegetarian and vegan soups, hot dishes, salads, filled bagels, foccacia, tomato breads, smoothies, fresh juices, organic coffee and homemade cakes (organic where possible). There are discounts for students.

Gallagher's Boxty House

20–21 Temple Bar, Temple Bar, D2, **t** (01) 677 2762 (*moderate*)
Open daily 12 noon–11.30

A 'traditional Irish' restaurant which has as its speciality 'boxty' – potato pancakes. They come with a big choice of fillings and dishes on the side. Reservations are recommended for evenings.

Gotham Café

8 South Anne Street, D2, **t** (01) 475 0888 (*inexpensive–moderate*)
Open daily 11am–12 midnight

Gourmet pizzas, speciality salads, pasta, vegetarian and noodle dishes are on offer at this popular American-style family café. Children's menu, baby-changing room and high chairs are all available.

Govinda's

4 Aungier Street, D2, **t** (01) 475 0309 (*inexpensive-moderate*)
Open Mon–Sat 11–10.30

An Irish-Indian vegetarian café-restaurant where you queue at the bar for tasty dishes.

Harry Ramsdens

Naas Road, D12, **t** (01) 460 0233 (*inexpensive*)
Open Mon–Sat 11am–11.30pm, Sun 12 noon–9

At weekends, this fish and chips institution has a resident face-painter on hand as well as a life-size version of Postman Pat. Children are offered colouring books and crayons.

Juice

73–83 South Great Georges Street, D2, **t** (01) 475 7856 (*inexpensive*)
Open daily 8–2.30, 6.30–10.30

Dublin's first juice bar has all sorts of healthy and refreshing food: good vegan and vegetarian snacks, meals and veggie burgers, and lots of tasty juices.

Kilkenny Restaurant

6 Nassau Street, D2, **t** (01) 677 7066 (*inexpensive*)
Open Mon–Wed and Fri–Sat 9–5, Thurs 9–7, Sun 11–5

Traditional home cooking is on offer for lunch at this excellent self-service restaurant that overlooks Trinity College.

Leo Burdock's

2 Werburgh Street, D8, **t** (01) 454 0306 (*inexpensive*)
Open Mon–Sat 12 noon–12 midnight, Sun 4–12 midnight

Next door to the Lord Edward pub and Christchurch Cathedral sits Dublin's best and oldest fish and chip shop. As is traditional, they only do takeaways.

Luigi Malones

The Friary, 5–6 Cecilia Street, Temple Bar, D2, **t** (01) 679 2723 (*inexpensive–moderate*)
Open daily 12 noon–11

A family-friendly restaurant with a children's menu, a relaxed atmosphere and friendly staff, serving modern Italian-influenced food including pizza. Note the arch as you enter the Temple Bar restaurant, as it is part of the original 12th-century Dublin Wall; ask about the origins of the other artefacts on display that now serve as interior decorations. There's another branch in the suburb of Stillorgan, D4.

Mao Café and Bar

2–3 Chatham Row, D2, **t** (01) 670 4899 (*inexpensive–moderate*)
Open daily 10am–12 midnight

Slightly hip, popular spot that's open daily for coffee, lunch and Sunday brunch. It tends to be very busy in the evenings, so dine early with kids. To eat there's Asian-based food plus salads, juices, smoothies and desserts. There's also a branch near the ferry terminal in Dun Laoghaire.

Milano's

Dawson St, D2, **t** (01) 670 7744 (*inexpensive*)
Open daily 12 noon–12 midnight

Reliable pizza, like the UK's Pizza Express chain. There's a supervised play area on Sundays, 12–5pm.

Nectar Juice Bar

53 Ranelagh Village, D6, **t** (01) 491 0934 (*inexpensive*)
Open daily 10am–11pm

For health-oriented children who like snacks and understated evening meals, this café-style restaurant creates nourishing juices, smoothies, wraps, salads and some hot dishes.

Nude

21 Suffolk Street, D2, **t** (01) 677 4804 (*inexpensive*)
Open daily 11–11

Good for freshly made juices, smoothies, paninis and organic snacks.

Outlaws

62 Upper George Street, Dun Laoghaire, **t** (01) 284 2817 (*inexpensive*)
Open daily 11.30am–11pm

A cheerful spot in Dun Laoghaire serving good steaks, chicken and burgers.

Thunder Road Café

Fleet Street, Temple Bar, D2, **t** (01) 679 4057 (*inexpensive*)
Open daily 12 noon–12 midnight

Staff dress in 1950s gear, and offer American style food at this fun café. Facilities include a baby-changing room, children's menu and high chairs.

Trentuno

Wicklow St, D2, **t** (01) 677 4190 (*inexpensive–moderate*)
Open Mon–Sat 11–11.30pm, Sun 12 noon–9

Traditional and contemporary Italian cuisine. It's open all day, and has friendly staff, a children's menu and a baby-changing area.

Wagamama

South King Stt, D2, **t** (01) 478 2152 (*inexpensive*)
Open Mon–Sat 12 noon–11pm, Sun 12 noon–10pm

For children who like oriental soups, noodle or rice dishes, this friendly, spacious branch of the well-known restaurant chain has benches at long refectory-style tables. Crayons and colouring paper are there to amuse the kids before the food arrives.

Yamamori Noodles

71/72 South Great Georges St, D2, **t** (01) 475 5001 (*inexpensive*)
Open Mon–Thurs 12.30–3, 5.30–11, Fri, Sat 12.30–3, 5.30–11.30, Sun 2–10pm

A very popular place with very authentic Japanese noodle and rice dishes, and which is also notably child-friendly, with high chairs, baby-changing facilities, extremely helpful staff and small portions for children.

Leinster

04

LEINSTER

Around 300 BC an Irish chieftain named Lavra the Mariner lost his kingdom to his thieving uncle, and hired mercenaries from France to help him regain it. The Gauls found his homeland so agreeable that they decided to stay on. They had triumphed in battle using special broad-pointed spears, called *Laighen* in Irish, and so the people of the kingdom began to refer to it as 'The place of the broad-pointed spear' – that is, *Laighenster*, or Leinster.

The province's fertile farmland, lush forests, lakes and mountains have always attracted outsiders, and each foreign invasion brought new techniques and skills. All along Ireland's east and southeast coasts, down to the tip of Hook Head in County Wexford, Vikings, Norsemen, French Normans and Englishmen settled and lived together peacefully enough, after an initial period of strife. Evidence of Ireland's Christian 'golden age' – when Irish monasteries were among Europe's greatest seats of learning – can be found in abbeys, churches and ruined monasteries dotted throughout Leinster. What makes Ireland's 'enlightenment' all the more noteworthy is the fact that it coincided with the Dark Ages in the rest of Europe.

Today Leinster is the most heavily populated province of Ireland. It includes two of Ireland's original provinces – *Mide* (now Counties Longford, Meath and Westmeath) and the original, but much smaller, Leinster (the other nine counties of present-day Leinster). The busiest county by far is, naturally, Dublin, and the influence of the Republic's capital reverberates outward via the tentacles of its new, sprawling highways. Ireland's laws have been made in Leinster for more than 2,000 years, first at the Hill of Uisneach and later at Tara (*see* pp.100, 106). The first parts of Ireland brought under English control were Dublin and the small area around it known as the 'Pale'. The border of the Pale changed, but at its biggest it stretched from Dundalk to Waterford. 'Beyond the Pale' the Irish tribal leaders were a law unto themselves, at least until the time of Elizabeth I. Not surprisingly, English settlers tended to congregate in the Pale. Leinster was also the favourite home of the Protestant Irish landed gentry, who left the region with many enormous stately homes. You can feel the influence of this community's writers, thinkers and men and women of action all around you.

Children can learn a lot from a visit to Leinster, as history seeps from every nook and cranny. There are some facilities specifically geared towards children, but they can be some distance from each other – the charm of this area lies in discovering things at your own pace and in your own way. Regal houses or ruins from its long-inhabited past can be found around each corner or bend in the road, and you can wander through farmland, forests, mountains and seascapes for days on end, letting the faeries, maybe, take you in circles around the place you thought you were looking for.

More specifically, the coastal areas from Hook Head, in Wexford, to Louth are great for children who like to swim and cycle; Kilkenny, Westmeath and Wicklow are lush counties to visit for fresh air and country walks, some in mountains. Dublin, Meath, Westmeath and Kilkenny are especially noteworthy for ruins and castles. Horse-lovers will want to see Kildare, while the spiritually and ecologically minded enjoy Wicklow and Kilkenny. Southeast Leinster is the sunniest part of Ireland. Its marshes teem with wading birds – so pack binoculars and good pairs of boots. Low-lying pasture drops down to golden, sandy beaches, so in summer make sure too that you bring along a bucket and spade and swimsuits.

On a single trip to Leinster, you might like to jump into the middle of Ireland first and visit its first-known ancient seat of power, the Hill of Uisneach in Westmeath. If you arrive via Dublin, you could first stay a couple of nights in Malahide. Not far from Uisneach is the Loughcrew cairn, near where a peaceful guesthouse, Mornington House, sits on the edge of Lake Derravaragh. This lake is where the Children of Lir are said to have lived as enchanted swans for a hundred years (*see* p.177). Drive back east to the Hill of Tara (Co. Meath), where later High Kings held counsel, and Newgrange, home of Aengus the Young, the Tuatha Dé Danaan god of love, in the Boyne Valley.

Highlights

All aboard for the Fry Model Railway Museum in Malahide, p.71
Walking in the Wicklow Mountains, p.81
Exploring the medieval delights of Kilkenny, p.83
Discovering Celtic ways at the Irish National Heritage Park, Wexford, p.85
Visiting Aengus Óg at Stone-Age Newgrange, p.99
Tracking the Vikings in Westmeath, p.106

Leinster

Leinster
MONAGHAN
CAVAN
Cavan
DOWN
Cullaville
Faughart
Carlingford
Cooley Peninsula
Cooley Point
Knockbridge
Dundalk
Louth
LOUTH
Castlebellingham
IRISH
SEA
Lough Gowna
Newtown Forbes
Killoe
Granard
Lough Sheelin
Lough Ramor
Nobber
Ardee
Dunany
Carrigglas Manor
Lough Kinale
Oldcastle
Sliab na Cailleach
Collon
Monasterboice
Clogherhead
Cloondara
Longford
LONGFORD
Lanesborough
Mostrim (Edgeworthstown)
Loughcrew
River Blackwater
Old Mellifont Abbey
Hill of Slane
Knowth
Drogheda
Kells
Ardagh
Tullynally Castle
Castlepollard
Fore
Fore Abbey
Lough Derravaragh
L. Leane
Fordstown
Slane
Newgrange
Bettystown
Laytown
Royal Canal
R. Inny
Navan
R. Nanny
Saint's Island
Ballymahon
Abbeyshrule
Delvin
MEATH
Balbriggan
Ardgillan Demesne
Lough Ree
The Pigeons
Lough Owel
Mullingar
Tara
Naul
Skerries
Inchmore
Glassan
WESTMEATH
Trim
Kilmessan
Killinure Lough
Hill of Uisneach
The Downs
Castle
Dunsany
Lusk
Lough Ennell
Belvedere House
Athlone
Castletown
Ratoath
Newbridge House
Donabate
Lambay Island
Kinnegad
Swords
Malahide Castle
River Shannon
Moate
Tyrellspass
R. Boyne
Dublin Airport
Malahide
Portmarnock
Clonmacnoise
Clara
Kilcock
Maynooth
Edenderry
Carbury
Leixlip
Douglas (Isle of Man)
Shannonbridge
Blackwater Bog
Durrow Monastery
Castletown House
Howth Castle
Howth
R. Brosna
Grand Canal
KILDARE
Celbridge
Lucan
Holyhead
DUBLIN
Liverpool
Tullamore
Bog of Allen
Prosperous
Straffan
Dublin Bay
Shannon Harbour
OFFALY
Lullymore
Robertstown
Clane
Rathfarnham
Blackrock
Dun Laoghaire
Monkstown
Dalkey
Dalkey Island
Banagher
Kilcormac
Rathangan
Sallins
Kill
Naas
Glencullen
Killiney
Portarlington
Newbridge
Punchestown
Bray
Birr
Kinnitty
Slieve Bloom Mtns
R. Barrow
Monasterevin
Kildare
Tully National Stud
Blessington
R. Liffey
R. Dodder
Enniskerry
Powerscourt Estate
Kilruddery Gardens
Sugar Loaf Mountain
Greystones
Leap Castle
Emo Court
Emo
The Curragh
Kilcullen
L. Tay
Wicklow Way
Aghancon Hill Fort
Portlaoise
Hollywood
Kilcoole
Roundwood House
Rock of Dunamase
Ardscull Motte
Wicklow Mountains
Gloster
Mountrath
Stradbally
Dunlavin
Wicklow Gap
Roundwood
Ballaghmore
LAOIS
Ardscull
Crookstown
Glendalough
Ashford
Mount Usher Gardens
Roscrea
R. Nore
Athy
Ballitore
Timolin
WICKLOW
Laragh
Wicklow
Borris in Ossory
Timahoe
Moone High Cross
Moone
R. Slaney
Morleygall
Abbeyleix
Kilkea
Avonbeg
Wicklow Head
R. Suir
Rathdowney
Ballinakill
Castledermot
Rathdrum
Rathvilly
Avondale Forest Park
Dunganstown Castle
Durrow
Killeshin
Carlow
Craiguecullen
Hacketstown
Brown's Hill Dolmen
Aughrim
Avoca
Vale of Avoca
Castlecomer
Tullow
Johnstown
CARLOW
Tinahely
Arklow
River Barrow
Freshford
Old Leighlin
Leighlinbridge
Thurles
R. Nore
Ballon
Clogga
Dunmore Cave
Bagenalstown
Kilmichael Point
Slieveardagh Hills
Tullaroan
Kilkenny
Myshall
Clonegal
TIPPERARY
South Leinster Way
Gorey
Ballymoney
Gowran
Mount Leinster
Courtown
Kings River
KILKENNY
Blackstairs Mtns
Ferns
Cashel
Kells
Graiguenamanagh
Ballycanew
Thomastown
R. Bann
Mount Juliet
Jerpoint Abbey
Ballyemund
Dysart Castle
Brandon Hill
Inistioge
Enniscorthy
WEXFORD
Wexford Coastal Path
River Nore
R. Slaney
NORTHERN IRELAND
ULSTER
Blackwater
CONNACHT
New Ross
Blackwater Harbour
Ballynabola
Curracloe
Dunganstown
Irish National Heritage Park
Ferrycarrig
Wexford Bay
Raven Point Peninsula (Nature Reserve)
REPUBLIC OF IRELAND
LEINSTER
J.F. Kennedy Park
Campile
Foulksmills
Wexford
N
Dunbrody Abbey
Fishguard
Waterford
Ballyhack
Tintern Abbey
Johnstown Castle
Rosslare
Arthurstown
Pembroke
Cherbourg
Roscoff
Duncannon
Bannow
Kilrane
Rosslare Harbour
Kilmore
MUNSTER
Fethard
Bannow Bay
Baginburn Head
Carne
Kilmore Quay
Wexford Coastal Path
20km
10miles
Waterford Harbour
Hook Head
Saltee Islands

Stop off at Newgrange Farm, then visit Dublin and drive south to Co. Wicklow to see St Kevin's monastery at Glendalough after climbing in the Wicklow Mountains. You could easily spend a few days wandering in the hills, or find out what life was like in a medieval town like Kilkenny. For big-city excitement you'll have to stay in Dublin (*see* pp.43–64), but, instead of battling with its traffic, you might prefer to take a bus tour round town or a trip out to a museum or a working farm. That way, you'll be able to relax and look around, play with your children, and find how easy it is to have a chat with the Irish, who have a habit of being welcoming, even in the age of the Celtic Tiger.

Tourist information for Leinster

Tourism Ireland, Freephones UK **t** 0800 039 7000, US and Canada **t** 1 800 223 6470, **www**.tourismireland.com (*see* p.300)
Dublin Tourism Centre, St Andrew's Church, Suffolk St, D2, **t** 1 850 230 330
Open Sept–June Mon–Sat 9–5.30, Sun (Sept only) 10.30–3; July–Aug Mon–Sat 9–7, Sun 10.30–3.
Dublin's central tourist office also provides all sorts of information and services (including accommodation advice) for the whole of Ireland as well as for the city itself. *See also* p.49
Dúchas, the Heritage Service, 51 St. Stephen's Green, Dublin 2, **t** (01) 647 3000/1890 321 421, **www**.heritageireland.ie
The Irish government department responsible for running many monuments and historic sites throughout the country (*see also* p.300).

Getting there and around

By air Dublin Airport is naturally the main flight arrival point for Leinster. *See* p.283.
By sea Leinster also contains Ireland's busiest ferry entry points: Dublin and nearly-adjacent Dun Laoghaire, and Rosslare, near Wexford. Rosslare is a very useful entry harbour for anyone travelling to the south and southwest of the Republic, and wishing to miss out the Dublin area. *See* pp.284–5.
By bus Bus Eireann coaches to every part of Leinster leave from Busáras bus station in Dublin. *See* p.46
By train In Dublin, trains along the east coast between Dundalk and Wexford/Rosslare and to northeast Leinster (Longford) leave from Connolly Station; trains to destinations further west and south (south Co. Kildare, Carlow, Kilkenny) leave from Heuston Station. *See* p.288

COUNTY DUBLIN

County Dublin is the area surrounding Dublin itself, and includes the suburbs a little to the west and south of the city, and a larger rural and coastal area to the north, up to Balbriggan on the border with Co. Louth. In ancient times, Howth, the point that closes off the north side of Dublin Bay, was named *Elta Edar*, and this is where Partholón (*see* p.29) is said to have arrived with the second wave of human immigrants to settle in Ireland. On a grimmer note, it is also where a boat landed that brought the Black Death plague to Ireland in 1348.

From Howth Head, and from Dun Laoghaire and Sandycove on the south side, there are wonderful views of Dublin Bay – in spite of the new plague of housing developments, which are sprouting everywhere in the county, blurring boundaries between the city and other towns. It is to be hoped the movers and shakers will stop before they build over all of this county's beautiful surroundings, whose forests, hills and clean waterways bring good health in mind and spirit to its children.

Everywhere in Co. Dublin is easy to get to from the city by public transport. The DART local rail line follows the coast around Dublin Bay all the way from Bray, Co. Wicklow (*see* p.76), to Howth, main-line trains run further north, and there's an ample choice of buses. Hence this is a good alternative to trying to drive and suffering the stress of getting lost due to maps that still don't have on them the roads to Dublin's brand new suburban realms.

Tourist information for Co. Dublin

Dublin Tourism Centre, St Andrew's Church, Suffolk St, D2, **t** 1 850 230 330, *see* p.49
Branch offices at: **Dublin Airport** Arrivals Hall
Dun Laoghaire Ferry Terminal
The Square, Tallaght, D24
As well as Dublin Tourism's offices there are local offices in:
Balbriggan George's Square, **t** (01) 841 4884
Malahide Malahide Castle, **t** (01) 845 0490

Getting around

For anywhere along the shore of Dublin Bay the **DART** local train is the easiest way to get there (*see* p.47). In central Dublin you can get DART trains at Connolly, Tara St or Pearse St stations. For Malahide and the coast north of Howth, take **Northern Suburban** trains on the Dublin–Dundalk line, from the same stations. Many Dublin city **buses** run to the suburbs and surrounding towns, so coach services are not usually necessary.

SPECIAL TRIPS

Dalkey

Once an important port on Ireland's east coast, Dalkey is nowadays better-known as Dublin's most fashionable suburb – the favourite hang-out for Ireland's top pop idols and film stars. It's easy to see why: it's the most charming of all the old villages around Dublin Bay, still with a good deal of the look and feel of a real fishing village, and has the best views over the bay, especially towards the neighbouring village of Killiney. Dalkey and Killiney also have a good choice of places to eat.

Dalkey Castle and Heritage Centre

Castle Street, Dalkey, **t** (01) 285 8366
Getting there DART to Dalkey station or bus 8
Open Daily Apr–Dec 9.30–5, Sat–Sun and public holidays 11–5 all year
Adm Adult €5, under-12s €3, family (2+4) €14

This is one of two tower castles left in Dalkey (there once were seven), and known as the Medieval Goat Castle. You enter through the larger castle on Castle Street, and from the top there is a fine view of Dalkey village. An adjoining 11th-century church is dedicated to a local saint called St Begnet, who also has a church dedicated to her on nearby Dalkey Island. Children can scramble over the tiny graveyard, and may be interested in Dalkey Castle's Murder Hole, through which boiling oil (or worse) used to be thrown upon unwanted intruders. Teenagers may be interested in the exhibition scripted by local writer and playwright Hugh Leonard and the theatre attached to the castle. The seaside is about 10 minutes' walk from here.

Dalkey Island

Getting there boats run regularly roughly May–Sept from Coliemore Harbour in Dalkey, most frequently at weekends and holidays.

In summer you can take a boat trip to this tiny island just offshore from Dalkey, where there is a Martello tower, a bird sanctuary and the medieval church of St Begnet.

Killiney Hill Park

Getting there DART to Dalkey or Killiney; from Killiney station, walk up Victoria Rd

A short, steep walk up the hill between Killiney and Dalkey will take you to beautiful views of Killiney Strand, Dublin Bay and much of Dublin.

> ***Tell me an Irish riddle –***
> **Question –** ***What has an eye but cannot see?***
> **Answer –** ***A needle***

Howth

Round off a day in Howth with a trip to Ireland's Eye – which has another lonely Martello Tower – and the other tiny rocky islands just offshore; boats leave regularly daily from East Pier in Howth Harbour Apr–Sept, if there are enough people.

Howth Castle and Demesne

Off Howth Road, Howth, D13, **t** (01) 832 2246
Getting there 5mins walk from Howth station; from Dublin city centre, take DART to Howth station or buses 31, 31B, making sure you sit on the top deck to admire the view.
Open Apr–Jun daily 8am–sunset. **Adm** Free

This 15th-century castle, currently being renovated by its inhabitants, is surrounded by giant oak trees, and rhododendrons and azaleas that bloom in May and June. Co. Mayo's 16th-century pirate queen Grace O'Malley (*see* below) is credited as the reason why the Castle's front gate is always left open, and a table is set every evening with linen, crystal and candelabras to await a visitor. In the Castle grounds are a portal tomb known as Aedeen's Grave and the Howth Transport Museum.

National Transport Museum

Howth Castle Demesne, Howth, D13, **t** (01) 832 0427, **www.nationaltransportmuseum.org**
Open Sept–May Sat, Sun and bank holidays 2–5, 2 Jun–Aug Mon–Sat 10–5, 6 Dec–1 Jan daily 2–5,
Adm Adult €3,child €1.50, family €8

Children fascinated by automobiles, models and moving things in general will love this very attractive and well-organized museum. On show are 60 of its 100 examples of historic means of transport, from military vehicles to trucks and cars. The buses, trams and fire engines of over a century ago are here, going right back to horse-drawn carriages and even handcarts. It may be a surprise to discover that at the start of the 20th century, Dublin's public transport system was well ahead of most other cities, as it was one of the first places to bring electric trams to its streets.

A story to tell: The ransom of Grace O'Malley

Do you want to know why, every evening, even to this day, a table is laid for dinner, waiting for a stranger to call at Howth Castle?

In the 16th century, after the 'pirate queen' of Connacht Granuaile, also known as Grace O'Malley, had gone to England to bargain with Queen Elizabeth I (*see* p.178), she landed on her return to Ireland at the port of Howth. She then walked up the slope to Howth Castle to ask for a place to spend the night – the logical thing to do, since she was of noble blood, and under Ireland's old Brehon Laws the local nobility were obliged to give her shelter.

When the door was opened by the Earl of Howth's butler, she said, 'I am Granuaile, Lady of the Isles. Would you be so kind as to ask the Earl of Howth to grant me hospitality this evening?'

'I beg your pardon, my lady,' he replied, 'Who are you?'

'I rule the waves of the islands to the far west of the big island.'

'The big island?' he queried, 'I am sorry, but his lordship has already dined this evening, and is not expecting visitors.'

'Such ways you have, sir,' Granuaile's face had turned red with anger. 'Have you no conscience about the rules of hospitality, especially to a lady of my birth?'

But already the door was slammed in her face.

According to the laws of her people, a stranger was always to be given food and lodging, even by the poorest in the realm. Granuaile spluttered with rage as she stomped down the hill to a tavern for her supper. Then, as fate would have it, she met the son of the Earl of Howth, who was friendlier to her than his butler had been. They ate and drank together for hours, until Granuaile had drunk him under the table. The next thing the Earl's son knew was when he woke up to hear the gulls circling Granuaile's ship, bound for a faraway place.

When the Earl of Howth was told about the kidnapping he sent word to Granuaile, promising whatever she wanted if she would only return his son. Her reply was this: 'That henceforth he honours the laws of hospitality. That the gates of Howth Castle are ne'er to be shut till after the dinner hour, and that an extra place always be set at his table just in case one shall come.' By the standards of those times this was a mild demand, so the Earl immediately gave his promise, and his son was duly returned to him.

Malahide

One of the most pleasant seaside towns around Dublin, Malahide is well prepared for tourists with good restaurants and up-market shops. The marina is lovely and there are good beaches, but if you want to swim look out for the strong currents. Because it's so close to Dublin and its airport it is quite busy, yet far enough away to allow visitors to escape into the green world of the castle grounds and get a taste of a more tranquil way of life.

Getting there Malahide is 8 miles (13km) northeast of Dublin City via Fairview and the Malahide Road, and 4 miles (6km) from Dublin Airport.

By bus Bus 42 from Beresford Place (near Busáras), or from Talbot St. Dublin Bus's 'Coast and Castle' tour also visits Malahide, *see* p.48

By car N1 Dublin-Belfast Road, turn right at Swords bypass roundabout for Malahide.

By train Some northbound Drogheda–Dundalk trains from Connolly Station, Dublin, stop in Malahide, or take suburban trains from Connolly, Tara St or Pearse St stations.

Getting around

Bike hire CGL, 9 Townyard Lane, Malahide, **t** (01) 845 4275.

Malahide Castle Demesne

Malahide, **t** (01) 846 2184/846 2516

Getting there The Demesne and sites within it are a 10–20mins walk through the park from Malahide station. Everything is well signposted.

Open Apr–Oct Mon–Sat 10–5, Sun and bank holidays 11–6; Nov–Mar Mon–Sat 10–5, Sat–Sun and bank holidays 11–5, winter times may vary

Adm Free, see below for individual attractions

Toilets, tourist office, bookshop, restaurant, café, disabled access, audio tours, playground, playing fields, cricket pitch, tennis courts, golf and pitch and putt course, parking

This vast expanse of 270 acres of rolling parkland just outside Malahide was once the home of the Talbot family, who occupied the Castle for 800 years after Prince John granted it to them in 1185. The castle is the longest to have been continuously inhabited by the same family in all of Ireland.

Cromwell displaced them briefly, but otherwise the Talbots lived here until 1975. The land around the Castle does not seem to have changed much over the years, apart from the beautiful gardens created by the last Lord Talbot of Malahide. Here you can sense the peace the owners enjoyed when not defending their realm, eight centuries ago.

Contained within the grounds are the Castle, the Fry Model Railway Museum, the Talbot Botanic Gardens, Tara's Palace Dolls' House, stable yards and many sports facilities. It is, in effect, nearly a town in itself. There are even ruins in the grounds, including an old chapel, so that you gain a sense of what it was like to live alongside a castle in days of yore. Plus, there are all the wide, empty grassy spaces where children can play after poring over the exhibits in the museums. You can stop for lunch or a picnic in the grounds, and shop for locally-made crafts in the former stable yard. If you've been stuck in Dublin traffic, it's a welcome relief to spend a day enjoying these grounds.

Malahide Castle

Malahide Castle Demesne, t (01) 846 2184
Open Apr–Oct Mon–Sat 10–5, Sun and bank holidays 11–6, Nov–Mar Mon–Fri 10–5, Sat–Sun and bank holidays 2–5
Adm Adult €6, under-12s €3.50, family (2+4) €16.50
Restaurant, disabled access, craft and souvenir shop, picnic areas, children's playground

A guide takes you into this well-preserved castle, its oldest part begun in 1185. It has an air of cloistered tranquility. The Great Hall – built in 1475, with additional parts added between the 15th and 19th centuries – is Ireland's only surviving original medieval great hall. Talbot family portraits hang on its walls. Fourteen Talbot cousins breakfasted here in 1690 before riding out to fight at the Battle of the Boyne; none returned (*see* p.35). The castle feels very much like a home, and gives children a good impression of what it was like to live there. They will probably be most curious about its nursery, library and bedrooms, but equally impressive are the oak room, Great Hall and drawing room, and the National Gallery of Ireland's national portrait collection, which adorns the walls.

Malahide Castle Craft Shop

Seaview, Yellow Walls Road, Malahide, t (01) 846 2516

Interesting pottery, musical instruments and woven cloth.

Fry Model Railway Museum

Malahide Castle Demesne, t (01) 846 3779
Open Apr–Sept Mon–Sat 10–1, 2–5, Sun and bank holidays 2–6
Adm Adult €6, child €3.50, family €16.50
Model shop, bookshop

The Fry Museum in the castle grounds is one of Ireland's most exciting places for model railway enthusiasts. The purpose-built museum contains one of the world's largest working miniature railways, covering 2,500 sq ft. Intricate handmade models of Irish trains from the beginnings of rail travel, with replicas of stations in Dublin and Cork and other well-known landmarks, convey the history of railways in Ireland. Look out for the giant model complete with stations, bridges, buses, trams and even barges on the River Liffey – all made to scale with incredible attention to detail. The collection was amassed in the 1920–30s by railway engineer and draughtsman Cyril Fry.

Talbot Botanic Gardens

Malahide Castle, t (01) 872 7777
Open Daily May–Sept 2–5, guided tour of walled garden Wed 2pm, groups by appointment only
Adm Adult €3.50, under-12s free; guided tour €3
Toilets, teashop, wheelchair access

Over 5,000 different varieties of trees and shrubs are on display. The gardens as they are today were laid out by Milo, the last Lord of Malahide Castle, between 1948 and 1973. A Victorian conservatory, 16 acres of shrubbery and 4 acres of walled gardens complete these refreshing botanic environs where children can play and adults can breathe easily.

Tara's Palace Dolls' House

Malahide Castle Demesne, t (01) 846 3779
Open Apr–Oct Mon–Sat 10–1, 2–5, Sun and bank holidays 2–6, Nov–Mar Sat, Sun and bank holidays 2–5. Adm Donations welcome – adult €2, child €1

Meticulously constructed over 10 years in the late 20th century, Tara's Palace combines the grandeur and elegance of three great 18th-century Irish mansions – Leinster House, Castletown House and Carlton House. It shows in miniature the best of Irish craftsmanship, worked into the interiors of a great Georgian house. Miniature porcelain and glassware, and even paintings by Tom Ryan, RHA, adorn its rooms. Girls who enjoy dolls, and budding architects, will find it fascinating. Accompanying the dolls' house is a collection of 18th- and 19th-century dolls, silverware and furniture.

AROUND AND ABOUT

Animal magic

Animal Farm

Reynoldstown, Naul, **t** (01) 841 2615
Getting there 19 miles (30km) north of Dublin, 5 miles (8km) west of the N1.

A working farm in an olde-worlde setting where children can stroke and feed the animals.

Dublin Butterfly House

Harap Farm, Magillstown, Swords, **t** (01) 840 1285, **www.dublinbutterfly.com**
Getting there About 3 miles (5km) north of Dublin Airport; by car, take N1 north around Swords town, then left onto the R125 (Ashbourne road)
Open May–Sept Tues–Sun and bank holidays 10–6
Adm Adult €5, child €2.50, family (2+2) €12

The natural habitats of hundreds of the world's most beautiful butterflies are remarkably recreated on this family-run farm.

North Bull Island

Dollymount, D5
Getting there Bus 130 from Lower Abbey St, D1
Open daily 7–4.30. **Adm** free

A nature reserve and bird sanctuary near Dollymount Beach, on a 740-acre island created by the build-up of sand behind a sea wall built in Dublin Bay. There are sand dunes, mudflats and salt marsh, plus birds and many interesting plants.

Buckets and spades – best beaches

Dubliners have plenty of favourite beaches around them, not far from town.

Balscadden Beach, Howth – sandy but shallow.
Donabate – just north of Malahide and famous for its sand dunes, but watch out for dangerous tides.
Killiney – good for long walks taking in the view, but part of it is stony.
Malahide – a long, sandy beach, but be aware of strong currents and undertows.
Portmarnock – donkey rides in the summer on this golden sand beach, between Howth and Malahide.
Portrane – has a bird sanctuary at the north end, and, like Donabate just next to it, has lovely dunes.

Bricks and mortar

Ardgillan Castle

Balbriggan, **t** (01) 849 2212
Getting there 19 miles (30km) north of Dublin. By car, N1; by bus, 33; by train, Northern Suburban from Connolly, Tara St or Pearse St Stations.
Open Castle: Apr–Sept Tues–Sun (daily Jul–Aug) and bank holidays 11–6: Oct–Mar Tues–Sun and bank holidays 11–4.30, closed 23 Dec–1 Jan. Park: daily dawn to dusk; Rose garden: Mon–Fri 9.30–5, Sat–Sun and bank holidays 11–5; Guided tours Jun–Aug Thurs 3.30pm or by arrangement
Adm Castle: adult €4, under-12s €3, family (2+3) €9; map exhibition and guided tours €3
Café, wheelchair access, parking

This was originally a Georgian country manor house, built in 1738 by Reverend Robert Taylor, which over time grew to become a castle. Children can explore its 198 acres of woodland and gardens, including a Victorian conservatory and a walled rose garden with a 20-alcove fruit wall. There is also an interesting permanent exhibition of 17th-century maps of Ireland.

Look at this!

Newbridge House, Demesne and Farm

Donabate Demesne: **t** (01) 843 6064,
House: **t** (01) 843 6534/5
Getting there 12 miles (19km) north of Dublin, off the N1. By car, turn east after Swords; by bus, 33B; by train, Northern Suburban to Donabate from Connolly, Tara St or Pearse St.
Open House: Apr–Sept Tue–Sat 10–1, 2–5, Sun and bank holidays 2–6, closed Mon; Oct–Mar Sat–Sun and public holidays 2–5. Grounds open all year
Adm House: adult €6, ages 12–17 €5, 3–11s €3.50, family (2+2) €16.50
Farm: adult €2.50, under-12s €1.50, family €6
Café, shop, children's playground, free parking

You could spend a full day looking around this 350-acre demesne, with a fine 18th-century manor house designed by George Semple. Built in 1737 for Charles Cobb, who later became Archbishop of Dublin, the house was sold to Dublin County Council with much of its original contents. Works of art and antiques that belonged to the

Archbishop are on show on the ground floor, and don't miss the wing added in 1760 by his daughter-in-law Lady Elizabeth Beresford, whose red drawing room is one of the finest Georgian rooms in Ireland. Children will enjoy the strange objects and souvenirs the Cobb family collected, though on a fine day they might prefer Newbridge's woodland and hilly pastures. There's also a playground and a farm with animals, managed with traditional methods. In the museum, in a cobbled courtyard, there's an old-time dairy, forge, carpentry shop, labourer's cottage with original furnishings, stable yard and the striking Lord Chancellor's Carriage.

Skerries Mills

Skerries, **t** (01) 849 5208
Getting there 19 miles (30km) north of Dublin. By car, off coast road (R126) or south from N1; by bus, 33 from Eden Quay; by train, Northern Suburban from Connolly, Tara St or Pearse St.
Open Apr–Sept daily 10.30–5.30, Oct–Mar daily 10.30–4.30, closed 20 Dec–1 Jan and Good Fri
Adm Adult €5, child €4, family €10
Guided tours, tearoom, craft shop, parking

In the seaside town of Skerries there are, next to each other, a watermill, 5-sail windmill and 4-sail thatched windmill, all in good working order. A fun place to see after visiting other sites nearby.

Nature lovers

Arnold's Fruit Farm

Corduff, Lusk, **t** (01) 843 8554
Getting there 4 miles (6km) north of Swords, off N1
Open Jun–Aug, pay for the fruit you pick

Children are always welcome to pick this farm's soft fruit.

Primrose Hill

Lucan, **t** (01) 628 0373
Getting there 8 miles (12km) west of Dublin in Lucan village; bus 25, 66, 67
Open daily Feb–Mar 2–5, Jun–Jul 2–6
Adm Adult €4, child €2.50
Guided tours, plants for sale

A Regency villa, attributed to architect James Gandon, amid 6 acres of grounds that include a garden with perennial plants, roses and lilies that provide continuous colour throughout summer, and a lovely spring garden and woods.

Sporty kids

Activity centres

Adventure Activities

t (01) 668 8047,
www.adventure-activities-ireland.com

Canoe or kayak in Dublin Bay, rock-climb in Dalkey quarry, walk in Wicklow: this agency organizes a raft of activities, all run by friendly, fully qualified instructors. Fees vary by activity; equipment is supplied, and transport is also available.

Fort Lucan Adventureland

Westmanstown, Lucan, **t** (01) 628 0166
Getting there 8 miles (12km) west of Dublin; bus 25, 66, 67
Open Daily 10–6

Outdoor adventure playground with trampolines, swings, slides, maze, a waterslide and crazy golf.

Golf

Willie Fox's Golf

Glencullen, **t** (01) 295 9260
Getting there 12 miles (19km) south of Dublin

A mature golf range with scenic views, plus a pitch and putt course for youngsters.

Horse riding

Ashtown Riding Stables

Navan Road, Ashtown, D15, **t** (01) 838 3807
Getting there North of Phoenix Park, 10 mins from central Dublin; bus 37, 38, 39, 70
Open Summer daily 9–5. **Adm** Adult €25 for lesson, child aged 7+ €16 for a lesson or a ride

Likeable riding centre just north of Phoenix Park.

Water sports

Fingall Sailing School

Upper Strand Road, Broadmeadow Estuary, Malahide, **t** (01) 845 1979
Getting there Malahide harbour, *see* p.70

Junior, youth and adult courses in sail training and windsailing.

Wind and Wave Watersports

16a The Crescent, Monkstown, **t** (01) 284 4177
Getting there DART to Salthill & Monkstown

Windsurfing tuition and gear.

WICKLOW AND CARLOW

Counties Wicklow and Carlow lie cheek by jowl just south of Co. Dublin. Wicklow is hilly, lush and has the most spectacular landscapes near Dublin, of mountains, steep valleys, forests and lakes – so that the county has long been known as an ideal place to visit from the city, for locals and outsiders. Carlow in contrast is open and flat, with tranquil rivers feeding its farmlands. In the quiet farming villages of Carlow (good cycling territory), there is a subtle French influence, a result of the influx of Anglo-Normans around the 12th century. Wicklow meanwhile remained 'rebel territory', full of people who could trace their ancestors back to folkloric warriors like Cúchulainn (*see* p.30). Some managed to secrete themselves away in hills and glens without ever quite giving up their freedoms to the waves of outsiders who arrived over the years.

Many myth-laden ruins are hidden among Wicklow's trees, lakes and mountains. The monastery of St Kevin at Glendalough (*see* p.77) is only the most famous. One of the oldest roads in Leinster is *Bearna na Sciath* (Gap of the Shields), and western Wicklow contains the Glen of Imáil (or Imaal), seat of power of Leinster's kings in the Iron Age. Along one of many winding roads is Donard (*Dún Árd* or High Fort), a tiny village (with a very friendly pub) that is the site of one of three churches founded in Wicklow, circa AD 430, by Palladius, St Patrick's predecessor in bringing Christianity to Ireland. Other landmarks include the ruins of the 14th-century St Mary de Hogges nunnery, and, not far away in a wood on one side of Kilranelagh Hill, 'St. Brigid's Headstone'. In Irish it's called *cloch na gceann* ('stone of the head'), as the son of 6th-century King Aed Ainmire lost his head here. According to local tales Cromwell also put the stone to use for getting rid of the nuns from the nunnery. At any rate, Wicklow people believe that putting your head in the hole cures a headache. The respectful and the hopeful leave rosaries, coins, holy medals and pictures in and around it, in thanks to whatever invisible force may be there that can cure illnesses or answer prayers.

Tourist Information

Arklow, t (0402) 32484, open Jun–mid Sept only
Avoca, t (0402) 35022
Bray, t (01) 286 7128/286 6796
Carlow Town, t (059) 9131554
Glendalough, t (0404) 45688, open Jun–Sept only.
Wicklow Town, t (0404) 69117

Getting there and around

By bus Bus Eireann coaches run to all the main towns in Co. Wicklow from Dublin, Rosslare and Waterford, and most towns in the north of the county are also served by Dublin Bus (*see* p.46) **St Kevin's Bus, t** (01) 281 8119, has direct buses twice daily from Dublin to Glendalough, via Bray.

Carlow Town has a few Bus Eireann connections each day with Dublin, Kilkenny and Waterford. Many villages have bus services provided by a local company, **Rapid Travel Express**, t (0503) 43081.

By train Dublin's **DART** trains run down to Bray and Greystones (*see* p.47). Towns further south along the coast (Wicklow Town, Arklow) are on the Dublin–Rosslare line, from Connolly or Pearse St stations in Dublin. Carlow is on the Dublin–Waterford line, from Dublin's Heuston Station.

Bike hire

Bray Sports Centre, 8 Main St, Bray, **t** (01) 286 3046
Coleman Cycles, 19 Dublin St, Carlow, **t** (059) 9131273
Celtic Cycling, Lorum Old Rectory, Bagenalstown, Co. Carlow, **t** (059) 9775282
Tommy McGrath, Rathdrum, Co. Wicklow, **t** (0404) 46172.

Horse-drawn caravans

Clissmann Horse-drawn Caravans, Carrigmore Farm, Wicklow, **t** (0404) 48188
Travel the old-fashioned way through the Wicklow Mountains.

Shopping

Avoca Handweavers

Avoca Village, Co. Wicklow, t (0402) 35105, **www**.avoca.ie

The lovely and original handwoven woollens made in Avoca are rightly famous, and there is an attractive outlet for them in Dublin (*see* p.49). In Avoca village itself, as well as visiting the shop you can take a tour, in the oldest weaving mill in Ireland (built 1732), and watch the whole weaving process and examine the yarns being used.

Cloydagh Woodcraft

Milford, Co. Carlow, **t** (059) 9132294

Fine carvings and other handmade woodwork; visits by appointment.

Honeysuckle Products

The Watermill, Hacketstown, Co. Carlow, **t** (059) 6471375

Herbal suppliers.

Special Events – Wicklow and Carlow

May

Bray Jazz Festival, Bray, **t** (01) 287 3992, **www**.brayjazz.com

A 3-day international music festival.

Avoca Melody Fair Fitzgerald's Bar, Avoca, Co. Wicklow, **t** (0402) 35108

A music and song festival, held at the end of May.

Spring Wicklow Mountains Walking Festival, **t** (0404) 20070

Boots and warm clothing are recommended; bring a packed lunch and water too.

Carlow Eigse Arts Festival, Bridewell Lane, Carlow Town, **t** (059) 9130065

Music, exhibitions, recitals and dances, from May into June.

Wicklow Gardens Festival, t (0404) 20070

Alongside public gardens over 30 privately owned ones join this event, from May into July.

June

Bray Seaside Family Festival, Bray, **t** (01) 286 1702

Fun festival with races, festival queen ball, GAA sports and soccer, live bands and fireworks, for one week at the end of June.

Dunlavin Arts Festival, Dunlavin, Co. Wicklow, **t** (045) 401 459

A 3-day village festival with a parade, flower and agricultural shows, horse and dog shows, music, street entertainment and crafts.

July

Arklow Seabreeze Festival, Arklow, Co. Wicklow, **t** (0402) 33356

This 4-day street festival, with plenty of music, includes a renowned pig race.

Wicklow Regatta Festival, Wicklow Town, **t** (086) 811 2809

Carnivals, treasure hunts and sports for 11 days.

August

Bray International Festival of Music and Dance, Bray, **t** (01) 286 0080

Always has varied, enjoyable programmes.

Greystones Arts Festival, near Bray, **t** (01) 287 7308, **www**.greystonesartsfestival.com

Street theatre from Europe, workshops and music at the east coast's largest 4-day arts festival.

Rathdrum Festival and Fireworks, Rathdrum, Co. Wicklow, **t** (0404) 46262

Spectacular family event in the Market Square, with a busking competition.

Tinahely Agricultural Show, Fairwood Park, Tinahely, Co. Wicklow, **t** (0402) 38953

Livestock, show-jumping, craft village, a dog show, food hall, dancing and music.

September

Music under the Mountains, Hollywood, Co. Wicklow, **t** (043) 867380

The east coast's premier traditional music event, which always presents some of Ireland's finest folk music artists.

October

Oscar Wilde Autumn School, Bray, **t** (01) 286 4943

Readings and talks by leading writers, for teenagers and above.

Autumn Wicklow Mountains Walking Festival, **t** (0404) 20070

As in Spring (*see* above), this event consists of a great range of organized and guided walks.

Pembroke Gallery

Pembroke Street, Carlow, Co. Carlow, **t** (059) 9141562.

An attractive gallery for local artists.

Wicklow Vale Pottery

Arklow, Co. Wicklow, **t** (0402) 39442

Arklow was built around the pottery industry, and this pottery keeps the tradition alive. Visitors can watch pots being made and all the many skills involved.

Wild Irish Crafts

Kilquigguin, Co. Wicklow, **t** (0503) 56228

At the foot of the Wicklow Mountains in the very south of the county (6 miles/10km east of Tullow, Co. Carlow), this craft centre has on display a wide range of products, all made in the same workshops, including decoupage, framed verses and Victorian jewellery, adorned with pressed flowers taken from the proprietors' own gardens. Around them they have also marked out well-maintained nature trails across five acres of the surrounding countryside (**adm**: adult €2, child free; accessible to wheelchairs) at the foot of the Wicklow mountains. The main path is ideal for short walks, and leads up to a unique viewing point with panoramic views of the Wicklow and Carlow countryside. There's also a picnic area.

TOURING TOWNS

Bray

Now almost a residential suburb of Dublin, the Wicklow coastal town of Bray has also long been one of Dubliners' favourite seaside towns, with a long shingle beach, traditional seaside-resort attractions and bracing sea air.

Things to see and do

Esplanade (Doona Lawn) Hotel

Bray, **t** (01) 286 2056

This hotel hosts country-rock and folk singing during the summer months, Thur–Sun evenings.

Killruddery House and Gardens

Bray, **t** (01) 286 2777/286 3405, **www.**killruddery.com

Getting there 2 miles (3km) south of Bray off Greystones Road

Open House: daily May–Jun and Sept 1–5; Gardens: daily Apr–Sept 1–5; other times by arrangement

Adm House and Gardens: adult €6.50, under-12s €2.50; Gardens only: adult €4.50, under-12s €1.50

This mansion has been the seat of the Earls of Meath since 1618, but was extensively remodelled in 1820. The gardens are the oldest formal gardens in Ireland, and date from the 1680s. Special events are often held here in summer – look out for Irish Heritage Week, in September – and *My Left Foot*, *Angela's Ashes* and *Dancing At Lughnasa* are among the movies that have used it as a location.

National Sealife Centre

Strand Road, **t** (01) 286 6939, **www.**sealife.co.uk

Open Mid-Mar–Oct daily 10–5, Jan–mid-Mar Sat–Sun 10–5

Adm Adult €6.99, child €5.02, family €25.40 (2+3)

Over 20 displays filled with Ireland's native fresh and saltwater marine animals from chub to stingrays are on show here, along with a 'theatre of the seas' presentation featuring sharks. Children can get a chance to hold some rockpool creatures.

Wicklow

County Wicklow is the home of many talented craftspeople, and their studios are often open to visitors, who can observe them at work. The county is known for pottery, weaving, jewellery, silverware, glasswork, sheepskin and traditional hand knitting (*see* p.74, Shopping). Wicklow town is a pleasant little place that makes a good base for touring the area. Facing a shingle bay, it has nice beaches on both sides and the remains of a castle built by one of the first Norman lords in the 12th century.

Things to see and do

Wicklow's Historic Gaol

Kilmantin Hill, Wicklow, **t** (0404) 61599

Open Daily Mar–Oct 10–6

Adm Adult €5.70, under-12s €3.50, under-5s free, family (2+3) €16

Gaol café, shop, pre-booking advised for groups

From 1702 to 1924 there was a jail here. The exhibition covers prisoners' stories from this time, including the 1798 rebellion, the famine and the 18th–19th-century transportation of prisoners to the penal colonies of Australia. The highlight is a reconstruction of a prison ship, which you climb aboard. A vivid insight into Ireland's social history.

Carlow

Carlow town lies where the Barrow and Burrin rivers meet. It is thought there was once a lake here, since the town's Irish name means 'quadruple lake' (*Ceathar Loch*). This unassuming place doesn't seem to mind that the world rushes past it, and appears happy to keep its treasures hidden among its musicians and artists, who quietly produce little gems. One part of the lively local music scene is the Carlow Traditional Singers Club, which brings together singers and storytellers in the Teach Dolmen pub in Tullow St every month.

Within the overlay of an ordinary old Irish town, little alleys lead to places like the Cathedral of the Assumption, off College St, and the 18th-century seminary of St Patrick's College. Nearby is the Browneshill Dolmen, for budding archaeologists (*see* p.80). Having been a border town on the edge of the Pale, Carlow was once heavily fortified, but today only a small part of the castle remains.

Things to see and do

Carlow County Museum

Town Hall, Centaur Street, **t** (059) 9140730

Open All year Tues–Fri 9.30–1, 2–5.30, Sat–Sun 2.30–5.30. **Adm** Adult €1.50, child €0.65

Displays on 19th-and early 20th-century folk life, local history and archaeology, with some rare Celtic artefacts.

SPECIAL TRIPS

Clara-Lara Fun Park

Vale of Clara, Rathdrum, Co. Wicklow,
t (0404) 46161
Getting there 8 miles (12km) inland from Wicklow
Open Daily May–Aug 10–6
Adm Adult €13, under-12s €7, under-4s free

This former army assault course, set in mountains beside the Avonmore River, has been transformed into an 100-acre outdoor adventure park. Children can play Tarzan on rope swings and climb about in tree houses, go rafting like Huckleberry Finn, play mini-golf or ride on an aqua shuttle, row a boat or go-cart. Bring a change of clothes and old shoes, as you'll get wet and muddy.

A story to tell:
Michael Dwyer the Rebel

Michael Dwyer is a legend around Wicklow. He was one of the United Irishmen, led by Wolfe Tone, who rose up against the British in 1798 (*see* p.36). Dwyer was at large in the Wicklow Mountains, and even after the main rebellion was over he continued the fight in a guerrilla campaign against the British troops. He was considered such an important adversary that the British built the 'Military Road' through the Glen of Imaal in an effort to capture him and his rebel followers, but he skilfully avoided them, since he knew the mountains and the Wicklow people so well.

Eventually they tracked him down to a small white stone cottage at Derrynamuck (*see* right). His colleague, a Presbyterian minister named McAllister, ran out of the cottage to draw the fire of the troops while Dwyer escaped. Eventually he decided to give himself up, but only on the understanding that he would be deported to America with his family. Once he was arrested, well-wishers lengthened Dwyer's journey to Kilmainham Jail in Dublin by several hours, cheering him along the route. Once there, he was mistreated by a sadistic jailer and eventually sent to Australia. He died there 20 years later, aged 53, just one week after his by-then grown children had finally arrived to join him. McAllister's grave is still tended and in 1999, on the 200th anniversary of his death, local people placed fresh flowers upon it.

Dwyer McAllister Cottage

Derrynamuck, Co. Wicklow, contact via Glendalough Visitor Centre, **t** (0404) 45325
Getting there Off the Donard–Rathdangan road, southwest of Glendalough
Open Daily mid-Jun–mid-Sept 2–6. **Adm** Free

A traditional thatched cottage of local stone, whitewashed inside and out, nestling in the shade of Kaedeen Mountain at the top of a grassy lane. Restored in the 1940s after lying in ruin for 150 years following a fire, it stands as a monument to the famed Irish rebel Michael Dwyer (*see* left), who in 1799 fought encircling British soldiers here before escaping over snow-covered mountains.

Glendalough

Forever associated with the figure of St Kevin, Glendalough was one of the most important religious centres in Ireland during Europe's 'Dark Ages' (*see* p.31). Even after Kevin died the monastery thrived as an educational and ecclesiastical centre. It contained stone cells, workshops for cabinet-makers and metal workers, a scribes' room, refectory, a dairy, bakery, corn-drying kiln and a grain mill. The community around Glendalough continued to grow until by the 12th century it had become a major trading centre, and home to about 6,000 people. This was despite continuous Viking raids between 800 and 1000, in answer to which the monks built Glendalough's famous round tower as a refuge. It still stands there today. The monastery was finally destroyed in the 14th century, by a fire set by an English army.

Since then the valley between Glendalough's two lakes (the Upper and the Lower) has generally remained the kind of quiet place that St Kevin would have approved of. It's a wonderful spot, amid the kind of countryside you probably imagined when you first thought of coming to Ireland. It gets very busy in summer, so visit early to catch the atmosphere and make time for a stroll by the lake.

Glendalough Visitors' Centre

Glendalough, Co. Wicklow, **t** (0404) 45325
Getting there 30 miles (50km) from Dublin
Open Daily mid-Mar–mid-Oct 9.30–6, mid-Oct–mid-Mar 9.30–5
Adm Adult €2.75, child €1.25, family €7
Car and bicycle park, self-guiding trails, picnic tables

The centre provides history and background information about the monastic site started by St

A story to tell: St Kevin of Glendalough

Saint Kevin (or *Caoimhín*, 'fair begotten') lived alone in the Wicklow Mountains, in Glendalough, in the 6th century AD. Scholars say that Kevin studied with monks from the age of 12, and became an abbot before he went to Glendalough to be a hermit. One story about St Kevin claims he was born at a tiny spot on the map in Wicklow, but even that was too big for him, so he went off walking in the Wicklow Hills until he discovered the most peaceful place he had ever seen, a valley that lay between two lakes – the Glen of the Two Lakes, or Glendalough. He decided to settle there, in the stump of a great hollow tree at the end of the glen next to the larger of the lakes (the Upper Lake), with wild fruits and nuts for food and the skins of animals that had died nearby for clothing.

The legend goes that the woodland animals soon befriended him, watching as he sat or stood motionless for hours, in deep contemplation. He would wade into the lake and stand with his arms outstretched in prayer for the longest time. One day he stood so still that a blackbird put a twig into one of his hands, and then another and another until she had built a nest, and then laid her eggs in it. Not wanting to disturb the mother bird and her babies, he remained motionless until they hatched and flew away. This is why Kevin is often portrayed with a bird in his hand.

A cow is also said to have visited him while he was meditating. The cow would lick his feet and clothes and then wander back home to give the farmer who owned her as much milk as 50 other cows. One day the farmer followed his cow to find out what she was eating, and was surprised to discover the cow licking the immobile saint's feet. He was so amazed that he told everyone in the village, and they all brought their cows to lick Kevin's feet as well.

Thereafter, people sought him out from far and wide. Monks settled near him to live as hermits, creating a beehive of stone cells you can still find throughout Glendalough. The remains of at least seven churches can be seen in the area. The most famous one is called St Kevin's Kitchen, because the locals thought the spire looked like a chimney rising from a hearth.

The monks who followed Kevin elected him abbot, and soon he found himself in charge of a small city that grew up around the monastery. St Kevin was known to be happy with animals, but not so much with humans, who disturbed the peace he sought. One day, during a drought, Kevin fed his monks with salmon brought to him by an otter that lived in one of the lakes. The otter overheard one of the monks say, 'T'would make a fine pair of gloves, that otter's pelt,' and so he left and never returned. Kevin was annoyed by this insult to one of his animal friends.

To get away from the crowds, St Kevin sometimes walked 12 miles (19km) west over the hills through the Wicklow Gap to a village now called Hollywood, where he stayed alone in a cave. Just above it today is a modern statue of St Kevin, erected in 1950. About 30 years ago a hermit lived in the cave and used to tell children that he was St Kevin, but the real Kevin had died on 3 July 618. In the Irish calendar, however, he died on 3 June, and this is the day when people celebrate his life.

Kevin. Places to look out for around Glendalough include St Kevin's Cave, St Kevin's Chair, the 12th-century Norman tower of Geoffrey de Marisco, a replica road used in the film *Michael Collins*, the 4,000-year-old Athgreany Stone Circle and the 'Seat of Finn', a 5,000-year-old passage tomb associated with the legendary hero Finn McCool.

Mount Usher Gardens

Ashford, Co. Wicklow, **t** (0404) 40116
Getting there 2 miles (3km) north of Wicklow town
Open Daily mid-Mar–end-Oct 10.30–6
Adm Adult €6, child €5
Limited wheelchair access, craft shops, tearoom

Woodland walkways and suspension bridges over babbling streams make these gardens, just off the Dublin road a little inland from Wicklow town, a tranquil, romantic place for wandering. The gardens are particularly lush, containing 5,000 trees and shrubs with rhododendrons, magnolias and maples. A clever mix of seasonal plants ensures the garden remains colourful throughout the year, and there's a particularly nice tearoom: its cakes are excellent, and there are lovely views over the gardens, the river and the green valley known as the 'Devil's Glen'.

Powerscourt Estate

Enniskerry, Co. Wicklow, **t** (01) 204 6000, **www**.powerscourt.ie
Getting there 12 miles (19km) south of Dublin off N11; bus 44 from Hawkins St, Dublin
Open Gardens and House daily 9.30–5.30; times vary, i.e. winter 10.30–dusk, midsummer 9.30–7
Adm House and Gardens: Mar–Oct adult €8, under-16s €4.50; Nov–Feb adult €6.50, under-16s €3.80; reductions for garden- or house-only visits
Terrace restaurant, shops, garden centre, picnic and play areas

One of the most beautiful estates in Ireland and a fine example of the enormous stately homes built in the safe vicinity of Dublin in the 18th century by the Irish Protestant landed gentry. The main house, sadly, burnt down in the 1970s and has never been fully restored, but the estate is still a great place to take the kids to show them something of the splendour in which the aristocracy lived. The grounds contain Ireland's highest waterfall – Powerscourt Waterfall, 3 miles (5km) from the entrance across the 47-acre gardens. It's easy to spend a whole day here with children, exploring the tree trail, pet cemetery, Japanese and Italian gardens and Pepper Pot Tower.

AROUND AND ABOUT

Animal magic

Annamoe Leisure Park and Trout Farm

Annamoe, Co. Wicklow, **t** (0404) 45470
Getting there 2 1/2 miles (4km) north of Glendalough on the R755 (Dublin) road
Open Jun–Aug daily, May, Sept Sat, Sun only 10.30–6.30; junior bait pond open Jun–Aug daily, Apr–May and Sept–Oct Sat, Sun only 12 noon–6
Adm Rod hire and bait: €5, fish caught must be bought at €2.50 each

A leisure park in 9 acres of woodland, containing a mile-deep lake with canoes and rafts, adventure play areas and a separate lake for fishing (rods and bait supplied). Children are welcome, but be prepared for lots of mud and wet clothes.

Ballykeenan House Pet Farm and Aviary

Myshall, Co. Carlow, **t** (059) 9157665
Getting there 10 miles (16km) east of Bagenalstown on R724 road
Open Mon–Fri 11–5, Sun 2–5. **Adm** Adult €3, child €2

The farm owners, the McCord family, give an enthralling guided tour on which kids can observe and pet a variety of animals and unusual birds.

Glenroe Open Farm

Kilcoole, Co. Wicklow, **t** (01) 287 2288, **www**.glenroefarm.com
Getting there 8 miles (12km) south of Bray
Open Apr–Aug Mon–Fri 10–5, Sat–Sun, bank holidays 10–6, Mar and Sept–Oct Sat–Sun only
Adm Adult €4.25, child €3.50, family €14
Indoor and outdoor picnic areas, gift shop

This family-run farm offers a pets' corner, aviary and a display of old Irish farm implements.

Greenan Farm Museums and Maze

Ballinanty, Greenan, Rathdrum, Co. Wicklow, **t** (0404) 46000, **www**.greenanmaze.com
Getting there 9 miles (14km) west of Rathdrum via a country lane through Ballinaclash
Open Easter weekend, May–Jun Tues–Sat and bank holidays 10–6, Jul–Aug daily 10–6, Sept–Oct Sun only 10–6, or by appointment
Adm Adult €6.50, under-16s €5, under-5s free, family €15.50 (1+ 3) or €19 (2+2), extra child €2.50; maze only: adult €4, child €3
Nature walk, craft shop, tearoom

Spend a pleasant afternoon in the Glenmalure Valley. A stream flows through a half-acre maze to a pond in the centre that is hard for adults to find, never mind children. Exhibits in the farmhouse (once a safe house used by Michael Dwyer, *see* p.77) show what life was like here in the 19th century. The large two-storey barn exhibits traditional hill-farming methods from the days when ploughs were drawn by horsepower.

Lalor's Open Farm

Ballykealey, Ballon, Co. Carlow, **t** (059) 9159130
Getting there 12 miles (19km) southwest of Carlow Town on the N80 Wexford road.
Guided tour followed by traditional lunch; ring for times

The Lalor Family take you on a tour of their accolade-winning 100-acre dairy farm surrounding the 1830 Ballykealey House, where they show off their very high farming and environmental standards.

Bricks and mortar

Avondale House

Rathdrum, Co. Wicklow, **t** (0404) 46111, **www**.coillte.ie
Getting there 1 mile (1.6km) south of Rathdrum on the R752 road towards Avoca and Arklow
Open Mar–Oct 11–6
Adm Adult €5, child €2.50, family (2+3) €15
House tour, forest walk, children's play area, café and restaurant, picnic area, shop, disabled access to ground floor, coach and car park

Set in Avondale Forest Park – 500 acres of exotic forest beside the Avoca River – this restored Georgian building was the home of the celebrated politician Charles Stewart Parnell (1846–91), one of the most important figures in 19th-century Irish history (*see* p.37). His career came to a disastrous end when it emerged that he was involved with a married woman. Exhibits at the house give you an idea of how and why Parnell, the son of a Protestant landowner, persuaded the British government to push through several laws called the Land Acts which greatly improved the lives of Irish tenant farmers, and of the later campaign for Irish Home Rule. When you've learnt enough, you can spend the rest of a very pleasant day here enjoying the lovely grounds and letting the kids run riot in the play area.

The Browneshill Dolmen

Rathvilly Road, Carlow
Getting there 2 miles (3km) east of Carlow Town on the R726

Here since 3500–2900 BC, this stone dolmen (also called Brown's Hill) has the largest capstone in Europe, weighing an estimated 100 tons.

Old Leighlin Cathedral

Old Leighlin, Co. Carlow, **t** (059) 9721411
Getting there West of the N9 Waterford road 9 miles (14km) south of Carlow Town
Open Jul–Aug Mon–Fri 10–5
Adm Donations welcome

The village of Old Leighlin actually has a cathedral, the 13th-century church of Saint Lazerian's, which replaced a 7th-century monastery that once had 1,500 monks. A church synod here in AD 630 decided on the formula that determined western Christianity's dates for Easter. The nearby holy well still attracts votive offerings today.

Did you know?
Avoca, Co. Wicklow, is the tiny village used as the setting a few years ago for the TV series 'Ballykissangel'. It is also the home of the oldest mill in Ireland at Avoca Handweavers, which has additional sites at Kilmacanogue and Powerscourt.

Nature lovers

If you're hindered by buggies and so unable to take on too many walks in the hills, the drive along the 'Military Road', the road built by the British to track down rebels 200 years ago (otherwise now classified as the R755), will give you a glimpse of how beautiful Ireland is. Join the road at Enniskerry just south of Powerscourt (*see* p.79) and roll down to Glendalough to stroll by the lake. Make time to do this even if you are on a short break in Dublin.

Altamont Gardens

Tullow, Co. Carlow, **t** (059) 9159128
Getting there Off the N80 Carlow/Bunclody Road
Open Summer Mon–Thur 9–5, Fri 9–3.30, Easter–Oct Sat–Sun 2–5
Adm Adult €2.75, child €1.25, family (2+2) €7
Garden centre, toilets (wheelchair accessible)

This beautiful garden has clipped yews sloping down to a lake, around which there are rare trees and a profusion of roses and plants. It was planted in the 19th century around Altamont House, parts of which are 16th-century. You can walk through its arboretum and bog garden to an Ice Age glen,where ancient oaks lead to the River Slaney. Birds, butterflies and squirrels are everywhere.

Kilmacurragh Gardens

Rathdrum, Co. Wicklow, **t** (01) 857 0909
Getting there 6 miles (9.5km) east of Rathdrum on local road towards Arklow
Open Mon–Sat 9–6, Sun 11–6 or dusk. **Adm** Free
Car park, limited access for people with disabilities

Budding botanists will find this 19th-century arboretum fascinating for its many species brought from around the world by David Moore and his son Sir Frederick, first curators of the National Botanic Gardens in Dublin (*see* p.61). Planted by Thomas Acton, it is especially famous for its conifers and calcifuges.

National Garden Exhibition Centre

Kilquade, near Bray, Co. Wicklow, **t** (01) 281 9890
Getting there 2 miles (3km) south of Bray
Open All year Mon–Sat 10–6, Sun 1–6
Adm Adult €4.50, under-16s free
Garden centre, tea house, guided tours

The 100-metre Harlequin Walk has eight rose arches with a rose garden in the middle.

Sporty kids

Activity centres

Blessington Lakes Leisure Pursuits Centre

Burgage, Blessington, Co. Wicklow, **t** (045) 865 092
Getting there 20 miles (32km) south of Dublin
Open Daily Mar–Dec 10–dusk

Activities for ages 8 and up: canoeing, board-sailing, tennis, sailing, orienteering, pony-trekking.

Tiglin National Mountain and White Water Centre

Ashford, Co. Wicklow, **t** (0404) 40169
Getting there 2 miles (3km) north of Wicklow town

Field courses in mountaineering, orienteering, canoeing, surfing and skiing.

Cycling

Celtic Cycling

Lorum Old Rectory, Bagenalstown, Co. Carlow, **t** (059) 9775282
Getting there 11 miles (17km) south of Carlow

Arranges cycling holidays in the region.

Horse riding

Brennanstown Riding School

Hollybrook, Kilmacanogue, Bray, Co. Wicklow, **t** (01) 286 3778
Getting there 1 1/2 miles (2km) inland from Bray

Rides in the hills behind Bray.

Carrigbeg Riding Stables

Bagenalstown, Co. Carlow, **t** (059) 9721962
Getting there 11 miles (17km) south of Carlow on Waterford road

Indoor and outdoor arenas, cross-country rides and tuition.

Fishing

The River Barrow in Co. Carlow is known for brown trout and coarse fishing. There are several angling centres in Bagenalstown and Tullow.

Dargle Anglers' Club

Bray Sports Centre, Main St, Bray, Co. Wicklow, **t** (01) 286 3046

For fishing salmon and sea trout on the Dargle.

Ray Dineen

Tara House, Redcross, Co. Wicklow, **t** (0404) 41645.
Getting there Near Blessington, 20 miles (32km) south of Dublin on N81 road

Trout fishing in the Blessington Lakes.

Watersports

Adventure Canoeing

t (0509) 31307

For canoeing trips on the Barrow River in Co. Carlow; phone for the current programme..

Walking in Wicklow and Carlow

The Wicklow Mountains are wonderful for walking, from easy walks through the woods to real hikes over the hills. There are well-marked long-distance footpaths. The Wicklow Way begins in Co. Dublin near Marley Park, not far south of Dublin city, and climbs rapidly into the Wicklow Mountains, switching from glen to glen. The Dublin Tourism Centre and local tourist offices have maps and details of footpaths, walking tours and festivals in the hills.

In Co. Carlow, the South Leinster Way is a good route, covering 64 miles (102km) through Carlow, Kilkenny and Tipperary, with many attractive sections along the way, and another lovely long-distance path is the Barrow Way (70m/113km), along the river through Carlow and Kildare. There is also a very nice forest walk by a canal at Bahana, in the southernmost point of Co. Carlow 3 miles (5km) south of Graiguenamanagh (on an unclassified road to St Mullins). Tourist offices, again, have details of all these routes.

Some agencies that offer guided walks, long and short, in the Wicklow Mountains are:

Barry Dalby, 1555 Beachdale, Kilcoole, Co. Wicklow, **t** (01) 287 5990
Damien Cashin Outdoor Activities, Tomdarragh, Roundwood, Co. Wicklow, **t** (01) 281 8212
Footfalls Hiking Tours, Trooperstown, Roundwood, Co. Wicklow, **t** (0404) 45152

Guided walks with accommodation en route.

KILKENNY AND WEXFORD

County Kilkenny presents to any visitor an embracing, hilly lushness, making it one of the greenest and most idyllic pieces of the Irish countryside. Birdwatchers and fishermen love this area's rivers, like the Slaney, which flows south through the county and down into Wexford Harbour. Centuries ago the Vikings made use of these same waterways, in their plundering raids. Sophisticated country grace mixes with eccentric whimsy in these counties, in a unique, particularly Irish combination. The Normans founded the town of New Ross and County Wexford's breweries, farms and mills. From this rich, gently undulating countryside the people – more Celtic and Viking than Anglo-Normans -– have exported fine produce and strong ales to the world.

County Wexford, Ireland's southeastern corner, is known for its birds, on the offshore Saltee Island and along the Wexford Slobs and Harbour. It also has many fine beaches and lovely old fishing villages, especially along its south coast, and rare coastal rock formations, especially near Hook Head.

Tourist information

Enniscorthy, The Castle, **t** (054) 34699, **www.northwexford.com**
Gorey, Lower Main St, **t** (055) 21248
Kilkenny, Shee Alms House, Rose Inn St, **t** (056) 7751500
New Ross, **t** (051) 21857
Wexford, Crescent Quay, **t** (053) 23111

Getting there and around

By bus There are at least 6 Bus Eireann coaches each day between Dublin and Cork that stop in Kilkenny, and less frequent services from Waterford. Bus Eireann in Kilkenny, **t** (056) 7764933. Many local bus routes are operated by **Kavanagh's**, **t** (056) 8831106.

Bus Eireann coaches run every hour daily from Dublin to Wexford Town and Rosslare, and there are also many services to Waterford and Cork.

By sea Rosslare Harbour is one of Ireland's busiest ferry ports, with sailings from Fishguard and Pembroke in Wales and the French ports of Roscoff and Cherbourg (*see* pp.284–6). There's not much in

Special Events – Kilkenny and Wexford

March–April

Spring Music Festival, Wexford, **t** (053) 23923
A lively classical music festival.

Viking Festival, Wexford, **t** (053) 23401
A celebration of Wexford's Viking past, running from April into May.

May

The Cat Laughs, Kilkenny, **t** (056) 7751254
Fun for all at this annual comedy festival in Kilkenny town, from late May to early June.

June–July

Strawberry Fair, Enniscorthy, **t** (054) 33256
Ten days dedicated to the celebration of the strawberry harvest.

Kilmore Quay Seafood Festival, Kilmore Quay, Co. Wexford, **t** (053) 29922
A celebration of seafood, horse races and music.

Wexford Hooves and Grooves Festival, **t** (053) 44634
Horse racing and live music and street entertainment, in and around Wexford town.

Sandworld, Duncannon, Co. Wexford, **t** (051) 389434
This international sand-sculpting event is inspiration for castle builders of all ages.

August

Blessing of the Fleet, Kilmore, Co. Wexford, **t** (053) 29922
An annual event to safeguard the fishing community when out at sea.

Kilmuckridge Mardi Gras Festival, Kilmuckridge, Co. Wexford, **t** (053) 30163
A fun non-traditional event.

Kilkenny Arts Festival, **t** (056) 7752175, **www.kilkennyarts.ie**
One of Ireland's most important arts festivals – opera, art exhibitions and music of all sorts, in the last week of the month

September

Blackstairs Blues Festival, Co. Wexford, **t** (054) 35364
Intimate blues music festival, best for teenagers and their parents.

October–November

Wexford Opera Festival, contact Wexford Festival Office, Theatre Royal, Wexford, **t** (053) 22400
A delightful event with an informal atmosphere that's much loved by opera fans.

Good to know...
Crossing Waterford Harbour
Waterford Harbour, between Co. Wexford and Co. Waterford in Munster (*see* pp.146–50), is a wide expanse of water. The quickest way to cross from Wexford to Waterford is via **Passage East Car Ferry**, not far from Arthurstown on the Wexford side.

Rosslare Harbour, but you can catch trains and Bus Eireann coaches to other parts of Ireland from directly outside the ferry terminal, and find taxis and buses for nearby Wexford.
By train Kilkenny Town is on the Waterford line from Dublin Heuston. Services are more frequent on the east coast line, from Rosslare and Wexford to Dublin, via Enniscorthy and other towns.
Bike hire
The Bike Shop, 9 Selskar St, Wexford, **t** (053) 22514
Hayes Cycles, 108 South Main St, Wexford, **t** (053) 22462
JJ Wall, 86 Maudlin St, Kilkenny, **t** (056) 7721236
Kenny's, Slaney St, Enniscorthy, **t** (054) 33255

Entertainment

Arm Breacha ('Our Roots')
Raheen, Ballyduff, Co. Wexford, **t** (054) 44148, **www.iol.ie/~story**
Traditional evenings of Irish stories, music and dancing are held at the 'House of Storytelling' on the first Tuesday of each month, and every Tuesday night in July and August. Always call ahead.

The Sky and the Ground
South Main St, Wexford, **t** (053) 21273
This was once an old shop and pub, and they've left everything the way it was, including the groceries. Good traditional music is played every night Sun–Thur.

Shopping

Badger Hill Pottery
Enniscorthy, **t** (054) 35060
Attractive and original ceramics.

Cushendale Woollen Mills
High Street, Old Road, Graiguenamanagh, Co. Kilkenny, **t** (059) 9724118
Handmade woollens, from the mill's own shop.

Kilkenny Crystal
Rose Inn St, Kilkenny, **t** (056) 7725132
Fine original glassware.

Kilkenny Design Centre
Castle Yard, Kilkenny, **t** (056) 7722118
An excellent selection of crafts from all over Ireland.

Kilkenny Irish Crystal
Canal Square, Kilkenny, **t** (056) 7761377
The factory at Callan can be visited in summer.

Kiltrea Bridge Pottery Ltd
Kiltrea Bridge, Cairn,Enniscorthy, **t** (054) 35107
You can watch clay earthenware being hand-thrown here.

Nicholas Mosse Pottery
Bennettsbridge, Co. Kilkenny, **t** (056) 7727505, **www.nicholasmosse.com**
Possibly the nicest pottery in Ireland: sponge-ware decorated with animals and flowers. Slight seconds are available and there's an exhibition of pottery through the ages. Bennettsbridge is about 5 miles (8km) south of Kilkenny town.

Stoneware Jackson Pottery
Ballyreddin, Bennettsbridge, Co. Kilkenny, **t** (056) 7727175
Lots of swirly bright patterns.

TOURING TOWNS

Kilkenny

One of the most attractive medieval towns in Ireland, with a lovely old centre of cobbled streets and a lively atmosphere – if a bit too much traffic. Kilkenny makes a good place for a stop-over, or to use as a base for exploring the region.

Things to see and do

Cityscope and Smallworld Miniatures
Shee Alms House, Rose Inn Street, **t** (056) 7751500
Open Daily Mar–Sept 9–5, Oct–Nov Mon–Fri 9–5
Adm Adults €1, child €0.50
The 16th-century Shee Alms House, which also houses Kilkenny Tourist Office, contains the Cityscope Exhibition, where you can spend an entertaining half hour learning about Kilkenny's history via a dramatic presentation combining a scale model of the city as it was in 1640 with some

state-of-the-art electronics. Then move on to the Smallworld Miniatures exhibition, to look at the collection of tiny models of traditional houses built here from the 16th century to the present.

Kilkenny Castle

The Parade, **t** (056) 7721450
Open Daily Apr–May 10.30–5, Jun–Sept 10–6.30, Oct–Mar Tues–Sat 10.30–12.45 and 2–5, Sun 11–12.45 and 2–5, closed Mon
Adm Adult €4.45, child €1.90, family €10.15
Café in summer, children's play area, shop, art gallery, wheelchair accessible on ground floor, by guided tour only, pre-booking recommended

Children who like faery tales enjoy visiting this castle, built in the 12th century and remodelled in the Victorian era. From 1391 it was the main seat of the Butler family, who were Earls, Marquesses and Dukes of Ormond, but the first castle here, still largely intact, was probably built about 1192. Acres of parkland surround it. Do have a look at the recently restored middle block of the castle.

Rothe House

Parliament St, **t** (056) 7722893
Open Mar–Oct Mon–Sat 10.30–5 and Sun 3–5, Nov–Feb Mon–Sat 1–5. **Adm** Adult €3, child €1

A typical Tudor Kilkenny house built in 1594–1610 for the merchant John Rothe, containing pictures and artefacts from Kilkenny's past, including fine oak furniture and paintings. A collection of period costumes and a large kitchen, bakery and brew house are also on view, and there's a nice shop.

St. Canice's Cathedral

Irishtown, **t** (056) 7764971
Open Easter–Sept Mon–Sat 9–1, 2–6, Sun 2–6, Oct–Easter Mon–Sat 10–1, 2–4, Sun 2–4
Adm Cathedral: adult €3, 12–16s €1.50, under-12s free; Tower: adult €2, 12–16s €1.50, under-12s free
Shop, disabled access, conducted tours on request

Did you know...?
Irish Protestants of the 18th century produced some very famous sons. The writer Jonathan Swift (1667–1745) went to school at Kilkenny College with fellow scholars William Congreve, the playwright, and the philosopher Bishop Berkeley, after whom Berkeley University, California, is named.

A story to tell...
The Kilkenny Cats

Some Kilkenny townspeople are said to have tied the tails of two cats together, and then watched them fight until only their tails were left behind. This – though some say the story referred to warring Co. Kilkenny towns – is most often said to be the origin of the Irish saying, 'To fight like Kilkenny Cats'. It's also why Kilkenny's hurling team, many times All-Ireland champions, are known as 'The Cats'.

This limerick is about the cats –

There wanst was two cats of Kilkenny
Each cat thought there was one cat too many
So they fought and they fit
And they scratched and they bit
Till instead of two cats there weren't any

Kilkenny's atmospheric Norman-Gothic cathedral is the second-largest medieval church in in Ireland. Completed in the 13th century, it still has some of its original carvings, and lovely, colourful stained-glass windows to look at. Next to the cathedral is a much older, 9th-century Irish round tower, which you can climb up in good weather, so long as you are steady on your feet and don't mind heights.

Enniscorthy

Known for its river angling, craft studios, good restaurants and annual Strawberry Fair, Enniscorthy is an excellent base from which to explore North Wexford. The craft of pottery especially has become synonymous with Enniscorthy, since one of Ireland's oldest potteries was established in the region over 300 years ago. Several potteries in the area are open to visitors (*see* p.75).

Things to see and do

Friar Murphy Centre

Boolavogue, Ferns, Enniscorthy, **t** (054) 66898
Open Daily May–Sept Mon–Sat 10–5, Sun 2–5
Adm free
Picnic area, guided tours, craft shop, café

Next to an 18th-century farmyard is a restored thatched house with period furnishings and farm implements. Stories and pictures decorate the walls, and there are scenic views from the gardens.

National 1798 Centre

Millpark Road, **t** (054) 37596/7, **www**.1798centre.com
Open Open Mon–Sat 9.30–5, Sun 11–5
Adm Adult €6, child €3.50, family (2+2) €16
Gift shop, café, audio-visual presentation

Vinegar Hill, outside Enniscorthy, was the site of the most important battle in Ireland's 1798 Rebellion (*see* p.36). This centre, near the battle-ground, tells the story of the rising and its aftermath via multimedia displays and interactive computers. The rebels' political strategy is conveyed via a chess game, in which six-foot chessmen represent political figures of the 18th century on a chequered floor – the 'king' on the Irish side is Wolfe Tone. A film relates how Wexford suffered 11 out of the 23 battles of 1798, and lost 20,000 people from a population of 120,000 in four weeks. The enormity of this tragedy for the Irish people becomes all the more apparent when Ireland's losses are compared to the first six years of the French Revolution, which cost France's population of 30 million merely 25,000 people.

Wexford County Museum

Town Centre, Enniscorthy, **t** (054) 35926
Open Daily Jun–Sept Mon–Sat 10–6, Sun 2–5.30, Oct–Nov Sun 2–5, Dec–May call for times
Adm Adult €4.50, child €1, family €11

Set in a magnificent Norman castle that was built in the 13th century by the Prendergast family, Co. Wexford's museum offers a fascinating insight into its agricultural, maritime, industrial, military and ecclesiastical history. There are commemorations of the uprisings of 1798 and 1916.

SPECIAL TRIPS

Irish National Heritage Park

Ferrycarrig, Co. Wexford, **t** (053) 20733
Getting there 2 1/2 miles (4km) north of Wexford off the Dublin road (N11)
Open All year daily 9.30–6.30
Adm Adult €7, 13–18s €5.50, under-13s €3.50, family (2+3 under 18) €17.50; discounts in winter
Restaurant (with Celtic banquets on some evenings), picnic areas, shop, café, parking, walks, guided tours on request

Wexford's star attraction for children has won the European Year of the Environment award. Families can spend a whole day exploring 9,000 years of Ireland's history in this outdoor park, which shows how people lived in the Stone and Bronze Ages and the Celtic, Early Christian and Early Norman periods. There are recreations of houses, communities and customs from 7000 BC to the arrival of the Normans in the 12th century, and of the ways in which the Celts, Vikings and Normans came together to create the unique Irish persona of today. Site attendants wear period costumes, and tell you all they can about how people lived. Children can explore all the replicas of historic homes freely, touching whatever they like.

A map shows you how to navigate the 35 acres of forest to each of 16 historical sites, designed by expert archaeologists. First you visit a site from the Mesolithic era, then move to an early farm where the crop-growing techniques of Neolithic times are displayed. Next is the Bronze Age, when more durable weapons and copper and bronze utensils were made. You can see pre-Celtic rituals and burials, and a re-created 'Stone Circle'. Then you walk into the Celtic era, and to the 4th century AD when Christianity came to Ireland, along with new foods, new cooking and water-milling methods, and writing. All this, plus the story of how Christian missionaries were sent here, is described inside a reconstruction of a 10th-century monastery. Nearby is a fascinating Viking home, with a shipyard and longboats for children to clamber over. Then there are round towers, which offered their owners some protection from Viking raiders, and then an early Norman castle and examples of the first Norman fortifications in Ireland.

At the end of your long walk, you'll probably want to rest and visit the park's Fulacht Fiadh restaurant, which serves traditional Irish specialities. Your children will enjoy a meal in the archaeologically-themed surroundings, overlooking a *crannóg* (a round house on an island in a lake, an early Irish way of protecting yourself from intruders.

Kilkenny and Wexford songs to sing...
Bunclody, Kilkenny's the Best of Them All, Highland Paddy, Kelly from Killane, The Croppy Boy, Come to the Bower.

Berkeley Costume and Toy Museum

Berkeley Forest House, New Ross, Co. Wexford, **t** (051) 421361
Getting there In New Ross town
Open May–Sept Thur–Sun 11–6
Adm Adult €4, child €2

On display inside this house are 18th- and 19th-century costumes, beautiful embroidered textiles, dolls and toys, while outside there are Victorian goat-carriages for children to ride in. The family of Bishop George Berkeley, after whom the California university town is named, own the property.

Dunbrody Abbey and Castle

Campile, New Ross, Co. Wexford, **t** (051) 388 603
Getting there 7 miles (11km) south of New Ross
Open Daily May–Sept 10–6
Adm Castle, maze, minigolf: adult €4, under-17s €2, family €10; Abbey: adult €2, under-17s €1, family €5
Maze, pitch'n'putt, picnic areas, tearoom, craft shop, walks, free parking

Spend a quiet day here at this 13th-century Cisterian Abbey while your children get lost in the yew hedge maze and amuse themselves in the visitor centre and museum. A large dolls' house replicates Dunbrody Castle in miniature, and there's an excellent teashop.

Dunbrody Famine Ship

JFK Trust, New Ross, Co. Wexford, **t** (051) 425 239, www.dunbrody.com
Open Daily Oct–Mar 10–5, Apr–Sept 9–6
Adm Adult €6.50, under-16s €4, family (2+3) €18
Disabled access, guided tour, café and souvenir shop

Experience firsthand the conditions that faced Irish emigrants in the years after the Great Famine on this floating museum ship – a full-size replica of a 19th-century sailing ship – moored on the waterfront at New Ross. You'll get your ticket for 18 March 1849, and follow in the footsteps of emigrants bound for New York. Onboard children find out what happened to those bound for America in the 1840s, and experience the smells and sounds of a wooden sailing ship full of people crossing an ocean. They might even encounter the ship's Captain, Mr Williams, or one of his crew or passengers, who will let them know in graphic detail what such a crossing was like. After imagining the lives of the emigrants and finding out what they experienced in the New World, you can cheer things up with a snack and hot drink in the modern café, and check on the computer to see if any of your ancestors sailed to America.

Pirates Cove Adventure Golf and Fun Centre

Courtown Harbour, Co. Wexford, **t** (055) 25555
Getting there On the coast near Gorey, 31 miles (50km) north of Wexford by the N11 Dublin road
Open Golf and Fun Cave, daily Jun–Aug 11–11, Sept–May bowling only Sun 2pm–late.
Adm Bowling, €21 for 1 hr, €11 for 1/2 hr; Golf, adult €5.50, child €4.20, family 2+2 €16.50, 2+3 €20; Fun Cave for ages 3–10 €4.20 per hour
Picnic areas, restaurant with children's menu

The tropical gardens and waterfalls create a magical atmosphere at this theme attraction for children and their adults. Explore the Fun Cave, play golf or bowling, and eat at the Lagoon Restaurant. A good place to spend an afternoon.

Wexford Wildfowl Reserve

North Slob, Co. Wexford, **t** (053) 23129
Getting there 3 miles (8km) from Wexford via Curracloe
Open Daily mid-Apr–Sept 9–6, Oct–mid-Apr 10–5, closed Christmas Day. **Adm** Free
Guided tour on request, picnic area

The land spit known as the Wexford Slobs, on the north side of Wexford Harbour is famous for the wild geese that winter there. Go birdwatching or explore the area on horseback; horses can be hired from Curracloe Equestrian Centre, *see* p.xx.

Yola Farmstead Folk Park

Tagoat, Rosslare Harbour, Co. Wexford, **t** (053) 32611
Getting there 2 miles (3km) south of Rosslare
Open Daily May–Oct 10–5
Adm Adult €5, under-16s €2, family (2+4) €11
Crystal craft shop, children's playground, café

Step back to a less complicated time when life was centred on the cycles of nature at this traditional Irish farmstead with thatched buildings, forge, church, schoolhouse, aviary and windmill. Kids can explore the enclosure for farm animals and rare breeds of poultry, and let off steam in the supervised play area. Take a stroll beside the flora and fauna of the past and find out about your own past at the genealogy centre.

AROUND AND ABOUT

Animal magic

Ballylane Open Farm Nature Reserve

New Ross, Co. Wexford, **t** (051) 425 666
Getting there 2 1/2 miles (4km) east of New Ross
Open Easter and May–Sept daily 10–6 (last entry 5)
Adm Adult €4.70, child €3.50, family €16
Tearoom/restaurant, play and picnic areas, wheelchair access, walks

This family-run 150-acre farm is one of Ireland's best rural attractions. City children enjoy seeing its woods, crops, farm animals and deer, and the farm walk is suitable for baby buggies too.

A story to tell...
The witches of Wexford

It is whispered there were, or are, witches in Kilkenny and Wexford. Some, of course, will have been of the good wise woman variety, but others may have been of the other sort. According to Irish tradition, there are still all kinds of good and bad beings out there, and you must be careful not to offend them. If you're untidy, dirty, discourteous, greedy or rude, you risk their ire. You need to have a few tricks up your sleeve to avoid spirits who mean you harm, or to counter their magic.

Christians had the *Lord's Prayer* and holy water as antidotes. Before that, the Irish used to carry a piece of iron or steel – a horseshoe or a fish hook – to protect them from supernatural powers. Salt and St John's Wort were said to counteract faery spells, and placing ash berries in a cradle would stop faeries from taking human babies and leaving one of their own (a 'changeling') in its place. Some Irish parents used to dress little boys as girls, as the faeries seemed to prefer stealing boys to girls.

One thing Irish country people knew better than to do, though, was to eat the faery food the Good People offered them, for if they ate even a morsel of it they would be trapped in Fairyland. If this happened, the horseshoe or bit of old iron could come in handy to wedge open the doorway of the faery fortress and make good your escape.

Kia Ora Mini Farm

Courteencurragh, Gorey, Co. Wexford, **t** (055) 21166
Getting there 31 miles (50km) north of Wexford
Open Mid-Mar–Easter Sat–Sun 1–6, Easter–Sept hours variable, around 10–6, ring in advance
Adm €5 per person

Most animals are indoors here, so this is a good place to visit when the rain comes down. Tropical birds, fish, Jacob sheep, pheasants, deer, turkeys, mules, pigs, chipmunks, ducks and geese are just some of those on show. Children can also meet some in the play area, while you have coffee in the pleasant café. Santa Claus visits at Christmas time.

Nore Valley Open Farm

Bennettsbridge, Co. Kilkenny, **t** (056) 7727229
Getting there 5 miles (8km) south of Kilkenny
Open Easter–Sept Mon–Sat 9–7
Adm €3.70 per person, guided tour extra
Café, shop, crazy golf, caravan and camping park

Children can help feed lambs or kids and hold chicks and rabbits, and a wooden American-style fort lets them watch animals from up above. They can also take a ride on a pony or donkey, play in a playground, sand pit and 'straw bounce', trundle off for a relaxed 2 mile (3km) walk by the river, picnic or have a home-baked scone in the café.

Bricks and mortar

Ballyhack Castle

Ballyhack, Co. Wexford, **t** (051) 389 468
Getting there 12 miles (19km) north of New Ross
Open Daily Jun–early Sept 9.30–6.30
Adm Adult €1.20, child €0.50, family €3.80
Guided tours on request, prior booking essential

This tower house stands on a steep slope overlooking Waterford Harbour. The Knights of Saint John built the castle in 1450. You'll also find the story of the marriage of Norman lord Strongbow to Aoife, daughter of the King of Leinster (*see* p.33).

Duiske Abbey and Abbey Centre

Graiguenamanagh, Co. Kilkenny, **t** (059) 9724238
Getting there 12 miles (19km) north of New Ross
Open All year Mon–Fri 10–5, Jun–Aug also Sat–Sun 2–5. **Adm** Donations invited

A restored Cistercian abbey originally built in 1204. The Centre next door has a display of local historic artefacts, including Christian art.

Jerpoint Abbey

Waterford Road, Co. Kilkenny, **t** (056) 7724623
Getting there Off N9, 2 miles (3.5km) from Thomastown and 11 miles (17km) from Kilkenny
Open Daily Mar–May 10–5, Jun–Sept 9.30–6.30, Oct–15 Nov 10–5, 16 Nov–30 Nov 10–4
Adm Adult €2.50, child €1.20, family €6.30
Shop, wheelchair access

This impressive 12th-century Cistercian abbey has a magnificent carved cloister arcade.

Tintern Abbey

Near Saltmills, Hook Peninsula, Co. Wexford, **t** (051) 562 321
Getting there 20 miles (32km) west of Wexford
Open Mid-Jun–late Sept 9.30–6.30
Adm Adult €2, child €1, family €4

The tranquil grounds of this 13th-century abbey, with walled gardens, a battlemented bridge, ancient woods, a ruined church and a mill on a stream, are perfect for relaxation and peace.

Look at this!

Bród Tullaroan and Lory Meagher Heritage Centre

Tullaroan, Co. Kilkenny, **t** (056) 7769107
Getting there 8 miles (12km) west of Kilkenny
Open Easter–Jun Sun 2–5.30, Jun–Aug Mon–Fri 10–5.30, Sun 2–5.30, Sept–Nov Sun 2–5.30
Adm Adult €3.90, family €7.70
Children's play area, café, craft shop

Sports buffs might be interested to see the old home of a hurling hero of the 1920s, Lory Meagher. Bród Tullaroan is a thatched farmhouse built in the 17th century, and beside it is a museum on the history of Gaelic games in Kilkenny.

Did you know...
What a 'croppy boy' was?
During the 1798 Rebellion, which was inspired by the French Revolution, the United Irish rebels showed their allegiance to the cause by cropping, or cutting, their hair very short in the style of French revolutionaries. So people called them 'croppies', and a 'croppy boy' was a rebel for the cause of Irish independence.

Craanford Mills

Craanford, Gorey, Co. Wexford, **t** (055) 28124
Getting there 2 miles (3km) west of the N1 Dublin road near Gorey, 31 miles (50km) north of Wexford
Open May and Sept Sat–Sun, Jun–Aug daily 11–6
Adm Adult €4, 8–16s €3, under-8s free

A 17th-century watermill restored to working order by the Lyons family. They will give you a guided tour, after which you can savour their homemade produce in the Kiln Loft.

Duncannon Fort

Duncannon, County Wexford, **t** (051) 389 454
Getting there 22 miles (35km) west of Wexford
Open Daily Jun–Sept 10–5.30
Adm Adult €4, child €2, family €10
Guided tours, café, shop, artists' studios, art centre

Older children will love exploring this intriguing star-shaped 16th-century fortress on a promontory at the mouth of Waterford Harbour. Built on top of a Celtic fort and Norman castle, the bastion was built in 1588 in anticipation of the Spanish Armada. It is noted for its dry moat, exterior walls and shape. There is a lament attached to Duncannon in which a 'croppy boy', who was betrayed, tried and hanged, is deeply mourned by his mother.

Guillemot Maritime Museum

Kilmore Quay, Co. Wexford, **t** (051) 561144
Getting there 15 miles (24km) south of Wexford
Open May and Sept Sat–Sun 12 noon–5.30, Jun–Aug daily noon–5.30
Adm Adult €4, child €2, family€10

A lightship converted into a maritime museum. Below deck there are pictures, nautical antiques and model ships, and up above you have panoramic views from Waterford Harbour to Hook Head and the Saltee Islands.

Hook Lighthouse

Hook Head, Fethard, Co. Wexford, **t** (051) 397 055
Getting there 33 miles (53km) from Wexford
Open Guided tours daily Mar–Oct 9.30–5
Adm Adult €4.75, 6–16s €2.75, under-5s free, family (2+2) €14
Restaurant, café, children's play area, craft shop

The 13th-century circular Hook Lighthouse is the oldest lighthouse in the British Isles. It was first built when a Welsh monk named Dubhan was so appalled to see the bodies of shipwrecked sailors on the rocks that he began to shine a light here to help ships avoid disaster. An automated system

Did you know...?
The saying 'by hook or by crook' relates to Hook Head peninsula and Crooke, across the bay near Waterford Town. It goes back to the 17th century, when Cromwell said that Waterford would be taken by assault at Hook in Wexford or at Crooke on the other side of the water.

now fills the almost intact stone lighthouse, perched on the tip of the Hook peninsula. You'll have to cover your ears if you find yourself below its foghorn when it sounds. The setting is magnificent, surrounded by roaring surf, and Hook Head is also a great place to spot seals and hunt for fossils.

Irish Agricultural Museum, Famine Exhibition and Johnstown Castle Gardens

Johnstown, Co. Wexford, **t** (053) 42888
Getting there 2 miles (3km) south of Wexford
Open Gardens: Dec–Mar Mon–Fri 9–12.30, 1.30–5, Sat–Sun 2–5, Apr–May Mon-Fri 9–5, Sat–Sun 2–5, Museum: Jun–Aug Mon–Fri 9–5, Sat–Sun 2–5, Apr–May Mon–Fri 9–12.30, 1.30–5, Sept–mid-Nov Mon–Fri 9–12.30, 2–5
Adm Adult €3.15, child €1.90, family €10.16
Grounds, craft shop, picnic area, café

Thousands of plant species are protected in the castle gardens here. Within the 50-acre grounds the rustic farm buildings, from around 1810, house one of the best museums of rural life in Ireland, with old farm furniture, machinery and household implements. A permanent exhibit commemorates the Great Famine. Johnstown Castle was owned by the wealthy Grogan family, but its last owner left it to the state. The house is not open to the public.

Kennedy Homestead

Dunganstown, Co. Wexford, **t** (051) 388 264
Getting there 4 miles (6km) south of New Ross
Open Daily May–Sept 10–5.30
Adm Adult €2.50, child €1.50, family (2 + 3) €6
Visitor centre, museum, café, craft shop, picnic area, toilets, disabled access, parking

Dunganstown was the birthplace of Patrick Kennedy, great-grandfather of President John F. Kennedy, who left in 1848 for the United States. His house is long gone, but a plaque on the wall marks the spot. The road leading to it remains unchanged since Patrick senior walked down it to the famine ship. In the museum you learn how Patrick moved from being one of Ireland's poorest migrants through the slums of Boston to build a dynasty that became one of the most influential families in America. As it's told here, the tale ends with his most famous descendant taking office in the White House in January 1961 – only to be assassinated in Dallas in 1963. Admission also gives you reduced rates at the Kennedy Arboretum (*see* below) and Dunbrody Famine Ship (*see* p.86).

Nature lovers

Dunmore Cave

Ballyfoyle, Co. Kilkenny, **t** (056) 776 7726
Getting there 7 miles (11km) north of Kilkenny
Open Daily Mar–May 9.30–5.30, Jun–Sept 9.30–6.30, Oct 10–5; Nov–Feb Sat–Sun and bank holidays only 10–5
Adm Adult€2.75, 7–12s €1.25, under-6s free, family €7

A limestone cave with many strange rock formations. Visitors also learn all about a terrible Viking massacre that happened here in 928.

John F. Kennedy Arboretum

Near New Ross, Co. Wexford, **t** (051) 388 272
Getting there 7 miles (11km) south of New Ross
Open Daily May–Aug 10–8, Oct–Mar 10–5, Apr and Sept 10–6.30
Adm Adult €2.75, 6–17s €1.25, under-6s free, family €7
Visitor centre, café, deck with picnic tables

Enjoy a peaceful morning or afternoon exploring these beautiful gardens, with 4,500 shrubs and forest plots covering 1,000 acres of Slieve Coillte.

Kilfane Glen and Waterfall

Kilfane, Thomastown, Co. Kilkenny, **t** (056) 7724558
Getting there 11 miles (17km) south of Kilkenny
Open May–Sept Tue–Sun 2–6
Adm Adult €5.50, under-12s €4.50, family €15
Teashop, guided tours, picnic area

This magical wild garden was created in 1790 and is perfect for letting children run free in lots of open space, although you'll need to watch younger and wilder kids on the clifftops. The cascading stream, hermit's grotto, waterfall and woodland trails combine to create a special atmosphere to feed the imagination and soothe the soul.

Kilmokea Country Manor and Gardens
Great Island, Campile, Co. Wexford, **t** (051) 388 109
Getting there 7 miles (11km) south of New Ross
Open Mar–Nov daily 10–6, all year by appointment
Adm Adult €5, 3–12s €2.50, under-2s free,
Seven acres of delightful, lush gardens.

Sporty kids

Activity centres

Aqua Club
Kelly's Resort Hotel, Rosslare Strand, Co. Wexford, **t** (053) 32222
Open to non-residents, with two swimming pools, sauna, jacuzzi, a plunge pool, and more.

Fun House Adventure Playcentre
Redmond Place, Wexford, **t** (053) 46696
If you need a break, this is the perfect place to leave children while having a cup of coffee. It's well supervised, and they can have fun on slides, bouncy castles, and in a mini-adventure area for under-5s.

Ramsgrange Shielbaggan Outdoor Education Centre
New Ross, Co. Wexford, **t** (051) 389550
Offers sailing, snorkelling, kayaking, orienteering, canoeing, archery, rock-climbing, team challenges and more. Residential and day courses available.

Buckets and spades – Wexford's beaches

The Wexford coast has some of Ireland's best beaches. North of Wexford town, the narrow R742 road winds behind the scenic east coast past many fine sandy beaches, especially around **Courtown** and **Curracloe**. The shallow waters of Curracloe and Ballinskar are where battle scenes for *Saving Private Ryan* were shot. On the other side of Wexford, **Rosslare Strand**, a long stretch of golden sand west of Rosslare Harbour, is one of the most famous of all Irish beaches.

On the south coast, the working fishing village of **Kilmore Quay** is charming, with thatched, white-washed cottages and a new Blue Flag marina, and good food is no problem here if you like seafood. On the shores of Waterford Harbour, **Arthurstown** is a pleasant town by the water that also offers exceptional cuisine, and the clean beaches of **Duncannon** are popular with families.

Boat trips

Saltee Princess
Kilmore Quay, Co. Wexford, **t** (053) 29684
Don't miss an opportunity to see Ireland's most famous bird sanctuary on the Saltee Islands, where puffins, gannets, many other birds and seals live.

Valley Boats
Barrow Lane, Graiguenamanagh, Co. Kilkenny, **t** (059) 972 4945
Cruises on the River Barrow.

Wexford Harbour Boat Club
Wexford, **t** (053) 22039
For water-skiing and sailing.

Fishing

Graiguenamanagh, Co. Kilkenny, has some of the best fishing on the lower River Barrow. These shops can provide equipment and information:
Hook, Line & Sinker, 31 Rose Inn St, Kilkenny, **t** (056) 7771699
Town and Country Sports Shop, 82 High St, Kilkenny, **t** (056) 7721517

Horse riding

Curracloe House Equestrian Centre
Curracloe, Co. Wexford, **t** (053) 37129
Excellent facilities for all ages and levels of experience, and rides on Curracloe Beach or Wexford Slobs. Curracloe is 5 miles (8km) north of Wexford.

Horetown Equestrian Centre
Foulksmills, Co. Wexford, **t** (051) 565786
Combine a hunting course, picnic rides or beginners' courses with a stay in a 17th-century manor.

Iris Kellett Equestrian Centre
Thomastown, Co. Kilkenny, **t** (056) 7724455
For riders of all standards, and tuition provided.

Walking

Guided walks of Kilkenny town are available through the tourist office. On summer evenings walking tours of Wexford town are given by the local historical society; the tourist office has details. In the rest of the county the Wexford Coastal Path stretches over 138 miles (221km) all the way round the shoreline from Kilmichael Point to Ballyhack.Maps are available at tourist offices.

Tynan Walking Tours
Kilkenny, **t** (056) 7765929
Tours of Co. Kilkenny; call for times and costs.

KILDARE, LAOIS AND OFFALY

Kildare means 'church of the oak' in Irish, but when people think of County Kildare it is usually two things that come to mind – horses, and St Brigid. Kildare town has the church in the whole of Ireland that is most closely associated with Brigid and the order of nuns that followed her. As you enter the town on the busy main road from Dublin, though, you cannot see much of anything, so park your car and visit the Japanese Gardens and Tully Stud Farm, before investigating the famous grassy heath known as the Curragh, Ireland's finest horse country and the site of its premier race course.

Neighbouring Co. Laois has the town of Stradbally, famous for its flower festival as well as for what's known as the Stradbally Banshee. Around 70 years ago, every single Stradbally villager swore they heard a banshee one night. Her cry was likened to a hare being killed by a hound.

County Offaly is mostly bog land, but its western border is the River Shannon, so it's good for boat trips. Many Offaly people make a living via farming, turf-cutting or old trades like clay pipe making.

One interesting aspect of Kildare is the fact that schools thrived there while most of Europe was stuck in the Dark Ages, and that long years later a similar pattern was repeated, in the 19th century. In 1176 Strongbow, first Norman king of Leinster, gave a Norman called Fitzgerald the Maynooth area of Kildare, where his family later set up a Catholic college. This was closed with all of Ireland's Catholic monasteries by Henry VIII, and later even the Fitzgeralds turned Protestant to survive.

The only place where Irish priests could train at that time was seminaries in Catholic countries of Europe, but many of these were shut down by the French Revolution. In 1793, however, while Britain was at war with France, the British government suddenly became concerned to appease Ireland's still-Catholic majority. So, when Irish Catholic bishops asked for permission to set up a seminary in Ireland, the government agreed, since they didn't want 'revolutionary' priests coming over from the continent. The son of Ireland's only Duke, whom no one dared oppose, welcomed the seminary at Maynooth. This Duke of Leinster happened to be of the Fitzgerald family of Maynooth. Today the Fitzgeralds' ruined fortress still stands outside the main gates of Maynooth College.

Tourist information

Birr, Co. Offaly, **t** (0509) 20110
Clonmacnoise, Co. Laois, **t** (090) 9674134
Kildare, Market House, Market Square, **t** (045) 522 696
Naas, Co. Kildare, 38 South Main St, **t** (045) 898 888
Portlaoise, Co. Laois, **t** (0502) 21178
Tullamore, Co. Offaly, **t** (0506) 25015

Special Events – Kildare, Laois, Offaly

January–February

Féile Bhríde, Kildare, **t** (045) 522890
Festival of St Brigid, at St Brigid's Cathedral.

March

Kildare Drama Festival, Kildare, **t** (045) 521 907.
A varied small theatre festival.

May

Leixlip Salmon Festival, Co. Kildare, **t** (01) 624 3085
Includes a mock battle with Vikings (late May).

June

Derby Festival, Kildare, **t** (045) 521858
A week of music, theatre and celebrations up to the big race at the Curragh (*see* p.96).

Durrow Carnival Weekend, Erkindale Drive, Durrow, Co. Laois, **t** (0502) 36327
Traditional music, dancing and street shows.

Music in Great Irish Houses, Co. Kildare, **t** (01) 278 1528
Festival held in various locations.

July

Maynooth Summer Festival, Maynooth, Co. Kildare
Music, drama, dance, football and a treasure hunt.

French Festival, Portarlington, Co. Laois, information from Portlaoise Tourist Office, **t** (0502) 21178
Celebrates the town's French Huguenot ancestry.

August

Birr Vintage Week, Birr, Co. Offaly, **t** (0509) 20293
An 'Old Time Fayre', with art shows, antiques, parades, street entertainment, fireworks and singing competitions.

Stradbally Steam Rally, Stradbally, Co. Laois, **t** (0502) 25444
Working steam engines, carousels and stalls, over August bank holiday weekend.

October

Laois Arts Festival, Dunamaise Theatre and Centre for the Arts, Portlaoise, Co. Laois, **t** (0502) 63355
Traditional music, dancing, and other events.

Getting there and around

By bus In Co. Kildare, Maynooth, Newbridge and Kildare town are stops on many routes into Dublin; services to Laois and Offaly are a bit less frequent.
By train Sligo trains from Dublin Connolly stop in Maynooth. Trains from Dublin Heuston on the Waterford, Cork, Limerick and Galway lines stop at Kildare town; Cork and Limerick trains go through Portlaoise, and Galway trains stop in Tullamore.
Bike Hire
The Raleigh Rent-a-Bike network operates in Kildare and Laois, via:
John Cahill and Son, Sallins Rd, Naas, Co. Kildare, **t** (045) 879 655
M. Kavanagh, Railway St, Portlaoise, Co. Laois, **t** (0502) 21357.

SPECIAL TRIPS

The Offaly town of Birr was one of many planned by Plantation landlords in the 17th century. An indelible graciousness has been left upon it by grand Georgian squares and streets. There's a fine walk by the river through the town, beside St. Brendan's Church and the Convent of Mercy.

Birr Castle Demesne

Birr, Co. Offaly, **t** (0509) 20336
Open Mid-Mar–Oct 9–6 and Nov–mid-Mar 10–4
Adm Castle: adult €8, child €4.50;
National Birds of Prey Centre: Adult €5.50, child €3
Café, shop, picnics, guided tours, parking

The neo-Gothic castle is not open to the public, but there are river gardens, parkland, a Historic Science Centre and a giant telescope. Astronomical instruments, photographic and scientific equipment from the 1800s are exhibited along with information on the botanical work in the gardens, planted with Chinese and Himalayan trees,

Can you spot...?
Silken Thomas's tree? It's beside the path leading to Maynooth College. Garrett Óg Fitzgerald, son of the Earl of Kildare, refused to be ruled by Henry VIII, and instead wanted to rule all of Ireland himself. He was called Silken Thomas because he wore fine silk clothes, and he is said to have played his lute under this tree.

Larchill Arcadian Garden

Dunsaughlin Rd, Kilcock, Co. Kildare, **t** (01) 628 7354
Getting there N4, 19 miles (30km) west of Dublin
Open May bank holidays and Jun–Aug Tues–Sun 12 noon–6, Sept Sat–Sun 12 noon–6,
6–23 Dec 3–7pm for Christmas grotto
Adm Adult €7, 5–12s €5, under-4s free, family (2+4) €25

Your children may not appreciate that this is Ireland's last 18th-century *ferme ornée* or ornamental farm, but they will enjoy exploring the grounds to find the 10 follies set in its 63 acres of parkland. Among them are a circular Greek temple and fortress on an island in an 8-acre lake, and a tower lined with shells inside a walled garden. The follies lie on a circular walk through beech avenues, with wonderful views. Rare farm animal breeds graze among the follies, including Kerry Bog ponies, cattle, four-horned sheep, exotic wildfowl, puck goats and old breeds of pig. Larchill is said to have the largest number of rare breeds in Ireland.

A special grotto is created for children at Christmas time with donkeys, farm animals, fairy lights in the trees and hot chocolate and marshmallows for after they meet Santa Claus.

AROUND AND ABOUT

Bricks and mortar

Castletown House

Celbridge, Co. Kildare, **t** (01) 628 8252
Getting there N4, 15 miles (24km) west of Dublin
Open Easter–Sept Mon–Fri 10–6, Sat–Sun 1–6, Oct Mon–Fri 10–5, Sun and bank holidays 1–5pm, Nov and bank holidays 1–5; closed Dec–Easter
Adm adult €3.50, child €1.25, family €8.25
Guided tours, coffee shop, disabled access

18th-century paintings and furniture fill Ireland's finest Palladian country house, built in 1722 for the speaker of the Irish House of Commons.

A story to tell: St Brigid and her magic cloak

There are actually two Brigids, although you'd think there were several, the name is spelled in so many different ways – Brigid, Brighid, Bridget, Bride, Brigit and more. All these names mean 'exalted one'. In Ireland Brigid is often called Mary of the Gael. In the days before Christianity, she was a goddess who looked after poets, scholars, metal-workers, blacksmiths and healers. People prayed to her for help with handicrafts, fertility, writing poems and when they wanted to learn something or heal someone. Some say she had two sisters with the same name, and the three became remembered as one goddess, named *Brigantia* and associated with nourishment and divination.

The first Brigid was called goddess of fire and illumination, and linked with the festival of Imbolg on 1 February, celebrated by pre-Christian Celts to welcome the beginning of spring and say goodbye to winter. It was a time to encourage the new growing season; today it's St. Brigid's Feast Day.

It is said that in County Kildare, in the house of the Daghda, leader of the Tuatha Dé Danaan, there was great rejoicing one morning, for at sunrise the Daghda's wife had given birth to Brigid. At that very moment a beautiful white cow appeared by the door in a puff of cloud, and her mooing made it clear she wanted to be milked. The cow nudged them to indicate that the new baby should have its milk to drink, and from then on that is what Brigid fed upon until she grew up into a lovely girl with cream-coloured skin, black curls and sky-blue eyes.

Every morning she lit the hearth fire. The house always seemed full of light whenever Brigid was about, for she always sang songs and whispered little poems as she did her work, and always with a smile in her eye. The only trouble was, she had a habit of giving away whatever she saw in the house to any poor person who came asking.

One day, the King of Leinster paused beside the family's well and asked Brigid for some water. She didn't know who he was, but Brigid treated him kindly, as she did everyone, and the king was smitten by her beauty and gentleness of manner. Unable to forget her, he returned and begged for her hand in marriage. Brigid was shocked, as she had no desire to become the wife of a king; she had decided to dedicate her life to the needy. But the king would not take no for an answer, and so she was forced to agree to an engagement.

Then, she prayed to be made ugly so that the king would no longer want her. She fell ill and sallow-skinned, and her eyes lost their shine. When the king came to see her again, she told him she did not wish to marry him, so he freed her from the engagement and went away.

The next day her bloom and health returned, as did the bounce in her step. When the king saw her later, he was very downhearted he had lost her and asked if there was anything he could do for her.

'There is one thing,' she said. 'If you would give me a bit of land, just enough that my cloak will cover, then I will be happy indeed. Then I can start my church for the poor.' The king protested that her request was too little, but Brigid assured him it was enough. The king reluctantly agreed. Then Brigid spread out her cloak on the ground, and spread it, and spread it, for it kept growing, doubling in size, and then tripling, and quadrupling, until it covered the grasslands of the Curragh as far as the eye could see. The king couldn't help smiling, and gave her all the land beneath the cloak. Thereafter he often sought her advice, and they remained lifelong friends.

Brigid built a church of oak, a sacred tree to the Druids, and 19 more women joined her to help minister to the poor. They dressed in simple white dresses so strangers would know them, and kept a fire going constantly at a shrine in a grotto in the grounds of what is now the Church of Kildare.

Clonmacnoise Monastic Site

Near Shannonbridge, Co. Offaly, **t** (090) 9674114
Getting there 10 miles (16km) south of Athlone
Open Daily Jun–Aug 9–7, Sept–May 10–6
Adm Adult €5, under–12s €2, family (2+4) €11
Café, visitor centre, multi-lingual audio-visual show

Tour buses from Athlone depart daily for this peaceful monastic setting beside the Shannon. This beautiful early Christian site was founded by Saint Ciaran in the 6th century, and includes the ruins of a cathedral, eight churches (10th–13th century) and two round towers. The original high crosses and grave slabs are on display in the Visitor Centre, where there is an audio-visual show as well as a number of exhibitions. The site gets very busy in the summer, so expect lengthy queues.

Durrow Monastery

Getting there Off the N52, 5 miles (8km) north of Tullamore, Co. Offaly

This ruined monastery is not open to the public, but you can stop to view the remains of the ancient buildings founded in the 6th century by St Columcille. It is famous for the 7th-century manuscript produced here, the *Book of Durrow*, which is now in Trinity College Dublin (*see* p.56).

A game for St. Brigid's Day, 1 February

This game is based on a traditional ritual. Parents can take part, or children can take on the roles of the 'parents'. Younger children might just like to join in the active parts of the game.

One child plays Brigid, wearing a veil or scarf and carrying rushes or straw, and knocks three times on the closed door of a 'house' where the 'family' sits around a table on which food is spread. The house's boundaries can be marked however the players wish, so long as there is enough space for the participants to move around. Each time Brigid knocks, she calls, 'Kneel and let Blessed Brigid enter the house'. When she says this for the third time, those inside the house kneel and say, 'Oh come in, you are a hundred times welcome.'

The girl enters the 'house' and places her rushes under the table. The 'father' and 'mother' inside the house recite this verse: 'Bless us, O God, bless our food and drink, and deliver us from evil!'

Then everyone tries to run out of the house while Brigid tries to stop them. If she touches someone, they must sit down and stay where they are until someone who is free touches him or her so they are released. Brigid must chase and touch each person three times, before a player is 'out', at which point he/she must stay sitting until everyone else is caught. Once everyone is caught, they all say in unison '1-2-3', to give Brigid the chance to run away. Then each person must touch or tag her before they can return to the 'house'. Those freed first have to prepare Brigid's seat and food at the table for her. Once Brigid is tagged by everyone, she can also return to the house.

Then the 'parent' gives a thanksgiving prayer and everyone eats their food, after which they may plait the rushes or straw into a St Brigid's cross, sprinkle it with 'holy' water and hang it up where it will remain until the next St Brigid's Day.

Emo Court Demesne

Emo, Co. Laois, **t** (0502) 26573

Getting there 13 miles (20km) west of Kildare, just north of the N7 Portlaoise road

Open Grounds, till dusk; House, Mar–Oct Mon only, mid-Jun–mid-Sept daily 10.30–5, guided tour only

Adm Adult €2.75, child €2

This lovely 18th-century house, recently restored, has an impressive domed rotunda room, but children may prefer the surrounding grassy spaces and walks near the large lough beyond it.

Leap Castle

Near Gloster, Co. Offaly, **t** (0509) 31115

Getting there 10 miles (16km) south of Birr

Open May–Sept daily 10–5, Oct–Apr by appointment. **Adm** €6, child €2

This large, spooky tower was built by the Darby family around 1750. It was famous for its smelly ghost, one of many that inhabited it, until the castle was ruined in the Irish Civil War in 1922.

St Brigid's Church, Kildare

Kildare Town, Co. Kildare

This church is linked with St Brigid, since it was built on an ancient pagan site where Brigid and her nuns kept alight their eternal sacred fire.

Look at this!

Irish Pewter Mill and Moone High Cross Centre

Timolin, Moone, Co. Kildare, **t** (0507) 24164

Getting there 20 miles (32km) south of Naas

Open Showrooms/museum all year Mon–Fri 10–4.30, plus Sat–Sun 11–4 in summer, closed Good Fri, Easter Sun and Christmas. **Adm** Free

Watch pewter jewellery and tableware being made here by hand at this 1,000-year-old mill.

Lullymore Heritage Park

Lullymore, Rathangan, Co. Kildare, **t** (045) 870 238

Getting there 17 miles (27km) north of Kildare

Open Easter–Oct Mon–Fri 9–6, weekends 12 noon–6, Nov–Easter Mon–Fri 9–4

Adm €7 per person + €2 crazy golf, family €15 (2+2)

This 13-acre community project has early Christian, 1798 Rebellion and Famine exhibitions, a train ride, a faery bower, Celtic mythology walk and kiddies' play area.

Rock of Dunamase

Getting there 3 miles (5km) east of Portlaoise, Co. Laois

Apparently a banshee and a hell hound (a big black mastiff with flaming breath) frequent this striking 13th-century ruin built on a Celtic ring fort. It has stood here since the Iron Age, and has been a ruin since Cromwell badly battered it in 1650.

Nature lovers

In the flood meadows on either side of the Little Brosna River in Co. Offaly, north of Tullamore, you can watch for golden plover, widgeon, whooper swans, curlews, lapwings and black-tailed godwits.

Celbridge Abbey Grounds

Celbridge, Co. Kildare, **t** (01) 628 8350
Getting there N4, 15 miles (24km) west of Dublin
Open Apr–Sept Mon–Fri 10–6, Sat 11-6, Sun 12–6, Oct–Mar Tues–Fri 10–5, Sat 11–5, Sun 12–5
Adm Adult €3.80, child €2.50, family €9.50
Disabled access, free parking, tearoom, garden centre, picnic area, playground

Families might want to spend a whole day exploring these grounds by the River Liffey, first planted in 1697 by the daughter of the Lord Mayor of Dublin for the author Jonathan Swift. You can follow a model railway past 300ft of 17th-century buildings and country landscapes, and even an island beneath a bridge. Children can take a donkey and trap ride or play in an adventure playground, then have a picnic or lunch or an afternoon snack in the tearoom in the 17th-century gatehouse.

Irish National Stud and Japanese Garden

Tully, Kildare Town, **t** (045) 522 963
Getting there Just south of Kildare town
Open Daily mid-Feb–mid-Nov 9.30–6
Adm Adult €8.50, under-12s €4.50, under-5s free, family (2+4) €18
Toilets with baby-changing room, restaurant, craft shop, Lego play area, disabled access, garden centre

Kildare is the hub of horse-lore in Ireland, and the museum on the stud farm's racehorses has a fine visitor centre. Also here is a real Japanese garden, created by landscape designer Tassa Eida, with Japanese plants, stone ornaments and a geisha house illustrating the symbolic journey of the soul through life on earth to eternity.

> ***An Irish proverb –***
> ***A light heart lives long.***

Morell Open Farm

Turnings, Straffan, Co Kildare, **t** (01) 628 8636
Getting there 5 miles (8km) south of N4
Open Daily 10.30–5.30. **Adm** Adult €4, child €3
Picnic area, animal hospital, access for disabled

Here your children can learn about many animal breeds and how they are looked after. They should wear wellies and old clothes, so they can touch rare breeds of sheep, pigs, cows and exotic birds.

Peatland World

Lullymore, Rathangan, Co. Kildare, **t** (045) 860 133
Getting there 17 miles (27km) north of Kildare
Open All year Mon–Fri 9.30–6, Sat groups only by appointment, Apr–Oct Sun 2–6
Adm Adult €7, family €15
Restaurant, crafts and bookshop

Exhibits on the fauna and flora of the bog lands and turf production since prehistoric times are here, together with an Irish farmhouse with a kitchen from the 1900s with a turf fire.

Sporty kids

Activity centres

Outdoor Education Centre

Birr, Co. Offaly, **t** (0509) 20029

For orienteering in the Slieve Bloom mountains.

Shannon Adventure Canoeing

The Marina, Banagher, Co. Offaly, **t** (0509) 51411

Canoeing trips on the Shannon.

Boat trips

Grand Canal Hotel

Robertstown, Co. Kildare, **t** (045) 860 260

The boat Eustace offers trips on the Grand Canal.

Lowtown Marine

Robertstown, Co. Kildare, t (045) 860 427

Rent a boat on the canal.

Celtic Canal Cruisers

Tullamore, Co. Offaly, **t** (0506) 21861

Cruiser hire.

Did you know...?
William Hill-Walker, founder of the National Stud at Tully, Kildare, in 1900, believed astrology could influence the outcome of horse races, so he had skylights installed in his stables so that his horses could feel the influence of the stars.

Historic Cruising Tours
17 Woodlands, Birr, Co. Offaly, **t** (0509) 51411

Cruises on Lough Derg.

Fishing
For equipment and information on fishing spots in these counties, contact:

Mrs Travers, Curryhills House, Prosperous, Naas, Co. Kildare, **t** (045) 868 728

Ballaghmore Lake, Ballaghmore House, Borris-in-Ossory, Co. Laois, **t** (0505) 21366

J Hiney's Pub & Tackle, Main Street, Ferbane, Co. Offaly, **t** (0902) 54344. For coarse fishing

Horse racing
Look for upcoming events in national newspapers, or in the racing calendar in the *Tourism Ireland Calendar of Events*, published every year.

The Curragh Racecourse
Co. Kildare, **t** (045) 441 205, **www**.curragh.ie

Ireland's foremost racecourse and home of the Irish Derby, every June.

Punchestown Racecourse
Co. Kildare, **t** (045) 897 704, **www**.punchestown.com

Horse riding

Birr Equestrian Centre
Kingsborough House, Birr, Co. Offaly, **t** (0509) 21961

Riding and tuition in the Offaly countryside.

Kill International Equestrian Centre
Kill, Co. Kildare, **t** (045) 877 208

Getting there 5 miles (8km) east of Naas

Purpose-built centre, open all year, offering riding tuition for all ages and levels of experience, and with very high-quality facilities.

Old Mill Riding Centre
Kill, Co. Kildare, **t** (045) 877 053

Tuition for children and adults, and also open all year round.

Walking and cycling
The Slieve Bloom Way, a circular route of 31 miles (50km), starts at Glenmonicknew Forest car park. Ask for information at any tourist office, or contact:

Slieve Bloom Walking Centre
Kinnitty Village, Co. Offaly, **t** (0509) 37299

Getting there 8 miles (13km) east of Birr

Guided walking tours programme, maps and information.

Wild Earth Trails Ltd
Contact B Doheny, The Elms, Spollenstown, Tullamore, Co. Offaly, **t** (0506) 22410

Eco tours, wildlife trails, cycling and walking.

Steam power!

Clonmacnoise and West Offaly Railway
Bord na Mona Blackwater Works, Blackwater, near Shannonbridge, Co. Offaly, **t** (090) 9674114

Getting there 18 miles (28km) north of Birr

Open Apr–Oct 10–5, departures hourly, on the hour

Tickets Adult €5.80, child €3.90, family €18

Guided train tours, picnic areas, café, craft shop, car park, wheelchair access

All aboard the Bog Train for a trip across Blackwater Bog to visit the turf bank and see a demonstration of turf cutting. It's a 6-mile (9km) circular journey through time that takes about an hour, while your guide tells you everything you could want to know about the ecology of bog land. There is a daily bus tour to the site from Athlone.

Lodge Park Heritage Centre and Steam Museum
Straffan, Co. Kildare, **t** (01) 627 3155

Getting there 5 miles (8km) south of N4 near Celbridge

Open Jun–Jul Tues–Fri, Sun and bank holidays 2–6, Aug 2–5.30; other times by arrangement

Adm Walled garden, €4 per person

Disabled access, park, shop, tearoom

Five big Victorian steam engines housed in this Gothic church actually work, as do the historic models of trains and plumbing systems. A hands-on area where your kids can climb on everything will give them a thrill, while outdoors you can visit an 18th-century walled garden and park.

MEATH AND LOUTH

Counties Louth and Meath are full of sites connected with Ireland's folklore and ancient history. The Boyne Valley and Hill of Tara in Meath are the most frequented tourist sites, but there are many others. Investigate the areas surrounding the Boyne Valley, Tara and Bective Abbey, or travel west to Oldcastle for ancient remains and delicious green spaces. Look around the peninsula beside the Irish Sea from Carlingford to Cooley Point, where there are many places to try water sports.

The Boyne Valley is the most important part of Co. Meath, historically and mythologically. It is filled with the homes of the Tuatha Dé Danaan, the Sidhe (pronounced 'shee') – or faeries, as they are better known. You will see the odd solitary 'faery tree' in the middle of a field, and 'faery raths' (grass-covered craters where ancient buildings stood) at nearly every turn in the road. The magnificent Hill of Tara has many earthworks, including the ancient tomb or passage cairn of Niall and the Nine Hostages, and the Lia Fáil, the stone of destiny that is said to roar when the rightful king of Ireland sits upon it. Newgrange, ancient home of Aengus Óg, is also in the Boyne Valley.

This is also the place where one of the most important battles in Irish history was fought: the Battle of the Boyne, in July 1690, where Protestant William of Orange decisively defeated the Catholic James II (*see* p.35). On a lighter note, teenagers might like to know that Irish pop lovelies The Corrs hail from Dundalk.

In County Louth, many sites are associated with the mythical hero-warrior Cúchulainn, and especially with the great Irish epic 'The Cattle Raid of Cooley', the *Táin Bó Cúailgne*. It is set in the Cooley Mountains in the northern part of the county, as is Muirtheimhne, where Cúchulainn is supposed to have been born. The county's name comes from the Tuatha Dé Danaan sun god Lugh of the Many Talents, who some stories claim was also the father of Cúchulainn. Louth village itself was a centre of a Lugh cult in St Patrick's time, and Louth also has a claim to be the county where St Brigid was born (at Faughart Hill), rivalling Co. Kildare for the honour.

Tourist information

Bru na Boinne, Donore, Co. Meath **t** (041) 988 0305
Carlingford, Co. Louth, **t** (042) 937 3888
Drogheda, Co. Louth, **t** (041) 984 5684
Dundalk, Co. Louth, **t** (042) 933 5484
Kells, Kells Heritage Centre, **t** (046) 49336.
Navan, **t** (046) 77273
Newgrange, **t** (041) 988 0300
Rathcairn, An Bradán Feasa, **t**(046) 32381
Trim, Co. Meath, **t** (046) 37111, and **Meath Heritage Centre**, Mill St, **t** (046) 36633

Getting there and around

By bus Bus Eireann buses run hourly to Navan, Drogheda and Slane, and many Belfast–Dublin buses stop in Drogheda and Dundalk.

By train The main Dublin–Belfast line from Dublin Connolly runs through Drogheda and Dundalk, and a branch line runs to Navan.

Bike Hire

The Raleigh Rent-a-Bike network operates at the following shops:

Irish Cycle Hire, Mayoralty St, Drogheda, **t** (041) 873 3622
Quay Cycles, 11 North Quay, by train station, Drogheda, **t** (041) 983 4256

Shopping

Bookwise Booksellers

Kennedy Road, Navan, Co. Meath, **t** (046) 27722

Maps, guidebooks and books on Irish history.

Claidhobh O'Gibne

Drogheda, Co. Louth, **t** (041) 41960

Celtic wood carvings.

Courtyard Craft Centre and Café

Cookstown House, Kells, Co. Meath, **t** (046) 40346

Locally handcrafted ceramics, linen, textiles, woodwork, glass, jewellery, baskets and metalwork.

Maguire's

Hill of Tara, Co. Meath, **t** (046) 26205

Celtic theme and mythology books – also for children – Aran sweaters, crafts, jewellery, and a café with homemade scones.

Mary McDonnell Craft Studio

4 Newgrange Mall, Slane, Co. Meath, **t** (041) 982 4722

Quilts, wall hangings, ceramics and jewellery. During the winter it houses the local organic food market, every Friday 3–6pm.

Trim Visitor Centre

Mill St, Trim, Co. Meath, **t** (046) 37227, **www.meathtourism.ie**

Handmade silver jewellery, ceramics, textiles, leather goods, crystal glass and soaps.

Special Events – Meath and Louth

May–June

Dundalk International Maytime Festival, Dundalk, Co. Louth, **t** (042) 933 5253

Art, theatre, dancing, concerts, sport, and events for children.

June

Moneley Oyster Pearl Regatta, Carlingford, Co. Louth; contact Dundalk and Carlingford Sailing Club, **t** (042) 937 3238

Races are held late in the month.

Blackrock Annual Raft Race, Promenade/beach, Blackrock, Co. Louth, **t** (042) 932 1098

Local event with carnival and fancy dress.

Laytown Races, Laytown, Co. Meath, **t** (041) 984 2111

July

Kells Heritage Festival, Kells, Co. Meath, **t** (046) 41097

Crafts, art, walking tours and other attractions.

Loughcrew Garden Opera, Loughcrew Historic Gardens, Oldcastle, Co. Meath, **t** (049) 854 1356, **www.loughcrew.com**

Le Chéile, Oldcastle, Co. Meath, **t** (049) 854 2197 **www.lecheile.com**

A mixed festival of arts and music.

August

Carlingford Oyster Fest, Carlingford, Co. Louth, **t** (042) 937 3033

Oyster festival with arts, crafts and family fun.

Moynalty Steam Threshing Festival, Moynalty, Co. Meath, **t** (046) 44390

Traditional farming festival showing vintage machinery, ploughing and tilling demonstrations.

September

Carlingford Medieval Weekend, Carlingford, Co. Louth, **t** (042) 937 3033

Knights on horseback, battle reenactments, dancing and music. Local people dress up as the town is transformed into a medieval market place.

October

O'Carolan Harp Cultural and Heritage Festival, Nobber, Co. Meath, **t** (046) 52115

A very fine festival of Irish music.

SPECIAL TRIPS

The Causey Experience

Lily or Angela Murtagh, Girley, Fordstown, Navan, Co. Meath, t (046) 34135, www.causeyexperience.com

Getting there The farm is about 8 miles (12km) west of Navan, south of Kells

Open Apr–Oct Sat 2–8, other times by arrangement

Adm Adult €5, child €3 50

Includes meals, tuition and Irish dancing, weekend camps available for teenagers.

This is a truly educational day out for children, as the family-owners of this farm, just outside Kells in Co. Meath, recreate and offer a hands-on experiences of Irish traditional country life. When you arrive, the matriarch of the Murtagh family, Lily, welcomes you with her homemade brown bread and scones. Ask her whatever you want to know about Ireland, whether it's the old mythologies or how people used to run a farm. If you have chosen to simply visit the farm rather than trek on the land, her husband, Tom, will take you with him on his tractor to cut turf. Upon returning to the stone cottage that has been especially converted for visitor activities, you don an apron and learn how to make the perfect brown bread. After that their son Matt will show you how Chip the sheepdog rounds up sheep , cattle or even Connemara ponies, and the Murtaghs' son-in-law Eoin Carton demonstrates how to hurl and shows how the hurley and ball, or *sliothar*, are made.

Maybe you'll milk a cow or pair up to make Sugán rope out of straw. Lessons in goatskin drum (or *bodhrán*) making and dancing follow. Your break for afternoon tea will be somewhere in the midst of all this activity, and at the end of your day you will have a delicious 4-course evening meal with the family. By this time you will have picked up a few Irish words to include in your chatter with the Murtaghs and loosened up enough to enjoy the lively *ceilidh* that ends the day. Bring a change of clothing and shoes, as you may get muddy and wet. For the geography trek, bring a packed lunch, raingear and old shoes or waterproof boots.

The Murtaghs are flexible and friendly, so if you'd prefer a shorter visit than this one, simply let them know. There are also bus tours from Dublin direct to the farm.

Loughcrew

Loughcrew Historic Gardens

Oldcastle, Co. Meath, **t** (049) 854 1922, **www**.loughcrew.com
Getting there 3 miles (5km) from Oldcastle off the Mullingar Road
Open 17 Mar–Sept daily 1–5, Oct–16 Mar Sun and bank holidays only 1–5
Adm Garden and St Oliver Plunkett Church, adult €6, child €3.50
Book and gift shop, parking, tearoom, wheelchair accessible, garden guide for walks in area available

Beside Loughcrew Cairns, Charles and Emily Naper (who conduct residential courses in gilding) have restored these 17th–19th-century gardens to their former grandeur. They have also added touches that will appeal to children, like the 'Celtic Legend' trail, watermill cascade, nature and history trails and a fairy grotto. It is a wonderland for children, but adult supervision is needed at all times, for the grounds are extensive and there are many water features to fall into and plenty of meandering paths on which to get lost. Within the grounds you can picnic, play outdoor games or investigate the family church and tower house of St Oliver Plunkett, among 350-year-old yews and many other varieties of trees. The new entrance lodge with its comfortable, tasteful café is inviting and very much in keeping with its surroundings.

St Oliver Plunkett was a 17th-century Catholic archbishop who was hung, drawn and quartered at Tyburn in London for going against the anti-Catholic laws of his time. His supporters managed to grab hold of his head, which after a long and complicated journey eventually ended up in St Peter's Church in Drogheda, where it is displayed as a relic. He was made a saint in 1975.

Loughcrew Cairns

Believed to be a Stone Age cemetery (3000 BC), this has around 30 passage tombs similar to the one at Newgrange, all of which sit on a hill called *Sliabh na Caillì* (the Hill of the Hag) in northwest County Meath. The best-preserved tomb is that of Ollamh Fodhla, believed to have been a poet-king at Tara around 1300 BC. The mound is known by local people as 'the witch's cave'; they say she will put a curse on those who enter it. Access to the cairns is steep, so it's not great for a hike with toddlers. Richard Marsh (*see* p.26) takes tours around the site.

Newgrange and Knowth

Brú na Bóinne (The Boyne Valley) Visitor Centre

Donore, Co. Meath, **t** (041) 988 0300
Getting there 2 miles (3km) off the N51, 8 1/2 miles (13km) west of Drogheda
Open Daily Mar–Apr 9.30–5.30, May 9–6.30, Jun–mid-Sept 9–7, mid–end Sept 9–6.30, Oct 9.30–5.30, Nov–Feb 9.30–5, last admission 1hr before closing
Adm Centre only, adult: €2.50, child, €1, family €6.30; Centre and Newgrange, adult €5.00, child €2.50, family €12.70; Centre and Knowth, adult €3.80, child €1.50, family €9.50; Centre, Newgrange and Knowth, adult €8.80, child €4.10, family €22.20
Tourist office, café-restaurant, parking

Newgrange is Ireland's best-known prehistoric monument. Built between 3500 BC and 2700 BC, 500 years before the Egyptian pyramids and 1,500 years before Stonehenge, it fills almost a full acre of ground. Made of white quartz and granite, it is 36ft tall and has a 6-ton capstone, with other stones weighing up to 16 tons each. Inside it, tri-spiral and other designs like chevrons and diamonds are carved into the stone. In Irish folk tales, it is the home of Aengus Óg, the Tuatha Dé Danaan god of love and birds.

All traffic for Newgrange is directed to the Centre, eliminating direct access to it or to the similar nearby prehistoric sites of Knowth and inaccessible Dowth (currently being excavated). Visitors register at the centre for tours to Newgrange and/or Knowth, where they are taken by minibus. In summer the wait can be as long as 3hrs for a 1hr (max 25-persons) tour. Exhibits at the centre include a 7-min introductory audio-visual show, and a walk-through replica of Newgrange with a simulation of the winter solstice.

Did you know...?
Aengus Óg, the ancient Irish god of love who lived at Newgrange, was always surrounded by birds, and he fell in love with a woman who was turned into a fly in one of her lives.

A story to tell:
The Burning of the Hill of Tara

In the days when the Tuatha Dé Danaan (*see* p.29) roamed the earth freely, Aengus the Young, Aengus Óg, had his home at Newgrange, while other Tuatha Dé lived on high places like the Hills of Tara and Uisneach. Then ordinary humans came along and took these over, with their High Kings. The Tuatha fought many battles, first against cruel magical beings that sought control of Ireland and later against humans, with whom they called a truce. The Tuatha agreed to let the humans take the upper surface of the world, while they themselves chose to move into the hills and the hidden realms of the Otherworld.

But there were some who disagreed with this truce, and did whatever they could to cause mischief for the upper-world dwellers. For a time, on every Samhain (Halloween) night an invisible enemy would burn down the palace at Tara. No one ever saw the enemy because every time it struck, they were fast asleep. All anyone could remember was hearing the most beautiful flute music and awakening in the morning to see the palace burned to a crisp. This was in about the 2nd century AD, and in those days the best palaces were made of wood, so nothing could stop them from burning down. At the time Ireland's highest king was Conn of the Hundred Battles – so named because he had won that many battles without being injured, making him the greatest warrior of Ireland. So on Samhain, Conn assembled his best warriors at Tara to protect the palace. However, no one could ever stay awake long enough to even see who their attacker was, much less defeat him.

One year, Conn's most powerful warrior came from the west of Ireland to defend Tara. His name was Goll mac Morna (the 'One-eyed son of Morna'); he had been called Aed ('fire'), but was renamed Goll after he lost an eye in a battle between his men and the Fianna, when he had slain the Fianna leader Cumall. Since then Goll had presided over the Fianna lands in eastern and southern Ireland. Their rightful leader, Cumhall's young son Finn, had been in hiding since his father's death because Goll's warriors, the Fir Bolg from Connacht, had sworn to kill him.

Now, this Samhain a great feast was being held at Tara, and again the assembled warriors awaited the attack. Just then there was a pounding on the gate of the palace, and in swept a tall, handsome young man with hair like spun gold.

'I am Finn, son of Cumhall,' he said. 'Since my father was leader of the Fianna, it is right that I should be leader, now that I am of age.'

Conn knew that if he didn't make Finn leader of the Fianna, Finn's faction would revolt, and there would be civil war. But if he took the leadership away from Goll, the Morna faction would revolt.

So Conn said, 'Not even the great Goll mac Morna can stop Tara from burning. Finn, you may be leader if you can prevent it.'

Soon the faery flute was heard and one by one each warrior fell snoring on the ground. Last to fall was Conn of the Hundred Battles – except for Finn, who had prepared himself with treasures from a Crane-skin Bag left to him by his father. It was made from the skin of Aoife, a warrior woman, who had been shape-changed into a crane by an enemy and then died. In the bag was a cap of silence and a poisonous spear.

Finn placed the cap on his head so as not to hear the music and watched as one of the Sidhe, named Aillén, opened his mouth and blew a flame at the palace. Quickly Finn caught the fire in a magic cloak and threw the fire back to Aillén, who fled in panic. Finn then hurled the magic spear at him, and it caught and slew him before he could return to the safety of the Otherworld. And that's how Finn became leader of the Fianna, so that now there are stories about Finn MacCool and the Fianna all over Ireland.

The Boyne Battlefield

Getting there Near Tullyallen, 2 1/2 miles (4km) west of Drogheda, signposted

The kids may wonder why you have brought them to see this green field when the country is covered in similar acres of verdant pasture, but this is no ordinary field. Here in July 1690 William of Orange defeated the deposed King James II, and secured the Protestant succession to the British throne. The battle soon entered into Protestant mythology and William of Orange became an Ulster Loyalist hero. This turning point in Irish history is commemorated annually in Northern Ireland on 12 July (*see* p.203). At the site, there is a small monument.

Newgrange Farm

near Slane, Co. Meath, **t** (041) 982 4119
Getting there 8 1/2 miles (13km) west of Drogheda on the N51
Open Daily Easter Sat–Aug 10–5
Adm adult €6, €5 per person in a family group
Café, disabled access, picnic areas, gift shop, pets' corner, rural life museum

This working farm offers tours around its 17th-century buildings and herb garden. See vintage farm machinery and crops, and hold and feed poultry and farm animals. Children may enjoy visiting this while you're near Newgrange. The café serves up tasty homemade soups and desserts.

Stephenstown Pond and Agnes Burns Visitor Centre

Knockbridge, Co. Louth, **t** (042) 937 9019
Getting there 4 miles (6km) west of Dundalk
Open Apr–Oct 9–8.30, Nov–Mar 9–4.30 (In winter hours may vary slightly)
Adm Free, parking €2
Children's playground with safety matting, picnic facilities, coffee and crafts shops, disability access

Five acres of woodland, water walkways, decks for fishing and a pond with wildlife surround this 18th-century cottage where the sister of Scotland's national poet, Robert Burns, lived for nearly 20 years. Inside the period-furnished cottage are artifacts and information on animals, birds and local history, as well as on the poet's life and works. Home-cooking and cakes are available in the café.

AROUND AND ABOUT

Animal magic

Grove Gardens Tropical Bird Sanctuary and Mini Zoo

Fordstown, Kells, Co. Meath, **t** (046) 9434276
Getting there About 5 miles (8km) south of Kells
Open Daily 10–6 except Nov–Jan
Adm Adult €5, child €3
Tearoom, barbecue and picnic areas, tree house, summer house, shop, garden centre

Grove Gardens have 4 acres of gardens with one of Europe's biggest collections of clematis and climbing roses. Children can have a look at the vegetable garden, bantams with their chicks and exotic and rare birds from around the world. There is a 10-acre enclosure full of friendly animals to meet and a soccer pitch where kids can play.

Bricks and mortar

Dunsany Castle

Dunsany, Co. Meath, **t** (046) 9025198
Getting there 10 miles (16km) south of Navan
Open Call ahead for times of tours and open days
Adm Variable

Today this castle is inhabited by the 20th lord of the estate, the artist Edward Plunkett, who inherited it after the death of the writer Lord Dunsany. It includes a 12th-century kitchen, a vaulted hall, a drawing room with fine plasterwork, family portraits, a distinguished library and the writing table where Lord Dunsany and writers like poet Frances Ledwidge worked. Its surrounding farm and parklands are enclosed within a stone wall.

Slane Castle

Slane, Co. Meath, **t** (041) 9824163
Getting there 8 1/2 miles (13km) west of Drogheda

This castle sits on top of the Hill of Slane, where a story claims St Patrick lit an Easter (Paschal) fire before Laoghaire, the High King, lit his Beltaine fire on the Hill of Tara. This gesture of defiance was a sign of the impending takeover of the High Kings' position by Christianity. Sadly in 1991 a fire gutted the interior of the 18th-century castle including its fine ballroom ceiling, and it is not open to visitors. The castle grounds, however, contain a natural amphitheatre where rock luminaries including the Rolling Stones, Robbie Williams, U2, Oasis, Red Hot Chili Peppers and REM have graced the stage, and which also hosts occasional 'medieval festivals'. For more information check **www**.mcd.ie.

Trim Castle

Mill Street, Trim, Co. Meath, **t** (046) 94372227
Getting there 9 miles (14km) southwest of Navan
Open May–Oct daily 10–6
Adm Adult €1.20, child €0.50, family €3.80; with tour of Keep: adult €3.10, child €1.20, family €7.60
Craft shop

Did you know...?
There were two great divisions of the year in the old Celtic calendar – Oíche Bheáltaine, the eve of 1 May (Beltaine), and Oíche Shamhna (Samhain or Halloween). On these two nights gateways between this world and the Otherworld are open. One gateway is the Hill of Tara.

Children need to be well supervised here, as there are all sorts of lumps and bumps in this part-restored ruined castle and grounds. Little ones might find the audio-visual a bit grizzly. Trim Castle was on the farthest edge of the Pale, the area the Anglo-Normans ruled, and was the seat of a notorious 12th-century Norman warlord, Hugh de Lacy

Old Mellifont Abbey

Near Drogheda, Co. Louth, **t** (041) 982 6459
Getting there 4 miles (6km) west of Drogheda
Open Daily May–mid-Jun and mid-Sept–Oct 10–5, mid-Jun–mid-Sept 9.30–6.30
Adm Adult €2, child €0.80 cents, family €5

St Malachy of Armagh founded the first Cistercian monastery in Ireland here in 1142. Families can explore the site and visitor centre.

Look at this!

Drogheda Heritage Centre

Mary St, Drogheda, Co. Louth, **t** (041) 983 1153
Open All year Tues–Sat 10–5, Sat–Sun 2–6
Adm Adult €3.17, child €1.90, family (2+3) €7.62
Craft shops, café, disabled access, parking nearby

This wonderful informative centre spans eight centuries of Drogheda life in a way that both children and adults will appreciate. Families are invited to don period costumes and step back in time. Less pleasant aspects of history, such as the Battle of the Boyne and Cromwell's bloodthirsty activities (he killed 3,000 people in the town in 1649), are brought to life via a chilling audio-visual display.

Hill of Tara

Getting there About 5 miles (8km) south of Navan off the N3

Centuries ago this hill was the social and political centre of Ireland's nobility (*see* p.100). Today it's covered in grass, but you can see the sites of the circular dwellings of Cormac mac Airt and Grainne, and the cairn, said to be the oldest of its kind in Ireland, where the Sons of Uisneach are said to be buried and where there may be an opening into the Otherworld of the faeries. A Lia Fáil stone here was reputed to roar whenever the rightful heir to the high kingship sat upon it, but whether it is the true Lia Fail is another matter, as some say the original was stolen away and became the 'Stone of Scone' on which Scottish kings were crowned, which is now in Edinburgh.

Kells Heritage Centre

Headfort Place, Kells, Co. Meath, **t** (046) 47840
Getting there 10 miles (16km) northwest of Navan
Open May–Sept Mon–Sat 10–5, Sun, Oct–Apr Tues–Sat 10–5, Sun and bank holidays 1.30–6
Adm Adult €4, child €3, family (2+4) €12
Gift shop

There's a fine Celtic High Cross in the grounds of this centre, while inside there are stone carvings, metalwork and a facsimile of the *Book of Kells*. Information on local sites is also available.

Ledwidge Cottage Museum

Janeville, Slane, Co. Meath, **t** (041) 982 4544
Getting there 8 1/2 miles (13km) west of Drogheda
Open Daily 10–1 and 2–5.30
Adm Adult €2.50, child €1, family €6.50

Frances Ledwidge (1887–1917) was a nature poet who lived in this stone cottage in the heart of the Boyne Valley, which is kept today as it was then. Ledwidge once got a job in Dublin, but grew so homesick that one night he walked all the way back to Slane under the light of a full moon, neglecting to tell anyone he was going home. Ledwidge died as a soldier in World War I.

Millmount Museum and Martello Tower

Drogheda, Co. Louth, **t** (041) 983 3097
Open Mon–Sat 10–5, Sun and bank holidays 2–5
Adm Museum: adult €3.50, child €2.50, family €8; Tower: adult €3, child €2, family €6; both: adult €5.50, child €3, family €12; reduction for groups
Craft and genealogy centres, restaurant

This multi-purpose museum set in an old 18th-century military strongpoint in Drogheda town houses a folk kitchen, medieval room, geological curiosities and exhibits on local history. There's also a good view over Drogheda and much of the Boyne Valley from its tower.

Monasterboice Round Tower

Near Drogheda, Co. Louth

Getting there 5 miles (8km) north of Drogheda

The ruins of this 5th-century monastery, amid fields just off the N1 road, contains a perfect Celtic high cross, known as Muireadach's Cross.

Proleek Dolmen

Cooley Peninsula, Co. Louth

Getting there About 4 miles (6km) north of Dundalk just east of the N1, on the R173

This is one of the most impressive of Ireland's late Neolithic portal tombs (c.2500–2000 BC). Its capstone weights 40 tons, and is one of around 350 dolmens spread all over Ireland that are said to be 'Gráinne and Diarmuid's bed' (*see* p.184).

Nature lovers

Bective Abbey

Bective, Co. Meath

Getting there About 5 miles (8km) south of Navan on the Trim road

Stop for a picnic, a runaround or a peaceful walk around the ruins of Ireland's second Cistercian monastery, built in 1147. You can have lunch overlooking the Boyne and then play hide and seek, but keep an eye on toddlers; most ruins have stone steps and precipices, and this one also has a river flowing by the hillock on which the abbey sits.

Butterstream Garden

Kildalkey Road, Trim, Co. Meath, **t** (046) 9436017

Getting there 9 miles (14km) southwest of Navan

Open Daily Apr–Sept 11–6. **Adm** €6 per person

Toilets, café, wheelchair access

Jim Reynolds began creating this garden in the 1970s, and it's considered one of the best in Ireland. There are integrated sections with themes such as colour, architectural features or plant species. Roses and yew, thorn and beech trees are key features here, leading to a kind of Pompeiian villa garden.

Cooley Hills

Cooley Peninsula, Co. Louth

Within these hills much of the action of the famous Irish epic poem 'The Cattle Raid of Cooley' – the *Táin Bó Cuailnge*, more often referred to as *The Tain* – took place. You can follow a 'Tain Trail' and find many landmarks mentioned in the 12th-

A Traditional Recipe – Irish Barm Brack

Every St Brigid's Eve (31 January), homemakers in Ireland would make a cake called Barm Brack. The same cake is also sometimes made for Halloween, but with a ring added into the mix too – so that whoever found it would get a wish to make.

Ingredients

450g/1lb/3 1/2 cups of flour
pinch of salt
1 tsp mixed spice
15g/1/2oz/1 tbsp fresh yeast
1 tsp sugar
300 ml/1/2 pt/1 1/4 cups of warm water
85g/3oz/6 tbsp of butter
2 eggs
30g/1 oz/2 tbsp of candied peel
110g/4 oz/3/4 cup of raisins
110g/4 oz/3/4 cup of sultanas
110g/4 oz/3/4 cup of currants
110g/4 oz/1/2 cup of castor sugar
For glaze, 2 tbsp of castor sugar, and 1 tsp water

This makes two bracks, which take about three hours to make, although the mixing up does not take too long. Cream the yeast with a teaspoon of sugar. Add water. Sieve the flour with salt and mixed spice, and mix to a stiff dough with the yeast mixture. Knead until smooth and springy for about 5 minutes. Leave this in a bowl covered with a cloth in a warm place for 1 hour or until it has doubled in size.

Now add beaten eggs, fruit, sugar and melted butter. Beat it all together well. Half-fill two greased bread tins with the mixture and put to rise in a warm place, covered with a cloth. Leave for approximately another hour to rise to the top of the tins. Have ready a moderately hot oven, at 190°C, 375°F/ or Regulo 6. Bake for approximately 50 minutes or until fairly firm and brown.

To make the bracks gleaming brown, dissolve 2 tablespoons of sugar in 4 teaspoons of water over heat, boil for half a minute, and then brush this glaze over the bracks as they come out of the oven. Once they cool, they're ready to enjoy.

Thanks to Myrtle Allen for her permission to use the above recipe, from The Ballymaloe Cookbook, *by Myrtle Allen, Gill and MacMillan Ltd.*

century book, with its battles between Conchobar, Cúchulainn and Queen Maeve. To get around the peninsula by car, take the R173 road from Dundalk to Carlingford.

Faughart Hill

Faughart, Co. Louth

Getting there Just north of Dundalk off the N1 road

St Brigid is supposed to have been born here and founded a church on this hill. Beside the church is the grave of Edward Bruce, brother of King Robert the Bruce of Scotland, who tried to become king of Ireland and died here in 1318.

Sporty kids

Activity centres

Carlingford Adventure Centre

Thosel St, Carlingford, Co. Louth, **t** (042) 937 3100

Open Feb–Nov

Professionally supervised windsurfing, sailing, tennis and canoeing lessons, as well as tours, hiking and other activities. Beginners' courses are available on a daily or half-day basis, and inexpensive dormitory accommodation is available.

Giraffes Play Centre

Kennedy Road, Navan, Co. Meath, **t** (046) 27379

A fully supervised indoor fun centre for ages from 1–12, with bouncy castles, slides and ball-pools.

Mosney Holiday Centre

Mosney, Co. Meath, **t** (041) 982 9000

Day visitors can use the babysitting, crèche and baby-changing facilities at this centre on the Meath coast (next to a train station). Activities include indoor and outdoor swimming pools, supervised playgrounds, pet farm, boating lake, nature walks, discos and a funfair.

Buckets and spades – Beaches in Meath and Louth

Meath's short stretch of coastline has wide, Blue Flag-status beaches at **Mornington**, **Bettystown** and **Laytown**. In Louth, there are enjoyable beaches at **Termonfeckin** and **Clogherhead**, only a few miles north and east of Drogheda, and, on the Cooley Peninsula, at **Shelling Hill** and **Templeton** near Greenore, and at **Carlingford**.

Tell me an Irish riddle...

Question – What has legs but cannot walk?

Answer – A table

Cycling

Irish Cycle Hire

Ardee, Co. Louth, **t** (041) 685 3772, **www.irishcyclehire.com**

Cycling holidays and bike hire.

Fishing

Bellingham Castle

Castlebellingham, Co. Louth, **t** (042) 937 2176

For salmon fishing on the River Glyde.

Peadar Elmore

North Commons, Carlingford, Co. Louth, **t** (042) 937 3239

Boats for fishing trips in Carlingford Lough.

Horse racing

Laytown Races

Laytown, Co. Meath, **t** (041) 984 2111

The only official strand (beach) races in Europe.

Horse riding

Bellingham Stables

Castlebellingham, Co. Louth, **t** (042) 937 2175

All-weather arena. Beginners must be over age 7.

Bachelor's Lodge Equestrian Centre

Kells Road, Navan, Co. Meath, **t** (046) 9021736

Riding lessons, farm treks, pony camps.

Rathe House

Kilmainhamwood, Co. Meath, **t** (046) 9052376

Horse riding, archery and other activities.

Walking and cycling

The Tain Trail is a superb, well-signposted 18-mile (30km) circular walking and cycling path through the Cooley Mountains in Co. Louth, from Carlingford almost round to Dundalk. A Tourism Ireland leaflet on the trail is available at all tourist offices. By car, take the R173 from Dundalk. In Carlingford itself there is an enjoyable town walk – ask at the local tourist office for information.

Kelltic Walking and Adventures

White Gables, Headford Place, Kells, Co. Meath, **t** (046) 40322

Tailor-made walks for groups and individuals.

WESTMEATH AND LONGFORD

The quiet farming counties of Longford and Westmeath hold history and magic in equal measure. Until the arrival of Christianity in the 5th century, Westmeath was part of *Mide*, or Meath. In about the year AD 300 the palace of the High King of Ireland (the *Ard Rí*, *see* p.31) was at Uisneach, a small hill in the middle of the flat Westmeath countryside. Around 350, the seat of the *Ard Rí* moved to Tara (*see* p.102), but in the early 11th century it returned to Uisneach for a brief period. In a fairy tale the children of King Lir were changed to swans on the shores of Westmeath's Lake Derravaragh, where they spent the first 300 years after their stepmother's curse (*see* p.177).

County Longford, which is also quite flat, is in the basin of the River Shannon and known for its trees and rivers, and the pretty islands that dot its lakes. Many famous writers of different eras, like Oliver Goldsmith (1728–24), author of the play *She Stoops to Conquer*, and Padraic Colum (1881–1972), who wrote the children's story *The King of Ireland's Son*, were born here, and Anglo-Irish author Maria Edgeworth (whose *Castle Rackrent* denounced the hardships of Irish peasants in the 19th century) lived in Edgeworthstown, where her father had a large estate.

Tourist information

Athlone, Co. Westmeath, **t** (090) 6494630
Longford, Co. Longford, **t** (043) 46566
Mullingar, Co, Westmeath, **t** (044) 48650

Getting there and around

By bus Bus Eireann buses from Dublin or Galway stop at Kinnegad, Mullingar, Moate and Athlone in Westmeath, and Longford and Granard in Longford. Many small-company local services to villages run from Athlone, Mullingar and Longford.

By rail The Galway line from Dublin Heuston stops in Athlone; the Sligo line from Dublin Connolly stops in Mullingar, Edgeworthstown (Mostim) and Longford town.

Bike Hire

Buckley Cycles, Main St, Athlone, Co. Westmeath, **t** (090) 6478989

Shopping

The Longford Bookshop

Ballymahon Street, Longford, Co. Longford, **t** (043) 47698

A good general bookshop with plenty of material on attractions in the region, and a nice children's section.

Tom McGuinness

Main Street, Longford, Co. Longford, **t** (043) 46305

Crafts and sweaters.

Mullingar Pewter Limited

Great Down, The Downs, Co. Westmeath, **t** (044) 48791

Interesting bronze and pewterware made with traditional methods; guided tours are also available.

Special Events – Westmeath and Longford

May

All Ireland Amateur Drama Festival, Deane Crowe Theatre, Athlone, Co. Westmeath, **t** (090) 6472333

Busy arts festival, with many shows and stalls.

July

Mullingar Festival, Mullingar, Co. Westmeath, **t** (044) 44044

A week of family and street entertainment, music, dance and talent competitions – plus the 'International Bachelor Competition'.

Ballymahon Budweiser Festival, Carrigdow, Ballymahon, Co. Longford, **t** (090) 6432143

Town festival catering for all ages with street tug of war, children's art and drama workshops, water sports and other street entertainment.

Brideswell International Celtic Festival, Brideswell, Athlone, Co. Westmeath

Popular folk music festival with musicians, singers and dancers from all over the Celtic world.

August

Granard Harp Festival, Granard, Co. Longford, **t** (043) 86643

Renowned festival dating back to 1781. The main events are on the second Saturday of the month.

November

John McCormack, the Golden Voice of Athlone, Athlone, Co. Westmeath

Athlone's international classical singing competition is named after a celebrated local son, John McCormack, a legend in Ireland and one of the greatest tenors in the world from the 1900s to the 1930s.

SPECIAL TRIPS

Adventure Viking Cruise

7 St Mary's Place, Athlone, Co. Westmeath, t (090) 6473383, www.vikingtoursireland.com
Cruises daily Jun–Sept, on request Mar–May, Oct–Nov, to Lough Ree (90 mins trip) and twice-weekly to Clonmacnoise (4 1/2hrs), departing from Strand Fishing Tackle Shop, **t** (090) 6479277

Dress up in Viking costumes, swords, helmets and shields for your adventure cruise in a replica Viking ship on the Shannon, and follow the trail of the marauders who once plundered villages and monastic sites along the river, accompanied by historic tales told by your friendly Viking guide.

Athlone Castle

Athlone, Co. Westmeath, **t** (090) 6492912
Open Easter/May–Sept Mon–Sat 10–4.30
Adm Adult €5, child €3, family €11.50
Folk and military museums, tearoom

Right on the River Shannon, this 13th-century castle houses a museum of folk artefacts and a separate historical museum, which focuses mainly on the Siege of Athlone in 1691, during the war between the forces of the deposed Catholic King James II and the Protestant William of Orange (*see* p.35). Soldiers' costumes and other exhibits complement an audio-visual display on the siege. More peacefully, there's information about the flora and fauna of the River Shannon, and also on Ireland's most famous tenor and one of Athlone's most famous sons, John McCormack (1884–1945).

Fore Abbey

Coffee Shop and Information Centre, Fore, **t** (044) 61780
Getting there About 15 miles (24km) north of Mullingar and the N4 Dublin–Sligo road
Open May–Sept. **Adm** Free
Tour guide available upon request

For a peaceful day out, take a picnic and drive to this sleepy village of ruins deep in the Westmeath countryside, near the valley where the Norman landlords, the De Lacys, built a Benedictine priory in the 13th century. Once there, you and the kids can find out about the 'Seven Wonders of Fore':

* The water that flows uphill (it really does!)
* The monastery built in a bog
* The mill without a race
* The water that won't boil (don't try it, or you'll be cursed)
* The tree that won't burn (don't try this or ditto)
* The hermit in a stone
* The stone raised by St Fechin's prayers (to sit above the entrance of the church)

A story to tell: The Hill of Uisneach

It is said that the first High King to sit upon the Hill of Uisneach was King Midhe. As all kings do, he started making pronouncements, and he even had the audacity to light the Beltaine fire. The Druids didn't like this, for they were the ones who always lit the bonfire every year, the one that all the other tribal chiefs took as the signal to light their own fires on the highest hilltops on the eve of 1 May. It was a sight to see – Ireland lit up from coast to coast as if little golden eyes were opening all over it. This was an important time for the Druids; they were inviting the summer sun back into Ireland to make sure crops were good, and cows healthy for the rest of the year. They'd throw a cow bone into the 'bone-fire' for the sake of their cattle, and then drive them between two fires for good measure. Both of these rituals were said to keep disease and misfortune at bay.

Lugh, the hero-king of the Tuatha Dé Danaan, had ruled from Uisneach, with the Druids as his advisors. Ériu – who some called a sun goddess, and who was promised by the Milesians' chief poet Amergin that Ireland would be named after her in exchange for her giving Ireland to them (*see* p.119) – is also said to be buried beneath the Cat's Stone on the southwestern slope of Uisneach hill. So it was no small thing that a king could take it upon himself to start the Beltaine fire, and the Druids came together on Uisneach to discuss the matter. King Midhe responded by cutting out all of their tongues and then sitting himself down above the spot where he buried them in the earth.

His mother looked on fondly and said, 'It is *uisneach* [which means proudly in Irish] you sit up there tonight!' And that is how the great Hill of Uisneach got its name – and, of course, County *Mide*, or Meath, also took its name from the very same king.

St Fechin founded a monastery at Fore around 630, and a community of 300 monks gathered around him. Today you can visit the old church of St Fechin (get the key in the Seven Wonders Pub) and above it a tiny chapel called the Anchorite's Church, where it is said the last hermit in Ireland lived in the 17th century.

Did you know...?
According to Geoffrey of Monmouth, the wizard Merlin advised England's King Arthur to move Stonehenge (then called 'The Giants' Ring') from the Hill of Uisneach to Salisbury Plain, and so he did. The stones were believed to have healing properties, and each one had a unique purpose.

AROUND AND ABOUT

Bricks and mortar

Belvedere House, Gardens and Park

Tullamore Road, Mullingar, Co. Westmeath, **t** (044) 49060, **www.belvedere-house.ie**
Getting there 3 miles (5km) from Mullingar on N52, the Tullamore road
Open Jan–Apr Mon–Fri 10.30–4.30, May–Aug 9.30–6, Sat–Sun 10.30–7, Sept–Oct 10.30–6, Nov and Dec 10.30–4.30 (last adm 1hr before closing)
Adm Adult €6, child €3.80, family €14–16
Restaurant, visitor centre, gift shop, play area, animal sanctuary, parking

Secluded woodland trails run from this 18th-century former home of the Earls of Belvedere and its lakeside and walled gardens. A multimedia presentation tells the story of how cruel and jealous Lord Rochfort imprisoned his wife for 31 years here behind Ireland's largest man-made folly, nicknamed the Jealous Wall. Younger children will enjoy the playground and animals, which are both near the visitors' centre.

Carrigglas Manor

Longford, Co. Longford, **t** (043) 45165
Getting there 1 mile (1.6 km) from Longford
Open May–Sept Mon–Tues, Fri–Sat 11–3, closed Wed–Thur, Sun, tours at 12 noon, 1 and 2
Adm Adult €9, child €6
Gift shop, meals available

This can be a pleasant brief interlude if you are in the area: fascinating exhibits fill a romantic Victorian manor house built in a castellated Tudor-Revival style, with stableyard buildings. Its original pictures, artefacts and furniture are intact, so the house exudes an atmosphere of Victorian life.

Tullynally Castle and Garden

Castlepollard, Co. Westmeath, **t** (044) 61159
Getting there on the Granard Road 1 1/2 miles (2.5km) outside Castlepollard, 12 miles (20km) north of Mullingar
Open Grounds, May–Aug 2–6; Castle, 15 Jun–31 Jul 2–6 and to pre-booked groups at other times
Adm Adult €3, child €1.50

These extensive pleasure grounds contain a Tibetan and Chinese garden. The Gothic Revival castle is still inhabited by the Earls of Longford, whose seat this is.

Look at this!

Mullingar Bronze and Pewter Visitor Centre

Greatdown, The Downs, Mullingar, Co. Westmeath, **t** (044) 48791
Open Mon–Sat 9.30–6, workshop tours Mon–Fri 9.30–4
Craft shop, showrooms, coffee shop

At this co-operative studio children can learn the secrets of making bronze- and pewterware, using methods unchanged for the past 800 years.

Dún na Sí Cultural Centre

Knockdomney, Moate, Co. Westmeath, **t** (090) 6481183
Getting there 10 miles (16km) east of Athlone
Open Apr–Oct Mon–Thur 9–5, Fri 9–4, or by appointment. **Adm** free
Tearoom-restaurant, ample parking, souvenir shop

An outdoor folk heritage park with farm machinery from days gone by. A restored farmhouse holds a cultural centre specializing in genealogical research, and featuring music, storytelling, song and dance evenings.

Nature lovers

Jonathan Swift Park

Lilliput, Lough Ennell, Mullingar, Co. Westmeath, **t** (044) 26457

Getting there 3 miles (5km) south of Mullingar

Café during summer, beach, children's playground, adventure centre

Swift was a regular visitor to Westmeath and this park was named after him. 'Lilliput' boasts one of Ireland's three inland Blue Flag lakeside beaches.

Sporty kids

Activity centres

Jonathan Swift Adventure Centre

Lilliput, Lough Ennell, Mullingar, Co. Westmeath, **t** (044) 26457 (as above)

Canoeing, kayaking, abseiling, orienteering, swimming, angling, archery and golf.

Wineport Sailing Centre and Restaurant

Glassan, Athlone,Co. Westmeath, **t** (090) 6474944

Open For sailing seasonally, restaurant all year

Sailing on Lough Ree, with instruction for beginning and experienced sailors (ages 10 and above).

Boat trips

Several companies offer trips on the Shannon and Lough Ree.

Athlone Cruisers

The Jolly Mariner, Athlone, Co. Westmeath, **t** (090) 6472892

Cruiser and rowing boat hire.

Lilliput Boat Hire

Jim Gavigan, Dysart, Mullingar, Co. Westmeath, **t** (086) 8286849

Boat hire on Lough Ennell.

Buckets and spades – Beaches in Westmeath

Athough Westmeath is an inland county it still has Blue Flag beaches, on two of the regions many beautiful lakes: at the **Cut** on **Lough Leane**, 3 miles (5km) southeast of Castlepollard, and at **Lilliput** on **Lough Ennell**, 3 miles (5km) south of Mullingar.

Did you know...?
Jonathan Swift used the name of Lilliput House on Lough Ennell, Co. Westmeath – now long demolished – for the country of the little people in his famous book Gulliver's Travels.

Fishing

Brown trout fishing is good on Lough Sheelin, Co. Westmeath, and for coarse fishing try Loughs Owel, Ennell and Derravaragh. There is very good pike fishing all over Lough Ree, and Lough Gowna in northern Co. Longford is a coarse fishing centre.

For equipment and information contact:

Denniston Edward & Co, Centenary Square, Longford, Co. Longford, **t** (043) 46345

Strand Fishing Tackle Shop, St Endas Place, The Strand, Athlone, Co. Westmeath, **t** (090) 6479277.

Information and boats for fishing Lough Ree.

Horse riding

Ladestown House

Mullingar, Co. Westmeath, **t** (044) 48218

Trail rides along the lake.

Mullingar Equestrian Centre

Athlone Road, Mullingar, Co. Westmeath, **t** (044) 48331/40569

Open all year for treks along Lough Derravaragh.

Steam power!

An Dún Transport and Heritage Museum

Doon, Ballinahown, Athlone, Co. Westmeath, **t** (090) 6430106

Getting there 7 miles (11km) south of Athlone

Open Daily Easter–end Oct Mon–Sat 10.30–6 and Sun 1–6

Video presentation, souvenir and coffee shop

On the *Slí Mór* or Chariot Way, one of the five ancient roads of Ireland, this private collection has forms of transport from trap cars to early cars, and old combine harvesters and other farm equipment. Its friendly owner, who has lovingly restored everything here, will give an informative tour if you ask.

WHERE TO EAT

Co. Dublin

Dalkey

PD's Woodhouse

1 Coliemore Road, Dalkey, **t** (01) 284 9399 (*moderate*)

Nice cosy atmosphere and food barbecued over oak fires. Early supper (6–7) is cheaper, and there's a children's menu and vegetarian specials.

The Queens

12 Castle Street, Dalkey, **t** (01) 285 4569 (*inexpensive*)

This pub serves good sandwiches and seafood chowder. Pleasant for lunch on a sunny day, when you can sit outdoors with your children.

Ragazzi

Coliemore Road, Dalkey, **t** (01) 284 7280 (*inexpensive*)

Italian restaurant that serves child-size portions, with attentive, welcoming staff.

Glencullen

Fox's Pub

Glencullen, **t** (01) 295 5647 (*inexpensive*)

Good seafood pub on the Wicklow border that's very enjoyable for lunch.

Howth

Big Blue Restaurant

Howth, **t** (01) 832 0565 (*moderate*)

This restaurant has a children's menu, high chairs, colouring paper and pencils available, plus a fish tank to help keep kids amused.

Casa Pasta

Clontarf Road, Howth, **t** (01) 833 1402 (*inexpensive*)

An Italian chain restaurant with a friendly atmosphere. A kids' menu and high chairs are available.

Malahide

Giovanni's Restaurant

Malahide, **t** (01) 845 1733 (*inexpensive–moderate*)

Italian restaurant with a relaxed, friendly atmosphere. Children can have small portions from the main menu, and high chairs are available.

Malahide Castle

Malahide, **t** (01) 846 3027 (*inexpensive*)

Good soups, snacks and desserts for lunch and afternoon call-ins.

Oscar Taylor's

Malahide, **t** (01) 845 0399 (*expensive*)

Known for steaks, seafood and vegetarian dishes. The carvery in the main bar is popular, bright and airy. No children's menu or prices, but high chairs are available, and there's a baby-changing area.

Skerries

The Red Bank Restaurant

5–7 Church Street, Skerries, **t** (01) 849 1005 (*expensive*)

This is a little upmarket and formal but still a great choice if you like fish. Families with small children who need high chairs usually have dinner in the adjoining Red Bank Guesthouse.

Wicklow and Carlow

Arklow

The Stone Oven

65 Lower Main Street, Arklow,Co. Wicklow, **t** (0402) 39418 (*inexpensive*)

Great bakery and coffee shop.

Avoca

Avoca Mill Stores

Avoca Village, Co. Wicklow, **t** (0402) 35105, (*inexpensive*)

A wide range of dishes, including homemade soups, vegetable bakes and cakes made from fresh produce are available at the café in the knitwear centre. Service is very child-friendly.

Ballon

Ballykealey House

Ballon, near Carlow, Co. Carlow, **t** (0503) 59288 (*inexpensive–moderate*)

This country-house-style restaurant serves homemade pizzas, ice cream and food that's as natural as possible. A children's menu is available in the bar, and in the dining room they offer half-portions from the main menu or a kids' menu and high tea.

Bray

Escape

1 Albert Avenue, Seafront, Bray, Co. Wicklow, **t** (01) 286 6755 (*inexpensive–moderate*)

Children are welcome at this friendly restaurant for tasty vegetarian and vegan food opposite the Sea Life Centre.

The Tree of Idleness

Seafront, Bray, Co. Wicklow, **t** (01) 282 8183 (*expensive*)

Renowned restaurant with Greek-Cypriot food.

Carlow Town

The Beams Restaurant

59 Dublin Street, Carlow, **t** (0503) 31824 (*expensive*)

A 300-year-old coaching inn with bistro-style modern Irish cuisine: fresh seafood, game and homegrown vegetables. Attached to the restaurant is an excellent wine and cheese shop.

Enniskerry

Poppies Restaurant

The Square, Enniskerry, Co. Wicklow, **t** (01) 282 8869 (*inexpensive*)

Good for salad lunches, and lively at weekends.

Glendalough

Glendalough Hotel

t (0404) 45135 (*moderate–expensive*)

A child-friendly hotel: kids choose between their own menu or small portions from the main menu.

Greystones

The Hungry Monk

Greystones, Co. Wicklow, **t** (01) 287 5759 (*expensive*)

This family-run fish restaurant has an impressive wine list and is a good spot for Sunday lunch.

Laragh

Lynham's Laragh Inn

Laragh, Co. Wicklow, **t** (0404) 45345 (*moderate*)

Family-oriented traditional restaurant.

Mitchell's Restaurant

Laragh, Co. Wicklow, **t** (0404) 45302 (*moderate*)

Family restaurant in a restored, rustic granite schoolhouse. The menu includes Wicklow lamb and lovely home-baked cakes, and there's a children's menu or small-size portions.

Leighlinbridge

The Lord Bagenal Inn

Main Street, Leighlinbridge, Co. Carlow, **t** (0503) 21668 (*inexpensive*)

Very popular hotel pub-restaurant with carvery, with a varied menu and an excellent wine list. A children's play area is beside the rather smoky bar.

Macreddin Village

The Brook Lodge Inn

Near Aughrim, Co. Wicklow, **t** (0402) 36444 (*expensive*)

Only free-range, organic and wild foods are served in this award-winning restaurant.

Rathdrum

Cartoon Inn

Rathdrum, Co. Wicklow, **t** (0404) 46774 (*inexpensive*)

Children will enjoy examining the walls of this inn, which are covered with the work of many famous cartoonists. Take along some paper and crayons for them to doodle on.

Roundwood

Roundwood Inn

Roundwood, Co. Wicklow, **t** (01) 281 8107 (*expensive*)

A 17th-century inn with bar food – filling Irish stews – or a restaurant menu. Helpings are ample.

Tullow

The Tara Arms

Church Street, Tullow, Co. Carlow, **t** (0503) 51305 (*inexpensive*)

Home-cooked bar food and carvery lunches.

Kilkenny and Wexford

There has long been a tradition of attention to cuisine in this part of Ireland, and around places like Inistioge in Kilkenny you will find several independent cooks offering sophisticated modern food. Specialities of the area include oysters, potatoes and strawberries.

Arthurstown

Dunbrody House Hotel

Arthurstown, Co. Wexford, **t** (051) 389 600 (*expensive*)

There's a kids' menu for families who appreciate good gourmet food at this superior hotel.

Ballynabola

Horse and Hounds Inn

Ballynabola, Co. Wexford, **t** (051) 428482 (*inexpensive*)

Gargantuan portions of simple food, good stews; and accommodation available.

Campile

Kilmokea Country Manor

Campile, Co. Wexford, **t** (051) 388109 (*expensive*)

Cream teas and organic food are prepared especially creatively for children in this health-oriented country hotel. High tea served in the conservatory.

Carne

Lobster Pot

Carne village, south of Rosslare, Co. Wexford, **t** (053) 31110 (*moderate*)

A popular bar and restaurant serving great seafood and pub grub all day.

Curracloe

Blake Restaurant

Hotel Curracloe, Curracloe, Co Wexford, **t** (053) 37308 (*moderate*)

This hotel restaurant and bar offers a children's menu and half-portions of the adult menu.

Graiguenamanagh

Waterside

The Quay, Graiguenamanagh, Co. Kilkenny, **t** (059) 9724246 (*expensive–moderate*)

Refined cooking and especially good seafood, in an atmospheric stone building by the River Barrow.

Inistioge

Circle of Friends

The Bank House, High St, Inistioge, Co. Kilkenny, **t** (056) 58800 (*moderate–inexpensive*)

Café and evening restaurant in a converted house on the village square; excellent cakes and snacks downstairs, and fine meals upstairs.

The Motte

Main St, Inistioge, Co. KIlkenny, **t** (056) 7758655 (*moderate–expensive*)

A charming little restaurant in this most picturesque of villages, with adventurous food and a cosy atmosphere.

Kilkenny Town

Edward Langton's

69 John St, Kilkenny, **t** (056) 7765133 (*expensive–moderate*)

An award-winning hostelry, with good pub lunches and dinners, including vegetarian dishes.

Kilkenny Castle

t (056) 7721450 (*inexpensive*)

This restaurant, in the old castle kitchen, serves delicious lunches and teas in summer only.

Kilkenny Design Centre

Castle Yard, Kilkenny, **t** (056) 7722118 (*inexpensive*)

Good soups, cooked meats and salads for lunch.

Lacken House

Dublin Road, Kilkenny, **t** (056) 7761085 (*expensive*)

Popular, family-run restaurant serving imaginative, perfectly cooked food.

Parliament House Restaurant

22–24 Parliament St, Kilkenny, **t** (056) 7763666 (*expensive–moderate*)

Pleasant food in one of Kilkenny's finest houses.

Tynan's Bridge House Bar

St John's Bridge, Kilkenny, **t** (056) 7721291 (*inexpensive*)

Unspoilt Victorian pub with original fittings.

New Ross

Clarion Brandon House Hotel

New Ross, Co. Wexford, **t** (051) 421 703 (*moderate*)

Award-winning restaurant in a family-friendly hotel.

Neptune

Ballyhack Harbour, New Ross, Co. Wexford, **t** (051) 389284 (*moderate*)

On the harbour: good-value menus with seafood as a speciality, and you can bring your own wine.

Cedar Lodge Restaurant and Hotel

Carrighbyrne, Newbawn, New Ross, Co. Wexford, **t** (051) 428386 (*inexpensive*)

Quality food on the Wexford–New Ross road.

Thomastown

Thomastown Water Garden and Café

Thomastown, Co. Kilkenny,
t (056) 24690 (*inexpensive*)

Teas served on the terrace of a lovely little water garden, beautifully planted with aquatic plants.

Wexford Town

Cappuccinos

23 North Main St, Wexford (*inexpensive*)

Very popular lunchtime snack spot, with hot ciabatta sandwiches among the options.

Conservatory

Ferrycraig Hotel, Enniscorthy Road, Wexford,
t (053) 22999 (*moderate*)

An idyllic setting and good food – try breast of duck in a strawberry vinaigrette sauce, and save room for the homemade ice cream and pastries.

Heavens Above

The Sky and the Ground, 112 South Main St,
t (053) 21273 (*moderate*)

This delightful restaurant above a well-loved pub serves excellent food and has an enormous wine list. A must if you're in striking distance.

Tim's Tavern

51 South Main St, Wexford, **t** (053) 23861
(*moderate–inexpensive*)

Lovely old-style, intimate restaurant, noted for traditional Irish cooking as well as French and vegetarian specials. Children welcome.

Kildare, Laois and Offaly

Abbeyleix

Morrissey's Bar

Abbeyleix, Co. Laois, **t** (0502) 31233 (*inexpensive*)

A charming pub and grocery shop with old cake tins and a stove; good for stout and sandwiches.

Preston House

Abbeyleix, Co. Laois, **t** (0502) 31432 (*moderate*)

Ivy-covered stone B&B, run by Allison Dowling, which was originally a school. Now furnished with antiques, and the restaurant is recommended.

Athy

Tonlegee House

Athy, Co. Kildare, **t** (059) 8631473 (*expensive*)

Imaginative and delicious cooking is on offer at this Georgian house restaurant in its own grounds. Children's meals and larger menus are available.

Banagher

The Vine House

Banagher, Co. Offaly, **t** (0509) 51463 (*moderate*)

Good value, simple cooking.

Birr

Spinners Town House & Bistro

Beside Birr Castle, Castle St, **t** (0509) 21673
(*moderate*)

Alongside this informal restaurant with high-chairs and wheelchair access is a courtyard play area. Local fresh ingredients are served modern-Irish style, with many vegetarian dishes. Rooms are available too (children under 2 stay free).

Castledermot

D'Lacy's

Kilkea Castle, Castledermot, Co. Laois,
t (059) 9145156 (*expensive*)

Local produce and fresh vegetables served in a dining room with a decidedly historic atmosphere.

Durrow

Woodview Restaurant

Bishopswood, Co. Laois, **t** (0502) 36433 (*moderate*)

There are baby-changing facilities and wheel-chair access in this casual establishment, which serves traditional, modern and vegetarian dishes.

Eustace

Ballymore Inn

Eustace, Co. Kildare, **t** (045) 864585
(*inexpensive–moderate*)

This child-friendly local serves traditional and Irish cuisine, pastas and pizzas.

Kildare

Silken Thomas

The Square, Kildare, **t** (045) 521 264
(*inexpensive–moderate*)

This is a large, child-friendly pub and restaurant with a reputation for good food.

Leixlip

Da Vinci's Restaurant

Leixlip, Co. Kildare, t (01) 624 4908 (*moderate*)

Italian restaurant with baby-changing facilities, high chairs and open-plan kitchen. Children are given dough to play with and there is a kids' menu.

Moone

Moone High Cross Inn

Bolton Hill, Moone, Co. Laois, t (059) 8624112 (*moderate*)

Friendly, old-fashioned pub serving better than average food, including home-cooked roasts, sandwiches and scrumptious apple pie.

Portlaoise

Dowling's Restaurant

77 Main St, Portlaoise, t (0502) 22770 (*moderate*)

This Irish bistro has a children's menu and high chairs, and is open for breakfast.

The Kitchen and Food Hall

Hynds Square, off Main St, Portlaoise, t (0502) 62061 (*inexpensive–moderate*)

This casual eaterie can make up food hampers to take on picnics, with home-produced products.

Meath and Louth

Carlingford

Ghan House

Carlingford, Co. Louth, t (042) 937 3682 (*moderate–expensive*)

Book ahead for excellent gourmet evening meals made from organic produce, at this period guest-house-hotel. Children are very welcome and small or special meals are available for them.

Collon

Forge Gallery Restaurant

Church St, Collon, Co. Meath, t (041) 982 6272 (*expensive*)

Open evenings only, but great for vegetarians.

Cooley

Riverstown Old Mill

Off Dundalk to Carlingford Road, Co. Louth, t (042) 937 6310 (*inexpensive–moderate*)

Make reservations in advance for late afternoon and evening. They have a kids' menu, and half portions from the adult menu are available.

Drogheda

The Buttergate Restaurant and Wine Bar

Millmount, Drogheda, Co. Louth, t (041) 983 4759 (*moderate*)

Good, plain food made more sophisticated by imaginative sauces. Children welcome until 7pm.

Kells

Vanilla Pod

Headfort Place, Headfort Arms Hotel, Kells, Co. Meath, t (046) 9240063 (*expensive–moderate*)

International cuisine, children welcome.

Kilmessan

The Station House Hotel

Kilmessan, Co. Meath, t (046) 25239 (*moderate*)

Tasty food: fish, lamb and beef with herbs and sauces in this former train station.

Navan

Dunderry Lodge Restaurant

Navan, Co. Meath, t (046) 31671 (*expensive*)

This little restaurant has acquired a tremendous reputation, and Dubliners think nothing of driving out to it for a meal. It's set in converted farm buildings, with good décor, Mediterranean-influenced food and wine.

Hudson's Bistro

30 Railway St, Navan, Co. Meath, t (046) 29231 (*moderate*)

Casual place with an international menu; desserts are a speciality.

Slane

Boyles Tea Rooms

Main St, Slane, Co. Meath, t (041) 982 4195 (*inexpensive*)

Very good homemade food for lunch.

Trim

Kerr's Kitchen

Haggard St, Trim, Co. Meath, t (046) 9437144 (*inexpensive*)

Coffee shop with homemade food using local produce, open for lunch.

Westmeath and Longford

Abbeyshrule

Rustic Inn

Abbeyshrule, Co. Longford, **t** (044) 57424 (*inexpensive*)

Good value, family-run restaurant with plain food and steaks.

Athlone

Conlon's Restaurant

5–9 Dublingate St, Athlone, Co. Westmeath, **t** (090) 6474376 (*moderate*)

A good traditional Irish restaurant adjoining a pub; children are welcome during the day.

The Left Bank Bistro

Fry Place (behind Athlone Castle), Athlone, Co. Westmeath, **t** (090) 6494446, (*moderate*)

This café by day, restaurant by night serves imaginative food with East/West flavours and excellent seafood, salads, dressings and vegetarian dishes. There's a heated walled garden, and children are welcome; half portions available.

Pavarotti's

Fry Place, Athlone, Co. Westmeath, **t** (090) 6493066 (*moderate*)

Child-friendly Italian restaurant but no high chairs available.

Restaurant Le Château

St Peters Port, The Docks, Athlone, Co. Westmeath, **t** (090) 6494517 (*expensive*)

Friendly, informal and good value, children welcome in the early evening.

Glassan

The Glassan Village Restaurant

Glassan, Co. Westmeath, **t** (090) 6485001 (*moderate*)

This restaurant offers lovely plain Irish cooking, with lots of seafood options. Children welcome for early dinners, wheelchair access.

Wineport Lodge Lakeshore Restaurant

Glassan, Co. Westmeath, **t** (090) 6485466 (*expensive*)

A very popular, casually elegant, friendly spot on the inner lakes of Lough Ree, north of Athlone. Families are welcome and there are early bird and special group menus.

Longford Town

The Longford Arms

Main St, Longford, **t** (043) 46296 (*moderate*)

Pub lunches and à la carte menu.

Café au Lait

Main St, Longford, **t** (043) 47483 (*inexpensive*)

Excellent salads, quiches and soups.

Aubergine

1 Ballymahon St (upstairs above Market Bar), Longford, **t** (043) 48633 (*moderate–inexpensive*)

Recommended highly by locals for lunch, vegetarian dishes, busy wine bar atmosphere.

Torc Café and Shop

Ballymahon St, Longford, **t** (043) 48777 (*inexpensive*)

Good light lunches, cakes, chocolates.

Mullingar

Crookedwood House Restaurant

Mullingar, Co. Westmeath, **t** (044) 72165 (*moderate–expensive*)

This cellar restaurant, which has won awards for its excellent country cooking, welcomes children for lunch and early evening dinners. The menu features modern Irish dishes, seafood, game and vegetarian meals. Accommodation also available.

Tyrellspass

Tyrrellspass Castle Restaurant

Tyrellspass, Co. Westmeath, **t** (044) 23105 (*inexpensive–moderate*)

Medieval castle banquets and delicious home-cooked breakfasts, lunch, snacks, grills and Sunday lunches in this historic building and museum site.

Munster

05

Munster

Atlantic
Ocean
Kilronan
Aran Islands
South Sound
Ballyvaughan Bay
Burren
Fanore
Ballyvaughan
Burren Way
Aillwee Cave
The Burren
Poulnabrone Megalithic Tomb
Lisdoonvarna
N67
Carran
Doolin
Cliffs of Moher
Kilfenora
Liscannor
Inchiquin Lough
Liscannor Bay
Lahinch
Corofin
N67
Dysert O'Dea
N85
Spanish Point
Miltown Malbay
The Hand Cross Roads
CLARE
Doonbeg
N68
Kilkee
Deer Island
N67
Kilrush
Killadysert
Killimer
Carrigaholt
Scattery Island
River Shannon
Foynes
Loop Head
Carrigafoyle Castle
Tarbert
Glin
N69
Mouth of the Shannon
Ballybunion
Cashen River
Listowel
Ardagh
Kerry Head
Newcastle West
Ballyheige
N69
N21
Magharee Islands
Banna Strand
Banna
Abbeyfeale
Kilflynn
Brandon Bay
Brandon Head
Dingle Way
Tralee Bay
Mullaghareirk Mtns
Broadford
Ballydavid Head
Brandon Mountain
Brandon
Fenit
Spa
Tralee
Cloghane
Castlegregory
N21
Smerwick
Blennerville
N21
Ballydavid
Camp
Crag Cave
Gallarus Oratory
DINGLE PENINSULA
N86
Slieve Mish Mtns
N70
N23
Castleisland
Dunquin
Dingle
Inch
Castlemaine
N22
Ventry
R. Maine
Ballydesmond
Blasket Islands
Slea Head
Doonbeg Fort
KERRY
Kanturk
Rossbeigh Creek
Dingle Bay
Killorglin
Kells Bay
Rossbeigh
Kerry
N72
Gap of Dunloe
KILLARNEY
River Blackwater
Glenbeigh
Ring of
Ross Castle
N72
Lough Coomasaharn
Lough Leane
Muckross
Macgillycuddy's Reeks
Muckross Abbey
Millstreet
Cahercirveen
PENINSULA
Killarney National Park
N22
The Paps Mountains
Valentia Island
N70
Kerry Way
IVERAGH
Derrynasaggart Mountains
Portmagee
N71
R. Finnihy
R. Roughty
Kenmare
St. Finan's Bay
Waterville
Macroom
Ballinskelligs
Staigue Stone Fort
Ring of Sneem
Kerry
Gougane Barra Forest Park
Carrigadrohid
Skellig Islands
Lough Currane
Inchiquin L.
Inishcarra Reservoir
Bolus Head
Caherdaniel
Shehy Mountains
Derrynane House
Castlecove
Kenmare River
BEARA PENINSULA
Scariff Island
Deenish Island
Ardgroom
Glengarriff
Ballycrovane Harbour
Beara Way
Cod's Head
Castletownbere
Whiddy Island
Bandon River
Ballydonegan Bay
Bantry
N71
Kilmichael
Sheep's Head Way
Rossmore
R. Argideen
Dursey Head
Bear Island
Bantry Bay
Durras
Clonakilty
N71
Sheep's Head
Ballydehob
N71
Rosscarbery
Inchydoney Island
Dunmanus Bay
Schull
Skibbereen
Drombeg Stone Circle
Three Castle Head
Goleen
Roaringwater Bay
Castletownshend
Crookhaven
Heir I.
Baltimore
Mizen Head
Clear Island
Lough Ine
Sherkin Island
Fastnet Rock
N
20km
10miles

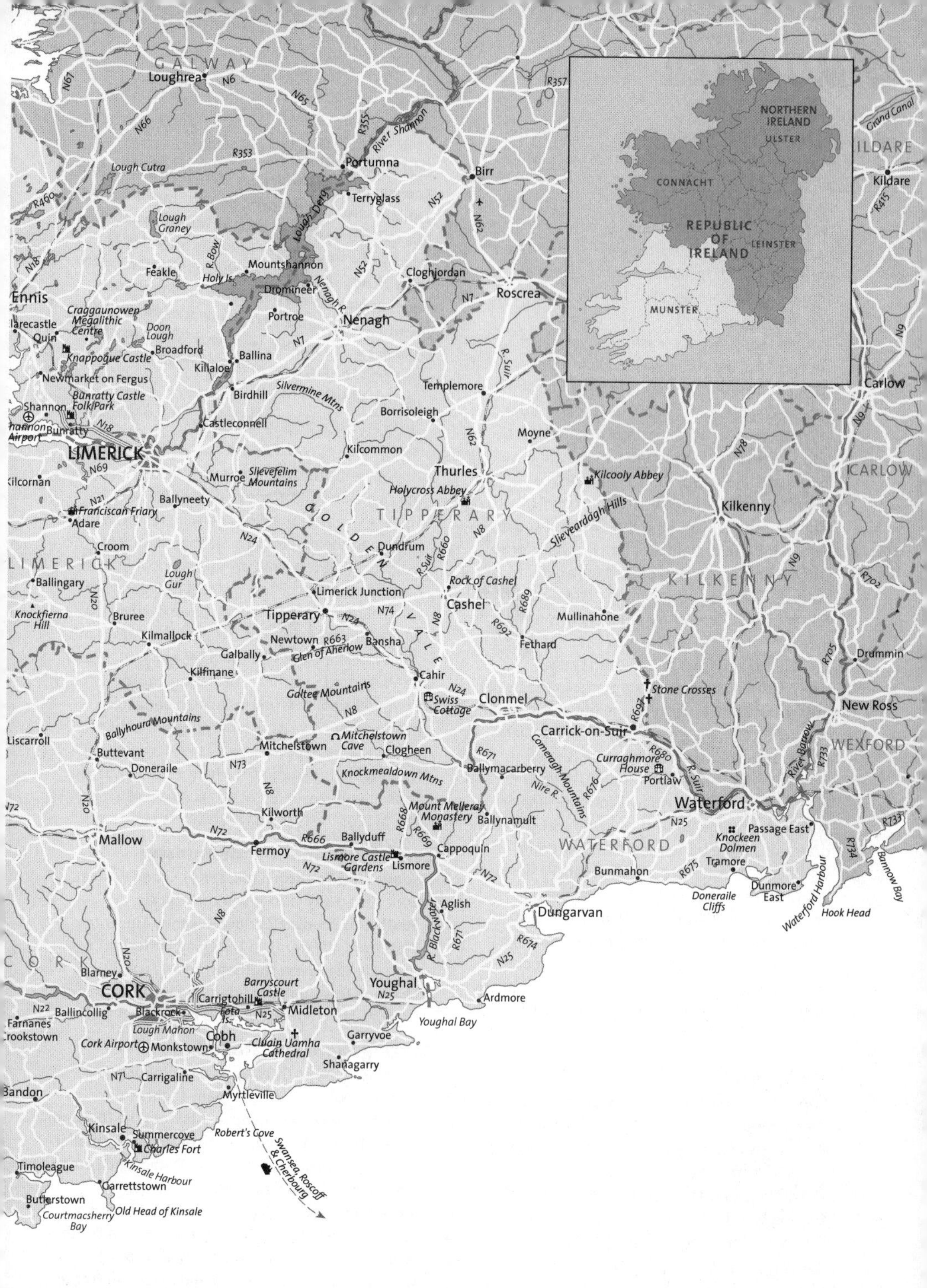

GALWAY
Loughrea
N67
N6
N66
N65
R355
River Shannon
R357
R353
Portumna
Birr
Lough Cutra
Terryglass
N52
N62
R460
Lough Graney
Lough Derg
R. Bow
Holy Is.
Mountshannon
Feakle
N18
Dromineer
Nenagh R.
Cloghjordan
Roscrea
N7
Ennis
Clarecastle
Quin
Craggaunowen Megalithic Centre
Doon Lough
Portroe
Nenagh
Knappogue Castle
Broadford
Ballina
Killaloe
Newmarket on Fergus
R. Suir
Templemore
Bunratty Castle Folk Park
Birdhill
Silvermine Mtns
Shannon
Shannon Airport
Bunratty
N18
Castleconnell
Borrisoleigh
Moyne
LIMERICK
Kilcommon
N69
Thurles
Kilcornan
Murroe
Slievefelim Mountains
Holycross Abbey
Kilcooly Abbey
N21
Franciscan Friary
Adare
Ballyneety
GOLDEN VALE
TIPPERARY
Slieveardagh Hills
Kilkenny
N24
N8
Croom
Dundrum
R660
LIMERICK
Lough Gur
Rock of Cashel
KILKENNY
Ballingary
Limerick Junction
Cashel
R689
N20
Tipperary
N74
Knockfierna Hill
Bruree
N24
R692
Mullinahone
Kilmallock
Newtown
R663
Bansha
Fethard
Galbally
Glen of Aherlow
Kilfinane
Cahir
N24
Galtee Mountains
Swiss Cottage
Clonmel
Stone Crosses
N8
Ballyhoura Mountains
Mitchelstown Cave
R697
Carrick-on-Suir
Liscarroll
Buttevant
Mitchelstown
Clogheen
R671
Comeragh Mountains
Curraghmore House
R680
Doneraile
N73
Knockmealdown Mtns
Ballymacarberry
Nire R.
R676
Portlaw
R. Suir
N8
N72
N20
Kilworth
Mount Melleray Monastery
R668
R669
Ballynamult
Waterford
N25
N72
Mallow
Fermoy
R666
Ballyduff
Cappoquin
WATERFORD
Knockeen Dolmen
Passage East
Lismore Castle Gardens
Lismore
N72
R675
Tramore
Bunmahon
N72
Aglish
Doneraile Cliffs
Dunmore East
Waterford Harbour
Hook Head
N8
R. Blackwater
Dungarvan
R671
R674
N25
CORK
N20
Blarney
Barryscourt Castle
Youghal
N25
Ardmore
CORK
Carrigtohill
Fota Is.
N25
Midleton
N22
Ballincollig
Blackrock
Youghal Bay
Farnanes
Lough Mahon
Crookstown
Cork Airport
Monkstown
Cobh
Cluain Uamha Cathedral
Garryvoe
Shanagarry
N71
Carrigaline
Bandon
Myrtleville
Kinsale
Summercove
Robert's Cove
Swansea, Roscoff & Cherbourg
Charles Fort
Timoleague
Kinsale Harbour
Garrettstown
Butlerstown
Old Head of Kinsale
Courtmacsherry Bay
KILDARE
Grand Canal
Kildare
R415
N9
Carlow
N9
N78
CARLOW
N9
R702
R705
Drummin
New Ross
WEXFORD
River Barrow
R733
R733
R734
Bannow Bay
NORTHERN IRELAND
ULSTER
CONNACHT
REPUBLIC OF IRELAND
LEINSTER
MUNSTER

MUNSTER

The first September morning I awoke on the west coast of Ireland's largest province – Munster (*Cuige Mumhan*) – in 1972, I recall looking out of my window with utter awe. It didn't seem possible that anything on earth could be more like paradise. Rainbow colours kaleidoscopically shifted across the Atlantic and the same unmoving island, altering its delicate beauty to a new beauty with each passing moment.

When I explored the seashore, I was delighted to discover that the water was so clean and clear that rocks, sand and seaweed on the ocean bottom appeared sharp and crystalline. This is not the case anymore in most other parts of Ireland, but the Gulf Stream still flows round this coastline, making its climate temperate throughout the year.

Because of its beauty, Munster is popular with families, especially in summer – when, if you're lucky, it even might not rain for two weeks or so. Come rain or shine, be prepared for weather changes. There is nothing more dramatic than an Atlantic storm here, although usually you will merely be treated to a fine mist that is gentle upon the skin, or perhaps a bit of ocean spray.

Be prepared for queues and traffic in the busier towns and attractions at the height of the summer season. For tourists, Kerry is the most popular county in Ireland, with Cork a close runner-up. Swimmers and hikers who enjoy lush greenery and environmental mysticism will love the Ring of Kerry's mountains, while those who seek the rocky drama of a more barren seascape will prefer Co. Cork's coastal walks around the Beara Peninsula.

Munster's other counties provide fantastic attractions for children, not to mention ideal settings for relaxing holidays and Ireland's best unspoiled beaches and areas for water sports. Birdwatchers shouldn't miss Co. Clare, and horse-lovers will find much to entertain them in Co. Tipperary. Youthful historians will be fascinated by the castle on a hill in the middle of Cashel, Co. Tipperary, seat of the Kings of Munster for over 700 years, and the medieval castle that dominates the neighbouring town of Cahir. Days out at Bunratty Castle and at the history parks of Cragganowen, Lough Gur and Muckross will be enjoyed by the whole family. Those on the trail of the Vikings must visit Waterford, the first town they built in Ireland. Co. Waterford's history of seafaring intruders like Cromwell's soldiers will fascinate youngsters nearly as much as its fishing villages and bird life.

If you come expecting rain as well as sun, you'll thoroughly enjoy your time here, especially if you to see rainbows, or leprechauns. And if you have 'the luck of the Irish', maybe it won't rain at all...

Did you know...?

Some believe the 'Milesians' described in Irish folk stories were actually the Celts. It's true that when the Celts first came to Ireland, they thought of the Tuatha as gods. But after the arrival of St Patrick and the spread of Christianity, the Tuatha gods became known as faeries, and their faery world was described as the realm of the spirits, or the dead. The monks, who wrote down most of the folk stories, were happy to retell the old tales with a Christian twist.

Highlights

Cork, Cobh and a bit of Blarney, pp.121–2
Island hopping on the wild west coast, p.126
Killarney National Park, Muckross and the Ring of Kerry, pp.129, 133
Down Dingle way with Fungi the dolphin, p.132
Getting back to nature in the Burren, p.141
Discovering the Rock of Cashel and Tipperary's horses, pp.147, 150

Tourist information for Munster

South West Tourism (Cork, Kerry), Grand Parade, Cork, **t** (021) 425 5100, **www**.corkkerry.ie
South East Tourism (Carlow, Kilkenny, Tipperary, Waterford, Wexford), 41 The Quay, Waterford, **t** (051) 875 823, **www**.southeastireland.com
Shannon Development (Clare, Limerick, North Kerry, North Tipperary), **t** (061) 471 664

Getting there and around

By air It's easy to fly to Munster without going through Dublin: there are many flights from Britain to **Cork**, and many flights from the USA and Britain land at **Shannon**, north of Limerick. Smaller airports also with direct links to Britain and Europe are **Kerry** and **Waterford**. *See* pp.283–4.

By sea Swansea–Cork Ferries (in Cork, **t** (021) 271 166) operate between Cork and Swansea in South Wales, and Brittany Ferries, **t** (021) 427 7801, has weekly ferries between Cork and Roscoff in France.

A story to tell:
The coming of the Sons of Míl

The Tuatha Dé Danaan were good and decent rulers over Ireland. Theirs was a time when kindness reigned and noble thoughts filled the minds of the people. But ominous predictions and forebodings came from the Tuatha's Druids. Oracles implied that the Tuatha's rule over Ireland was nearing an end. Some Druids had seen visions of ships bringing men to their shores. The Tuatha leaders – the Daghda and his wife Ogma, Lugh and Aengus Óg among them – lived for a long while with the shadow of what was to come.

Then, one feast of Beltaine (May Day), the Druids prophecies seemed to be coming true. Ships were seen on the horizon. There was a flurry at Uisneach, where the Druids and high chieftains held counsel. 'What did it mean? Was this the time?', they asked themselves again and again.

Every Druid in every part of Ireland began chanting in the hope that it would make the strangers return whence they came. The drumbeat of their chanting filled every nook and cranny until a mist formed that rose and thickened until heavy fog covered the island. Suddenly Ireland was no longer there, and there was only a cloud.

'What's this?' cried a captain on the leading ship. 'The island was there and now suddenly it is not. The Sons of Míl should not be deceived so in battle or in peace.'

'It is Druid magic, Captain Midhir,' murmured the dignitary sitting in the prow of the boat.

'Druid magic!' the crew gasped, a hush falling upon the ship, apart from the knock of ropes against the mast.

'Well then, Amergin,' said Midhir, 'do what you can do.'

So Amergin stood on the prow of the ship. Carefully arranging his robes and steadying himself, he began, in a tone soft and sonorous:

I am the wind on the sea
I am the wave of the sea
I am the bull of seven battles
I am the eagle on the rock
I am a flash from the sun
I am the most beautiful of plants
I am a strong wild boar
I am a salmon on the water
I am a lake in the plain
I am the world of knowledge
I am the head of the spear in battle
I am the god that puts fire in the head
Who spreads the light in the gathering on the hills?
Who can tell the ages of the moon?
Who can tell the place where the sun rests?

The moment Amergin stopped chanting, a great wind rose and pushed the giant cloud away from Ireland in one big whoosh. The sun shone powerfully upon the three glistening ships of the Milesians. And then it was that the Tuatha Dé knew that the Druids had predicted the truth about the arrival of Men. After the Sons of Míl set foot upon Ireland, it quickly became obvious that no trick or magical device could repel their advances, and the Druids had to accept that the Milesians' poet Amergin had a magic stronger than their own. His was the greater gift. Amergin knew, as did the Druids, that the best words conjure the best spells.

The Tuatha had to accept that their time for ruling the great island was at an end. And so they formed a truce with the Milesians, agreeing to take the hidden half of Ireland, the part that lay in the hills and otherworld regions, while leaving the Sons of Men the rest. Ever since, the Tuatha Dé have kept to themselves, while Men (the Milesians) have roamed Ireland's surface and treated the Tuatha with respect... until recently.

By bus There are frequent Bus Eireann services between Dublin, Wexford/Rosslare and Cork, Limerick and all the other main towns in Munster. Many regional services run out from Cork. Bus Eireann also runs a service between Cork city and Cork airport. For Bus Eireann details, *see* p.284.

By car From Dublin, take the N7 for Limerick, and turn south onto the N8 in Portlaoise for Cork or Kerry. Allow plenty of time, as the roads are busy.

By train Irish Rail trains run from Dublin's Heuston station to Cork, Killarney, Tralee, Limerick, Ennis, Tipperary and Waterford, with many stops en route on slower trains. There are also many trains from Cork to other places in Munster.

For more information on Irish Rail/Iarnród Eireann, *see* p.288. They can be contacted in Ireland on **t** 1 850 366 222 or **t** (01) 703 4070, or check **www**.irishrail.ie.

COUNTY CORK

County Cork has some of Munster's finest green countryside, and some of its most dramatically rugged, rocky coasts, laid along winding bays with many small islands to add extra fascination to the view. One of the greatest reasons for coming to Cork City and its county is that their inhabitants are known for humour, spontaneity, love of parties and generous hospitality. Teenagers and young people will find lots to do in Cork City, with its vibrant street life. If you want a more languid holiday, though, base yourself outside the town, maybe in somewhere like the seaside town of Cobh, or in Ireland's gastronomic capital, Kinsale.

Tourist information

Cork City, Grand Parade, Cork, **t** (021) 427 3251, **t** 1 850 230 330
Blarney, t (021) 438 1624
Bantry, t (027) 50229
Cobh, t (021) 813 301
Fermoy, Fermoy Resource Centre, **t** (025) 33699
Kinsale, Pier Head, **t** (021) 477 2234
Macroom, Castle Gates Lodge, **t** (026) 43280
Mallow, Bridge St, **t** (022) 42222
Midleton, t (021) 461 3702
Skibbereen, North St, **t** (028) 21766
Youghal, Market House, **t** (024) 20170

Tours

Archaeological and Historical Tours of West Cork, Teach Dearg, Ballydehob, **t** (028) 37282.

Titanic Trail Guided Tours, Michael Martin, The Bookcase, Riverside Wharf, West Beach, Cobh, **t** (021) 481 5211, **www.titanic-trail.com**

A guided tour around Cobh visiting locations connected with the *Titanic* – including the White Star Line Office and the pier where passengers embarked – plus other aspects of the port's history.

West Cork Special Guided Tours, The White House, Lough Hyne, Baltimore, **t** (028) 20566.

Getting there and around

By air Cork Airport is 3 miles (5km) south of Cork City on the Kinsale road (N27). There is a regular 20-min shuttle bus service to and from the airport from the city. Airport information **t** 021 431 3131, **www.cork-airport.com.**

Special Events – County Cork

May

Cork International Choral and Folk Dance Festival, Cork City, **t** (021) 484 7277

One of Ireland's foremost music festivals.

June

Cork Midsummer Festival, Firkin Crane Centre, Shandon, Cork City, **t** (021) 455 0946

West Cork Chamber Music Festival, Bantry, **t** (027) 52788

July

Cahirmee Horse Fair, Buttevant, **t** (022) 23100

Young equestrians must see at least one community horse fair in Ireland during their stay, and this is a very good one.

July–August

Youghal Premier International Busking Festival, Upper Strand, Youghal, **t** (024) 92640

This 4-day event of music, storytelling, mime, street and puppet theatre includes performances by artistes from the US to China.

August

Clonakilty Music Festival, Clonakilty, **t** (086) 604 3455

A decade-old annual family-orientated festival with free activities for all ages, and music nightly.

Regattas: Cobh, Glandore, Glengarriff, Schull and Baltimore

Plenty of boats and salty tales for budding mariners of all ages, throughout August.

September

Kinsale Arts Festival, The Gallery, The Glen, Kinsale, **t** (021) 477 4558

Annual event to foster new artistic talent.

International Storytelling Festival, Cape Clear Island, **t** (028) 39157

Children enjoy hearing these tales as told by professional storytellers. It's an event that's fun for the whole family; there's also a puppet theatre, boat trips around Fastnet Rock, and archaeological and ornithological explorations. A daily ferry service is available from Baltimore.

November

Long Weekend of Music in Ireland, Ballymaloe House, Shanagarry, **t** (021) 464 6785

This three-day musical event features workshops and performances by local musicians. Visitors can also choose to stay in the superb Ballymaloe House Hotel (*see* p.258).

By bus The main bus station is Cork City Depot, Parnell Place, **t** (021) 506 066. Most local buses pass St Patrick's Street. During summer, open-top bus tours of Cork and Blarney are available.
By train Trains run from Kent Station, including local lines to Cobh. Information, **t** (021) 504 888.
By boat A car and passenger ferry crosses Cork Harbour at Ringaskiddy, 7 miles (11km) from Cork.

CORK CITY

Cork City is an important port and second-largest city in the Republic. About AD 650, St Finbarr founded a monastery here. Cork grew slowly until the Georgian era in the 18th century, when fine buildings were constructed over the old town's narrow alleyways, giving it a graceful appearance.

Until the last decades of the 20th century, Cork City remained a beautiful port without much interference from the outside world. Today, Cork is undergoing unprecedented changes. It has grown in recent years, with many cars on new roads, and has become known for a vibrant arts community. It's an interesting place to shop and explore, and in the meanwhile you may happen upon its native inhabitants' way of talking in riddles, not to mention their great humour and generosity.

Things to see and do

Butter Exchange Shandon Craft Centre

John Redman St, **t** (021)430 0600
Open Daily 9–5.30
Adm Adult €3.50, child €2.50

In the 1980s, part of this 1770 building – where butter was graded before being exported – was re-opened as Shandon Craft Centre. Children can watch artists, crystal cutters and weavers doing their work. The Shandon area on the northern shore of the River Lee is one of the most interesting parts of the old city of Cork.

Cork City Gaol Heritage Centre and Radio Museum

Sunday's Well, **t** (021) 430 5022
Open Mar–Oct daily 9.30–6; Nov–Feb daily 10–5 (last admission 1hr before closing)
Adm Adult €4.44, child €2.54, family €12.7 for Gaol or Radio Museums; joint tickets for both available
Souvenir shop, teashop, car and coach parking

Find out what 19th-century Cork was like inside this old prison, the majestic appearance of which belies the wretched conditions in which prisoners were kept. Sound effects bring to life wax figures in cells furnished as they once were, and a film conveys why people turned to crime at that time. The Radio Museum in the Governor's House, ex-residence of the prison governor, displays the collection of Ireland's national radio and TV network RTE. Dummies portray workers using old machines in the early days of Irish and world broadcasting, and exhibits convey the impact these new technologies had on the way we live.

Cork Public Museum and Fitzgerald Park

Fitzgerald Park, North Cork City, **t** (021) 427 0679
Open All year Mon–Fri 11–1 and 2.15–5 (until 6pm Jun–Aug), Sun 3–5 (except bank holidays)
Adm Free

This 18-acre park holds a museum covering 18th–20th-century political history and Cork's evolution and development. Set in a Georgian house, the museum holds many interesting items and information on some of Cork's most famous citizens.

Crawford Municipal Art Gallery

Emmet Place, near Lavitt's Quay, **t** (021) 427 3377
Open All year Mon–Sat 10–6. **Adm** Free
Wheelchair accessible

The city's most important art gallery is housed in what was Cork's original customs house, built in 1724. Named after the 19th-century art patron William Horatio Crawford, it became the Cork School of Art in 1884 and today houses some of the best work by 19th- and 20th-century Irish artists. There are also three windows by Ireland's premier stained-glass artist Harry Clarke (1889–1931), and a small collection of international paintings. Afterwards, don't miss the gallery's restaurant, run by the Ballymaloe School of Cookery, which serves some of the best of modern Irish gourmet cuisine at very decent prices.

St Ann's Shandon Church

Church Street, Shandon, **t** (021) 450 5906
Open Daily except 25 Dec

Near the Butter Exchange (*see* above) north of the River Lee is Shandon Steeple, built in 1720, which dominates the city. Here visitors may ring the famous 'bells of Shandon'.

An Irish Proverb –
The older the fiddle, the sweeter the tune.

St Finbarr's Cathedral

Library House, Dean St, Cork City, **t** (021) 496 3387
Open Oct–Mar Mon–Sat 10–12.45 and 2–5; Apr–Sept Mon–Sat 10–5. **Adm** free

St Finbarr is said to have founded Cork City on this very spot in the 7th century, but the Church of Ireland cathedral – even though it may look medieval – was built in the middle of the 19th century, in extravagant Victorian Gothic style with giant spires that tower over the city.

Entertainment

Cork Opera House

Emmet Place, **t** (021) 270 022

Despite the name, this grand building hosts theatre more often than opera – mostly new plays by Irish writers. Its season lasts for about 8 weeks every summer, often with children's shows in the programme.

Everyman Palace Theatre

McCurtain St, **t** (021) 501 673

There are no restrictions at this imaginative theatre: any play can be produced – tragedy or comedy – by any author, so long as it's good. Go prepared for anything and you won't be disappointed.

Leisureplex Coliseum

t (021) 450 5155
Open Daily. **Adm** Prices according to activity

Indoor bowling, snooker, pool, quasar, Zoo Adventure Land, video games.

Triskel Arts Centre

Tobin St, off South Main St, **t** (021) 427 7300

This attractive centre hosts a wide range of lively events – film seasons, music, exhibitions, drama, poetry and more – with plenty in among them to engage kids.

Shopping

Easons

Patrick St, **t** (021) 427 0477

Cork's branch of Ireland's biggest bookshop chain, with a good children's section.

SPECIAL TRIPS

Blarney Castle

Blarney, **t** (021) 385 252
Getting there 5m (8km) west of Cork City
Open May Mon–Sat 9–6, Sun 9.30–5.30; Jun–Aug Mon–Sat 9–7, Sun 9.30–5.30; Sept Mon–Sat 9-6.30, Sun 9.30–5.30; Oct–Apr Mon–Sat 9–dusk (around 6pm), Sun 9.30–dusk
Adm Adult €7, under-14s €2.50, family (2+2) €16
Gift and souvenir shop, toilets with disabled and baby-changing facilities, park walks, parking

According to tradition you can get 'the gift of the blarney' by kissing the Blarney Stone here – but it could be dangerous for young children as they have to clamber to the top of the 1446 castle. 'Blarney' is the ability to talk your way out of any kind of difficult situation and give someone the runaround, and the phrase was coined by Queen Elizabeth I when she told the castle's owner that he was speaking nothing but 'blarney' as he tried by devious means to avoid doing what she demanded. The surrounding 1,000 acres of woodland are magical to walk in – excellent for playing faeries – and the castle itself has real charm.

Cobh Visitor Centre: The Queenstown Story

Cobh Railway Station, Cobh, **t** (021) 481 3591, **www.cobhheritage.com**
Getting there Great Island, Cork Harbour, 15m (24km) from Cork City; frequent buses and trains run from Cork
Open Jan Mon–Fri 10–5, Feb–Dec daily 10–6
Adm Adult €5 , child €2.50, family (2+4) €15.50
Multimedia exhibition, café, gift shop

Cobh was the *Titanic*'s last port of call before it set sail for its encounter with an iceberg in 1912, and this is where many of its victims embarked on their last voyage. This attractive seaside town, not far from Cork, has a fascinating museum which tells the story of how the fishing village of Cobh came to prominence during the French Revolution and Napoleonic Wars (1792–1815). It was an important ship-refuelling point, where you sometimes saw up to 300 ships at anchor. It was renamed Queenstown after Queen Victoria visited in 1849, and in the following years it serviced the tall ships that transported convicts to Australia and Irish emigrants to North America, and later transatlantic steamers and ocean liners. Over 2.5 million people emigrated through Cobh between 1848 and 1950, more than from any other port in Ireland. The multimedia exhibition inside Cobh's Victorian railway station brings its history to life, with real artefacts and a rolling ship's interior that will show you why people become seasick. Afterwards, you can relax in the extremely friendly railway café and take a look at a more modern means of transport.

Fota Wildlife Park

Carrigtohill, near Cobh, **t** (021) 481 2678/481 2736, **www.fotawildlife.ie**
Getting there 10m (16km) east of Cork City off N25, with access by rail: Fota station is by park entrance
Open Mid-Mar–Oct Mon–Sat 10–6, Sun 11–6; Nov–Mar Sat 10–3, Sun 11–3; 6 Jan–11 Mar and 10 Nov–16 Dec Sat 10–4 and Sun 11–4
Adm Mid-Mar–Oct, adult €8, under-16s €5, under-3s free, family (2+4) €29; Nov–Mar Sat–Sun, adult €6.80, child €4
Playgrounds, wildlife train (adm extra), picnic areas, coffee shop, gift shop, restaurant, first aid, toilets with disabled and baby-changing facilities, car park

This is one of Europe's best modern animal parks, with over 90 species of wildlife wandering freely in 70 acres of open grass and woodland. There are no obvious restraints or cages (apart from the cheetah breeding area), yet everything is completely safe. You can easily spend a day exploring the grounds and meeting animals from five different continents. Bring good walking shoes, or else make sure the train is running so that you can look around without overtaxing little legs. Fota aims to conserve wildlife through education, the breeding of endangered species and promoting and supporting international conservation programmes. After you've spent some time communing with the animals, visit the Fota Arboretum and Gardens nearby for a picnic.

County Cork Songs to Sing...
Blackwater Side, Bold Thady Quill, Skibbereen, The Wild Rover, Whiskey in the Jar, Goodbye Mursheen Durkin, O'Donnell Abu, The Holy Ground.

AROUND AND ABOUT

Animal magic

The Donkey Sanctuary

Knockardbane, Liscarroll, Mallow, **t** (022) 48398, **www.thedonkeysanctuary.org.uk**
Getting there About 10 miles (16km) northwest of Mallow, 30 miles (48km) north of Cork
Open Mon–Fri 9–4.30, Sat–Sun, bank holidays 10–5

Rescued donkeys are rehabilitated and protected at this welfare centre, where they never turn away any donkey that needs a home or veterinary care. Some are placed in new homes, but welfare officers continue to check up on their wellbeing. There are educational programmes on donkey care.

Millstreet Country Park

Millstreet, **t** (029) 70810
Getting there 5 miles (8km) from Millstreet, 27 miles (42km) northwest of Cork
Open Mar–Oct Mon–Fri 10–7, or by arrangement
Adm €7.50 per person, €20 per car/family
Restaurant, visitor centre, gardens, deer farm, picnic area, disabled access, gift shop, free parking

This 500-acre park in the Boggeragh Mountains has nature trails, ornamental grounds, waterfalls, rivers, wetlands, moorlands and reconstructions of archaeological sites that you can explore via park transporters or on foot, using the map you are given on arrival. Wild animals including birds and 700 red deer live in this park, which has a 4,000-year-old stone circle, and *crannóg* at the base of Musheramore Mountain. Meals are available in the visitor centre, along with a gift shop, theatre and state-of-the-art interactive displays.

Bricks and mortar

Bantry House and Gardens

Bantry, **t** (027) 50047
Getting there 54 miles (86km) west of Cork
Open Gardens, Mar–Oct 9–6
Adm Adults €4; accompanied children free
B&B, craft shop and tea room

In the gardens of this mid-18th-century house, with French and Flemish tapestries, works of art and furniture from 1800 to 1868, is the 1796 French Armada Exhibition Centre, a small exhibition about the failed French landing at Bantry Bay in 1796.

Barryscourt Castle

Carrigtohill, **t** (021) 488 2218
Getting there 10m (16km) east of Cork City off N25
Open Jun–Sept daily 10–6, Oct–May Fri–Wed 11–5
Adm Adult €1.90, child €0.76 cents, family €5.07
Guided tours only, restaurant-teashop, craft shop, car park

This 15th-century tower-house with 16th-century additions has a bawn wall with three nearly intact corner towers. The remains of the keep house an exhibition telling the story of the Barry Family, who inhabited the castle until the 17th century. Sir Walter Raleigh lived here for a time.

Desmond Castle (French prison)

Cork Street, Kinsale, **t** (021) 477 4855
Getting there 16m (26km) south of Cork City
Open Mid-Apr–mid-Jun Tues–Sun 10–6 (also Mon bank holidays); mid-Jun–early-Oct daily 10–6
Adm Adult €2.53, child €1.26, family €6.34
Wine museum, guided tour on request

A custom house built by the Earl of Desmond in about 1500, occupied by the Spanish in 1601 and used as a prison for American sailors captured during the American War of Independence. It became known locally as 'the French prison' after a fire in which mainly French prisoners died in 1747. During the Great Famine in the 19th century it was used as a workhouse. An exhibition tells the story of Ireland's wine links with Europe.

Look at this!

Argideen Valley Heritage Park

Near Timoleague, **t** (023) 46107
Getting there About 1 mile (1.6km) east of Clonakilty towards Timoleague;from Cork, 32 miles (51km) southwest on N71 towards Clonakilty
Open Mid-Jun–mid-Sept Mon–Sun 10.30–5; other times by arrangement
Adm Adult €4, under-12s free
Historical, mythological and music tours can be arranged, including 3 1/2 hr Michael Collins tour: €50 for private guide

The history, traditions and folklore of southwest Cork are conveyed via dramatic re-enactments, exhibitions, video shows and other presentations in traditional white-washed surroundings. There's an Archaeology Trail with full-sized replicas of ancient monuments, and in the park, there is a *Gallaun* (standing stone) and a *Fulachda Fiadh* (an ancient open-air cooking pot), along with a circular ring fort, holy well and the ruins of a church and a watch house. On Crowley Way, a scenic tour and hill walk, park staff guide you round sites connected with Michael Collins (*see* pp.38–9).

Charles Fort

Summercove, Kinsale, **t** (021) 477 2263
Getting there 2 miles (3km) east of Kinsale
Open mid-Mar–Oct daily 10–6, Nov–mid-Mar Sat–Sun 10–5
Adm Adult €3.17, child €1.26, family €6.34
Guided tours available on request, exhibition centre, restricted disabled access, parking

This huge star-shaped fort beside Kinsale Harbour was built in 1677, and used for coastal defence until British withdrawal in 1921. It's an impressive sight in this lovely coastal town.

Schull Planetarium

Schull, **t** (028) 28552
Getting there On Roaringwater Bay, 69 miles (111km) southwest of Cork near Skibbereen
Open Jun Tues and Sat 3–5pm, Thurs 4; please ring to check for times of other shows
Adm Adult €4.50, child €3.20, family (2+2) €12

Each summer regular star shows are offered to the public at the Community College in Schull.

Youghal Heritage Town Exhibition Centre

Market House, by tourist office, Youghal, **t** (024) 20170
Getting there 29 miles (46km) east of Cork on N25
Open Daily 10–6. **Adm** free

The exhibition here consists of reconstructions and an audiovisual display on the area's history. Sir Walter Raleigh stayed in Youghal for a while just before setting sail on one of his voyages to America, and this was also where he first landed on his return. He brought with him the potato, and is said to have been the first person to plant it in Irish soil. He also brought tobacco, and soon after he got back, he lit up a smoke, but his servant thought he had set himself on fire, and threw a bucket of water over him.

West Cork Model Railway Village

Inchydoney Rd, Clonakilty, **t** (023) 33224
Getting there 32 miles (51km) southwest of Cork
Open Daily 5 Feb–Oct 11–5 (extended in summer)
Adm Adult €5, 5–12s €2.50, under-5s €0.70, family €13

This miniature copy of West Cork villages in the 1940s includes a 1:24-scale working model of the West Cork railway line. Four towns are depicted – Bandon, Clonakilty, Dunmanway and Kinsale.

Prince August Toy Soldier Factory Visitor Centre

Kilnamartyra, Macroom, **t** (026) 40222
Getting there 23 miles (37km) west of Cork
Open Jun–Aug Mon–Fri 9–5,30, Sat 10–4. **Adm** Free

Find out how to make toy soldiers: watch a craftsman follow an artist's design for a figure and then have a go yourself at casting a model and making a mould of it. Afterwards, have a look at hundreds of hand-painted figures, and you can buy a casting kit to make your own at home.

Nature lovers

Cork Heritage Park

Bessboro, Blackrock, **t** (021) 358 854
Getting there 2 miles (3km) from Cork City
Open Apr Sun only 12 noon–5.30, May–Sept Sat–Sun 12 noon–5.30, Mon–-Fri 10.30–5.30
Adm Adult €4.45, child €1.91, family €9.53
Restaurant, play areas, baby-changing facilities, toilets with disabled access, car park

Six acres of grounds around the 19th-century Bessboro Estate in which you can explore Cork's heritage. Displays feature local ecology, maritime history, the fire service, transport and archaeology. Its children's play areas are great, with a playhouse and sandpit. Relax here for an afternoon with lunch in the restaurant, or tea after a picnic.

Doneraile Court and Wildlife Park

Turnpike Road, Doneraile, **t** (022) 24244
Getting there North of Mallow, 27 miles (43km) north of Cork City
Open Mid-Apr–Oct Mon–Fri 8am–8.30pm, Sat 10–8.30, Sun, bank holidays 11–7, Nov–mid-Apr Mon–Fri 8–4.30, Sat, Sun, bank holidays 10–4.30
Adm Park: adult €2.55, child €1.27, family €6.36; House: adult €2.50, child €1.20, family €6.30

This elegant park was landscaped in the early 18th century in the Capability Brown style, so that it looks to have been created by nature and not the landed gentry. The 395-acre site is dotted with stone bridges and water features, and mature groves of deciduous trees, including one of the best collections of old oaks in Ireland, and herds of deer and other Irish wildlife.

Sporty kids

Activity centres

Trabolgan Holiday Village

Midleton, **t** (021) 466 1551, **www.trabolgan.com**
Getting there South of Midleton (14 miles/22km east of Cork) on the R630; turn south on to an unclassified road, the site is signposted
Open mid-Mar–Oct
Adm Priced per activity, or day or half-day

This self-catering and caravan village offers day visitors aged 4+ activities divided by age like: archery, outdoor' wooden wonderland' pool with wavemaker, adventure sports and crazy golf.

> ***A story to tell: 'Them'***
>
> Under their truce with each other, the Tuatha Dé Danaan and the Sons of Mil agreed that neither would interfere in the affairs of the other, and that they would dwell alongside each other in peace so long as they treated each other with respect. In the centuries after the truce, too, certain places in Ireland were recognized by country people as 'theirs' – that is, the land of The Gentry, The Good People, Them or the Sidhe (pronounced *shee*). If you say the word 'faery' outdoors at twilight, which is the time when they come out, one of 'them' might overhear you and play a trick on you, as it is said they do not like to be called 'faeries'.
>
> In the west of Ireland, people still exercise caution about Them. For instance, just a while ago a farmer who merely swept clear the moat around a fairy whitethorn bush was given a scare when on his way home, driving his familiar lorry along a road he knew like the back of his hand, the lorry suddenly fell sideways into a ditch – leaving him unharmed (like the bush) but warned!

Good to know...
Getting to the islands of County Cork

Cruises are run to offshore islands from Kinsale by **Shearwater Cruises**, Seaview Farm, Kilbrittain, **t** (023) 49610. The regular local ferries are these:

Bere Island: Off Castletownbere, Bantry Bay. Ferries are frequent in summer: contact Colm Harrington, **t** (027) 75000; Patrick Murphy, **t** (027) 75004

Cape Clear Island: May–Sept, the island has two ferries, from Schull, one daily, **t** (028) 28138, and from Baltimore, twice daily, **t** (028) 39119

Hare Island: Departs Cunamore Pier, Skibbereen, **t** (028) 38144. West Cork Coastal Cruises, **t** (028) 39153, sails from Schull to Baltimore via Hare Island and Cape Clear, and vice versa.

Sherkin Island: From Baltimore seven times daily May–Sept, **t** (028) 20125.

Whiddy Island: Off Bantry in Bantry Bay. Contact Danny O'Leary, **t** (027) 50310.

Boat trips

Carrig Water Ski Club

Carrigadrohid, Macroom, **t** (021) 487 3027
Open May–Oct

Waterskiing on Inishcarra Reservoir.

Cork Harbour Cruises

t (021) 427 7085

In summer, boats depart from Penrose Quay in Cork and the main pier in Cobh.

Kinsale Harbour Cruises

t (021) 477 3188

Enjoyable trips around the bays near Kinsale.

Fishing

The Kinsale Angling Co-op

1 The Ramparts, Kinsale, **t** (021) 477 4946

For fishing in the Blackwater River.

Horse riding

Bantry Horse Riding

Coomanore South, Bantry, **t** (027) 51412

Blarney Riding Centre

The Paddock, Killowen, **t** (021) 385 854

Qualified instruction for all abilities.

Valley View Equestrian Centre

Gooseberry Hill, Newmarket, **t** (029) 68026

Cross-country trekking and pony camps.

Walking

There are miles of great long-distance paths in Co. Cork, which you can follow a long way or for just a short stroll: the **Beara Way**, a 122-mile (195km) circular route around the Beara peninsula from Glengarriff; the **Sheep's Head Way**, a 56-mile (90km) circular trail from Bantry; the **Ballyhoura Way**, 56 miles (90km) from Limerick Junction to John's Bridge near Kanturk; and the **Blackwater Way**, 104 miles (166km), all along the Blackwater river from Clonmel to Muckross.

Good places for short walks include Charles Fort, Kinsale, and Clear Island.

Water sports

Aquaventures

Lifeboat Road, Baltimore, **t** (028) 20511

This is an impressive new dive centre with abundant marine life and wrecks, including a German U-boat and the infamous Kowloon Bridge.

Baltimore Diving and Watersports Centre

Baltimore, **t** (028) 20300

The Baltimore Sailing School

The Pier, Baltimore, **t** (028) 20141

Courses on ketches and day boats.

International Sailing Centre

5 East Beach, Cobh, **t** (021) 481 1237, **www.sailcork.com**

Schull Watersports

Schull, **t** (028) 28554

Dinghies and windsurfing.

Buckets and spades – Beaches in Co. Cork

Around the Cork coastline there are many fine beach spots, many now with Blue Flag status.

Bantry Bay: one of Ireland's most beautiful beach areas.

Clonakily to Skibbereen: Inchydoney, Long Strand, Owenahincha (near Roscarbery) and Red Strand are some of the best Cork beaches for swimming, and there are more nice beaches at Tragumna, Tralispean, Sandycove and Sherkin Island.

Kinsale area: try the sandy beaches at Summercove and Castlepark; Harbour View and Coolmain (near Garretstown); or Garrylucas, on the Old Head of Kinsale.

Youghal: East Cork's best beaches are Front Strand and Claycastle, near Garryvoe.

COUNTY KERRY

The lush county of Kerry is known for its mountains, lakes and folklore, which encourage story-making. This was one of the last large Irish-speaking parts of Ireland, and its *shenachie* storytelling tradition continued well past the first half of the 20th century. Most of its people were fishermen and farmers who understood nature better than the machinations of Dublin society, before their children were caught up in pop music and all the blow-ins arrived from other countries.

Kerrymen don't have the attitude that one must entertain children all the time, but the genial kindness they offer them, alongside the great beauty of these surroundings, will make city people relax. So many tourists visit in July and August, though, that you'll need to book accommodation in advance.

For many people, Kerry's coastal scenery is second to none. The famous 'Ring of Kerry' on the Iveragh Peninsula is hauntingly beautiful, with one of Ireland's earliest monastic settlements offshore on the Skellig Islands, but the Dingle Peninsula's Mount Brandon and Gap of Dunloe are more dramatic. Half of the Beara Peninsula, shared with Co. Cork, is also part of Kerry. Iron Age stone forts and beehive huts are scattered on private land, which sometimes you have to pay farmers to visit.

This is a place to ride bikes or hike in the hills and along the ocean shore.Play a musical instrument in a pub here and, so long as there's no football on TV, it will attract glances and the noise machines will be turned off. Before you know it, you'll have tourist-hardened Kerrymen asking you questions.

Despite all the foreign traffic, Kerry holds a sense of being cut off from the rest of the world, especially in winter, and Kerrymen often say the 'next stop', across the Atlantic, is America. The periodic wild storms that bash its shores intensify that feeling. And when rainbow colours dance upon sky and water, or heavy giant clouds fly fast across the mountains, it is easy to imagine that one is very close to the Otherworld of the Fairies.

Tourist Information

Caherciveen, t (066) 947 2589
Castlegregory, Strand St, **t** (066) 713 9422
Dingle, t (066) 915 1188
Kenmare, beside Heritage Centre, **t** (064) 41233
Killarney, Town Hall, **t** (064) 31633
Listowel, St John's Church, **t** (068) 22590
Tralee, Ashe Memorial Hall, **t** (066) 712 1288
Waterville, t (066) 947 4646

Special Events – County Kerry

April

Samhlaiocht – Kerry Arts Festival, t (066) 712 9934 **www**.samhlaiocht.com

This annual 10-day community arts festival held in various Kerry venues provides a global platform for established and emerging artists.

July

Féile Lunasa, Cloghane and Brandon, **t** (066) 713 8137/713 8142

A fine traditional festival. Dates vary each year.

August

Puck Fair, Killorglin, **t** (066) 976 2366, **www**.puckfair.ie

One of Ireland's oldest – and wildest – annual festivals; it includes traditional cattle and horse fairs, the coronation and dethronement of a goat, and free family entertainment including busking, parades, fireworks, street entertainment, concerts, traditional dancing and kids' competitions.

Rose of Tralee International Festival, Tralee, **t** (066) 712 1322, **www**.roseoftralee.ie

This 5-day international festival boasts carnivals, street parades, fireworks and free outdoor concerts alongside its fashion and beauty show and Rose Ball to choose the year's 'Rose of Tralee'.

Tours

Donkey Rambles, Slattery's, Russell St, Killarney, **t** (066) 712 4088

Hire a donkey, saddle and maps for €30 a day.

Fios Feasa Holyground, Dingle, **t** (066) 915 2465

Archaeological tours.

Gap of Dunloe Tour, t (064) 31068/33483, **www**.killarneydaytour.com

Book ahead for day trips in the Kerry countryside, combining hiking and/or cycling with boating, coach, pony or horse-drawn trap transportation.

Getting there and around

By air Kerry Airport is at Farranfore, 9 miles (14km) north of Killarney on the road to Tralee (N22); there are shuttle buses to Killarney. Airport information: **t** 066 976 4644, **www**.kerryairport.ie (*see* p.283). Flights to Kerry are operated by Aer Arann and Ryanair, *see* pp.280–2.

By bus Long-distance buses run to Killarney and Tralee. From Tralee, regular buses go to Dingle, from where there are infrequent services to other points on the peninsula. From June–Sept Bus

Eireann runs daily coach tours round the Ring of Kerry and Dingle between Killarney, **t** (064) 34777, and Tralee, **t** (066) 712 3566.

By train Kerry is linked to Dublin Heuston by a rail line from Tralee via Killarney. Information, Tralee, **t** (064) 31067, Killarney, **t** (066) 712 3522

By boat In North Kerry, you can avoid Limerick with the car ferry over the Shannon at Tarbert, to Killimer, Co. Clare. It sails hourly each way.

There is a ferry service around the Ring of Kerry from Dingle, every day except Mon and Fri.

Bike Hire

Cycle Ireland, St Mary's Terrace, Killarney, **t** (064) 32536

Foxy John Moriarty, Main St, Dingle, **t** (066) 915 1316

A bar, hardware store and cycle hire centre.

Kerry Cycle Tours, Tralee, **t** (066) 712 3376

Killarney Rent-a-Bike, Old Market Lane, Main St, Killarney, **t** (064) 32578

Gives out a free map with rentals.

Good to know...

Getting to the islands of Kerry

The situation with regard to insurance in boats for hire from local boat owners is complicated, so bear in mind that if you take such a trip you may do so at your own risk; check your insurance policy or ask about cover before you embark.

Blasket Islands: The **Blasket Island Boatmen** take day-trippers from Dunquin Harbour every half-hour in summer, **t** (066) 915 6422. Ask in Krugers Bar, Dunquin, **t** (066) 915 6127, about hiring a boat to the Great Blasket. **Mountain Man**, Main Street, Dingle, **t** (066) 915 2400, offers bus and boat trips.

The Skelligs: Boats can be hired from Waterville, Caherdaniel, Derrynane Pier, Portmagee or Valentia Island – it's a matter of trying your luck with the local fishermen. Michael O'Sullivan does the trip from Waterville, and fishing cruises; ask at the Oyster Bar, **t** (066) 947 4255. Sean Feehan arranges angling, diving and boat hire at Ballinskelligs Pier, and trips to the Skelligs, **t** (066) 947 9182.

Due to the popularity of the Great Skellig, and the fragile nature of its ruins and paths, a limit has been set on how many people can visit at once – book ahead in July and August. A waterbus tour is available from the **Skellig Experience Heritage Centre**, **t** (066) 947 6306 (*see* p.133).

Mountain Man, Main St, Dingle, **t** (066) 915 2400

O'Gorman's Cycle Hire, Ballydavid, Dingle, **t** (066) 915 5162

O'Neills, Plunkett St, Killarney, **t** (064) 31970

Standard and tandem bikes for rent, as well as fishing and camping gear.

Tralee Bike Hire, Ashe St, Tralee, **t** (066) 712 7527

Shopping

An Grianan

Dykegate Lane, Dingle, **t** (066) 51910,

Excelllent wholefoods shop.

Billy Clifford's Farm

Cork Road, Kenmare, **t** (064) 41693

Fresh vegetables and salad-makings are supplied to many Kenmare households by this farmer.

Gorthbrack Organic Farm

Near Tralee, **t** (066) 37042

Boxes of fresh produce from this organic farm are delivered locally on order.

Killarney Bookshop

32 Main St, Killarney, **t** (064) 34108, **www**.killarneybookshop.ie/

Has a good selection of books for kids and adults.

TOURING TOWNS

Killarney

Kerry's most popular tourist town, Killarney and its surroundings offer a multitude of sights. The town itself is quite small, but can get very busy in summer. It has a wonderful park, a range of accommodation and plenty of restaurants to visit.

Things to see and do

Coolwood Wildlife Sanctuary

Coolcaslagh (off Cork Road), **t** (064) 36288

Open Apr–Oct daily 10–6

Adm Free except for children's zoo: adult €2.60, child €1.20

Children's play and craft areas, pet shop, scenic walk, children's zoo, coffee shop, picnic area, parking

Take your family here for a day of hiking in 50 acres of parkland, where you may well see a big range of wild birds and mink.

Killarney National Park

t (064) 31440
Getting there 4 miles (6km) from Killarney via N71
Open Park daily, visitor centre daily mid-Mar–Jun and Sept–Oct 9–6, Jul–Aug 9–7. **Adm** Free
Nature trails, lake swimming, restaurant, toilets with disabled access and baby-changing areas

This is Ireland's premier tourist attraction, so it attracts large crowds in high season. Still, your kids will enjoy the mystical, often misty, beauty of this giant park, encompassing the three Lakes of Killarney and set within thousands of acres of mountains and lush landscape. Muckross Abbey (a friary built in 1448 by Fransciscan monks), Dinis Cottage and the Torc Waterfall lie within yew and oak woodland inhabited by Ireland's only native herd of red deer. The park's fresh sweet air will leave you exhilarated even on the dampest days.

Queen Victoria put the place on the map when she visited in 1861. Ladies View, a prime place to stop for a picnic, is so called because her ladies in waiting were delighted by the stunning view.

You can hire a traditional 'jaunting car' or a horse-drawn 'side-car', or cycle around the vast 26,000-acre grounds. There are places to snack along the official 15-mile (24km) route, but a better idea would be to bring a picnic.

Muckross House, Gardens and Traditional Farms

t (064) 31440, **www.muckross-house.ie**
Getting there 4 miles (6.5km) from Killarney
Open House and gardens: daily mid-Mar–Jun, Sept–Oct 9–6, Jul–Aug 9–7, Nov–mid-Mar Tue–Sun 11–5. Farms: 17 Mar–end Apr Sat–Sun and bank holidays 1–6; daily May, Oct 1–6, Jun–Sept 10–7
Adm House: adult €5.07, child €2.03, family €12.70; Farms: adult €5.07, child €2.03, family €12.70; joint ticket (house and farms) adult €7.61, child €3.49, family €19.04, gardens free
Restaurant and craft shop (open daily 9–5.30), vintage coach trip, information centre, restricted access, toilets with disabled access, parking

Families visiting Killarney mustn't miss this vast estate. Muckross House is a splendid Victorian museum where in summer you can watch a blacksmith, bookbinder, potter and weaver working at their trades and see an informative film about the environment and geology of the park, which you can traverse by horse and cart to visit sites like Muckross Friary or Muckross Traditional Farms.

Boats on the Lakes of Killarney

Killarney Waterbus, t (064) 32638

Beginning at Ross Castle, this trip offers a 1hr commentary about the Killarney Lower Lakes.

Lily of Killarney, book via Killarney Boating and Tour Centre, **t** (064) 31068, or Dero's Tours, **t** (064) 31251

Cruise around the lakes of Killarney from Ross Castle – with 5 departures daily – with entertaining folklore and history of the area from your guide.

In the latter, a history park-style is applied to a community in the countryside, where children can absorb the atmosphere of a way of life that has all but vanished in Ireland today. No machine noise pollutes a wide expanse of land in this recreated early 20th-century rural community, where traditional organic farming methods are employed and dirt roads lead between farmhouses and farms. You smell the air and hear birds sing the way people did in Ireland until half a century ago, and suddenly find you have a spring in your step and a song on your lips just as people there used to. In each house you'll meet a lady who will tell you how people used to live. Talk to them about life and people's perspectives in Ireland then, while bread bakes over a turf fire. Out of doors you'll probably find a farmer who looks after the land and animals in the traditional manner, without chemical pesticides. Maybe you'll meet an elderly Irish visitor who comes here just to remember the peace of living in this kind of houses without the noise of modern houses, TVs and computers. Survival in those days demanded that people be in tune with their surroundings. Today we can escape the hard work and damp houses of the past, but what price do we pay for it? How can we retrieve the good things in the past we have lost and sometimes have never even experienced? Visit this place and maybe you or your children will come up with some answers.

Museum of Irish Transport

Scotts Gardens, Killarney, **t** (064) 34677
Open Daily May–Sept 10–6; Apr–Oct 11–5
Adm Adult €5, child €2, family (2+2) €12

The entire history of bicycles is presented here, from the Hobby Horse of 1825 to modern bikes. Also on show is a unique collection of Irish vintage, veteran and classic cars, fire engines and motorcycles, including a very rare 1907 Silver Stream.

A story to tell: Oísín and Tír na n'Óg

The son of Finn McCool was Oísín, meaning 'fawn'. He was so named because a sorceress jealous of his mother's beauty had transformed her into a deer. For a long time, Oísín was watched over by an invisible faery presence, a warmth that cushioned him from the blows of training as a warrior of the Fianna (*see* p. 30). He did not know he was being admired by a faery princess called Niamh of the Golden Hair, who often rode far from her home in Tír na n'Óg, the Land of Eternal Youth.

No sorrow or death disturb the Tuatha Dé Danaan's merrymaking there – a place where there is always feasting and never famine. The Tuatha still have their work to do, regenerating and caring for the earth, which is how Niamh one day came to see Oísín. She saw him as his horse ran upon the white-sand shore, his cheeks as red as rowan berries. She began spying upon him, invisibly, and his manner was so gentle that love couldn't help rising in her heart. Oísín would wake in the night to see a bowl of stars glittering down upon him, or a curtain of moonbeams on his face from a silent sky, little knowing that faery magic was about.

One day Niamh decided to meet him. As Oísín rode along the shore, he saw the most beautiful shining woman, with hair like spun gold, floating above the ocean on a pearl white mare. She was smiling, too, with an exquisite look in her eyes.

'I am Niamh,' she said, 'of Tír na n'Óg. Perhaps you have heard of it?'

Oísín could barely speak. 'Until now I had thought it an old man's fantasy.'

'Well indeed it is not,' Niamh laughed. 'Would you like to see it?'

Her fingers touched his hand, and he was lost to ordinary mortals forever. Without a doubt in his heart, he answered, 'I would. Who would not?'

For a moment, a pang of memory made him hesitate. Didn't he recall that people usually never returned from Tír na n'Óg? 'But,' he murmured, 'perhaps not at this very moment.'

Niamh, smiled, 'Well, later then,' and dashed off on her steed before vanishing into thin air.

It was months before Oísín saw Niamh again, and still his love for her grew. The Fianna worried about him, whispering that he must be terribly lonely to be dreaming he had met a faery lady. They introduced him to the prettiest girls they could find, but they could not take away the spell that Niamh had cast upon Oísín's heart.

So when he saw Niamh again, his heart leapt into his eyes and she knew she had him. With barely a word, he joined her on her steed and off they flew to Tír na n'Óg.

There was much sorrow among the Fianna when they found Oísín's horse. They thought Oísín must have gone mad and cast himself into the sea.

Oísín was happier in the land of his heart's desire than he had ever been. But after a time, he remembered his home and worried how his fellow Fianna were doing without him. He begged Niamh to let him return, just for a visit. She put off replying but couldn't refuse him, saying, 'My horse will take you.' Then, her eyes turning dark, she warned, 'But do not dismount or touch the earth of Ireland, or never more will you return to Tír na n'Óg.'

He promised her that he would return, and flew back across the waves to Ireland. But it was a changed land. Nothing looked familiar and the people were so small. There were only weak little men struggling to lift what to him was a small rock he could move with one hand.

He looked at the ragged men, then asked them, 'Where might I find King Finn and the Fianna?'

One of the men sat down and wiped the sweat from his brow, unable to believe the giant he saw before him really existed. 'Where indeed?' he replied, 'just when you need them!' and waved his hand at his building work. A near-toothless man beside him piped up, 'Come here now, would ye ever be able to help us lift this boulder?'

'What? That stone?' Oísín started to dismount, then heard Niamh's voice in his ear, '...never more will you return to Tír na n'Óg,' so instead he leaned over from his saddle to pick it up, but, stretching too far, he lost his balance and fell to the earth.

In that moment, Niamh's horse fled and the young giant shrank to a white-haired old man nearly as small as the men he had pitied. He lay in a heap on the ground silently weeping, knowing what he had lost.

'Whisht! Did you see that, man?', the men cried to each other. 'Are ye all right, sir?', one said to Oísín. And then the men heard the story of Oísín, and the tales of the Fianna – from the last there has been on earth of that proud race.

Ross Castle

Killarney, **t** (064) 35851/2
Getting there 11/2 miles (2.5km) outside Killarney off Kenmare Road
Open Daily April 10–5, May and Sept 10–6, Jun–Aug 9–6.30; Oct Tue–Sun 10–5
Adm Adult €3.80, child €1.58, family €1.58
Disabled access to ground floor with prior arrangement, toilets and car and coach park near site

A grand example of a medieval Irish stronghold. It was probably built in the 15th century by one of the O'Donogue Ross tribal chieftains, and was one of the last of its kind to fall to Cromwell's forces in the 17th century. It has 16th-17th-century furniture and is one of Kerry's finest castles, with a tower house inside a bawn (fortified enclosure). Boats from here will take you to Innisfallen Isle in the middle of Lough Leane (book ahead in high season, *see* p.129). *The Annals of Innisfallen* were written there, in Innisfallen Abbey, founded around AD 600.

Tralee

Famous for its annual 'Rose of Tralee' festival, for which the whole town turns out – usually in August or September – Tralee boasts several attractions to interest children. It's a good place from which to travel around the whole of Kerry and Co. Limerick, as it's slightly off the main tourist track of Killarney and the Ring of Kerry.

Things to see and do

Aqua Dome

Ballyard, **t** (066) 712 8899 (summer); info line for other seasons: **t** (066) 712 9150,
Open Daily Jun–Aug 10–10, call for Sept–May opening times
Adm Adults €8, 4–16s €7, under-4s free, off-peak and family discounts available
Swimming pool, kiddies' pool, sauna, steam rooms, cool pool, toilets with baby- changing facilities, lazy river, restaurant with children's meals and snacks

This ultra-modern swimming pool and leisure centre is the biggest and reputedly best water-based complex in Ireland. A separate toddlers' pool has a bubble slide fountain and mushroom spray, while older children can play in the medieval castle with water cannons, bubblers, gushers and geysers, whirlpools, rapids, a wave pool and the giant 90m water chute. Adults can relax in the luxurious Sauna Dome with its two large saunas, steam room, cool pool and relaxation area. Aqua Golf, with an 18-hole miniature golf course, is next door.

Fenit Sea World

The Pier, Fenit, **t** (066) 713 6544
Getting there 8 miles (13km) west of Tralee
Open Daily Jun–Aug 10–6; Apr–May and Sept–Oct Tues–Sun 10–6
Adm Adult €6, 4–16s €4, under-4s free, family (2+up to 5) €16.50
Gift and craft shop, café, toilets with disabled access and baby-changing facilities, parking nearby

Some of the hundreds of underwater creatures who live in Tralee Bay and the Atlantic can be observed at close quarters in this modern aquarium. Youngsters will be interested in the submarine labyrinth and the shipwreck. Native species are shown in reconstructed natural habitats: rock pools, salt marshes and sandy seabeds.

Kerry the Kingdom Museum

Ashe Memorial Hall, Denny St, **t** (066) 712 7777
Open Daily Mar–end Oct 9.30–5.30, Nov–Dec 11.30–4.30
Adm Adult €8, 5–15s €5, under-4s free, family (2+3) €22
Café, shop, free coach and pay car park

This museum offers exceptional attractions, which detail the last 8,000 years of Irish (particularly Kerry) history: a panoramic audio-visual tour of the county, where children can play with interactive devices; and the 'artefacts zone', with reconstructions from the Stone Age to modern times, including a street scene of medieval Tralee. As you pass through the Abbey and Castle of old Tralee in 'time cars', you're confronted by authentic sounds, sights and smells of the age.

Siamsa Tíre – National Folk Theatre of Ireland

Godfrey Place, **t** (066) 712 3055
Shows Apr–May Mon–Thur and Sat 8.30, Jun–Oct Mon–Wed 8.30; specials at other times
Adm From adult €16, child €14
Coffee shop, bar, souvenir shop, gallery, parking for cars, coaches nearby

The theatre offers a regular programme of evening entertainment based on Irish music, folklore and dance. Shows are suitable for all the family and contain Irish stories and songs.

SPECIAL TRIPS

The Dingle Peninsula

The most famous resident of Dingle, west of Tralee, is Fungi the dolphin, who has lived in Dingle Bay for some years and can be visited on boat trips or by swimming out to him. Out in the country and the smaller villages of the peninsula, the land is flat enough to ride bikes or go horse riding along much of the coast. There are caves and souterrains to explore, and the beehive huts around Slea Head, and Dunbeg Fort west of Ventry, or you can take boats out to wind-blasted islands like now-uninhabited Great Blasket. Dingle is a walker's paradise too. You can walk along the sea for glorious views, or swim off protected sandy beaches like the one at Inch. Get the kids in the mood by renting the 1970 film *Ryan's Daughter*, which was filmed here.

Things to see and do

Dingle Oceanworld Aquarium

The Wood, Dingle, **t** (066) 915 2111, **www**.dingle-oceanworld.ie
Getting there 31 miles (49km) west of Tralee
Open Daily 10–5
Adm Adult €8, child €5, family (2+4 under 16) €22, additional child €2.50, weekly family pass €40,
Aquarium, gift shop, café overlooking the harbour

Before you go to see Fungi the dolphin, have a look at local sea life in the underwater tunnel here and learn about the various creatures inhabiting the ocean off the west coast of Ireland. There is also a display about St Brendan the Navigator's voyages of discovery in the Atlantic Ocean.

Fungi the Dolphin

The Pier, Dingle; contact **t** (087) 285 8802; Dingle Boatmen's Association, **t** (066) 915 2626; Flannery's Wet-Suit Hire, **t** (066) 915 1967
Times All operate in summer, daily 8–10am
Cost around €10.50 per person

For an experience that youngsters won't forget take them to meet Fungi, the wild bottlenose dolphin who has chosen to live in Dingle Harbour since 1984. He normally comes to greet the boats that go out to see him. They say he really likes people, but be sensitive as he is not a pet.

Some people claim that swimming with dolphins is therapeutic and that these unique sea creatures have a special empathy for humans in trouble or need. A meeting with Fungi is not a cure-all, but becoming closer to animals and nature is likely to have a positive effect. If you want to swim with Fungi, you need to hire a wetsuit. You can rent one from Flannery's (above), with whom you also can book an early morning swim with Fungi. The swimming trip is about 2hrs long.

Gallarus Oratory

Kilmalkedar, Dingle Peninsula
Getting there 2 miles (3km) south of Kilmalkedar or west from Dingle on the road to Ballydavid
Open All year. **Adm** Free
Craft shop, tearoom

This impressive stone hut, built using the drystone corbelling technique of Neolithic tomb-makers, is still watertight after over 1,000 years of existence, and resembles an upturned boat. It is an Early Christian miniature church, built between the 6th and 9th centuries.

Kids interested in archaeology will also want to see Doonbeg Fort, an Iron Age construction south of Ventry that sadly is inaccessible because it's falling into the sea.

Ionad an Bhlascaoid Mhóir (The Blasket Centre)

Dunquin, **t** (066) 915 6444
Getting there At the end of the peninsula 10 1/2 miles (17km) west of Dingle
Open Daily Easter–Jun and Sept–Oct 10–6, Jul–Aug 10–7, last adm 45 mins before closing, available for bookings during winter
Adm Adult €3.17, child €1.26, family €7.61
Guided tour (45 mins) on request, coffee shop/restaurant with light lunches, bookshop, toilets with disabled access, car and coach park

Before a visit to the Blasket Islands you can learn about them at this modern heritage centre, which sticks out like a sore thumb in front of the beautiful Great Blasket. The centre commemorates the

> ***Thoughts from Peig Sayers –***
> ***Youth slips away as the water slips away from the sand of the shore... A person falls into old age unknown to himself. And a word is more lasting than the wealth of the world.***

Irish-speaking people of the seven islands that comprise the Blaskets. Their last inhabitants left for the mainland in 1953, but the islands are best known for their Irish-speaking storytellers, notably Tomás Ó' Crohan, Maurice O'Sullivan and Peig Sayers (a stone commemorating her can be found in the graveyard just outside Dunquin), who documented the last years on Great Blasket. Today, the books of Sayers, O'Sullivan and Ó' Crohan are part of the Irish national curriculum. A video features islanders talking about their old way of life.

Scanlon's Pet Farm

Slea Head Drive, near Ballydavid, t (066) 915 5135
Getting there 5 miles (8km) west of Dingle
Open Apr–Sept Mon–Sat 10–6, Sun 12 noon–6
Adm Adult €2.50, child €1.20
Children's playground, picnic area, guided tours, refreshments, parking

This family-owned petting farm houses many kinds of animals and birds. You can either walk around independently or follow a guided tour round this gorgeous, windswept part of Ireland.

The Ring of Kerry

The 'Ring' is one of the most famously beautiful roads in all Ireland, a 112-mile (180km) circuit all the way around the shores of the Iveragh Peninsula. The full round trip – clockwise or anti-clockwise – makes a natural excursion from Killarney.

Derrynane House

Derrynane National Historic Park, t (066) 947 5113
Getting there 1 miles (1.6km) from Caherdaniel, near the southwest corner of the Ring
Open Nov–Mar Sat–Sun 1–5, Apr and Oct Tue–Sun 1–5, May–Sept Mon–Sat 9–6, Sun 11–7
Adm Adult €2.53, child €1.26, family €6.34
Disabled access to ground floor only, guided tours available, coffee shop with home-baked snacks, toilets with disabled access, parking

Spend a while exploring the ancestral home of Daniel O'Connell, the 19th-century nationalist and campaigner for Catholic emancipation (*see* p.36), and its beautiful surroundings – 296 acres of land in a giant national park beside sand dunes and Derrynane Bay. Many relics of Ireland's 'Liberator' are on display, notably his writing desk, rosary and duelling pistols. A film tells you more about this eminent lawyer, politician and statesman. His old Gaelic family – hereditary constables of Ballycarberry Castle in the Middle Ages – managed to get along with their Protestant neighbours despite fighting against Cromwell and William of Orange; they were even able to buy land in Penal times with the help of friendly Protestants.

The wild west of Ireland was far from the forces of law and order in the east, and before Daniel's birth the O'Connells made money from smuggling in France and Spain. He was born in Caherciveen, but was fostered out to some island people, an ancient Irish custom. He stood for parliament to challenge the law that no Catholic could take a seat in the House of Commons, and won so decisively that the law was repealed in 1829.

After touring Derrynane House, you can wander the grounds or go further afield for a walk along the rocky and sandy shore and in the national park. You can also swim from the beach (*see* p.135).

An Irish Proverb –
It is the quiet pigs that eat the meal.

Skellig Heritage Centre

Valentia Island, t (066) 947 6306, or Killarney Tourist Office, t (064) 31633
Getting there A boat trip is available for the Skelligs via Sea Quest, Seanie, Valentia Island, t (066) 947 6214
Boats depart from Valentia at 10am, Renard at 10.05 and Portmagee at 10.30
Open Apr–Jun and Sept 10–7, July–Aug 9.30–7
Adm Adult €4.40, under-12s €2.20, family (2+4) €12.70
Refreshment area, shop, toilets with disabled and baby-changing facilities, free parking

Using sound effects, models and graphics, this exhibition tells how early Christian monks lived on the Skelligs, 7 miles (11km) southwest of Valentia Island. There's also information about the Skellig Michael Lighthouses (built in 1820 and 1987), and the many species of sea birds and marine life that inhabit the area. Gannets and kittiwakes arrive here every February, while razorbills, guillemots, puffins, and others arrive in April. Boat trips to the Skellig Islands – whose impressive rock-hewn dwellings were carved by monks seeking solitude – depart daily from the pier below this centre; you can circle the island rather than disembark on it if you prefer. Afterwards, enjoy lunch in a nice room overlooking the channel towards Portmagee.

Staigue Fort

Near Castlecove, **t** (066) 947 5127
Getting there 27 miles (43km) west of Kenmare
Open Visitor Centre, daily Easter–end Sept 10–9; Fort, open all year dawn to dusk
Adm Adult €3.50, child €1.50
Animated audio-visual display, coffee shop

Thought to be 2,500 years old, this is probably the best stone fort in Ireland. The exhibition centre houses a complete model of the fort as well.

Valentia Island

Off Portmagee, **t** (066) 947 5127
Getting there You can cross to the island over a causeway at Portmagee, but in summer there is a ferry to the opposite end of Valentia from Renard Point near Caherciveen, **t** (066) 947 6141, or via Valentia Island Car Ferry, **t** (066) 947 6141
Open Apr–Sept 10–7, Oct–mid-Nov 10–5.30
Adm Adult €4.40, under-12s €2.20, family €12.70

The Valentia Island Car Ferry operates a shuttle service to the Island and its picturesque 1800s planned village of Knightstown. The island contains well-preserved pre-Christian remains, a famous grotto, slate quarry and colourful flora and fauna. Places to visit include the Skellig Centre (*see* p.133) and Valentia Heritage Museum.

AROUND AND ABOUT

Animal lovers

Farm World

Slieve Annascaul, Camp, Tralee, **t** (066) 915 8200
Getting there on Dingle road 9 1/2 miles (15km) west of Tralee
Open May–Sept 10–6, Feb–Apr by appointment
Adm Adult €3, child €1.50
Pets' corner, children's playground, nature trail, coffee shop, picnic area

On rainy days you can visit the indoor exhibit all about the animals that live on this 160-acre hill farm on the Dingle peninsula. There's a pets' corner for little kids to get to know the animals and a rare breeds tour. Stop for a rest by the lake to enjoy its panoramic, ethereal bogland views.

Look at this!

Blennerville Windmill and Visitor Centre

Blennerville, near Tralee, **t** (066) 712 1064
Getting there 2 miles (3km) from Tralee on N86
Open Daily Mar–Oct 10–6
Adm Adult €2.50, child €1
Craft shop, workshops, toilets with disabled access

An 18th-century windmill beside Tralee Bay. Displays explain all aspects of processing grain into flour. Also within the 5-storey building is an exhibit on emigration, with models of the 'coffin ships' on which Irish people travelled to escape the famine.

Seanchaí

Kerry Literary and Cultural Centre, 24 The Square, Listowel, **t** (068) 22212
Getting there 15 miles (24km) north of Tralee
Open Daily Apr–Sept 10–6; Oct–Mar Mon–Fri 10–5
Adm Adult €5.10, under-12s €2.60, family €12.70
Café, gift shop, free car parking at rear

Ireland's storytelling tradition is celebrated in this museum in a 19th-century Georgian residence beside Listowel Castle. It's a must for young authors-to-be who want to learn how to tell stories themselves, or who are perhaps already telling a few tall tales. There is an audio-visual display on North Kerry and its writers, and in July and August you can enjoy evenings of traditional Irish music, song and dance by top musicians.

Nature lovers

Crag Cave

Castleisland, **t** (066) 714 1244
Getting there 12 miles (19km) east of Tralee
Open Daily mid-Mar–Jun, Sept–Nov 10–5.30, July–Aug 10–6
Adm Adult €5.50, 5–16s €3.25, under-5s free, family (2+4) €15.50
Guided tour only, restaurant, gift shop, children's play area (separate fee), toilets with disabled access

Learn about stalagmites and stalactites in this ancient limestone cave system that may well be over a million years old. Coloured lighting effects and sounds add drama to the tour. The excellent gift shop and café has home-baked specialities.

Glen Inchaquin Waterfall Park

Tuosist, Kenmare, **t** (064) 84235
Getting there Kenmare to Castletownbere; left after 8 miles (13km) at sign to Inchiquin Lake; then 5 miles (8km) to amenity area
Open Daily all year
Adm Adult €4, 12–16s €1.50, under-12s free
Picnic areas, car park

A good place for a day out when the weather is fine: there are nice walks around the waterfall, streams, lakes and woodlands and you see all kinds of farm animals. The café has home-baked snacks.

Sporty kids

Activity centres

Activity Ireland and Skelligs Aquatics

Caherdaniel, **t** (066) 947 5277

Scuba-diving lessons and equipment, and sea angling and guided hill walking on the Kerry Way.

Golf

Deerpark Pitch'n'Putt

Lewis Road, Killarney, **t** (064) 36768

Children can test out their putting and driving skills in this open country park; all kids must be accompanied by an adult.

Horse riding

Killarney Riding Stables

Ballydowney, near Killarney, **t** (064) 31686, **www**.killarney-reeks-trail.com

For treks in Killarney National Park.

Muckross Riding Stables

Mangerton Road, Muckross, **t** (064) 32238

Hard hats, boots, ponies and horses for all ages.

Water sports

Dingle Sailing Club

The Wood, Dingle, **t** (066) 915 1984

Contact this club for week-long courses for children in the summer and Easter holidays. In the same area, you can hire wetsuits and body boards on Ventry beach.

Kenmare Seafari

The Pier, **t** (064) 831 7120, **www**.seafariireland.com

Guided cruises introducing local marine life, plus fishing, kayaking and water-skiing.

Buckets and spades – Kerry's Beaches

Kerry has some of Ireland's finest beaches, of which the following is just a selection.

Dingle Peninsula You can swim on Ventry Beach (4 miles/6km west of Dingle), where lifeguards are on duty during summer, and you can dive in Ventry Bay. Other good places to try swimming are Beenbawn, near Dingle; Cappagh Strand, near Brandon; Wine Strand between the villages of Ballydavid and Ballyferriter; Smerwick Strand, near Ballyferriter; and Slea Head or Stradbally.

There's also a Blue Flag beach at Maherabeg, near Castlegregory in the north of the peninsula, and on the south side there's good surfing at Inch Strand (15 miles/24km east of Dingle) and Srudeen Strand, nearer Dingle, but bring your own board.

Ring of Kerry Waterville is the main resort of the Ring of Kerry: its beach and St Finan's Bay are beautiful. Other Blue Flag beaches are at Derrynane (west of Caherdaniel) with glorious sand dunes and a lovely 1-mile strand, Ballinskelligs (west of Waterville), Kells Bay (7 miles/11km northeast of Caherciveen), Rossbeigh (Glenbeigh) and White Strand near Castlecove.

North Kerry Banna (9 miles/14km northwest of Tralee), Ballyheigue (12 miles/19km northwest of Tralee), Ballybunion (northwest of Listowel)

Waterworld

Castlegregory, **t** (066) 713 9292, **www**.waterworld.ie

Ireland's largest scuba-diving centre, which offers visits to the Blasket and Magharee Islands. Dive holiday packages for all levels available, as well as hill-walking and other energetic activities.

Steam power!

Tralee and Blennerville Steam Railway

Ballyard Station, Tralee, **t** (066) 712 1064/712 8888
Operates Daily May–Sept
Adm Adult €5, child €2.50, family €12.50

The Tralee and Dingle Steam Railway, which ran from 1891 to 1953, was one of the world's most famous narrow-gauge lines. Now you can ride in one of its old carriages on the short (2 miles/3km) trip between Ballyard Station, near the Aqua Dome in Tralee, to the Blennerville Windmill (*see* left).

A ghost in the town of Macroom
One night found a ghoul in his room
They argued all night,
As to which had the right,
To frighten the wits out of whom.

Scholars haven't yet proved that the Limerick five-line poem originated here, but it's certain that in the 18th century the taverns of Mungret, Co. Limerick, were renowned for their performing rhymers. This charming county of undulating farmland is known for picturesque villages like Adare and old abbeys like Kilmallock. You can take cruises on the River Shannon and fish for salmon, or go on family walks in the history park at Lough Gur and explore a Neolithic settlement that has been here since 3000 BC, not to mention the 4,000-year-old stone circle outside it. There's plenty of space here for children to play traditional Irish games (*see* p.25), and to pick blackberries from country lanes.

Tourist Information

Adare, Heritage Centre, Main St, **t** (061) 396 255
Limerick City, Arthur's Quay, **t** (061) 317 522
Shannon Airport, **t** (061) 471 664

Tours

***Angela's Ashes* Walking Tours of Limerick**, from Tourist Office, Mon–Fri 2.30, Sat by appointment.
Tickets €8 per person

Getting there and around

By air Shannon Airport is just into Co. Clare, 16 miles (26km) along the N18 northwest of Limerick. There are shuttle buses to the City (40 mins, *see* p.283). Information, **t** 1 890 742 6666, **t** 061 712 400
By bus Limerick's bus station for all services is on Parnell St. Bus Eireann, **t** (061) 474 311/313 333
By car Parking isn't easy in Limerick, and most of the city centre is a disc parking zone.

By train There are trains daily to Dublin, Cork, Waterford and Rosslare. Information **t** (061) 315 555.
Bike Hire
Emerald Cycles, 1 Patrick St, Limerick, **t** (061) 416 983

Entertainment

Belltable Arts Centre

69 O'Connell St, Limerick, **t** (061) 319 866
Open All year Mon–Fri 9–7, Sat 10–9

Limericks's main live arts centre hosts very good theatre and films, and a gallery of local artists.

Irish Rambling House

Sessions in various locations in Limerick and Adare, **t** (068) 48353, **www.irishramblinghouse.com**
Open Summer shows in different venues
Adm €12 show only, €30 show and dinner

Sample some traditional Irish entertainments with music, song, dance and storytelling.

Shopping

O'Mahony's Bookshop

120 O'Connell St, Limerick, **t** (061) 418 155
Open Mon–Wed, Fri–Sat 9–6, Thur 9–7

Ireland's oldest independent bookshop, a local institution which has lots for children and on local interests. Branches in Tralee and Ennis.

Special Events – County Limerick

August

All-Breeds Championship Dog Show, Fitzgerald's Woodlands House Hotel, Adare, **t** (061) 304 433

Dog-loving families will enjoy this event where over 2,500 dogs are judged.

October

Halloween Storyfest, Lough Gur Heritage Centre, information from HoneyFitz Theatre, **t** (061) 385 386

Storytelling, music and dancing.

LIMERICK CITY

Limerick is a city cloaked in the colour grey, from the stones of its dwellings to its Custom House where you'll find the impressive Hunt Museum beside the blue River Shannon. Founded in the 9th century by the Vikings, who originally named it *Laemrich*, 'rich soil or land', it is the Republic's third largest city. Having recently gained notoriety as the home of Frank McCourt, who wrote the autobiography *Angela's Ashes* that became a film about his poverty-stricken early days there, it still has the charm of the past lurking in its alleyways and streets. So go on a walking tour with your children, and investigate its historic sites. For some, the town's rugby ardour makes it Ireland's sports capital. For others, it is a regional entertainment centre with its heritage precinct, where you can visit the 'Treaty Stone', on which was signed the treaty that ended the bloody Jacobite-Williamite war in 1691 (*see* p.35), and visit King John's Castle.

Things to see and do

The Georgian House and Garden

2 Pery Square, **t** (061) 314 130
Getting there 5min walk from Tourist Office
Open Mon–Fri 10–4, other times by appointment
Adm Adult €4.45, 5–16s €1.90, under-4s free, family €12.70

A faithfully restored house with Georgian furnishings, architectural details and decorations.

The Hunt Museum

Custom House, Rutland St, **t** (061) 312 834
Open May–Oct Mon–Fri 10–5, Sun 2–5; Nov–Apr Tues–Sat 10–5, Sun 2–5, closed Mon
Adm Adult €5.70, 6–16s €2.80, under-5s free, family (2+5) €14

Art and artefacts from the Stone Age to the 20th century, donated by noted art historians and Celtic archaeologists John and Gertrude Hunt. Teenagers interested in art find its early Celtic brooches and medieval crucifix figures fascinating, and there's also a bronze horse by Leonardo da Vinci and a cross belonging to Mary, Queen of Scots.

King John's Castle

Nicholas St, King's Island, **t** (061) 360 788
Open Daily mid-Apr–Oct 9.30–4.30, Nov–Mar Mon–Sat 10.30–4.30, Sun 12–3 or by appointment, closed Good Friday and 24–26 Dec
Adm Adult €6.65, 6–18s €4, under-5s free, family (2+6) €16.70
Souvenir shop, tearoom, toilets with disabled access

There is a lot to see and explore in this authentic medieval castle, built between 1200 and 1210 and in the middle of Limerick's medieval heritage precinct. A state-of-the-art interpretative centre covers 800 years of local history from the 13th century onwards. The most family-friendly displays are reconstructions of medieval courtyards, crewed by actors demonstrating 16th-century trades. On other floors the castle's role in history is brought to life via audio-visual effects, 3-D images, models and displays of early weapons, as well as excavated Norman fortifications and houses. See what King John says about himself, and how he made his own coins, on your way up to the battlement walk-ways on top of the castle's walls and towers. Find out what soldiers used in battle before gunpowder and cannons were available, and explore the southwest tower to learn what happened here in the 17th century. You can also see the archaeological excavations below, which show that houses existed here before the castle was built.

A Limerick from Limerick, 1 –
A mouse in her room woke Miss Doud,
Who was frightened and screamed very loud,
Then a happy thought hit her,
To scare off the critter –
She sat up in bed and just meowed.

Can you spot?
Look out for the shapes of imaginary animals like the griffin and cockatrice on the 15th-century choir stalls in St Mary's Cathedral.

Limerick Museum

Castle Lane, off Nicholas St, **t** (061) 417 826
Open Tues–Sat 10–1 and 2.15–5. **Adm** Free

This museum won the first Gulbenkian award in 1992. It sits beside King John's Castle and houses Neolithic, Bronze and Iron Age artefacts and fragments of Limerick's civic and natural history, archaeology and traditional lace and silver crafts.

St Mary's Cathedral

Bridge St, **t** (061) 416 238
Adm Donation

Built in 1172 by the King of Munster, Donal Mor O'Brien, this is both the oldest and the last ancient church left in Limerick City, and its most architecturally important building.

SPECIAL TRIPS

Celtic Park and Gardens

Cloonagulleen, Kilcornan, **t** (061) 394 243
Getting there Off the N69 10 miles (17km) west of Limerick and 5 miles (8km) northwest of Adare
Open Daily mid-Mar–Oct 9.30–6, other times by appointment
Adm Adult €5, free for up to 4 children under 12, family (2+4 children under 12) €10
Tearoom, bookshop, free car and coach parking

Visit this landscaped garden and see whether you can tell the difference between the original and reconstructed Celtic buildings here. Sited on one of Cromwell's plantations, this is an excellent place to teach children something about Ireland's ancient buildings – with a lake dwelling (*crannóg*), ring fort, communal tomb and stone church along with a dolmen, stone circle, mass rock, cooking site, lime kiln and holy well, dotted within the beautiful gardens. End the day well by walking among the rockeries, lily ponds and roses in the ornamental garden and having tea amid beautiful views.

Lough Gur Heritage Centre

Ballyneety, **t** (061) 360 788,
www.shannonheritage.com
Getting there 12 miles (19km) south of Limerick
Open Daily May–end-Sept 9.30–5.30
Adm Adult €4.20, child €2.40, family (2+4) €10.50
Guided tours available, visitor centre, audio-visual

This outdoor park on the shore of Lough Gur is possibly the most important Stone Age site in Ireland. The exhibition explores the history of the area over the last 5,000 years. At the ends of the horseshoe-shaped lake are two castles built by the Earls of Desmond. Around them lie the remnants of stone circles, including the 4,000-year-old Grange Stone Circle, which has 113 stones and may be the largest in Ireland. There are also standing stones, wedge-shaped cairns, a ring fort, Neolithic house and a *crannóg*. Visit reconstructions of the ritual, burial and dwelling places of this region's first farmers. Wear good shoes and rainwear, as the pathways can get muddy.

AROUND AND ABOUT

Animal magic

Buttercup Farm

Ballygrennan, Croom, **t** (061) 397 556
Getting there 18 miles (29km) south of Limerick

Meet lambs, rabbits, pigs, peacocks and other farm animals at this old-fashioned farm. It offers a tree trail, nature quiz and picnic area.

Bricks and mortar

Glin Castle

Glin, **t** (068) 34173 **www.glincastle.com**
Getting there 31 miles (50km) west of Limerick
Open Mar–Oct 10.30–3.30, strictly by appointment
Adm Castle and gardens, €7 per person
Guided tours every half hour

This Georgian Gothic castle is the ancestral home of the Knights of Glin, part of the Fitzgerald family. A walled garden with fruit, herbs and vegetables slopes beyond the romantic house, where a few guests can stay. The splendid Gothic-styled grounds feature a headless Ariadne statue in a rustic temple, a yew tree walk and hens roaming freely.

Croom Mills Visitor and Heritage Centre

Croom, **t** (061) 397 130, **www.croommills.com**
Getting there 18 miles (29km) south of Limerick
Open Exhibition: all year 9–5, Shop and bistro: daily 9–6, Restaurant: Thurs–Sat 5–9.30. **Adm** free
Crafts and gift shop, restaurants, parking

An old grain mill – with a huge 16-foot-diameter cast-iron waterwheel built in 1852 and a 1900s steam engine – has been restored and converted into this centre, where you can meet the descendants of local people who once worked it. First watch the film on the history of Croom Mills, then explore the mill itself, with interactive exhibits that enable visitors to get involved in the corn-grinding process. Children can try turning a heavy stone quern and touching freshly milled grain as it is prepared via methods used more than a century ago. Afterwards, stroll along the Maigue river and return to the mill's restaurant for a home-baked meal. Sunday lunches are especially good.

De Valera Museum and Bruree Heritage Centre

Bruree, **www.bruree.net**
Getting there 30 miles (48km) south of Limerick off N20 Cork road
Open Mon–Fri 10–5, Sat–Sun 2–5. **Adm** free

Older children may be interested in this museum, in the National School attended by the late president of Ireland, Eamon de Valera (1882–1975). He was born in Manhattan, New York, to a Spanish father and an Irish mother. Following the death of his father, when Eamon was only two, he was sent to live in Ireland with his grand-

A Limerick from Limerick, 2 –
A landlady mean in Ardee,
Served little of honey at tea.
A new lodger said,
As he shook a sad head,
'I'm glad, Ma'am, to see you've one bee."

mother. As an adult, De Valera became a maths teacher, then joined the Gaelic League and became a lifeling champion of the Irish language. There are displays of his belongings and articles recording life in Bruree in the early 20th century. The cottage where De Valera spent his youth is nearby.

Tarbert Bridewell Courthouse and Jail

Tarbert, **t** (068) 36500
Getting there 38 miles (58km) west of Limerick on the N69
Open Daily Apr–Oct 10–6, other times by appointment
Adm Adult €5, 4–12s €2.50, under-4s free, family (2+4) €10.50
Coffee and gift shops, ample parking

This restored jail of 1831 gives an insight into the harsh penal system in Ireland in the 1830s and recreates the atmosphere of those tough times. Dummies in period dress with recorded voices and sounds of the time bring to life the experiences of the inhabitants of these tiny jail cells.

Look at this!

Flying Boat Museum

Foynes, **t** (069) 65416
Getting there On N69 23 miles (37km) west of Limerick
Open Mar–Oct 10–6, last entry 5.15
Adm Adult €4.50, 6–14s €2.50, under-6s free, family (2+4) €12
Tearoom, gift shop, free car and coach parking

A fascinating museum focusing on the famous seaplane airliners of the 1930s. Flying boats were used to carry all kinds of passengers, from celebrities to refugees, and this port beside the Atlantic was a stopping-off and refuelling point for air traffic between the US and Europe from the 1920s to the 1940s. 'Irish coffee', it is said, was created here to comfort cold passengers. Older children may be intrigued by the radio and weather room with original transmitters for Morse code, and the 1940s-style cinema with original footage.

Nature lovers

Ballyhoura Mountain Park

Kilfinane, Golden Vale
Getting there N20 south from Limerick to Killmallock, then southeast to Kilfinane (35 miles/56km)
Open All year
Interpretive panels, marked walking routes, fitness and orienteering routes, car parking

There is enjoyable birdwatching and walking in this natural woodland area covering approximately 25,000 acres. Within it there are mountains, peat bogs, wild berries and flowers, and it also has waymarked trails and nature walks.

Sporty kids

Horse riding

Clonshire Equestrian Centre

Adare, **t** (061) 396 770

A friendly and well-equipped riding centre.

Hillcrest Riding Centre

Galbally, **t** (062) 37915

Choose from cross-country, show jumping and trekking. See the Glen Of Aherlow on horseback on the new Ballyhoura/Glen of Aherlow Trail.

Walking

Knockfierna Hill

Getting there 6 miles (10km) southwest of Croom, 24 miles (39km) from Limerick

This hill is the home of the Tuatha Dé Danaan King of the Otherworld, whose name is Donn Forinne. A vast expanse of Ireland can be viewed from its summit, including the Shannon Estuary and the distant Blue Mountains. This is also the home of the National Famine Commemoration Park, and it contains 15 buildings associated with the famine; ask for directions in Ballingarry.

COUNTY CLARE

The Irish say that if you turn over a rock in County Clare (*Conndae an Chlair/An Clár*, 'a level surface or plain'), there's a story under it. It wouldn't be a surprise if music didn't sing out from under it as well. Near the Cliffs of Moher, Doolin has a fine tradition of Irish music and Ennis is home to the *Fleadh Nua*, an annual celebration of folk music.

Clare is a wonderful big-sky kind of place. Here, bird colonies can be observed off Loop Head in shale rock 'apartments', each inhabited every summer by the same bird until it dies. Dolphins leap in Kilrush Harbour for no reason at all, apparently, but to show themselves to a dying child whose foremost wish is to see a real dolphin, as I saw happen. A gentler kind of people inhabit this county, where protests about chopping down a faery tree in Ennis forced the council to reroute a new highway. Such occurrences are common in Clare, perhaps because its people's imaginations still dance with the natural world around them.

From the seaside towns of the west and castles of the south to the rugged Burren and Cliffs of Moher, there is remarkably good pasture in Clare. Numerous lakes and turloughs (lakes or ponds that disappear in dry periods) lie in land that's often fissured limestone, or a treeless terrain weathered to form peat bogs and rush-infested pastures.

Cromwell dismissed the Burren as 'a country where there is not water enough to drown a man, wood enough to hang one, or earth enough to bury him'. But there is a peace in Clare, especially in the Burren, that cannot be created by anything but nature, something the Cromwells (and faerytree choppers) of this world may not even notice.

Tourist Information

Bunratty, **t** (061) 360133
Cliffs of Moher, Liscannor, **t** (065) 708 1171
Ennis, Arthur's Row, off O'Connell St, **t** (065) 682 8366
Lahinch, **t** (065) 708 2082
Kilkee, The Square, **t** (065) 905 6112
Kilrush, Town Hall, **t** (065) 905 1577
Shannon Airport, **t** (061) 471664

Getting there and around

By air Shannon Airport is 13 miles (21km) from Ennis along the N18 towards Limerick (*see* p.283). Information, **t** 1 890 742 6666, **t** 061 712 400

By bus Most buses leave from alongside Ennis train station, with regular connections to Shannon airport, Limerick, Galway and Dublin. There are a few buses daily to Lahinch and Doolin, Lisdoonvarna and the Cliffs of Moher.
Bus Information, Ennis, **t** (065) 682 4177, or Burren Coaches, **t** (065) 707 8009

By train Ennis is on the Galway–Limerick rail line and many trains continue on to Dublin.

By boat The Clare–Kerry ferry runs from Killimer to Tarbert: Shannon Ferries, **t** (065) 905 3124.

Bike Hire

Burren Cycling Holidays, t (065) 707 4300
David Monks, Monks Bar, Ballyvaughan, **t** (065) 707 7059
Gleeson's Cycles, Henry St, Kilrush, **t** (065) 905 1127
Irish Cycle Hire, Ennis Station, **t** (065) 682 1992
Shannon Cycle Hire, Bunratty, **t** (061) 364 696
Williams Rent-a-Bike, Kilkee, **t** (065) 905 6141

Special Events – County Clare

May

Fleadh Nua, Ennis, **t** (065) 684 0406, **www.fleadhnua.com**

A festival of traditional music, dancing and singing that takes over the whole town for a week.

June

Shannon Dolphin Festival, Kilrush, **t** (065) 905 2522

Live street theatre for all the family.

July

Feile Brian Boru, Killaloe, **t** (061) 376 866

Weekend of music, song, parades, dancing and barbecues to honour the reign of Brian Boru.

Willie Clancy Summer School, Milltown Mowbay, **t** (065) 708 4281

Concerts and workshops in Irish traditional music and dance are held as a tribute to Ireland's greatest uillean piper, Willie Clancy (1921–73).

August

Carrigaholt Family Festival, Carrigaholt, **t** (065) 905 8186

There's a fun fair, fancy-dress parade and other entertainments for the whole family.

September

Matchmaking Festival of Ireland, Lisdoonvarna (late Sept–early Oct), **t** (065) 707 4005, **www.matchmakerireland.com**

Single women come all the way from America for the fun; Mr Lisdoonvarna and the Queen of the Burren are the stars of the show.

ENNIS

Clare's county town straddles the River Fergus (*Inis* means an islet or river meadow). A market town dating back to the 11th century, it's famous today for traditional music. It's a friendly town whose historic buildings and narrow streets, not to mention its inhabitants, give it great charm. In the centre is a memorial to Daniel O'Connell, and another to Eamon de Valera, who represented Clare in the Irish Parliament from 1918 to 1959.

Things to see and do

Ennis Friary

Abbey St, **t** (065) 682 9100
Open Daily mid-Jun–Sept 9.30–6.30

The O'Briens, Kings of Thomond, founded this 13th-century Fransciscan friary, now in ruins.

The Riches of Clare

Clare Museum, Arthur's Row, off O'Connell Square, **t** (065) 682 3382
Open Jan–Feb Mon–Fri 9.30–1, 2–5.30, Mar–May and Oct, Dec Mon–Sat 9.30–1, 2–5.30, Jun–Sept daily 9.30–5.30. **Adm** Adult €3.80, child €1.90

Housed in a former convent built in 1861, this museum tells the story of Co. Clare from 6,000 years ago to the present day. There are impressive historical artefacts, imagery, special effects and original works of art, all organized along themes of Earth, Power, Faith and Water.

SPECIAL TRIPS

Bunratty Castle and Folk Park

t (061) 360 788, **www.**shannonheritage.com
Getting there 8 miles (13km) from Limerick off the N18 to Shannon and Ennis
Open Sept–May castle 9.30–4, park 9.30–5.30, Jun–Aug both 9–6.30, closed Good Fri, 24–26 Dec
Adm May–Sept, adult €9.50, under-18s €5, family (2+ up to 6) €25, Oct–Apr, adult €8, under-18s €4.70, family €22
Tearoom, shop, Irish Nights Apr–Oct at 7pm and Medieval Castle Banquets twice nightly, at 5.30 and 8.45pm, year-round subject to demand

If you arrive in Ireland at Shannon, this is one of your first must-sees. It's a microcosm of Irish history with a replica 19th-century Irish village, complete with people dressed as Irish country folk used to 100 years ago. There are eight farmhouses, two watermills, a blacksmith's forge and a church, plus a pub, post office, school, doctor's house, hardware shop, printers, drapery store, pawn shop and hotel, whose informative attendants will tell you all about their work and times.

The exhibits are as authentic as possible – roofs are thatched and stone walls are white-washed – and you may see animals and fields being tended as they were before the days of machines, or milk being churned and bread baked over an open fire.

Children can go even farther back into history by investigating the tower house known as Bunratty Castle, built in 1425 by the MacNamara clan. It has been magnificently restored so that visitors can imagine what it was like to live in such a place, with its dungeon, great hall and huge kitchen. To really appreciate its past, you must indulge in the castle's medieval banquet, where you are treated to a sumptuous feast while being enchanted by the songs and stories of the Bunratty Entertainers. The early feast at 5.30 would most suit children.

The Burren

In the north of Clare is one of Ireland's most rare and magical landscapes – the Burren ('the stony district'), a giant limestone plateau. Apparently barren, the Burren is full of life amid its strangely-shaped rocks, with ancient ruins, old villages, animals and an amazing range of scented plants.

Aillwee Cave

The Burren, Ballyvaughan, **t** (065) 707 7036, **www.**aillweecave.ie
Getting there 23 miles (37km) north of Ennis
Open Jul–Aug 10–6.30, Sept–Jun 10–5.30, Nov–Feb, 3 tours daily
Adm Adults €7.50, 4–14s €4.50, under-3s free, family (2+2) €21, (2+4) €24, cheese tour €2
Guided tours, tearoom, farm shop, parking

The Burren has the most important and extensive cave systems in Ireland, but only one is safe enough for the general public to explore (with a guide). Aillwee Cave was formed millions of years ago by an underground river that cut through the limestone left behind after the Ice Age. Older children who have never been inside a cave will enjoy seeing the rock formations caused by dripping water, and the hibernation indentations caused by brown bears sleeping there through long winters.

After exploring the cold grey hollows of the underworld, you can eat a baked potato back on ground level in the café and shop for minerals or fossils. Outdoors you can picnic or climb over the Burren limestone pavements, or walk in coppice woods on a nature trail. After that pay a visit to the dairy and watch cheese being made or honey extracted from combs, then try fudge or chutney made in the farm kitchen. It's important that your children are not afraid of the dark, as the tour is quite slow. Have a warm jumper to hand too.

The Burren Centre

Kilfenora, **t** (065) 708 8030,
www.theburrencentre.ie
Getting there 15 miles (24km) from Ennis on R476
Open Daily Mar–May, Sept–Oct 10–5, Jun–Aug 9.30–6
Adm Adult €5, 5-12s €3, under-4s free, family (2+2) €15
Guided tours on request, shop, tearoom, toilets with disabled and baby-changing facilities, garden

Here in the village that has more Celtic crosses than you can shake at a Druid, you will find one of the most thoughtfully planned and impressive small museums in Ireland. Discover how 350 million years of life on earth have shaped the limestone of the Burren. Fascinating exhibits explain its archaeology, flora, fauna, geography and geology and the effects of people on the landscape.

Most notable are the history sections, with life-size models showing ancient Irish people in their habitats, plus atmospheric sound recordings of traditional music and local folk stories recounted by children. Don't miss this centre if you want to appreciate the Burren and its unique features.

Burren Exposure Exhibition

Whitethorn, outside Ballyvaughan, **t** (065) 707 7277, **www.**burrenexposure.com
Getting there 23 miles (37km) north of Ennis
Open Week before Easter–Oct daily 10–6
Adm Adult €4.45, child €2, family €13

Three rooms show videos explaining how the Burren was formed, which plants grow there and when its various manmade structures were erected. It's a good introduction for older children: the approachable, friendly attendants are very knowledgeable. For example, they explain that a governmental drive to stop farmers grazing cattle on the Burren's flowers is, in fact, allowing brambles to grow more, inhibiting wildflower growth.

Burren Perfumery and Floral Centre

Carran, **t** (065) 708 9102,
www.burrenperfumery.com
Getting there 14 miles 22km) north of Ennis
Open Daily Mar–Jun, Sept–Oct 9.30–5, Jul–Aug 9–7, Nov–Feb open most days but phone first
Adm Free

This small centre now imports its floral essences due to new laws on the local environment, but you can watch an audio-visual exhibit on the history of perfume-making in the Burren. Then head outside to visit the essential oil distillery and the garden.

Gregan's Wood

Getting there On N67 between Lisdoonvarna and Ballyvaughan

A gold mine for amateur archaeologists, as you'll find cairns, ring forts, megalithic tombs and the like everywhere. It's also a great look out over the Burren, and the surrounding hills are good for fishing, swimming and walking.

Poulnabrone Portal Dolmen

Getting there 5 miles (8km) south of Ballyvaughan on the R480 road

This 5,000-year-old portal tomb was excavated in 1986 and is one of Ireland's finest dolmens. It's a huge three-legged tomb, standing alone on the rocky landscape.

The Salmon of Knowledge Experience

Burren Smokehouse, Lisdoonvarna, **t** (065) 707 4432, **www.**burrensmokehouse.ie
Getting there 20 miles (32km) from Ennis on R476
Open All year daily 9–7. **Adm** Free
Visitor centre, exhibition, audio-visual tour, crafts and gourmet food store and pub, parking

This is worth visiting to hear the story of the 'Salmon of Knowledge' (*see* p.29) and learn about the ancient Irish custom of oak-smoking salmon.

Craggaunowen – The Living Past

Quin, **t** (061) 360 788, **www.**shannonheritage.com
Getting there 10 miles (16km) east of Ennis
Open Daily Apr–Oct 10–6 (call ahead, as dates may vary), last adm 5pm. **Adm** Adult €7, child €4.20
Guided tours, teashop, craft shop, picnic areas

The past is brought to life at this award-winning museum on all aspects of Celtic life. Guides in authentic period shoes and rough-hewn costumes demonstrate the daily work of the people who lived in Ireland 1,000 years ago. They know all sorts of fascinating details, like how to spin wool or dry animal skins, or make Celtic crosses out of reeds. You may get the chance to do some of these things yourselves. Imagine what it was like to be a Celtic chieftain, peeking at intruders through the stick walls of a *crannóg* (lake dwelling). See a ring fort and Iron Age roadway, and learn how Finn McCool and the Fianna cooked whole deer in man-made pools filled with hot stones. Look around to spy on the Soay and Jacob sheep, Kerry cattle and tusked, wild Irish boars (cordoned off behind a fence).

Don't miss 'The Brendan' – the recreation of a leather curragh used in the 6th century by St Brendan the Navigator and other Irish mariners on the high seas. In 1980s the late Tim Severin sailed in it to North America to show that St Brendan could, indeed, have reached America first, long before the Vikings. When you've finished walking through the ancient woods, pay a visit to the shop and the cottage coffee shop, with a traditional decorated hearth, for an excellent Irish afternoon tea. Be sure to telephone Craggaunowen before you go, to ask for their best guide for children.

A story to tell:
The Way to Sing a Song

One twilight, a hunchback who had been watching over sheep all day heard strange high-pitched singing in the wind, as if from far, far away. He followed the sound towards a faery hill. And he saw an orange-gold light shining out from it, as if from the last rays of the evening sun.

As he ventured nearer, the words of the song became clearer. Many voices seemed to be singing, in Irish, 'Monday, Tuesday, Wednesday', over and over again. Then he saw them – the Little People, the Sidhe – all merrily repeating the verse as they danced around together in swirls of colour.

After a time, he thought maybe the Sidhe didn't know the next day of the week and so, to help them, he took his courage into his voice and sang, 'Monday, Tuesday, Wednesday, Thursday', adding a new twist in the melody for good measure.

Suddenly all was silent. The hunchback broke into a cold sweat. What would they do to him, he wondered? Then the voices sang again, adding his melody and 'Thursday' to their song, immediately after which he found himself surrounded by them.

A tiny, elegant fellow with a golden crown strode up. 'Thank you, kind sir, for your addition to our song. We have been singing it for hundreds of years and couldn't find the next bit of it.'

Another little plump man piped up, 'Do you think you could add something more to it for us?'

'Certain so', replied the hunchback, singing, 'Monday, Tuesday, Wednesday, Thursday, Friday', adding yet another melody to the end, which was repeated by the faery people, who cheered and tossed the hunchback into the air.

The next thing he knew, it was pitch dark and he was alone and there were millions of diamond stars smiling down on him from the night sky. He rose quickly, thinking he must have fallen asleep and dreamt of the faeries, worrying where his sheep were. But somehow he felt lighter, straighter – yes, for the first time in his life he was standing up straight! He rubbed his back where his familiar hump always was and – it was gone!

The hunchback's story spread, and another hunchback heard it. Determined to find these faeries and get them to take away his hump, he arrived at the faery hill one afternoon, muttering that the faeries were taking their sweet time arriving. Finally, at twilight, he heard them singing their song, with the other hunchback's melody. This went on and on til he could stand it no longer and finally burst out, 'Would ye stop your infernal racket! It's Saturday and Sunday next!'

Again, there was silence. Only this time the song was not sung again and the hunchback was surrounded by hundreds of tiny angry faces. The fellow with the crown rushed up to him and said, 'How dare you disturb our songmaking!'

The plump one added, 'Would you mind adding a tune to that Saturday and Sunday of yours?'

'If you'll take off this hump of mine, I will,' sneered the hunchback.

At that point he was thrown into the air, and the next thing he knew it was night and thick clouds were dripping rain upon him. He found he could barely stand at all, so heavy had his hump become. And, when he rubbed the usual spot where it ached, he found he had two humps instead of one!

Scattery Island dolphin tours

Scattery Island Ferries/Gerald Griffin Boat Tours
The Marina, Kilrush, **t** (065) 905 1327
Getting there 27 miles (43km) from Ennis by N68
Open Summer season; call at other times
Adm Dolphin watching: adult €14, under-16s €7; Scattery Island Ferry, adult €8, under-16s €6

Boat hire and cruises from here take you dolphin-watching or out to Scattery Island's monastic sites; call for sailing times. Ferries run from Kilrush Creek Marina to the uninhabited island in the Lower Shannon, weather permitting. There are 3–4 trips per day in peak season, but booking is advisable.

There is something very special about seeing dolphins frolicking in the waves around Scattery Island with its ruined churches, round tower and lighthouse. The boat's friendly crew can tell you all about Ireland's only known resident group of bottlenose dolphins. This Shannon Estuary haven allows more than 100 to breed each year, between May and August. Even getting through the elaborate locks from the bay into the Atlantic is exciting to those unused to such things, on a rough day with thick foam on the water. Once the dolphins see your boat, they may swim alongside it.

Scattery Island Centre

Merchants Quay, Kilrush, **t** (65) 905 2139
Open Daily Jun–mid-Sept 10–1, 2–6. **Adm** Free

In the 6th century, St Senan defeated a horrible monster on an island called *Inis Cathaig*, and founded a monastery on the same spot. It was destroyed in times of Elizabeth I, when the island became known as Scattery Island, and a castle was built there. Today you can see the ruins of the monastery, seven churches and a round tower.

Did you know?
Lisdoonvarna has the only active spa, from iron and magnesium springs, in Ireland. Because of this farmers long came to relax here when they finished harvesting each year, and here they looked for wives. The tradition by which women and men of marriageable age were 'matched' by a matchmaker was common in Ireland until quite recently, and still thrives at the matchmaking festival held every September in Lisdoonvarna.

AROUND AND ABOUT

Bricks and mortar

Dysert O'Dea Castle and Clare Archaeology Centre

Corofin, **t** (065) 683 7722/683 7401
Getting there 5 miles (8km) north of Ennis
Open Daily May–Sept 10–6, other times by appointment
Adm Adult €3.81, child €1.91, family €8.89
History trail, 1–3 hr guided walks, shop, tearoom

Follow the archaeology trail to find out more about the history of this 15th-century castle. Under the 12th-century Dysert O'Dea Church sits an early Christian monastery founded by St Tola in the 8th century. With an illustrated guide from the shop kids can have fun tracking 25 historical and archaeological sites within 2 miles (3km) of the castle.

Knappogue Castle

Quin, **t** Bunratty Folk Park: (061) 360 788, **www.shannonheritage.com**
Getting there 8 miles (13km) east of Ennis
Open Daily Apr–Oct 9.30–5
Adm adults €4.20, child €2.40
Craft shop, picnic area, toilets with disabled access

An audio-visual display tells the story of this 15th-century castle. There are medieval banquets twice nightly April–Oct, subject to demand, similar to those at Bunratty (*see* p.141). Knappogue's speciality is a show with music, song and dance about famous women of Ireland through the ages.

Nature lovers

Cliffs of Moher (Ailltreacha Mothair)

Visitor Centre, **t** (065) 81171
Getting there 20 miles (32km) northwest of Ennis
Open Site all year; Visitor Centre, Sept–May 9.30–5.30, Jun–29 Aug: 9–8; O'Brien's Tower, Mar–Oct (weather permitting) 9.30–6

You can't visit Clare without seeing the Cliffs of Moher – but hold on to young children, as it's a dangerous area beyond the fences, especially when winds are high. These dramatic 600ft cliffs, confronting the might of the Atlantic Ocean, are horizontal layers of flagstones that extend for 5 miles (8km) from Hag's Head to beyond O'Brien's Tower. Hag's Head resembles a seated woman looking out to sea, and is linked with the story of an old witch named Mal of Malbay at Loop Head.

Aill na Searrach (Cliff of the Colts) is the northernmost point of the Cliffs. It is linked with a story about some colts of faery origin that leaped over the cliffs to the sea. To view the cliffs, walkers should start at O'Brien's Tower. Watch for ravens and the puffins (with highly coloured beaks) that nest on Goat Island and near the Tower.

Loop Head Birdwatching

NatureQuest Centre, Kilkee, **t** (065) 905 6789
www.naturequest.ie
Getting there 36 miles (57km) northwest of Ennis
Call to arrange guided tour; booking essential

NatureQuest's proprietor, Kilrush lawyer Eugene O'Kelly, has lived in this part of the world all his life and knows the secrets of its terrain, history and people extremely well. Nature lovers can go on field trips to look at the abundant birdlife, animals, and geology of the Loop Head peninsula. Day trips can be arranged. Take warm clothing and good shoes; children need to be watched closely near Loop Head's unfenced cliff edges, as they are highly dangerous due to their geology and high winds.

Sporty kids

Boat trips

Dolphinwatch

Carrigaholt, **t** (065) 905 8156
Operates Apr–Oct, but always book in advance

Two-hour cruises from the old fishing port of Carrigaholt, between Kilrush and Loop Head. The boat is custom-built for watching the dolphins of the Shannon and eavesdropping on their conversations (via a hydrophone). An evening cruise goes around Loop Head to observe dolphins, sea-birds and cliffs, and early morning trips are available.

Shannon Castle Line

Williamstown Harbour, Killaloe, **t** (061) 927 042,
www.shannoncruisers.com

Daily sailing in summer from Killaloe on the Shannon and Lough Derg on a 48-seat river bus.

Buckets and spades – Clare's Beaches

Clare has both sea- and freshwater beaches.
Lahinch (16 miles/26km northwest of Ennis) is a popular seaside resort with a fine, Blue-Flag beach, good surfing and a fun-packed leisure centre with a sealife centre and indoor full-size and kids' pools.
Other Blue Flag beaches: at **Kilkee**, **White Strand**, **Spanish Point** (Milltown Malbay), **Lough Graney**, **Fanore** and **Doonbeg**.
Freshwater swimming: **Lough Derg** is the largest and of the River Shannon's lakes, and at Killaloe (*see* below) there are several points where you can swim (children should always be supervised).

Horse riding

Burren Riding Centre

Fanore, t (065) 707 6140

Clare Equestrian Centre

Deerpark, Doora, near Clarecastle, **t** (065) 684 0136

A well-organized centre with ponies for children.

Walking

The **Burren Way** stretches 20 miles (32km) west of Ballyvaughan over the Burren to the Cliffs of Moher, with superb ocean views. Other fine walks are at **Ballyalla Lake**, near Ennis, **Ballycuggaran**, north of Killaloe on the Shannon, and **Doon Lough**, between Ennis and Lough Derg.

Burren Hill Walks, Ballyvaughan, **t** (065) 707 7168

Able guides lead a varied range of walks.

Water sports

Killaloe (Shannonside) Activity Centre

Killaloe, **t** (061) 376 622

A centre custom-built for a big range of land- and water-based activities. Special weeks are organized in summer for different age groups.

Steam power

West Clare Railway

Moyasta Junction, **t** (065) 905 6789
Getting there On the N67 Killrush to Killkee Road
Open Daily 10–6, otherwise by appointment
Tickets Adult €6, child €3, free in Sept

A narrow-gauge steam locomotive, the No.5 Slieve Callan, runs for 3 miles (5km) through an area rich in birdlife. Please call at the adjoining Taylor's Pub before entering the site.

TIPPERARY AND WATERFORD

County Tipperary is known for horses and lakes. It's perfect for a quieter family holiday – just far enough from cities to avoid traffic, yet close enough to popular tourist sites in nearby counties. A riding tour with overnight stays planned in advance is a pleasant, leisurely way to holiday here, but if you prefer to see sights, Tipperary's rambling country roads are ideal for touring unhurriedly by car, and Bus Eireann also offers many bus tours.

Lough Derg is a pleasant spot for a boating trip. With an abundance of salmon, trout, roach, bream, perch, pike and eels, it's also an angler's paradise. Other fine places to visit are Cashel, with the Rock of Cashel as its centerpiece; the village of Bansha, for horse lovers; the Glen of Aherlow, if you prefer forest views, or Cahir, a characterful market town.

Just to the south, the rather flat southeastern county of Waterford is known for its scenic coast and fishing villages. Within it is one of the most famous and most curious Irish-speaking areas of Ireland – far away from other such areas on the west coast – An Rinn (Ring), south of Dungarvan on Helvick Head. Noteworthy for being the first part of Ireland to have a city established by the Vikings, County Waterford has a history beset with invasions, thanks to the easy access its geography gives to seafarers. Interestingly, once people settled here, they became very peaceful – a quality you will find today throughout Waterford.

Tourist Information

Ardmore, Co. Waterford, **t** (024) 94444
Cahir, Co. Tipperary: Castle St, **t** (052) 41453
Cashel, Co. Tipperary: Main St, **t** (062) 61333
Clonmel, Co. Tipperary: Sarsfield St, **t** (052) 22960
Dungarvan, Co. Waterford: The Square, **t** (058) 41741
Lismore, Co. Waterford, **t** (058) 54975
Nenagh, Co. Tipperary: Connolly St **t** (067) 31610
Tramore, Co. Waterford: Railway Square, **t** (051) 381 572, **www**.tramore.ie
Waterford, 41 The Quay, **t** (051) 875 823, **www**.waterfordvisitorcentre.com

Tours

Walking Tours of Historic Waterford, Waterford Tourist Services, Jenkins Lane, **t** (051) 873 711
Guided tours daily Mar–Oct at 12 noon and 2pm

Local historian and storyteller Jack Burtchaell takes you through the history of his home town and Ireland's oldest city. The 1hr tour brings to life the town's 'gallery of rogues and rascals' and departs from the Waterford Treasures Museum.

Getting there and around

By air Waterford has an airport, 8 miles (13km) south of the town on the road to Clohernagh (*see* pp.280, 284). Information, **t** 051 875 589, **www**.flywaterford.com.

By bus There are frequent Bus Eireann buses from Dublin and Cork to Tipperary, Cashel, Waterford and other towns. From Cashel, Kavanagh's, **t** (062) 51563, runs other local services.

In Waterford, most buses leave from the Quay opposite the tourist office; as well as Bus Eireann services, Suirway, **t** (051) 382 422, runs buses to places all along the River Suir. Bus Eireann in Waterford, **t** (051) 879 000.

By train The Dublin–Cork line passes through Tipperary, and Waterford has frequent trains on the Dublin–Kilkenny and Rosslare/Wexford–Cork lines. Tor Tipperary town trains stop at Limerick junction, a few miles north. Local information, Tipperary, **t** (062) 51206, Waterford, **t** (051) 873 401.

Bike Hire

The Raleigh Rent-a-Bike network operates via:
Altitude Cycle and Outdoor, 22 Ballybricken, Waterford, **t** (051) 870 356/850 228
Classic Cycles, 8 Mary St, Clonmel, Co. Tipperary, **t** (052) 27827
McInerneys, Cashel, Co. Tipperary, **t** (062) 61225
Murphy's Toys and Cycles, Main St, Dungarvan, Co. Waterford, **t** (058) 41376

Entertainment

Brú Ború Heritage Centre

Beside the Rock of Cashel, Cashel, Co. Tipperary, **t** (062) 61122, **www**.comhaltas.com
Open Mid-Jun–mid-Sept Tue–Sat 9–6, evening performance at 9pm, pre-show dinner at 7.30pm
Adm Free, shows individually priced

Comhaltas Ceoltóirí Éireann runs a traditional Irish music and dance show here every summer. At other times it is a centre for the study of Irish traditions. A recent addition is a visit to subterranean chambers running 7 miles (11km) underground at the base of the Rock of Cashel.

Waterford Show

City Hall, The Mall, Waterford, **t** (051) 381 020
Performances 4 May–Sept Tue, Thur, Sat 8.45pm, plus Wed July–Aug. **Adm** €12 per person

Older children might enjoy this presentation of the story of Waterford in a historic setting. Performers in Georgian costume sing and dance in a comic tale full of Irish music and folklore.

Special Events – Tipperary and Waterford

February

Merriman Winter School, Dungarvan, Co. Waterford, **t** (098) 27758, **www**.merriman.ie

Celebrates all aspects of Irish culture.

April

Sean Dunne Literary Festival, Waterford, **t** (051) 309 983

Readings, workshops and music to celebrate the works of Waterford's writers.

June

Clonmel Show, Clonmel, Co. Tipperary, **t** (052) 22611

A lively horse show, with showjumping.

July

Cashel Cultural Festival, Cashel, Co. Tipperary, **t** (052) 22611

Families will enjoy this arts-based town festival.

Munster Fleadh Cheoil, Co. Tipperary, **t** (01) 280 0295

Traditional Irish music, song and dance festival for families, held in a range of venues.

Kilcommon Festival, Kilcommon, Co. Tipperary, **t** (062) 78103

An 8-day affair in the rural highlands between Nenagh and Thurles: traditional music and dance, Gaelic games, sheepdog trials and street entertainment make it fun for all the family.

August

Aonach Paddy O'Brien, Newtown, Co. Tipperary, **t** (067) 42900

Traditional music and arts festival, named after a local composer and accordionist.

Spraoi Street Festival, Waterford, **t** (051) 841 808

'Ireland's biggest street festival', held in Waterford town for the whole of the bank holiday weekend in August.

September–October

Waterford International Festival of Light Opera, Theatre Royal, Waterford **t** (051) 357 437, **www**.operafestival.com

A charming festival of high quality music.

TOURING TOWNS

Cashel

Once the home of the High Kings of Munster, Cashel is just small enough to be manageable for those who want to explore an Irish town in a day. Take a tram tour from the Cashel Heritage Centre and visit the Rock of Cashel and Cashel Folk Village. There are several other attractions within easy reach and it's a good place to take a break if you're driving from Dublin to Cork – and don't forget to try some Cashel Blue cheese too.

Things to see and do

Cashel Folk Village

Dominic St, **t** (062) 62525

Open Daily Mar–Apr 10–6, May–Oct 9.30–7

Adm Adult €4.40, child €1.90, family €10.10

Guided tour available, wheelchair access

Behind a wall near the Rock of Cashel lies a reconstruction of a group of traditional thatched shops, a forge and other businesses complete with old signs and historical displays. At Dominic's Well you can wish yourself back in time or visit Widow Breen's House and the Wild Rover Pub. Find out how old tools were used in the Trades Hall and try out a Tinker's Caravan, then learn about the famine before meditating in the movable chapel that was hidden from official view in Penal times.

Cashel Heritage Centre/Tram Tour

Town Hall, **t** (062) 62511

Open Daily Mar–June 9.30–5.30, July–Aug 9.30–8, Sept–Feb Mon–Fri 9.30–5.30, Sat–Sun on request; tram operates Jun–Sept

Adm Adult €1.27, child €0.63 cents, famly €3.81

Disabled access

A large-scale model of Cashel dominates this centre, which tells you the history of this ancient site. The royal relics of the MacCarthy Mur kings are on permanent display, alongside changing exhibitions on the area. The Heritage Tram takes guided tours of Cashel's many historic sights.

Rock of Cashel

Cashel, **t** (062) 61437

Open Daily mid-Mar–mid-Jun 9.30–5.30, mid-June–mid-Sept 9–7.30, mid-Sept–mid-Mar 9.30–4.30

Adm Adult €4.40, child €1.90, family €10.10

Guided tour available, shop

Don't miss this medieval castle, which sits spectacularly above the Golden Vale and town of Cashel on a great mound, the Rock of Cashel itself. The rock was the seat of the Eóghanachta clan from the 4th century, from where they conquered much of Munster to become its High Kings. For 400 years, Cashel rivalled Tara as Ireland's centre of power. In the 10th century the clan lost it to the O'Briens, led by Brian Boru, and in 1101 King Muircheartach O'Brien gave Cashel to the Church. It was a great ecclesiastical centre until Cromwell's army killed 3,000 Catholic devotees here in 1647. Visitors see a film, 'Strongholds of the Faith' and some relics are on display. While inside the Castle keep an eye on young children, as there are lots of rocky surfaces to negotiate.

Waterford Town

Waterford is the oldest town in Ireland, created by the Vikings before they settled in Dublin. A lovely old-fashioned quiet hovers above its grey streets, reminiscent of Irish towns in the 1970s. Families can enjoy folk performances in summer, and fun walking tours are available (*see* p.146).

Things to see and do

Reginald's Tower Museum

The Quay, **t** (051) 873 501
Open Apr–May and Sept–Oct Mon–Fri 10–5 and Sat–Sun 10–1 and 2–5, Jun–Aug daily 8.30–8.30
Adm Adult €2, child €1, family €5
Shop, guided tour

A round tower has stood here for 1,000 years, but the current round, fat building has been here since the 12th century. Around that time, in this place, the Norman warrior Strongbow first met Aoife, the daughter of the King of Leinster (*see* p.33). Viking-era and medieval artefacts are on show.

Waterford Treasures at the Granary

The Granary, **t** (051) 304 500,
www.waterfordtreasures.com
Open Daily Apr–May, Sept 10–5, June–Aug 9.30–9
Adm Adults €6, 6-16s €3, under-5s free, family €12
Shop, restaurant. tourist office

This excellent museum has many interactive and audio-visual presentations to appeal to school-age children, and some fun activities for younger ones too. As you enter, there is a short film about how Viking settlers first came to Waterford. The benches you sit on begin to roll as if you're on a ship, to give you a taste of Viking life at sea. You move on to a reconstruction of the wedding between Strongbow and the King of Leinster's daughter Aoife, and later Georgian Ireland and its artefacts, including Waterford crystal and other treasures of the town's 1,000-year history. There are interactive computers and a child-friendly entertainment of music, song, dance and storytelling called **The Waterford Viking Show** (**t** 051 303 500, shows June–mid-Sept Mon, Wed, Fri 8pm).

Waterford Crystal

Kilbarry, t (051) 373 311,
www.waterfordvisitorcentre.com
Open **Apr–Oct Mon–Sun 8.30–4 (showrooms 8.30–6), Nov–Mar Mon–Fri 9–3.15 (9–5)**
Adm **Adult €6.50, students €3.50, under-12s free**
Guided tours, toilets with baby-changing facilities and disabled access, coffee shop

Learn how this world-famous crystal is made via a film and a tour of this glass-making factory, one mile (1.6km) west of Waterford on the Cork road. The informative, friendly staff are known for welcoming children and making visits interesting for them. See every aspect of how glass is made by master blowers, cutters and engravers, who use modern technology alongside traditional skills.

SPECIAL TRIPS

Cahir Castle

Castle St, Cahir, Co. Tipperary, **t** (052) 41011
Getting there 11 miles (18km) from Cashel by N8
Open Daily mid-Mar–mid-Jun 9.30–5.30, mid-Jun–mid-Sept 9–7.30; mid-Sept–mid-Oct 9.30–5.30, mid-Oct–mid-Mar 9.30–4.30, closed 24–31 Dec
Adm Adult €2.50, child €1.20, family €6.30

Sitting on a rocky island on the River Suir, this impressive castle is one of Ireland's largest and best preserved. Founded by Conor O'Brien in 1142 and passed on to the Butler family in 1375, it defines the town that has grown up around it with medieval grandeur. It has survived nearly intact through the centuries, largely because it surrendered to Cromwell in 1650 without a fight.

AROUND AND ABOUT

Animal magic

Holycross Rare Breeds Farm

Holycross, Thurles, Co. Tipperary, **t** (0504) 43173
Getting there 9 miles (15km) north of Cashel
Open Daily May–Sept 10–7, Apr and Oct Sat–Sun and bank holidays only, and also by appointment
Adm Adult €3.50, child €2.50
Pets' corner, picnic areas, toilets with disabled access

Children can learn about 70 or more breeds of birds and animals at this farm's interpretative centre, in the Gate Lodge. After that they meet the animals: of note are the Kerry Bog Ponies, once used to pull carts of turf from the bogs, and also here are rare Irish Moiled Cattle, tiny brown Soay and blue Herdwick sheep (rescued from extinction by Beatrix Potter), living alongside exotic birds.

Touraneena Heritage Centre

Ballinamult, Co. Waterford, **t** (058) 47353
Getting there 12 miles (19km) north of Dungarvan
Open Daily May–Oct 10–7
Adm Adult €4, child €1, family €10
Pet farm, pony and tractor rides, café, picnic area

The whole family will enjoy going back in time at this 300-year-old thatched farm. Irish farm life of the 1890s is recreated, with bread baking over a turf fire, butter-making, a forge, hatchery and tinkers' wagon. Little kids can pet the animals and climb around the playground, and on Sunday afternoons in July and August there is Irish dancing

A story to tell:
A true story of the Galtees

There is a lake in the Galtee Mountains of Tipperary where a serpent is said to live. The story goes that a saint put it there, promising to let him out every Monday morning. However, the saint never came back, so before dawn every Monday the serpent sticks his head out of the water and says, 'It is a strange fact that Monday morning is so long coming.' Once upon a time, local people planned to drain the lake to channel its water to their town, but when they got to the shore they looked back and saw that their town was on fire and burning fiercely. They hurried frantically down the hill to quench the fire but, on arriving home, they couldn't see any fire there at all. They took the hint, and never tried to drain the lake again.

Bricks and mortar

Ormond Castle

Carrick-on-Suir, Co. Tipperary, **t** (051) 640 787
Getting there 16 miles (25km) from Waterford
Open Daily mid-Jun–Sept 9.30–6.30
Adm Adult €2.50, child €1.20, family €6.30
Guided tours only, shop

The best Elizabethan manor house in Ireland. Begun by the Earls of Ormond in the 14th century, it has two 15th-century towers and rooms with beautiful plasterwork. Anne Boleyn is said to have been born here, just before Black Tom Butler, the 10th Earl, built the Elizabethan mansion.

Look at this!

Fethard Folk Farm and Transport Museum

Cashel Road, Fethard, Co. Tipperary, **t** (052) 31516
Getting there 9 miles (14km) southeast of Cashel
Open Sun all year 12.30–5
Adm Farm: adult €1.50, child €1;
Museum: adult €1.50, child €1
Playground, shop, tearoom, disabled facilities

This museum is in a former railway station near the medieval walls of Fethard. It houses thousands of exhibits of folk and farm life, and transport is a speciality, so Thomas fans feel right at home.

Nature lovers

Lismore Castle

Lismore, Co. Waterford, **t** (058) 54424
Getting there 15 miles (24km) from Dungarvan
Open Mid-May–Sept daily 1.45–4.45pm (11am opening in high season)
Adm Grounds only: adult €5, under-16s €2.50

This castle can only be viewed from outside but its magical gardens are open to visitors. Built in 1185, it was presented to Sir Walter Raleigh in 1589 along with a huge area of countryside. Many famous writers have walked in these gardens.

Mitchelstown Caves

Burncourt, Cahir, Co. Tipperary, **t** (052) 67246
Getting there 10 miles (16km) west of Cahir on N8
Open May–Sept daily 10–6
Adm Adult €4.44, child €1.90, family €11.43

These limestone caves, discovered in 1833, extend over 16 kilometres between Mitchelstown and Cahir, with impressive stalagmites and stalactites like the Tower of Babel, 10 metres tall.

Parson's Green Pet Farm and Caravan Park

Clogheen, Co. Tipperary, **t** (052) 65290
Getting there 8 miles (13km) south of Cahir
Open 17 Mar–Sept daily 10–8
Adm Adult €3, child €2, family (2+3) €10
Pet farm, picnic area, café and fast-food restaurant

This has a Viking sweat lodge on site, along with pigs, emus, goats, cattle and old farm equipment. You can spend a day here with children playing in the garden, on the beach, or taking a trap, boat and pony rides. Little kids are very well catered for.

Sporty kids

Boat trips

Shannon Sailing Centre

New Harbour, Dromineer, Nenagh, **t** (067) 24499

Cruises on Lough Derg with lunch or dinner. The centre also offers boat hire, water-skiing, sailing, windsurfing and canoeing.

Buckets and spades – Beaches in Tipperary and Waterford

In Co. Waterford there are excellent beaches for swimming at **Dunmore East**, **Ardmore** and around Dungarvan – especially **Clonea Bay**, 5 miles (8km) to the east. The seaside resort of **Tramore** is typically touristy but is a popular spot for surfing.

In Co. Tipperary there is enjoyable lake swimming on Lough Derg at **Ballina**, opposite Killaloe in Co. Clare, and around **Portroe**.

Ireland Line Cruisers

Ballina, Co. Tipperary, **t** (061) 375 011,
www.irelandlinecruisers.com

Cruise on Lough Derg and the River Shannon.

Horse riding

Homeleigh Horse and Trekking Centre

Ballinacourty, Aherlow, Co. Tipperary, **t** (062) 56228

Trap rides and pony treks in the Glen of Aherlow.

The Irish Horse Experience

Lismore, Co. Waterford, **t** (058) 53111
Open End May–Sept Thur at 10am

The Ballyrafter Equestrian Centre offers a 30min show on the legends, history and origins of the Irish horse, along with information on the way in which horses are bred and used for sport today.

Melody's Riding Stables

Ballymacarberry, Co. Waterford, **t** (052) 36147

Ride in the beautiful Nire Valley south of Clonmel. Caters for novices and experienced riders.

Walking

Ballyhoura Way, part of the O'Sullivan Beara trail, stretches 56 miles (90km) from John's Bridge in west Limerick to Limerick Junction in Co. Tipperary. The **Cahir Way** is another signposted path from Cahir to Ballydavid through the Galtee Mountains. There are also fine paths between Carrick-on-Suir, Clonmel and Clogheen in the Knockmealdown Mountains. In Co. Waterford, walk through the Comeragh Mountains south of Clonmel on the **Munster Way**, or **St Declan's Walk**, a popular pilgrimage route from Lismore to Ardmore.

Water sports

Dunmore East Adventure Centre

The Harbour, Dunmore East, Co. Waterford,
t (051) 383 783

Sailing, windsurfing, canoeing.

Splashworld

Tramore, Co. Waterford, **t** (051) 390 176
Open Seasonally, daily 10am–10pm
Disabled access, toilets with baby-changing facilities, café, under-10s must be accompanied by adult

An aqua-adventure playground with bubble pools, a river ride, wave machine and waterslides.

T-Bay Surf Centre

The beach, Tramore, Co. Waterford, **t** (051) 391 297

Surf hire, beach facilities, activity camps.

WHERE TO EAT

County Cork

Baltimore

Custom House Restaurant

t (028) 20200 (*moderate–inexpensive*)

Imaginative fresh dishes in a seaside setting.

Bantry

The Snug

The Quay, **t** (027) 50057 (*inexpensive*)

An eccentric bar by the harbour with simple home-cooked dishes.

Castletownbere/Bere Island

Lawrence Cove House

Bere Island, **t** (027) 75063 (*moderate*)

Fabulous fish restaurant.

The Old Bakery

West End, Castletownbere, **t** (027) 70790 (*moderate*)

The last espresso machine till New York.

Clonakilty

Fionnuala's Little Italian Restaurant

30 Ashe Street, **t** (023) 34355 (*moderate*)

Lasagne and pizza are specials here.

Cork City

Café Paradiso

16 Lancaster Quay, Western Road, **t** (021) 427 7939 (*inexpensive–moderate*)

Great vegetarian food made solely from organic ingredients. Many consider it the best vegetarian restaurant in Ireland.

Crawford's Art Gallery Café

Emmet Place, **t** (021) 427 4415 (*inexpensive*)

Run by one of the Allen Family of Ballymaloe (*see* p.258), with light, original food for lunch or supper. Excellent fresh orange juice and gooey cakes.

The Gingerbread House

Paul Street Plaza, **t** (021) 427 6411 (*inexpensive*)

A very popular café and bakery that's good for breakfast, lunch or coffee and welcomes children.

Gino's

Winthrop St, **t** (021) 427 4485 (*inexpensive*)

Fabulous pizzas for large and small appetites; this is a famous diner amongst Corkonians.

Kelly's

64 Oliver Plunkett St, **t** (021) 427 3375 (*inexpensive*)

Friendly, charming and simple surroundings for home-style Irish lunches. Children welcome.

Tony's Bistro

69 North Main St, **t** (021) 427 0848 (*inexpensive*)

Open for breakfast, lunch and dinner, with great fry-ups, and popular with all ages.

Glandore

The Baybery

Union Hall, **t** (028) 33605 (*inexpensive*)

Serves wholesome food, and has handcrafted pine furniture and pottery for sale.

Kinsale

The Blue Haven

3 Pearse Street, **t** (021) 477 2209 (*expensive*)

This very good restaurant is in a cosy hotel. Seafood is a speciality, and the steaks are good too.

Fishy Fishy Café

t (021) 477 4453 (*inexpensive–moderate*)

Kinsale's best and busiest restaurant, with an outside terrace in good weather..

Macroom

The Auld Triangle

Killarney Road, **t** (026) 41940 (*moderate*)

Popular for its extensive dinner menu.

Midleton

The Farm Gate

Coolbawn, **t** (021) 463 2771 (*moderate–inexpensive*)

Fresh local ingredients and traditional dishes.

Schull

Adele's

Main Street, **t** (028) 28459 (*inexpensive*)

A bakery and restaurant offering excellent lunches, salads and desserts.

The Courtyard

Main St, **t** (028) 28390 (*inexpensive*)

Combined restaurant, bar, craft shop and deli.

Youghal

Aherne's Pub and Seafood Restaurant

North Main St, **t** (024) 92424/92533 (*moderate*)

Good atmosphere and delicious seafood dishes: perhaps the best pub-restaurant in the south.

Browne's County Restaurant

Killeagh, **t** (024) 91373 (*moderate*)

This family-run restaurant offers breakfast, brunch, lunch, tea and Sunday lunch in a snug ambience beside Browne's Equestrian Centre.

County Kerry

County Kerry is known for good local produce. Fenit and Castlegregory are renowned for vegetables, Cromane for mussels, Tralee Bay for oysters, Dingle for seafood and North Kerry for beef.

Brandon

O'Shea's Bar & Restaurant

near Castlegregory, **t** (066) 713 8154 (*inexpensive*)

Food is served all day at this pub. Outside there's a beer garden and a children's play area.

Caherdaniel

The Blind Piper

t (066) 9475126 (*inexpensive*)

Good, lively atmosphere in this pretty village. The pub has a kiddies play area and a garden.

Castlegregory

O'Riordan's

t (066) 713 9379 (*inexpensive*)

Wonderful lunch spot – unusual dishes, memorable breads and a good atmosphere.

Dingle

An Café Liteartha

t (066) 915 2204 (*inexpensive*)

A combined bookshop and café serving delicious open sandwiches.

Doyle's Seafood Bar and Restaurant

John St, **t** (066) 915 1174 (*expensive*)

In a room like an old Irish kitchen, with stone floor and simple furniture, and fine seafood chosen by very welcoming owners John and Stella Doyle.

The Forge

Holy Ground, **t** (066) 915 2590 (*moderate*)

Popular family-owned pub in the centre of Dingle with children's menu, decent steaks and seafood.

Murphy's Ice Cream

Strand Street, **t** (066) 915 2644 (*inexpensive*)

Malteasers ice cream and chocolate cakes for that perfect summer children's treat.

Kenmare

An Leath Phingin

35 Main Street, **t** (064) 41559 (*moderate*)

The Italian chef, Maria, makes fresh pasta, scrumptious sauces and stone-baked pizzas.

Café Indigo and the Square Pint

Henry St, **t** (064) 42350 (*inexpensive*)

This wholesome café serves imaginative food and organic wine and is a treat for vegetarians.

The Wander Inn

2 Henry Street, **t** (064) 42700 (*inexpensive*)

Perfect for the classic combination of a plate of Irish stew, a pint of Guinness and traditional music.

Killarney

The Celtic Cauldron

27 Plunkett St, **t** (064) 36821 (*moderate*)

Although at first it seems to cater for the tackiest type of tourism, this restaurant is redeemed by the food, inspired by traditional Celtic cookery.

Foley's Seafood and Steak Restaurant

23 High St, **t** (064) 31217 (*moderate*)

Delicious seafood, lamb and vegetarian dishes.

Gaby's Restaurant

27 High St, **t** (064) 32519 (*moderate*)

A Mediterranean-style café with tasty seafood, and very popular. No bookings, so arrive early.

The Strawberry Field

Blackwaterbridge, **t/f** (064) 82977 (*inexpensive*)

Restaurant and tearoom with a terrace, located just beyond Molls' Gap outside Killarney Town.

Killorglin

Nick's Restaurant and Pub

Lower Bridge Street, **t** (066) 976 1219 (*expensive*)

Serves large portions of seafood and steaks. Often packed with local people singing around the piano, it's a very friendly place and great fun.

Tralee

Ashes Bar

Upper Camp, **t** (066) 713 0133 (*inexpensive*)

Seafood platters for lunch, a more elaborate dinner menu, and traditional music in summer.

County Limerick

Adare

The Wild Geese

t (061) 396 451 (*expensive*)

A mix of classic French and modern Irish cooking.

Limerick City

Belltable Arts Centre Café

69 O'Connell Street, **t** (061) 319 866 (*inexpensive*)

Limerick's arts complex is good for tasty lunches.

Greene's Café Bistro

63 William Street, **t** (061) 314 022 (*inexpensive*)

The beautiful stained-glass features and wholesome dishes make this a very nice spot for lunch.

The Parlour Restaurant

Ennis Road, **t** (061) 322 777 (*moderate*)

A cosy atmosphere and classic, creative dishes.

County Clare

Ballyvaughan

An Fear Gorta

t (065) 707 7023 (*inexpensive*)

In a garden, this is a nice place for a hearty lunch.

Gregan's Castle Hotel

t (065) 707 7005 (*moderate*)

Delicious food served all day in the Corkscrew Bar, where there's a warm fire beneath a low-beamed ceiling. It's an especially welcoming sight after a long hike, and family friendly.

Bunratty

Gallagher's of Bunratty

t (061) 363363 (*moderate*)

Charming thatched cottage with local seafood.

The Burren

Linnane's Lobster Bar

New Quay, **t** (065) 707 8120 (*moderate*)

This pub specializes in lobster and oysters.

Cassidy's of Carran

t (065) 708 9109 (*inexpensive*)

A remote pub in the wildest part of the Burren, with excellent lunches using local produce.

The Burren

Carran, **t** (065) 708 9109 (*inexpensive*)

Burgers, steaks, baked potatoes and sandwiches are sold here. It's a great spot in the middle of the Burren, with beauty all around (and a play area).

Doolin

Aran View House Hotel and Restaurant

Coast Road, **t** (065) 7078 4061, (*inexpensive–moderate*)

This hotel restaurant specializes in fresh seafood and the best local produce. It's also family friendly, has good vegetarian dishes and has superb views.

Ennis

The Cloister Restaurant and Bar

Club Bridge, Abbey St, **t** (065) 682 9521 (*inexpensive–moderate*)

In a medieval building, this offers good soups, local cheeses and nutty brown bread by day (away from the smoky bar it is fine for children); at night it's a more formal restaurant.

Lahinch

Bartrá Seafood Restaurant

t (065) 708 1280 (*expensive–moderate*)

A simple but good restaurant just outside Lahinch, with fine views of the bay.

O'Looney's

On the Promenade, **t** (065) 708 1414 (*moderate*)

Good seafood, bar food, sandwiches and music.

Liscannor

The Mermaid

t (065) 708 1076 (*inexpensive–moderate*)

A snug restaurant with an open fire in one room of a building on the outskirts of Liscannor village. Its hard-working owners serve mainly fish, but also inventive vegetarian dishes of local ingredients.

Lisdoonvarna

Roadside Tavern

Kincora Road, **t** (065) 707 4494 (*inexpensive*)

This charming wood-panelled pub-cum-smoking house specializes in delicious smoked fish.

Spanish Point

The Cape Restaurant

Armada Hotel, **t** (065) 708 4110 (*moderate*)

Hearty, traditional Sunday roasts or informal bar food, and uninterrupted views over the Atlantic.

Tipperary and Waterford

Ballina

Galloping Hogan's

Ballina, Co. Tipperary, **t** (061) 376162 (*moderate*)

Dine al fresco overlooking tranquil Lough Derg.

Molly's Bar and Restaurant

Ballina, Co. Tipperary, **t** (061) 376 632 (*inexpensive*)

Children are welcome for lunch and early-evening meals at this restaurant by Lough Derg.

Cahir

Clifford's at The Bell

2 Pearse Street, Cahir, Co. Tipperary, **t** (052) 43232 (*moderate–expensive*)

Superb, interesting food, and a great view.

Crock of Gold

1 Castle St, opposite Cahir castle, Co. Tipperary, **t** (052) 41951 (*inexpensive*)

Above a craft shop, and handy for snacks and tea.

Cappoquin

Barron's Bakery and Coffee House

The Square, Cappoquin, Co. Waterford, **t** (058) 54045 (*inexpensive*)

Stock up on picnic treats here or call in for lunch.

Cashel

Cashel Palace Hotel

Cashel, Co. Tipperary, **t** (062) 61411 (*moderate–expensive*)

There are two restaurants in this old house, built in Queen Anne-style in 1730. The formal Three Sisters is more adult, while the Bishop's Buttery is welcoming for children.

The Bakehouse

7 Main St, Cashel, Co. Tipperary, **t** (062) 61680 (*inexpensive*)

An irresistible choice for breakfast, lunch or snacks, with gourmet coffee and goods baked daily on the premises. Children welcome.

Mother Hubbard's Truck Stop and Family Restaurant

Cork Road, Cashel, Co. Tipperary, **t** (062) 62122 (*inexpensive*)

Mother Hubbard's offers kiddies' meals with a soft drink and a toy, and 4-course lunch specials.

Clonmel

Abbey Restaurant

Abbey St, Clonmel, Co. Tipperary, **t** (054) 36060 (*inexpensive*)

This wholefood and vegetarian restaurant is open in the daytime only and is situated in an old warehouse: a good range of soups and stir-fries.

Dunmore East

The Ship Restaurant and Bar

Dunmore East, Co. Waterford, **t** (051) 383141 (*moderate*)

Casual, fun atmosphere, which is fine for children during the day and early evening. Good seafood.

Waterford Town

Dwyer's Restaurant

8 Mary St, **t** (051) 877 478 (*moderate*)

In a fomer barracks, Dwyer's offers a cosy setting and fine food. Children are welcome early evening.

Haricots Wholefood Restaurant

11 O'Connell St, **t** (051) 841 299 (*inexpensive*)

Comfortable and relaxing surroundings for vegetarians, vegans and omnivores alike, as freshly cooked wholefood recipes are created daily. Very good homemade soups, and freshly squeezed juice.

The Olde Stand

45 Michael St, **t** (051) 879 488 (*inexpensive*)

This charming inn offers excellent pub food for lunch and has a good restaurant upstairs. Children are welcome during the day.

Connacht

06

Connacht

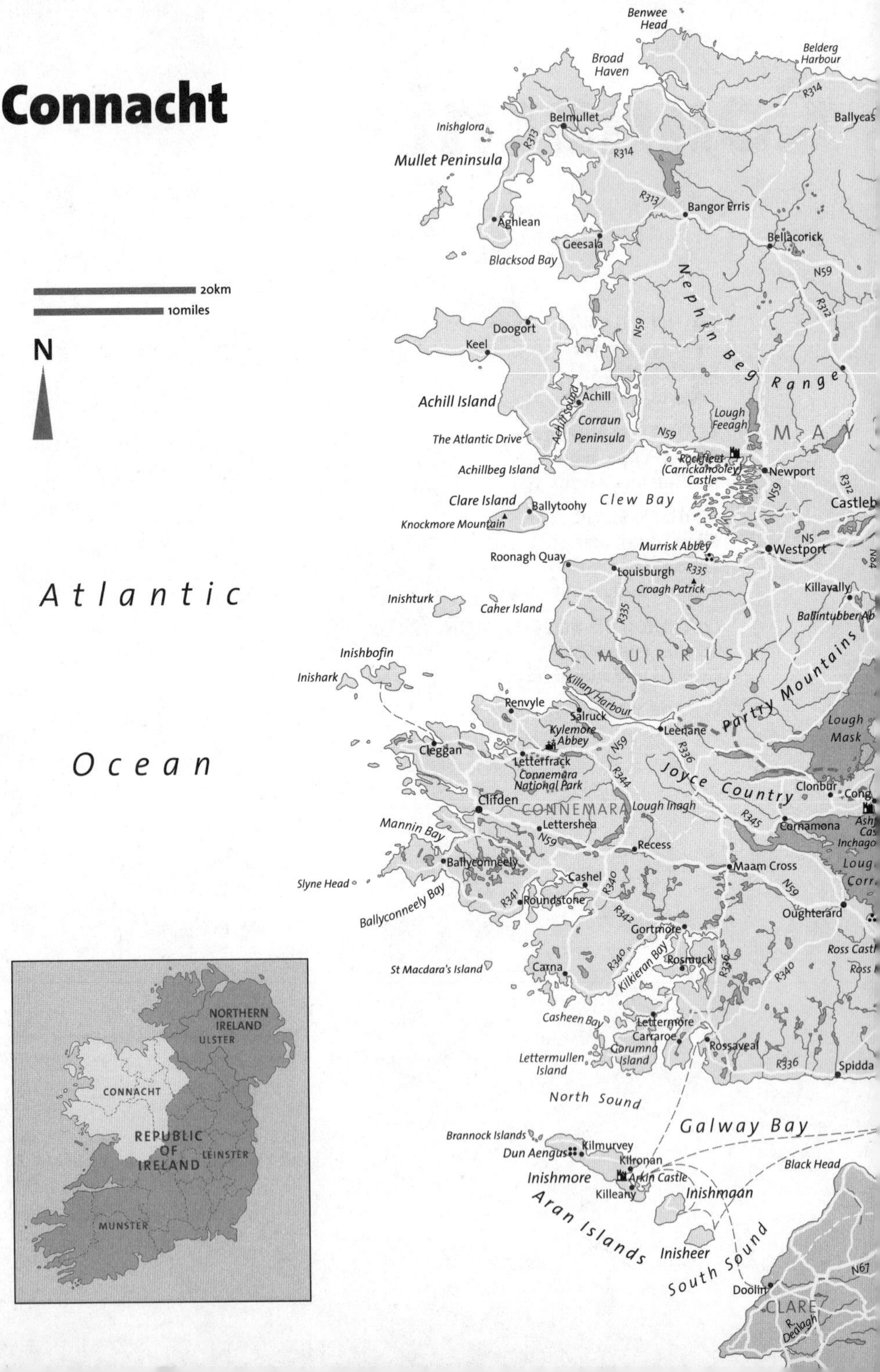

20km
10miles
N
Atlantic
Ocean
Benwee Head
Broad Haven
Belderg Harbour
R314
Ballycas
Inishglora
Belmullet
Mullet Peninsula
R313
R314
R313
Bangor Erris
Aghlean
Bellacorick
Geesala
Blacksod Bay
Nephin Beg Range
N59
R312
Doogort
Keel
N59
Achill Island
Achill Sound
Achill
Corraun Peninsula
Lough Feeagh
MAY
The Atlantic Drive
N59
Achillbeg Island
Rockfleet (Carrickahooley) Castle
Newport
R312
N59
Clare Island
Ballytoohy
Clew Bay
Castleb
Knockmore Mountain
N5
Murrisk Abbey
Westport
Roonagh Quay
R335
Louisburgh
Croagh Patrick
N84
Inishturk
Caher Island
Killavally
Ballintubber Ab
R335
MURRISK
Inishbofin
Inishark
Killary Harbour
Partry Mountains
Renvyle
Salruck
Lough Mask
Kylemore Abbey
Leenane
Cleggan
N59
R336
Letterfrack
Connemara National Park
R344
Joyce Country
Clonbur
Cong
Clifden
CONNEMARA
Lough Inagh
R345
Cornamona
Mannin Bay
Lettershea
N59
Inchago
Recess
Ballyconneely
Maam Cross
Slyne Head
Cashel
R340
N59
Ballyconneely Bay
R341
Roundstone
Oughterard
R342
Gortmore
Ross Castl
St Macdara's Island
Carna
R340
Kilkieran Bay
Rosmuck
R336
R340
Casheen Bay
Lettermore
Carraroe
Gorumna Island
Rossaveal
Lettermullen Island
R336
Spidda
North Sound
Galway Bay
Brannock Islands
Kilmurvey
Dun Aengus
Kilronan
Black Head
Inishmore
Arkin Castle
Killeany
Inishmaan
Aran Islands
Inisheer
South Sound
N67
Doolin
CLARE
R. Dealagh
NORTHERN IRELAND
ULSTER
CONNACHT
REPUBLIC OF IRELAND
LEINSTER
MUNSTER

Mullaghmore
Bundoran
N15
River Erne
Lower Lough Erne
A35
A46
Inishmurray
Kinlough
Lough Melvin
Downpatrick Head
Lissadell House
Benbulben Mountain
N15
B81
Rossinver
Sligo Bay
Drumcliff
Ulster Way
FERMANA
Easky
Killala Bay
R. Easky
R281
N15
N16
R280
R283
Manorhamilton
Enniskillen
A32
R297
Strandhill
Ballysadare Bay
Sligo
R286
River Bonet
N16
Killala
Inniscrone
Dromore West
Carrowmore
R292
Lough Gill
N59
N59
Dromahair
R287
R289
Collooney
R280
A509
R314
Ballina
Slieve Gamph/The Ox Mountains
SLIGO
R284
Riverstown
R200
R294
Lough Talt
N4
Ballymote
Lough Allen
Arigna Mountains
CAVAN
Lough Conn
Tubbercurry
Castlebaldwin
Lough Arrow
N26
R294
Ballinafad
Lough Meelagh
LEITRIM
Drumshanbo
Ballinamore
Waterway
Pontoon
Lough Cullin
Foxford
Curlew Hills
Gorteen
Lough Key
R284
R202
Corrawaleen
N26
Charlestown
Boyle
Leitrim
Straide
N5
Swinford
Lough Gara
Lough Key Forest Park
Carrick-on-Shannon
N4
Knock Airport
Kiltimagh
Ballaghaderreen
Ballinameen
Mohill
Cloone Grange
N5
Frenchpark
Clougher
Knock
Elphin
R202
Dromod
Clonalis House
Castlerea
Claremorris
R367
Tulsk
Strokestown
N60
N60
N4
Lough Carra
ROSCOMMON
N5
Lough Forbes
R. Camlin
Killoe
Longford
R194
N84
Cloonfad
Ballintober
Ballymore
Four Mile House
N4
Ballinrobe
LONGFORD
R334
Roscommon Castle
Royal Canal
R332
Roscommon
N84
N83
Glennamaddy
Castlestrange Stone
R366
Athleague
Knockcroghery
Lisacormack Fort
Tuam
R333
River Clare
Saint's Island
R332
Lough Ree
Mount Bellew
N61
Inchmore
Curraghboy
WESTMEA
Moycullen
N84
Claregalway Abbey
Claregalway
GALWAY
Athlone
N17
N6
Galway (Carnmore)
N6
River Shannon
N6
Salthill
Athenry
Moyode Castle
R348
Ballinasloe
GALWAY
Oranmore
Aughrim
N6
N6
N18
R. Suck
Grand Canal
N52
Clarinbridge
R355
Clonfert Cathedral
Clonfert
Tullam
Loughrea
N6
Doorus House
N67
R357
N52
Lough Rea
N65
OFFALY
Dunguaire
Kinvarra
Banagher
N66
Slieve Aught Mountains
River Shannon
R355
Thoor Ballylee
Coole Park
R353
R. Barrow
Gort
Portumna
Priory
Lough Cutra
Glendine Gap
Portumna Forest Park
R460
N52
N62
CLARE
TIPPERARY
LAOIS

CONNACHT

Arthur Colaham's old song *If You Ever Go Across the Sea to Ireland* speaks of a time in Galway when children would run barefoot from May to September to save their shoes for the winter, and women would work in the fields digging potatoes and harvesting hay. It is a world that no longer exists, but still echoes in modern Connacht.

The province's recent history includes great poverty. Connacht was deeply harmed by the Great Famine in the middle of the 19th century. Already the majority of its people were struggling to survive, often under landlords of a different culture and faith. Many of the ancestors of Connacht's inhabitants had been dumped there by Cromwell in the 17th century. Life was hard, so you made the best of it with music and stories. The rock-filled vastness of Connemara can be seen to symbolize its people's struggle, and the tiny colourful wild-flowers that grow every year in the gaps between the rocks their spirit.

Known for the barren sweep of its rocky land and thin topsoil, this was a part of Ireland where few chose to live, and those who did do so tended to be fishermen, farmers or turf-cutters. In the 19th century, life was not made any easier for Connachtmen by the developing industrialization of Europe. The arrival of the mass market in Ireland was made manifest in its wool and textile industries, where the money to be made rarely trickled down to the handknitters of Connemara and the Arans, whose human-speed artistry was not then and still is not a particularly lucrative trade. Foreign landlords with no loyalty to the land were deeply resented by those whose lives depended upon it for survival. This and the arrival of the Famine triggered mass migration to America. After that, young and old grew ever more determined to find gold in the streets of the New World, so that for generations of displaced Connachtmen Ireland became a distant, nagging memory.

Today Connacht is a much more cosmopolitan province, even if it is still much less so than the towns around Dublin. As more natives return home after years of working abroad, a mixture of European, British and American influences are coming with them, affecting the buildings and look of the countryside and transforming once-peaceful towns like Galway into cities with all their attendant problems.

But still the old habits linger in the countryside, where traditional music and culture are nearer ordinary life, and rarely ever are things that are merely done cynically 'for the tourists'. In Connacht you will find a more careful approach to strangers than in other provinces, but perhaps a less contrived one too, with the old Irish laws of hospitality still working as they have for centuries.

Highlights

Discovering how Galway crystal and traditional *bodhrán* drums are made, pp.162, 169
Wandering in wild Connemara, p.170
Sailing to the magical Aran Islands of Galway or Clare Island, Co. Mayo, pp.164, 179
A day of fun at Westport House, Co. Mayo, p.176
Horse riding around Ashford Castle in Co. Mayo, p.180
Visiting Sligo's faeries at Knocknashee and Gillighan's World, p.183

Tourist information for Connacht

Ireland West Tourism (Galway, Mayo, Roscommon), Aras Failte, Forster St, Galway, **t** (091) 537 700, **www**.irelandwest.travel.ie
Self-catering information, t (091) 537 777
North West Tourism (Sligo, Leitrim, Cavan, Monaghan and Donegal), Aras Redden, Temple St, Sligo, **t** (071) 61201, **www**.ireland-northwest.travel.ie

Getting there and around

By air Connacht has two airports with direct links with Britain, **Galway** (used by Aer Arann) and **Knock** (British Airways, MyTravelLite, Ryanair). Galway is also the airport for Aer Arann flights to the Aran Islands. For travellers from North America the best airport to use is **Shannon**. *See* pp.280–4.
By bus Frequent Bus Eireann coaches run between Dublin and Galway, Westport, Sligo and other towns. Many local services operate from Galway. For Bus Eireann details, *see* p.286.
By car From Dublin, for north Connacht follow the N4 via Longford; for Galway, take the N4 as far as Kinnegad, then the N6 via Athlone.
By rail Trains to Galway run from Dublin Heuston, and there are also west coast lines to Ballina or Westport, via a change in Athlone or Athenry. Trains to Sligo run from Dublin Connolly, via Longford. For more on Irish Rail/Iarnród Eireann, *see* p.288. They can be contacted in Ireland on **t** 1 850 366 222, or check **www**.irishrail.ie.

COUNTY GALWAY

County Galway will be most enjoyed by families who love active holidays – fishing, cycling, horse riding, or walking along spectacular Atlantic beaches and through unique landscapes. Junior archaeologists and geologists will especially enjoy exploring the wind-blown Connemara peninsula, its landscape bereft of most things but rocks dotted with strikingly blue eyelet lakes. This is the land that Cromwell was thinking of when he banished Catholic landowners from the rest of Ireland 'to Hell or Connacht' in the 17th century. Apart from these cosy fishing holes, anglers can visit Connemara's largest lake, Lough Corrib, and the numerous bays leading to the Atlantic Ocean, which holds the special world of the Aran Islands.

Connemara is loosely defined as the area between Lough Corrib and the Atlantic Ocean, with a northern boundary at Killary Harbour and its southern coastline beside Galway Bay. Hours can be spent traversing it looking for forgotten cairns, and visitors might be interested to know that this is the largest area of Ireland that is still a *Gaeltacht*, a place where Irish is spoken as a first language. In the far west of Connemara, road signs and directions are often only in Irish, perhaps something of a political statement stretching back to the 17th century, when Irish people are said to have been hanged for speaking in their native tongue.

Traditional culture was a lively part of life on the Arans and in western Connacht until near the end of the 20th century. Vestiges of the old habits can still be found here, and there is a quiet renaissance going on that is regenerating communities, with folklorists the new holders of tradition and ecologists bringing new vigour and support for organic farming. Faerylore is still present here also, although it might take some uncovering, which you can only do through getting to know the often-cautious country people.

County Galway's greener eastern region is a place of farms and romantic woodland, among which Ireland's greatest 20th century poet WB Yeats chose to live. His magical home, Thoor Ballylee, sits beside a rushing stream in the middle of a countryside that, comfortingly, doesn't seem to have changed for a very long time. Not far from there are the vast grounds of Coole Park, once the home of the folklorist Lady Gregory, co-founder with Yeats of Dublin's Abbey Theatre and the wealthy benefactress behind the early 20th-century's Irish Literary Renaissance.

Good to know...

Try to find a real storyteller to tell you all about what might happen if you mix with the Gentry (faeries), or listen to stories recorded by Irish storytellers (*see* p.26).

Tourist information

Aran Islands, Comharchumann Forbartha Arann, **t** (099) 61354, **www**.visitaranislands.com, also **Kilronan**, Inishmore, **t** (099) 61263
Ballinasloe, **t** (0905) 42131
Clifden, Galway Road, **t** (095) 21163
Galway, Aras Fáilte, Forster St, **t** (091) 537 700
Oughterard, **t** (091) 552808
Salthill, Promenade, **t** (091) 520 500
Thoor Ballylee, **t** (091) 631436
Tuam, **t** (093) 25486/24463

Tours

Bus Eireann (*see* below) also offers bus tours of Connemara in summer, from Galway.

The Famous Connemara Bus,
Old Galway, Connemara, **t** (091) 85780

Sightsee in Galway City and Connemara aboard a vintage bus.

Lally Tours, **t** (091) 593 034/562 905

Connemara day tours by bus with a guide depart from Galway and Salthill daily.

O'Neachtain's, **t** (091) 553 188

Getting there and around

By air Galway Airport is 4 miles (6km) east of the city in Carnmore. Buses are infrequent, but Aer Arann often provides its own shuttle buses, or there are taxis (*see* p.283) between the airport and the city. Galway Airport, Carnmore, **t** (091) 755 569, **www**.galwayairport.com.

By bus In Galway City buses depart from the train station, in the centre off Eyre Square. Galway is one of Bus Eireann's main hubs, and you can get to almost every town in Connacht and the surrounding counties quite easily. Other private operators provide services to Co. Galway towns, especially in summer. Galway Bus Information, **t** (091) 562 000; Nestor Bus, **t** (091) 797 144; Bus Eireann, **t** (091) 562 000, **www**.buseireann.ie.

By train Galway has a few trains daily from Dublin via Athlone. Information, **t** (091) 564 222

Bike Hire

Celtic Rent-a-Bike, Queen St, Galway, **t** (091) 566 606

Chieftain's Cycle Hire, Victoria Place, Galway, **t** (091) 567 4554
Europa Bicycles, Earls Island, Galway, **t** (091) 563 355
Flaherty Cycles, Upper Dominic St, Galway, **t** (091) 589 230
Irish Cycle Hire, Victoria Place, Galway, **t** (091) 561 498
John Mannion, Bridge St, Clifden, **t** (095) 21160
Kearney's Bicycle Hire, Headford Road, Galway, **t** (091) 563 356
Renvyle Stores, Tullymore, **t** (095) 43485
Rothar Arainn TEO, Frenchman's Beach, Kilronan, Inishmore, Aran Islands, **t** (091) 61132/61203

Special Events – County Galway

April

Cadbury's Easter Egg Hunt, Turoe Pet Farm, Loughrea (*see* p.167), **t** (091) 841 580

Seasonal fun for youngsters.

May

Ballinasloe Coarse Angling Festival, t (0905) 42619

A real catch for budding fishermen.

Fleadh nag Cuach ('Cuckoo Festival'), Kinvarra, **www.kinvarra.com**

A traditional festival that's fun for all the family.

Walks through Ancient Times, Inishmore, Aran Islands, **t** (099) 61263

The shorter walks are good for youngsters: teenagers might enjoy the longer walks.

May

Children's Day, Aughrim Interpretative Centre (*see* p.168), **t** (090) 9673939

On the second Sunday in June there are special educational and fun events for families.

Festival of Saints Peter and Paul, Inishmore, Aran Islands, **t** (099) 61263

Music and curragh (traditional boat) races.

Ragus, Halla Ronain, Kilronan, Inishmore, Aran Islands, **t** (099) 61515

A 1hr show of traditional Irish music, song and dance, presented through the summer (May–Sept).

July

Traditional Echoes in Song and Dance, Inishmore, Aran Islands, **t** (099) 61424

A ten-day programme of dancing, Gaelic songs, boat trips, walks and partying with islanders.

August

Crinniu na mBad ('the Gathering of the Boats') Kinvarra, **t** (091) 637 579

Traditional boat festival with curragh-racing, arts, sports, children's events and traditional music.

Connemara Pony Show, Clifden, **t** (095) 21863

Annual show of the world famous Connemara ponies, by Connemara Pony Breeders Society. A lovely event for horse-struck kids.

September

Clarinbridge Oyster Festival, t (091) 796 359

Oyster-opening competitions, traditional music, dance and fun during the day for families.

Clifden Community Arts Festival, t (095) 21644, **www.connemara.net/artsweek**

Top-quality arts events – poetry, recitals, exhibitions – with some family friendly activities.

Lady Gregory of Coole: An Autumn Gathering, t (091) 521 836

A weekend of lectures, discussions and drama, highlighting the ideas of Lady Gregory.

The Quiet Man Festival, Clonbur, **t** (092) 46155

This celebrates the 1952 John Ford movie *The Quiet Man* with John Wayne and Maureen O'Hara, in the villages where it was filmed.

October

Baboró International Arts Festival for Children, t (091) 509 705

Irish and international theatre, dance, music, workshops for 3–12 year-olds. Held in Galway and around the county.

Ballinasloe International Horse Fair and Festival t (090) 9643453/9644132

This traditional festival, dating back to 1772, includes a children's workshop along with puppet shows and other street entertainments.

Cooley-Collins Traditional Music Festival, Gort, **t** (091) 632 370

Traditional music, ceili and stories for children.

Maam Cross October Fair, t (091) 552 306

Sale of sheep, cattle and Connemara ponies via stalls, trailers and cars parked for miles on each of the four roads leading to Maam Cross village.

December

Christmas Winter Wonderland, Turoe Pet Farm, Loughrea, **t** (091) 841 580

Thurs–Sun evenings: a chance to meet Santa.

Woodford Mummers' Feile, Woodford, **t** (090) 9749326 (held 26–27 Dec)

Traditional folk activities for all the family.

GALWAY CITY

Galway is a provincial college town whose enterprising citizenry have long traded wine with Spain, and encouraged tourism. Built on the Corrib River, which runs from Lough Corrib north of the city, it is the gateway to the Connemara Gaeltacht. Also the home of University College Galway, it has long been a favourite of students and foreign visitors. The arts are very much alive here, with fine traditional music and the internationally renowned Druid Theatre Company.

Busy with traffic that is reminiscent of Dublin at times, central Galway's Eyre Square is no longer a peaceful empty expanse you can just walk across to the shops, and where someone may speak to you curiously because they know you're a stranger since they haven't seen you before. It is now even difficult to park a car there (car parks can be found beside the new centrally located hotels). Galway's main tourist office stands on an offshoot of the Square, but if you get lost, orientate yourself via Galway Bay. At the west end of the town (right, looking bay-wards) you will find the seaside resort area of Salthill, with a tourist office open in summer near Atlantaquaria and Leisureland.

If you want to hear some Irish music in one of Galway's lively pubs, you'll need a babysitter. Sessions don't start until about 9 or 10pm.

A story to tell: The Claddagh Ring

Once upon a time there was a king who so loved a woman he could not be with that it drove him mad. Since she was a peasant and therefore of lower status than him, society would not allow him to marry her. He instructed his servants that after he died they should cut off his hands and place them around his heart as a symbol of his undying love for her. This macabre little tale may not be true, but it conveys the strong feelings people have in this part of the world and describes the origins of the famous Claddagh ring.

Another story claims the symbol was worn and painted on ships and sails by fishermen from Claddagh, a poor fishing village that stood on the outskirts of Galway town in the Middle Ages. They are said to have killed fishermen they found in their waters not wearing it.

Whatever the truth of the symbol's beginnings, to the fishing kings of Claddagh it meant 'in love and friendship let us reign'. Two hands (signifying friendship) hold a heart (indicating love) on which sits a crown (symbolizing loyalty).

In the 17th century a goldsmith named Richard Joyce – who had earlier learnt his craft when he had been captured by North African pirates and sold as a slave to a Moroccan goldsmith – returned to Galway and opened a shop in the Claddagh. He began to make Claddagh rings, and they became popular as wedding rings, with the heart pointed towards the wearer's fingers when betrothed, and towards the body upon marriage. According to tradition, love and friendship will reign supreme in the life of its wearer.

The ring's fame spread with the vast exodus from the west of Ireland after the Great Famine. Kept as heirlooms, Claddagh rings were passed from mother to daughter all over the world. Today they are still worn all over Ireland.

Things to see and do

Atlantaquaria

National Aquarium of Ireland, Toft Park, The Promenade, Salthill, t (091) 585 100
Open Daily Mar–Oct 10–6
Adm Adult €7, child €4, under-3s free, family (2+2) €21
Guided tours available, gift shop, café

A small shock awaits you just after you enter Atlantaquaria on the ground floor, but don't worry – you won't get wet! Suddenly you feel as though you have been submerged in a ship deep in the ocean, where sea creatures dwell in tanks behind glass and in open-surfaced saltwater pools. This is the place to meet Galway's underwater inhabitants – from starfish to conger eels, sea anemones to mussels. The conditions that sea creatures normally inhabit are recreated in some tanks, while others protect the young of certain species. Baby plaice come to the surface of their pool periodically and cling to the sides, while starfish lie on the sandy gravel bottom beneath them. Accompanying text panels provide information about feeding patterns, tides and the size, habitat and habits of the many species that are exhibited in each tank.

Young children will enjoy the small submarine-like Deep Submergence Vehicle. They can crawl into it for a 'fish-eye' view of what life is like under the water for fish, starfish and crabs (the crabs eat anything, including fish excrement, and so are

Special Events – Galway City

April

Cuirt Literary Festival, t (091) 565 886, **www.galwayartscentre.ie**

Readings and performances are held in venues across the county.

Siamsa, Galway Folk Theatre, Claddagh Hall, **t** (091) 755 479

Irish music, singing, dancing and folk plays, with plenty for young audiences. The programme continues with performances a few times each week all through the summer (April–Sept).

May

Galway Early Music Festival, t (091) 846 356, **www.galwayearlymusic.com**

Traditional music and song festival incorporating art and drama; an attractive option for music-loving families.

June

Bloomsday, Nora Barnacle House, Bowling Green, **t** (091) 564 743

Open-air readings from the works of James Joyce, on 16 June: one for teenagers who may be studying Joyce for exams!

July

Galway Races, Ballybrit Racecourse, **www.iol.ie/galway-races**

The most exciting meetings are at the end of July, and feature the Galway Plate and the Galway Hurdle – a mixture of high society and smooth-talking bookies. Races go on through August.

Galway Arts Festival, t (091) 562 480/509 700. **www.galwayartsfestival.ie**

Ireland's biggest arts festival lasts 15 days and includes a children's festival with clowns, puppets and events especially for them.

Galway Film Fleadh, Town Hall Theatre, **t** (091) 751 655

Previews of high-quality movies.

Salthill Air Show, Seafront at Salthill, **t** (091) 526 158

A fun free air show on Galway Bay.

September

Galway Oyster Festival, Galway City, **t** (091) 527 282

The oyster-opening championships attract international participants. Children are a bit peripheral, as the affair snowballs into dances, shows and speeches, but you may spot a celebrity or two.

generally put in tanks to clean the place up). Skeletons of the fin whale and porpoise are on view, as are models of canal gates, a curragh and lighthouse, and deepwater corals.

Staff can tell you all about Ireland's marine ecosystem and the efforts now being made to protect and support it. After exploring the range of displays, you can have a snack or buy a souvenir in the shop, then go outside to walk along Galway Bay or have a swim at Leisureland next door.

Galway Irish Crystal Heritage Centre

Merlin Park, **t** (091) 757 311, **www.galwaycrystal.ie**
Open Daily 9–5.30
Adm Adult €4, child €3, family €10
Guided tours only

Visit this glass-making factory and find out what etching and acid polishing are and how beautiful lead crystal glassware is made. Watch glass blowers at work, and see the complete range of Galway Irish Crystal, displayed in the showroom. Then visit the 'Hall of the Tribes' museum, where you can learn about the merchants and artists who were the original leading families of Galway, known as the 'fourteen tribes', and the history of the Claddagh ring and Claddagh Village. Don't miss the boatbuilders' workshop and exhibit on Galway's fishing vessels, known as the 'Hooker'.

Galway Leisureland

Headford Road, Salthill, **t** (091) 562 820
Open Daily 10am–midnight
Adm According to activity
Adventure rides, bowling, laser games, full-size and learners' swimming pools, disabled access, baby-changing and buggy storage, café, shop, outdoor funfair in summer

A great place to go after visiting Atlantaquaria next door. Different sections cater for different age groups; under-7s must be accompanied by an adult in the water, and there's a learner area for toddlers with an adjustable floor for controlling water depth. For older children, the Treasure Cove has pirate ships on a beach-style pool with a water cannon, bubble pool and 65m waterslide.

Leisureland sits on the Galway Bay seaside promenade at Salthill. In summer there's an outdoor funfair with miniature train rides, a ghost train, giant wheel, virtual reality games, fun house, crazy golf, carnival rides, adventure playgrounds and bumper cars.

Royal Tara China Visitor Centre

Tara Hall, Mervue, **t** (091) 751 301, **www**.royal-tara.com

Open All year Mon–Sat 9–6, Sun 10–6. **Adm** Free

Café, free guided tours, showrooms

Take a guided tour of this china and pottery factory: it's best to visit Mon–Fri before 4.30 if you want to see craftspeople in action.

Entertainment

Druid Theatre

Chapel Lane, **t** (091) 568617, **www**.druidtheatre.com

Producing very exciting performances, Druid have built up a high international reputation.

Galway Children's Theatre

The Kids Kafé, Seapoint, Salthill, **t** (091) 524 388

Open Summer only. **Adm** According to show

Fun shows tailor-made for little ones.

Taibhdhearc na Gaillimhe

Middle St, **t** (091) 562 024/530 291/755 479

Intriguing Irish-language theatre that also hosts traditional music and bilingual folk presentations. Home to the acclaimed Siamsa festival (*see* p.162).

Shopping

Charlie Byrne's Bookshop

The Cornstore, Middle St, **t** (091) 561 766

A characterful local bookshop.

A story to tell: The Tuatha Dé Danaan, or People of the Goddess Dana

Long ago the People of the Goddess Dana – or Danu, or Anu – flew within clouds from far northern lands to Ireland. They called themselves the Tuatha Dé Danaan.

A fine white mist spread below them over County Leitrim as they landed on the mountain of Sliabh an Iarainn, and around Mayo and Lough Corrib, near what may have been their blood-kin, the Fir Bolg. Some say they were all of the race of Nemedians, who had escaped centuries earlier from the Fomorian monsters (*see* p.29).

The Tuatha asked the Fir Bolg if they could share Ireland. The Fir Bolg leader Eochai said 'no' quite boldly as he cowered below the tall, shining Tuatha. Little did he know how much magic they had. He soon found out, during what became known as the First Battle of Moytura (*see* p. 175).

The Tuatha were a handsome race – tall, fair, with blue or grey eyes, and round heads. Well-versed in the mystic sciences and medicine, they were skilled horsemen and excellent inventors. They were fond of music and brought to Ireland new musical and poetic arts, metal-working skills, and a kind of magic for healing the earth and living things, as well as winning battles.

Head of the Tuatha was the Daghda ('the great father'), who brought along Oghma his wife, and four talismans:

The Stone of Destiny or *Lia Fál*, which roared when the rightful candidate sat upon it as he was made king on the Hill of Tara, where some claim it is still (others say it became the Stone of Scone on which Scottish kings were crowned, recently returned to Scotland after being kept in Westminster Abbey in London for several centuries).

The Spear of Lugh, whose bearer never failed in battle.

The Sword of Nuadhu, from which no attacker escaped.

The Cauldron of Plenty, from which no hunger went unsatisfied (also called the Cauldron of the Daghda)

Later the Tuatha had to fight the Fomorians again, in the Second Battle of Moytura (*see* p.183), and later still resist the humans when they arrived (*see* p.119). The Tuatha called for a truce, as they knew it was their fate to lose any battle with the Milesians. They agreed that the Milesians could have the surface world of Ireland so long as they, the Tuatha, were left in peace to inhabit the interior of its hills. Some say the Tuatha moved to the Otherworld, where dreams and magic intermingle.

Irish country people maintained this truce as best they could for centuries afterwards, by offering the Tuatha respect and leaving 'them' alone as much as possible. But today many people aren't keeping the Tuatha's secret places sacred... which perhaps isn't such a good idea.

Just because you don't see something doesn't mean it isn't there. A hill may be just mud and rock to you, but, for the Tuatha, it could be home. What fool can say that those who live in a world unseen (that is, the one that you yourself cannot see) are not affected by your actions and whatever else goes on in the dimension you occupy?

Claddagh Jewellers

Eyre Square, t (091) 563 282

Where to buy your souvenir claddagh rings.

Easons

Shop St, t (091) 562 284

A branch of the bookshop chain with a stock that covers all areas, including a big children's range.

Galway Woolen Market

21 High St, t (091) 562 491

Tweeds and knitwear.

Hughes & Hughes

Galway Shopping Centre, Headford Road, t (091) 563 903

Excellent modern bookshop with a comprehensive stock for kids, and also special events.

It's Magic

Eyre Square Shopping Centre, t (091) 563 313

Unusual toys from around the world.

Kenny's Bookshop

Tuam Road, t (091) 773 311, www.kennys.ie

This famous bookshop stocks Irish literature and children's books and more, and has an art gallery.

Smyths Toy Shop

Galway Shopping Centre, Headford Road, t (091) 561 520

Largest toy shop in Galway .

SPECIAL TRIPS

The Aran Islands

The Arans are made up of three main islands – Inishmore, Inishmaan and Inisheer – and a few smaller ones. For native Aran islanders English is their second language, if they speak it at all.

Riding a bike is probably the best means of independent travelling on the islands, although the weather can be unpredictable (so the best thing to carry with you is a lightweight plastic poncho that covers your head and leaves your arms free). You also need strong legs and lungs for cycling here, although the air is invigorating for the out-of-shape. Otherwise, you'll have a choice of a bus tour or horse-and-cart, which is a fantastic experience on a sunny day, even if you don't cover as much ground as on the bus.

Inishmore

Inishmore, or *Inis Mór*, the 'Big Island', is the largest of the three Aran Islands. The islanders' traditional way of life is still maintained a great deal, and Irish is still the majority language – although the Islanders speak English as well. There is a regular public bus service, but you may want to take one of the minibuses that meet the boats arriving in Kilronan, its main town. Minibus tours of the whole of Inishmore cost about €10 – good value if you want to find your way to all of its archaeological sites, ruined churches and bays where the seals live.

Inishmore has a wealth of historic ruins and sites, dating back to the Iron Age. Dún Aonghasa is the largest, but others are Dún Eoghanachta, a circular stone fort northwest of Kilronan, Dún Eochla, between Kilronan and Dún Aonghasa, Dún Duchathair, south of Kilronan, and Teampall Bheanain and Chiarain. The tourist office stocks an excellent guide to the archaeological jewels of Inishmore – *Legends in the Landscape, a Pocket Guide to Araínn*, by Dara O'Maoildhia. The book's author has started organic training courses so that the Islanders can successfully grow vegetables unique to Inishmore without using pesticides.

Should you choose to visit Kilronan first, head for the Aran Heritage Centre (*see* right), and then have a look at the locally made and imported Aran knitwear. There are also restaurants on the island, but take a picnic (and drinks) if you don't want to stay in town but prefer to roam about the island.

Dun Aonghasa Visitor Centre

Kilmurvey, Inishmore, t (099) 61008
Open Mar–Oct daily 10–6, Nov–Feb daily 10–4
Adm Adult €1.20, child €0.50 cents, family €3.80
Limited parking for bicycles only, exhibition and disabled access to toilets, local coffee shops nearby

This Iron Age fort is the most famous and spectacular of the island's national monuments: an ancient stone ruin so old that no one knows when it was built. Situated right on the edge of the cliff, part of it appears to have fallen into the sea, although some scholars have suggested that fort-dwellers there built it this way on purpose in order to evade intruders (you will need to hang onto your younger children, as there are no barriers to stop them from going over the edge). You may want to take advantage of the wonderful guided tours on offer at the visitor centre, as they employ excellent

Good to know...

Getting to and around the Aran Islands

Tourist information Comharchumann Forbartha Arann, **t** (099) 61354, **www**.visitaranislands.com. The main tourist office is in Kilronan, **t** (099) 61263.

By air Aer Arann (*see* p.280) flies to all three islands, with several flights daily all year from Galway and from Connemara Airport in Inverin (19m/30km west of Galway, with buses to the city). Flights take about 10 mins; fares are around twice the cost of the ferry – but look out for special packages, which include a night's stay on the islands. Galway Airport, **t** (091) 755 569; Inverin, **t** (091) 593 034; Inishmore, **t** (099) 61109; Aer Arann, Galway, **t** (091) 593 034, **www**.aerarann.ie.

By boat From three mainland harbours: Galway, Rossaveal, 23 miles (36km) west of Galway City, and Doolin, Co. Clare. The main island port is Kilronan on Inishmore. Crossings from Rossaveal take 40mins–1hr; return tickets on all lines are about €20. Tourist offices have current timetables.

Aran Ferries, t (091) 568 903, **www**.aranislandferries.com. Two boats: the Galway Bay runs between Galway and Inishmore, late May–Oct daily, and the Aran Flyer between Rossaveal and Inishmore, April–Sept daily.

Doolin Ferries, t (065) 74455. Ferries run from Doolin to Inisheer and Inishmore, Easter–Sept. You can arrange through tickets to make the islands a stepping-stone from Clare to Galway.

Island Ferries, t (091) 561 767. Ferries between Rossaveal and all three islands year round; in summer there may be six boats a day to Inishmore. Day trips are also available.

O'Brien Shipping, t (091) 567 283. Services to all three islands from Galway, June–Sept daily.

Queen of Aran II, t (091) 566 535, **www**.queenofaran2.com. Nov–Mar, Rossaveal to Inishmore.

By bus There is a regular bus service on Inishmore, from Kilronan around the island. Many islanders also offer inexpensive minibus tours.

Bike Hire Bicycles can be hired at several places in Kilronan: **Aran Bicyle Hire, t** (099) 61132.

folklorists. Before you go, tell your children about the Fir Bolg (*see* p.29), who allegedly built this fort after losing Ireland to the Tuatha Dé Danaan.

At the bottom of the hill where Dún Aonghasa is located, you can have tea and shop at the crafts stores congregated together there for woollen goods, or visit the site's tourist office, where you can sometimes get hold of the noted Aran folklorist Padraigín (pronounced pora-geen) Clancy, a woman who often guides tours there – in Irish as well as English (her book *Celtic Threads*, Veritas Publications, Dublin, 1999, is a collection of essays on Ireland's Celtic spiritual heritage by well-known scholars and celebrities).

Afterwards, look for the seals that sometimes lounge off the coast of Inishmore, and contemplate what life must have been like – and the way it still is – for islanders here. You may even catch a glimpse of the enchanted island of *Hy Brasil* ('island of the blessed'), which some say appears every seven years west of Inishmore. Others claim it appears elsewhere or is the modern name for Tir na n'Óg, the land of eternal youth, or is merely an optical illusion created by weather conditions. However, it has been on maps since the 16th century, and the 6th-century sailor-monk St. Brendan the Navigator is said to have discovered America long before Columbus while seeking this illusive isle.

Ionad Arann/Aran Heritage Centre

Kilronan, Inishmore, **t** (099) 61355
Open Daily Apr–May and Sept–Oct 11–5, Jun–Aug 10–7; other times by appointment
Adm Adult €3.50, under-16s €2
Book/craft shop, restaurant, toilets

This small exhibition centre constantly runs Robert Flaherty's classic film *Man of Aran,* and displays old boats and artefacts found on the largest of the Arans. Older children will enjoy seeing the vintage boats used for fishing and transport that are displayed, and part of the movie, but it is more of a classic film for adults, so youngsters may grow restless after a while.

Inishmann and Inisheer

The middle of the three islands that make up the Arans is Inishmann, and the smallest, most southern one is Inisheer. These are less popular with tourists, and people who do go there generally rent bicycles or hire spots on horses and carts. The largest, best preserved of the Arans' stone forts is on Inishmann, while the best beach is on lonely little Inisheer.

But before you leave the Arans, or the Gaeltacht, you may like to surprise the shopkeepers by speaking in Irish: 'go rev muh hah gut' (thank you) and 'shlan' (good health to you/goodbye).

Dunguaire Castle

Kinvarra, **t** (091) 637 108,
www.shannonheritage.com
Getting there 17 miles (28km) south of Galway City: N6 and N18 to Kilcolgan, then N67 to Kinvarra
Open Daily mid-Apr–Sept 9.30–5.30
Adm Castle: adults €4.20, 5–12s €2.40, under-5s free, family (2+4) €10.50; Banquet: adults €44, 9–12s €33, 6–9s €22, under-5s free
Guided tours, banquets twice nightly

In an ocean-side corner of Co. Galway you'll see this fascinating 400-year-old castle, on the outskirts of Kinvarra. After exploring the restored castle – built by the Hynes Clan in 1520 – go to the early evening medieval banquet with your children, to be transported back to a time of candlelight and kings, cold grey stone walls, acoustic music and hosts in medieval attire. A harpist opens the evening with a serenade, then your regal host welcomes you and takes you to the time of King Guaire, who was renowned for his banquets in the 7th century. Your first course follows, and then there are intervals of serving and performing, as your servers illustrate the castle's history through a series of playlets incorporating faery stories, Irish poems and music. Other works cited include those of past owners of the castle like writer Oliver St John Gogarty and his visiting friends: WB Yeats, Lady Gregory, George Bernard Shaw and JM Synge all visited here in the early 20th century.

The ambience makes it easy to chat with neighbours on the wooden benches at long oak tables. Food is the one thing that could be improved here – maybe with more authentic dishes from the Middle Ages – as the feast is a bit too 20th-century. However, sweet mead and wine are served to adults to ensure that the evening is merry, while children receive something less potent.

Thoor Ballylee

Near Ballaba, outside Gort, **t** (091) 563 081/631 436
Getting there From Galway, N6 then N18 to Gort (23 miles/38km). From Gort, take the N66 north.
Open Jun–Sept Mon–Sat 10–6
Adm Adult €4.45, child €1.27, student €3.81
Audio presentations, book/craft shop, gardens, picnic area, tearoom, toilets

It is obvious why Ireland's best-loved lyric poet WB Yeats chose this fairytale tower house (pronounced 'toor bahh-lilee') as a place to live and write. Its pastoral surroundings remain much as they were when he lived there with his family in the early 20th-century. Yeats never allowed his son or daughter to enter his writing alcove, above the rest of the house, nor to make noise while he was writing. He generally left his wife 'George' to settle any squabbles. Only once did he come down from his study to discipline his children, his daughter claimed, by reciting a poem about little dogs that bark and bite, which so shocked them that they fell silent for the rest of the day.

The tower has been kept true to its original, rather bare condition, so that one can understand Yeats's complaints about floods and drafts. Press a button to learn how each room was used in his time; the best people to talk to about this, though, are the locals, whose relations knew him. Take note of the inscription on the tower, which goes:

I, the poet William Yeats
With old millboards and sea-green slates
And smithy work from the Gort forge
Restored this tower for my wife George;
And may these characters remain
When all is ruin once again.

A story to tell: A Galway folk tale

Galway is known for its folktales, and stories about giants and faeries from the Otherworld are common around the Ballylee and Gort area.

One story filed at the Kiltartan Gregory Museum near Gort is about a poor old woman with only a piece of bread left in her press (larder or cupboard). On the day of her worst poverty ever, a poor stranger appeared at her door begging for bread. The kind old lady had only a small bit left but she gave it gladly to 'the poor craithur' (creature), who was hobbling on two sticks and seemed so much worse off than herself. At twilight she fell asleep with the pangs of the hunger upon her and had a dream in which she was wandering in a wood looking for berries to eat. There she met a faery lady who told her to go home, where she would find her fortune in the press. The next morning, remembering the dream, she opened the press. In it, she found bread, faery cakes and a cupboard full of food, which never emptied until she died many years later. In the evening, a purse filled with gold was left at her door that, no matter how much she took out of it, always remained full.

AROUND AND ABOUT

Animal magic

Oceans Alive Visitor Centre

Renvyle Peninsula, Connemara, **t** (095) 43473
Getting there 22 miles (35km) north of Clifden
Open All year daily 10–6
Adm Centre: adult €5, child €2, under-6s free, family €20; Cruise: Adult €16, child €8, family €20
Children's play and picnic areas, telescope, toilets

Connemara's marine life and heritage are the focal point of this centre, which includes an aquarium, maritime museum, seaside park and a restaurant. Scenic and wildlife cruises and short sea angling trips are available, and it hosts traditional Irish music on summer evenings.

Turoe Pet Farm and Leisure Park

Turoe House, Bullaun, **t** (091) 841 580
Getting there 25 miles (40km) east of Galway; N6 to Loughrea, then north 4 miles (6km) to Bullaun
Open Daily Easter and May–Sept 10–8, Apr and Oct Sat–Sun and bank holidays, 1–24 Dec 4–9pm for Christmas Village, other times by appointment
Adm Adult €5, child €10
Farm tour, shop, café, BBQs and entertainment, picnic areas, pets' corner, playground, indoor play area, football pitch, nature walk, guided tours, disabled access, toilets, baby-changing room

Meet an Irish farming family here and take the opportunity to feed and cuddle farm animals or enjoy special events like the Easter Egg Hunt, Halloween Party and Christmas Village. Bring the right footwear to walk the nature trail that winds around this tranquil farm and the famous Turoe Stone, a beautifully carved standing stone made around 300 BC. Children have a great time here, making a wish at the wishing well, feeding ducks, playing on the swings and slides in the play area or petting the animals. There are two playground areas, one for little kids and another for older ones. Have a look at the old farm machinery before stopping at the teashop for home-baked goodies. Or, for more excitement, you can book to have Irish music, song and dance with lunch or dinner, as a buffet or barbecue, on the patio in good weather.

A Connemara proverb –
Every short dog is bold in the doorway of its own house.

Bricks and mortar

Athenry Castle

Athenry, **t** (091) 844 797
Getting there 15 miles (23km) north of Clifden
Open Apr–May Tues–Sun 10–5, Jun–mid-Sept daily 10–6, mid-Sept–Oct Tues–Sun 10–5
Adm Adult €2.50, child €1.20, family €6.30

This medieval walled town was made famous by the popular song, 'The Fields of Athenry', and this 13th-century Norman castle ruin is worth a look.

Aughnanure Castle

Oughterard, **t** (091) 552 214
Getting there 17 miles (27km) north of Galway
Open Mid-Jun–mid-Sept 9.30–6, Oct and May–mid-Jun 9.30–6
Adm Adult €2.50, child €1.20, family €6.30

A 15th-century tower built by the Norman De Burgo clan, but captured by the rival O'Flaherty's, as their stronghold beside Lough Corrib.

Clonfert Cathedral

Clonfert Village
Getting there 55 miles (88km) east of Galway by the River Shannon
Open Daily all year, hours vary

This atmospheric ruined church – known as a 'cathedral' despite being small – is thought to have been built in the 12th century over a monastery founded in 563 by St Brendan the Navigator, who some think discovered America before Columbus.

Kylemore Abbey

Kylemore, Connemara, **t** (095) 41113/41146
Getting there 11 miles (18km) north of Clifden
Open Oct–Mar 10–4.30, Easter–Sept 10.30–6, except Christmas week and Good Friday
Adm Abbey and Garden: adult €7, under-16s free, students €4
Visitors' centre, abbey, restaurant (open Easter–Oct), craft shop and pottery (open Mar–Oct), toilets

One of few human-built monuments in this wild part of Connemara, the abbey is also a place where you can pause for some home cooking and excellent freshly-baked desserts. This is Ireland's only convent of Benedictine nuns, who also run an international girls' boarding school here. The nuns fled here from their parent convent in Belgium during World War I. Today they generously open the grounds and part of the house to the public, along with the neo-Gothic chapel. Kylemore Abbey was built in 1868, and its chapel is a beautiful miniature cathedral. After seeing the exhibition and the rooms that are open to visitors, stroll along the Lake Walk and see how the Victorian walled garden, once one of the most impressive in Ireland with flower and kitchen gardens separated by a mountain stream and woodland, is being restored. Distinctive pottery is made in the Abbey's studio.

Look at this!

Aughrim Interpretative Centre

Near Ballinasloe, **t** (0905) 73939
Getting there 36 miles (58km) east of Galway
Open Daily Easter–end Sept 10–6. **Adm** €4
Book/craft shop, restaurant, toilets

Older children fascinated by history may enjoy reliving one of Ireland's most important and bloodiest wars. The 1691 Battle of Aughrim, which is reconstructed very well here, took place after the Battle of the Boyne and the Siege of Athlone during the war between Catholic James II and his Jacobite followers and the Protestant William of Orange (*see* p.35). At the height of the battle, just as the Jacobites were about to win, a cannonball killed their French general St Ruth, and panic ensued. The Williamites got the upper hand, and killed 6,000 Jacobites that day, against 2,000 of their own men. This decisive Protestant victory was Ireland's last great land battle. The centre has a Children's Day on the second Sunday in each June (telephone for precise times).

Galway songs to sing...
Connemara Cradle Song, Galway Is Where I Want to Be, Sweet Marie, The Galway Races, The Hills of Connemara, The Waxies Dargle, Dan O'Hara, The Galway Shawl, The Fields of Athenry.

Athenry Arts and Heritage Centre

St Mary's Church, The Square, Athenry,
t (091) 844 661, **www.athenryheritagetown.com**
Getting there 15 miles (23km) north of Clifden
Open Apr–May Tues–Sun 10–5, Jun–mid-Sept daily 10–6, mid-Sept–Oct Tues–Sun 10–5
Adm Adult €3.20, child €1.90, family (2+2) €10.16
Archery lessons, guided tours of Athenry, toilets

This display on Athenry's medieval past will provide you with all the details you need for exploring the 13th-century walled town.

Dan O'Hara's Homestead Farm

Lettershea, **t** (095) 21246/21808
Getting there 5 miles (8km) inland from Clifden, Connemara, on the N59 road from Galway.
Open Daily Apr–Oct 10–6; off-season on request
Adm Adult €7, child €3.50, student €6, family (2+4) €17
Audio visual display, guided tours, turf-cutting and other demonstrations on request, craft shop, tearoom, accommodation available, toilets

This 8-acre organic farm is run today exactly as it would have been in the 19th century. Teach your children the 'Ballad of Dan O'Hara' in honour of your visit here, where they can learn about the sad tale of a tenant farmer whose eviction after the famine ruined his life. Reconstructions of a *crannóg* (island house), a ring fort and a *clochaun* (stone hut) and the exhibition about how farming began here 6,000 years ago, with a bit of history of Connemara thrown in, give them a context in which to consider Dan O'Hara's thatched stone cottage and deepen their insight into the life of a non-English speaking 19th-century tenant farmer. They will be able to find out how turf was cut in the nearby bogs and used to fuel the hearth, around which O'Hara's family and friends gathered to tell stories and dance céilis (group dances).

People of O'Hara's time lived quite well on a diet of potatoes and buttermilk, supplemented with fish, seaweed, eggs and a little meat from animals they raised. Self-sufficient, O'Hara rented the house in which they lived and the land on which they worked. One day he enlarged his windows, not realizing he would have to pay a higher rent for them. This and the arrival of the potato blight and the Famine in the 1840s made it impossible for him to pay his landlord, and eventually he and his family were evicted. They got a ship to New York, one of the terrible coffin ships (so called because people were crammed together in appalling conditions). On the voyage, his wife and three of his children died. Arriving in America broken and destitute, O'Hara had to put the rest of his children into an orphanage and ended up selling matches on the streets of New York, far from home.

Kiltartan Gregory Museum

Kiltartan Cross, north of Gort, **t** (091) 631 069
Getting there 23 miles (38km) from Galway on N18
Open Jun–Aug 10–6; Sept–May Sun 1–5. **Adm** free
Souvenirs shop

A little museum housed in a former schoolhouse where a dedicated (plain-clothes) nun can tell you lots of stories about the mementoes of Lady Gregory, the Great Famine and the Celtic Revival on display. It offers a history of Lady Gregory's life and times, covering everything from records of the famine on the vast lands that her family owned to her correspondence with many renowned Irish artists. Of special note is a letter from James Joyce to Lady Gregory just before he left Ireland for Paris. Children will perhaps be most interested by the replica of an early 20th-century Irish classroom, with its mannequin teacher in period costume, old maps of Ireland and the world, textbooks and other accoutrements.

Leenane Cultural Centre

Leenane, **t** (095) 42323
Getting there 40 miles (65km) north of Galway via Oughterard
Open Apr–Sept daily 9–6 (times may vary)
Adm Adult €4, child €2, family €8
Craft shop, audio-visual display, restaurant, toilets

This centre overlooks Killary Harbour and on a good day is a wonderful place to show children something about sheep and the wool industry in Ireland. Kids see how wool gets from sheep to humans, and all the related processes (carding, spinning, weaving, felting, dyeing).

Roundstone Music and Crafts

IDA Park, Roundstone, Connemara, **t** (095) 35808, **www**.bodhran.com
Getting there 13 miles (21km) south of Clifden
Open Mar–Oct daily 9–7, Nov–Feb Mon–Sat 9–7
Craft shop, workshop, coffee shop, toilets

The famous *bodhrán* (pronounced bow-rawn) is one of Ireland's oldest known instruments, a drum made of goatskin stretched across a round Irish beech tree rim. You'll often hear it played in traditional Irish music, and Irish traditional musicians worldwide use bodhráns that were made here. You can book a time to watch Malachy Kearns make one for you, which can be decorated with a Celtic design, family crest or even your child's initial or name while you wait, free of charge. Malachy also specializes in smaller custom-made instruments (wooden flutes, harps, tin whistles). Another of their shops may be found in Main Street, Clifden, but is open only in summer. Afterwards, you might be inspired to climb Mount Errisbeg, a 300m (984ft) mountain overlooking the Atlantic, to which you can walk from Roundstone village, or take a walk along the beach at Dog's Bay.

A story to tell: Knockma: The Great Hill

The very first people to live in Ireland, allegedly, were a daughter of Noah named Cessair and her companions, who came to avoid the Great Flood (*see* p 29). Cessair, it is said, was buried under a cairn on top of Knockma (*Cnoc Meadha*, 'the great hill'), near Belclare, west of Tuam, in Co. Galway. Later, Knockma became known as the home of Fionnábar (or Finnveara), the King of the Faeries. Rumour has it that it's a good idea not to disturb this place or you may attract the ill will of the immortal King who lives there, and it's a certainty that if you throw something into a hole on the top of Knockma, it will be thrown right back out at you with as much force as it dropped.

Now, why is the King of the Faeries living inside a hill? The answer goes back to long, long ago before the days of Men (the Sons of Míl, *see* p.119), deep in the mists of time when magic was taken as a real and common thing in the world. The best magicians of all were the Tuatha Dé Danaan, later known as the faeries among country people. Fionnábar is one of the Tuatha, and therefore dwells in the shadowy nether regions of the earth.

Teach an Phiarsaigh (Patrick Pearse's Cottage)

Near Ros Muc (Rosmuck), **t** (091) 574 292
Getting there On Kilkieran Bay, 21 miles (34km) southwest of Oughterard
Open 30 Mar–Easter Sat–Sun 10–5, mid-Jun–mid-Sept daily 10–6, mid–end-Sept Sat–Sun 10–6
Adm Adult €2, child €1, family €5
Guided tours on request, toilets

This cottage is a bit difficult to find on Connemara's winding roads and doesn't contain a lot of information, apart from some memorabilia belonging to its owner. However, it's notable for being the modest thatched house where the poet-teacher Pádraic Pearse (1879–1916), leader of the 1916 Easter Rising, spent several summers. Pearse was an ardent supporter of the Irish language, and improved his knowledge of it by talking to local people in the lonely village of Rosmuck.

Nature lovers

Connemara National Park

Visitor Centre, Letterfrack, **t** (095) 41054/41006
Getting there 10 miles (16km) north of Clifden
Open All year, visitor centre daily May–Sept 10–5.30, Jun 10–6.30, Jul–Aug 9.30–6.30
Adm Adult €2.75, child €1.25, family €7
Disabled access, indoor picnic area with kitchen, coffee shop, toilets with disabled access and baby-changing room, free parking, summer events

One of Ireland's six National Parks, covering 2,000 hectares of Connemara's mountains. Extra activities in July–August include 2–3hr guided walks, nature mornings (for children aged 5+) and evening talks. There are also self-guided trails, including two short ones. In the visitor centre children can watch an audio-visual show and see 3-D models and plans of the park, and get to grips with interactive exhibits. Summer Tuesdays and Thursdays are activity days – involving games, the arts, animals and nature – for ages 4 and up.

Coole Park

Gort, **t** (091) 631 804
Getting there 23 miles (38km) south of Galway
Open Visitor Centre: Easter–May Tues–Sun 10–5, Jun–Aug daily 10–6, Sept Mon–Sun 10–5; Park: all year
Adm Adult €2.50, child €1.20, family (2+2) €6.30
Visitor centre, disabled access, tearoom, toilets

Just northeast of Gort lie the vast grounds of Coole Park. This estate used to hold the former home of the great folklorist Lady Gregory. She offered it as a haven to Yeats, Synge and many other writers. The house was demolished in the early 1940s, and now only fragments of it remain, but the park is a nature reserve with majestic yew trees. The Coole Visitor Centre provides historical background and maps of the area. You can spend a whole day here exploring Coole's nature trails and lakeside walks among graceful trees. Take a break to enjoy the centre's excellent café, and to watch the video about the days when Lady Gregory and her friends planned a better future for Ireland in this very setting. In the walled garden you can still find the famous copper chestnut tree known as the 'autograph tree' on whose trunk many of Coole Park's illustrious visitors carved their names.

Portumna Forest Park

Portumna, Lough Derg

A big area beside Lough Derg on the Shannon in eastern Co. Galway, with lakeside and forest walks, a nature trail to follow, an observation point and a tower that children can climb to look down upon the beautiful lough and the surrounding forest.

Sporty kids

Activity centres

Delphi Adventure Sports Centre

Delphi, Leenane, **t** (095) 42208/42307
Adm Price according to activity
Indoor sports hall with climbing wall, tennis court, shop, café, sauna, instruction, equipment included

Buckets and spades – Beaches in County Galway

There are fine beaches all along the twisting Galway coast, scattered around its hundreds of inlets and coves. In particular, **Ballyconneely** in western Connemara is surrounded by beaches: **Aillebrack** is good for swimming, and **False Bay** is better for surfing.

Omey Strand is a huge, magnificent sandy beach near **Cleggan** in Connemara. At low tide you can also drive over to the beautiful Omey Island, where there's a freshwater lake near the beach on the western edge. The island is a paradise for walkers – but watch the tides, or you'll get cut off.

Other beaches that stand out in the county are at **Salthill** just west of Galway, **Traught Beach**, further south at **Kinvarra**, **Tra na mBan** beach at **Spiddal**, and **Tra na Doilin** beach on the inlet at **Carraroe**. More unusual options are **Cill Muirbhthe** beach on **Inishmore** in the Aran Islands, and, for freshwater swimming, **Loughrea Lake** beach.

Tell me an Irish riddle...
Question – How many 'o's can you put in potatoes?
Answer – Put eight o's

Adventure holidays for ages 8–17: day or half-day activities include sailing, raft-building, canoeing, rock-climbing, surfing, hillwalking and snorkelling, plus evening events like céilis.

Killary Adventure Centre

Renvyle, Salruck, near Leenane, t (095) 43411/42276

Provides half-day, day, weekend, or week-long sea or land-based activities, including archery, canoeing, sailing and rock-climbing.

Peter Pan Funworld

Corbett Commercial Centre, Wellpark, Galway, t (091) 756 505

This excellent fully supervised indoor playcentre has areas for children of different age groups: soft play for under-5s, a junior adventure zone for 4–8 year-olds; and Captain Hook's area for the 8–12s.

Boat trips

Several companies offers cruises on Lough Corrib, in the heart of Connemara. Most cruises last about 90 mins; single tickets are around €9–10 for adults, €4–5 for children under 16, and a family ticket (2+2) costs around €24–25.

Aran Watersports

Kilronan, Inishmore, The Arans, t (087) 904 2777

Fishing trips or boats for hire – even a traditional curragh. Open May–Sept.

Corrib Cruises

Oughterard, t (092) 46029/46292

Guided commentary, open-top deck, bar

Cruises twice-daily in summer (May–Sept) on the Irish Republic's largest lake, the surface of which reflects the sunlight like polished glass. One of the cleanest and most scenic of Ireland's lakes, it has 365 islands, one for every day of the year.

Corrib Princess River Cruises

Furbo Hill, Furbo and Woodquay, Galway, t (091) 592 447, www.corribprincess.ie

Twice-daily cruise tours in the summer season around Lough Corrib from the Woodquay on the north side of Galway city, with a bar on board, optional buffet and dinners.

Island Discovery

Cleggan, Connemara, t (095) 44642/21520

Several sailings daily to Inishbofin Island, leaving from Cleggan, just north of Clifden.

Fishing

For brown trout, sea trout, and salmon fishing on Lough Corrib, contact the tourist office in Galway City for details and regulations.

Galway Fishery

Nun's Island, t (091) 562388

Horse riding

Aille Equestrian Centre

Aille Cross, Loughrea, t (091) 841 216

Also organizes week-long trails in Connemara.

Cashel House Hotel Riding Centre

Cashel, Connemara, t (095) 31001

Shorter or longer rides in Connemara.

Cleggan Trekking Centre

Cleggan, Connemara, t (095) 44746

Trek on sandy beaches or, if you prefer, for two hours on one of the offshore islands.

Clonboo Riding School

Corandulla, t (091) 791 362

Small family-owned riding school with day and week-long courses, or half-hour sessions for very small children.

Feeney's Riding School

Tonabrucky, Bushypark, near Salthill, t (091) 527579

Friendly centre just outside Galway city.

Rockmount Riding Centre

Claregalway, t (091) 798 147

Located a few miles north of Galway, this centre with indoor arena offers instruction and trekking.

Walking

There are naturally many wonderful walks in Connemara and the rest of Co. Galway, but the beautiful wildness of the terrain itself makes it still more important than in other parts of Ireland to go with a good map and orientation, and it's a good idea to go with a guided walk.

Michael Gibbons' Walking Ireland

Connemara Walking and Cycling Centre, Dun Gibbons Inn, Clifden, t (095) 21379/21492, www.walkingireland.com

A choice of guided walks, with accommodation arranged en route.

COUNTY MAYO

Mayo (*Mag nEo na Sacsan*) in Irish means 'The Plain of the Yew Trees of the Saxons', which indicates how long ago it got its name. The secrets County Mayo holds are found in quiet places where the past is still relatively unbothered by tourism. Archaeological treasures and ancient monuments in the form of standing stones, *fulachta fiadh* (outdoor water cooking troughs), ring forts and intriguingly shaped hills like the pointed Croagh Patrick will draw your attention.

There are welcoming amateur historians everywhere in Mayo who want to talk about the old stories of this part of the world, but you may not meet them if you don't take your time and slow down to the gentler pace of its people, who prefer slower ways to the glitz of the city. You will be able to relax in this part of Ireland, walking in its gardens, riding horses, climbing mountains, exploring prehistoric settlement sites and just making conversation. Taking the time to talk will lead to unexpected adventures. Often these will have something to do with the Mayo landscape, where you'll find lakeland scenery, the highest sea cliffs in Europe, safe beaches and islands like Inishglora, where four small graves are alleged to be those of the Children of Lir, or Clare Island, the home of the 16th-century pirate queen Grace O'Malley. Families can fish for salmon on the River Moy in the middle of Ballina, take part in outdoor sports, or make a pilgrimage to Croagh Patrick on Reek Sunday in August for a sense of what pagans and Christians have long experienced there. Try to understand how Irishmen felt after the Great Famine when so many saw the Knock apparition, while the practical joined Michael Davitt's Land League. Then discover the proud Gaelic heritage that people in Mayo have never quite forgotten, and the sense that women are not on Earth to be meek or mocked, as their High Queen Grace O'Malley demonstrated (*see* p.178).

Beneath Mayo natives' generosity and easygoing hospitality burns a special independence of spirit and love for freedom. They are not slow to tell you about the terrible Famine, which they remember annually with a long-distance 'famine walk'. Nor are they embarrassed when they speak of their nature-based remedies that heal people when modern medicine does not. There is great respect here for the traditions and lessons of the past, allied with a staunch determination not to dwell on what has been but to make the most of what is.

Ballina, Castlebar and Westport are Mayo's main towns. Ballina is a lively grey town through which heavy lorries pass, while the more anglicized Castlebar is bigger, with modern buildings. Princess Diana's ancestors, the Spencers, were landowning gentry here – given land in Castlebar during a British loyalist plantation after Cromwell's takeover. Westport still retains the charm of its Georgian past, as its town leaders have heroically combatted 'development', which outsiders, as usual, claim is necessary if Ireland is to keep up with the rest of the world. Westport's strength is that its people know better. That is why it is still a beautiful, inviting town, while its counterparts in other places have fallen to the drill. It is an ideal base, with pleasant shops, restaurants and hotels.

Did you know...?

Over each joint and sinew of the buried corpse of the Tuatha healer Miach grew 365 herbs, each one growing above the spot in the body that it could cure. His sister collected them, carefully noting the position of each one on her cloak, but when her father the healer Dían Cécht discovered this he was so jealous of his dead son's greater powers that he mixed them up – and so today we do not have the cures known by the Tuatha healers – all because of one man's selfish heart.

Tourist information

Achill, t (098) 45384
Achill Tourism, Achill Island, **t** (098) 47353, **www**.achilltourism.com
Ballina, t (096) 70848
Belmullet, t (097) 81500
Castlebar, t (094) 9021207
Cong, t (092) 46542
Knock, t (094) 9388193
Knock Airport, t (094) 9367247
Westport, James St, **t** (098) 25711/28288, **www**.visitmayo.com

Tours

Mayo Experience, Enterprise House, Aiden St, Kiltimagh, **t** (094) 9381494, **www**.mayoexperience.com
Tours of Counties Galway and Mayo.

Mayo Island Tours, t (098) 26015
Guided tours of the islands off the Mayo coast.

Special Events – County Mayo

June

Westport Horse and Pony Show, t (098) 26206
Children who love horses will enjoy this; only don't be surprised if they want you to buy one.

Westport International Sea Angling Festival and Horse Show, t (098) 27297/27344
Late June – only of interest to really keen youthful fishermen and riders.

Achill Archaeological Field School, t (098) 43564
Explore the deserted village of Slievemore on Achill Island, best for teenagers and young adults.

Castlebar International Blues Festival, t (094) 23111
Held over the bank holiday weekend, and fun for parents and (maybe) older kids.

July

Ballina Street Festival and Arts Week, t (096) 79814/79862/70905
For the whole family.

Ballinrobe Agricultural Show, Green Park, Ballinrobe, **t** (92) 41523
For future farmers and animal lovers.

Castlebar International Walking Festival, t (094) 24102
Walkers need to be fit, so be ready to carry small children on their walks.

Croagh Patrick Pilgrimage, Westport, **t** (098) 25711
At the end of the month. A harsh climb for the super-fit, and serious pilgrims.

Feile Iorras, Erris region of the Mullet Peninsula, **t** (097) 81500
A local traditional festival for families to visit.

Mulranny Mediterranean Heather Festival, t (098) 36287
Sheepdog trials, community sports, angling and rural entertainment for families to enjoy.

August

Geesala Festival, Ballina, **t** (097) 86742
A traditional community festival with riding and other horse-related sports, as well as music and folklore.

Westport Horse Fair, t (098) 25616/26206
A real fair for those seeking horses to buy.

September

Westport Arts Festival, t (098) 66502
Fun for teenagers but families enjoy it also.

October

Westport Harbour Seafood Festival, t (098) 29000/26534
For families with a taste for seafood.

Getting there and around

By air Mayo has an international airport at Knock, in the countryside near Charlestown by the N17 Galway–Sligo road, 24 miles (38km) east of Castlebar (*see* p.283). It has flights from airports in Britain with British Airways, MytravelLite and Ryanair (*see* pp.280–2). The only transport from the airport is by taxi or airline bus. Knock information, **t** 1 850 67 22 22, **www**.west-irl-holidays.com.

By bus Bus Eireann coaches from Dublin and other cities run to Ballina, Castlebar, Westport and several other towns. You can also get around by bus to almost anywhere within Mayo, or points beyond, but they are never as frequent or convenient as they might be. There are a number of obscure local lines; tourist offices are the best sources for bus information. Bus Eireann, Ballina, **t** (096) 71800, **www**.buseireann.ie.

By car Dublin to Castlebar takes about 5 hours (by the N4, then the N5 from Longford). A car is the best way to get around Mayo with children, but journey times are long and roads are narrow and bumpy. Don't expect to get anywhere fast!

By train Rail services are infrequent: Westport, Castlebar and Ballina each have about 3 trains daily to and from Dublin Heuston, and there are also trains down the west coast to Galway and Limerick. Stations: Westport, **t** (098) 25253; Castlebar, **t** (094) 9021222; Ballina, **t** (096) 71818.

Bike Hire

Achill Sound Hotel, Achill Island, **t** (098) 45245

Bike World, Castlebar, **t** (094) 9025220

P. Breheny and Sons, Castlebar St, Westport, **t** (098) 25020

Gerry's Cycle Centre, Crossmolina Road, Ballina, **t** (096) 70455

Mayo Leisure Cycling, Newantrim St, Castlebar, **t** (094) 9025220
Self-guided cycling tours, with accommodation.

O'Connor's, Main St, Cong, **t** (092) 46008

O'Malleys Island Sports, Dooagh, Achill Island, **t** (098) 43125

Sean Sammons, The Fuel Yard, James St, Westport, **t** (098) 25471

Good to know...
Getting to Mayo's offshore islands
Clare Island: O'Malley Ferries, t (098) 25045, make five runs a day from Roonagh Quay; tickets can also be bought from Westport Tourist Office.
Chris O'Grady also operates boats out to Clare Island, and can organize sea-fishing and boating via **Clare Island Ferry and Clew Bay Cruises,** Westport, **t** (098) 25212 (or via Westport Tourist Office). They have two boats, the Pirate Queen and the Clare Island mail boat, and also operate from Roonagh Quay. Both boat operators run all year round, but with much less frequency from October to April.
Inishturk and Caher: Boats also run from Roonagh. Service is somewhat informal; negotiate with local fishermen, or Chris O'Grady (*see* above). The Caher Star and Lady Marilyn make trips in summer from Roonagh via Inishturk, **t** (098) 45541.
Inishglora and Inishkea: There is no regular service to these islands, and you'll have to find someone with a boat to take you over, such as **Matthew Geraghty** in Belmullet, **t** (097) 85741.

SPECIAL TRIPS

Hennigan's Heritage Centre

Killasser, near Swinford, **t** (094) 9252505
Getting there North of Swinford about 19 miles (30km) east of Castlebar by N17
Open Daily Apr–Oct 10–6
Adm Adult €7, child €2; with (recommended) guided tour: adult €9, child €4, family (2+2) €22 + €4 per extra child
Guided tours, boat-hire, fishing, tearoom, toilets

Proprietor Jim Hennigan offers what is most likely the best folklore tour in Mayo. He tells the story of the way life used to be here for him and his family, who lived in a thatched cottage on this 10-acre farm for 200 years. Human-sized models hold farm tools, exhibiting in 3-D the working, as well as bad, habits of the past. A mannequin waits for illegal alcohol, *potcheen*, to distill in a real potcheen still. To avoid dying from its lethal, normally potato-based, brew, it was important to distill it at least three times before you drank it. The finer points of similar matters Hennigan can provide you with, like why boys were made to wear dresses and their hair wasn't cut until they were old enough to look after themselves (to make the faeries think they were girls so they wouldn't steal them, as boys were much sought after by the faery realm). Here you can see the real way of life of Mayo people, and how they lived in frugal, self-sufficient communities and used a 'barter and meitheal' system of exchange without money in order to survive the terrible conditions they lived under during Penal times and in the 19th century. There's a comprehensive collection of agricultural implements, while outdoors spuds grow in fields as they used to do, with fowl and animals in an unchanged farm yard. A tour around the lake, with more from Mr Hennigan about local history, rounds off your personalised tour, with home-baked scones and fresh coffee on offer in the tearoom. Tours are available at 12 noon, 2, 4 and 5.30pm (later on request).

Knock

Knock, Ireland's National Marian Shrine

Knock, **t** (094) 9388100, **www.knock-shrine.ie**
Getting there By N17 7 miles (11km) north of Claremorris
Open Daily. **Adm** Free

A total of 15 people of different ages – some of them children – saw an apparition of the Virgin Mary in 1879 in the Mayo village of Knock, in the pouring rain. It lasted for more than two hours. On her left was the spirit of St John the Evangelist holding an open book in his left hand, his right hand raised as if he were preaching, and a lamb on an altar to his left with a large cross behind it. To her right was St Joseph. Around the altar were hovering angels, and the vision was enveloped in a bright light that could be seen from miles away. No message was given and no word spoken. Today a modern complex of buildings stands on the site, with holy water available from lines of outdoor water fountains. If you want to learn about the apparition and Knock, do visit the on-site Knock Folk Museum, which will also interest children.

Knock Folk Museum

Knock, **t** (094) 9388100, **www.knock-shrine.ie**
Open Daily May–Jun, Sept and Oct 10–6, July–Aug 10–7. **Adm** Adult €5, child €4
Guided tours on request, shop, access for disabled

This small, excellent museum tells the story of the Knock Apparition of 1879 and places it in the context of life in Ireland at that time. It was not long after the Great Famine, when poverty was rife and there was a lot of social unrest in Ireland, manifested in the formation of the Land League (*see* p.37). It was against this background that people in Knock saw a vision of the Virgin Mary. The museum's exhibits include reconstructions of rooms, with information on crafts, education, clothing and transportof the time, and religious life and traditions.

Museum of Country Life

Turlough Park, Castlebar, **t** (094) 9031589, **www.**museum.ie
Getting there 5 miles (8km) from Castlebar
Open Tues–Sat 10–5 and Sun 2–5; closed Mon
Adm Free
Guided tours on request, full disabled access, shop, café, gardens, workshops, craft demonstrations and activity sheets for children (book in advance)

This new, modern museum looks out of place in its beautiful 19th-century setting beside a lake in the grounds of Turlough Park, next to the carefully restored 18th-century Turlough Park House. But once you get inside, you can immerse yourself in an unmissable exhibition on Irish rural life from the 19th to the 20th centuries. Here you can find out how furniture, utensils and even thatched roofs were made. Films of real people making things like curraghs and straw ropes fascinate anyone, and there are free teaching sessions in Irish craft skills. Modern city kids are impressed with the skill, patience and strength required to make traditional products, and it's an education for them to realize the importance of knowing how to look after oneself in the wilds of nature, and how helpless modern civilization makes many of us. The demands of living with the elements are emphasized in displays on hunting, fishing and farming. Equally interesting are exhibits on religion and education, where you listen to lessons as they were taught in Irish schools, and on how clothes and shoes were made. Your children can find out more about the games Irish children played; what they did on holidays like St Bridget's Day, May Day, Samhain or Christmas; and how people mourned at wakes. Highlighted are the political history of the time and Ireland's geography. Home to the National Folklife Collection, this is the first branch of the National Museum of Ireland outside Dublin.

A story to tell: The First Battle of Moytura

When they arrived in Ireland, the Tuatha Dé Danaan challenged the Fir Bolg for control of the island (*see* p.29). These 'Bag Men' were busy digging turf and husbanding the bogland at the time, and were overwhelmed by these god-like, glittering magicians – with their golden torcs and jewellery, their fine cloaks embroidered in yet more gold. But the Fir Bolg and their king, Eochaí, still fought the Tuatha proudly on the Plain of Moytura in Mayo, around Cong and along the shore of Lough Corrib.

They managed to cut off the arm of the Tuatha King, Nuadhu, but then three Tuatha warriors caught King Eochaí bathing at a well near a little hill (now called *Tulach an trír*, 'The Hill of the Three'). A small monument called *Carn an éinfhir* ('Cairn of the One Man') stands where they killed him. Of course the Tuatha won after this, especially with their superior magic, herbal medicines and special healing baths they used for their wounded.

After losing the First Battle of Moytura, the Fir Bolg retreated to find freedom in the faraway places of Ireland, like Rathlin Island in Antrim, and the Aran Islands of County Galway. On Inishmore, their leader Aonghus built a fort you can still see, at Dún Aonghasa ('Fort of Aonghus', *see* p.164).

According to Tuatha laws, no king was allowed to have a bodily imperfection, so now that Nuadhu had only one arm he gave the kingship to the half-Tuatha warrior Bres the Beautiful, whose father was a Fomorian. However, Bres was unkind to the Daghda, and proved stingy and inhospitable to visitors to his fort. His Fomorian genes must have got the better of him, because he showed none of the kingly virtues valued by the Tuatha, and grew very unpopular.

Meanwhile, Nuadhu was given a silver arm by the Tuatha's great healer, Dían Cécht, whose son Miach, though, was a still better healer and restored Nuadhu's natural arm. Dían Cécht grew so jealous of his son for this that he had him killed.

Now whole again, Nuadhu told Bres that he wanted to take back his kingship, especially since Bres had been wreaking havoc among the Tuatha by his mean-spirited behaviour. But Bres refused to comply, and turned to his evil relatives the Fomorians for help, and so began the Second Battle of Moytura (*see* p. 183).

Westport House

Westport House Estate, Westport, **t** (098) 25430
Getting there 2 miles (3km) north of Westport
Open Hours vary for different attractions (call to check what's operating on the day of your visit); most are open 6 Apr–21 Sept: Apr–May Sat–Sun 2–5, Jun daily 1.30–5.30, Jul–24 Aug daily 11.30–5.30, 25 Aug–21 Sept daily 1–5.30
Adm All attractions: adult €24, child €15, family (2+6) €75; House and Gardens only: Adult €11.50, child €6.50, family (2+6) €40
Exhibition, shop, tea room, restaurant, baby-changing facilities, toilets, disabled access

Combining a historic house with a 'Children's Animal and Bird Park', this makes a perfect family day trip. Westport House is set within delightful grounds and owned by the 13th great-grandson of Grace O'Malley, legendary pirate queen of Clare Island (*see* p.178). Little kids especially enjoy the animal farm with its llamas, camels, deer, monkeys and ostriches, not to mention the ball pond, playground, boating area, miniature railway, hill slide, dungeons, pedal boats, pitch'n'putt and flume ride. You could spend all day here, and even try fishing, on the lake or the river. The grand interior of 18th-century Westport House should be seen too, with its statue of Grace O'Malley nursing a baby.

AROUND AND ABOUT

Animal magic

Island Otterwatch

Claggan, Kilmeena, Westport, **t** (098) 41048
Getting there 5 miles (8km) north of Westport

Spend a day on the lookout for otters, dolphins and seals around Clew Bay with Shay Fennelly.

Partry House

Partry, **t** (094) 9543004
Getting there 12 miles (19km) south of Castlebar
Open Jul–Aug daily 2–6. **Adm** €4.50 per person

A pleasant outing may be had at this ecologically friendly organic farm and garden with abundant wildlife in its peaceful grounds.

Bricks and mortar

Ballintubber Abbey

Ballintubber, **t** (094) 9030934
Getting there 8 1/2 miles (14km) south of Castlebar
Open Daily all year 9am–12 midnight; guided tours May–Sept 10–6, at other times by appointment
Adm By donation
Video, interpretative centre, shop, guided tours available with advance notice

This historic abbey, founded in 1216 by Cathal O'Connor, King of Connacht, is overseen by the charismatic Father Fahey, renowned locally for his knowledge of the history of the Abbey and local folklore. Appearing a bit like a white-haired John Lennon, he leads pilgrims on cross-country walks to ancient shrines and local places, like Croagh Patrick (*see* p.178). A panel display describes how Ballintubber became known as 'the Abbey that wouldn't die' – where, despite robberies and the abbey being left roofless for 250 years, local people continued to attend Mass in rain, wind and snow. Guides here are as entertaining as professional actors, and tell you all sorts of stories about the Abbey, which, with its cemetery, retains a feel of bygone times.

Father Fahey also oversees the nearby Celtic Furrow museum when he is not busy with retreats and his duties for local parishioners, not to mention weddings, often for famous people like the actor Pierce Brosnan, who was married here.

Celtic Furrow

Visitor Centre, Ballintubber Abbey, **t** (094) 9030934
Getting there 8 1/2 miles (14km) south of Castlebar
Open May–Sept daily 10.30–5 (but call in advance)
Adm Adult €4, child €2.50, family €9, students €2.50, tour of Celtic Furrow and Ballintubber €4
Exhibition, toilets, teashop

This small museum brings to life the past 5,000 years in Ireland via models of Neolithic farmers (c.3000 BC), paintings of Celtic celebrations (c.600 BC); an outdoor maze tracing the early Christian period and displays on Irish folklore and customs.

Michael Davitt Memorial Museum

Straide, **t** (094) 9031022,
www.museumsofmayo.com/davitt
Getting there 12 miles (19km) north of Castlebar
Open Daily all year 10–6, including bank holidays
Adm Adult €3.50, child €1.50, family €8

A story to tell:
The Children of Lir

King Lir, the Tuatha Dé Danaan father of sea god Manannan mac Lir, married the eldest daughter Aebh (or Ava, or Eve) of King Bodh Dearg. Their union brought a daughter and a son, and then twin sons, at which point Aebh died in childbirth.

Lir would have died himself of grief, but for his children, whose beauty and singing soothed his heart, and made their grandfather Bodh Dearg and all their peoples love them. Lir was so miserable that when Aobh's younger sister Aoife attracted him with her magic arts, he married her. But Lir loved his children and their singing more than Aoife, and she grew very jealous.

One day, she told Lir, 'I'm taking the children to see their grandfather.'

But on the way she paused at Lough Derravaragh (the 'lake of the oaks' in Co. Westmeath, *see* p.105), and cursed the beautiful children with a Druid rod, saying, 'As swans with feathered companions will you live through the length of your lives.'

The children wept as a white cloud rose from the lake and moved to envelop them within its mist. Lir's eldest child, his daughter Fionnuala, begged Aoife to limit their time on the lake.

Aoife declared, 'It is bad for you that you have asked me, but, since you ask, you will remain here at Lough Derravaragh for 300 years, and on the Sea of Moyle[between Antrim and Scotland] for 300 years, and then 300 more on the island of Inishglora [off the coast of Mayo].'

The children, now swans, mourned, and their pitiful sounds made Aoife's heart soften a little, so that she declared, 'You may keep your own speech and continue singing the sweet music of the Sidhe, and there will be no music in the world equal to yours until your swan shapes leave you when you hear the first bells of a new religion in Ireland. But go away out of my sight now, children of Lir, with your white-feather faces and stammering Irish.'

Aoife went on to Bodh Dearg and lied, 'I'm sorry, my father, but Lir would not let your grandchildren come visit you.'

King Bodh Dearg did not believe her and sent word to Lir, who, fearing something terrible, set out to follow them. But on the way, he heard the singing of his children over Lough Derravaragh. The swans flew to him and he slumped in sorrow as he heard what Aoife had done.

After Bodh Dearg heard the story, he went to Aoife, not telling her what he knew, and asked her, 'What shape do you fear most?'

'A witch of the air in the cold north wind.'

To which Bodh Dearg replied, 'It is that you will be until the end of time, Aoife, for your cruel deed to Lir's children,' and Aoife immediately flew away as a witch of the air, where you can still hear her screaming when a north wind blows.

After 900 years, the swans followed the ringing of church bells on Inishglora, where they returned to their human forms as withered ancient people before dying. Graves for them were tended on Inishglora until the 20th century.

The hardships of Irish nationalist hero Michael Davitt (1846–1906) and how he overcame them may be inspirational for kids. Born in Straide at the height of the Famine, he was thrown out of his home with his parents for being unable to pay rent, which marked him for life. They went to England and aged 11 he began working in a cotton mill, but after an accident his right arm had to be amputated. Later, he joined the Irish Republican Brotherhood, and was sentenced to 15 years prison for arms running. Returning home, he decided peaceful political action was the best way to help Ireland, and founded the Land League (*see* p.37).

Davitt later travelled the world, collecting and spreading humanitarian ideas and campaigning for the rights of all oppressed peoples. Opposite the museum there is a ruined Fransciscan Abbey.

Look at this!

Ballymagibbon Cairn

Cross village, near Cong
Getting there 25 miles (40km) south of Castlebar

Cross (An Crois), on the Plain of Moytura, marks the site of the battle between the Tuatha and the Fir Bolg (*see* p.175). Oscar Wilde roamed this area as a youngster, while holidaying nearby.

Céide Fields

Ballycastle, **t** (096) 43325, **www.**heritageireland.ie
Getting there 5m (8km) west of Ballycastle
Open Daily mid-Mar–May 10–5, Jun-Aug 9.30–6.30, Sept 9.30–5.30, Oct 10–5, Nov 10–4.30,
Adm Adult €3.50, child/student €1.25, family €8.25
Guided tours, tearoom, toilets, disabled access

The modern pyramid-shaped interpretative centre has a viewing area overlooking this Stone Age site, where people farmed long before the bog was formed. Dating from 5,000 years ago, it is the most extensive settlement of megalithic tombs and field systems discovered anywhere in the world. Try out the archaeologists' technique for finding old fence poles by pushing a rod of wood into the bog (guides show you how). In the visitor centre you can warm up with a hot drink before examining the huge tree trunk in the middle of the hall, whose discovery here proved that this barren area was once a forest of giant trees. Friendly, well-informed guides here tell you all you could want to know about the site and more – just ask.

Croagh Patrick (the Reek)

Information Centre, Murrisk, near Westport, **t** (098) 64114, **www.croagh-patrick.com**
Getting there 5 1/2 miles (9km) west of Westport
Open All year daily. **Adm** free
Craft shop, café, guided tour (book ahead), toilets

The pointed summit of this mountain, 2,510ft (765 metres) high, dominates the north Mayo coast. It gained its holy status because St Patrick fasted there for 40 days in AD 441, when it was called the Reek. From the summit he prayed to God to be allowed to intercede for all Ireland's sinners. While there, blackbirds tormented him, perhaps seeking the food they were used to receiving from Druids during their rituals (in some folk stories, blackbirds are Druids who have 'shape-shifted'). The birds surrounded Patrick and turned into demons and serpents that attacked him. He threw his holy bell at them, and banished them to the hollow called Lag na nDeamha ('Hollow of the Demons'), on the north side of the mountain. The story grew to include all the snakes of Ireland, and this is said to be why no poisonous snake or reptile can live wild in Ireland today.

Thereafter the Reek was named Croagh Patrick, after Ireland's most famous saint, and became one of the foremost shrines of Irish Catholicism. But megalithic peoples had held an annual festival

A story to tell: Connacht's Pirate Queen

Did you know there was a pirate queen of Ireland? Her name was Granuaile, in Irish, or Grace O'Malley in English. The English called her a pirate, which the Irish found gaulling, as Granuaile was one of Ireland's last tribal chieftains, controlling the waters off the coast of Connacht from Mayo to Clare. She was well-matched against England's queen, only not so rich or powerful.

For 200 years Granuaile's family the O'Malleys had been Lords of the Isles, seafarers who ruled the islands of Clare, Inishturk, Inishbofin and Caher. In Granuaile's time, English feudalism was replacing Ireland's system of clan chiefs, and English law displacing Ireland's ancient Brehon Laws. Irish lords had very little power. So Granuaille resorted to unusual methods to get her taxes, which foreigners never seemed to want to pay.

From her Clare Island stronghold, Granuaile told her lads to row out to the merchants in their ships on their way to sell wines and such in Galway.

'Failté,' one of Granuaile's men would cry out from their boat, 'I thought I should warn you, sir, that your ship is in dangerous waters.'

'But the sea appears quite calm here', the Captain would reply.

'Ach, sure your honour, but there's trouble down below,' the boater would say. 'Many's the captain whose goods have been washed up ashore because he broke his craft upon our rocky secrets.'

'Hmph, thats very hard to believe,' came back.

'Well, suit yourself,' Granuaile's seaman would then say, preparing to row away, 'but if I was you I'd pick meself as your captain to guide you in.'

A long silence began as the sailor rowed and the Captain weighed his options, then shouted, 'Err, look here, how much will you take us in for?'

'A mere pittance,' Granuaile's man grinned.

'Right then,' says the Captain, 'up aboard.'

And that is how many a ship ended up wrecked on the shores of Connacht, which, oddly enough, did not prevent their goods from turning up at Galway market.

Granuaile felt that her seafaring warriors were merely demanding the taxes due from the ships trading in her domain. In 1593, aged 63, she went all the way to the Queen of England to tell her so. Amazingly, Elizabeth I let her out of her sight without taking off her head, and even agreed to allow Granuaile to police the waters off Ireland's western shore without interference from British soldiers. On her way back to Ireland, she had a famous encounter at Howth Castle (*see* p.70).

here for the God Lugh at least 3,000 years before Christ was born (about 5,000 years ago), so it is possible that the tradition of every pilgrim carrying a rock to its summit and leaving it there started that long ago. The present Christian Pilgrimage to Croagh Patrick begins in Murrisk on the last Sunday of July, which is called Reek Sunday.

Foxford Woollen Mills

Visitor Centre, Foxford, t (094) 9256756
Getting there 15 miles (24km) north of Castlebar
Open May–Oct Mon–Sat 10–6, Sun 2–6; Nov–Apr Mon–Sat 10–6, Sun 2–6
Adm Adult €6, child/student €5, family €18
Tours, mill/craft shop, restaurant, baby-changing room, tourist information, toilets

Founded by a nun in 1892, this woollen mill has been producing Foxford tweeds, rugs and blankets ever since. The fascinating story of how Mother Agnes Morrogh Bernard began this factory in an impoverished post-famine village is told via an ingenious self-guided exhibition, part of the tour of the factory where you see woollens being made. Afterwards, you can have a snack in the restaurant or perhaps buy something made in the mills.

Granuaile Centre

Louisburg, t (098) 25711
Getting there 14 miles (22km) west of Westport
Open Jun–mid-Sept 10–6 (but phone to check) or by appointment. **Adm** Adult €3.20, child €1.60
Bookshop, crafts centre, coffee shop, toilets

On your way to Roonagh to take the boat to Clare Island (*see* p.174), find out here about its 16th-century 'Pirate Queen of Clew Bay' Grace O'Malley (1530–1600). Born to a clan with lands from Achill Island to Inishbofin, she married a neighbouring clan member, but when he was murdered by the rival Joyce family she established a base on Clare Island, from which her galleys attacked shipping. When the English viceroy in Ireland, Sir Richard Bingham, tried to halt the activities of local chieftains, Granuaile went to England to appeal to Queen Elizabeth I for protection (*see* left).

Murrisk Abbey

Murrisk, near Westport
Getting there 5 1/2 miles (9km) west of Westport

In the shadow of Croagh Patrick, this ruined abbey was built in the 1450s by the Augustinians, and destroyed in the 17th century by Cromwell's soldiers.

The Quiet Man Heritage Cottage

Cong, t (092) 46089, www.quietman-cong.com
Getting there 25 miles (40km) south of Castlebar
Open 17 Mar–Oct daily 10–5
Adm Adult €3.75, child €1.50, family €6.50, student €2.25

This is an exact replica of a typical Irish cottage of the 1920s, exactly like the set (filmed in Hollywood) for the 1952 movie *The Quiet Man*. Cong, chosen for much of the location shooting, remembers the film fondly, and hosts an annual 'Quiet Man' festival.

Nature lovers

Clare Island

Getting there *see* p.174

Synonymous with Grace O'Malley, this 6-square-mile (1,500 hectare) island at the mouth of Clew Bay has quartzite hills that rise to the 1,510ft (460m) peak of Knockmore. The island's archaeological remains include a court-tomb at Lecarrow, ancient cooking sites, standing stones, forts and many other sites from later times. One of the most interesting places to visit is the remains of the 15th-century Cistercian Friary, originally founded by monks from Abbeyknockmoy, Co. Galway. Substantial patches of frescoes remain in a faded condition in the chancel vault. Local legends say that after O'Malley's death in 1600 her body was buried in the decorated O'Malley wall-tomb in the Friary. Overlooking the harbour, note the O'Malley Castle, which in 1831 became a coastguard station. Pack a picnic if you're making a day trip and head for the lovely sandy beaches, where you might be able to spot otters, seals and dolphins offshore.

Sporty kids

Activity centres

Glenans Sailing Centres

Collanmore Island, Westport, t (098) 26046

Residential courses in sailing offered.

Mayo Leisure Point

Moneen, Castlebar, t (094) 9025473

Indoor swimming pool, jacuzzi, sauna, steam-room, gym, cinema, bowling, go-karts and more.

Buckets and spades – Mayo's Beaches

Achill Island: Keel Beach, in Keel village; Keem Strand, near the western tip of Achill; Dugort Beach, in Doogort village; Golden Strand; and Dooega Beach in Dooega village.

Clare Island: many fine beaches around the island, *see* p.179

Clew Bay: Bertra Beach, near Westport; Old Head Beach and Carrowmore Beach near Louisburgh

Mullet Peninsula: Belmullet, at Elly Bay Beach and Mullaghroe Beach.

North Coast: Ross Strand, Killala northwest of Ballina

Tir Na n'Og Venture Fun Park

Enterprise House, Aiden St, Kiltimagh, **t** (094) 9381494

The play areas for children aged 3–13 here are environmentally friendly, safe, supervised and free. There are nice picnic areas, and the sculptures in the park will also draw your kids' attention.

Westport Leisure Park

James St, Westport, **t** (098) 29160

Indoor children's fun pool, swimming pool, gym, sauna, plunge pool, and other facilities. Under-8s must be accompanied when using the pools.

Horse-drawn caravans

Mayo Horse-drawn Caravan Holidays

Belcarra, Castlebar, **t** (094) 9032054, **www**.horsedrawn.mayonet.com

Caravans come with full self-catering facilities and instruction in managing your horse. Stops are planned for three hours travelling time per day.

Horse riding

The centres below offer 1hr to full-day rides with experienced guides for all ages in the Mayo countryside. Headgear and other essentials supplied.

Ard Chuain Equestrian Centre

Corballa, near Ballina, **t** (096) 45084

Carrowholly Stables

Carrowholly, Westport, **t** (098) 27057, **www**.carrowholly-stables.com

Claremorris School of Equitation

Galway Road, Claremorris, **t** (094) 9362292

Drummindoo Stud and Equitation Centre

Castlebar Road, Knockranny, Westport, **t** (098) 25616

Walking

Local tourist offices (*see* p.172) have excellent guidebooks for all Mayo's walks. Especially enjoyable are **Westport town walks** and the **Foxford Way**, 52 miles (84km) long, which links Western Way in the Ox Mountains to Loughs Conn and Cullin via many sites of archaeological interest. Others are the **Bangor Trail** (29 miles/48km) from Newport through Nephin Beg to Bangor, and the **Western Way**, from Killary Harbour and the Ox Mountains across Croagh Patrick to Westport.

The **North Mayo Sculpture Trail** consists of 15 outdoor sculptures by living artists, created in 1993 during the 'Mayo 5000' celebration to draw attention to the beauty of the coastline. The trail stretches from the Moy Estuary through Erris to the southern tip of the Mullet peninsula.

Cong Wood

Just north of the border with Co. Galway is Cong, celebrated as the location for the 1952 film *The Quiet Man* (*see* p.179). Long before that Cong Abbey was the home of the last High King of Connacht, Rory O'Connor. The surrounding woods, from Cong to Ashford, are a maze of roads, forest walks and high stone walls where you will even find an old tower. In Cong Park, note the romantic spot where the Monk's Fishing Cottage sits and picnic in the park in the nearby village. Enter it via Cong Abbey so that you do not have to pay a fee for entry.

Walking tours

Clew Bay Heritage Centre, The Quay, Westport, **t** (098) 26852

Historical walking tours in summer.

Croagh Patrick Walking Tours, Westport, **t** (098) 26090

Guided hill-walking tours for adults, with selected walks for older, accompanied children.

Doon Peninsula Nature Archaeological Walk, Burriscarra, **t** (094) 9360287

Gerry Greensmyth, Cloona, Westport, **t** (098) 26090

Tochar Phadraig, **t** (094) 9030934

An ancient pilgrim cross-country path from Ballintubber Abbey to Croagh Patrick.

Watersports

Glenans Irish Sailing School

Collanmore Island, Kilmeena, Westport, **t** (098) 26046

Sailing and other water sports facilities.

COUNTY SLIGO

Perhaps the Tuatha Dé Danaan still wander in the clouds in County Sligo, or the ghost of the poet Yeats haunts visitors to this place he loved so well. Whatever the reason, the county hangs heavy with mystical enchantment. Here you can almost hear the ancient lovers Diarmuid and Grainne whispering to each other as they hide from jealous Finn McCool, or Diarmuid rasping for water somewhere on the high mist-hidden plateau of Benbulben.

You will see traffic-stopping trains of cars following funerals in slow solemn procession here, pall-bearers walking before them, and giddy bridesmaids dressed to the nines giggling with their wedding flowers next to young bucks in their tuxedos, and somehow it seems the past is no different from today in this dreamy place. Only the rush of cars, new bungalows built outside towns and the colder modern bridge development inside Sligo town remind you of the march of time.

Sligo has beaches to swim beside, woods to walk in, waterfalls to discover, ancient stone megaliths to stumble over and the occasional hill to climb like Knocknarea, where the grave of Queen Maeve is covered by a cairn, to which every pilgrim should add their own stone. Near enough to Donegal to make its wilds and the woodlands of Fermanagh accessible, yet close to Mayo and the Gaeltacht, Co. Sligo is a peaceful place to base yourself if you wish to listen for the slow heartbeat of a lore and an old, old spirit now much besieged by the 21st century.

Tourist information

Sligo Town: Temple St, **t** (071) 9161201; Douglas Hyde Bridge, Yeats Building, **t** (071) 9138772

Tours

There are signposted walking tours around Sligo town and guided tours every weekday in summer; contact the tourist office for details.

Sacred Island Tours, Carrowkeel, Castlebaldwin, **t** (079) 9666241

Martin Byrne offers guided tours of ancient and mythical sites with the eye of an artist, by car or coach. Some walks unsuitable for small children.

Sligo Minibus Tours, Tourist Office, **t** (071) 9147488

Getting there and around

By air Sligo has an airport, 5 miles (8km) west of town at Strandhill, **t** (071) 9168280/9168318. It only has domestic flights from Dublin and Cork.

Special Events – County Sligo

June–July

Sligo Arts Festival, Sligo Town, **t** (071) 9169802

A festival mixing the contemporary and the traditional.

Sligo County Fleadh, Ballintogher, **t** (071) 9164250

A classic country festival of traditional music, dance and *craic*.

Seisiún, Sligo Town, **t** (071) 9164250

Traditional festival of music, storytelling and dance for children to enjoy.

South Sligo Summer School of Traditional Music and Dancing, Tubbercurry, **t** (071) 9185010

A festival where dancing, musical children may want to get up and take part.

August

Ballymote Heritage Weekend, t (071) 9183380

Good for families.

Gurteen Agricultural and Horse Show, Gurteen, **t** (071) 9165082

Held at the end of the month, and fun for animal-lovers.

Joe Fallon Traditional Festival, Collooney, **t** (071) 9130962

A family music event and party.

Michael Coleman Traditional Festival, Gurteen, **t** (071) 9182250/9182599

A similar event: they don't usually coincide.

Warriors Festival, Strandhill, **t** (071) 9168633

This incorporates the Culleenamore Horse and Pony Races and the Warriors' Run to Queen Maeve's legendary grave, on Knocknarea Mountain. Horse-lovers won't want to miss this community festival.

October

Ballintogher Feis, Ballintogher, **t** (071) 9164250

Community family festival.

Sligo International Choral Festival, Sligo Town, **t** (071) 9160780

Some choral events for children.

November

Sean Nós Singing, Coleman Heritage Centre, Gorteen, **t** (071) 9182599

This music school-based event is interesting for young singers who want to learn about Ireland's unusual unaccompanied traditional singing techniques. It's fun for everyone, too, especially anyone intrigued by Irish small town and country culture. Plenty of laughter ensues at such events.

By bus Sligo bus station is on Lord Edward St. Bus Eireann has daily buses between Sligo and Dublin, Ballina, Derry and Galway. Local buses link the county's villages. Bus information, **t** (071) 9160066
By car N4 from Dublin via Longford
By train There are several trains daily between Sligo and Connolly Station in Dublin via Longford. Sligo information, **t** (071) 9169888.

Bike Hire

North West Tourism, **t** (071) 9143149, produces a very good local *Hiking and Biking Guide*, available from tourist offices. For bike hire, try:
Conway Brothers, 6 High St, Sligo Town, **t** (071) 9161370
Flanagan Cycles, Market Yard, Sligo Town, **t** (071) 9144477
Gary's Cycles, 5 Quay St, Sligo Town, **t** (071) 9145418
West Coast Cycles, Quigabara, Inniscrone, **t** (096) 36593

SLIGO TOWN

The face of County Sligo's main town has been altered in recent years by modern shopping centres and cars, and, while the sleepy romanticism of the quiet town that entranced Yeats and Yeatsian scholars until the late 20th century still exists, it is no longer quite the charmer that it once was. But, get out of your car and you will find people who are very friendly and happy to get to know you, and who enjoy conversation and the new perspectives strangers bring into what is essentially still a small town. Here you will sniff a bit of the 'old romantic Ireland' that is not quite dead and gone, which can be missed altogether in a big city like Dublin. Yet, enough outsiders pass through Sligo all the time to make it a little bit cosmopolitan, especially thanks to its place on the literary map.

Things to see and do

Model Arts and Niland Gallery

The Mall, **t** (071) 9141405
Open All year Tues–Sat 10–5.30
Adm Free exhibitions but charges for courses
Atrium coffee bar, toilets

This large modern building hosts international artists and a daring mixture of local, national and international works – from Sligo youth theatre groups to Baroque and contemporary music festivals. It also has a permanent exhibit of paintings by Jack B Yeats, brother of the poet WB Yeats, and one of the largest collections of Irish artwork, the Niland Collection of Contemporary Irish Art.

Sligo Abbey

Abbey St, **t** (071) 9146406, **www**.heritageireland.ie
Open Apr–Oct daily 10–6,
Nov–Mar Sat–Sun 10–6, phone first
Adm Adult €2, child €0.70 cents, family €5
Guided tour on request, visitor centre, toilets (also for disabled), coach/car park nearby

This Dominican Friary, built in the mid-13th century, holds Gothic and Renaissance carved tombs, cloisters and the only 15th-century sculptured high altar left in any Irish monastic church.

Sligo Art Gallery

Yeats Society, Yeats Memorial Building, Douglas Hyde Bridge, **t** (071) 9142693/9147264, **www**.yeats-sligo.com
Open Mon–Fri 10–5. **Adm** Free

This small gallery in the Yeats Society's building host related arts shows, as well as a library, summer schools and other events.

Sligo County Museum and Branch Library

Stephen St, **t** (071) 9142212
Open Tues–Fri 10–12.45, 2–4.45. **Adm** Free

This small museum in the branch library building displays artefacts related to the prehistory of Co. Sligo along with a special section on Yeats and his family's connections with Sligo.

Entertainment

The Factory

Sligo, **t** (071) 9170431.

Productions by the Blue Raincoat Theatre Company.

The Hawk's Well Theatre

Temple St, **t** (071) 9161526, **www**.hawkswell.com

Revivals and contemporary Irish theatre.

Did you know... What a geis is?
In Irish tradition, it was a binding spell or obligation put upon someone from birth to death that was much stronger than honour or faith.

SPECIAL TRIPS

Carrowmore Megalithic Cemetery

Sligo, **t** (071) 9161534
Getting there About 2 miles (3km) south of Sligo Town; ask at tourist office for directions.
Open Daily May–Oct 10–6
Adm Adult €2, child €1.50, family €5.50
Guided tours on request, exhibition (restricted access for those with disabilities), toilets, car park

This lofty, windy ancient site is said to be where the warriors of the Second Battle of Moytura (*see* right) are buried, and where some of the battle itself was fought. It contains the largest collection of megalithic monuments or tombs in Ireland. They are also among the country's oldest prehistoric relics, predating Newgrange by some 700 years. Archaeologists have identified over 60 stone constructions, and excavations are ongoing.

Older children will be engaged if you provide some historical background, as well as stories about the area; younger kids may be entranced by the faerylore associated with the megaliths. There is little shelter here, so long treks can be tiring and you need to bring along water and a snack. Be sure to wear clothing and shoes suitable for changeable and wet weather, and for uneven, rocky terrain too.

Gillighan's World

Knocknashee, near Lavagh, **t** (071) 9130286, **www**.gillighansworld.com
Getting there Near Lavagh village 17 miles (26km) south of Sligo Town
Open Easter–Sept Mon–Fri 12 noon–6 and Sat–Sun 2–7 (phone ahead to check times and activities)
Adm Adult €6, child/student €5
Shop, picnic areas,, adventure playground, disabled access, baby changing, toilets

From Sligo town, drive out to the impressive hill of Knocknashee, whose name means 'hill of the faeries'. At its base you'll find this adventure centre for young children. Older kids will be interested to hear the stories associated with the hill, smaller ones will feel big as they come upon tiny houses and toy creatures hidden like Easter eggs among the trees, rocks and streams, and everyone will enjoy petting the small animals and meeting the tame pig who wanders freely in the hope of finding titbits, or the donkey who may neigh to you as you arrive. There are little model faery villages, competitions and quizzes for children, and special magical events at Christmas and Easter.

A story to tell: The Second Battle of Moytura

After refusing to let Nuadhu take back the kingship of the Tuatha Dé Danaan (*see* p.163), King Bres sought the help of his evil relatives the Fomorians, who asked for taxes from the Tuatha. They of course refused to pay the Fomorians anything at all, and war ensued.

While the Tuatha were waiting to fight Bres and the Fomorians, a young, handsome warrior with all the virtues of the most noble of beings called Lugh, 'the shining one', arrived to help them. Lugh had survived the attempt of his grandfather the one-eyed Balor, leader of the Fomorians, to kill him. Balor had been told by Fomorian prophets that he would die at the hands of his own grandson, and so had ordered all his grandchildren to be drowned. But Lugh was rescued and raised by the sea god Manannan mac Lir ('son of the ocean'). Lugh was better than anyone at every skill, which he proved when he won every test the Tuatha gave him. Nuadhu made him King of the Tuatha Dé Danaan, so that he could lead the Tuatha in battle against the Fomorians. This was the Second Battle of Moytura.

The Fomorians' most deadly weapon was the eye of Balor, whose lid it took several men to lift. Any man it looked upon disintegrated into nothing.

Lugh cast a slingshot straight into Balor's eye, and killed him. So, the prophecy was fulfilled, and Balor fell at the hands of his own grandson. This is how the Tuatha Dé Danaan won the battle and the Fomorians were expelled from Ireland. For years afterwards Ireland prospered, with Lugh or the Daghda taking turns to be King.

Sligo Folk Park

Riverstown, **t** (071) 9165001, **www**.sligofolkpark.com
Getting there 10 miles (16km) south of Sligo
Open Apr–Oct Mon–Sat 10–5.30, Sun 12.30–6, Nov–Apr by appointment or for special events
Adm Adult €5, child €3, family (2+3) €14
Adm Special group rates (prices under discussion)
Disabled access, free parking, craft and coffee shops, exhibition, toilets

For a special trip down memory lane visit Sligo's largest and newest attraction. In the beautiful village of Riverstown, the Folk Park offers a range of rural-life exhibits around a recreated streetscape of a small Irish town, a traditional cottage, a working forge, the restored 19th-century Millview House and many vintage and farmyard implements. A museum and exhibition hall has displays on rural history, and the 'village street' has the kinds of shops that once existed in every Irish village. Visitors can also watch local craftspeople at work, buy craftwork and souvenirs and have homemade snacks in the restaurant or coffee shop. Through the year the park also holds many special events, such as Vintage Day.

AROUND AND ABOUT

Bricks and mortar

Lissadell House

Drumcliffe, **t** (071) 9163150
Getting there 11 miles (18km) north of Sligo
Open Jun–mid-Sept Mon–Sat 10.30–1, 2–5
Adm Adult €6, child €3

You mustn't visit Sligo without seeing this house, where WB Yeats and other early 20th-century lumi-

A story to tell: Diarmuid and Grainne

King Finn McCool was due to marry a young woman half his age – Grainne (pronounced 'grawn-yuh'). When she was born, Druids had predicted her beauty would cause great trouble in the land, so Finn decreed he would marry her to keep his kingdom safe. But when Grainne saw her future husband just before their wedding, her heart sank, as he was old, very old. She drifted off to her chambers, wondering how she might avoid what seemed a fate worse than death.

Finn's famous warriors, the Fianna, had come to the castle to join in the wedding festivities and were playing games in the courtyard beneath Grainne's window. Among them was Diarmuid, an honourable character, without fault or blemish. Apart from being very handsome, he had a 'love spot' on his forehead, which made any woman who saw it fall instantly in love with him. Knowing the trouble it caused, Diarmuid always wore a cap to hide it. But, as Grainne gazed wistfully at the young men her own age, leaping about with the blush of health upon them, Diarmuid's cap fell off, and the inevitable happened.

That evening in the King's banqueting hall, Grainne waited until the old men were dozing over their mead and made her way to Diarmuid. Before he knew it, she was asking him to take her away from Finn and marry her himself. He cried, 'Oh no, that is not possible. I am loyal to King Finn. A man of the Fianna never breaks faith with his own kin.'

'Then I put geis upon you,' wept Grainne, 'you must take me away from here this very night. Steal out of the castle now and I will follow you.'

Now Diarmuid was ruined. Grainne had put *geis* upon him – a binding demand that a faithful member of the Fianna could not refuse (*see* p.182). So Diarmuid and Grainne ran away from King Finn, sleeping in a different place each night for many moons to avoid his warriors, leaving behind their 'beds' (flat smooth stones on top of earthworks) all over Ireland, before finally settling beside Benbulben in County Sligo.

At last King Finn found out where they were, and sent word he wanted to see them. Suspicious, Grainne sent a servant to spread the rumour she had lost her looks, from years of hard living. But Finn sent a spy to find out the truth, and he reported back that she was even more beautiful, and that the pair were as happy as two swans on a lake. This enraged the king, but he kept it secret.

Grainne encouraged Diarmuid to make peace with Finn, and eventually, after many entreaties, Diarmuid agreed to hunt with him on Benbulben, as in old times. However, Finn conjured up a magical boar, which chased Diarmuid and gored him. The king found his former warrior gasping for breath upon the ground, and his heart softened as Diarmuid begged for water from his hands, for Finn had the gift of healing in them. He rushed to a well to carry water back to Diarmuid. Three times he tried, but each time anger rose in his heart about his former warrior's deceit and the water fell through his fingers. And then Diarmuid died.

At first Grainne was inconsolable – but, after a while, Finn won her affection. And do you know, the terrible truth of it all is that in the end, Grainne married King Finn...

naries exchanged ideas with suffragette Eva Gore-Booth and her sister Constance. The latter married a Polish count to become Countess Markievicz, and also an ardent Irish nationalist who took part in the 1916 Easter Rising. Spared execution because she was a woman, in 1918 she was the first woman ever elected to the British House of Commons, although she did not take her seat.

The Gore-Booths have lived near Drumcliffe since the time of Elizabeth I, but Sir Robert Gore-Booth built this house in the 1830s in a Greek Revival style. It still is the family home, and holds the legacy of generations of colourful Gore-Booths. This idealistic family gave away much of its fortune to the poor in the Great Famine. If you take time to walk in the well-loved parkland around the house, you may sense a bit of old Ireland's quiet nobility.

Look at this!

Yeats' Grave

Drumcliffe Church, Drumcliffe, **t** (071) 9144956
Getting there 6 miles (10km) north of Sligo
Open All year Mon–Fri 8.30–6, Sun 1–6. **Adm** Free

Beneath Benbulben, outside the little white Protestant church at Drumcliffe, you will find a plain gravestone on which is inscribed –

Cast a cold eye on life, on death;
Horseman, pass by

This is the simple message WB Yeats left to posterity (although the Sligo tourist industry has not passed it by). Yeats died in France in 1939, and his body was brought here, in accordance with the poet's wishes, by Sean MacBride, son of Maude Gonne, with whom Yeats had been desperately in love. In the grounds of the churchyard, there is a crafts shop, tearoom and a children's play area.

Nature lovers

Benbulben

Getting there 10–15 miles (16–24km) north of Sligo

This unmissable flat-topped mountain marking the view north of Sligo town, rising up like some great upturned ship left by giants long ago, is where Diarmuid is said to have died after a false reconciliation with Finn McCool (*see* left).

Buckets and spades – Sligo Beaches

Inniscrone: Almost in Mayo on Killala Bay, about 30 miles (48km) west of Sligo, this big beach has a well-developed seaside look, with good facilities and play areas for small children, and a fairground in summer. **Easky**, further north, is quieter and a bit of a surfing centre.
Mullaghmore: Near the Leitrim border; a broad beach that's safe for smaller children.
Strandhill: Sligo's 'town' beach, 5 miles (8km) to the west, with little shops and beach cafés, and also good for surfing. For information and equipment, try **Malibu Surf Shop, t** (071) 9168302.

Sporty kids

Boat trips

Boat tours are available on Lough Gill, or trips can be made to Inishmurray Island (April–Oct; contact Rodney Lomax, Mullaghmore, **t** (071) 9166124, or Tommy McAllion, Rosses Point, **t** (071) 9142391).

Blue Lagoon Bar, Sligo, **t** (071) 9142530
Boat hire on Lough Gill.

Lough Arrow Boats, t (071) 65491
Boat rental on one of Sligo's inland loughs.

Wild Rose Waterbus (or **Yeats Waterbus**), **t** (071) 9164266
Tours of Lough Gill with readings of Yeats' poetry, visiting the 'Lake Isle of Innisfree' and other sights.

Horse riding

Ard Chuain Equestrian Centre

Corbally (near Ballina), **t** (096) 45084
Children's riding holidays for all abilities.

Markree Castle Riding Stables

Collooney, **t** (071) 9130727
Rides on the Markree estate and forest trails.

Sligo Riding Centre

Carrowmore, **t** (071) 61353
One of Ireland's major equestrian complexes.

Walking

Some of the best walks in Co. Sligo are around Lough Gill. On the north side of the lake there are forest paths at **Carns, Deerpark** and **Hazelwood**; on the south side at **Slish Wood**, on the R287, there is a kids' paddling pool in a small river by the car park.

Alainn Tours, 12 Stephen St, Sligo, **t** (071) 9144536
Guided and self-guided walks.

LEITRIM AND ROSCOMMON

The unassuming strip of Ireland known as Leitrim, the place where in legend the Tuatha Dé Danaan are said to have first settled when they came to Ireland, and its next-door inland county of Roscommon, once coal and iron mining centres, are today known for fishing and farming. Visitors come to them to cruise on their rivers and lakes, or to cycle along picturesque roads observing these counties' rolling hills, pastures and boglands. Leitrim lies between County Sligo and the province of Ulster, with just 2 1/2 miles (4km) of Atlantic coastline. Roscommon has more level plains and blends into the midlands of Leinster.

Quiet farmers fill this area, with German settlers doing a good job of regenerating the land, so the locals claim. Notably, near Rossinver, Co. Leitrim, lies what may be Ireland's only true official organic farm. Health is not a new concern in this vicinity. People with aches and pains used to go to Lough Allen, for instance, to indulge in sweathouse therapy. This consisted of sitting on a pile of straw inside a stone hut, in which a fire burned steadily for hours, and then taking a dip in the stream.

Perhaps past-smallpox sufferers – like Jonathan Swift and his friend, Meath-born musician Turlough O'Carolan, who set up home for his wife and children in Mohill, Co. Leitrim, while he travelled around the country as a blind harpist – also found better health here. In fact we have smallpox to thank for O'Carolan's music. He caught the disease while a teenager, but survived, after which his Roscommon benefactor, a Mrs MacDermott, felt sorry for him and financed his musical education. She set him on a horse with a guide to ply his trade as a blind harpist roaming 18th-century Ireland. The first place O'Carolan is known to have performed was the house of a certain Seóirse Ua Raghnall (George Reynolds) on the banks of Lough Scur in Leitrim. Apparently he wasn't such a great harp player and, after hearing him, Reynolds suggested perhaps he might be more successful if he wrote music well, as opposed to playing it badly. That night O'Carolan composed his first tune, naming it after a local story of warring faeries – *Sí Beag Sí Mór*, still one of his most famous compositions and a favourite of Irish traditional musicians.

Special Events – Leitrim and Roscommon

May–June

Community Arts Festival, Carrick-on-Shannon, Co. Leitrim, **t** (071) 9620673

Josie McDermott Memorial Festival, Ballyfarnon, Boyle, Co. Roscommon, **t** (071) 9647024

Traditional music.

Strokestown International Poetry Festival, Strokestown, Co. Roscommon, **t** (071) 9633759

Poetry competitions and international poets giving readings and workshops.

Douglas Hyde Summer School of Traditional Irish Music and Dance, Ballaghaderreen, Co. Roscommon, **t** (094) 9860013

July–August

Joe Mooney School of Traditional Music, Song and Dance, Drumshanbo, Co. Leitrim, **t** (071) 9644091

Sliabh an Iarainn, Drumbshanbo, Co. Leitrim, **t** (071) 9641522

Music and singing festival.

Mohill Arts Festival, Mohill, Co. Leitrim, **t** (071) 9631174

Boyle Arts Festival, Greatmeadow, Boyle, Co. Roscommon, **t** (071) 9662066, **www.boylearts.com**

Boyle Heritage Festival, Boyle, Co. Roscommon, **t** (071) 9662193

O'Carolan Harp and Traditional Irish Music Festival, Keadue, Boyle, Co. Roscommon, **t** (071) 9647204, **www.keadue.harp.net**

Harp competition and traditional Irish music summer school that runs through July and August.

Tulsk Summer Fair, Tulsk, Co. Roscommon, **t** (071) 9639195

Ballinamore Annual Festival, Ballinamore, Co. Leitrim, **t** (071) 9644091

Michael Shanley Traditional Weekend, Kiltyclogher, Co. Leitrim, **t** (071) 9620489

Rosfest, Roscommon Summer Festival, Roscommon Town, **t** (086) 232 6419

Music, arts, culture and street entertainment.

Castlerea International Rose Festival, Castlerea, Co. Roscommon, **t** (094) 9620067

Top bands perform in the street.

September

Carrick-on-Shannon Fishing Festival, Carrick-on-Shannon, Co. Leitrim, **t** (071) 9620489

October

Eileen Og Harvest Festival, Castlerea, Co. Roscommon, **t** (094) 9655175

North Leitrim Walking Festival, **t** (071) 9644091

Halloween Magic, King House, Boyle, Co. Roscommon, **t** (071) 9663242

A story to tell:
Cruachan and the Brown Bull of Cooley

The legendary Cruachan was once a Royal Palace, the inauguration site and burial place of the Kings of Connacht. At one time, Cruachan was also the home of Maeve, or Mebh – 'the drunken one' – the famed warrior queen (some say earth goddess) whose burial mound is on top of Knocknarea near Strandhill in Co. Sligo. Fierce and proud, Maeve was responsible for launching the famed cattle raid of Cooley, as recounted in one of the greatest works of early Irish literature, the *Táin Bó Cuailnge* or 'The Brown Bull of Cooley'. Born queen of the southern part of Ireland, she married Ailill, who was king of the northern part. Their alliance made them the most powerful people in the country.

But that was not enough for Maeve. One morning she had an argument with her husband over which of them held the greatest power in Ireland. Agreeing that their wealth should be the deciding factor, they separated their fortunes and counted everything against the other. They found that they were equal in every respect but one. Ailill had one thing more than she had – the finest bull of their combined stocks. However, in Ireland there was one bull finer even than Ailill's, and that was owned by a farmer in Louth – the 'Brown Bull of Cooley'. Secretly, Maeve asked the farmer to let her borrow it. Intending merely to make her husband think she had more than he, she planned to return the bull to the farmer immediately afterwards. But he grew suspicious of her motives, and didn't let her have it. For no money would he part with it, even temporarily. So Maeve turned her army upon the farmer to steal the bull from him. This started a terrible war, which ended in her husband Ailill's white bull and the brown bull of Cooley fighting to the death, and tearing each other to bits.

Tourist information

Athleague, Co. Roscommon, **t** (090) 6663602
Boyle, Co. Roscommon, **t** (071) 9662145
Carrick-on-Shannon, Co. Leitrim: The Marina, **t** (071) 9620170, **www**.leitrimtourism.com
Roscommon Town, **t** (090) 6626342, **www**.roscommon.ie, **www**.visitroscommon.com

Getting there and around

By bus Bus Eireann's Sligo–Dublin and other routes stop in Carrick-on-Shannon, Roscommon, Boyle, Strokestown and other towns. There's also a good local network. For Bus Eireann information phone Sligo, **t** (071) 9160066, or Athlone, **t** (090) 6473322.
By train Carrick-on-Shannon and Boyle are on the Sligo line from Dublin Connolly; the Dublin Heuston–Ballina line passes through Roscommon Town and Castlerea. Carrick-on-Shannon, **t** (071) 9620036; Roscommon Town, **t** (090) 6626201.

Bike Hire

For cycle routes in Roscommon, contact Athleague tourist office or check the Suck Valley Tourism website, **www**.suckvalley.firebird.net.
Brendan Sheerin, Main St, Boyle, Co. Roscommon, **t** (071) 9662010
Buckley's Cycles, Astor Buildings, Roscommon Town, **t** (090) 6627318
Gerharty's, Main St, Carrick-on-Shannon, Co. Leitrim, **t** (071) 9621316
Riverside Cycles, Bridge St, Boyle, Co. Roscommon, **t** (079) 63777

SPECIAL TRIPS

Cruachan Ai Visitor Centre

Tulsk, Co. Roscommon, **t** (071) 9639268, **www**.cruachanai.com
Getting there 22 miles (35km) west of Longford
Open Jan–Mar and Nov–Dec Mon–Sat 10–5, closed Sun and bank holidays; Apr–Oct daily 10–6
Adm Adult €5, under-18s €2.75, family (2+4) €11
Café, exhibition, toilets

In this legendary home and inauguration-place of the Kings of Connacht there is said to be an opening that leads straight into the Otherworld. Deep in the crevice of Crúachain lies the Owenygat (or Cat Cave) of the faeries, which is protected by a giant King of the Cats, whose minions travel through it between this world and that of the faeries. Myths aside, school-age children with any curiosity about archaeology will think this little exhibition centre a real find. Ask at the desk for information on other sites in the area. There is a good exhibition about how a Galway University project has determined – through ground-probing radar and other modern techniques – that the area around Tulsk, Rathcroghan and Carnfree holds some 60 Iron and Bronze Age earthworks.

The visitor centre also has exhibits about later buildings, such as Tulsk Castle and a 15th-century Dominican Abbey on the Ogulla River. At Ogulla there is a well that is said to be where St Patrick converted to Christianity the daughters of the High King of Ireland, who immediately died and went to heaven. It is still a place of pilgrimage.

Children won't want to spend long indoors here, though, while their parents read all the displays, as they will be eager to explore the surrounding sites. You have to tour these independently, on foot, by car, or with a guide. Major sites include:
Rathcroghan Mound, a large circular mound thought to have been used in pre-Christian ceremonies, possibly also containing a passage tomb.
Rathmore (opposite Rathcroghan School), an impressive raised ring fort.
Rathnadarve (*Ráth na dTarbh*), the site in the Táin where the brown bull of Cooley and the white horned bull of Connacht did battle.
Relignaree (*Relig na Rí*), the burial ground of the kings, a large enclosure in Glenballythomas.
Dathí's Stone, where the last pagan king of Ireland is reputedly buried.

Educational visits for groups of children can be arranged in advance.

Who was... Douglas Hyde?

Connachtman Douglas Hyde, a Protestant Anglo-Irishman, planted the seed for the revival of the Irish language with a lecture he gave in 1892 on de-Anglicizing Ireland. He said, 'In Anglicizing ourselves wholesale, we have thrown away with a light heart the best claim which we have upon the world's recognition of us as a separate nationality.'

In 1893, with the poet Yeats, he co-founded an organisation in Dublin called Conradh na Gaeilge, the 'Gaelic League', to promote a revival of the Irish language. Though not a political group, it was very influential in creating Irish national consciousness. Hyde later became disillusioned when other members like Padráic Pearse took up a more political stance. An opponent of the 1916 Easter Rising, Hyde believed in building identity through education about Irish history, arts and traditions.

Still, he took political office himself, becoming a member the Irish Parliament. This enigmatic figure was so popular that De Valera asked him to become the first President of Ireland in 1938, an office he kept until 1945, aged 85. During his Presidency he lived in Dublin's Phoenix Park, but returned to his native Frenchpark in Roscommon afterwards, ending his days there in 1949.

Derryglad Folk Museum

Curraghboy, Co. Roscommon, **t** (090) 6488192
Getting there 7 miles (11km) north of Athlone on the Roscommon Road
Open May–Sept Mon–Sat 10–6, Sun 2–6
Adm Adult €3.50, child €2.50, family €11
Full wheelchair access

Be sure to talk to the friendly proprietor of this award-winning rural artefacts museum. He grew up and worked on a traditional Irish farm, and has a passion for conveying to people what he feels was a superior way of life to that lived in modern Ireland. He makes the implements that Irish farmers once used come to life for the visitor, and is accustomed to teaching school groups all about how to make butter, iron and wash clothes, cook food and harvest crops. He also plays old records on a wind-up gramophone to bring voices of the past to life for bored children weaned on computers. His knowledge and enthusiasm make this a gem.

King House

Main St, Boyle, Co. Roscommon, **t** (071) 9663242
Getting there 24 miles (38km) south of Sligo
Open Apr and late Oct Sat–Sun 10–6, May–mid-Oct daily 10–6; open at other times by request
Adm Adult €4, child €2.50, family (2+2) €10
Guided tours on request, restaurant, shop, full disabled access, adventure playground and park, special events all year

The life-size models and dynamic effects used in this 18th-century mansion combine to help you explore the world of landlords, monks, soldiers and craftsmen in the Ireland of 1600–1800. The story of the house, its inhabitants and the locality is told in an informative, entertaining manner, focusing on dramatic episodes such as the King family's lives, Gaelic Ireland, the construction and restoration of the house and its military history. The King family were Earls of Kingston in England and arrived in 1603 to control nearby Rockingham Estate, which is now Lough Key Forest Park. Sir Henry King built the present Georgian mansion about 1730, and its grand scale was created to impress outsiders with the wealth of its owners. Visitors are led through stunning tableaux and interactive exhibits like building part of a brick vault like craftsmen of the time. Children might enjoy banging the Regimental Drum of the Connaught Rangers, based here when it became a barracks in 1788.

Strokestown Park House

Strokestown, Co. Roscommon, **t** (071) 9633013, **www**.strokestownpark.ie
Getting there 14 miles (22km) west of Longford
Open Daily Apr–Oct 11–5.30
Adm Gardens and Museum: €12 per person; two of the three sites: €8.50; one site: €5
Shop, guided tours, tearoom, disabled access

Strokestown Park House was the family home of the Pakenham Mahon family from the 1600s to 1979. The 18th-century mansion has been restored with virtually all its original furnishings intact. Most impressive is the cavernous kitchen, which will amaze kids with its facilities. They will also enjoy seeing the clothing and toys used by 18th-century children in the nursery. Built in the Palladian style, this mansion also houses the Irish National Famine Museum. Outside the house there's an impressive 6-acre walled garden, faithfully restored to its 1740s layout. You can buy some of its organic produce in the shop by the entrance.

The village of Strokestown ('Ford of the Blows') is a curiosity itself. Peculiarly grand for a country village, it probably has the widest village street in Ireland, the ends of which are marked by an octagonal church and Strokestown House. The street was created by a local landowner, Lord Hartland, who was inspired by the Ringstrasse in Vienna.

AROUND AND ABOUT

Bricks and mortar

Boyle Abbey

Boyle, Co. Roscommon, **t** (071) 9662604
Getting there 24 miles (38km) south of Sligo
Open Apr–Oct daily 10–6, guided tours hourly 10–5
Adm Adult €1.20, child €0.50 cents, family €4
Visitor centre in restored gatehouse, toilets

Founded in 1161 by the MacDermott family, Boyle Abbey is a fairly well-preserved ruin, considering its history: it was built as a companion house to the first Irish Cistercian monastery at Mellifont, and consecrated in 1220, after which it was attacked many times by the MacDermott and O'Conor clans.

A story to tell... Carolan's last tune

The musician Carolan returned one day to the home of his first patron, Mrs MacDermott of Ballyfarnon. She was the lady who had first taught him the harp, and the one who had suggested he tour professionally, giving him a horse to travel with. After telling her that he had come to her house to meet his maker, he asked her for whiskey and composed his heartbreaking *Farewell to Music* before retiring to bed. A week later, he died. Carolan is buried in Kilronan Church, a few miles from his own home in Mohill over the border in Leitrim, in the MacDermott family vault.

Clonalis House

Castlerea, Co. Roscommon, **t** (094) 9620014
Getting there 6miles (9km) west of Castlerea
Open Jun–mid-Sept Tues–Sat 11–5
Adm Adult €5.50, child €3.50
Afternoon teas available in the tearoom

The descendants of the last High Kings of Ireland lived here, in the ancestral home of the O'Connors, kings of Connacht. The harp of O'Carolan, who often played here, is also on display, along with the O'Connor inauguration stone. The house itself was built in 1880 but stands on ground which has been in the O'Connor family for 1,500 years. Owen O'Connor was dispossessed for short periods in the 17th century, but their remarkable tenure survived even wars and penal laws. A fascinating archive of over 100,000 documents is maintained at Clonalis. Other exhibits include uniforms belonging to the O'Connor family, and Louis XV-style furniture.

Lough Rynn House

Mohill, Co. Leitrim, **t** (071) 9631427
Getting there 11 miles (17km) east of Carrick-on-Shannon
Open Daily May–mid-Sept 10–7. **Adm** €4.44 per car
Playground, boat rides, craft shop, restaurant

Children will enjoy the boat rides, playground, arboretum and the grounds here, leading to a 16th-century tower, a Bronze Age dolmen and a wishing seat. A 600-acre lake sits within 100 acres of woodland for families to explore, and nearby is a walled garden, originally made to grow vegetables, with terraces designed to catch the sun and replanted like a Victorian pleasure garden. It's one of the largest walled gardens in Ireland, with splendid views over Lough Rynn, and nature trails.

Look at this!

Cavan and Leitrim Railway

Dromod, Co. Leitrim, **t** (071) 9620089, **www**.cavanandleitrimrailway.com
Getting there 11 miles (17km) south of Carrick-on-Shannon
Open Mon–Sat 10–5, Sun 1–5.30
Adm Adult €6, child €4, family €14 (prices vary if you travel on a steam or diesel train)

There's a small exhibition with pictures of the old railway in this period ticket office and waiting room. Here you can catch the old-fashioned train, which ran on a narrow-gauge line to the Leitrim towns of Drumshanbo, Mohill and Ballinamore.

Douglas Hyde Interpretative Centre

Frenchpark, Co. Roscommon, **t** (094) 9670016
Getting there 9 miles (14km) south of Boyle
Open Daily May–Sept, but phone ahead
Adm Free, donations accepted

Douglas Hyde was the first President of the Republic of Ireland and co-founder of the Gaelic League (*see* p.188). This centre, dedicated to him, is in the church where his father was rector, and has an informative exhibition on his life and times.

Elphin Windmill

Ballyroddy, Elphin, Co. Roscommon, **t** (071) 9635695
Getting there 6 miles (9km) north of Tulsk
Open All year daily 10–6. **Adm** Adult €3, child €1.50
Guided tours offered all year by arrangement

This early 18th-century windmill is in full working condition and the only one of its kind in the west of Ireland. Restored as a local community project, the tower was built to grind oats and wheat.

Hell's Kitchen Bar and Railway Museum

Main St, Castlerea, Co. Roscommon, **t** (094) 9620181, **www**.hellskitchenmuseum.com
Getting there 40 miles (64km) west of Longford
Open Pub hours, or on request
Adm Adult €2, child €1

This Aladdin's cave of a place in a small country town has a very friendly proprietor, Sean Browne, who thoroughly enjoys showing people his collection of memorabilia in the rooms behind his pub. There are old-fashioned knick-knacks both in the pub and beyond – including an impressive diesel locomotive. Children find it fascinating, especially given the unstoppable enthusiasm of its owner.

Nature lovers

Lough Key Forest Park

Boyle, Co Roscommon, **t** (071) 9662363
Getting there 24 miles (38km) south of Sligo
Open Dawn–dusk daily. **Adm** €5 per car

With woods, a lake and several islands, this is one of Ireland's most attractive forest parks. It has lots of facilities and great walks, and on the lake, which connects with the Shannon, there are boats for hire.

Organic Centre

Near Rossinver, Co. Leitrim, **t** (071) 9854338
Getting there 24 miles (38km) northeast of Sligo
Open May–Sept Sat–Thurs 11–4 (but phone ahead)
Adm Adult €5, child free

This organic farm offers educational visits around its demonstration garden and centre.

Sporty kids

Boat trips

The most popular waterways are the Shannon, from Carrick-on-Shannon, Lough Garadice, from Ballinamore, and Lough Key (*see* above) from Boyle.

Ballinamore Boats, Ballinamore, Co. Leitrim, **t** (071) 9644079
Carrick Craft, The Marina, Carrick-on-Shannon, Co. Leitrim, **t** (071) 9620236
Tara Cruisers, The Moorings, Knockvicar, Boyle, Co. Roscommon, **t** (071) 9667777

Horse riding

Moorlands Equestrian Centre, Drumshanbo, Co. Leitrim, **t** (078) 41500

Unaccompanied children are catered for.

Una Bhan Rural Tourism Cooperative, King House, Boyle, Co. Roscommon, **t** (071) 9663033

They also organize fishing and bike tours.

Walking

Suck Valley Visitor Centre, Athleague, **t** (090) 6663602, **www**.suckvalley.com

On the banks of the River Suck, this centre has full information on local attractions and walks: the **Suck Valley Way** is a 60-mile (100km) path through woods, bogs and wetlands, and there's also a 135-mile (217km) **Green Heartlands Cycle Route**, in a paradise of unspoiled countryside.

WHERE TO EAT

County Galway

The Arans

An tSean Cheibh ('The Old Pier')

Kilronan, Inishmore, t (099) 61228 (*moderate*)

Good home-baking and fresh fish, and a good fish and chip shop in the same building.

Aran Fisherman's Restaurant

Kilronan, Inishmore, t (099) 61363 (*inexpensive*)

A children's menu available during the day, with dishes made from organically grown vegetables.

Fisherman's Cottage

Inisheer island, near the pier, t (087) 904 2777 (*inexpensive*)

Inisheer has this one good and reasonably priced seafood restaurant.

Teach Osta

Inishmaan, t (099) 73003 (*inexpensive*)

This is the only pub on Inishmaan, and offers good bar food and conviviality.

Mainister House Hostel

Kilronan, Inishmore, t (099) 61322 (*inexpensive*)

Wonderful vegetarian buffets, but be sure to book and turn up for 8pm, for food disappears fast.

Ballinasloe

Haydens

Dunlo St, t (090) 9642347 (*moderate*)

Good pub snacks and an excellent dining room.

Barna

O'Grady's on the Pier

Barna Pier, t (091) 592 223 (*inexpensive–moderate*)

Breton- and French-style seafood.

Clarinbridge

Moran's on the Weir

Kilcolgan, near Clarinbridge, t (091) 796 113 (*inexpensive*)

This seafood bar is tucked away in an old cottage overlooking its own oyster beds in Galway Bay.

Clifden

Fire and Ice Restaurant

Station House Courtyard, t (095) 22946 (*moderate–expensive*)

A strong following is growing locally for this restaurant, which serves inventive dishes made with local organic produce – in an eclectic, international mix of styles.

Quay House

Beach Road, t (095) 21369 (*expensive*)

Here you'll find a very high standard of cooking and a friendly, relaxed atmosphere.

Galway City

An Gabhar Orga (The Golden Goat)

37 Newcastle Road Lower, t (091) 523 966 (*inexpensive–moderate*)

Good vegetarian restaurant.

Antonios

Salthill Road, t (091) 581 100 (*inexpensive*)

New York-style pizza, children's menu and high chairs provided. Closed Sun.

Busker Browne's

Cross St, t (091) 563 377 (*inexpensive*)

An all-day bright and breezy seafood bar.

Delight

29 Upper Abbeygate St, t (091) 567 823 (*inexpensive*)

Light lunches, snacks and takeaways are available in this little café.

Eddie Rocket's

Egliton Street, t (091) 566 026 (*inexpensive*)

1950s-style American diner with good service and very child friendly.

The Galleon

Salthill, t (091) 522 963 (*inexpensive–moderate*)

Plain yet substantial food served up by efficient and family-friendly staff. High chairs, children's menus, baby-changing facilities and colouring pads are all provided.

Goya's Fine Confectionery and Pastry Shop

3 Kirwans Lane, t (091) 567 010 (*inexpensive–moderate*)

Delicious cakes and coffee, and excellent meals for children too.

McDonagh's Seafood House

22 Quay Street, **t** (091) 565 001 (*inexpensive*)

Excellent eat-in or takeaway fish and chip meals; McDonagh's has a reputation as one of Ireland's best fresh fish restaurants.

Milano's

Middle St, **t** (091) 568 488 (*inexpensive*)

Helpful staff, high chairs and baby-changing facilities make for a winning combination at this contemporary child-friendly pizza restaurant.

Sev'nth Heav'n

Courthouse Lane, Quay St,
t (091) 563 838 (*inexpensive–moderate*)

Award-winning modern Irish-Cajun-Mexican restaurant with children's menu, vegetarian options and good desserts and ice creams.

Gort

The Blackthorn

Crowe St, Gort, **t** (091) 632 127
(*moderate–expensive*)

The bar and upstairs restaurant open for dinner and good-value lunches. Live music on Saturdays.

Inishbofin Island

Day's Hotel Bar

Inishbofin, **t** (095) 45809 (*inexpensive*)

Good seafood and soups.

Kinvarra

Kinvarra Coffee and Wholefood Shop

Kinvara Harbour (*inexpensive*)

Good for snacks and wholesome takeaways.

Kylemore

Kylemore Abbey Restaurant and Teahouse

t (095) 41146 (*inexpensive*)

Lunch and snacks with hot and cold dishes and home baking made on the premises are served here. Children are welcome.

Moycullen

Drimcong House Restaurant

Moycullen, **t** (091) 555 115 (*expensive*)

The owners create delicious original combinations of flavours, yet never overdo it. It's known as one of the best eateries in the west of Ireland, but vegetarian and children's meals are still available.

Roundstone

Beola Restaurant

Roundstone, **t** (095) 35871 (*moderate*)

Seafood is a speciality.

Spiddal

Boluisce Seafood Restaurant

Spiddal Village, **t** (091) 553 286 (*inexpensive*)

Try the fish chowder with homemade bread.

Tuam

Cre-na-Cille Public House

High St, **t** (093) 28232 (*inexpensive-moderate*)

An intimate, relaxing family-run restaurant that specialises in seafood, game and local produce.

County Mayo

Achill Island

The Beehive Craft and Coffee Shop

Keel, **t** (098) 43134 (*inexpensive*)

Open daily for snacks and light lunches.

The Boley House

Keel, **t** (098) 43147 (*inexpensive–moderate*)

Good, well-prepared menus served in a stone cottage: fine salmon, seafood and steaks.

The Chalet

Keel, Achill Island, **t** (098) 43157 (*inexpensive*)

Fish and chips.

Ballina

BJ's Bistro

Bury Street, **t** (096) 73097 (*inexpensive*)

Pasta, fish, meat dishes and a children's menu.

Ballycastle

Mary's Cottage Kitchen

Main St, **t** (096) 43361 (*inexpensive*)

Home cooking in a comfortable, casual setting.

Castlebar

Garden Restaurant

Breaffy House Hotel, Breaffy Road, **t** (094) 9022033 (*moderate*)

Good hotel restaurant.

Charlestown

Riverside Restaurant

Church St, **t** (094) 54200 (*inexpensive–moderate*)

Children's menus and even baby dinners are available in this quaint family-friendly restaurant specializing in seafood, steak and Irish cuisine.

Cong

Ashford Castle

Cong, **t** (094) 9546003 (*luxury*)

Irish food in a sumptuous setting. Families might prefer afternoon tea to a full meal; of most interest to youngsters will probably be the evenings in the Dungeon Bar, where a resident storyteller tells stories and myths from Irish folklore.

Echoes

Main St, **t** (094) 9546059 (*moderate*)

Children are welcome at this family-run restaurant, which serves cheerful home cooking.

Foxford

The Sun House

Swinford Road, **t** (094) 56506 (*inexpensive*)

This casual café is fine with kids and serves good coffee and light snacks.

Louisburgh

Durkan's Weir House and Restaurant

Chapel St, **t** (098) 66140 (*moderate–expensive*)

Children's meals and bar menus are available in this family-run seafood restaurant.

Newport

Newport House

Newport, **t** (098) 41222 (*expensive*)

It is a treat just to see inside this house, with its elegant furniture, and the food is good too. This is a good place for a treat with teens, but younger kids may be a bit fidgety around the fine china.

Westport

Bernie's Café

High St, **t** (098) 27797 (*inexpensive*)

Vegetarian and children's menus for lunch.

Quay Cottage

The Harbour, **t** (098) 26412 (*moderate*)

Folksy seafood restaurant. Very cosy, with good bread and a vegetarian menu as well.

County Sligo

Castlebaldwin

Cromleach Lodge

Lough Arrow, **t** (071) 9165155 (*expensive*)

In the hills above Lough Arrow, close to Boyle in Roscommon. Traditional, hearty Irish cooking.

Castlegarron

Ben View Restaurant and Mullarkey's Bar

Castlegarron, Drumcliffe, **t** (071) 9163149 (*inexpensive–moderate*)

Families and children welcome. Straightforward, simple meals.

Collooney

Glebe House

Coolaney Road, **t** (071) 9167787 (*moderate–expensive*)

This award-winning country house restaurant offers homely French-based cooking with lots of herbs and vegetables from the garden. Children are welcomed, and there's a children's menu.

Drumcliffe

Yeats Tavern

Drumcliffe, **t** (071) 9163117 (*inexpensive–moderate*)

Casual dining with good home cooking and salads, and good facilities for children.

Mullaghmore

Eithna's Seafood Restaurant

The Harbour, **t** (071) 66407 (*moderate–expensive*)

Organic coastal ingredients are used with fresh fish and shellfish, and vegetarian dishes.

Sligo Town

Bistro Bianconi

44 O'Connell Street, **t** (071) 9141744 (*moderate*)

Pasta and pizza to eat in or takeaway. An informal pizza joint with a pleasant modern interior.

Crazy Jane's

Rockwood Parade, **t** (071) 9141976 (*inexpensive–moderate*)

Families are welcome here, beside the River Garavogue in the middle of town. There's a children's menu, colouring books and lollipops.

Hargadon's
O'Connell St, **t** (071) 9170933 (*inexpensive*)

Atmospheric pub with cosy snugs and mirrors decorated with gold Guinness slogans. The lunchtime pub fare goes down well with kids.

Harmony Hill Cafe and Wine Bar
Harmony Hill, **t** (071) 9144362 (*inexpensive*)

Light lunches and snacks, from herbal teas to salads and BLTs, and they cater for food allergies.

Hillside
Kilsellagh, Enniskillen Road,
t (071) 9142808 (*inexpensive*)

Comfortable old farmhouse, home cooking and log fires in the company of the Stuart family.

Hy-Brasil Espresso Bar
Bridge St, **t** (071) 9161180 (*inexpensive*)

Good for coffee, juices, snacks and lunch.

Penthouse
Tobergal Lane, **t** (071) 9145030
(*inexpensive–moderate*)

Unpretentious food for lunch and dinner, especially geared to families.

Primrose Grange House
Knocknarea, outside Sligo,
t (071) 9162005 (*inexpensive–moderate*)

This farmhouse, built as a school in the 18th century, has a splendid position overlooking the glen and the sea.

Leitrim and Roscommon

Ballinamore

Glenview
Ballinamore, Co. Leitrim, **t** (071) 9644157
(*moderate*)

This restaurant, part of a B&B, is in a lovely setting beside the river at Woodford; call ahead.

Boyle

Donnellan's
Clarendon House, Knockvicar, Boyle, Co. Roscommon, **t** (071) 9667016 (*moderate*)

Good children's menu.

The Royal Hotel
Bridge St, Boyle, Co. Roscommon,
t (071) 9662016 (*moderate*)

The coffee shop serves salads and snacks.

Carrick-on-Shannon

Barge Steakhouse
Leitrim Village, Carrick-on-Shannon, Co. Leitrim,
t (071) 9620807 (*moderate*)

Steaks are a speciality; there are good children's menus and daytime bar menus.

Dromahair

Stanfords Village Inn
Main St, Dromahair, Co. Leitrim, **t** (071) 9164140
(*inexpensive–moderate*)

Cosy pub with a simple restaurant and a garden.

Drumshanbo

Maguire's Cottage
Drumshanbo, Co. Leitrim, **t** (078) 41033 (*moderate*)

A friendly restaurant with an open fire, traditional furnishings, and good steaks, seafood and salads.

Frenchpark

Sheepwalk Bar and Restaurant
Frenchpark, Co. Roscommon, **t** (094) 9870391
(*moderate*)

Open all year. Children are welcome in this recommended restaurant south of Boyle. High chairs and a special children's menu are available.

Kinlough

Courthouse Restaurant
Kinlough, Co. Leitrim, **t** (071) 9842391
(*moderate–expensive*)

Mixture of Italian and Irish, with organic produce.

Roscommon Town

Abbey Hotel
Abbeytown, Galway Road,
t (090) 6626240 (*expensive*)

Comfortable, bright 18th-century house with fine French-style cuisine, Irish dishes and a children's menu in a 60-seat restaurant; one for a treat.

Gleeson's Restaurant
Market Square, **t** (090) 6626954 (*moderate*)

Try breakfast in the 'Manse' restaurant, or eat in the café for lunch, afternoon tea or dinner.

Ulster

07

20km
10miles
N
Malin Head
Ballyhilfin
Lag Sand Dunes
Doagh Isle
Fanad Head
Tory Island
Culdaff
Ballyliffin
Tory Sound
Horn Head
Sheep Haven
Carndonagh
Inishbofin
Dunfanaghy
Downings
Portsalon
Marblehill
Carrigart
Dunree Head
Lough Swilly
INISHOWEN
Redcastle
Gweedore
Gortahork
Buncrana
Crana River
White Cas
Bunbeg
Millford
Rathmullan
Lough Foy
Aranmore Island
Donegal Airport
Derryveagh Mountains
Glenveagh Nat. Park
Inch Island
Inch
Burnfoot
Derry City Airp
The Rosses
Kilmacrenan
Burt
Burtonport
Newtown-cunningham
Grianan Aileach
DERRY
Dungloe
Letterkenny
River Swilly
Ardmore
Ness Wood
Gweebarra Bay
Lough Finn
River Foyle
Dunmore Head
Portnoo
Naran
Convoy
Maas
DONEGAL
River Deele
Ballyneaner
Loughros Beg Bay
Glenties
Lifford
Strabane
Blue Stack Mountains
Ulster Way
Maghera
Ardara
Ballybofey
Dergalt
Glencolmcille Folk Village
Glencolmcille
River Finn
Sperrin
Glengesh Pass
Lough Mourne
Plumbridge
Glenelly Valley
Malin Bay
Mourne River
Lough Eske
Castlederg
Newtownstewart
Gortin
Kilcar
Killybegs
Bruckless
Donegal
Ulster History Park
Gortin Glen Forest Park
Greenca
Ulster American Folk Park
Mountfield
Doorin Point
TYRONE
St John's Point
Lough Derg
Omagh
Camowen
Rossnowlagh
Carn
Donegal Bay
Pettigo
Ballyshannon
Boa Island
Kesh
Bundoran
Lower Lough Erne
White Island
Dromore
Belleek
Tully Castle
Castle Archdale
Irvinestown
Ballygav
Blaney
Augher
Devenish Island
FERMANAGH
Fivemiletown
Upper Lough Macnean
Enniskillen
Castle Coole
Ulster Way
Sligo
Lower Lough Macnean
Brookeborough
Lough Gill
Blacklion
Bellanaleck
Marble Arch Caves
Gubaveeny
Florence Court Forest Park
Florence Court
Lisnaskea
Knockatallon
Monagha
Upper Lough Erne
Rossmore Forest Park
SLIGO
Dowra
Crom Estate
Drumswords Church
Lough Allen
Arigna Mountains
Ballyconnell
Annagh-makerrigh House
Rockcorry
Blackwater River
Belturbet
LEITRIM
Milltown
Cootehill
NORTHERN IRELAND
ULSTER
CONNACHT
Killykeen Forest Park
Leitrim
Killashandra
CAVAN
Carrick-on-Shannon
REPUBLIC OF IRELAND
LEINSTER
Cavan
MAYO
River Erne
Baileborough
MUNSTER
Lough Gowna
LONGFORD
Ballymachugh
Virginia
Lough Sheelin
Lough Ramor
River Easky

Ulster

Rathlin Island
Rathlin Sound
Campbeltown
Fair Head
Inishowen Head
Greencastle
Giant's Causeway
Dunluce Castle
B146
Portrush
A2
Bushmills
Ballycastle
Downhill
Portstewart
Ballyvoy
Torr Head
Magilligan
Castlerock
Coleraine
Ballypatrick Forest
Runabay Head
N
O
R
T
H
Benvarden
Dervock
ANTRIM MOUNTAINS
Limavady
Ulster Way
A29
A54
A26
Layde Church
Ringsend
Balleymoney
Cushendall & Hill of Tivereagh
Glens of Antrim
B68
A26
River Main
Glenariff Forest Park
Garron Point
ONDONDERRY
A6
Dungiven
B64
Carnlough
Glenarm
Glenshane Pass
Carntogher
River Bann
Carnagee
Glenarm
Cairnryan
Broughshane
Slemish Mountain
Mountains
B40
Maghera
Ballymena
M2
B94
Ballygalley
ANTRIM
Larne
B47
Portmuck
Draperstown
Castledawson
Magee Island
A26
Magherafelt
C
M22
Balleyclare
Whitehead
Stanraer
Beaghmore Stone Circles
Moneymore
B18
Springhill
Antrim
M2
B58
Carrickfergus
Liverpool
H
Cookstown
Belfast International Airport
A6
A57
Douglas (Isle of Man)
Belfast Lough
Drum Manor Forest Park
Ardboe High Cross
Newtownabbey
Helen's Bay
Copeland Islands
Crumlin
Holywood
M5
A
Lough Neagh
Cultra
Bangor
Belfast City Airport
Donaghadee
M2
N
Coalisland
Mountjoy
Glenavy
BELFAST
Newtownards
Dungannon
Upper Ballinderry
Coney Island
Giant's Ring
Mount Stewart
N
Maghery
Temple of the Winds
Comber
A4
Lisburn
Strangford Lough
Ballywalter
Grey Abbey
E
Ards Peninsula
Moy
Ardress House
Moira
A22
A20
A24
River Lagan
L
Blackwater
Lurgan
Hillsborough
Kircubbin
Benburb
Portadown
Craigavon
B28 R.
Loughgall
A28
A1
N1
Dromore
Rowallane Gardens
Navan Fort
Killylea
Armagh
Gilford
Ballynahinch
Glaslough
Tandragee
Banbridge
DOWN
B7
Portaferry
ARMAGH
Castle Ward
Strangford
A28
Cusher River
A24
Milltown
Saul
Markethill
Downpatrick
Newry Canal
Ballyquinton Point
Ballynaskeagh
B1
B25
Seaforde
A28
Keady
A25
Castlewellan Forest Park
B176
A1
A20
Castlewellan
Tyrella
Dundrum
HAN
Ardglass
Tullymore Forest Park
Newtownhamilton
Newry
Ulster Way
Newcastle
B27
Dundrum Bay
B183
Ballybay
Slieve Gullion Forest Park
Mourne Mountains
Silent Valley
A2
Castleblaney
Narrow Water Castle
R173
Mullaghbane
Dunmore
Warrenpoint
B30
Rostrevor
Crossmaglen
Annalong
Carlingford Lough
A2
Mannan Castle
Kilkeel
Fane River
Greencastle
Inishkeen
Cranfield Point
Carrickmacross
Dundalk
Dún a Ró Forest Park
Kingscourt
LOUTH
MEATH
N2

Ever since the time of Macha (*see* right, *The Curse of Ulster*), Ulster has had its share of political ups and downs. Its High Kings held out longest against outside invaders, until the 17th century when English and Scots 'planters' set up shop there. Their descendants, the tough 'Scots-Irish', were later welcomed with open arms by the United States to settle its frontier.

For nearly a century, Ulster has been divided, with the consequences that are well known. You might not think of Ulster as a good holiday destination for children, but if you want to stimulate an interest in politics and history in them, this is the place to go – some of the finest museums on the whole island can be found here.

And, intriguingly, some of the loveliest and most peaceful countryside and landscapes in the whole of Ireland can be found here too – in Antrim, Down, and Fermanagh in Northern Ireland, or in Cavan and Donegal in the Republic. And, with the peace process now in place – despite its glitches – there has never been a better time to come and enjoy them. Northern Ireland is experiencing a social renaissance, with new gourmet restaurants and cultural ventures springing up in main towns. People are helping each other to rebuild communities and businesses. Some of the world's most forward-thinking humanitarian efforts have begun here too, like Antrim's Corrymeela Community near Ballycastle, which brings together Catholic and Protestant children for holidays. You also may find things – especially accommodation – less expensive in Northern Ireland than in the Republic.

Although many Northern Irish towns have been redeveloped in recent years, you might prefer to stay in the countryside or villages with children in tow, and make day trips to museums and tourist sites, which are often outside its major cities. Perhaps the most peaceful, pleasing landscapes are in Antrim, Down, Derry and Fermanagh, but very worth discovering are less well-known areas like the Sperrins forest area in Co. Tyrone.

Highlights

Talking to the animals at Belfast zoo, p.204
Exploring Finn McCool's bridge: the Giant's Causeway, p.207
Visiting the faeries in the Glens of Antrim, p.208
Discovering St Patrick in Downpatrick and Armagh, pp.212, 216
Island-hopping on Lough Erne and walking the forests of Fermanagh, pp.229–32
Playing on remote beaches and horseriding in Donegal, pp.235–9

Did you know...?

Six of the nine counties of historic Ulster make up Northern Ireland, while three (Cavan, Monaghan and Donegal) are in the Republic. A few border towns are still dominated by fortress-like police stations, and remnants of guard posts can sometimes be seen, but otherwise movement between the Republic and Northern Ireland is unrestricted.

Older children will find a visit to Northern Ireland fascinating, particularly if they've grown up in Britain, but seeing an ordinary street transformed by political murals, or the (now much rarer) army patrols, will get anyone asking questions. Most likely they'll never have seen anything like the Red Hand flags and multicoloured pavement curbs that show you're in a Catholic or Protestant area.

In the mainly loyalist counties of Antrim and Down, you can have a great time wandering through the pristine Nine Glens of Antrim, north of Belfast, and the Giant's Causeway along the glorious shores of the northern coast, not to mention Rathlin Island, where you may glimpse puffins. Blatant child-pleasers like Co. Antrim's high-tech Dunluce Centre and the 5W's (who-what-where-when-why) science museum in Belfast are worth visits, and don't miss Downpatrick's St Patrick's Centre, Cultra's Ulster Folk Museum and Portaferry's Exploris Aquarium.

Moving west into Co. Armagh, you'll find the Hill of Navan, where King Conchobar and his Red Branch Knights lived, near Armagh City. In Armagh City itself youngsters will be delighted with the Gulliver's Travels show at St Patrick's Trian Museum and meeting living history characters at the Palace Stables, before moving on to Armagh Planetarium. Nearby on Lough Neagh, Ireland's largest lake, is Oxford Island's Lough Neagh Discovery Centre, for outdoor sports. In Fermanagh, you will find delicious woodland walks, rich Irish folklore and the intensely peaceful Lough Derg. Storytelling and traditional music festivals abound in the southern part of County Armagh and places like Magherafelt, Co. Derry.

In the countryside of Co. Derry (or Londonderry), you will find beautiful nature spots on the coast like those near Mussenden Temple and the impressive Mountsandel Estate. Londonderry/Derry City itself is fascinating, with its virtually intact ancient walls and award-winning Tower Museum.

For a real interactive experience, combine visits to the Ulster History Park and fantastic Ulster American Folk Park in Co. Tyrone. Nearby are Gortin Forest Park and the Sperrin Mountains, where you can pan for gold (but watch out for leprechauns, if you try to take away their hidden pots of it!).

Over the border in the Republic, Co. Donegal's people are much closer psychologically to Ireland's ancient high kings than anywhere else in Ireland. At the mouth of the Inishowen Peninsula, just north of Londonderry, you'll find the prehistoric seat of Ulster's high kings. Said to have been built by the Daghda, leader of the Tuatha Dé Danaan, before them, the Grianán Aileach is an awe-inspiring stone ring fort. Its nearby museum at Burt should not be missed by young children who like faery tales mixed with a bit of history. Donegal has some of the most magical mountain- and seascapes in Ireland, and after travelling for miles to the county's coastal towns, at the end of long, winding roads, you will be rewarded with magnificent views, open skies and plenty of time for storytelling. In South Donegal, Ardara embraces those who want to know about folklore and woven crafts, while nearby Bruckless offers young riders country and seaside treks. South of Northern Ireland lies the 'buffer zone'of Cos. Cavan and Monaghan, where there is nothing to attract wild holidaymakers, but a huge amount of unfussy tranquility. Once an important flax and linen area, fishermen and equestrians tend to keep it as their secret holiday hideaway.

A story to tell: The curse of Ulster

One morning an Ulster farmer rose with the sun, as he did every day, but such a shining light lay upon the land that he decided to stroll through the woods to find some wild berries for his breakfast. Named Crunnchu, he was a practical, hardworking man, especially now that his wife had died, but today, the truth was, some strange magic had drawn him out of his dreams and into the wood.

Suddenly the early morning chatter of the birds stopped, and Crunnchu saw something flash past the trees beyond the clearing where he was picking berries. It was fast as lightning: it couldn't be a horse, he thought – the trees were too close together for an animal that size to run between them, and the golden-red flash he'd seen was too light on its feet. It must be some strange animal, he concluded, and went back to his berry-picking.

Little did he know that he had attracted the interest and attention of the goddess Macha, who stopped and peeked at him from behind the trees while he wasn't looking. Eventually Crunnchu glanced up, and saw a beautiful red-haired woman gazing at him.

Well, one thing led to another, and Macha went to live with him, and eventually fell pregnant. They were very happy together, but he did notice his wife had one small quirk. At times, she would dash out of the house without a word and run faster than any horse he had ever seen.

One day Crunnchu was invited to a feast of Ulster's powerful King Conchobar mac Nessa, whose hospitality was well known. His greatest warrior, Cúchulainnn, would be there too, so Crunnchu was very excited. Knowing her husband well, Macha warned him not to boast, especially since she couldn't be there to keep an eye on him because she was about to have their baby.

The banqueters grew merry with drink, and Crunnchu was no exception. Then King Conchobar began to boast about the speed of his horses, until Crunnchu burst out with, 'My Macha runs faster than any horse I have ever seen, including your own, King Conchobar.'

Blood rushed to the king's face as he demanded, 'Then so. Your wife must race my horses.'

Crunnchu, unable to refuse the King, brought a raging, pregnant Macha to the palace.

'Please, your majesty,' said she, 'May I not participate in this race, as I am weighty with child.'

But none of Conchobar's men would listen to her, and they made her race. So Macha ran, and ran – faster than all King Conchobar's horses put together. And while the cheers flew about her, she fell to the earth, went into labour and bore twins.

Then she said, 'Men of Ulster, hear me! From this day forward, in times of great danger, you will become as weak as a woman in labour. Her pains will be yours in every battle.'

And then she died upon the dusty ground.

Tourist information for Ulster

Tourism Ireland, freephones UK **t** 0800 039 7000; US and Canada **t** 1 800 223 6470; **www**.tourismireland.com

The joint travel information service for the whole of Ireland, north and south.

Northern Ireland Tourist Board (NITB), 59 North St, Belfast BT1 1NB, **t** (028) 9023 1221, **f** (028) 9024 0960, **www**.discovernorthernireland.com

Affiliated to Tourism Ireland.

Belfast Welcome Centre, 47 Donegall Place, BT1 5AD, **t** (028) 9024 6609, **f** (028) 9031 2424, **www**.discovernorthernireland.com

Causeway Coast and Glens Ltd, 11 Lodge Road, Coleraine, BT52 1LU, **t** (028) 7032 7720, **f** (028) 7032 7719, **www**.causewaycoastandglens.com

Derry Visitor and Convention Bureau, 44 Foyle Street, Derry, BT48 6AT, **t** (028) 7137 7577, **f** (028) 7137 7992 or (028) 7136 9501, **www**.derryvisitor.com

Fermanagh Lakeland Tourism, Wellington Road, Enniskillen BT74 7EF, **t** (028) 6634 6736, **f** (028) 6632 5511, **www**.soeasygoing.com

Kingdoms of Down, 40 West Street, Newtownards, BT23 4EN, **t** (028) 9182 2881, **f** (028) 9182 2202, **www**.kingdomsofdown.com

North West Tourism (Cavan, Monaghan, Donegal), Aras Redden, Temple St, Sligo, **t** (071) 9161201, **f** (071) 9160360, **www**.ireland-northwest.travel.ie

Tours

Minicoach From Belfast Welcome Bureau (*see* above), or Belfast International Youth Hostel, 22 Donegall Road, Belfast, **t** (028) 9032 4733, **www**.minicoachni.co.uk

These one-day tours by minibus cover the whole of Northern Ireland from Belfast: the Giant's Causeway, Belfast City, St Patrick's Tour in Co. Down, Carrickfergus Castle, the Antrim coast and more.

Good to know... Phoning Northern Ireland

The whole of Northern Ireland has the UK area code **028**. You do not need to use this code with the individual number within Northern Ireland. To call a Northern Ireland number from the Irish Republic, you have to change the code to **048**. Phoning the Republic from the North still counts as an international call, but at low rates: dial **00**, then **353**, then the number, **omitting** the first 0 from the area code.

Good to know... Pounds and euros

While the euro is the currency used in the Irish Republic, in the six counties of Northern Ireland it is the British pound sterling (£). However, many businesses across the North will accept and/or exchange both currencies – especially in border towns like Derry or Newry. *See also* p.294

Getting there and around

By air There are a great many flights between Britain and Belfast, with several airlines, and some have direct flights to Northern Ireland's 'other' airport, **Derry**. Note that Belfast has two airports, **Belfast International** and **Belfast City**, and you need to be clear which one your airline is using. Derry is also the best airport for Donegal and the northeast Republic. At present there are no scheduled flights between North America and Northern Ireland, so the best way to get there is via a change in Britain or Dublin or Shannon in the Republic. For all airline and airport details, *see* pp.280–4.

By bus Most public transport in Northern Ireland is run by **Translink**, which has several sub-divisions: **Ulsterbus** operates most buses across the six counties, with a comprehensive network. In Belfast, buses heading west and south (Armagh, Tyrone, Derry, Fermanagh and West Down, the Republic) leave from the **Europa Centre**; buses to Antrim and North Down leave from the **Laganside Bus Centre** (*see* p.202). Both Ulsterbus and Bus Eireann also have plenty of long-distance coaches between the North and many towns in the Republic. For more on buses and ticket information, *see* p.286.

By rail Another part of Translink is **Northern Ireland Railways** (NIR), which has suburban lines around Belfast and trains to Coleraine, Portrush and Derry. **Enterprise** trains, run by NIR with Irish Rail, provide a very well-priced service between Belfast and Dublin, with several trains each day. For more on trains and fares, *see* pp.287–8.

Translink, for bus and rail information, **t** (028) 9066 6630, **www**.translink.co.uk

By sea There's a wide choice of ferry routes and companies from Britain: from Cairnryan and Troon in Scotland and Fleetwood, near Blackpool, to Larne; from Troon, Stranraer and Liverpool to Belfast; and from spring to autumn there's also a ferry between Campbeltown in Argyll, Scotland, and Ballycastle, Co. Antrim. For companies and further details, *see* pp.284–5.

COUNTY ANTRIM

This is one of the most visited parts of Northern Ireland, not least because it contains the capital, Belfast. Places that children enjoy are dotted all over Antrim, and include Northern Ireland's most famous tourist site, the Giant's Causeway – originally named *Clochan na bhFómharach* ('the stones of the Fomorians'). In legend it was once inhabited by the giant seafaring race called the Fomorians, who were known for preying on others and feature as monsters in many of Ireland's mythological tales. Antrim has castles, gardens and museums, not to mention many opportunities for walking, riding and watersports. For fairy-lore enthusiasts, the 'capital' of Ireland's faeries is said to be near Cushendall, as is the grave of Oisín (*see* p.130).

Tourist information

Antrim, 16 High St, **t** (028) 9442 8331
Ballycastle, 7 Mary St, **t** (028) 2076 2024
Ballymena, 76 Church St, **t** (028) 2563 8494
Ballymoney, **t** (028) 2766 2280
Belfast Welcome Centre, 47 Donegall Place, **t** (028) 9024 6609, **www**.discovernorthernireland.com
Tourism Ireland/NITB Information Centre , 59 North St, Belfast, **t** (028) 9023 1221, **www**.discovernorthernireland.com
Carrickfergus, Knight Ride, Antrim St, **t** (028) 9336 6455, **www**.carrickfergus.org
Cushendall, 25 Mill St, **t** (028) 2177 1180
Giant's Causeway, Visitor Centre, 44 Causeway Road, Bushmills, **t** (028) 2073 1855
Larne, Narrow Gauge Road, **t** (028) 2826 0088
Portrush, Dunluce Centre, Sandhill Drive, **t** (028) 7082 3333

Getting there and around

By air For information on Belfast's two airports (Belfast International and Belfast City) and transport into town, *see* p.284.

By bus Ulsterbus, **t** (028) 9066 6630, in addition to its regular services, operates the Antrim Coaster, which runs in summer between Belfast and Portstewart, stopping at most towns around the Antrim coast. Ulsterbus and the Bushmills Distillery operate an open-topped bus, 27 Jun–28 Aug, from Coleraine along the Giant's Causeway, via Portstewart, Portrush, Portballintrae, Bushmills, and back. For bus stations in Belfast, *see* p.202.

By train From Belfast (Central Station or Great Victoria St) there are trains along the north side of Belfast Lough via Carrickfergus to Larne Ferry Port, and on a line through Antrim town and Ballymena to Coleraine. Larne trains always connect with ferry arrivals and departures. NIR information, **t** (028) 9066 6630.

A Belfast Skipping Game...

Cinderella dressed in yella,
went upstairs to kiss a fella.
How many kisses did she get?
1... 2... 3... 4...
(Count until misstep)

By car

Roads are often in much better condition in Northern Ireland than in the Republic. The M2 motorway provides a fast route out of Belfast towards the north; turn off at Antrim onto the A26 for the Glens and the Giant's Causeway. Note that if you arrive and hire a car at Belfast International Airport, you do not need to go into Belfast at all.

Car hire

The best places to hire a car are at the airports and in Belfast. Rates often work out lower than those in the Republic, especially in Dublin.

AVIS, 69–71 Great Victoria St, Belfast, **t** (028) 9024 0404; Ferry Terminal, Larne Harbour, **t** (028) 2827 0381
Budget, 96–102 Great Victoria St, Belfast, **t** (028) 9023 0700
Dan Dooley, 175B Airport Road, Aldergrove (near Belfast International), **t** (028) 9445 2522
Europcar, City Airport, **t** (028) 9045 0904; International Airport, **t** (028) 9442 3444
Hertz, International Airport, **t** (028) 9442 2533
McCausland Car Hire, 21–31 Grosvenor Road, Belfast, **t** (028) 9033 3777

Bike Hire

Many bike hire shops in Northern Ireland are part of the linked Raleigh Rent-a-Bike network.

Ardclinis Outdoor Adventure Centre, 11 High St, Cushendall, **t** (028) 2177 1340
RF Linton and Sons, 31 Springwell St, Ballymena, **t** (028) 2565 2516
The Skerries Pantry, 6 Bath St, Portrush, **t** (028) 7082 4334
Check too with Portrush tourist office (*see* left) for other cycle shops in the summer season.
Cushendall Activity Centre, **t** (028) 2117 1340 Well-placed for the Glens of Antrim.

BELFAST

Belfast, from *Beal Feirste*, 'mouth of the sandy ford', can seem more peaceful than Dublin these days – apart from the odd boom around Halloween, when youngsters like to frighten every one with fireworks. As a parent, if you've never been to Northern Ireland, you'll be surprised what a friendly place it is and how normal life is here. If you have been before but not for some years, you'll be amazed how much the city has been redeveloped around beautifully preserved examples of Georgian, Victorian and Edwardian architecture.

However, one of the things that has been most exceptional about Belfast is how verbally clever its people have been, especially its children, in rhymes and street games. There was also something about the unique constellation of qualities the city possessed that produced inventive adults in arts like literature, and more mechanical pursuits like engineering. Today, Belfast's shipping industry, which built the *Titanic* and many British battleships, is scarcely a memory, but evidence of the money being poured into the city shows in the new buildings that have sprung up on the dockside in recent years. All the big British shopping chains are present here, and if you go around Belfast to see the Catholic and Protestant wall murals, you'll find busy shopping streets and residential areas where people live and work. As to the political situation, the peace process is firmly underway and, while there are still occasional disputes, tourists are most unlikely to encounter any problems.

Much of the city centre is pedestrianized, and teenagers will find its nightlife pretty lively (young girls should be sensible visiting pubs or clubs at night, and go out in pairs or a group). Queen's University attracts an international student population, which fills the 'Golden Mile' – from Donegall Square down Great Victoria Street to Dublin Road and University Road – of clubs, pubs and restaurants on weekend evenings.

Belfast and Antrim songs to sing...
Belfast Town, I'll Tell Me Ma,
The Belle of Belfast City, The Great Shipyard
Protest Parade, Carrickfergus

Children will have fun visiting the exceptional Zoo, the W5 centre and Sandra's Candy Factory, and the special events for youngsters in Dixon's Park. The Botanic Gardens is a nice green place to walk after a visit to the Ulster Museum. Give your kids *The Lion, the Witch and the Wardrobe* and other tales of Narnia to read before you go to Belfast, then let them know that the author, CS Lewis, grew up there. As did singer Van Morrison, among many other luminaries of this fascinating city.

Getting around

On foot Much of the city centre is pedestrianized, and the main shopping streets and many city attractions are within easy walking distance of each other. To get to some places such as Stormont or the Zoo it's best to make use of buses or cabs.

By bus Another branch of Translink, **Citybus**, runs all buses in Belfast, with over 60 routes around the city. Most routes run around 7am–12 midnight daily, and on Saturday nights there are Nightlink late-night buses. If you travel more than a few journeys it might be worth buying one of two types of **Smartlink** card, the MultiJourney (MJ) card, valid for five to 50 journeys (the minimum 5-journey card costs £5.75) or a weekly Travelcard (from £13.50 for adults, £7.50 children). They can be bought from Citybus offices and many shops.

Citybus Ticket and Information Kiosk, Donegall Square West; phone information, **t** (028) 9066 6630, **www.translink.co.uk**

For **Ulsterbus** coach services the main stations are the **Europa Bus Centre**, Great Victoria St, **t** (028) 9032 0011 (for the west and south) and **Laganside Bus Centre**, Donegall Quay, **t** (028) 9032 0011 (for Down and Antrim).

By car Parking is heavily restricted in central Belfast, but there are plenty of parking meters, and car parks and pay-and-display areas ring the centre of the city; the tourist office has a list and map.

By train Central Station, East Bridge St, near the Albert Bridge over the Lagan, is the hub of NIR rail services, but most trains also pass through Great Victoria St Station, on the west side of the city centre. Information, **t** (028) 9066 6630, **www.translink.co.uk**

By taxi Ranks can be found at City Hall in Donegall Square, Upper Queen St, Wellington Place and Castle St.

Belfast Taxi, t 0786 090 1899
Black Taxi, t (028) 906 2264

Tours

Information on a range of walking tours of Belfast can be found in Belfast Welcome Centre's free leaflet *Walk this Way*. Bus tours include:

Citybus Tours, t (028) 9030 1732/9024 6485

Main sights of Belfast (Stormont, Belfast Castle, etc.) and 'Troubles' hotspots.

Leprechaun Tour Guiding, 6–8 Main St, Gilford, near Banbridge, Co. Down, **t** (028) 3883 1236

Tours of Belfast by car with a fascinating commentary, by arrangement with actor-playwright Ken McElroy.

Things to see and do

Aunt Sandra's Candy Factory

60 Castlereagh Road, Belfast, **t** (028) 9073 2868
Getting there Bus 32, 5mins from city centre
Open Mon–Fri 9.30–4.30, Sat–Sun 9.30am–1pm
Adm Free

This is a fascinating confectionary factory, where honeycomb, chocolate macaroon cake and traditional fudge are made from 100-year-old recipes. Through a viewing window, children can watch the sweets being made in a building kitted out with the original fittings, brick walls, wooden ceilings and the slate floors of a small candy shop of 1958.

Special Events – County Antrim

May

Ballyclare May Fair, t (028) 9034 0000

Horse trading, community fair and other equestrian events.

Feis nGleann, t (028) 2076 2024

A feast of Gaelic music, crafts and sports held through May and June in the Glens of Antrim for all the family to enjoy.

Larne Irish Dancing Festival, t (028) 2826 0088

A week of Irish dance competitions, for all ages.

July

Lughnasa Medieval Fair and Craft Market, Carrickfergus Castle, **t** (028) 9336 6455

For young damsels and brave knights.

August

Ould Lammas Fair, Ballycastle, **t** (028) 2076 2024

Families will enjoy Northern Ireland's oldest traditional market fair; last weekend in August.

Events and Festivals – Belfast

May

Belfast City Summer Festival, t (028) 9032 0202

Family fun including the Lord Mayor's Show, through May and June.

Cathedral Quarter Arts Festival, t (028) 9023 2403

An impressive arts programme.

Ulster Drama Festival, The Lyric Theatre, **t** (028) 9038 1081, **www.lyrictheatre.co.uk**

For young thespians.

July

12 July The Boyne Anniversary

Parades are held and bonfires lit in Protestant areas of Belfast and throughout Northern Ireland to commemorate William of Orange's victory at the Boyne in 1690 (*see* p.35). Note that watching the Orange March along Belfast's Lisburn Road is quite safe, but it's best to avoid marches on controversial routes. If you don't know if a place is safe ask someone; people are very friendly and will almost certainly give you the right advice.

August

Ardoyne Fleadh, Ardoyne, **t** (028) 9075 1056

Local and international performers, ceili (dance) – for families seeking the Irish traditional arts.

Feile an Phobail, t (028) 9031 3440

Annual festival of Irish music, drama, Irish language events, carnival and a parade.

September

Belfast Film Festival, t (028) 9032 5913, **www.belfastfilmfestival.org**

More for teenagers and adults than little ones, though big kids movies feature in the line-up.

November

Belfast Arts Festival, Queens University, information **t** (028) 9066 7687, bookings **t** (028) 9066 5577, **www.belfastfestival.com**

Three weeks of music, films, plays, poetry and art exhibitions, fringe shows from Edinburgh and international stars. Events take place mainly around the university area.

Cinemagic Festival, t (028) 9023 0606

This children's film festival, usually held in November or December, offers free film workshops, acting, production and screen-writing sessions in addition to a children's film programme.

Belfast City Hall

Donegall Square, **t** (028) 9027 0456
Getting there Via Centrelink bus
Open All year Mon–Sat. **Adm** Free
Guided tours by appointment (book in advance)

Belfast City Council sits in this 1906 Edwardian building, where the parliament of Northern Ireland held its first meeting in 1921. It was built with Portland stone in Renaissance style after Queen Victoria gave Belfast city status in 1888, in recognition of its growth from a mere village in the 17th-century. Today this rectangular monolith dominates central Belfast, covering some one and a half acres within gardens open to the public.

Belfast Castle and Cave Hill Country Park

t (028) 9077 6925/bookings: **t** (028) 9037 1013, **www.belfastcastle.co.uk**
Getting there 3 1/2 miles (6km) north of Belfast city centre, off Antrim Road; entrances at Belfast Castle and near zoo, via Citybus 45–51
Open Visitor centre (2nd floor of Castle): Mon–Sat 9am–10pm, Sun 9–6;
Playground: Apr–May Mon–Fri 2–5, Sat–Sun 10–6; Jun Mon–Fri 2–8, Sat–Sun 10–8; Jul–Aug Mon–Sun 10–8; Sept Mon–Fri 2–7.30, Sat–Sun 10–7.30; Oct Sat–Sun 11–4.30; Nov–Dec Sat–Sun 11–3.30; Jan Sat–Sun 11–4; Feb–Mar Sat–Sun 11–4.30
Adm Park: free; Playground: £1.30
Waymarked trails, visitor centre, restaurant

Spend a sunny day at this 740-acre park. Two nature reserves surround the castle (c.1870) on the slopes of Cave Hill, overlooking Belfast Lough. Five caves on its east side contain evidence of prehistoric occupation, as does its highest point, McArt's Fort. There's an elaborate adventure playground for 3–14 year olds (only) with supervisory staff, but children must be accompanied by an adult. Its junior area has cradle swings, slides, spring rockers, a sand pit, bicycle roundabout and play ships. Older children can climb a space net, whizz down an aerial runway or explore tunnels and tube slides.

Belfast Zoo

Antrim Road, Belfast, BT36 7PN, **t** (028) 9077 6277, **f** (028) 9037 0578, **www.belfastzoo.co.uk**
Getting there 5 miles (8km) north of the city on the A6, and located in the park below the slopes of Cave Hill; via Citybus 9, 45–51 from City Hall
Open Daily except Christmas Day, Apr–Sept 10–5, Oct–Mar 10–2.30
Adm Apr–Sept adult £6, child (4–18) £3, family (2+2) £16.50; Oct–Mar adult £5, child (4–18) £2.50, family £13.50
Restaurant, shop, tea house, children's playground, facilities for the disabled, free parking

Children will love this 50-acre world-class zoo and adults will appreciate its perfect position on the side of Cave Hill just outside Belfast, from where they can have panoramic views over the city and Belfast Lough. Highly regarded for its conservation and education programmes, it looks after over 160 rare or endangered species as part of national and international breeding programmes. Enclosures replicate natural environments. Chimpanzees and spider monkeys can be seen on their island, alongside slower-moving gorillas. Watch penguins and sea-lions swimming underwater from the viewing enclosure. One of the newest attractions is a big group of pelicans. There is a very rare white tiger called Jack and another called Jill, as well as lemurs and tamarins.

Botanic Gardens

Stranmillis Road/Botanic Avenue, next to Ulster Museum
Getting there Citybus 71, 69
Open Daily till dusk. **Adm** free

Delightful for a stroll, these formal gardens (c.1827) hold a 'tropical ravine' with a fish pond full of giant water-lilies and a jungle glen whose centrepiece is the restored Palm House with its exotic trees and flowering plants.

Lagan Lookout Visitor Centre

Donegall Quay, **t** (028) 9031 5444
Open Mar–Sept Mon–Fri 11–5, Sat 12–5, Sun 2–5; Oct–Feb Mon–Fri 11.30–3.30, Sat 1–4.30, Sun 2–4.30
Adm Adult £1.50, child 75p, family £4
Disabled access

Take a boat trip to see Belfast old and new along the River Lagan from this high-tech exhibition about the city's industrial and folk history.

Queen's University Visitor Centre

University Road, **t** (028) 9033 5252
Open May–Sept Mon–Fri 10–4, Sat 10–4; Oct–Apr Mon–Fri 10–4. **Adm** Free

Northern Ireland's most prestigious university was built in 1845–49 and designed by Charles Lanyon. It was founded by Queen Victoria as the first university in the north of Ireland, as part of a trinity of 'Queen's Colleges', the other two being in

Cork and Galway. Today it's one of the most respected universities in the British Isles, and Nobel-prizewinning poet Seamus Heaney is just one of its distinguished ex-students.

Sir Thomas and Lady Dixon Park

Upper Malone Road, **t** (028) 9032 0202
Getting there Citybus 71
Open Daily dawn to dusk. **Adm** free

This park has a playground, Japanese gardens and Rose Garden, and in summer it hosts a 'Teddy Bears Picnic'.

Stormont

Getting there Just outside Belfast on the A55 east of town (between the A2 and A20)

Older kids will be interested to see the home of the Northern Ireland Assembly at Stormont. It's an impressive neoclassical building at the end of an imposing avenue, and the huge park around it is a good place to let the kids run off some excess energy. The statue at the front of the entrance is of Lord Carson, who led the Protestant opposition to Home Rule a hundred years ago.

Ulster Museum

12 Malone Road/Stranmillis Road, **t** (028) 9038 3000, **www**.ulstermuseum.org.uk
Getting there Citybus 69
Open Mon–Fri 10–5, Sat 1–5, Sun 2–5
Adm Free except for special exhibitions
Museum, art gallery, shop, café

Spend at least half a day exploring this great museum with its large collections of archaeology, art, history and the natural sciences. Children may not entirely appreciate the variety and quality of its collection, but they might be taken by the steam engines from old mills and factories, the treasures of the Spanish Armada, relics from prehistoric to medieval Ireland, ethnography exhibits on subjects like Native Americans, and the natural history displays. Its gallery houses a collection of Irish paintings, and there are always family activities to complement the changing programme of temporary exhibitions, lectures, films and workshops. The café is good and overlooks an ancient graveyard.

West Belfast Wall Murals

Getting there The Falls and Shankill Road are 5 mins from the centre by car. To see them with children you'll need a car or to take a tour. It's a long walk with children, and it's hard to find your way without a guide.

West Belfast by black taxi cab or tour:
Black Taxi Tour, t (028) 9064 2264, **www**.belfast-tours.com. Tours from £7.50 per person, min 3 people, for a 90-min tour, which takes in the murals on the Shankill and Falls Roads and other places around the city.
Leprechaun Tour Guiding, *see* p.203

It would be a pity to visit Belfast and not take a look at the city's most famous area. Over the last 30 years the Catholic Falls Road and Protestant Shankill Road have become household names as the battlefronts of the Troubles. These days they're safe enough during the day, and over-8s will find them fascinating, above all for the huge murals that are all over this part of town. On the Falls Road they commemorate events like the 1981 Hunger Strike and the Famine (*see* p.36), while on the Shankill Road they commemorate the Battle of the Boyne and Protestant heroes (see p.35). The Peace Line that divides the two communities and the massive police stations will get kids asking questions.

Black cabs, called 'people's taxis', were used during the Troubles as a substitute bus service, since normal buses didn't run in this part of town. You'll still see them today, and there are many to choose from if you feel like taking a tour. They now have something of a cult status and songs have even been written about Falls Road taxi drivers.

Whowhatwherewhenwhy – W5

2 Queen's Quay, at The Odyssey Centre, **t** (028) 9046 7700, **www**.w5online.co.uk
Getting there Centrelink bus
Open Daily Mon–Sat 10–6, Sun 12 noon–6
Adm Adult £5, child £3, family £14

This new science and discovery centre contains over 100 interactive exhibits that have something for the whole family. It's divided into five areas, including the 'Wow, Start' exhibition for children up to age 8, and 'Go, See and Do' for older children, where they can see a laser harp and watch a fire tornado rise to the ceiling. You also can try creating cloud rings, build a house, try a lie detector, design a robot or a bridge, play with a flying machine or make music by walking on a floor piano.

The museum is inside the Odyssey, a multifunctional venue which has within it an indoor arena seating up to 10,000, a 12-screen multiplex cinema, IMAX® Cinema and a big range of bars, restaurants and other leisure facilities.

Entertainment

Belfast Waterfront Hall

2 Lanyon Place, **t** (028) 9033 4455/9033 4400
www.waterfront.co.uk

Concert hall where 2,200 people watch performances by stars of classical and pop music.

Grand Opera House

2–4 Great Victoria St,
t (028) 9024 1919/9024 0411, **www.goh.co.uk**

Matinees and early performances (11am on) of musical and theatrical entertainment in architect Frank Matcham's Victorian 'pleasure dome'.

The Ulster Hall

Bedford Street, **t** (028) 9032 3900

Lunchtime recitals, concerts and comedy shows.

SPECIAL TRIPS

Carrickfergus

Carrickfergus Castle

Antrim St, Carrickfergus, **t** (028) 9335 1273
Getting there Train from Belfast (Larne line)
Open Daily Apr–May and Sept–Oct Mon–Sat 10–6, Sun 2–6; Jun–Aug Mon–Sat 10–6, Sun 12–6; Nov–Mar Mon–Sat 10–4, Sun 2–4 (closed 25 Dec)
Adm Adult £3, child £1.50, family (2+2) £8
Visitor centre, gift shop, guided tours, disabled access, café, activity room, baby-changing room

On the coast just north of Belfast you'll find this impressive 4-storey rectangular tower built in 1180 by the Anglo-Norman John de Courcy to guard the entrance to Belfast Lough. He had led an invasion of Ulster in 1177, and he and his kinsmen conquered much of Down and Antrim. The best-preserved Norman castle in Ireland, it is enclosed in a way that makes it easier to keep track of wandering children. The castle was besieged by King John in 1210 and Edward Bruce in 1315, and briefly captured by the French in 1760. A film tells the castle's history in a way young people will absorb easily, and models of soldiers stand poised with real cannons. There are medieval games for children to play, or perhaps they'll get the chance to don some armour. Periodic pageants or military tattoos are held here, especially in summer. After this, visit the Knight Ride, especially with young kids in tow.

Knight Ride and Heritage Plaza

Antrim St, Carrickfergus, **t** (028) 9336 6455, **www.carrickfergus.org**
Open Apr–Sept Mon–Sat 10–6, Sun 12–6, Oct–Mar Mon–Sat 10–5, Sun 12–5
Adm Adult £2.70, child £1.35, family £7.30
Exhibition with monorail cars (special car available for wheelchair users), disabled access, shops, café

Old and young children will have fun riding in the little Disney-like pods that slide through 1,000 years of the history of Carrickfergus. This small museum is in a historic building, whose hall you observe at one point in the ride. Youngsters can imagine time-travelling as they listen to a voice-over conversation between a child and his grandfather, as you pass from one chamber to another. Even if they miss the details, they'll still gain a flavour of Irish history. And parents tired of walking or driving will enjoy it even more!

Dunluce

Dunluce Centre

10 Sandhill Drive, Portrush, **t** (028) 7082 4444, **www.touristnetuk.com/nidunluce**
Getting there On A2 east of Portrush
Open Sept–May Sat–Sun 12 noon–5, Easter (2 weeks) daily 10.30–7, Jun–Aug daily 10.30–6
Adm All-inclusive ticket (all 3 areas): per person £7, family (2+2) £21 plus £6 per person for extra members to max. 3; Finn McCool's Playground only: child aged 0–4 £2.75, 4–14 £3.95; Treasure Fortress or Turbo Tours only: child to age 14 £2.75
Shop, restaurant, viewing tower, tourist office

Children could spend the whole of a rainy day quite happily at Dunluce with its three themed game areas (aimed at ages 6–13). The Finn McCool Adventure Playground has three floors of themed games that a spectrum of ages can play alone or in a group, including 'Shadow Cave', 'Echo Well', 'Ball Swamp' and 'Make Your Own Weather'. Treasure Fortress is a high-tech treasure hunt set in a real castle, where players must find quiz clues hidden in secret portals, to collect enough 'magic' to free the spellbound princess and acquire her dowry of Spanish treasure. Once they are ready to sit down for a bit they can take the Turbo Tour ride, which synchronizes moving seats with sound and imagery from top action films. Then, after you've had a look in the shop for a souvenir and the excitement of the day has been discussed over a good meal, maybe your kids will go to bed early.

Dunluce Castle

Portrush, **t** (028) 2073 1938
Open Apr–Sept Mon–Sat 10–6, Apr–May and Sept Sun 2–6, Jun–Aug Sun 12–6, Oct–Mar Tues–Sat 10–4, Oct and Mar Sun 2–4, also open Mons and bank holidays. **Adm** Adult £2, child £1
Shop, guided tours, limited wheelchair access

Dramatic ruins on a rocky chalk headland date from the 16 and 17th centuries. Located west of Portballintrae, parts of the castle date from the 14th century.

The Giant's Causeway

Giant's Causeway and Causeway School Museum (Visitor Centre), 44 Causeway Road, Bushmills, **t** (028) 2073 1855, **www**.giantscausewayofficialguide.com
Getting there 2 miles (3km) east of Bushmills
Open Causeway: daily, shop and tearoom: daily Mar–May 10–5, Jun 10–6; Jul–Aug 10–7; Sept–Oct 10–5; Nov–Feb 10–3, bank holidays and Good Fri, closed 25 Dec and 1 Jan; School: daily Jul–Aug 11–5
Adm Visitor centre free; guided tours of stones: Jun–Aug £2, shuttle bus: free for National Trust members but Ulsterbus fee for others; parking £5
Visitor centre with disabled access, shop, restaurant, toilets with baby-changing facilities, picnic tables

Northern Ireland's number one tourist attraction and a World Heritage site. You could spend a long afternoon or more exploring these polygonal columns of layered basalt rocks and caves, formed by a volcanic eruption 60 million years ago. There are various legends describing the chunks of basalt as 'stepping stones' to Scotland, which are usually

A story to tell: Finn McCool and the Giant's Causeway

Like many warriors, Finn was the size of a giant, and one day he decided to build a bridge of stones between the coast of Antrim all the way to Scotland across the narrow Sea of Moyle, in case he ever wanted to walk over in a hurry to buy the good whisky that he had heard was there. But a Scottish giant named Benandonner got wind of his plan and thought, 'Hmph, he's going to bring his Fianna warriors over this bridge and try to conquer my lands,' so he went stomping through the waters from Scotland with the idea of stopping Finn from building his bridge.

With his special long-distance sight, Finn saw big Ben approaching and realized he was much larger than himself, so he fled home and asked his wife Oonagh for advice. Fearing for her husband's life, she told him, 'Quickly now, build a baby's cradle large enough to hold a man your size.' And then she sewed some giant baby clothes and a bonnet and put her husband in them.

When Finn's wife saw big Ben bounding through the waves her heart sank at his size. 'He is much bigger than you, Finn McCool,' she whispered to her husband.

'Don't I know it,' Finn replied as big Ben's shadow darkened their shore like a great grey storm cloud.

'Whist, husband, keep your mouth shut and close your eyes here in this cradle. No matter what the Giant says to me, no matter what he does, behave as if you are asleep. Mind yourself now...'

As the Scottish giant came to shore, Oonagh was humming to herself and gently rocking the cradle with her husband in it.

'Pleased to meet you,' Ben boomed on reaching the place where Finn's bridge began.

'Shhh,' whispered Finn's wife, placing her forefinger to her lips. 'You'll wake the baby.'

The giant peered at the supposed baby, marvelling at its size. 'And whose child might this be?' he whispered to Finn's wife.

'Finn McCool, the great leader of the Fianna,' she replied with pride.

Finn couldn't help but manufacture a little extra baby snore to further emphasize his high status.

Mightily nervous, the Scottish giant began to shake as he considered how big Finn McCool must be to have such a large baby, but only the merest tremble was in his voice as he said, 'And where might this Finn McCool be at the moment?'

'Oh not far. He's hunting but should be back this noon. Will you come in for tea?'

'Well,' said the Scot, 'I must be off to my own dinner myself. It'll take some walking to get there from here.'

Oonagh laughed heartily as she watched the Scottish giant splashing away as fast as he could back towards Scotland.

As soon as he was out of sight, Finn kissed his wife for her cleverness and then tore up the parts of the bridge nearest to Scotland, to make sure that the huge Scottish giants would never venture Ireland's way again.

associated with a giant named Fionn McCumhail (Finn McCool, *see* p.207). Similar rock formations can be found on the Scottish island of Staffa, which features in some of the stories. Watch the fun film that tells one of these Finn stories before you hike out to the stones. Be prepared for lots of walking, or just take the shuttle bus to the place where the Causeway's famous octagonal geological formations start and take a gentle stroll. Do bring along a snack or picnic, water and a windcheater or raincoat and wear good walking shoes that won't slip easily on wet or rocky surfaces. Next door to the Visitor Centre, the Causeway School Museum recreates a 1920s Irish classroom. Desks with inkwells and playground toys are featured.

Giant's Causeway and Bushmills Railway

Runkerry Road, Bushmills, **t** (028) 2073 2594, www.giantscausewayrailway.org
Open Summer (call for running times)
Adm Return: adult £5, child £3.50, family (2+3) £12; Single: adult: £3, child £2

An old steam train along the coast between the Giant's Causeway and the Old Bushmills station.

The Glens of Antrim

Glenballyeamon, Glenaan and Glencorp are especially beautiful glens near Cushendall, north of Belfast. Maps for 14 different walks in the Glens are available, and you can also ride, visit beaches, cycle (if you don't mind steep roads) and enjoy many sports events and festivals, not to mention search for the hideouts of the Good People, whose main haunts are said to be Lurigethan Mountain and Tiveragh Hill. On the slopes of Tieve Bulliagh, about 2 miles (3km) west of Cushendall in Glenaan, you'll find **Oisín's Grave**, the supposed burial site of Finn McCool's son.

Glenariff Forest Park

Glenariff, **t** (028) 2175 8232
www.forestserviceni.gov.uk
Open All year daily 10–dusk
Adm Per car: £3, Pedestrians: adult £1.50, child 50p
Visitor centre, shop, restaurant, picnic areas

For families tired of the city, a day spent exploring this 2,927-acre park at the heart of the 'Nine Glens of Antrim' won't go amiss. Some people call it 'the Queen of the Glens', the most beautiful of the nine. There are mountain views along the waymarked trails and its waterfall walk offers spectacular views along the Glenariff River.

AROUND AND ABOUT

Animal magic

Brookhall Historical Farm

2 Horse Park, Ballinderry Road, Magheragall, near Lisburn, **t** (028) 9262 1712
Getting there 5 miles 8km) southwest of Belfast off the A3
Open Easter–Oct Wed–Sat 11–5, Sun 2–6
Adm Adult £2, child (aged 4+) £1, under-4s free
Museum, cottage garden, gift shop, nature walks, country farm tea-house, guided tours for groups available, no dogs allowed

Artefacts used on Irish farms in the past are displayed on this historical farm with gardens and a wildlife pond. Children may see and pet farm animals, including some rare breeds, then follow nature walks and visit the enclosed garden – an ancient burial ground – fishing lake, 12th-century church and a holy well that never runs dry, with waters reputed to have healing powers. Before you leave, stop for refreshments in the teahouse.

Leslie Hill Open Farm

Macfin Road, Ballymoney, **t** (028) 2766 3109
Getting there 7 miles (11km) of Coleraine
Open Apr–May and Sept Sun and bank holidays 2–6, Jun Sat–Sun 2–6, Jul–Aug Mon–Sat 11–6, Sun 2–6, House only open to groups (book in advance)
Adm Adult £2.90, child £1.90, family £8.50

Visit 18th-century farm buildings here, including the Bellbarn (a threshing barn), a dovecote, a typical cattle byre and old stables that may house piglets. The estate has been lived in by the Leslie family for 350 years, and the Big House is a classic Georgian stone-cut building dating from 1760.

Did you know?
The Hill of Tivereagh, near Cushendall, is alleged to be the capital of the faeries, who live inside the hill – a rounded volcanic plug. From here there are good views of the coast.

Watertop Open Farm

188 Cushendall Road, Ballyvoy,
t (028) 2076 2576
Getting there 2 miles (3km) east of Ballycastle
Open Easter, May and Jun Mon–Fri 11–5.30, mid-Jun and Sept Sat–Sun 11–5.30, Jul–Aug daily 10.30–5.30, caravan and camp site open all year
Adm Adult £2, child £1
Caravan and campsite, tearoom open Jul–Aug, electric hook-ups, showers, toilets, washing machine

A family activity centre in a scenic area beside a lake. You can ride ponies, fish or take a boat out, walk along the historical trail and take a farm tour, then pet and feed the small animals. Your children may even have the chance to watch a shearing demonstration or take part in an assault course. Afterwards, you can refresh yourself in the tearoom beside the lake. If you want to stay longer, you can camp if you have a tent or caravan.

Look at this!

The Giant's Ring

Getting there Off B23, 1 mile (1.6km) south of Shaw's Bridge, near the Lagan Valley, Belfast

An impressive prehistoric hill fort, a giant earth mound almost within the city of Belfast, and over 600ft (180m) wide.

Irish Linen Centre and Lisburn Museum

Market Square, Lisburn, **t** (028) 9266 3377, **www.**lisburn.gov.uk
Getting there 9 miles (14km) south of Belfast
Open All year Mon–Sat 9.30–5. **Adm** Free
Exhibition, guided tour, linen and crafts shop, café

This is a must if your children are interested in crafts. They can talk to weavers in the damask handloom workshop and watch as they spin and weave, then try it themselves. The old-fashioned factory and 'Flax to Fabric' exhibition show Northern Ireland's world-renowned linen industry from the past to the present, and include Egyptian linen from the tomb of Tutankhamun as well as Irish damask napkins made for European royal courts. After the factory, be sure to visit the spinner's cottage and hear the tape of Victorian mill girls gossiping before learning how modern linen fashions are created via a combination of traditional skills and high technology.

Patterson's Spade Mill

Near Templepatrick, **t** (028) 9443 3619
Getting there 11 miles (17km) north of Belfast
Open Mid to end-Mar Sun 2–6, Apr–May and Sept Sat–Sun 2–6, Jun–Aug daily 2–6, bank holidays and Good Fri. **Adm** Adult £3.25, child £1.50, family £8.50

The only water-driven spade mill left in Ireland, its forge produces nine kinds of spades, although in its heyday it made around 300 types. A fascinating tour takes you to a busy, glowing workshop full of bangs and clangs where people make things the way they used to – you can even take away your own sturdy spade to show the neighbours.

Nature lovers

Benvarden Garden

26 Benvarden Road (off B67), Dervock, Ballymoney, **t** (028) 2074 1331
Getting there 7 miles (11km) north of Ballymoney
Open Jun–Aug Tues–Sun 1.30–5.30 except bank holidays. **Adm** £2.50 per person

One of the few fully maintained walled gardens in Ireland, Benvarden has an attractive 18th-century rose garden and pleasure grounds. Its river is spanned by a Victorian iron bridge, and a woodland pond surrounded by gardens.

Carnfunnock Country Park

Drains Bay, Coast Road, Larne, **t** (028) 2827 0541, **www.**larne.gov.uk
Getting there 3 miles (5km) north of Larne
Open Spring/summer 9–dusk, Jul–Aug 9–9, autumn/winter 9–4.30, closed Christmas Day and New Year's Day; Attractions open from Easter–Oct: times vary, call to check.
Adm Park: free but charges for each activity
Wildlife garden, partial wheelchair access/hire, toilets (also for disabled), walks, café, shop

On a fine day, this is a fine place for a family outing. There are lots of activities for all ages in over 473 acres of mixed woodland, gardens, ponds, walking trails, beaches and coastline. Many of the original features remain, including an icehouse and lime kilns. Outdoor man-made attractions include a maze shaped like Northern Ireland, and a walled garden with sundials from different eras. Little ones who can't read clocks will enjoy seeing where their shadows fall on the Human Sundial.

Ecos Centre Millennium Centre

Kernohans Lane, Broughshane Road, Ballymena, **t** (028) 2566 0300, **www.ecoscentre.com**
Getting there Off Junction 11 of the M2
Open All year except 24 Dec–1 Jan, phone for times
Café and gift shop, nature trails, play areas, caravan park, baby-changing and disabled facilities

This centre underlines how fragile our world is and promotes natural energy sources like wind and sun. Its interactive exhibits on environmental issues are geared to older children and teenagers.

Rathlin Island

Getting there There are daily boat crossings from Ballycastle, Jun–Sept. Boats leaves Ballycastle about 10.30am and return in the afternoon. The rest of the year, contact the Tourist Office in Ballycastle. Rathlin Island Ferry, **t** (028) 2076 9299

The island lies 6 miles (9km) off Ballycastle and 16 miles (26km) from the Mull of Kintyre in Scotland. It is 8 miles (13km) long and less than a mile wide. You can see some of the endangered species of puffins nesting on the cliff.

Sporty kids

Activity centres

Dundonald International Ice Bowl

111 Dundonald Road, Belfast, **t** (028) 9048 2611

This entertainment complex has an Olympic-size ice rink, bowling centre, IndianaLand jungle-themed play paradise for children, and more.

Lagan Valley LeisurePlex

12 Lisburn Leisure Park, Lisburn, **t** (028) 9267 2121, **f** (028) 9267 4322, **www.lisburn.gov.uk**

An impressive complex with a swimming pool with various thrills and spills, a diving pool, fitness suite, four squash courts, main hall and restaurant.

Did you know...?
Throughout the Middle Ages, Ireland and Scotland disputed the ownership of Rathlin Island. The argument was finally settled in Ireland's favour in 1617 on the grounds that on Rathlin, as in Ireland, there weren't any snakes.

Buckets and spades – Beaches in Co. Antrim

From Larne northward, there are golden stretches of sand all along the Antrim Coast Road. **Cushendall** has a particularly lovely beach, and **Ballycastle** is definitely worth a visit – lovely and quiet and with cliffs and caves to explore. You can camp, park a caravan or dock a boat, as well as swim on a Blue Flag beach and take a boat to Rathlin Island, *see* below. Other Blue Flag beaches are at **Portrush** and **Magilligan.**

Horse riding

Castlehill Equestrian Centre

86a Fenaghy Rd, Cullybackey, Ballymena, **t** (028) 2588 1222

A very well-equipped centre with expert staff.

Drumaheglis Riding School

89 Glenstall Rd, Ballymoney, **t** (028) 2766 5500

Tuition in all the riding disciplines for all ages.

Fishing

The Bann, Main, Braid, and Glenwhirry rivers and Lough Neagh are renowned for trout and salmon. Sea fishing is also good all along the Antrim coast. For a list of centres contact Tourism Ireland.

Ulster Cruising School

Carrickfergus Marina, **t** (028) 9336 8818

Boats available with expert fishing guides.

Walking

As well as the Glens of Antrim or the Giant's Causeway, there are many more great walks in the county. One spot is the **Slemish Mountain**, 4 miles (6km) east of Ballymena. The **Ballypatrick Forest Drive**, between the Glens and Ballycastle, is excellent for combining a scenic drive with stops for leisurely walks. Tourist offices have full guides.

Steam Power!

Railway Preservation Society of Ireland

Whitehead Station, York St, Whitehead, **t** (028) 2826 0803

The Portrush Flyer, a charming vintage train that takes two hours to run between Whitehead and Portrush, only operates on Sunday afternoons in June–August. Phone for times and fares.

COUNTY DOWN

One of Ireland's most famous, and most poignant, emigrant songs comes from Co. Down. *The Mountains of Mourne* compares the life that's lived 'digging for gold in the streets' in foreign cities (there are different versions, where the migrant is in London or New York) with the satisfactions of being in a place where mountains 'sweep down to the sea.' In other words, in a foreign land you have to dig for the beauty you already have in your own country, and most of the 'gold' you find there is no more than fairy dust.

A little ironically, in terms of the song, Down was one of the two most densely 'planted' counties of Northern Ireland in the 17th century, giving it and Antrim the heaviest Protestant population. Long before that, even St Patrick hailed from England; he landed in Saul, Co. Down in AD 432. A local chieftain called Dichu, who was his first convert, gave him a barn where he preached. Later he founded a church in Armagh, and his remains are buried on top of a hill outside Down Cathedral in Downpatrick, where he shares a grave with Sts. Brigid and Columcille.

As well as for the Mourne Mountains Down is known for lush woods and quiet coastal towns, and the wetlands around Strangford Lough. Families wanting a leisurely holiday will find many attractions, from the Ulster Folk Museum in Cultra to the Exploris aquarium and Castle Espie wildfowl centre. For a more active time, try watersports on the east coast or riding in the Mournes.

Tourist information

Ards, t (028) 9182 6846
Banbridge: Newry Road, **t** (028) 4062 3322
Bangor, t (028) 9127 0069
Downpatrick, t (028) 4461 2233
Groomsport, t (028) 9145 8882
Hillsborough, t (028) 9268 9717
Kilkeel: 6 Newcastle St, **t** (028) 4176 2525
Newcastle, t (028) 4372 2222
Newry, t (028) 3026 8877
Newtownards: Kingdoms of Down, 40 West St, **t** (028) 9182 2881, **www.kingdomsofdown.com**
Portaferry: Castle St, **t** (028) 4272 9882
Warrenpoint, t (028) 4175 2256

Special Events – County Down

March–April

St Patrick's Day, information **t** (028) 4461 2233

The county's biggest celebrations on 17 March are in Downpatrick, Newry and Cultra.

Easter Celebrations, Ulster Folk and Transport Museum (UFTM), Cultra, **t** (028) 9042 8428

Seasonal fun for the whole family.

The Best of Ireland, UFTM, Cultra, **t** (028) 9042 8428

Another festival at the museum, with traditional music and crafts geared in part to children.

June

Castle Ward Opera, Castle Ward, **t** (028) 4461 2233

An opera festival in the lovely setting of Castle Ward and its gardens (*see* p.214).

Green Living Fair, Castle Espie, **t** (028) 9187 4146

Ireland's biggest environmental event, in the Castle Espie wetlands centre (*see* p.213).

July

As in all Protestant areas of Northern Ireland, there are big celebrations on 12 July (*see* p.35).

Booley Fair, Hilltown; information from tourist offices

Demonstrations of vanishing skills like weaving, stone-carving and shoeing horses, with traditional music and dancing, street stalls and a sheep fair. It's held early–mid July. Good for the whole family.

Scarva Sham Fight, Scarva, **t** (028) 3883 2163

Symbolic re-enactment of the Battle of the Boyne on 12 July, between two horsemen in period costume – William of Orange and James II.

Kingdom of Mourne Festival, Kilkeel, Cranfield and Annalong, **t** (028) 4176 2166

Community festival for families.

Northern Ireland Game Fair, Ballywalter Park, Ballywalter, **t** (028) 9048 3873

Illustrates how farming, sport and conservation can work together to preserve the countryside.

Storytelling Weekend, UFTM, Cultra, **t** (028) 9042 8428

Storytelling and traditional music.

August

Fiddlers Green Festival, Rostrevor.

Five-day community festival.

Heart of Down Pipe Band Championship, **t** (028) 4461 2233

For pipers piping.

Rare Breeds Show and Sale, UFTM, Cultra, **t** (028) 9042 8428

Future farmers will enjoy seeing Ireland's largest rare breeds show.

Tours

Mourne Countryside Centre, 91 Central Promenade, Newcastle, **t** (028) 4372 4059

For guided walks in the Mourne Mountains.

Getting there and around

By bus Ulsterbus has excellent services to all parts of Co. Down, from Laganside Bus Centre, Belfast.

By rail NIR has a suburban line from Belfast along the south side of Belfast Lough through Holywood to Bangor, and the Belfast–Dublin line runs down the west of the county via Newry.

Bus and train information, **t** (028) 9066 6630, **www.translink.co.uk**

Bike Hire

Ross Cycles, 44 Clarkhill Road, Castlewellan, **t** (028) 4377 8029.

Quinn Cycles, Kilkeel, **t** (028) 4176 2654.

Mike the Bike, Newtownards, **t** (028) 9181 1311.

DOWNPATRICK

The county's main market town, Downpatrick bears the weight of its many associations with St Patrick. After landing in Ireland near Strangford Lough, the saint spent a lot of time around here, converting the warrior-heathen to a gentle form of Christianity and casting demons into oblivion. Locally, Patrick is also strongly associated with Saul, just east of the town near Slieve Patrick.

Things to see and do

Down County Museum

The Mall, English St, **t** (028) 4461 5218

Open Sept–May Tue–Fri 10–5, Sat, Sun 1–5, closed Mon; Jun–Aug Mon–Fri 10–5, Sat, Sun 1–5. **Adm** free

A brief history of the area is given and carved stones from Saul are displayed inside an old gaol. Model inmates wear 17th-century costume in the cells. Kids can also try on costumes of various religions, learn about an ancient chess game played by the Vikings and make simple brass rubbings.

Downpatrick Railway Museum

The Railway Station, Market St, **t** (028) 4461 5779

Open for train rides Jul–Aug Sat–Sun 2–5, and first 2 weekends Sept; special trains for St Patrick's Day, Easter Sun–Mon; May Day; Halloween and Dec weekends with Santa Claus; guided tours of carriages and workshops Jun–Sept Mon–Sat 11–2

Model-train-mad children will love this restored station building, with a museum of old railway carriages and a steam train that runs to a place called King Magnus's Halt, near the grave of a Viking king called Magnus Barefoot. Work is under way to extend the track south towards a restored corn mill at Ballydugan and on to Quoile River and Inch Abbey, where it's hoped to build a new station.

The Saint Patrick Centre

Market St, **t** (028) 4461 9000, **www.saintpatrickcentre.com**

Open Jun–Aug Mon–Sat 9.30–6, Sun 1–6; Apr–May and Sept 9.30–5.30, Sun 10–5.30; Oct–Mar Mon–Sat 10–5; St Patrick's Day 9.30–7

Adm Adult £4.50, child £2.25; free entry to restaurant, shops and art shows

Internet café, crafts and gift shop, restaurant

Were there two Patricks? What kind of world did he live in? Was he crazy or a visionary? These and other questions will be answered as you explore this state-of-the-art museum. Its modern audio techniques combine with innovative visuals and interactive technology to absorb you in a world where a man's dreams led him to sainthood.

When you enter the museum, you are greeted by a hallucinatory film covering an entire wall, its kaleidoscopic narrative taking you over a 'bridge of time' into the past and turning your mind to St Patrick's Ireland of 1,500 years ago, when heathen warriors and Christian men of peace lived side by side in occasional harmony. Children may not have the patience to wait for it to end, before moving on to the more interactive part of the museum.

If we are to believe the stories about him, St Patrick overcame all doubters with great miracles and banished many a pagan demon to the deep. He bettered the Druids in every respect, and overcame the magical beings that inhabited Ireland with even stronger magic – a magic that came not from him, he said, but from God.

Although folklore portrays Patrick as a being of mythic proportions, he was not a mythological character. We have proof, because he left two pieces he wrote himself: the *Letter to Coroticus*, in which he upbraided a chieftain who had murdered newly baptised Christians; and his *Confession*, a detailed account of his life's work and thoughts.

Don't miss this top-rate museum, perfect for a rainy day. Allow a couple of hours at least, and then have lunch or a snack in the excellent restaurant.

A story to tell:
How St Patrick came to Ireland

It's a great irony that Ireland's greatest saint came from England. It appears he was kidnapped as a boy by Niall of the Nine Hostages, and brought to these shores to tend the sheep of an Irishman. He was not a particularly holy lad at first, but after his Irish adventure and return to his homeland, he began to have visions. This led him towards the Church, and so he took a monk's vows.

Then, one night in a dream, he heard all the voices of Ireland as if they were one voice. 'Come and walk among us again,' they called out. And so when the Church asked Patrick to take the place of Palladius, the ageing missionary sent to Ireland before him, he did not hesitate to return.

He arrived at the mouth of the River Slaney on Strangford Lough, and landed at Slán (which means 'health' in Irish) – now the Struell Wells area, whose waters have an ancient reputation for healing. St Patrick's first church in Ireland was in a great barn in the village of Saul, which the local Gaelic chieftain Dichu, his first convert, gave him.

SPECIAL TRIPS

Castle Espie

The Wildfowl and Wetlands Trust, Castle Espie, Ballydrain Road, Comber, **t** (028) 9187 4146
Getting there On Strangford Lough 3 miles (5km) south of Comber and 13 miles (21km) southeast of Belfast, signposted from A22
Open Daily, summer: Mon–Sat 10.30–5, Sun 11.30–6; winter: Mon–Sat 11.30–4, Sun 11.30–5; closed 24–25 Dec
Adm Adult £4, child £2.50, family £10.50
Coffee shop, gift shop, walks, organic garden, guided walks by arrangement, picnic area, free parking

Children come into close contact with birds and wetlands here. The landscaped gardens, kilns, quarries and over 30 acres of woodland are home to Ireland's largest collection of ducks, geese and swans, as well as otters, badgers and foxes, amid rare flowers and grasses, moths and butterflies. From May to August you can see hundreds of fluffy ducklings and goslings. Probably the best nature park in Northern Ireland, it takes one hour to walk around it fast, but you could spend hours here. The views of Strangford Lough are wonderful.

Exploris

The Ropewalk, Castle St, Portaferry, **t** (028) 4272 8062, **www**.ards-council.gov.uk/exploris
Getting there 28 miles (46km) south of Belfast by A20 around Strangford Lough
Open Sept–Feb Mon–Fri 10–5, Sat 11–5, Sun 1–5; Mar–Aug till 6
Adm Adult £3.60, child £2.50, family £11.50 (2+4)
Shop, café, picnic area, playground, toilets with baby-changing facilities, disabled access

Perhaps Ireland's best aquarium, Exploris has a huge open sea tank housing rays and sharks. A virtual journey takes you out into Strangford Lough and the Irish Sea to encounter underwater creatures, then you can see real ones for yourself as you enter the walk-through tanks. Around 2,000 species are on show. There are feeding shows and touch tank sessions at 10.30, noon, 1.30, 3 and 4.30.

Exploris also rehabilitates orphaned, injured and sick seals – which can sometimes be seen – and is in a park and wildfowl reserve, with a caravan park, tennis, mini-golf and bowling green.

Seaforde Tropical Butterfly House, Maze and Garden

Seaforde Nursery, Seaforde, **t** (028) 4481 1225
Getting there Off the A24 between Ballynahinch and Newcastle, just outside Seaforde
Open Butterfly House: Apr–end-Sept Mon–Sat 10-5, Sun 1–6; Gardens: all year
Adm Butterfly House or Garden: adult £2.50, under-16s £1.50; Butterfly House and Gardens: adult £4.30, under-16s £2.50, family (2+2) £12
Maze, children's playground, nursery, gift shop

Hundreds of free-flying exotic butterflies fill the Tropical Butterfly House, where you can see their lifecycle firsthand. Insects and reptiles from every continent are displayed, behind glass. Young kids enjoy following the maze to its central 'treasure'.

The Ulster Folk and Transport Museum

Cultra, **t** (028) 9042 8428, **www**.nidex.com/uftm
Getting there 8 miles (13km) north of Belfast by A2, near Holywood.
Open Summer Mon–Sat 10.30–6, Sun 12 noon–6; spring and autumn Mon–Fri 9.30–5, Sat 10.30–6, Sun 12 noon–6; winter Mon–Fri 9.30–4, Sat–Sun 12.30–4.30

Adm Folk or Transport Museum: adult £4, 5–16s £2.50, under-4s free, family (2+3) £11; Joint ticket: adult £5, 5–16s £3, under-5s free, family (2+3) £13
Craft and gift shops, tearooms, Sunday carvery, toilets with baby-changing facilities, disabled access

Across the road from the indoor 'transport' part of this museum is an outdoor 'folk' part. A whole village – shops, a school, a church, houses – has been set in over 60 acres to look like an Ulster town in the early 1900s. There is even a sweet shop where kids can buy old-fashioned sugar candies.

The transport exhibition shows everything from horse-carts, unicycles and Belfast trams of the 19th century to the DeLorean car, old Ulster buses and railway carriages. There are life-sized models of people on the buses and trams, cleverly depicted as if they're taking part in little everyday dramas. Look out for the very funny tableau of the last bus home in 1950s Belfast. Kids love sitting in an early aeroplane, to watch a film of man's earliest attempts at flight. There's also a moving exhibition about the Titanic. This double-museum also hosts great family-orientated events throughout the year.

AROUND AND ABOUT

Animal magic

Ark Open Farm

296 Bangor Road, Newtownards, **t** (028) 9181 0445
Getting there 11 miles (17km) east of Belfast
Open Mon–Sat 10–6, Sun 2–6
Adm Adult £1.95, child £1.40
Coffee shop, wheelchair access

Rare breeds including Irish Moiled Cattle live here. Petting farms like this tend to rotate the animals on show so that they stay as healthy as possible, but you're likely to see pigs, a midget pony kitted out with a saddle ready to take a toddler for a ride and some very intelligent-looking llamas.

Did you know...?
Ireland's famous shamrock emblem came from St Patrick. After a contest of magical power against the Druids, which he won, St Patrick plucked a shamrock to illustrate the Trinity, the 'three in one' idea he was trying to convey as a means of understanding God.

Bricks and mortar

Castle Ward Castle and Gardens

Strangford, **t** (028) 4488 1204,
www.nationaltrust.org.uk
Getting there 30 miles (48km) south of Belfast
Open Castle: Apr, Sept–Oct Sat–Sun 1–6; May–Aug Fri–Wed 1–6; Grounds: all year dawn–dusk
Adm House and grounds: adult £4.70, child £1.80, family £9.90; Grounds only: £3.10, child £1.30, family £7.30
Restaurant, shop, toilets, disabled access, baby-changing and feeding facilities, children's play area

Crafts fairs, cultural and music events and historical re-enactments are held on this 700-acre estate of beautiful formal and landscaped gardens, woods, lakes and seashore. The 'castle' is an 18th-century house with classical and Gothic façades, a theatre in the stable yard, fortified tower house, sawmill and Victorian laundry. An interpretative centre offers historical background too.

There are woodland and lough-side paths to explore, plus horse trails, the gardens and the Strangford Lough Wildlife Centre (**t** (028) 4488 1411), where kids can learn all about the seals, otters and many species of birds who live on the lough.

Grey Abbey and Nendrum Monastic Site

Ards Peninsula, **t** (028) 9054 3037
Getting there 18 miles (29km) south of Belfast by A20 around Strangford Lough
Open Apr–Sept Tues–Sat 10–6, Sun 2–6 only; Oct–Mar Sat 10–4, Sun 2–4 (last adm 5.30)
Adm Free (under-16s must be accompanied)
Guided tours, picnic area, disabled access toilets

The beautiful 12th-century Grey Abbey – ruined, but with many intact rooms – has an exhibition on what life was like for monks here and demonstrating the skills of building and stone carving. Nearby is another monastic ruin at Nendrum. The visitor centre has displays about St Mochaoi, and a film on Nendrum and Grey Abbey.

Look at this!

North Down Heritage Centre

The Castle, Bangor, **t** (028) 9127 1200, **www**.northdown.gov.uk/heritage
Getting there 14 miles (22km) from Belfast
Open Tues–Sat 10.30–4.30, Sun and bank holidays 2–4.30; Jul–Aug 10.30–5.30. **Adm** Free
Disabled access, restaurant (Jul–Aug) in courtyard

Set at the back of Bangor town hall in the former outbuildings of the castle (1852), amid wooded grounds, this centre offers children a discovery quiz sheet to take with them as they look at the displays and audio-visual presentations. There is an observation beehive and also summer 'fun days' for children. As well as archaeological artefacts there are intriguing large-scale models of Bronze Age and Early Christian settlements.

Nature lovers

Castlewellan Forest Park

Main St, Castlewellan, **t** (028) 4377 8664
Getting there 4 miles (6km) north of Newcastle
Open All year daily 10am–sunset
Adm Per car £3.50
Caravan and campsites, picnic and barbecue areas, café, walks, riding trails, fishing, guided tours

A 19th-century Scottish baronial-style castle sits among trees here, in grounds that are delightful for family walks. You can explore the walled garden, established in 1740, with hothouses, rhododendron beds and woodlands, around a lovely pond in the foothills of the Mountains of Mourne.

Delamont Country Park

Mullagh, near Downpatrick, **t** (028) 4482 8333
Getting there 6 miles (10km) north of Downpatrick
Open Winter daily 9–5; summer daily 9–dusk
Adm Per car £1.50
Shop, picnic areas, tearoom, licensed restaurant, playground, miniature railway

Summer events such as magic shows, concerts and puppet plays are held in this wooded park.

Mount Stewart House and Gardens

t (028) 4278 8387, **www**.nationaltrust.org.uk
Getting there 5 miles (8km) south of Newtownards

Open House: Apr and Oct Sat–Sun 1–6; May–Sept Wed–Mon 1–6; Gardens: Mar Sun 2–5, Apr–Sept daily 10.30–6, Oct Sat–Sun 10.30–6
Adm House, garden, Temple of Winds: adult £4.95, child £2.35, family £10.15; Garden only: adult £3.90, child £2.10, family £8.85
Shop, teas, toilets with baby-changing room, disabled access, seasonal exhibitions and events

This 18th-century house and its garden are especially enjoyable for families with young children and the elderly. It contains shrubs cut into shapes – like the magnificent one of the Irish harp above a blanket of red-leaf plants in the shape of a Red Hand, created to symbolize reconciliation between Catholic/Gaelic and Protestant Ireland. There are stone images of all kinds of animals, including memorials to late family pets, decorating the grounds. Families could have fun by challenging children to spot the different stone sculptures and make up stories about them, such as why there's a monkey sitting on top of a Green Man (the one with grapes on his head), or why the Stewart family put sculptures of rabbits, boars, cats and even a stone ship in the garden. And the comfortable tearoom has good home-made cakes.

Rowallane Gardens

Saintfield, Ballynahinch, **t** (028) 9751 0131
Getting there 15 miles (24km) south of Belfast
Open Apr–Oct Mon–Fri 10.30–6, Sat–Sun 2–6; Nov–Mar Mon–Fri 10.30–5
Adm Apr–Oct: Adult £3, child £1.25, family £6.25; Nov–Mar: Adult £1.40, child 70p, groups 80p
Shop, tearoom, disabled access

Special events – concerts, fun days – are occasionally arranged for families, and this beautiful, flower-filled garden is great for easy walks.

Buckets and spades – Down's Beaches

Going from north to south, there are two lovely, and popular, beaches at **Helen's Bay**, just west of Bangor, and there's an attractive Blue Flag beach at **Millisle**, just south of Donaghadee.

South of Downpatrick, one of Northern Ireland's best is **Tyrella Beach** on Dundrum Bay, long, sandy and backed by dunes, and also good for swimming is **Dundrum** itself.

Cranfield Bay, Co. Down's southernmost point near Kilkeel, has long been a favourite summertime swimming and holiday spot, with Haulbowline Lighthouse not far away.

Tollymore Forest Park

Tullybrannigan Road, Newcastle, **t** (028) 4372 2428
Getting there 2 miles (3km) west of Newcastle
Open All year dawn to dusk
Adm Adult £1.50, child 50p, per car £3
Visitor centre, gift/craft shop, picnic areas, restaurant, caravan and camping park, disabled access

This impressively lush park of woodlands and mountains is huge, and a family could spend all day wandering along its lovely paths. Pick up a map on arrival. Look out for the White Fort rath, perhaps built around AD 500, the bridges across the two rivers, the grotto and the flower-filled arboretum.

Sporty kids

Activity centres

Pickie Family Fun Park

The Promenade, Bangor, **t** (028) 9127 4430

Ride in swan boats on the lake, paddle in pools, play in the sandpits, take a miniature train, explore the fairground arcades and walk by the shore.

Tropicana Pleasure Beach

Central Promenade, Newcastle, **t** (028) 4372 5034

Children will enjoy the bouncy castle, heated outdoor pool, flumes and adventure playground.

Boat trips

Weather permitting, boats leave from Bangor and Donaghadee in summer at 10.30, 2.30 and 7.30pm for short cruises along the coast. Information is posted on the piers. Boats from Bangor also go out to uninhabited Copeland Island; Bangor Tourist Office has details.

Horse riding

Mount Pleasant Equestrian Centre

15 Banannstown Road, Castlewellan, **t** (028) 4377 8651

For beginners and experienced riders.

Walking

The **Ulster Way** footpath goes along the shores of Strangford Lough, around the coast and into the Mourne Mountains. Tourist offices have guides.

Water sports

Bangor and Strangford Sailing School

13 Gray's Hill, Bangor, **t** (028) 9145 5967/9754 1592

For sailing in Strangford Lough.

COUNTY ARMAGH

The name Armagh comes from *Ard Macha*, 'Macha's Height', which refers to the fortress built on top of a hill by a legendary queen called Macha around the first millennium BC. For 700 years the High Kings of Ulster held court at what is now Armagh City, and their capital was at Navan Fort, very near the town. These kings were always at war with Connacht, at least until the 5th century AD when Christianity arrived in Ireland and St Patrick himself, supposedly, chose Armagh as his seat.

Armagh is known as the Orchard of Ireland, because its rich and beautiful landscape is renowned for its apples.

Tourist information

Armagh: St Patrick's Trian Centre, 40 English St, **t** (028) 3752 1800, **www.armagh-visit.com**
Craigavon: Civic Centre, Lakeview Road, **t** (028) 3831 2400

Tours

Armagh Guided Tours, **t** (028) 3755 1119, **www.armaghguidedtours.com**, or via Armagh Information Centre, **t** (028) 3752 1800

Barbara Ferguson can tell you all about Armagh, from folklore to history, and take you all around its most fascinating corners.

Getting there and around

By bus Ulsterbus Express buses run from Belfast to Armagh, Mon–Sat every hour 6.30am–6.30pm; on Sundays there are only two.
Armagh Bus Station, **t** (028) 3752 2266
By rail The **Enterprise** trains (*see* p.288) between Dublin and Belfast stop at Portadown and Newry, and there also slower trains with more stops.
Bus and train information, **t** (028) 9066 6630, **www.translink.co.uk**

ARMAGH CITY

The City of Armagh is steeped in Ireland's ecclesiastical history. Little is known about it before the middle of the 7th century, when it was the centre of the cult of St Patrick and fast becoming the religious capital of Ireland, but we do know that King Conor and his Red Branch warriors had occupied Navan Fort, just outside the town.

The famous *Book of Armagh* was written here in 807 by a scribe named Ferdomnach. It contains the New Testament plus St Patrick's *Confession* and some of the earliest documents about the saint, including the *Book of the Angel* (c.640), a unique glimpse of 7th-century Armagh.

The heart of Armagh is called 'the Rath', and it is surrounded by 'The Trians', part of the monastic settlement that grew up around the centre of the city. Armagh's most famous homegrown saint was the 12th-century St Malachy, portrayed holding 'Armagh apples' in sculptures and on the stained-glass inside St Patrick's Catholic Cathedral.

Today a strong military police presence occupies the city fairly benignly, a vestige of the Troubles. Mostly, it's a quiet town: shops close early in Armagh and restaurants do slow trade off-season.

Just to the west of Armagh City stands Navan Fort, the ancient Emain Macha of Irish history and legend and the earliest capital of Ulster. It is the setting for the tales of Macha, Cúchulainn and the heroes of the Red Branch. On the hill of Emain Macha, where traces of a giant Celtic temple (128ft in diameter) have been found, you are enveloped by the mysteries of Celtic rituals and prehistoric people's beliefs in the 'Otherworld'. Navan Fort, the cultural, political and spiritual capital of the Kings of Ulster from 600 BC, serves as the backdrop for a number of legends first written in the 7th century. Even today as you walk up the low hill, small in comparison to the weight of its mythology, you can sense an atmosphere of gravity and importance. King Conchobor McNessa ruled from here, with his Red Branch Knights assisted by Co. Louth's demigod Cúchulainn; the stories surrounding them are similar to those of Britain's King Arthur and his Knights of the Round Table, with Cúchulainn a rougher version of Lancelot. A few years ago an attractive visitor centre was installed next to the hill, but it has been closed for some time due to funding problems. Check with the tourist offices as to what tours or other activities may be available at Navan when you visit.

A story to tell: Queen Macha

Macha was sovereign of an area west of Armagh City, marked by a hill called *Emain Macha* – which most agree means 'the Twins of Macha'. Like many a mythical goddess in Ireland, this queen seems to have had three sides to her character, and three main stories have been handed down about her. In one she was the wife of Nemedh, who built a fort in South Armagh called *Ard Macha* or 'Macha's Height' (*see* p.29). When she foresaw the sorrows of the future of Ireland, she died of heartbreak. In another, Macha was the only child of a king of Ulster. When he died, she challenged her father's two brothers, who refused to let her succeed to the throne because she was a woman. She challenged them to a fight, which she won, and so became Queen. For the third story, *see* p.199.

Special Events – County Armagh

March

St Patrick's Day, 17 March

There's a huge parade in Armagh City, with a concert in St Patrick's Hall.

May

Apple Blossom Festival, Armagh City, **t** (028) 3752 2282.

Street concerts, games and a 'jail break' from Armagh gaol – fun for all the family.

June

Fleadh Ceol Comhaltas Ceoltori

Traditional music festival, all over the county.

Things to see and do

Armagh County Museum

The Mall East, **t** (028) 3752 3070
Open Mon–Sat 10–5. **Adm** Free

Costumes, natural history and maps of the city and county sit here, in a building that includes a library and art gallery. The Newry tram that carried coal, flax and linen is amid memorabilia of the Clogher Valley Railway and the lines that linked Armagh city to Belfast and with the rest of Ireland.

Armagh Planetarium and Observatory

College Hill, **t** (028) 3752 3689,
www.armagh-planetarium.co.uk
Open Planetarium: all year Mon–Fri 10–4.45, Sat–Sun 1.15–4.45 (check for show times which vary seasonally); Observatory: Apr–Sept 9.30–4.30
Adm Planetarium: adult £3.75, child £2.75, family £11; Observatory: free
Shop, café, disabled access

Mature grounds surround the 18th-century Astropark, an observatory with a model solar system, and the Eartharium, an earth science centre where children can find out all about volcanoes, earthquake activity and ozone depletion. Beyond the gardens you can visit the 20th-century planetarium, with a star show under a silver dome and interactive exhibits that allow you to look back through time to the 'big bang' that many scientists believe created our universe millions of years ago.

Palace Stables Heritage Centre

The Palace Demesne, **t** (028) 3752 9629
Open Mon–Sat 10-5, Sun 2–5
Adm Adult £3.75, child £2, family (2+2) £9.50
Restaurant, shop

Meander through the exhibit, with life-size models and audio commentary, explaining a day in the life of a lady visiting this grand house in the 18th century, and then get a guide to lead you through the stables, house, chapel and grounds. Converse with one of the 'living history' interpreters who act, speak and dress in the Georgian style of 1786. Don't miss the ice house, and make sure your guide explains how it was once used. During the winter, snow would be shovelled into it from a window near the top, so that the thick-walled round 'house', partially underground, would remain cold throughout the rest of the year. The adventure playground, 'sensory garden' and perhaps a horse-drawn carriage ride will round off your visit. Also, once a month the Armagh Pipers Club meets here to play music (**t** (028) 3751 1248).

St Patrick's Cathedral (Church of Ireland)

Cathedral Close, **t** (028) 3752 3142
Open Apr–Oct 9.30–5, Nov–Mar 9.30–4. **Adm** Free
Small car park, bookshop, toilets

St Patrick founded his bishopric and chief church on the high Hill of Armagh, once a prehistoric settlement, in AD 444, and the city spreads out below it. There is little left of a 13th-century cathedral that was built over the remains of St Patrick's original church, as it was 'renovated' by the English architect LN Cottingham in the 1830s. Note the 11th century Market Cross (one carved stone cross mounted on top of another). A nearby plaque claims that the body of Brian Boru, the High King of Ireland who died in 1014, lies in the vicinity.

> ***Did you know...?***
> ***Archaeologists think that Navan hill fort may have been more of a ceremonial than a defensive site. Its importance must have lasted into the Middle Ages, as Brian Boru camped there in 1005. Navan Fort was abandoned after St Patrick's Church was built in Armagh City.***

> ***Did you know...?***
> ***Trians (pronounced 'tree-anns') means 'three sections', an ancient name for the way central Armagh was divided; Christian monks and their followers later settled in these three sections.***

St Patrick's Cathedral (Roman Catholic)

Cathedral Road, **t** (028) 3752 2802
Open All day to dusk. **Adm** Free

Like most Catholic churches in Ireland, Armagh's Catholic cathedral could only be built after the laws against Catholics were relaxed in the 1820s (*see* p.36). It was begun in 1840, but work was suspended during the Great Famine of the 1840s. It began again in 1854, but it wasn't completed until the 20th century. There are very impressive interior decorations.

St Patrick's Trian Visitor Complex

40 English St, **t** (028) 3752 1801
Open Mon–Sat 10–5, Sun 2–5
Adm Adult £3.75, child £2, family (2+2) £9.50
Tourist office, shop, periodic craft workshops, restaurant, disabled access, enclosed car parking

Two exhibitions trace the development of Armagh from prehistoric times to its present incarnation as a world centre of Christianity. There's a film on this and displays on St Patrick and his effect on the city. The third exhibition is the one that will most interest young children, though – called 'The Land of Lilliput', it's a grand extravaganza based on Jonathan Swift's famous *Gulliver's Travels*. Children are invited into a brightly coloured wooden fairytale castle where they can put on play costumes before entering the land of Lilliput. There they will encounter the sleeping giant, tied down by the tiny natives who wait to feed him with tiny loaves of bread. The adventures of Gulliver are told in the next room with hi-tech atmospherics and 3-D, as you take part in his trial and Gulliver talks to you. A great way to interest children in a literary classic, and a must on a trip to Armagh.

Entertainment

Market Place Theatre and Arts Centre

t (028) 3752 1821/3752 1820

Arts centre, with drama, music and dance, two theatres, a gallery and restaurants and bars.

Shopping

A craft fair is usually held every last Sunday of the month at the Palace Stables Centre (*see* left).

Shambles Market

Cathedral Road, **t** (028) 3752 8192
Open Tues and Fri 9–5
Large food, clothing and general market.

AROUND AND ABOUT

Animal magic

Ardress House

64 Ardress Road, Portadown, **t/f** (028) 3885 1236, **www.**nationaltrust.org.uk
Open Mid-Mar–May and Sept Sat, Sun and bank holidays 2–6, Jun–Aug Wed–Mon 2–6
Adm Adult £2.70, child £1.35, family £6.75
Guided tours, shop, wheelchair access

This 17th-century manorhouse and its outbuildings contain rare farm animals, farm implements and a blacksmith's shop. The surrounding woods and gardens are lovely, and children can make the most of the adventure playground, special family events and riverside walks.

Tannaghmore Gardens and Farm

Silverwood, Craigavon, **t** (028) 3834 3244
Open All year daily; Gardens: dawn to 1 hour before dusk; Farm: 10–2 hours before dusk
Adm Free, small charge for bouncy castle
Picnic area, organized treasure hunts

Victorian rose garden, rare animal breeds and nature walks alongside an adventure playground.

Bricks and mortar

The Argory

Derrycaw Road, Moy, Dungannon, **t** (028) 8778 4753/8778 9598, **www.**nationaltrust.org.uk
Open April–May and Sept Sat,Sun, bank holidays 2–6; Jun and Aug Wed–Mon 2–6, July daily 2–6
Adm Adult £3, child £1.50, family rate available; £1.50 car park
Guided tours, shop, tearoom, toilets with baby-changing facilities, wheelchair access

Everything in this 1820s mansion is the same as it was at the start of the 20th century. There is no electricity, and family possessions from four generations are on show. The house stands in 315 acres of woodland overlooking the River Blackwater, and also has a children's playground.

Dan Winter's Cottage

1 The Diamond, Loughgall, **t** (028) 3885 2777
Open Spring/summer: Sat–Sun and bank holidays
Adm Free

A monument of Protestant Ulster, located at the crossroads where the 'Battle of the Diamond' took place in 1795 – and so the birthplace of the Orange Order. It all began when the 'Orange Boys', a Protestant club, heard that the Catholic 'Defenders' planned to burn all the Protestant homes in Richhill, Kilmore and Loughgall, and set out to catch them first. A short fight ensued next to Dan Winter's pub, between the 'Defenders' and many Protestant groups. The 'Defenders' were defeated in this 'Battle of the Diamond', and right afterwards, the leaders of the Protestant groups in the battle – notably three pub owners, James Wilson, Dan Winter and James Sloan – formed an umbrella organization supposedly to protect their faith, the Orange Order, which is still in evidence today.

The timbers of the cottage, said to have been Dan Winter's pub (although some say it was his

A story to tell: Cúchulainn

Chulainn was a man who held a feast for the Red Branch and King Conchobar. Setanta, the son of the god Lugh, who was half-god and not from Ulster at all but from Louth, arrived late at the banquet. The gates of Chulainn's palace were shut, and so Setanta simply scaled the walls and climbed over them – unfortunately straight into the vicinity of Chulainn's deadly guard dog, whose jaws were wide enough to swallow a man. Setanta wasn't too bothered by this, though, and simply threw a stone into the hound's mouth, which lodged in its throat and killed it instantly. Hearing all the commotion, Chulainn came out of the palace, and was most upset that his best protector had been killed. The honourable Setanta then promised to take the guard dog's place and be Chulainn's personal protector, so thereafter he came to be called 'the hound of Chulainn', or, in Irish, 'Cúchulainn'. Later he became the greatest hero of the Red Branch warriors, and of Ireland.

Did you know...?
Two Celtic warlords agreed to a contest for ownership of Ulster. The first to place his hand on the land would own it, after a race across the Irish Sea from Britain. One, named O'Neill, was behind in the race and, desperate to claim Ulster for himself, he cut off his hand and threw it ashore before his opponent could land. That is the origin of the Red Hand symbol you see in Ulster today.

neighbour James Sloan's pub, and that Winter's was burned to the ground) still bear scorch marks from when it was set alight in the battle. Thought to be the longest thatched cottage in Ireland, this 94ft home contains 18th-century furnishings in an area for selling alcohol, and a working loom.

Look at this!

Tayto Castle and Crisp Factory

Tandragee, **t** (028) 3884 0249, **www.tayto.com**
Getting there 11 miles (17km) east of Armagh
Open All year Mon–Fri 10–5, Sat 10–1 and 2–5
Adm Free (not suitable for children under age 5)

A 300-year-old castle that is also a factory producing one million packets of crisps and snacks every day. Children can sample many of them, including new products being developed.

Nature lovers

Gosford Forest Park

7 Gosford Demesne, Markethill, **t** (028) 3755 1277
Open Daily 8am–dusk
Adm Adult £1.50, child 50p, car £3
Guided tours and orienteering (book in advance), walled garden, deer paddock, caravan and camp site, horse riding routes, disabled toilets

Gosford Demesne is home to this park and a fine neo-Norman 18th-century castle that isn't open to visitors. The vast forest is ideal for a family walk, though, with plenty of trees, lakes, ducks, space and a magnificent round tower with attendant ghost. You can picnic or eat at the very good restaurant.

Loughgall Country Park

11–14 Main Street, Loughgall, **t** (028) 3889 2906
Open Dawn to dusk
Adm Park: £2, Fishing: £3 per day
Light refreshments at reception

This 464-acre estate of open farmland and orchards has a children's play area, bridle path, 18-hole golf course, 37-acre coarse fishery, country walks, formal gardens and the lake of Loughgall.

Lough Neagh Discovery Centre

Oxford Island, Lurgan, Craigavon, **t** (028) 3832 2205, **www.oxfordisland.com**
Open Centre: Oct–Mar Wed–Sun 10–5, Apr–Sept Wed–Sun 10–7
Adm Centre: adult £4, child £1.50; Park: free

Scenic boat and birdwatching trips are available on Lough Neagh, and there is an award-winning exhibition in the Centre. Cycling also available.

Sporty kids

Activity centres

Waves Leisure Complex

Robert St, Lurgan, **t** (028) 3832 2906

Wave and child's fun pool, adventure play area, crèche and restaurant; open all year.

Boat trips

Lough Neagh

Paddy Prunty, Harbour Master, Kinnego Marina, Oxford Island, **t** (028) 3832 7573

Boats depart from Kinnego Bay, Lough Neagh; Mr Prunty can also arrange sailing courses.

Horse riding

Ring of Gullion Centre

Lough Road, Mullaghbane, west of Slieve Gullion, **t** (028) 3088 9311

Walking

The **Ulster Way**, a well signposted trail, also goes through Armagh. There is an especially scenic stretch along the Newry Canal between Newry and Portadown. Carnagh and Slieve Gullion Forest Park also have fine paths. Details from tourist offices.

Water sports

Craigavon Water Sports Centre

Lakeview Road, Craigavon, **t** (028) 3834 2669

Water sports of all types can be enjoyed here.

COUNTY LONDONDERRY

The name of this county and its city can always confuse outsiders. It originally came from the Druids' sacred island of Derry, from which the city grew. Then, in the 17th century, after the 'Plantation' of Protestant settlers here, King James I renamed it Londonderry (*see* p.34). Co. Londonderry is a lively place of great beauty that is steeped in history and folklore. Mythology, Christian legends and dramatic landscapes entwine and wrap around the imagination.

Visit Derry City's Tower Museum for an introduction to its secrets, then stroll along the City Walls before going further afield to see plantation settlements at Springhill House and Mussenden Temple. Then investigate country folklore at the storytelling festival at Magherafelt, and show your children how Christianity affected Ireland by following some of the legends about St Columcille and St Patrick, which permeate the countryside.

Tourist information

Coleraine: Railway Road, **t** (028) 7034 4723; Causeway Coast and Glens, 11 Lodge Road, **t** (028) 7032 7720, **www**.causewaycoastandglens.com

Derry/Londonderry: Derry Visitor and Convention Bureau, 44 Foyle St, **t** (028) 7126 7284, **www**.derryvisitor.com

Limavady: 7 Connell St, **t** (028) 7776 0307

Tours

City Tours, 11 Carlisle Road, **t** (028) 7127 1996

McNamara's Famous Guided Walking Tours, **t/f** (028) 7134 5335

Top Dog Tours, Tirmacool, Buncrana, **t** 0868 046134
Tours of Derry City.

Getting there and around

By air City of Derry Airport is 7 miles (11km) north-east of the city on the Coleraine road (A2). It has flights from Britain with British Airways and Ryanair (*see* pp.281–2, 284). From the airport there are taxis and many buses, to Derry, Coleraine and many places in Donegal. Airport information, **t** (028) 7181 0784, **www**.cityofderryairport.com

By bus Ulsterbus has regular buses between Derry and every part of Northern Ireland (in Derry, **t** (028) 7126 2261). There are also many Bus Eireann coach services from Derry to Dublin and other destinations in the Republic. The **Londonderry and Lough Swilly Bus Company**, **t** (028) 7126 2017, runs local buses from Derry to most of the loughs and small towns across the border in Donegal.

By train Derry is the terminus of the main NIR line from Belfast via Antrim town and Coleraine, with several trains daily in each direction.
Ulsterbus and NIR train information, **t** (028) 9066 6630, **www**.translink.co.uk

Bike Hire

Happy Days Cycle Hire, 245 Lone Moor Road, Derry City, **t** (028) 7128 7128

Special Events – County Londonderry

March

St Patrick's Day, 17 March, **t** (028) 7136 5151
Parades and events around the county.

City of Drama Festival, Derry City, **t** (028) 7136 5151
A dynamic theatre festival.

Buth an Earraigh, Derry City, **t** (028) 7176 4132
Irish language festival.

June

Walled City Festival, Derry City, **t** (028) 7136 5151.
Outdoor carnival for the family.

July–August

Maiden City Festival, Derry City, **t** (028) 7134 6677

Foyle Cup, Derry City, **t** (028) 7126 7432
Youth soccer tournament.

Gasyard Wall Feile, Derry City, **t** (028) 7126 2812
Events around the city including music, workshops and exhibitions for the whole community.

Sperrins Summer Storytelling Festival, Bridewell TIC, 6 Church St, Magherafelt, **t** (028) 7963 1510; Rural College and Derrynoid Centre, Draperstown, **t** (028) 7962 9100
One of the most enjoyable showcases for Irish storytelling.

October

Flowerfield Arts Centre Festival, 185 Coleraine Road, Portstewart, **t** (028) 7083 3959
Fun for children.

Banks of the Foyle Halloween Carnival, **t** (028) 7126 7284
Quite a spectacle, with young and old dressing up for old-Gaelic Samhain revelry, down by the lough. After sunset, the very young might want to move away from the loud music after the fireworks display and so avoid the scarey spirits of the dark.

November

Foyle Film Festival, Derry City, **t** (028) 7126 7432

Craft Fair, Derry City, **t** (028) 7136 5151

DERRY CITY

This town's first name was *Doire*, meaning 'oak grove'. It is thought to have grown up around a sacred grove of the Druids, for whom oak trees were especially significant. After AD 546, when St Columcille established a religious settlement here, it was known as Derry-Columcille. It became 'Londonderry' in 1613, when King James I enlisted support for the Ulster Plantation (*see* p.34) by giving the London livery companies privileges in the town in return for sending young workmen (many of whom probably had little choice in the matter) to populate the country with loyal Protestants. During Northern Ireland's Troubles, you instantly gave away your political stance by the name you called it: Protestants called it Londonderry, and Catholics Derry. In local papers they began to call the town Londonderry/Derry (or vice versa) to try to avoid offending anybody. Local radio presenter Gerry Anderson is credited with first suggesting just calling it 'Stroke City' instead, and this has been eagerly taken up by local wags.

Whatever its name, it's an important city for two reasons. It lies between Ireland's cosmopolitan east and rural, romantic west, and it had a prominent role in the events leading up to the outbreak of 'the Troubles'. The Bogside, where riots began in 1969, was a famous Republican/Catholic enclave famous for its 'Free Derry' monument and murals. Today Catholics are in the majority in Derry, but there is some crossover in residential areas as Catholics and Protestants are beginning to integrate.

The acclaimed Field Day Theatre Company began here, and kids mustn't miss the award-winning Tower Museum in the rejuvenated tourist area of the city, where there are plenty of shops and cafés.

Things to see and do

Cathedral of St Columb

London St, t (028) 7134 2303, www.stcolumbscathderal.org
Open Summer, Mon–Sat 9–5; winter, 9–1, 2–4
Adm £1
Audio-visuals on local history; wheelchair access but shallow steps at entrance to chapterhouse

The most historic site in Derry is this Protestant 'plantation gothic' cathedral, built in the name of St Columba/Columcille by the Corporation of London in 1633. Stained-glass windows depict the life of the saint. You can also see the Catholic-fired cannonball that fell inside the cathedral during the Siege of Derry (1688–9), along with stained-glass scenes of the battle. The keys of the gates that were closed against the Jacobites are displayed in the chapterhouse; also on display are flags and artefacts from the various brigades that protected the Protestant camps in Ireland.

In 546, Aimire, a prince of Columcille's clan the O'Neills, granted an oak-clad hill in another part of Derry to St Columcille, the early missionary whose name is associated with ancient Christian sites all over Ireland and on the Scottish island of Iona.

A Derry song to sing...
Like everything else here, the song most closely associated with Derry has two names – the Londonderry Air, or Danny Boy. It's probably the most famous of all Irish songs.

City Walls

Derry tourist office, t (028) 7126 7284
Open All year daily dawn to dusk
Adm Free; guided tours £4

Derry is the only remaining completely walled city in Ireland, and one of the finest examples of its kind in Europe. These famous walls were built during the Plantation Period in the early 17th century, when Derry was one of the British Crown's new settlements of English and Scots Protestants. There are fine views from the tops of the walls encircling the old city, a circuit of a mile (1.6km), over the River Foyle and to the hills of Donegal. If you head for the area near the Apprentice Boys' Lodge you can look down on the Bogside.

The Fifth Province or Calgach Centre

4–22 Butcher St, t (028) 7137 3177
Open All year Mon–Fri 9.30–4
Adm Adult £3, child £1, family £6
Audio-visual showings at 11.30am and 2.30pm

This genealogical centre houses a library with a multimedia attraction that brings to life the times and culture of the old Celts in Ireland's west. 'The Fifth Province' mentioned in the presentation is not merely mythical; it suggests that those of Irish descent are connected through a shared heritage and state of mind, as well as referring back to Ireland's ancient fifth province.

Foyle Valley Railway Centre

Foyle Road, **t** (028) 7126 5234,
www.nwonline.demon.co.uk
Open All year Tues–Sat 10–1 and 2–4.30
Adm Adult £2.50, child £1.25, family £7

Train enthusiasts won't want to miss this display of railway artefacts. You can ride on a diesel train through Riverside Park in summer (book ahead).

Harbour Museum

Harbour Square, **t** (028) 7137 7331
Open All year Mon–Fri 10–1 and 2–4.30. **Adm** Free

The museum has exhibits on maritime history and interesting Victorian artefacts – highlights are old ship models, and a replica of a 30ft curragh in which St Columcille sailed to Iona in 563.

Tower Museum

O'Doherty Tower, Union Hall Place, **t** (028) 7137 2411, **www**.derry.net/tower
Open Sept–Jun Tues–Sat 10–5; Jul–Aug Mon–Sat 10–5, Sun 2–5; last adm 4.30; open bank holidays excluding Christmas and New Year
Adm Adult £4, child £1.50, family (2+2) £8
Exhibition, filmshop, guided tour, disabled access

From a modern square, you enter the darkness of a 17th-century grey stone tower and this award-winning museum within underground tunnels filled with treasures and relics, like those from the wrecked Spanish Armada ships of 1588. The museum helps you grasp the complex history of Derry – from geological origins through the Celts and St Columcille's arrival, and on to why the City Walls were built and the origins of the Troubles.

Workhouse Museum

23 Glendermott Road, **t** (028) 7131 8328
Open Jan–Jun and Sept–Dec Mon–Thurs and Sat 10–4.30; Jul–Aug Mon–Sat 10–4.30. **Adm** Free

Teach your children about what happened to people who fell on hard times in the past by showing them this museum's famine and work-house displays. Upstairs is the original workhouse dormitory, much as it was for the poor souls who were sent there. In another room is the Atlantic Memorial Exhibition, which shows the importance of Derry and the River Foyle during World War II.

Entertainment

Comhaltas Ceoltóiri Éireann

15 Crawford Square, **t** (028) 7128 6359

Organizes fleadhs (festivals) of Irish music, dance and storytelling, sometimes at this centre.

SPECIAL TRIPS

The Forge

Castledawson, **t** (028) 7946 8310 or (028) 7938 6812
Getting there 2 miles (3km) north of Magherafelt
Open Visitors welcome at any time, but phone in advance. **Adm** Free but gifts appreciated

Seamus Heaney's poem *The Forge* was about this blacksmith's cottage, which its owner Barney Devlin can tell you all about, since he's related to Heaney's wife. Barney will tell you how people preferred to wash in cold water because they thought hot water would destroy the skin, or how putting your hand in the blacksmith's water (used for cooling hot metals) cures warts. If he likes you, he might give you some of his ironwork.

Springhill House

20 Springhill Road, Moneymore, **t** (028) 8674 7927, **www**.nationaltrust.org.uk
Getting there 1 mile (1.6km) east of Moneymore
Open Jul–Aug Fri–Wed 2–4, Apr–Jun and Sept, Sat, Sun 2–6
Adm Adult £3, child £1.50, family £6.50
Guided tours, tearoom, caravan park

This charming 17th-century house was built for the Lennox-Conynghams, a Plantation family. Around it are Dutch-style outbuildings, walled gardens and lovely grounds for walks. Well-trained guides tell of tragedies, triumphs and the resident ghost. It has a display of historic clothing and a camomile lawn: to make feet smell better, people walked barefoot on it if they didn't want to wash their feet. Also events with 'living history' actors.

***What was...*The Siege of Derry**

Derry's walls have weathered a few sieges, but the best known is the Siege of Derry of 1688–9, which lasted 105 days. After Catholic King James II had lost the throne of England to Protestant William of Orange in 1688 (*see* p.35), he fled to Ireland and raised an army among his Catholic supporters, known as Jacobites. In Londonderry, when James's soldiers were about to enter and conquer the city, a group of apprentice boys – lowly trainee workers sent mostly from London to join the Protestant Plantation – famously locked a gate in the city walls just in time to keep them out.

Ulster Plantation Centre/The Flight of the Earls Experience

50 High St, Draperstown, **t** (028) 7962 7800, **www.flightoftheearlsexperience.com**
Getting there 17 miles (27km) north of Cookstown
Open Easter–Sept Mon–Sat 10–5, Sun 1–5; Oct–Easter Mon–Fri 10–5; open bank holidays (excluding Christmas and New Year)
Adm Adult £3, child £1.50, family (2+2) £7.50

An engaging and imaginative audio-visual exhibit on events of the 17th century – both the 'Flight of the Earls' and the Protestant Plantation.

AROUND AND ABOUT

Look at this!

Amelia Earhart Centre

Ballyarnet Country Park, **t** (028) 7135 4040
Getting there Just outside Derry City
Open All year Mon–Fri 10–4. **Adm** Free

This exhibition commemorates Amelia Earhart's historic flight across the Atlantic and her unexpected landing in Derry on 21 May 1932. She was the first woman to fly the Atlantic solo. Mistaking Derry for Paris, she began speaking French on arrival, which amused the locals no end.

Mountsandel Fort

Getting there Outside Coleraine

This large oval mound dominates the Bann River beside the remains of the oldest houses in Ireland (from 6000 BC), on the outskirts of Coleraine. This is an intriguing, beautiful place to explore. There's a riverside walk and an area perfect for picnicking.

Nature lovers

Palace of Downhill and Mussenden Temple

Castlerock, **t** (028) 7084 8728, **www.nationaltrust.org.uk**
Getting there 5 miles (8km) west of Coleraine

Buckets and spades – Derry's Beaches

A multiple recipient of European Blue Flag awards, **Benone Beach** on Lough Foyle near Limavady offers 7 miles (11km) of golden sand with dramatic scenery of mountains, cliffs and views of Co. Donegal, and many leisure and sports facilites.

Between Portstewart and the mouth of the River Bann lies the 2-mile (3km) **Portstewart Strand**, now a sand dune reserve as well as a tourist beach. On the west side of Portstewart is **Downhill Strand**, which is popular for surf fishing, and there's a fine beach and sandhills at **Castlerock**.

Open Downhill Palace and Temple: mid-Mar–May and Sept, Sat–Sun and bank holidays 1–6, Jun–Aug and Easter daily 1–6; Glen and grounds: always
Adm Free to sites, car park charge at Lion's Gate: £3

The 18th-century estate of Downhill is set on a stunning wild headland with fabulous views over the Inishowen Hills and the Antrim and Derry coasts. The area around the ruined 'palace' (also called Downhill Castle) is superb for walks. It and the temple and mausoleum were built in the 18th century by the famous Earl of Bristol and Bishop of Derry, Frederick Augustus Hervey (1730–1803).

Sporty kids

Horse riding

Hill Farm

Castlerock, **t** (028) 7084 8629

Fishing

You'll find good coarse fishing on the Bann. Fishing for brown trout and salmon is available on the Agivey, Clady, Roe, Bann and Faughan Rivers.
Foyle Fisheries Commission, 8 Victoria Road, Derry City, **t** (028) 7134 2100. Provides game-rod licences.

Walking

The **Sperrins Sky Way**, a 20-mile (32km) route, starts at Barony Bridge, near Draperstown, and runs along the Sperrin Ridge, finishing at Eden, east of Plumbridge, in Co. Tyrone. To the north, the **Ulster Way** runs towards the **Banagher Glen**, with fine walks and panoramic views. Not far south of Derry City is the **Ness Wood Country Park**, which has Ulster's highest waterfall, and near Limavady is the **Roe Valley Country Park**, with a lovely riverside walk through sites associated with St Columcille.

COUNTY TYRONE

Dominated in much of the north of the county by the lofty, little-populated Sperrin Mountains, Tyrone is the heart of Ulster. It's one of Ireland's lesser-known counties, but holds two of Northern Ireland's most impressive attractions that are worth the trip on their own: the Ulster History Park and the Ulster American Folk Park.

A kind of folk memory exists in Tyrone, with traditional walks like the one held on Cairn Sunday, the last Sunday in July, at Mullaghcarn (or *Mullach an Chairn*, 'the summit of the heap of stones') near Gortin Glen north of Omagh. It probably dates back to pagan times and the worship of the god Lugh, when people walked to the tops of hills on Lúghnasa for religious rituals, sports, picking bilberries, picnics, singing and dancing. On Mullaghcarn this practice was phased out by disapproving Victorians and discontinued during the Great Famine, but today the custom is being revived as a way of restoring the Cairn. Walkers leave a stone when they reach the summit, as they have done intermittently for 1,000 years.

Omagh is Tyrone's capital, but it might be more enjoyable for families to base themselves in the hills and forests outside the town. Astride the River Strule, it is best known as a centre for exploring the Sperrin Mountains, which lie to the north and northeast. Omagh is ringed by beautiful, dense woodlands: Seskinore Forest, close to Fintona, Dromore Forest, further west, and Gortin Glen.

The Omagh bombing in August 1998, which killed 28 and injured 200, was the worst single atrocity of the Troubles. It so shocked the community in Northern Ireland – and around the world – that it is said by many to have brought the effective end of large-scale terrorist activity.

Tourist information

Castlederg: 26 Lower Strabane Road, **t** (028) 8167 0795
Cookstown: 48 Molesworth St, **t** (028) 8676 6727
Cranagh: Sperrin Heritage Centre, 274 Glenelly Road, Plumbridge, **t** (028) 8164 8142
Dungannon: Killymaddy Tourist Information Centre, 190 Ballygawley Road, **t** (028) 8776 7259
Omagh: 1 Market St, **t** (028) 8224 7831, **www.omagh.gov.uk/tourism**
Strabane: Abercorn Square, **t** (028) 7188 3735

Getting there and around

There is no rail line in Tyrone, so buses are the only means of public transport.

By bus Ulsterbus has good services to all parts of the county, and Bus Eireann coaches link Co. Tyrone to many destinations in the Republic.

Ulsterbus information, **t** (028) 9066 6630, **www.translink.co.uk**; Omagh bus station, **t** (028) 8224 2711; Strabane bus station, **t** (028) 7138 2393

Bike Hire

Conway Cycles, 1 Market Place, Omagh, **t** (028) 8224 6195

Special Events – County Tyrone

March

St Patrick's Day, 17 March

Parades and celebrations around the county.

Mid-Ulster Drama Festival, Omagh, **t** (028) 8224 0537

Strabane Drama Festival, **t** (028) 7138 3111

June

Fair Day Carnival, Strabane, **t** (028) 7138 2204

Street entertainment in vintage Strabane for the whole community.

The Strawberry Fair, Sion Mills, Strabane, **t** (028) 8165 8350

Traditional village fête with music, dancing and lots of entertainments for kids.

June

Midsummer Festival, Ulster History Park (*see* p.226)

A fine day out for families.

Ulster American Folk Park Festival, Ulster American Folk Park, **t** (028) 8225 6330 (*see* p.226)

Another good event with a big choice of fun things to do.

August–September

Glenelly Sheep and Dog Trials, Plumbridge, Strabane, **t** (028) 8164 8744

Fun for dog-loving kids.

Johnny Crampsie Weekend, Strabane, **t** (074) 914 1106, **www.johnnycrampsie.com**

Traditional Irish music and workshops, with musicians of all ages. Note that the phone contact number is in the Republic.

Storytelling Festival, Rural College, Draperstown, **t** (028) 7962 9100

Always of interest to children who like stories.

SPECIAL TRIPS

The Ulster American Folk Park

Mellon Road, Castletown, **t** (028) 8224 3292, **www.folkpark.com**
Getting there Off A5 4 1/2 miles (6km) north of Omagh
Open Apr–Sept Mon–Sat 10.30–6, Sun and bank holidays 11–6.30; Oct–Mar Mon–Fri 10.30–5, closed Sat–Sun and bank holidays
Adm Adult £4, 5–16s £2.50, under-5s free, family (2+4) £10
Restaurant, special events, picnic areas, craft and gift shops, disabled access, parking

This wonderful museum depicts the life that emigrants of the 18th and 19th centuries left behind in Ulster, and the New World they found in America. The best days to visit are when the period-costumed guides put on storytelling, music or festival events. Children can take part in hands-on activities like spinning, open-hearth cooking and traditional corn craft, or feed the ducks at Mellon House.

Visit the indoor museum first for an introduction. It describes emigrants' reasons for leaving home for a new land and what they encountered there – in the 18th century, many Ulster Protestants left for America, where they became known as the 'Scots Irish'. It tells how some rose to fame and fortune, while others sank into penury. Children find the life-sized dioramas fascinating, as well as the Conestoga covered wagon, black bear, wooden dancing dolls, hobby horses and traditional games.

Then walk through the 18th-century Ulster farming village, to see, smell, touch and taste the past – the smell of soda bread cooking over a turf fire (the 'living history' guide may hand out warm bread with home-churned butter), the sound of a hammer on metal or the whirr of the spinning wheel in a weaver's cottage. On a special event day, kids may hear someone playing music in a cottage. There might be storytelling beside a cottage fire or by a teacher in the Castletown National School where the kinds of slates and slate pencils used in 1845 may be seen, along with old maps and traditional games like skittles and hoop-and-a-stick.

Leaving rural Ulster, turn left towards Shipbouy Street and wander through the shops with original signs and interiors. Then go to the dockside gallery and board the emigrant ship 'Brig Union', bound for the New World. The smells and sounds of the creaking timbers provide a small insight into the conditions experienced by thousands of emigrants on an ocean crossing that took up to 12 weeks.

After 'arriving' (on the other side of the ship) at an American port like that of Boston or Baltimore, wander through a 19th-century American street. Notice the heady scents of cinnamon and coffee. Imagine the sense of unreality these people experienced after surviving their horrific sea journey. As you leave the 'city', with its flea- and rat-infested flop houses where the poorest of the poor spent cold winter nights, you move 'west' and encounter a log cabin typical of the dwellings built by emigrants on the American frontier.

After a long walk through so much history (wear comfortable shoes and take raincoats), you may well want a snack in the museum restaurant.

Did you know...?
The parents of American frontiersman Davy Crockett were from Castlederg, Co. Tyrone.

Ulster History Park

Cullion, near Gortin Glen Park, **t** (028) 8164 8188
Getting there 7 miles (11km) north of Omagh on the B48
Open Apr–Aug Mon–Sat 10.30–6.30, Sun 11.30–7; Sept Mon–Sun 10–5.30; Oct–Mar Mon–Fri 10.30–5 (last adm one hour before closing)
Adm Adult £3.75, child £2.50, family (2+2) £12
Visitor centre with display; café

For an educational experience that will knock the socks off children, not to mention adults, visit this exciting outdoor museum before going to the Ulster American Folk Park. On a sunny day you'll have a grand time wandering on foot here through the past. Reconstructed dwellings help you to trace human settlement and society in Ireland from 8000 BC to the 17th century. History is absorbed easily from the atmospheres created here, although you also meet guides who can tell you facts about the buildings and the people who built them. Let your children imagine themselves back in the days before electricity, computers and aeroplanes. They can play along dirt pathways between the well-spaced historical periods, gaze at the houses from a distance, move closer to peer at the way people tilled their fields, then touch and explore the authentic stone huts and wooden houses. There is plenty of space for children to enjoy the fresh air, country fields and river walks, but keep an eye on toddlers who may tend to wander, and be sure to pack a picnic.

Did you know...?
Poets in ancient Ireland were forbidden by law from taking part in any physical combat, so instead they composed poetic curses which they recited at their enemies before battle.

AROUND AND ABOUT

Animal magic

Barrontop Funfarm

35 Barron Road, Dunnamanagh, Strabane, **t** (028) 7139 8649
Getting there 8 miles (13km) north of Strabane on the B49
Open Apr–Aug Mon–Sat 9.30–5.30, Sun 2–5; Jul–Aug Mon–Sat 9.30–5, Sun 2–5; Dec Sat 9.30–5, Sun 2–5; 17 Mar–Aug
Adm Adult £2.20, child £2
Bouncy castle, adventure playground, gift shop, tearoom, disabled facilities

Young children will have a fun time here bottle-feeding a lamb or cuddling calves, chicks, rabbits and puppies. Exotic breeds like emus, pot-bellied pigs and ostriches may be seen alongside deer, as kids are taken around the farm on a cart drawn by a horse named Rolo. Afterwards they can explore the playground or, if the weather turns bad, jump on the indoor bouncy castle. In December there's a nativity scene, and Santa Claus visits the farm.

Bricks and mortar

Beaghmore Stone Circles

North of Dunnamore, near Cookstown
Getting there 10 miles (16km) west of Cookstown, signposted off A505

Seven impressive Bronze Age stone circles and cairns have been excavated from the bog land.

Grant Ancestral Home

Dergina, Ballygawley, **t** (028) 8555 7133
Getting there 13 miles (20km) west of Dungannon
Open Apr–Sept Mon–Sat 12 noon–5, Sun 2–6
Adm Adult £1.50, child 75p

See a video and exhibit on the American Civil War and Ulysses S Grant, the Union General and later 18th US president. His great-grandfather, John Simpson, was born here in 1738. There are also agricultural implements, a butterfly garden and wildlife pond.

Wilson Ancestral Homestead

Plumbridge Road, Dergalt, **t** (028) 7138 2204
Getting there 2 miles (3km) southeast of Strabane
Open Jul–Aug Tues–Sun 2–5. **Adm** £1

US President Woodrow Wilson was another distinguished American of 'Scots Irish' stock. His grandfather was reared in this humble, now carefully conserved abode before he set off for the States to become a newspaper editor.

Look at this!

Benburb Valley Heritage Centre

Milltown Road, Benburb, **t** (028) 3754 9885
Getting there 8 miles (13km) south of Dungannon
Open Easter–Sept Tues–Sat 10–5 and Sun 2–5
Adm Adult £2, child £1.50

Take a tour around this 19th-century linen mill on the banks of the Ulster Canal to learn about the linen industry in Ireland and the Battle of Benburb, which took place nearby in 1646. Superbly sited on the River Blackwater, the mill has an excellent collection of dramatic-looking old machinery. The harsh conditions workers endured while busily warping, weaving, dyeing and beetling are recaptured in separate exhibitions. Not far from here you can also explore Benburb Valley Park, and follow the river downstream as it flows over a series of cascades beneath Benburb Castle.

Wellbrook Beetling Mill

20 Wellbrook Road, Corkhill, Cookstown, **t** (028) 8674 8210
Getting there Minor road through Dunnamore
Open Apr–Jun and Sept daily 2–6; Jul–Aug daily exc Tues 2–6; Oct–Mar Sat–Sun and bank hols 2–6
Adm Adult £2.50, child £1.25, family £5
Shop, walk, guided tour

This water-powered 18th-century hammer mill was an important centre for beetling, the final process used in manufacturing linen. Try scutching, hackling, weaving and beetling by hand and on the old machines inside this mill. Then take a walk in the lovely glen surrounding it, on paths that follow the Ballinderry River and the millrace.

Nature lovers

An Creagán Visitor Centre

Creggan, Omagh, **t** (028) 8076 1112
Getting there 12 miles (19km) east of Omagh
Open Apr–Sept daily 11–6.30, Oct–Mar 11–4.30

This visitor centre at the foot of the Sperrin Mountains provides an introduction to the history of the area, with bog trails and a small exhibition, including archaeological exhibits.

Drum Manor Forest Park

By the A505, **t** (028) 8676 2774
Getting there 3 miles (5km) west of Cookstown
Open All year daily 8am–dusk
Adm Car £3, Pedestrians: adult £1, child 50p

A walled butterfly garden, arboretum and forest trail for the disabled, near lakes and a heronry.

Gortin Glen Forest Park

t (028) 8164 8217
Getting there 7 miles (11km) north of Omagh, B48
Open Daily 10–dusk. **Adm** Per car £2.50

Nature trails pass through 5 miles (8km) of conifer woods here, as does the Ulster Way, where gorse and primroses bloom in spring.

The Sperrin Heritage Centre

274 Glenelly Road, Plumbridge, **t** (028) 8164 8142
Getting there 24 miles (38km) north of Omagh
Open Apr–Oct Mon–Fri 11–6, Sat 11.30–6, Sun 2–7
Adm Adult £2.15, child £1.25, family £6.70; Pan hire: adult 65p, child 35p
Craft shop, Glenelly Kitchen café

Between the villages of Cranagh and Sperrin in the Glenelly Valley, this centre tells the story of how gold was discovered in the Sperrins, and describes the making of the illicit spirit potcheen. Try panning for gold in the iron pyrite stream, after you find out about Sperrin wildlife in the exhibition. Outside you can walk in the glens and look for all their animals, birds and plants.

Sporty kids

Horse riding

Clanabogan Riding Stables

85 Clanabogan Road, **t** (028) 8225 2050

Crocknagrally Forest Stables

100 Croneen Road, Fivemiletown, **t** (028) 8952 1991

Walking

As well as those listed on the left, forest parks with good walks include **Favour Royal**, just south of Caledon, **Gollagh Woods**, and **Fardross Forest** near Clogher, where you can see lots of red squirrels. The **Ulster Way** also goes through the Sperrins, and there are lovely riverside walks by Wellbrook Mill (*see* above). Contact Omagh and Strabane tourist offices or the Sperrin Centre (*see* left) for information on walking in the Sperrins. The **Gortin Loop** path is one of the best walks that's easy to get to.

Steam power

Peatlands Park

The Birches, Dungannon, **t** (028) 3885 1102
Getting there 7 miles (11km) east of Dungannon
Open Park: Easter–Sept daily 9–9, Oct–Easter daily 9–dusk; Visitor centre: Easter–Sept Sat–Sun and bank holidays 2–6, Jun–Aug daily; Railway: times vary so check
Adm Adult £1, child 50p, under-3s free

A circular railway with open-top carriages pulled by a modern diesel engine moves through woods and peat bog on a narrow-gauge track near Lough Neagh, once used to carry turf from the bog. In the middle of the bog you can wander along an unusual boardwalk with a hide that allows you to peer at its flora without endangering it.

COUNTY FERMANAGH

Fermanagh (*Firmanach*) means 'men of Manach'. It is thought a man named Manach, or Monach, a member of the family of a High King, settled beside Lough Erne around the 3rd century AD. Later the Maguire clan took control of the area, and fought off potential usurpers for centuries until losing Fermanagh in the 17th century to the British.

A wonderland of woods and lakes, Fermanagh holds a serenity and intense peace at its heart, which the visitor occasionally senses in ancient settlements around and on the two Lough Ernes. One-third of the county is underwater, and is divided by the Lough Erne Waterway, which is linked by canals and locks to the Shannon, forming Europe's largest navigable inland waterway network, the Shannon-Erne Waterway.

Ancient carvings and stone heads can be seen on the Devenish and White islands on Lough Erne. Children who enjoy boat trips and maybe fishing will find Fermanagh magical, as will those who like folk tales, long walks in woods and making things. Craftspeople will be drawn to this county's old pottery and crystal-making traditions, still alive at Belleek Pottery and Fermanagh Crystal factory. Other sights not to be missed are Castle Coole, Florence Court Park and Marble Arch Caves, where you can float beneath stalactites on a boat.

Tourist information

Enniskillen: Fermanagh Tourist Information Centre, Wellington Road, **t** (028) 6632 3110, **www.**fermanagh-online.co.uk

Tours

Clonaog Heritage Tours, 18 Clonaog Valley, Derrylin Road, Lisnaskea, **t** (028) 6772 1730

Guided walks and bus tours to sites between Belturbet, Lisnaskea and Newtownbutler.

Heritage Tours of Fermanagh, t (028) 6862 1430

Blue Badge Guide and broadcaster Breege McCusker leads fine tours through county history.

Getting there and around

By air Enniskillen has a small airport, at Trory, 4 miles (6km) north of town. At present it does not have scheduled international flights, but they have been planned. Airport, **t** (028) 6632 3110.

By bus There are at least six Ulsterbus expresses daily between Belfast and Enniskillen, and good services around the county. Bus Eireann runs to Sligo and several other towns in the Republic. Enniskillen Bus Station, Wellington Road, **t** (028) 6632 2633.

Special Events – County Fermanagh

There are lots of tiny festivals and sporting events around Fermanagh's villages thoughout the summer. Ask at the tourist office.

February–March

Enniskillen Drama Festival, t (028) 6634 1449

Community fare for theatre-mad youngsters.

May

Scottish Pipe Band Competition, t (028) 6638 8202

The place to be if your family thrills to the sound of pipes.

June

Fiddlestone Festival, Belleek, **t** (028) 6865 8201

Traditional festival with great music.

Lisnaskea Feis, t (028) 6772 1610

A fun, friendly town festival.

July

Lady of the Lake Festival, Irvinestown, **t** (028) 6862 1656, **www.**ladyofthelakefestival.com

Named after a mystical figure sometimes seen making her way among the islands of Lower Lough Erne, carrying wildflowers and clad in a flowing gown filled with light. In her honour there's a varied and lively arts programme.

Summer Drama Season, Ardhowen Theatre, Enniskillen, **t** (028) 6632 5440

Imaginative fare for theatre-lovers.

August

Enniskillen Agricultural Show, t (028) 6632 2509

For outdoor types and animal-lovers.

By Bike

A way-marked trail stretches 230 miles (368km) through Fermanagh, Leitrim, Cavan, Donegal and Monaghan. Enniskillen Tourist Office has details: ask for the *Hiking and Biking Guide to the Waters and the Wild* or consult **www.**cycleireland.com.

Kingfisher Cycle Trail Tour, t (028) 6632 0121, **www.**cycleireland.com

A 30–40-mile (48–64km) ride from Belleek, over Boa Island to Kesh, down through Irvinestown to Enniskillen and over to Florence Court.

Did you know...?

Fermanagh people believe that if you see the Lady of the Lake floating in the air above Lower Lough Erne in May, good times are ahead.

ENNISKILLEN

Enniskillen (*Inis Ceaithleann*) means 'the island of Kathleen'. It is said to be named after the legendary wife of Balor, who fled here from battle. Enniskillen Castle was the medieval seat of the Maguires, High Kings of Fermanagh, who policed the lough with a private navy of 1,500 boats.

Chosen as the area's main town during the 17th century Ulster Plantation (*see* p.34), it played a major role in wars and rebellions, in 1641 and 1689. Later on, Enniskillen was the place where both Samuel Beckett and Oscar Wilde went to school (at Portora Royal School). Today it has about 14,000 people. The town's Buttermarket is a an attractive craft centre, and children will want to sample Maude's ice cream (the shop is near the tourist centre) before leaving to explore the countryside.

Things to see and do

Enniskillen Castle and Museums

Castle Barracks, **t** (028) 6632 5000, **www**.enniskillencastle.co.uk
Open All year Tues–Fri 10–5, May–Jun and Sept Mon and Sat 2–5, Jul–Aug Mon, Sat and Sun 2–5, Oct–Apr Mon 2–5, all bank holidays 10–5
Adm Adult £2.25, child £1.25, family (2+2) £5.25
Gift and book shop, children's activity corner, full disabled access in heritage centre, partial in castle

Enniskillen Castle houses exhibitions in the Castle Keep, and Fermanagh County Museum. Together they offer a good overview of the county's history from prehistoric times to the two world wars and into the 1950s. Be sure to see the audio-visual display on the Maguires, the Gaelic clan who built the castle on the River Erne in the 15th century and ruled Fermanagh up until the 1600s. Soldiers' uniforms, medals and memorabilia span the history of the famous Inniskilling regiments in the British Army since their formation in 1689.

Enniskillen Craft and Design Centre (The Buttermarket)

Down St, **t** (028) 6632 3110, **www**.fermanaghlakelands.com
Open All year Mon–Sat 9.30–5.30

Watch traditional crafts being made by local craftspeople, designers and artists, and pick up lace, knitwear and Belleek china as souvenirs.

SPECIAL TRIPS

Belleek Pottery Factory

Belleek, **t** (028) 6865 9300, **www**.belleek.ie
Getting there 25 miles (40km) north of Enniskillen
Open Apr–Sept Mon–Fri 9–6, Sat 10–6, Sun 2–6 (Jul–Aug 11–6); Oct Mon–Fri 9–5.30, Sat 10–5.30, Sun 2–6; Nov–Mar Mon–Fri 9–5.30; tours every half hour Mon–Fri 9.30–4.15
Adm Adult £4, under-12s free
Guided tours book in advance, showroom/shop, café

Fermanagh is known for its crafts traditions. Belleek Pottery was established in 1857 and still uses its original techniques. Watch a film on how pottery is made, then take a tour to see how skillfully craftspeople make pottery baskets and flowers, and delicately paint them. Before you leave, buy a reminder of your visit in the showroom, which has many items at discount prices.

Florence Court

t (028) 6634 8249, **www**.nationaltrust.org.uk
Getting there 8 miles (13km) south of Enniskillen
Open House: Apr–May and Sept Sat–Sun and bank holidays 1–6, Jun–Aug Wed–Mon 1–6; Grounds: Oct–Apr 10–4; May–Sept 10–7
Adm Adult £3, child £1.50, family £8
Restaurant, tearoom, gift shop, children's play area

For an enjoyable afternoon, visit this fine 18th-century house belonging to the Earls of Enniskillen, which was originally built for Lord Mountflorence. The house has fine rococo plasterwork and is set in woodland with views of the Cuilcagh Mountains. Free guided tours of the Forest Park are available (book in advance): Forest Office, **t** (028) 6634 8497.

Can you spot...
The white limestone outline of a horse that shows through the scree at the foot of the eastern cliff of the steep mountain of Benaughlin ('peak of the horse'), above Florence Court?

Benaughlin is said to be the dwelling place of a Tuatha 'faery' called Donn Binn, who had a talking horse. At some point the horse was engraved on the side of the hill.

Lough Erne

What Fermanagh people refer to as Lough Erne is actually two lakes, connected by the River Erne in the middle (where Enniskillen sits). A network of more than 150 islands fills Upper and Lower Lough Erne. Some are inhabited, such as Belle Isle, credited as the place where the *Annals of Ulster* were compiled in the 15th century. These waterways are home to a huge variety of birds.

ExplorErne Centre

Erne Gateway Centre, Belleek, **t** (028) 6865 8866
Getting there 25 miles (40km) north of Enniskillen
Open May–Sept daily 11–5, or by appointment
Adm Adult £1, 5–16s 50p, under-5s free, family £2.50

Travel through the past in this small museum with displays that give an inviting sense of the lushness of Fermanagh and its lakes. Children enjoy its models of local places and the folklore behind them, and it's a great information centre.

Boa Island

Along the north side of Lower Lough Erne, this 'island' is accessible by road, between Kesh and Belleek, 16 miles (26km) north of Enniskillen. Here is the famous Janus Stone, in Caldragh Cemetery (signposted beside the island's road), about which Seamus Heaney wrote a poem. These stone figures are thought to be Celtic in origin, but their shape and style seem closer to the prehistoric inhabitants of Ireland than its modern ones, with two different faces and a hole in the top of its head that collects water. Nearby is the 'Lusty Man', a smaller figure brought here from nearby Lustymore Island.

Devenish Island

Open Devenish Island Museum: Apr–Sept Tues–Sat 10–6, Sun 2–6. **Adm** Adult £2.25, child £1.20 (for museum and ferry)

This island in the Lower Lough has extensive ruins, including a 12th-century round tower, abbey and St Molaise's House. The island was one of Ireland's most important monasteries, and remained a key religious site till the 17th century.

White Island

Open Apr–Jun Sat–Sun 10–1 and 2–6, Jul–Aug daily 10–6. **Adm** Adult £3, child £2

On White Island, 3 miles (5km) south of Kesh, there are the ruins of a 12th-century church, with impressive stone figures from the 6th century.

Getting around Lough Erne

Devenish Island

The main ferry, **t** (028) 9023 5000, embarks at Trory Point (Easter–Sept daily at 10am, 1, 3 and 5); another, the Devenish Island Ferry Service, **t** (028) 7702 2873, runs Apr–Sept. Devenish is also visited by a boat tours from Enniskillen, the MV Kestrel waterbus (Erne Tours), **t** (028) 6632 2882, from the Round 'O' Quay in Enniskillen, daily Jul–Sept.

White Island

Ferries run from Castle Archdale, **t** (028) 6862 1588; also White Island Ferry Service (Apr–Sept), **t** (028) 6862 1333.

Cruises

To explore these islands via one of the least congested waterways in Europe, you can rent cruisers by the day or week. Prices range from around £385 per week for a 4-berth cruiser in low season to £1,000 for an 8-berth in high season. Free lessons on how to handle boats for novices.

Erincurrach Cruising, Blaney, Enniskillen, **t** (028) 6864 1737. One-way boat rental between the Erne and the Shannon.

Lakeland Canoe Centre, Castle Island, Enniskillen, **t** (028) 6632 4250. For canoeing, rowing, sailing, mountain biking, and a campsite.

The Viking Longship

Departs from Share Centre, Lisnaskea, **t** (028) 6772 2122; Sailings Easter–Oct, booking essential. Spend an hour touring Upper Lough Erne in (roughly) the same way the Vikings did – in a fully powered, canopied replica longship – noting their discoveries and plunders. It starts from Lisnaskea (11 miles/17km south of Enniskillen), an interesting little market town.

The Share Centre also runs guided tours of the Lower Lough (with bewitching folk stories about the lake) on the **Inishcruiser**, from the Inishclare Restaurant, Killadeas, **t** (028) 6862 8550, daily.

Water sports

Drumrush Watersports Centre, Drumrush Lodge, Boa Island Road, Kesh, **t** (028) 6863 1578. Waterskiing, jetskis, paddle boating, canoeing, sailing, and other activities on the lake, and the centre also has a 10-bed guesthouse, restaurant, tennis court, caravan and camping site.

Marble Arch Caves
Blacklion Road, **t** (028) 6634 8855,
www.fermanagh-online.com
Getting there On the 'Marlbank Scenic Loop', 8 miles (13km) north of Florence Court
Open Mar–Sept daily 10–4.30, Jul–Aug 10–5 (advance booking essential)
Adm Adult £6, child £3.50, family £14
Disabled access, shop, restaurant, parking area

An exciting 75-minute boat journey through an underground wonderland of cave formations and lofty chambers with rivers and waterfalls. Wear a sweater and good shoes; here are 120 steps at one point, so it isn't suitable for tired toddlers.

AROUND AND ABOUT

Bricks and mortar

Castle Coole
t (028) 6632 2690, **www.nationaltrust.org.uk**
Getting there 2 miles (3km) south of Enniskillen
Open House: Apr–May and Sept Sat–Sun and bank holidays 1–6; Jun–Aug Fri–Wed 1–6; Estate: May–Sept daily 10–8, Oct–April daily 10–4
Adm Adult £4, child £2, family £10
Guided tours, disabled access to ground floor and visitor centre, gift shop, tearoom, car and coach park

A very grand and beautiful neoclassical house, built in 1790–97. It retains its 18th-century furniture and magnificent woodwork, fireplaces, furniture and a library. There are family days in the school holidays and baby-slings are available.

Tully Castle
Blaney, **t** (028) 9023 5000
Getting there 9 miles (14km) north of Enniskillen
Open Apr–Sept Tues–Sat 10–6 Sun 2–6
Adm Adult £1, child 50p
Formal garden, visitor centre

Although it was the site of a bloody massacre by the Maguires in the 1640s, the ruins of this fortified house and bawn, built in 1613, are nearly intact.

Look at this!

Drumskinney Stone Circle
Getting there 41/2 miles (7km) north of Kesh

One of the best stone circles in Northern Ireland.

Fermanagh Crystal
Main St, Belleek, **t** (028) 6865 8631
Getting there 25 miles (40km) north of Enniskillen
Open Mon–Sat 9.30–5.30. **Adm** Free

Demonstrations of hand-cutting lead glass.

Nature lovers

Castle Archdale Country Park
Irvinestown, **t** (028) 6862 1588
Getting there 3 miles (5km) south of Kesh
Open Park: daily 9am–dusk; Museum and Visitor Centre: Easter–Jun Sun 12 noon–4, from May bank holidays 11–6, Jul–Aug Tues–Sun 11–7. **Adm** Free
Tearoom, pony trekking, ferry to White Island

Walk beside Lough Erne in this beautiful woodland, with a butterfly garden, wildfowl ponds, a wildflower meadow, and an old ruined castle. Camp or fish, or go by boat to the lake's islands.

Clonaveel Organic Garden
Letterbreen, **t** (028) 6634 1308
Getting there 6 miles (9km) west of Enniskillen
Open Daily. **Adm** Adult £2, child 50p

See how organic flowers, fruit and veg are grown.

Crom Estate
Newtownbutler, **t** (028) 6773 8118
Getting there 17 miles (27km) south of Enniskillen
Open Mar–Sept Mon–Sat 10–6, Sun 12 noon–6
Adm free

Walk on the shores of Upper Lough Erne among 1,000 acres of woodland, parkland and wetland.

Sporty kids

Activity centres

Corralea Activity Centre
Belcoo, **t** (028) 6638 6668

Archery, canoeing, caving, climbing, orienteering, windsailing, and more, with qualified instructors.

CAVAN AND MONAGHAN

The low-key counties of Cavan and Monaghan are the southernmost counties of Ulster but, since most of their people were Catholic rather than Ulster Protestants, they stayed part of the Republic when Ireland was divided in 1921. Infrequent tourist destinations, they nonetheless have great charm. If your family enjoy riding, Monaghan may be your preferred stop, but if you want to fish in pristine lakes amid clean air and lush woodlands with manicured villages, you will love Cavan, one of Ireland's least polluted counties, with a countryside steeped in Ireland's ancient past. It is perfect for families who need peace and quiet, and prefer outdoor activities to rushing about seeing sights.

Pleasant undulating landscape surrounds Cavan town, and it is conveniently situated for reaching Ireland's lake district, although Belturbet is even better placed if you want to spend a lot of time across the border on Lough Erne. Monaghan town is a more convenient location if you want to pop across to Belfast and the core of Northern Ireland.

Tourist information

Cavan: Farnham St, Cavan, **t** (049) 433 1942, **www**.cavantourism.com
Monaghan: Market House, Monaghan, **t** (047) 81122, **www**.monaghantourism.com

Getting there and around

By bus Bus Eireann runs to Cavan and Monaghan from Dublin, Belfast, Enniskillen and other towns. In both counties there are excellent local services. Cavan Bus Depot, **t** (049) 433 1353; Monaghan Bus Station, **t** (047) 82377.

Bike Hire

The Bicycle Shop, Shopping Arcade, Main St, Carrickmacross, Co. Monaghan, **t** (042) 31967
Emyvale Cycles, Knockafubble, Emyvale, Co. Monaghan, **t** (047) 63653
Fitzpatrick Cycles, Castle Hill, Belturbet, Co. Cavan, **t** (049) 952 2866
On Yer Bike Tours, Abbeyset Buildings, Farnham St, Cavan, **t** (049) 31932

Special Events – Cavan and Monaghan

March

Castleblayney Drama Festival, Castleblaney, Co. Monaghan, **t** (042) 974 0454.
An entertaining small-scale festival.

Cavan Drama Festival, Cootehill, Co. Cavan, **t** (049) 555 2241
Local event for families who enjoy theatre.

May

County Cavan Fleadh Cheoil, Co. Cavan
Traditional music events for the whole family, all around the county.

June

Festival of the Lakes, Killashandra, Co. Cavan, **t** (049) 433 4429
Music, dance, children's entertainment, power-boat racing and angling competitions.

Virginia Street Fair, Virginia, Co. Cavan, **t** (049) 854 8299
Vintage cars, machinery, music. Lovely village where you can enjoy the music even if you're not interested in the cars.

July

Belturbet Festival of the Erne, Belturbet, Co. Cavan, **t** (049) 952 2781
Large family festival with water-sports, music and heritage events, held in late July–early Aug.

Muckno Mania, Castleblayney, Co. Monaghan, **t** (042) 974 6087
Arts and music festival.

August

Ballybay Celtic Festival, Ballybay, Co. Monaghan, **t** (042) 974 1050
Fun celebration of all things Celtic.

Ballybay Festival of the Lakes, Ballybay, Co. Monaghan, **t** (047) 81122
Week-long town fair for all ages.

September

Rhythm and Blues Festival, Monaghan, **t** (047) 71114, **www**.harvestblues.net
Monaghan rocks.

October

Cootehill Arts Festival, Cootehill, Co. Cavan, **t** (049) 555 2150
Music, arts and crafts, drama, literature for crafts/arts-oriented families.

November

Patrick Kavanagh Weekend, Iniskeen, Co. Monaghan, **t** (042) 937 8560
Friendly literary event commemorating Monaghan's famous 20th-century poet.

Castleblayney Heritage Week, Castleblaney, Co. Monaghan, **t** (042) 974 6087
A community event for the education and edification of the whole family.

AROUND AND ABOUT

Look at this!

Belturbet Railway Station

Belturbet, Co. Cavan, **t** (049) 952 2074
Getting there 10 miles (16km) north of Cavan
Open Visitor centre: daily 9.30–5
Adm Adult €2.54, under 12s €1.27, family (2+2) €6.35

Part of the Cavan and Leitrim Railway (*see* p.190), this restored station also has a display on the history of these local lines through rural Ireland.

Cavan Crystal

Dublin Road, Cavan, **t** (049) 433 1800, **www.cavancrystaldesign.com**
Getting there Just south of Cavan town
Open Mon–Fri 9.30–6, 10–5 Sat, 12 noon–5 Sun
Adm Free; book visits in advance

Centuries-old glass craftsmanship is maintained here. A wide range of other crafts is also on show.

Maudabawn Cultural Centre

Cootehill, Co. Cavan, **t** (049) 555 9504
Getting there 15 miles (24km) north of Cavan

This centre arranges guided tours of Cos. Cavan and Monaghan, music, singing, dancing and story-telling evenings, and even pony-and-trap rides.

A story to tell:
Finn McCool and the Salmon of Knowledge

The Druid Finegas had long prepared himself for gaining the clairvoyant powers of the Salmon of Knowledge (*see* p.29), and one day he finally caught the fish. He asked his assistant Finn McCool, then still a boy, to guard it while it cooked in the pan, but to be certain not to let anyone taste it – neglecting to mention that the first person who did so would acquire its powers. After faithfully watching the salmon for a while, Finn noticed it was beginning to burn, and quickly turned it with his thumb. Finn burned his thumb on the hot grease, and so sucked it to cool it down.

Soon after Finegas returned, and immediately noticed that a great change had come over Finn. He saw the whole salmon still frying in the pan and said, 'Finn, lad, have you tasted the salmon?' 'Well, sir, I turned it with my thumb because it was burning and I burned my thumb and...'

...at which point Finegas went white with rage and shouted, 'You tasted MY salmon!'

Finn immediately braced himself for blows, not knowing what he had done, but well knowing the temper of his master. Finegas, though, calmed down enough to explain that Finn was now in grave danger, since he was untrained and in possession of powers he could not control.

Thereafter Finegas looked after Finn's education in Druid ways. The boy learned quickly, and so when Finn visited King Conn at the Hill of Tara (*see* p. 100), he was well-prepared to take his place as leader of Ireland's best warriors, the Fianna.

Sporty kids

Activity centres

Lough Muckno Leisure Park

Castleblaney, Co. Monaghan, **t** (042) 974 6356

Water-skiing, fishing, tennis, windsurfing, canoeing and riding are just some of the activities possible in this 900-acre lake and forest park.

Fishing

There is good coarse fishing in Loughs Oughter, Inchin, Gowna and Bunn in Cavan, and Ooney, Muckno, and the lakes by Ballybay in Monaghan.

Irish Angling Services, Ballyconnell, Co. Cavan, **t** (049) 952 6258

Jimmy McMahon, Carrick Sports Centre, Carrickmacross, Co. Monaghan, **t** (042) 61714

Horse riding

There are many riding centres around this area.

Cavan Equestrian Centre, Shalom Stables, Lath, Co. Cavan, **t** (049) 433 2017

Greystones Equestrian Centre, Castle Leslie, Glaslough, Co. Monaghan, **t** (047) 88100

Lessons for kids, and rides on Castle Leslie Estate.

Walking

The **Cavan Way** is a 15-mile (24km) path from Blacklion to Dowra, passing wonderful views. It goes close to the Shannon Pot, source of the Shannon. There are easier walks in **Killykeen Forest Park**, north of Killashandra; around **Lough Gowna**; and at **Castle Lake**, north of Bailieborough. The **Ulster Way** runs into Co. Monaghan near Clones.

COUNTY DONEGAL

There is a kind of lonely magic in Donegal (or *Dún na nGall*, 'the fort of the foreigners'), that you feel you can almost touch when you see double and even triple rainbows forming arcs across its barren mountains. You can sail from the port of Killybegs, ride horses just about everywhere, swim or splash around on superb beaches, learn how to make tapestries and explore Ardara's woollen shops. Donegal also contains one of the last of the Gaeltacht areas of Ireland, so if you want to hear Irish and like traditional music and folklore, it's a great place to go. Nothing moves fast in this part of the world, apart from summer tourist traffic.

Donegal town is the 'capital', but the main market town of northern Donegal is Letterkenny. It's a good place to stock up, and see sights nearby.

Tourist information

Buncrana, t (074) 936 2600
Bundoran, t (071) 984 1350
Donegal Town, t (074) 972 1148
Inishowen: Carndonagh, **t** (074) 937 4933
Letterkenny: Blaney Road, **t** (074) 912 1160

Getting there and around

By air Derry Airport (*see* pp.200, 284) is the most convenient airport for most of Donegal, with good bus connections across the border. Donegal has its own airport, on the coast near Crolly, but so far it only has Irish domestic flights and some charters.
Donegal Airport, Carrickfinn, **t** (074) 954 8284, **www.donegalairport.ie**.

By bus Bus Eireann coaches run from Dublin and other towns to Letterkenny and Donegal Town. To get around the villages of Donegal, you need a car, or to use one of several local companies.
John McGinley, t (074) 913 5201. Between Inishowen, Letterkenny, Donegal and Dublin.
Londonderry and Lough Swilly Bus Company, Derry, **t** (028) 7126 2017. Links Derry with various towns such as Ballyshannon, Burdoran, Donegal, Killybegs and Letterkenny. Note: the area code is 048 if you call from the Republic.
McGeehan's, t (074) 954 6150. Regular services from Donegal town to Glencolmcille, Dunglow, Ardara, Killybegs, Kilcar and Carrick.

Special Events – Donegal

Donegal is the location for some of the most renowned events in all Ireland in the world of traditional music – especially those held in Buncrana, Letterkenny and Glencolmcille.

March

Hill-walking Festival, Ardara, **t** (074) 954 1518
Mid-month. Families are welcome to join walks in this lovely part of south Donegal.

April

Hill-walking Festival, Glencolmcille, **t** (074) 973 0248
A similar 'festival' for western coastal walks. Book ahead.

June

Buncrana Folk Festival, Inishowen tourist office, **t** (074) 937 4933
Classic, very friendly Irish folk festival in Inishowen.

Weavers' Fair, Ardara, **t** (074) 924 1103
For budding craftspeople.

Donegal International Arts Festival, Donegal Town, **t** (074) 922 2312
Summer family festival with storytelling, dancing, magic, music, street performers and entertainment for children.

July

Buncrana Music Festival, t (074) 936 2737

Ballyshannon Folk and Traditional Music Festival, t (071) 985 1088, **www.donegalbay.ie**
Fun for visitors and locals alike in South Donegal.

Donegal Town Summer Festival
Runs through July and August.

Mary from Dunglow Festival, Dunglow, **t** (074) 912 1254
Puppet shows, art workshops, sports, music and dancing.

August

Fiddle Festival and Fiddle Music Summer School, Glencolmcille, **t** (074) 973 0248
For music lovers and musicians of all ages.

Letterkenny Folk Festival, Letterkenny, **t** (074) 912 7856
Family events including music, concerts, dancing and street performers.

Busking Festival, Milford, **t** (074) 913 3137
For traditional music lovers.

Muff Festival, Inishowen, **t** (074) 937 4933
One of the oldest and largest country fairs in Ireland for music and singing.

Good to know...
Getting to the islands of Donegal
Arranmore Island: There is a regular ferry from Burtonport that takes approximately 25 mins; there are about 6 sailings per day, year-round, **t** (074) 952 0532.
Tory Island: A passenger ferry operates daily from Bunbeg, Meenlaragh and Portnablagh (Wed only). Contact **Donegal Coastal Cruises** for times of sailings, **t** (074) 953 1991, or **t** (074) 913 5061, which are subject to the weather and tide.

North West Busways, t (074) 938 2619. Links Buncrana and Letterkenny.
Bike Hire
The Bike Shop, Waterloo Place, Donegal Town, **t** (074) 912 2515
Buncrana Community Leisure Centre, Shore Front, Buncrana (Inishowen), **t** (074) 937 0020
Church Street Cycles, Letterkenny, **t** (074) 912 6204

Shopping and Crafts

Glencolumcille Woollen Mill
Malin More, **t** (074) 973 0070
Watch traditional and contemporary knitwear being made in this shop.

Simple Simon
Anderson's Yard, The Diamond, Donegal Town, **t** (074) 972 2087
Wholefoods, organic produce and cheeses.

DONEGAL TOWN

Co. Donegal's county town is a pleasant small town – an active place to refuel and relax before travelling on to more remote coastal areas.

Things to see and do

Donegal Bay Waterbus Tour
Harbour Office, Donegal Pier, **t** (074) 972 3666
Open Sailing times vary and are posted on the pier
Adm Adult €10, child €5
Take this 70-minute boat trip around Donegal Bay. Your friendly guide will be happy to talk to children on board about the history and tales of the area. Hear stories about Red Hugh O'Donnell as you visit his burial place, and find out about *The Annals of the Four Masters* compiled around the Old Abbey in 1632–36. Then you'll learn about the famine years as you visit the embarkation point where emigrants left for North America. Look out for wildlife and seals, a wind farm and Magherabeg Abbey, among many other magical things.

Donegal Castle
Tyrconnell St, **t** (074) 972 2405
Open Daily May–Oct 9.30–5.45
Adm Adult €3.80, child €1.50, family €9.50
Built in 1505, this was the stronghold of the Princes of Tyrconnell, the O'Donnells. Last of them was Red Hugh O'Donnell, who tried to stop the English taking over Ireland in the 1590s. Finding their rule insufferable, Red Hugh fled to Europe with Co. Tyrone's Hugh O'Neill in the so-called 'Flight of the Earls' (*see* p.34). A 'planted' colonist named Sir Basil Brooke took over the castle in 1601, adding a Jacobean house to the stone tower and turrets of the O'Donnells. Today it contains historical displays and beautiful antique furniture.

Donegal Railway Heritage Centre
Old Station House, Tyrconnell St, **t** (074) 972 2655
Open Jun–Sept Mon–Sat 10–5.30, Sun 2–5
Adm Adult €3, child €1.50, under-5s free, family €6.50
A small exhibition about the narrow-gauge railways of Donegal, with a model train for children.

SPECIAL TRIPS

Glenveagh

Getting there 15 miles (24km) northwest of Letterkenny

Glenveagh Castle (also Glenveigh)
Glenveagh Park, Church Hill, **t** (074) 913 7088
Open Easter–last Mon in Oct daily 10.30–6.30 (Jun–Aug Sun till 7.30)
Adm Adult €2.54, child €1.27, family €6.35
Tearoom, visitor centre, parking at visitor centre
Morning and afternoon teas are served in a tearoom in this castle (built 1870–73), a four-storey keep with ramparts, turrets and a round tower, and, inside, the furniture of the last private owner. Surrounding it by a lake are gardens of Scots pine and tall rhododendrons, and a lovely section called the 'Pleasure Ground', from where you can take the Belgian Walk to a walled garden.

Glenveagh National Park

Church Hill, near Letterkenny, **t** (074) 913 7090
Open Mid-Mar–7 Nov daily 10–6.30 (last adm 5)
Adm Adult €2.50, child €1.90, family €6.30

This 40,873-acre park contains lakes, oak and birch-clothed glens and woodlands, red deer, lots of bird life on the upper slopes of its mountains and Glenveagh Castle. Landscapes are magnificent, and Ireland's highest peaks, Mount Errigal and Slieve Snaght, are here. A visitor centre introduces you to the wildlife and flora of the area.

A story to tell: The Fomorians and the arrival of Lugh

Possibly the first indigenous natives of Ireland, the Fomorians (*see* p.29) treated others very cruelly, demanding crops and even children from those who lived on the land they considered their own. They were misshapen, and some say they often had only one leg or arm. They fought wars against the Nemedians, then the Fir Bolg and finally the Tuatha Dé Danaan. They were helped in these wars by Balor of the Evil Eye, whose one eye instantly killed every living thing it looked upon. In battle, when he grew tired, the Fomorians kept his eye propped open with planks of wood.

A Druid predicted that Balor's daughter Eithne would bear a son who would kill him, so Balor put her in a tower where men were forbidden to enter. But one day Cian, a son of the Tuatha's great healer Dian Cécht, disguised himself as a woman and entered the tower, and secretly married her.

Shortly afterwards Balor found out Eithne was pregnant, and slew Cian on a white stone. Eithne bore triplets, and Balor cast them into the sea to drown. But the Tuatha sea god Manannan mac Lir rescued one of the babies and raised him in secret. His name was Lugh – the father of Cúchulainn, *see* p.219. At the time that Lugh reached manhood, the Tuatha Dé Danaan were suffering greatly at the hands of the Fomorians. Lugh went to the court of the Tuatha to offer his help, and killed Balor in the Second Battle of Moytura, fulfilling the prophecy (*see* p.183).

Thus, the Tuatha Dé Danaan remained rulers of Ireland, and they banished the Fomorians to Ireland's most northerly outpost, Tory Island off Donegal. Ever afterwards, they were reduced to raiding coastal areas, often drowning seafarers and fishermen off Ireland's northwestern coasts.

Glebe House and Gallery

Church Hill, near Letterkenny, **t** (074) 913 7071
Open Easter daily 11–6.30, mid-May–Sept Sat–Thurs 11–6.30 (last tour 1hr before closing)
Adm Adult €2.50, child €1.20, family €6.30

Teenagers will find this Regency house (built in 1828) more interesting than young children, but its beautiful wooded grounds are delightful for any age. Budding painters and designers will be intrigued by the house with its Morris textiles and artwork from around the world, including work by leading 20th-century artists. They were amassed by former owner Derek Hill, a bohemian British theatre designer who bought this place, renovated it, and then invited famous friends to visit.

Grianán Ailigh

Near Burt, Inishowen Peninsula
Getting there 5 miles (8km) north of Derry City

From this stone ring fort, only just across the border from Derry, you can look out over seven of Ireland's counties. It's name means 'Stone Temple of the Sun'; it may originally have been a temple where prehistoric peoples worshipped the sun goddess Gráinne (or Ainé or Anu). During Penal times, Catholics came here for secret Masses. On the top of Grianán Hill, 800ft (245m) above sea level, this magnificent circular rampart of rock is thought to have been built about 1700 BC. In legend it was created by the king of the Tuatha Dé Danaan, the Daghda. It originally consisted of a central 74ft 'cashel' or circular fortification, with a series of outer earthen ramparts 17ft high and 12ft thick. Today, two inner terraces, reached by a stone staircase, are set into the circular wall.

There's an Irish saying that any secret whispered inside the Grianán will not remain secret. And indeed, an archaeologist has noticed that, despite the sounds of gusting wind, conversations within its walls can be heard outside them quite easily.

Grianán Ailigh Visitor Centre

Inside the church, Burt, Inishowen Peninsula, **t** (074) 936 8000, **www.**griananailigh.ie
Getting there 1 mile (1.6km) below Grianán Ailigh
Open Summer daily 10–6, winter 12 noon–6
Adm Adult €2, child €1.50, family €5
Crafts/bookshop, restaurant

The story of the ancient stone ring fort of Grianán Ailigh is told here with an exhibition geared to children, although adults interested in

Irish folklore will also find it fascinating. Find out more about the end of the old pagan faith and the coming of Christianity, the founding of the O'Neill dynasty by Eoghan and Conal, and other legendary figures of Donegal. If you want to know the difference between a leprechaun and a cluricaun, you can find out here, as well as about some of the more scary creatures in Donegal. And don't forget to stop by the 'cave' beside the wishing pond.

AROUND AND ABOUT

Animal magic

Deane's Open Farm and Equestrian Centre

Darney, Bruckless, **t** (074) 973 7160
Getting there 12 miles (19km) west of Donegal
Open Farm: Easter–Aug; Horse riding: 10–5; ring in advance to check as hours can vary
Adm Farm: approx €3.80 per person

A welcoming, relaxing place to visit with children near Donegal town and the Atlantic. You can feed and walk farm animals, take a farm tour, stroll around the forest, or pony trek along country roads.

Donegal Organic Farm

Glenties, **t** (074) 955 1286, **www.esatclear.ie**
Getting there 19 miles (30km) north of Donegal Town, 2 miles (3km) outside Glenties village
Open daily. **Adm** free, donations appreciated

Biodynamic organic farm with dairy, meat and vegetable produce for sale, which also has a 'Highland Ecocamp Nature Trail'.

Millbridge Farm

Gobnascale, Convoy, **t** (074) 914 7125
Getting there 14 miles (22km) south of Letterkenny, signposted off the N13 road
Open Jul–Aug Tues–Sat 11–5, Sun 1.30–5, bank holidays except Good Fri
Pets' corner, playground, picnic area, tearoom

A 200-acre dairy farm by the River Deele, where children can pet pigs, goats, sheep and Clydesdale horses. The play area has trampolines and swings, and a museum has curiosities of old farm life.

Look at this!

Colmcille Heritage Centre

Gartan, Church Hill, **t** (074) 913 7306
Getting there 10 miles (16km) north of Letterkenny
Open Easter week and first Sun in May–last Sun in Sept, Mon–Fri 10.30–6.30, Sun 16.30
Adm Adult €2, child €1.50

Illustrated panels tell the story of St Columcille (or Columba), patriarch of Irish monasticism and the Scottish Church. Artefacts and models in period clothing of Colmcille's time are on display.

Doagh Visitor Centre, Famine Museum and Lapland Santa's Island

Doagh Island, Inishowen, **t** (074) 937 8078
Open Famine Museum: Easter–Oct 10–5.30; Santa's Island: 19 Nov–24 Dec: two shows (5pm, 7pm)
Adm €4 per person

You'll have to drive a long way to see this attraction on a beautiful coastal plain on the northern edge of Inishowen, but it's worth it. For much of the year there is an exhibition set up in traditional cottages to represent a village during Ireland's famine. A guide can tell you all about the traditions and history of the period, from wakes to entertainment, how people lived and ate, and whatever else you want to know. Small animals and a pond make up the outdoor part of the museum, and children can play with them in summer. For Christmas, the buildings are transformed into a magical 'North Pole' with reindeer and snow, where Santa Claus comes to give a gift to each visiting child.

Flight of the Earls Heritage Centre

Rathmullan, Lough Swilly, **t** (074) 915 8178
Getting there 10 miles (22km) north of Letterkenny
Open Easter–Sept Mon–Sat 10–5, Sun 12 noon–5
Adm Adult €2.50, child €1.20, special group rates

This small museum, best for older children, is very near the spot where the last two Gaelic High Kings of Ireland departed from their homeland in 1607 (*see* p.34). It is inside a fort built in 1810 by the British as a defence against a French invasion.

Tell me an Irish riddle...
Question – *What has teeth but cannot eat?*
Answer – *A comb*

Seat of Power Visitors Centre

The Old Courthouse, Lifford, **t** (074) 914 1733
Getting there 1 mile (1.6km) west of Strabane
Open All year Mon–Fri 9–4.30, Sun 12.30–4.30
Adm Adult €3.50, child €2.20, family (2+3) €11.50

An excellent introduction to Donegal, this exhibition – in a historic courthouse – describes what happened to Ulster in the 17th century when English and Scottish people were 'planted' here. As you enter, you see a film narrated by Manus, grandfather of Red Hugh O'Donnell. He tells the story of those who held power in Lifford from the time of St Columcille through to 1938, when the last court was held in this courthouse. The O'Donnells themselves built a castle at Lifford in 1527. On the second level the story is carried on up to the Siege of Derry, and an audio-visual show in the courtroom tells of the severe sentences meted out to criminals in the 18th century. After this, you go down to the dungeons, to be charged and fingerprinted by prison warders/tour guides before a visit to the cells. Your visit is completed with the sounds of gaolers' keys clanking and conversations between prisoners and their visitors and guards.

Nature lovers

Ardnamona

Lough Eske, **t** (074) 972 2650
Getting there 5 miles (8km) north of Donegal Town
Open Jan–Aug 10–5 (phone ahead). **Adm** €3

Children will love wandering these lovely landscaped grounds with their ponies, rabbits, birds and small animals, beside glittering Lough Eske. It's also a delightful guest house (*see* p.278).

Sporty kids

Activity centres

Donegal Adventure Centre

Bundoran, **t** (071) 984 2844,
www.donegal-holidays.com

Accommodation and guided or self-guided walking and cycling tours, plus surfing, canoeing, golfing, mountain biking, and other activities.

Buckets and spades – Beaches in Donegal

Once voted the 'second most beautiful beach in the world', the Blue Flag beach at **Portsalon** near Millford, north of Letterkenny, has a backdrop of heather-covered mountains that plunge into the blue seas of Ballymastocker Bay. However, visitors are asked not to walk on its sand dunes so that they can recover from overuse.

Rossnowlagh Beach is regarded by many as the most scenic beach in northwest Ireland, with miles of golden sand, 10 miles (16km) south of Donegal town. Popular for water-sports like surfing and windsurfing, it's also excellent for safe swimming.

Other Blue Flag beaches can be found at **Bundoran, Rathmullan, Naran** and **Portnoo** and **Marble Hill** and **Dunfanaghy**. Best for swimming are Silver Strand at **Malin Bay** and **Glencolmcille**.

Malinmore Adventure Centre

Malin Bay, Glencolmcille, **t** (074) 973 0123

Diving, canoeing, boat trips.

Waterworld

Bundoran, **t** (071) 984 1172

An award-winning aqua-adventure playground, swimming pools, a wave pool, and a slide pool.

Horse riding

Tourist offices have information on all the many riding centres in Donegal, often in great settings.

Dunfanaghy Riding Stables, Arnold's Hotel, Dunfanaghy, **t** (074) 913 6208
Golden Sands Equestrian Centre, Rathmullan, north of Letterkenny, **t** (074) 915 8124
Inch Island Stables, Inch Island, near Burt, **t** (074) 936 0335

Walking

There are many great walks in Donegal, often through wild and remote landscapes – there are many areas that newcomers shouldn't try without a guide and proper preparation. Organizations below offer guided walks. Glenveagh is one of the best places for more accessible walking (*see* p.236).

North West Walking Guides, Clunarra, Letterbarrow, **t** (074) 973 5967, **www.northwestwalkingguides.com**
The Blue Stack Way, Ardara, **t** (074) 954 1518, **www.thebluestackway.com**
SOS Walking Tours, Gortahork, **t** (074) 913 5206, **www.sosdonegal.com**

WHERE TO EAT

Belfast

Alden's
229 Upper Newtownards Road, **t** (028) 9065 0079 (*moderate–expensive*)
Comfort, service and ambience combine with good food to make this an excellent dining experience. Children are made very welcome.

Café Renoir
95 Botanic Avenue, **t** (028) 9031 1300 (*moderate*)
Sunday brunch and lunch are offered at this all-day restaurant, which has a wood-burning pizzeria and a café. Families are welcome and high chairs available, and dishes are made with fresh organic ingredients.

Cargoes
613 Lisburn Road, **t** (028) 9066 5451 (*inexpensive*)
Enjoyable modern café with nice Mediterranean salads and other light meals.

Cayenne
Ascot House, 7 Shaftesbury Square, **t** (028) 9033 1532 (*moderate–expensive*)
Very child-friendly and casual restaurant owned and run by Northern Ireland's celebrity chef Paul Rankin, with imaginative food and many vegetarian dishes, plus high chairs, wheelchair access. Good value set lunches.

Equinox
32 Howard Street, **t** (028) 9023 0089 (*inexpensive*)
Café with sophisticated interior design and gift shop. Excellent salads, coffee, milkshakes.

Maggie May's
50 Botanic Avenue, **t** (028) 9032 2662 (*inexpensive*)
Big servings, good value veggie meals, and breakfast served all day; it's in the university area.

Nick's Warehouse
35 Hill St, Cathedral Quarter, **t** (028) 9043 9690 (*moderate–expensive*)
Popular, informal restaurant owned by renowned chefs Nick and Kathy Price, and recommended. Until 9.30pm Nick's offers smaller portions and will change dishes on the menu according to a child's wishes; it also has high chairs. A special treat.

The Other Place
79 Botanic Avenue, **t** (028) 9020 7200 (*inexpensive*)
Good hamburgers, chips and Ulster fry all-day breakfasts.

Rain City
33–35 Malone Road, **t** (028) 9068 2929 (*moderate*)
Paul Rankin's new American-style restaurant attracts long queues, so kids might not have the patience to wait, but it's a great place for them, with fine food and excellent children's menus.

Tong Dynasty
82 Botanic Avenue, **t** (028) 9043 9595 (*moderate*)
Excellent Chinese food and fast service: children can play with chopsticks to their hearts' content, and their needs are genially accommodated.

Thai Village
50 Dublin Road, **t** (028) 9024 9269 (*inexpensive*)
Good vegetarian and vegan dishes and Thai classics. Children are welcome earlier in evening.

Around Co. Antrim

Ballycastle

Marine Hotel
t (028) 2076 2222 (*moderate*)
Simple but good cooking, and kids are welcome in this hotel restaurant overlooking Ballycastle Bay.

Bushmills

Bushmills Inn
25 Main St, **t** (028) 2073 2339 (*inexpensive–moderate*)
Children are well catered for in this superior Victorian-style coaching inn near the Bushmills Distillery, with enjoyable bar food and restaurant meals. Children can choose from their own menu or have half-portions.

Carnlough

The Londonderry Arms Hotel
20–28 Harbour Road, **t** (028) 2888 5255 (*expensive*)
This very child-friendly restaurant serves good fish and has a wide choice of dishes for children. They also provide things to do so kids don't grow bored while adults finish their meals, and there are wonderful views of the sea and the Glens.

Carrickfergus

Dobbins Inn

6 High St, **t** (028) 9335 1905 (*inexpensive*)

Rich à la carte food and bar meals in this old hotel. There's a children's menu in the evenings.

Cushendall

Harry's Restaurant

10–12 Mill St, **t** (028) 2177 2022 (*inexpensive–moderate*)

This family-friendly restaurant in a little town at the foot of the Antrim Glens is worth seeking out for its reasonably priced specialities, which include monkfish, sizzling grills, lamb, steaks and scampi.

Portrush

Ramore Restaurant

The Harbour, **t** (028) 7082 4313 (*inexpensive–moderate*)

Children are welcome in this upstairs nook overlooking Portrush Harbour until about 9pm, when a noisier crowd appears. Nearby, the less expensive Coast (phone as above) has pizzas and pasta.

County Down

Bangor

Shanks Restaurant

Blackwood Golf Club, 150 Crawfordsburn Road, **t** (028) 9185 3313 (*moderate–expensive*)

Rich, varied menu; one of the best in the area. High chairs, special menus and wheelchair access.

Comber

Castle Espie Coffee Room

Wildfowl and Wetlands Trust, Ballydrain Road, **t** (028) 9187 4146 (*inexpensive*)

Good food in a perfect setting – the middle of the nature reserve on Strangford Lough.

Donaghadee

Grace Neill's Bar and Restaurant

33 High St, **t** (028) 9188 2553 (*moderate*)

Adventurous food in ample portions. Said to be Ireland's oldest pub (founded 1611), and Russian Tsar Peter the Great stopped for a pint in 1694.

Downpatrick

The Slaney Inn

64 St Patrick's Rd, Raholp, **t** (028) 4461 2093 (*inexpensive–moderate*)

Children are welcome in this relaxed, family-owned restaurant. There is even an enclosed playground area and small animal farm.

Dundrum

The Buck's Head Inn

77 Main St, **t** (028) 4375 1868 (*moderate*)

This restaurant in an 18th-century building is renowned for its warm atmosphere, with a cosy panelled bar, open fire and imaginative menus. Children go for its fantastic fish cakes, home-made burgers and fish and chips, and there's a garden.

Holywood

Baytree Coffee House

Audley Court, 118 High St, **t** (028) 9042 1419 (*inexpensive*)

Fabulous desserts and own-made food put together with fresh ingredients and a gourmet touch. Children are especially welcome: fantastic breakfasts, and delicious mashed spuds and cakes.

Killinchy

Daft Eddys

Sketrick Island, Whiterock, **t** (028) 9754 1615 (*inexpensive*)

Pub on an island on Strangford Lough reached by a causeway. Good soups and steaks.

Newtownards

Roma's

4 Regent Street, t (028) 9181 2841 (*inexpensive*)

Italian dishes that most kids can't get enough of.

Portaferry

Portaferry Hotel

10 The Strand, **t** (028) 4272 8231 (*moderate*)

Seafood, delivered straight from the fishing boats of Portavogie.

Strangford

Cuan Bar and Restaurant

6 The Square, **t** (028) 4488 1222 (*moderate*)

Venison, quail, plus hot and cold buffet.

County Armagh

Armagh City

Café Papa Deli Bar and Bistro

15 Thomas St, **t** (028) 3881 1239 (*inexpensive*)

Very good deli and patisserie counter.

Pilgrim's Table Conservatory Restaurant

St Patrick's Trian visitor complex,
38–40 English St, **t** (028) 3752 1814 (*inexpensive*)

Self-service but said to be the best lunch in town, with quality cooking. Set in pleasant Georgian surroundings, it is good for the whole family for morning coffee, lunch and afternoon tea.

Loughgall

The Famous Grouse

6 Ballyhagan Road, **t** (048) 3889 1778 (*inexpensive–moderate*)

Reasonably priced, relaxed and cosy restaurant that is welcoming to families. Try the pub grub at lunchtime, or the main menu in the evening.

Markethill

The Court Rooms Restaurant

7 Main St, **t** (028) 3755 2553 (*inexpensive*)

Children will love the excellent selection of delicious home-baked desserts on offer here.

Portadown

Yellow Door Rugger's Bistro

Portadown Rugby Club, Chambers Park, **t** (028) 3839 4860 (*inexpensive–moderate*)

A children's menu is available during the week, with baby pizzas, soups, burgers and fish; half portions of the adult menu can be ordered on Sundays. It's so relaxed in this rugby club restaurant that kids play quietly on the wooden floor.

Co. Londonderry

Coleraine

Salmon Leap

53 Castleroe Road, **t** (028) 7035 2992 (*moderate*)

Good buffet lunch, and a reputation for salmon. Children are welcome for lunch and early dinners.

Strawberry Fayre

1 Blagh Road, **t** (028) 7032 0437 (*inexpensive*)

Excellent food, with quality lunches and teas made from fresh produce and natural ingredients.

Derry City

Beckett's Bar

44 Foyle St, **t** (028) 7136 0066 (*moderate*)

Good pub lunches and evening meals.

Indigo

27 Shipquay St, **t** (028) 7127 1011 (*inexpensive*)

Relaxed café-bar with tasty Asian-influenced dishes on the menu, and vegetarian options.

Linenhall Bar

3 Market St, **t** (028) 7137 1665 (*moderate–expensive*)

A lively place popular with locals for relaxed lunches, with or without Guinness, that nods to Derry's past as a linen centre. Children feel comfortable here.

O'Brien's American Steakhouse and Grill Bar

59 Strand Road, **t** (028) 7136 1527 (*inexpensive*)

Whether it's a special occasion or you're just hungry, this friendly restaurant, with steaks, burgers and other Americana, is a handy standby.

Limavady

Coast Road Inn

t (028) 7776 1620 (*inexpensive–moderate*)

This excellent pub-restaurant is a haven for hikers and great for families, offering high chairs and comfort, with traditional and slightly adventurous dishes, made with very good ingredients.

Magherafelt

Café Slice

Rainey St, **t** (028) 7963 3980 (*inexpensive–moderate*)

Open daily, as a bakery–café by day and a restaurant/wine bar at night, with nouveau-Irish cooking and excellent starters. Well-priced children's menu.

Portstewart

Morelli's

54–57 The Promenade, **t** (028) 7083 2150 (*inexpensive*)

With the Italian name, what else could be served here but good ice cream and pasta? Children are welcome, and there's a children's menu.

County Tyrone

Cookstown

The Otter Lodge

Dungannon Road, **t** (028) 8676 5427 (*inexpensive*)

Pleasant pub grub and home cooking.

Cookstown Courtyard

56A William St, **t** (028) 8676 5070 (*inexpensive*)

There's a good set lunch in this rustic farm-themed coffee shop with home-made pies and puddings. Closed Sundays. Children very welcome.

Dungannon

Viscount's Restaurant

Northland Road, **t** (028) 8775 3800 (*moderate*)

This popular restaurant in a renovated church is decorated in medieval style, complete with suits of armour. Extensive main and children's menus.

Omagh

Carlton Restaurant

High St, **t** (048) 8224 7046 (*inexpensive*)

Children are made very welcome here: there's a full children's menu and colouring books, and on the menu there are tasty favourites like home-baked scones, lasagnes, quiches, the traditional Ulster Fry (breakfast) and more substantial dinners.

County Fermanagh

Bellanaleck

The Sheelin

t (028) 6634 8232 (*moderate*)

Children welcome for large, good-quality meals near the loughs, in a traditional cottage with climbing roses round the door. Very enjoyable.

Enniskillen

Franco's Pizzeria

Queen Elizabeth Road, **t** (028) 6632 4424 (*moderate*)

Pizzas are always popular with children and you won't find better ones than at this locally recommended, family-friendly restaurant, which also offers seafood, salad, steak and chicken dishes.

Oscar's

Belmore St, **t** (028) 6632 7037 (*moderate*)

Salmon and local trout are served in this small, popular restaurant with its fine atmosphere and good food. Children welcome.

Pat's Bar

1 Townhall St, **t** (028) 6632 7462 (*inexpensive*)

Good pub lunches, and families welcome.

Florence Court

Florence Court House

t (028) 6634 8249 (*inexpensive*)

Light lunches are served all day in an old barn: quiches, salads, wheaten bread. Families welcome.

Lisnaskea

Donn Carragh Hotel

t (028) 6772 1206 (*moderate*)

Bar food is available all day, and the restaurant is open evenings and for Sunday lunch.

Cavan and Monaghan

Ballyconnell

Polo D Restaurant

Main St, Ballyconnell, Co. Cavan, **t** (049) 952 6228 (*inexpensive–moderate*)

Light meals are served all day at this country-style restaurant, which also offers an imaginative dinner menu in the evenings. Children welcome.

Blacklion

MacNean Bistro

Blacklion, Co. Cavan, **t** (071) 985 3022 (*moderate–expensive*)

Children are welcome in this top-class restaurant (linked with MacNean House B&B), which creates imaginative dishes, mainly with locally grown organic produce, and highly lauded desserts.

Cavan

Casey's Steak Bar

Main St, Ballinagh, **t** (049) 433 7105 (*inexpensive–moderate*)

Children's menu, high chairs and the best steaks in Ireland, according to some.

Monaghan

Andy's Bar and Restaurant

12 Market St, **t** (047) 82277 (*inexpensive–moderate*)

Children's menu offered alongside a dinner menu with specialities: Monaghan mushrooms, steak in whiskey and beer sauce and good desserts.

Virginia

The Park Hotel

t (049) 854 6100 (*moderate*)

Children can have half portions or fast-food and high chairs are available. Imaginative, ambitious Irish and European cooking makes up the menu.

County Donegal

Ardara

Nesbitt Arms Hotel

Main St, **t** (074) 954 1103 (*inexpensive–moderate*)

High chairs are available, and there's a kids' fast-food menu alongside filling Irish food.

Burtonport

Lobster Pot

t (075) 42012 (*inexpensive*)

Families are welcome in this casual seafood restaurant in a tiny harbour village opposite Arranmore Island. High chairs and a kids' menu.

Donegal Town

Hyland Central Hotel

The Diamond, **t** (074) 972 1027 (*moderate*)

A children's menu, and exceptional Sunday lunches. Very family-friendly.

The Blueberry Tearoom

Castle Street, **t** (074) 972 2933 (*inexpensive*)

A lively casual café fine for children, with vegetarian dishes like quiche and lasagne.

Dunfanaghy

Dunfanaghy Workhouse

t (074) 913 6540 (*inexpensive*)

Seasonal coffee shop that's a wine bar with traditional music in the evening.

Dunglow

The Riverside Bistro

Main St, **t** (074) 952 1062 (*inexpensive*)

They offer a special children's menu and serve food to satisfy all tastes.

Glencolmcille

An Chistin

Ulster Cultural Foundation, **t** (074) 973 0213 (*inexpensive*)

Specializes in seafood, salads, soups.

Killybegs

The Fleet Inn

t (074) 973 1518 (*moderate*)

Children are welcome to try the menu in this snug little place – single upstairs room, with very friendly service. Portions are generous, and the cooking delicious. Reservations are recommended.

Letterkenny

Bakersville

Church Lane, **t** (074) 912 1887 (*inexpensive*)

Delicious fresh croissants, cakes, bread and sandwiches for light daytime meals and snacks.

Portnoo

The Dolmen Centre

Kilcooney, **t** (074) 954 5010 (*inexpensive*)

Soup, sandwiches and home baking in a smoke-free eco-centre that uses renewable energy.

Rathmullan

Rathmullan House Hotel

t (074) 915 8115 (*expensive*)

Fresh, original cooking with vegetables from the walled garden. Sunday lunches are good value.

Tory Island

Ostan Thoraigh

t (074) 913 5920, **www.toryhotel.com** (*inexpensive–moderate*)

Tory Island's one hotel was awarded Ireland's 'Dining Pub of the Year' award not long ago, and has great fresh seafood, in a wonderful location. Children welcome any time.

Sleep

08

WHERE TO STAY

Irish attitudes on what visitors expect in accommodation have changed enormously in the past decade. But then, so has the cost to the traveller. You will find more superior hotels that only the super-wealthy can afford than ever before, and more rooms with their own en suite baths, even in hostels. At the same time, you can also find more of the lowest form of budget accommodation.

Hotels and guesthouses in Ireland usually cater pretty well for children's needs, but you may prefer to rent a cottage or house for yourselves with its own kitchen and facilities instead (*see* right). Self-catering accommodation certainly offers more privacy and independence, although it can also make you feel a bit isolated, especially if you are driving your family around Ireland in a car.

Hotels

Tourism Ireland (which now unites the tourist offices of northern and southern Ireland) grades all types of accommodation with a system of stars and commendations. Lists of all the categories can be found in pamphlets available at local tourist offices, which will also make bookings for you. Prices in the Republic of Ireland will be listed in euros, while in Northern Ireland they will be in British pounds. In cities, some hotels cater mainly for business and/or older independent travellers, so it is a good idea to get clear whether children are welcome (and what is provided for them) when you're booking. Hotels oriented to the young-adult market, in trendy areas like Dublin's Temple Bar, can also be a problem for families. Check too if hotels offer discounts for children and longer stays; sometimes small children stay free, especially off-season. High season usually means Easter, July to mid-September, and maybe Christmas. At these times, it's best to book well in advance.

Only the larger Irish hotels usually have a lot of leisure facilities and particularly indoor pools, so this is something else you might want to bear in mind – you may have to balance the range of facilities against a loss of local character due to staying in a new, international-style hotel. Ireland's tourist boards do a fantastic job of grading and listing the massive amount of accommodation available in the country, but when you're looking for hotel ideas there's now a huge range of other information sources – specialist accommodation guides, websites, local organizations and independent hotel associations or marketing bodies. They vary a great deal, but independent groups like Blue Book and Hidden Ireland pay close attention to standards. For suggestions to check out, *see* p.248.

Bed and breakfasts and guesthouses

B&Bs can be a good choice if you are on a budget, but they often charge per head rather than per room, which can make prices rise to a level that makes a family hotel room more economical. Note, also, that while most hotels will have a restaurant and offer breakfast and evening meals, traditionally B&Bs offer breakfast only. However, nowadays many country guesthouses will also provide evening meals (and packed lunches) if you give advance notice, especially in more remote places where there may not be many alternatives.

Many farmhouses, like B&Bs, accommodate families, but Ireland also now has quite a few more upmarket guesthouses and country-house hotels which are geared more to business travellers and especially couples, and so not so family-friendly. Again, check this when booking.

Self-catering

Renting a self-catered cottage can often be the most amenable and economic option for a family. Self-catering allows you to come and go as you please without being restricted to set mealtimes, and gives kids room to spread out. However, it does tie you to one place, so make sure it's somewhere you want to spend the entire holiday. Choose accommodation in an area you want to visit, and consider places you want to explore and things you want to do and whether they are nearby.

Be a little cautious, also, if you don't want to spend your holiday in a new, purpose-built bungalow community. Many have sprung up all over Ireland, and you can find whole towns made up of holiday homes that are empty for most of the year. These new housing developments are pretty functional in look and atmosphere, though they will have all the modern conveniences.

If a house is described as 'modern' or 'purpose-built' this generally means it's not an old-fashioned kind of country place with any period details. Rental homes like this fit the bill if you want the assurance of certain conveniences but aren't too concerned about atmosphere, and may sometimes be cheaper than more characterful old houses.

Horse-drawn Caravans around Ireland

A distinctively Irish option combining travelling with a place to stay is to tour Ireland in a horse-drawn caravan. You get a trustworthy and solid horse, a barrel-shaped caravan which sleeps four, and you can travel at a relaxing pace, usually about 9 miles (15km) a day. Cost per week is from around €260 low-season to €700 in July and August. For more information contact Tourism Ireland, or:

Dieter Clissmann Horse-drawn Caravans, Carrigmore Farm, Wicklow, Co. Wicklow, **t** (0404) 48188

Into the West Horse Drawn Caravans, Ballinakill, Kylebrack, Loughrea, Co. Galway, **t** (090) 9745211

Kilvahan Horse Drawn Caravans, Kilvahan, Cullenagh, Portlaoise, Co. Laois, **t** (0502) 27048, **www**.horsedrawncaravans.com

Mayo Horsedrawn Caravan Holidays, Belcarra, Castlebar, Co. Mayo, **t** (094) 9032054, **www**.horsedrawn.mayonet.com

Slattery's Horse Drawn Caravans, 1 Russell St, Tralee, Co. Kerry, **t** (066) 718 6240, **www**.slatterys.com

Private homes

Owners of 'period houses' in Ireland who take paying guests are usually committed to a high standard of hospitality – of a kind that is traditional and natural to the Irish. However, in such circumstances you need to be especially conscious that you are visiting people's homes, no matter how professionally they are run. If you're planning to visit with children, do ask about their policy towards kids and check details like furnishings and whether they have outdoor play areas. If you have a baby, you naturally need to ensure that hoteliers and guesthouse owners know this in advance; sometimes they can accommodate you in special wings or cottages outside their main houses where you and your children can enjoy more freedom.

'Home baking' usually means the owners take care over their food and bake their own cakes and breads, but standards differ. The best places offer inventive gourmet spreads for breakfast.

'Special diets' implies that your hosts will do what they can to provide particular foods for you, if you give them advance notice. Owners of private homes will often provide or arrange babysitting, and advise on activities you and your children can enjoy in their area, or even organize them for you.

Activity centres

Centres with built-in leisure activities or facilities often cater for families as well as school and youth groups. Accommodation can be anything from basic dormitory-style to fully-equipped apartments, but normally a laundry and washing area are provided, along with a communal kitchen.

Hostels

Several independent hostelling associations have sprung up in Ireland in recent years, in addition to the traditional An Oige and YHANI (*see* p.248). Standards vary enormously. It's best to investigate before committing yourself to a stay of more than a night in one. People of all ages and types stay in hostels, but those who most enjoy them are budget travellers on walking and outdoor holidays. Visitors usually still have to leave the hostel during the day, and be in by a certain time at night. Self-catering is possible in some hostels with kitchen facilities, and breakfast and even dinner are sometimes offered. Washing machines, drying rooms, and Internet access may be found in some too. But anyone travelling with children should ensure first, before booking, that a hostel offers family rooms and not just dormitory-style accommodation.

Camping and caravanning

The amenities provided in Irish caravan and camping sites vary a lot, but electrical link-ups, toilets, showers and laundry areas are usually the bare minimum offered, while the best-equipped parks add kitchens, restaurants and games rooms.

Price ranges

All the accommodation listed in this chapter is categorized in one of the price bands below, based on prices for B&B per person, per night. In low seasons most hotels, and often guesthouses and B&Bs, offer 'discounts' for families or family rooms.

Be careful to find out how spacious family rooms are, as sizes and standards vary significantly.

High season = Easter, July–Aug, Christmas and New Year; Mid-season = April–June, Sept; Low season = the rest of the year.

Luxury	Over €130 (UK£90)
Expensive	Over €80 (UK£60)
Moderate	€35–80 (UK£25–60)
Inexpensive	under €35 (UK£25)

Useful Addresses and Sources

General Information

Tourism Ireland

Freephones UK **t** 0800 039 7000; US and Canada **t** 1 800 223 6470; **www**.tourismireland.com

The joint travel information service for the whole of Ireland. Affiliated to it are Bord Fáilte/the Irish Tourist Board (ITB, **www**.travel.ireland.ie) and the Northern Ireland Tourist Board (NITB, **www**.discovernorthernireland.com) and it has links to all the regional and local tourist bodies.

Guides, brochures and websites

Bed & Breakfast Ireland
Ireland Accommodation Guide
Ireland Self Catering Guide

Available from Tourism Ireland or the ITB.

Accommodation for Visitors on a Limited Budget
A Complete Guide to Self-catering Holiday Homes in Northern Ireland
Bed & Breakfast Guide, Northern Ireland
Northern Ireland Hotels and Guesthouses

From Tourism Ireland or the NITB.

Be Our Guest Hotels and Guesthouses Guide, from the Irish Hotels Federation, **www**.irelandhotels.com

Camping and Caravan Ireland, from **www**.camping-ireland.ie

Friendly Homes of Ireland, Tourism Resources Ltd, **www**.tourismresources.ie

Hostels Ireland, by Paul Karr, from An Oige, **www**.irelandyha.org

Independent Holiday Hostels of Ireland, **www**.hostels-ireland.com

Ireland Farmhouse Bed and Breakfast, **www**.irishfarmholidays.com

Lóistín Gaeltachta (Accommodation in the Gaeltacht), Freephones, **t** IR 1800 621 600, **t** UK 0800 783 5708; **www**.gaelsaoire.ie

Hotel and tour organizations

Country House Tours, 71 Waterloo Road, Dublin 4, **t** (01) 668 6463, in the US, **t** 1 800 688 0363, **www**.tourismresources.ie

Tours of grand houses and castles.

Ireland's Blue Book, t (046) 9023416, **www**.irelands-blue-book.ie

Individual, opulent country house hotels.

Irish Hotels Federation, www.irelandhotels.com

Access to over 1,000 hotels and guesthouses online, plus advice on specialist short breaks.

Holiday rentals and self-catering

Dream Ireland Holiday Rentals, Lodge Wood, Kenmare, Co. Kerry, **t** (064) 41170, **www**.dreamireland.com

Friendly Homes of Ireland, **www**.tourismresources.ie

This site features plenty of affordable, family-run accommodation.

The Hidden Ireland, t (01) 662 7166, in the US **t** 1800 688 0299, **www**.hidden-ireland.com

Self-catering rentals often in country houses of character, some so grand they'd be hard put to stay hidden.

Irish Country Holidays, The Discovery Centre, Rearcross, Co. Tipperary, **t** (062) 79330, **www**.country-holidays.ie

An association of rural homes all over Ireland offering a range of self-catering homes for visitors.

Irish Farmhouse Holidays Association, 2 Michael St, Limerick, **t** (061) 400 700, **www**.irishfarmholidays.com

Kerry Cottages, 3 Royal Terrace West, Dun Laoghaire, Co. Dublin, **t** (01) 284 4000, **www**.kerrycottages.com

Killarney Lakeland Cottages, Muckross, Co. Kerry, **t** (064) 31538, **www**.killarneycottages.com

Rent-an-Irish Cottage, 51 O'Connell Street, Limerick, **t** (061) 411 109, **www**.rentacottage.ie

Rural Cottage Holidays Ltd, St. Anne's Court, 59 North Street, Belfast BT1 1NB, **t** (028) 9024 1100, **www**.cottagesinireland.com

Shamrock Cottages, 13 Clifford Terrace, Wellington, Somerset TA21 8QP, UK, **t** (01823) 660 126, **www**.shamrockcottages.co.uk

An excellent company that can advise on country and beachside rentals suitable for young families.

Hostels

An Oige (Irish Youth Hostel Association), 61 Mountjoy Street, Dublin 7, **t** (01) 830 4555, **www**.irelandyha.org

The Republic's main hostel association.

Independent Holiday Hostels of Ireland, 57 Lower Gardiner Street, Dublin 1, **t** (01) 836 4700, **www**.hostels-ireland.com

Offers a 'bed search' service. Some of their hostels are very rudimentary.

Youth Hostel Association Northern Ireland, 22 Donegall Road, Belfast, BT12 5JN, **t** (028) 9032 4733, **www**.hini.org.uk

Has fine hostels on the Ulster Way footpath.

ACCOMMODATION

DUBLIN

Dublin's entrance into the club of the world's most popular tourist cities has brought a real explosion in new hotels and guesthouses. Below is simply a sample of what you will find. Dublin is a very popular city, so it's best to book well ahead.

Hotels

Ashling Hotel

Parkgate Street, D8, t (01) 677 2324, f (01) 679 3783, www.ashlinghotel.ie (*expensive*)

This big 3-star hotel with 150 rooms and a multi-storey car park is very near Phoenix Park and its attractions. It also offers discounts for children, kids' meals and a babysitting service. Adapted rooms are available for guests with disabilities.

Buswells Hotel

Molesworth St, D2, t (01) 676 4013, www.quinn-hotels.com (*expensive–luxury*)

This old-fashioned family hotel is very central and offers price reductions for families, children's meals and babysitting.

Camden Court Hotel

Lower Camden St, D2, t (01) 475 9666, f (01) 475 9677, www.camdencourthotel.com (*expensive*)

Not far from St Stephen's Green, this 246-room hotel has family rooms specially fitted with all amenities, and many other useful facilities: high chairs, babysitting service, children's menus and an indoor swimming pool – a rarity in Dublin hotels.

Georgian House Hotel

18–22 Baggot St Lower, D2, t (01) 634 5000, f (01) 634 5100 (*luxury*)

Children under 17 are charged less in this central Georgian house next to St Stephen's Green, with snug, pastel-coloured rooms. Babysitting and children's meals are available, and there's a car park.

The Gresham

Upper O'Connell St, D1, t (01) 874 6881, f (01) 878 7175, www.gresham-hotels.com (*expensive*)

Built in the days when a first-class hotel had big bedrooms and huge baths, this classic hotel still has the atmosphere of the 1930s. There are discounts for children, and the new restaurant offers children's meals.

Harcourt Hotel

60 Harcourt St, D2, t (01) 478 3677, f (01) 475 2013, www.harcourthotel.ie (*luxury*)

A five-minute walk from St Stephen's Green and Grafton Street: children are welcome in this former home of George Bernard Shaw, now an 86-room hotel with babysitting service and evening entertainment. Car parking is available locally for a fee.

Jurys Ballsbridge Hotel

Pembroke Road, Ballsbridge, D4, t (01) 660 5000, f (01) 660 5540, www.jurysdoyle.com (*expensive*)

Part of the reliable Jurys chain, this 5-star hotel has interconnecting rooms, restaurants, babysitting, children's meals and price reductions for kids. There's a fully equipped leisure centre on site, swimming pools and entertainment.

Mount Herbert Hotel

Lansdowne Road, Ballsbridge, D4, t (01) 668 4321, f (01) 660 7077, www.mountherberthotel.ie (*expensive*)

Stay in style at this smart Victorian residence in the upmarket Ballsbridge area. It has extras that kids enjoy: an outdoor play area with climbing frames, swings, sea-saws and tree houses, and children's meals and half portions in the restaurant. Also babysitting and access to a health club.

Sachs Hotel

19 Morehampton Road, Donnybrook, D4, t (01) 668 0995, f (01) 668 6147 (*expensive–luxury*)

This small, traditional hotel in a quiet Georgian terrace has ample parking, price reductions for kids, children's meals and babysitting are available.

School House Hotel

2–8 Northumberland Road, D4, t (01) 667 5014, f (01) 667 5015, www.schoolhousehotel.com (*moderate–expensive*)

One child aged 2–12 may stay free with parents when using existing beds in a twin/double room. Children's meals and babysitting are also available.

Shelbourne Hotel

St Stephens's Green, D2, t (01) 676 6471, f (01) 661 6006 (*luxury*)

Dublin's oldest, grandest 5-star hotel, where the Irish Constitution was drafted, offers babysitting and has a very elegant drawing room, bar, a gymnasium and an indoor pool.

The Westbury

Clarendon St, off Grafton St, D2, t (01) 679 1122, f (01) 679 7078, www.jurysdoyle.com (*luxury*)

One child up to age 12 stays free when sharing a double/twin room with two parents here. This is a modern, 5-star, top of the range hotel that's conveniently central, with children's meals and babysitting service available.

B&Bs and guesthouses

Aberdeen Lodge

53 Park Avenue, Ballsbridge, D4, t (01) 283 8155, f (01) 283 7877, www.halpinsprivatehotels.com (*expensive*)

Two family rooms are available in this small, sedate hotel in a quiet, leafy neighbourhood of embassies and Regency houses – a pleasant home away from home yet not far from central Dublin. Proprietor Pat Halpin ensures that everything is delivered promptly and with a smile, from room service to advice about what to do in Dublin. High teas and breakfasts are good too.

McMenamins Townhouse

74 Marlborough Road, Donnybrook, D4, t (01) 497 4405, f (01) 496 8585, www.irishwelcome.com (*moderate*)

A warm welcome awaits you here from helpful, hospitable host Padraig McMenamin, who knows all about Donnybrook's history and local sports activities. His wife Kay makes excellent home baking and special breakfasts are available for vegetarians. You can book a family room containing a double and single bed, along with an adjoining small room with another single bed, and sleep peacefully in this residential street not far from University College Dublin.

Simmonstown-house

Sydenham Road, Ballsbridge, D4, t (01) 660 7260, f (01) 660 7341, www.simmonstown-house.com (*moderate*)

Children under 3 share their parents' bedroom for free here while those aged 3–12 are charged 50% of adult rates.

Waterloo House

8-10 Waterloo Road, Ballsbridge, D4, t (01) 660 1888, f (01) 667 1955 (*expensive*)

Two fine Georgian town-houses contain a four-star guesthouse on a residential street within walking distance of the city centre. Friendly, efficient Mayo-born proprietress Evelyn Corcoran welcomes children of any age. There is a wicker-furnished conservatory and a plush dining room facing the back garden, which is a luxurious oasis of peace. This is perfection for those who require privacy in the easygoing gentility of old Dublin.

Self-catering

Baggotrath

Off Landsdowne Road, D4, t (01) 668 6463 (*moderate*)

A purpose-built apartment complex offering private parking and security, between the sea at Sandymount and the city centre. There is a minimum stay of two nights.

Hostels

Hostel facilities can be very rudimentary, and clientele and staff changes can alter the service significantly. Those listed here are only a few of the hostels open in Dublin.

Avalon House

55 Aungier Street, D2, t 475 0001, f 475 0303, www.avalon-house.ie (*inexpensive*)

Dublin's safest, most central hostel is more suited to families than some of the backpacker hostels. This old building has been converted into a well-run modern hostel with no-smoking twin, family and dormitory rooms, self-catering facilities, high chairs and, a great plus, no curfew.

Dublin International An Oige Youth Hostel

Mountjoy St, D7, t (01) 830 1766, f (01) 830 1600 (*inexpensive*)

The headquarters-hostel of Ireland's traditional youth hostel association has a café, tourist information, Internet access, bureau de change, self-catering kitchen and clothes-washing facilities, along with private, family and en-suite rooms. Supplements are charged for private facilities and stays longer than two nights or over bank holidays or major event weekends. Very popular.

Isaacs Hostel

2–5 Frenchman's Lane, D1, t 855 6215, f 855 6574 www.isaacs.ie (*inexpensive*)

Built as a wine warehouse on the Liffey in the 1700s, this is beside the central bus station and is clean and cosmopolitan, with a restaurant that's good value. It has a patio, garden and family rooms.

LEINSTER

County Dublin

Hotels

Gresham Royal Marine Hotel

Marine Road, Dun Laoghaire, **t** (01) 280 1911, **t** 1850 298298, **f** (01) 280 1089, **www.gresham-hotels.com** (*luxury*)

Children will like the suites facing Dun Laoghaire Pier with their four-poster beds, separate sitting rooms, wide windows and high ceilings. This 3-star Victorian seaside hotel overlooking Dublin Bay, with a garden, is comfortable and friendly, if a tad smoky in the bar areas. Non-smoking rooms are available and there are fine old-fashioned Dublin breakfasts. Babysitting service, children's meals and children's discounts.

B&Bs and guesthouses

Chestnut Lodge

2 Vesey Place, Dun Laoghaire, **t** (01) 280 7860 (*moderate*)

Gracious Georgian house with lovely comfortable rooms, good breakfasts and a very friendly atmosphere in which nothing is too much trouble. It is situated close to Dun Laoghaire ferry port.

Druid Lodge

Killiney Hill Road, Killiney, **t** (01) 285 1632, **f** (01) 284 8504, **www.druidlodge.com** (*moderate*)

Children are welcome in this ivy-clad house high above Killiney Bay, with lush flower-filled gardens. Inside, you are surrounded by an eclectic array of paintings, artefacts and sculptures from Ken and Cynthia McClenaghan's world travels. On a sunny morning, the view from the windows is more like northern Italy than a suburb of Dublin. A gourmet Irish breakfast prepares you for a morning's trek to Killiney Hill for an even better ocean view. Cynthia will advise on local restaurants or show you the way down to nearby Dalkey, and where to take a boat trip out to Dalkey Island during the summer.

Sandycove Guesthouse

Sandycove Seafront, Dun Laoghaire, **t** (01) 284 1600 (*inexpensive*)

Tidy B&B close to the DART station, beaches and Dun Laoghaire ferry port.

Self-catering

Harap Farm

Magillstown, Swords, **t** (01) 840 1285, **www.dublinbutterfly.com** (*moderate*)

Family-owned self-catering homes, with gardens and a tennis court. There are sports facilities and restaurants nearby, but you need to have a car.

Wicklow and Carlow

Hotels

The Brooklodge Inn

Macreddin Village, near Aughrim, Co. Wicklow, **t** (0402) 36444, **f** (0402) 36580, **www.brooklodge.com** (*moderate–expensive*)

This new holiday village-style hotel, where B&B is offered to guests in individual houses, uses organic produce in its food. They offer the option of a babysitter to take the children to their country pub for meals while parents dine at the Strawberry Tree Restaurant. There are good rates for families, and a smokehouse, organic bakery, wine and outdoor-wear shops on site, plus kids' meals, garden and games room. It's only 15 mins from Glendalough, with riding and fishing nearby.

The Lord Bagenal Inn

Main St, Leighlinbridge, Co. Carlow, **t** (059) 972 1668, **f** (059) 972 2629, **www.lordbagenal.com** (*moderate*)

A small hotel with the owner's collection of paintings decorating the walls, and helpful staff who prepare generous breakfasts. There's a good restaurant with fine wines and a bar serving snacks and carvery meals. Amenable to families, with a children's menu, family rates and an enclosed playroom open until 8pm. It also offers a private marina, fishing boat hire, riding and walking in the Blackstairs Mountains.

Powerscourt Arms Hotel

Enniskerry, Co. Wicklow, **t** (01) 282 8903, **f** (01) 286 4909 (*moderate*)

An attractive town hotel at the foot of the Wicklow Mountains where they serve good Guinness, and it also has kids' meals and price reductions for families.

Country houses

Ballyknocken House

Glenealy, near Ashford, Co. Wicklow, **t** (0404) 44627, **f** (0404) 44696, **www**.ballyknocken.com (*inexpensive–moderate*)

Pretty, romantic farmhouse with iron beds and claw feet baths, built in 1850. Advice is given on walks, and pony rides on the farm. Kids welcome, price reductions, gardens and fishing available.

Lorum Old Rectory

Kilgreaney, Bagenalstown, Co. Carlow, **t** (059) 9175282, **f** (059) 9175455, **www**.lorum.com (*expensive*)

An ideal place for those with children; there's plenty to do on Mrs Smith's farm, plus outdoor toys, dogs, pet sheep and croquet in the garden. Plus tasty meals and pretty, old-fashioned rooms.

Sherwood Park House

Kilbride, Tullow, Ballon, Co. Carlow, **t** (059) 915 9117, **f** (059) 915 9355 (*moderate*)

Children are welcome in this elegant Georgian farmhouse in rolling parkland. This accessible country retreat offers cosy log fires, candlelit dinners, quaint bedrooms with brass beds, excellent home cooking, fishing, riding and a pet farm for children, and there's good golf nearby.

B&Bs and guesthouses

Avonbrae Guesthouse

Rathdrum, Co. Wicklow, **t** (0404) 46198, **f** (0404) 46198 (*inexpensive*)

This family-run village guesthouse will help to arrange hill-walking and other activities.

Bel Air Hotel and Equestrian Club and Holiday Village

Ashford, Co. Wicklow, **t** (0404) 40109, **f** (0404) 40188 (*expensive*)

An equestrian village with a hotel and 4-star self-catering for those taking horse riding courses.

Old Rectory

Wicklow Town, Co. Wicklow, **t** (0404) 67048 (*inexpensive*)

Cosy rooms, delicious breakfasts and dinners.

The Watermill

Rathvilly, Co. Carlow, **t** (059) 9161392 (*inexpensive*)

Delightful restored 16th-century mill on the River Slaney, with home cooking and vegetables from Mr and Mrs Tononi's garden, plus free fishing.

Self-catering

Devil's Glen Holiday and Equestrian Village

Devil's Glen, Ashford, Co. Wicklow, **t** (0404) 40637, **f** (0404) 40638, **www**.devilsglen.ie (*moderate*)

Apartments, bungalows and 4-star cottages are available at this equestrian centre where guests may ride from morning to night.

Hostels

Glendalough An Oige

Glendalough, Co. Wicklow, **t** (0404) 45342, **f** (0404) 45690 (*inexpensive*)

A straightforward, traditional youth hostel.

Camping and caravanning

Avonmore Riverside Caravan and Camping Park

Rathdrum, Co. Wicklow, **t** (0404) 46080, **www**.avonmoreriverside.com (*moderate*)

Open Easter–Sept, this camping and caravan site on the banks of the Avonmore also has self-catering timber chalets available.

Kilkenny and Wexford

Rosslare Harbour and the road that leads into Wexford have a huge number of hotels and B&Bs. Even so, in summer it's best to book ahead.

Hotels

Dunbrody Country House Hotel

Arthurstown, New Ross, Co. Wexford, **t** (051) 389 600/1 800 323 5463, **f** (051) 389 601, **www**.dunbrodyhouse.com (*expensive–luxury*)

This antique-filled hotel in spacious parkland not far from the sea on the Hook Peninsula offers delicious, delicately flavoured cuisine from Kevin Dundon, ex-chef at Dublin's top Shelbourne Hotel, along with courteous service. Babysitting, price reductions for kids, gardens and a children's menu are available too, plus riding and fishing nearby.

Kelly's Resort Hotel

Rosslare Strand, Co. Wexford, **t** (053) 32114, **f** (053) 32222, **www**.kellys.ie (*expensive*)

A 4-star 100-bedroomed hotel on 5 miles (8km) of safe, sandy beach – near several golf courses. Children are catered for all day and activities are available for all ages: there's an indoor playroom, outdoor playground and special kids' dinner at 5.30pm. There's also entertainment, a leisure centre, swimming pool, tennis and crazy golf. You can book full board, or go self-catering (book well in advance). They will arrange a minibus to collect you from Rosslare Strand Station if you wish.

Whites Hotel

George Street, Wexford Town, Co. Wexford, **t** (053) 22311, **f** (053) 45000 (*moderate*)

Central and comfortable; this was the smartest hotel in town for years. It is now largely modern but incorporates part of an old coaching inn. Facilities include a health and fitness club, children's meals, price reductions and babysitting.

Country houses

Ballinkeele House

Ballymurn, Enniscorthy, Co. Wexford, **t** (053) 533 8105, **f** (053) 533 8468, **www**.ballinkeele.com (*luxury*)

Children are welcome to enjoy the peaceful atmosphere at this old family home in 350 acres of farm and woodland with ponds, mature trees and rhododendrons.

Ballyduff House

Thomastown, Co. Kilkenny, **t** (056) 775 8488 (*moderate*)

This 18th-century manor house is set in wooded parkland overlooking the River Nore. A family suite is available, and all the bedrooms are furnished with antiques and white linen. Your hostess Breda Thomas runs a pony club for youngsters and can arrange activities for visitors, young and old.

Belmore

Jerpoint Church, Thomastown, Co. Kilkenny, **t** (056) 772 4228 (*moderate*)

Fine old family home with gardens and a working farm on the site of a hunting lodge built in 1790. Children are welcome, but you may not want to tell them that St Nicholas is reputedly buried nearby.

Cullintra House

The Rower, Inistioge, Co. Kilkenny, **t** (051) 423614 (10am–2am), **www**.indigo.ie/~cullhse/ (*moderate*)

A magical place (especially for cat lovers) set in beautiful, flower-filled grounds, with antiques and bohemian furnishings. Lively proprietress Patricia Cantlon paints as well as runs her ancestral home and 230-acre estate at the foot of Mount Brandon. There is a separate building for those who prefer more private quarters, and a plant-filled art studio conservatory for conference and guest use. Superb dinners may last late into the night and breakfast can be served until mid-day.

Garranavabby House

The Rower, Inistioge, Co. Kilkenny, **t** (051) 423 613 (*inexpensive*)

One family room is available in this farmhouse, parts of which were built in the late-17th century. It's in a scenic farm setting near charming Inistioge, on the outskirts of Rower village.

Horetown House

Foulksmills, Co. Wexford, **t** (051) 565 771 (*moderate*)

Old-fashioned 17th-century manor house in beautiful parkland setting. Mrs Young offers good plain food in the Cellar Restaurant, and facilities include an equestrian centre in the courtyard.

B&Bs and guesthouses

Ballaghtobin

Callan, Co. Kilkenny, **t** (056) 772 5227, **f** (056) 772 5712 **www**.ballaghtobin.com (*moderate*)

Children are welcome in this Georgian home set in lovely grounds, where the bedrooms are tastefully decorated and luxurious.

Butler House

16 Patrick St, Kilkenny Town, **t** (056) 22828/65707, **f** (056) 65626 (*moderate–expensive*)

Smart guesthouse rooms are provided in this Georgian building, both central and comfortable.

Danville House

New Ross Road, Kilkenny Town, **t** (056) 772 1512 (*moderate*)

Family rooms are available in this Georgian farmhouse hidden behind trees just outside Kilkenny.

Self-catering

Blanchville House

Dunbell, Maddoxtown, Co. Kilkenny, **t** (056) 27197, **f** (056) 27636 (*moderate*)

Three self-catering apartments in a converted coach house, one with wheelchair access; they each sleep 4–6.

Kilmokea Coachhouse and Garden-suite

Kilmokea Country Manor and Gardens, Great Island, Campile, Co. Wexford, t (051) 388 109, f (051) 388 776, www.kilmokea.com (*expensive*)

Beside a walled garden on Great Island in the Barrow Estuary, two apartments are available in private trout-fishing and horse-riding grounds that also have a tennis court, indoor pool and games room. Cream teas, organic food and aromatherapy are offered, and children are specially catered for.

Killowen House

Dunganstown, New Ross, Co. Wexford, t (027) 51184 (*moderate*)

An attractive cottage and an apartment, with the use of tennis court and gardens.

Somers' Fort Cottages

Coolroe, Ballycullane, Co. Wexford, t (051) 562 335, www.somersfort.com (*moderate*)

Three 19th-century tenant farmers' cottages.

Hostels

Arthurstown An Oige Youth Hostel

Coastguard Station, Arthurstown, Co. Wexford, t (051) 389 411 (*inexpensive*)

Small family rooms available (summer only, opens 1 June). Good area for cycling and walking.

Rosslare Harbour An Oige

Goulding Street, Rosslare, Co. Wexford, t (053) 33399, f (053) 33624 (*inexpensive*)

This 85-bed hostel is bigger and busier than Arthurstown, and is open all year. It has its own courtyard where toddlers can play, and nearby you can swim, ride horses or play golf. Meals can be taken at a nearby hotel.

Kildare, Laois and Offaly

Hotels

Castle Durrow

Durrow, Co. Laois, t (0502) 36555, f (0502) 36559 (*luxury*)

Families are welcome in this country house hotel with a 30-acre orchard on its estate.

Kilkea Castle

Castledermot, Co. Kildare, t (059) 9145156, f (0503) 45187, www.kilkeacastle.ie (*luxury*)

Built by Hugh de Lacy in 1180, this is the oldest inhabited castle in Ireland and has views over tranquil gardens. Good health and sporting facilities.

Kinnitty Castle

Kinnitty, Co. Offaly, t (0509) 37318, f (0509) 37284, www.kinnittycastle.com (*luxury*)

Atmospheric rooms in a 17th-century neo-Gothic mansion. It hosts medieval banquets, and its Ely O'Carroll Banqueting Hall commemorates the clan who once lived here. A large luxury cottage is also available for rent. Dinner is served in the Georgian restaurant; other facilities include children's meals, babysitting, gardens, tennis and gym. Falconry, riding, fishing and golf also available nearby.

Country houses

Griesemount

Ballitore, Co. Kildare, t (059) 86481205 (*expensive*)

Families are welcome at this small, genteel B&B in a Georgian house.

Ivyleigh House

Church St, Port Laoise, Co. Laois, t (0502) 228081, f (0502) 63343, www.ivyleigh.com (*moderate*)

Children are welcome but no family rooms or cots are available. Breakfast is magnificent in this antique-furnished Georgian town-house.

The Manor House

Ballaghmore Castle, Borris-in-Ossory, Co. Laois, t (0505) 21453, www.castleballaghmore.com (*expensive*)

One of the oldest houses in Ireland; families are welcomed and they serve unbeatable breakfasts.

Roundwood House

Mountrath, Co. Laois, t (0502) 32120, f (0502) 32711, www.hidden-ireland.com/roundwood/ (*moderate*)

This Palladian mansion built in the 1740s near the Slieve Bloom Mountains is run by a delightful couple, Frank and Rosemarie Kennan, who instantly make you welcome. The atmosphere is relaxed and comfortable; antiques, books and paintings fill the house to absorb you on cold, wet afternoons. For good-weather days, riding and golf are on hand locally. There's lots for kids to do – animals to feed, woods to explore and games to play in the nursery. A self-catering apartment is available as well.

B&Bs and guesthouses

Kilkea Lodge Farm

Castledermot, Co. Kildare, t (059) 9145112 (*moderate*)

Charming 18th-century farmhouse, and riding holidays can be arranged; contact Mrs Greene.

Preston House

Abbeyleix, Co. Laois, t (0502) 31432, f (0502) 31432 (*moderate*)

Children are welcome in this ivy-covered Georgian B&B, just as they were when it was a school. Its award-winning restaurant serves Sunday lunches, where vegetarians and the health-conscious find nutritious options.

Spinners Townhouse and Bistro

Castle Street, Birr, Co. Offaly, t (0509) 21673, f (0509) 21673, www.spinners-town-house.com (*moderate*)

Set in a garden courtyard, this modern, stylish B&B has 13 rooms decorated in muted tones with a backdrop of Birr Castle. The bistro offers tasty dishes made from locally produced ingredients.

Self-catering

Kilrush Holiday Homes

Narraghmore, Athy, Co. Kildare, t (059) 8626631 (*moderate*)

One and 2-bedroom apartments are available in this 18th-century house on a 120-acre estate.

Meath and Louth

Hotels

Ballymascanlon House Hotel

Dundalk, Co. Louth, t (042) 935 8200, f (042) 937 1598, www.ballymascanlon.com (*moderate–expensive*)

Victorian country house set in an 18-hole parkland golf course. In the grounds is a fine example of a portal dolmen, as well as a pool, gym and tennis courts. Families are welcome, and there are price reductions for kids, children's meals, babysitting and riding and fishing nearby.

Smarmore Castle

Smarmore, Ardee, Co. Louth, t (041) 685 7176; t/f (041) 685 7650 (*luxury*)

This 14th-century building has been completely refurbished and now incorporates a fitness and leisure complex with a 22-metre indoor heated swimming pool, toddler's pool, gym, sauna, steam room and jacuzzi.

The Station House Hotel

Killmessan, Co. Meath, t (046) 902 5239, f (046) 902 5588, www.thestationhousehotel.com (*moderate*)

A converted 1850s railway station that's now a very pleasant hotel with price reductions for kids; also children's meals, gardens, plus fishing nearby.

Country houses

Ghan House

Carlingford, Co. Louth, t (042) 937 3682, f (042) 937 3772, www.ghanhouse.com (*luxury*)

You'll find luxury and comfort at this 18th-century Georgian manor in the medieval town of Carlingford, with views over Carlingford Lough and the Mountains of Mourne. Owners Paul and Joyce Carroll go out of their way to make you welcome. It's the variety and quality of the cooking that really makes this place special, though. The proprietors also run a cookery school and hold gourmet nights in their renowned restaurant. Everything is perfectly judged, and children are offered their own choice of simple gourmet-style foods. More independent and quieter en-suite family accommodation is available in a converted dairy next door, where youngsters can sleep in bunk beds. A good base for water-sports and hill walking.

Loughcrew House

Oldcastle, Co. Meath, t (049) 854 1356, f (049) 854 1921, www.loughcrew.com (*expensive*)

The Napers run a school for gilding and painting restoration as well as this B&B in their grand house on an estate that's been in the family for centuries. Children are welcome and families find the house and nearby Loughcrew refreshing and fascinating.

Mountainstown

Castletown, Kilpatrick, Navan, Co. Meath, t (046) 9054154/9054195 (*moderate*)

Children are welcome in this beautiful 17th-century house, on a wooded estate with peacocks on the lawn.

B&Bs and guesthouses

The Gables

Dundalk Road, Ardee, Co. Louth, **t** (041) 685 3789 (*inexpensive*)

Families welcome for simple accommodation.

Ravensdale Lodge Equestrian Centre

Ravensdale, Dundalk, Co. Louth, **t/f** (042) 937 1034 **www.ravensdalelodge.com** (*expensive*)

Accommodation with horse riding tuition – from beginners' trails to mountain treks.

Hostels

Slane Farm Hostel

Harlinstown House, Slane, Co. Meath, **t** (041) 988 4985, **www.slanefarmhostel.ie** (*inexpensive*)

This independent hostel is in the middle of the Boyne Valley on a working farm with a fairy fort. Ensuite family and dormitory rooms are available.

Self-catering

Kiltale Cottage

Kiltale, Dunsany, Co. Meath, **t** (046) 9436679, **www.irishholidayhomes.com** (*moderate*)

This self-catering 16th-century cottage in rural surroundings sleeps six. There's a children's playground, pony rides and a farm to visit nearby.

Camping and caravanning

Gyles Caravan and Camping Park

Riverstown, Co. Louth, **t** (042) 937 6262 (*moderate*)

Set in the Cooley peninsula beneath the Slieve Foy mountains overlooking Dundalk Bay. Facilities include a poolroom, leisure centre with gym, bar, sauna, children's playground and a nearby beach.

Westmeath and Longford

Hotels

The Village Inn

Tyrellspass, Co. Westmeath, **t** (044) 23171 (*moderate*)

A cosy, period townhouse hotel offering excellent service and food. The building forms part of an elegant crescent around the village green.

Country houses

Mornington House

Mornington, Multyfarnham, near Mullingar, Co. Westmeath, **t** (044) 72191, **f** (044) 72338, **www.mornington.ie** (*moderate*)

Teenagers and parents seeking quiet will enjoy this lovely country house whose two dogs act as the welcoming party and whose proprietors Anne and Warwick O'Hara will ensure your stay is restful. Their own vegetables and homegrown herbs flavour delicious, candlelit dinners served before a peat fire. The beautiful grounds are near Lake Derravaragh, to which you can walk.

B&Bs and guesthouses

Shannon Side House

Termonbarry, near Cloondara, Co. Longford, **t** (043) 26052 (*inexpensive*)

Comfortable house on the edge of the Shannon. Mr Keenan is an expert on fishing matters and has a boat available.

Toberphelim House

Granard, Co. Longford, **t** (043) 86568, **f** (043) 86568, (*moderate*)

Pleasant old farmhouse owned by a friendly family, the Smyths, who are also family-friendly.

Woodlands Farm

Streamstown, Mullingar, Co. Meath, **t** (044) 26414 (*inexpensive*)

Very typical of Irish farmhouses, Mrs Maxwell's is crammed with holy pictures, welcoming and has delicious food.

Self-catering

Mullingar Equestrian Centre

Athlone Road, Mullingar, Co. Westmeath, **t** (044) 48331/40569, **f** (044) 49004, **www.mullingare-questrian.com** (*moderate*)

Self-catering cottage that sleeps 8, and also 4 en-suite rooms at a well-equipped riding centre.

Camping and caravanning

Lough Derravaragh Camping and Leisure Park

Multyfarnham, near Mullingar, Co. Westmeath, **t** (044) 71500 (*inexpensive*).

Good facilities in a lovely location near the lough: excellent for walks, riding, sailing and other sports.

MUNSTER

County Cork

Cork City

Hotels

Jurys Cork Hotel

Western Road, **t** (021) 427 6622, **f** (021) 427 4477, **www.jurysdoyle.com** (*moderate–expensive*)

Lovely wood-panelled hotel with sports facilities including indoor and outdoor pools, a riverside garden and squash court. There are discounts for children, an outdoor playground and children's meals in the restaurant.

Metropole Ryan Hotel

McCurtain St, **t** (021) 450 8122, **f** (021) 450 6450, **www.metropoleh.com** (*moderate*)

Old-fashioned charm and excellent facilities are available, including three pools, two dining areas with views over the River Lee, and the Met Tavern.

Country houses

Farran House

Farran, Cork, **t** (021) 733 1215, **www.farranhouse.com** (*luxury*)

Families are welcome at this elegant country house, set in 12 acres of mature beech woods just west of Cork City. The rooms have huge bathrooms.

B&Bs and guesthouses

D'Arcy's

7 Sidney Place, Wellington Road, **t** (021) 450 4658/450 4522, **f** (021) 450 2791, **www.darcysguesthouse.com** (*expensive*)

Families are welcome at this ex-brewery now run by a friendly family who provide home cooking and fresh baking for breakfast in the basement. It's tough climbing to the top, but the views of the city from the larger bedrooms are worth it.

Garnish House

Western Road, Cork, **t** (021) 427 5111, **f** (021) 427 3872, **www.garnish.ie** (*inexpensive–moderate*)

In the morning at Garnish House you will find tables covered in crisp white linen tastefully laid with fresh flowers and china, and be amazed by an extraordinary breakfast – an array of stewed and fresh fruits, homemade breads and yogurts, Irish cheeses and anything you could possibly think of. If even that isn't enough, a very extensive menu is also on hand. Even the most fussy vegetarians will feel they are in hog heaven in this surprising jewel of Cork guesthouses, and children are made very welcome. The only drawback can be that parking is sometimes tight.

Hostels

Cork International An Óige

1/2 Redclyffe, Western Road, **t** 454 3289, **f** (021) 434 3715 (*inexpensive*)

Just across from the University of Cork, this central hostel has ensuite family rooms, a kitchen, and laundry. It's a bit bare, but clean and private.

Sheila's

4 Belgrave Place, Wellington Road, **t** (021) 450 0940 (*inexpensive*)

Conveniently central – north of the river – with family rooms.

Around County Cork

Hotels

Blarney Park Hotel

Blarney, **t** (021) 438 5281, **www.blarneypark.com** (*moderate*)

Not far from Cork city, this hotel has an especially ample kid-friendly leisure centre, with toddler pools, waterslide, pool, saunas, steam room, gym and playroom, plus a therapy centre with alternative therapies, and a babysitting/listening service.

The Blue Haven

Pearse Street, Kinsale, **t** (021) 477 2209 (*moderate*)

A strong candidate for best hotel (3-star) in Kinsale: cosy and comfortable with excellent food.

Casey's

Baltimore, **t** (028) 20197 (*moderate*)

The best type of small hotel: welcoming and comfortable, with excellent food in the bar and restaurant.

Midleton Park Hotel

Midleton, t (021) 463 1767 (*moderate–expensive*)

This is quite a luxurious residence for the price, with a leisure and 'wellness' centre, and indoor pool. The décor is beautiful, the atmosphere relaxed and the restaurant food is superb. Low rates for children sharing with parents.

O'Donovan's Hotel

44 Pearse Street, Clonakilty, t (023) 33250 (*moderate*)

Old-fashioned hotel in the town centre, with a public bar, and family rates.

Sea View House Hotel

Ballylickey, t (027) 50073, f (027) 51555 (*moderate*)

Cots, high chairs and babysitting are provided in this hotel with old-fashioned Irish hospitality as well as good food. Two cottages available to rent.

Westlodge Hotel

Bantry, t (027) 50360, f (027) 50438, www.westlodgehotel.ie (*moderate*)

A scenic location just outside town and activities for children from June–Aug, along with a leisure centre with toddler and children's pools, sauna, jacuzzi and gym, and also gardens, pitch'n'putt, tennis courts and playground. Self-catering cottages, babysitting and kids' meals also available.

Country houses

Assolas Country House

Kanturk, t (029) 50015, www.assolas.com (*luxury*)

Children are welcome in this superb 17th-century house among mature trees that run right down to the river. Monks lived here until the 16th century. Tennis, fishing and croquet, and delicious food.

Ballymaloe House

Shanagarry, t (021) 465 2531, f (021) 465 2021, www.ballymaloe.com (*expensive*)

A special trip to Myrtle Allen's Georgian house paradise is well worth it, for elegant rooms, friendly service, fabulous food and generous helpings served in a room decorated to create a French-style country atmosphere. Chefs from all over Ireland come here to learn at the celebrated Ballymaloe School, which sparked the current revolution in Irish cuisine. The whole Allen family are involved in the enterprise, and have created organic gardens that curl around greystone farmhouses and a summer house covered in seashells. Children can dine early on special fare made for them and in summer they can swim in an outdoor pool (not supervised) or play in a sand pit and on a slide. There's a small golf course and tennis court, plus a craft and kitchen shop, and fishing and riding can be arranged. Babysitting also available.

Ballyvolane House

Castlelyons, near Fermoy, t (025) 36349, f (025) 36781, www.ballyvolanehouse.ie (*luxury*)

Run by Mrs Merrie Green and her friendly family, this lovely old Georgian house is set in beautiful grounds, and locally produced vegetables are used in the cooking. Children are welcome.

Bantry House

Bantry, t (027) 50047 (*luxury*)

Children are welcome in this converted wing of one of Ireland's most beautiful stately homes, with a plush library, snooker room and extensive gardens at guests' disposal.

Lettercollum House

Timoleague, t (023) 46251 www.lettercollum.ie (*moderate*)

Families are welcome in this ex-Sisters of Mercy convent with fine food, prepared with homegrown organic produce by Karen Austin, who also runs cookery classes. Beaches for swimming are nearby.

Rock Cottage

Barnatonicane, near Schull, t (028) 35538, f (028) 35538 (*moderate*)

A Georgian hunting lodge renovated with bright bedrooms, wicker furniture and wooden floors by a German lady chef who spent happy holidays in Ireland as a child, and welcomes families.

B&Bs and guesthouses

Avonmore House

South Abbey, Youghal, t (024) 92617 (*inexpensive*)

Elegant old house with beautiful rooms; a good bargain.

Ballymakeigh House

Killeagh, Youghal, t (024) 95184, f (024) 95379, www.ballymakeighhouse.com (*expensive*)

Margaret Browne, award-winning cook and owner of Browne's Restaurant, runs this guest-house with aplomb, ensuring you feel at home. In the middle of her husband's dairy farm, the plant-filled conservatory welcomes you into a farmhouse with nouveau Irish dinners and breakfasts sprinkled with herbs. You'll have a peaceful time here.

Castle Salem

Near Rosscarbery, t (023) 48381 (*inexpensive*)

A family room is available in this atmospheric B&B, where William Penn once slept. Donations are gratefully received to preserve this impressive 15th-century castle owned by the Daly family.

Grove House

Ahakistra, Durras, t (027) 67060 (*inexpensive*)

An old and pretty farmhouse on the Sheep's Head Peninsula. Sample the delicious honey from the garden and the free-range eggs.

Magannagan Farm

Derryconnery, Glengarriff, t (027) 63361 (*inexpensive*)

Good high teas in this small, good-value cottage.

Sovereign House

Newmans Mall, Kinsale, t (021) 477 2850, **www.**sovereignhouse.com (*expensive*)

Striking Queen Anne house converted into a very comfortable guesthouse, with cobbled streets leading to the harbour.

Schull Central B&B

Schull, t (028) 28227 (*inexpensive*)

Efficiently run, comfortable B&B, handy for Schull harbour and with all rooms en-suite.

Seacourt

Butlerstown, t (023) 40151 (*inexpensive*)

Beautiful historic house (1760), with views of the Seven Heads Peninsula.

Self-catering

Courtmacsherry Coastal Cottages

Courtmacsherry, t (023) 46198 (*inexpensive-expensive*)

Eight luxury cottages, with use of hotel facilities.

The Castle

Castletownshend, t (028) 36100 (*moderate*)

Mrs Cochrane-Townshend has a choice of apartments in 18th-century buildings.

Glenview House

Midleton, t (021) 463 1680, **f** (021) 463 4680, **www.**glenviewmidleton.com (*expensive*)

Beside a Georgian guesthouse sit two self-catering coach-house cottages, one with disabled facilities, which sleep 2–6. Guide dogs welcome.

Green Lodge

Trawnamadree, Ballylickey, Bantry, t (027) 66146 (*inexpensive*)

A single-storey terrace in an enclosed courtyard, with disabled access, next to an organic garden on 10 acres in a beautiful part of West Cork.

Hostels

Cape Clear Island An Oige

Cape Clear Island, t (028) 39144 (*inexpensive*)

Basic family rooms available for summer only (opens 1 June) in this isolated place.

Maria's Schoolhouse

Cahergal, Union Hall, t/f (028) 33002, **www.**mariasschoolhouse.ie (*inexpensive*)

An English couple run this converted school as a B&B-style upmarket hostel that makes it perfect even for the largest family. Family and dormitory rooms with bunkbeds are available.

Shiplake Mountain Hostel

Dunmanway, t (023) 45750, **www.**shiplakemountainhostel.com (*inexpensive–moderate*)

Vary Knivett's restored traditional farmhouse in the mountains has a self-catering kitchen where you can cook the organic vegetables sold by the owners. They also serve home-baked breads, pizzas, vegan and vegetarian meals in their restaurant. Families and children are welcome. Excellent walking and cycling area, plus bikes for hire and camping available.

Camping and caravanning

Barleycove Holiday Park

Crookhaven, Skibbereen, t (028) 35302, **f** (021) 430 7230 (*inexpensive*)

Full camping site facilities, from laundry to fast-food restaurant, are available here.

County Kerry

Hotels

Brandon Court Hotel

Traylee, t (066) 712 9666, **f** (066) 712 5019, **www.**brandonhotel.ie (*expensive*)

Guests here have access to a swimming pool, and there are babysitting and listening services, price reductions and children's meals, plus other sports and leisure facilities. Cots and high chairs are also available.

Butler Arms Hotel

Waterville, **t** (066) 947 4144, **f** (066) 947 4520, **www.butlerarms.com** (*moderate–expensive*)

There are fantastic sea views from this intimate, family-run, pleasantly old-fashioned hotel. A lovely place to stay for salmon or trout fishing, and there's also a sandy beach and riding for the kids, plus children's meals, babysitting, price reductions and gardens to run around in.

Castlerosse Hotel and Leisure Centre

Killarney, **t** (064)31144, **f** (064) 31031, **www.castlerossehotelkillarney.com** (*moderate*)

Great lake and mountain views from the self-catering suites or the main hotel, which caters well for disabled guests. Golf and hotel packages and an inviting leisure centre offering Swedish massages. Children's meals, price discounts, gardens, swimming pool, babysitting and tennis are all available, plus riding and fishing nearby.

The Climbers' Inn

Glencar, **t** (066) 976 0101, **www.climbersinn.com** (*moderate*)

Get away from it all at this wild mountain location, 30 mins and a million miles in some respects from Killarney. There are cottagey bedrooms in the inn and a hostel behind. The on-site walking and climbing centre offers wilderness walking tours.

Dingle Skellig Hotel

Dingle, **t** (066) 915 0200, **f** (066) 915 1501 **www.dingleskellig.com** (*moderate–expensive*)

Family-friendly hotel with leisure facilities that include a children's pool with waterfall and bubble feature, Fungi Kids Club at weekends and school holidays, indoor and outdoor play areas, playroom, crèche, interconnecting rooms, babysitting and separate kids' menus and mealtimes.

Dromquinna Manor

Kenmare, **t** (064) 41657, **www.dromquinna.com** (*moderate*)

Playground, babysitting, children's rates and menus at this very comfortable house with lovely views over the water, and water-skiing and horse-riding and pony-trekking nearby.

Glencar House Hotel

Glencar, **t** (066) 976 0102, **f** (066) 976 0167, **www.glencarhouse.com** (*moderate*)

Remote, comfortable, clean and efficient country house hotel in stunning surroundings and with boats to hire on nearby lakes. Mountains frame this area of Special Conservation, an ethic mirrored in the largely organic menu. Children's facilities include price reductions, kids' meals, games room, tennis and gardens.

Killarney Park Hotel

Kenmare Place, **t** (064) 35555, **f** (064) 35266, **www.killarneyparkhotel.ie** (*expensive*)

Modern luxury in the heart of Killarney – marble floors, antique furniture, pool and huge suites. A brand new health spa complements the existing games room, library and billiard room. Children's meals, price reductions, babysitting and playroom.

Killarney Ryan Hotel and Leisure Centre

Killarney, **t** (064) 31555, **f** (064) 34001, **www.ryan-hotels.com** (*luxury*)

Leisure and family facilities include a children's activity programme in school holidays and at weekends, crèche (up to age 3), supervised activities (ages 3+), family events, 24-hour parents' kitchen , babysitting, playroom and outdoor playground, laundry service and leisure centre.

The Park Hotel

High Street, Kenmare, **t** (064) 41200, **f** (064) 41402, **www.parkkenmare.com** (*luxury*)

For a taste of the high life, this château-style, award-winning hotel has every modern comfort in rooms furnished with fine antiques. Thoughtful extras are left in your bedroom; children will exult over the nuts and delicious homemade biscuits. Views are exemplary and you feel a deep sense of rest as you breathe in the soothing Kerry air. Meals are made with organic local produce. There are very good babysitting and baby-listening services, and price reductions for families, games room, gym, gardens, tennis and numerous sports facilities.

Sheen Falls Lodge

Kenmare, **t** (064) 41600, **f** (064) 41386, **www.sheenfallslodge.ie** (*luxury*)

Popular with families because it has a leisure centre and lots of activities that children enjoy. This hotel is in a beautiful location with sunny, low-key décor. The rooms are elegant, the food is lavish and imaginative and there's even a helipad for visiting dignitaries. Parents can enjoy health treatments in the spa and fine dining overlooking the Sheen Waterfalls, plus gardens and an outdoor play area for kids, children's meals, price reductions, games room and babysitting.

Country houses

Glendalough House

Caragh Lake, Killorglin, t (066) 976 9156 (*moderate*)

Josephine Roder-Bradshaw is an excellent hostess and has furnished her house lovingly. There are great views over the lake.

B&Bs and guesthouses

Aisling House

Castlegregory, t (066) 713 9134 (*inexpensive*)

Clean and comfortable, with good breakfasts.

Castlemorris House

Ballymullen, Tralee, t (066) 718 0060 (*expensive*)

Children are welcome in this big 18th-century house in extensive gardens, a short walk from Tralee centre. A pleasant drawing room, spacious bedrooms, open fires and a friendly atmosphere.

Doyle's Townhouse

John Street, Dingle, t (066) 915 1174, www.doylesofdingle.com (*moderate*)

One of the most enjoyable places to stay in the country; rooms are full of individuality, and sitting-room shelves groan with books over which you can linger by a warm fire. The bar and restaurant next door are famous for their conviviality and food.

Fuchsia House

Muckross Road, Killarney, t (064) 33743, f (064) 36588, www.fuchsiahouse.com (*moderate*)

Children are welcome in this newly built Victorian-style house whose owners have made it into a peaceful, welcoming home.

Hawthorne House

Shelbourne Street, Kenmare, t (064) 41035 (*inexpensive*)

Families are welcome at this comfortable B&B, with all bedrooms en-suite and delicious food.

Inveraray Farm Guesthouse

Killarney, t (064) 44224 (*inexpensive*)

Playground, playroom, pony rides for children, babysitting, home baking and tours arranged.

The Phoenix

Shanahill East, Boolteens, Castlemaine, t (066) 976 6284 (*moderate*)

This slightly hippie B&B serves vegetarian and vegan foods only in a little café run by its Swiss-trained cook/owner and her Kerry-born husband.

Suan na Mara

Camp, t (066) 713 9258 (*moderate*)

Award-winning Laura Ashley-style home with mountain views, private walk to sandy beach, extensive breakfast menu, own pitch'n'putt course, cot and babysitting available.

Self-catering

Stone House

Ventry, t (066) 915 9962 (*inexpensive–moderate*)

A traditional three-bedroom stone house; the owner also has other comfortable properties.

The Cottage

Patrick O'Leary, Sneem, t (064) 45132 (*inexpensive*)

Two bedrooms, pleasantly placed near the sea.

Hostels

There are An Oige Hostels at Dunquin with family rooms, Ballyferriter, Beaufort, Killarney and on Valentia Island.

Ballintagart Hostel

Dingle, t (066) 915 1454 (*inexpensive*)

Converted 18th-century hunting lodge with family rooms available.

Collis Sandes House

Oakpark, Tralee, t/f (066) 712 8658, www.colsands.com (*inexpensive*)

Family rooms, self-catering kitchens and a laundry are available in this imposing 19th-century country house set in 15 acres of woodland on the edge of Tralee, with camping areas. It hosts traditional music sessions in the evenings.

Westward Court

Mary Street, Tralee, t (066) 718 0081, f (066) 718 0082 (*inexpensive*)

Family-friendly purpose-built hostel with en-suite and family rooms, private car park, breakfast and cots available, superior disabled access.

Camping and caravanning

Campail Teach An Aragail Oratory House Camping

Gallarus, Dingle, t (066) 915 5143, f (066) 915 5504, (*inexpensive*)

Killarney Flesk Caravan and Camping Park

Killarney, t (064) 31704, f (064) 35439 (*moderate*)

County Limerick

Hotels

Adare Manor Hotel

Adare, **t** (061) 396 566, **f** (061) 396 124, **www.adaremanor.ie** (*luxury*)

The former house of the Earls of Dunraven is a mix of Victorian, Gothic and Tudor fantasy architecture styles, with beautiful grounds, riding, clay-pigeon shooting and an 18-hole golf course. There's an indoor pool and fitness centre, plus children's meals, family discounts and babysitting.

Castletroy Park

Dublin Road, Limerick, **t** (061) 335 566, **f** (061) 331 117, **www.castletroy-park.ie** (*expensive*)

Modern 4-star hotel that's the best in the city, with fine food. Children's meals, price reductions, swimming pool and gardens are also available.

Dunraven Arms Hotel

Adare, **t** (061) 396 633, **f** (061) 396 541, **www.dunravenhotel.com** (*expensive*)

Old-world hotel, with appealing rooms, friendly staff and a huge pool and garden. Children's meals, price reductions and babysitting are available.

Country houses

Ash Hill Stud

Kilmallock, **t** (063) 98035, **f** (063) 98752, **www.ashhill.com** (*expensive*)

Children are welcome in this imposing 18th-century mansion with big, comfortable bedrooms, glorious plasterwork and shades of Anglo-Irish splendour – the front door leads straight into the stable yard. Set on a working horse-breeding farm; one self-catering apartment is also available.

Ballyteigne House

Rockhill, Bruree, **t** (063) 90575 (*inexpensive*)

Families are welcome at Mrs Johnson's warm and hospitable home; it has good food, and a convenient location for Shannon Airport.

B&Bs and guesthouses

Alexandra Guesthouse

5–6 O'Connell Avenue, Limerick, **t** (061) 400 433 (*inexpensive*)

Attractive Victorian house with en-suite rooms and only 5 mins walk from the city centre.

Cussens Cottage

Ballygreennan, Bulgaden, Kilmallock, **t/f** (063) 98926 (*inexpensive*)

Nearly two acres of organic gardens supply the kitchen here. Breakfasts and dinners are vegetarian, and vegan and macrobiotic foods are available. Children are welcome; disabled access.

Mount Gerard

O'Connell Ave, Limerick, **t** (061) 31498 (*inexpensive*)

Family B&B conveniently close to the city centre.

Self-catering

Springfield Castle

Drumcollogher, **t** (063) 83162 (*expensive*)

Fabulous historic home available for holiday lets.

Hostels

Barrington's Lodge and Hostel

Georges Quay, Limerick, **t** (061) 415 222, **f** (061) 416 611 (*inexpensive*)

These family-friendly premises offer children's meals, a playground and indoor playroom, babysitting service, cots and high chairs.

County Clare

Hotels

The Falls Hotel

Ennistymon, **t** (065) 707 1004, **f** (065) 707 1367, **www.fallshotel.net** (*moderate*)

With a high reputation of 50 years standing, this attractive hotel sits above the river that runs through Ennistymon. Its faded charm is perked up by a lively bar but there are quiet rooms for families. The grounds cover 50 acres of woodland and glen. Riding, fishing and river walks are available, plus children's meals, family rates and babysitting.

The Old Ground Hotel

O'Connell Street, Ennis, **t** (065) 682 8127, **f** (065) 682 8112, **www.flynnhotels.com** (*moderate*)

Built in 1749, this pretty ivy-covered hotel in the middle of Ennis has 83 rooms with antiques, and a garden. The Old Ground pub has entertainment from cabaret to Irish music in summer. Babysitting, children's meals plus price reductions are offered, as well as high chairs in the restaurant.

Temple Gate Hotel

The Square, Ennis, t (065) 682 3300, f (065) 682 3322, www.templegatehotel.com (*moderate*)

Built on the site of a 19th-century convent, this excellent modern hotel still has a sense of its former inhabitants' prayerful peace. Well-placed in central Ennis, it has an award-winning restaurant and an enjoyable pub, where you can have light meals or snacks. Family rooms, children's meals, babysitting, and riding and fishing nearby.

Country houses

Berry Lodge

Annagh, Milltown Mowbay, t (065) 708 7022, f (065) 708 7011, www.berrylodge.com (*moderate*)

Good food and lodgings from a lady who teaches home economics for local schools in her kitchen.

Clifden House

Corofin, t (065) 683 7692, www.clifdenhouse-countyclare.com (*moderate*)

Children are welcomed to this highly eccentric 18th-century house by Lake Inchiquin, near the Burren. It is associated with Richard Burton, translator of *The Arabian Nights*, and has been described as 'being slowly coaxed into compromise with the 20th century'. Two charming if basic apartments in the carriage house sleep 6–8. Children and romantics love this place with a tree house and walled garden of organic vegetables, which are used in the cooking.

Fergus View

Kilnaboy, Corofin, t (065) 683 7606, f (065) 683 7192 (*moderate*)

Families are welcome, and there's great food (give notice for special diets) and a garden sloping to a river. Also a self-catering cottage next door.

Gregan's Castle

Near Ballyvaughan, t (065) 707 7005, www.gregans.ie (*expensive*)

Not actually a castle but an old manor house, which serves delicious food and has comfortable rooms. Set at the top of the Corkscrew Hills amid green gardens, this makes a fantastic contrast to the Burren's moonscape, with wonderful views.

Lismacteigue

Ballyvaughan, t (065) 707 7040 (*inexpensive*)

Children are welcome in this 500-year-old thatched farmhouse in a ring fort, on a green road in the Burren.

Tinarana House

Killaloe, t (061) 376 966, f (061) 375 369, www.tinaranahouse.com (*inexpensive–moderate*)

Older children may enjoy this most, but small ones love the grounds. In 300 acres of woods and open countryside with deer, pheasants and other wildlife, this Victorian mansion has bedrooms with magnificent views across a valley by Lough Derg. Organic cuisine and health treatments are offered.

B&Bs and guesthouses

The Burren Haven B&B

St Brendan's Road, Lisdoonvarna, t (065) 74366 (*inexpensive*)

Children are welcome at this peaceful family home in Lisdoonvarna. Vegan, macrobiotic and vegetarian diets are catered for but non-vegetarians are welcome, as are well-behaved pets. Massage and aromatherapy can be arranged.

Doolin Activity Lodge

Doolin, t (065) 707 4888, f (065) 707 4877 www.doolinlodge.com (*inexpensive–moderate*)

For outdoor types who don't place too much importance on fine breakfasts and the like, these restored stone buildings near Doolin Pier have modern ensuite bedrooms and self-catering apartments (available weekly or nightly). Helpful staff can book (preferably in advance) many local sports activities: caving, diving, walking, cycling and golf.

Lahardan House

Crusheen, Ennis, t (065) 682 7128 (*inexpensive*)

Dilly Griffey's old family house has comfortable rooms with en-suite baths and home cooking.

Self-catering

The NatureQuest Centre

Blackweir Bridge, Kilkee, t (065) 905 6789, f (065) 905 1843, www.naturequest.ie (*moderate*)

Serenity is assured as you gaze out from these five superbly furnished, wooden-floored apartments onto Poulnasherry Bay. Binoculars are provided so you can observe wildlife from your living room. NatureQuest's naturalists also lead field trips, and can tell you all about the natural history of Loop Head. Dolphin-watching, walks, riding and birdwatching and photography workshops can be arranged. An indoor swimming pool and some exercise machines are also on-site, and the owners often offer guests freshly baked bread.

Tipperary and Waterford

Hotels

Cashel Palace Hotel

Main St, Cashel, Co. Tipperary, t (062) 62707, f (062) 61521, www.cashel-palace.ie (*luxury*)

Here you will find elegant living in a beautiful 18th-century house, just off the main street. They do not have family rooms, but there is a mews house with rooms with interconnecting doors.

O'Shea's Hotel

Strand St, Tramore, Co. Waterford, t (051) 381246, f (051)390144, www.osheas-hotel.com (*moderate*)

Small family-run hotel close to the beach, with price reductions, children's meals and babysitting.

Round Tower Hotel

College Road, Ardmore, Co. Waterford, t (024) 94494 (*inexpensive*)

Simple accommodation is on offer in this old former convent, with a restaurant. Also children's meals, family rates, a playroom and babysitting.

Waterford Castle Hotel

The Island, Ballinaskill, Waterford, t (051) 878 203, f (051) 878 342, www.waterfrodcastle.com (*luxury*)

Three miles (5km) downstream from Waterford, this Anglo-Norman castle sits on its own 310-acre island. The interior is luxurious, with indoor pool and sports facilities. Children's price reductions, meals and babysitting are offered, as well as a golf course, tennis courts and beautiful grounds.

Country houses

Ballycormac House

Aglish, Borrisokane, Co. Tipperary, t (067) 21129, f (067) 21200 (*moderate*)

A 300-year-old farmhouse lovingly restored by American ex-pats; exceptional breakfasts, they do dinners too, and will organize activities for guests.

Bansha House

Bansha, Co. Tipperary, t (062) 54194, f (062) 54215 (*moderate*)

Children will love this early Georgian farmhouse covered in ivy, where a tiny terrier may greet them inquisitively upon arrival. After you settle in, it's likely you'll be given a hot drink and homemade cake or biscuits. Then you can look out at some of the 100 acres of farmland owned by hosts John and Mary Marnan. In the morning, after a fine Irish breakfast, Mary may encourage you to explore the walker's paradise beyond the house, or perhaps show you some of her horses. If you're not careful, you may find yourself renting their guest cottage and staying longer in this charming village

Lismacue House

Bansha, Co. Tipperary, t (062) 54106, f (062) 54126 (*luxury*)

A beautiful lime-tree avenue leads to this gracious 17th-century house. The owners offer a warm welcome, with delicious dinners and breakfasts and a sense of Anglo-Irish tradition – not to mention local advice, particularly about horses. This is horse country: trekking parties often stay here and people come looking for horses to buy.

B&Bs and guesthouses

Brown's Townhouse

29 South Parade, Waterford, t (051) 870 594, f (051) 871 923, www.brownstown-house.com (*expensive*)

This charming late-Victorian house is decorated in period style and has a family room for four at the top of the house. Helpful proprietor Leslie Brown and his Labrador give a warm welcome. A hearty breakfast – of fresh fruit salad, homemade bread and jams accompanying a full fry-up, vegetarian if preferred – is served at a long table. Conveniently located for Waterford centre; you couldn't find a better spot from which to discover the town.

Castle Farm

Milstreet, Cappagh, Co. Waterford, t (058) 68049, f (058) 68099 (*moderate*)

Not as grand as it sounds, but it has a lovely restored 15th-century wing and is very homely. Tennis, trout fishing and riding are available.

Sion Hill House

Ferrybank, Waterford, t (051) 851 558, f (051) 851 678 (*moderate*)

Families are welcome in this early 19th-century house with beautiful views of Waterford and the River Suir. Its lovely gardens have been restored to their original condition of 250 years ago, and the house itself is full of antiques and memorabilia. For children the house and garden will be a fairy palace full of treasures.

Self-catering

Anner Castle

Ballinamore, near Clonmel, Co. Tipperary, t (052) 33365, www.annercastle.com (*moderate*)

Accommodation in a romantic 19th-century folly, set in landscaped parkland.

Garrykennedy Cottage

Garrykennedy, Co. Tipperary, **t/f** (01) 633 5487, **www.garrykennedycottage.com** (*moderate*)

Not far from Killaloe, this small village on Lough Derg has a lovely terraced cottage (c.1780). Flowers on the table meet you, and maybe a crackling fire. There's a small garden; bathrooms and two of the bedrooms are up a spiral staircase. As much of its original fittings as possible have been kept, and the cottage is a great place to settle into a small community – it's between two pubs, one of which has food, and often music. It's also ideal for boat trips, and morning walks by the lake are wonderful.

Eco Booley

Clogheen, Co. Tipperary, t (052) 65191, www.ecobooley.com (*inexpensive*)

A pioneering eco-friendly cottage.

Killaghy Castle

Mullinahone, Co. Tipperary, t (052) 53112 (*inexpensive*)

An 18th-century manor farmhouse with a Norman castle attached, and horse-riding close by. The castle accommodates 18 people, self-catering.

Riverrun Cottages

Terryglass, Co. Tipperary, t (067) 22125, f (067) 22187, www.riverrun.ie (*moderate*)

Three and 4-star cottages in the middle of the country near a small village with two pubs, a craft shop, post office, village store and a church. There are outdoor activities on and around Lough Derg.

Hostels

Cashel Holiday Hostel

John St, Cashel, Co. Tipperary, t (062) 62330 (*inexpensive*)

Cheerful hostel in an old town-house.

Rock House

Dundrum Road, Cashel, Co. Tipperary, t (062) 61003 (*inexpensive*)

A restored 18th-century coach house; hostel and self-catering accommodation available.

CONNACHT

County Galway

Hotels

Ardilaun House Hotel

Taylors Hill, Galway City, t (091) 521 433, www.ardilaunhousehotel.ie (*luxury*)

Large mansion in wooded grounds with a leisure centre and indoor swimming pool. There are good rates for children under age 15 sharing a room with their parents, and under-3s stay free.

Brennan's Yard Hotel

Lower Merchant's Road, Galway City, t (091) 568 166, f (091) 568 262, (*moderate*)

A nice town hotel with stripped pine surroundings decorated with locally-made pottery. Children aged 2–12 are charged half-price staying in a room with their parents, while those under 2 stay free.

Day's Hotel

Inishbofin Island, t (095) 45809 (*moderate*)

A hotel in a very special location on remote Inishbofin, a family-run, clean and friendly place right on the island's pier. The son of the house runs music nights, children are welcome, and facilities for divers are also available.

Doonmore Hotel

Inishbofin, t (095) 45804 (*moderate*)

A simple and clean alternative on Inishbofin with good local seafood.

Galway Ryan Hotel

Dublin Road, Galway City, t (091) 753 191, f (091) 753 187, www.ryan-hotels.com (*expensive*)

Children are welcome at this modern hotel on Galway's outskirts. Its leisure centre has swimming and toddlers' pools, games room, sports hall, gym, tennis courts and an organized activity programme for all ages; the restaurant has children's menus.

Ostan Inis Meáin

Inishmann, Aran Islands, t (099) 73020, www.galway.net/pages/inismeain/ (*moderate*)

Family rooms are available at the only hotel on the island, which was made famous by the playwright JM Synge when he came here in the 1900s.

Zetland House Hotel

Cashel Bay, Connemara, t (095) 31111, f (095) 31117, www.zetland.com (*expensive*)

A converted hunting lodge in an isolated setting overlooking Cashel Bay; the old wing has more character than the new. Owner John Prendergast trained at the Ritz in Paris and offers award-winning cuisine. Tennis, billiards and other activities are available, and children are welcome.

Country houses

Cregg Castle

Corrandulla, near Galway City, t (091) 791 434, www.creggcastle.com (*moderate*)

Children are welcome to explore this estate-sized farm with friendly dogs, a cat, donkey, chickens, sheep and cattle, around what looks more like a manor house than a traditional castle. Its family rooms are big and airy, with space for 2–3 youngsters. Board games are on hand to entertain on wet evenings, and friendly proprietors Pat and Ann Marie often play Irish music, usually inspiring a few budding musicans to join them for a session.

Crocnaraw House

Moyard, near Clifden, t/f (095) 41068 (*moderate*)

Small, cosy country house with an otherworldy atmosphere – not surprising, since Crocnaraw means 'hill of the faery fort'. Children and families are welcome. Delicious food is prepared by owner Lucy Fretwell, with local organic produce.

Delphi Lodge

Leenane, t (095) 42222, f (095) 42296, www.delphilodge.ie (*expensive*)

A beautiful old house run along traditional lines with tea and biscuits in your room on arrival. Fly-fishing can be arranged and owner Peter Mantle makes every dinner conversation unique. Prince Charles wrote thanking him for his visit. Children are offered early dinners, separate from adults. Self-catering cottages are available.

Dolphin Beach House

Lower Sky Road, Clifden, t (095) 21204, f (095) 22935 (*moderate*)

Children are welcome in this luxurious 19th-century farmhouse where the owners grow their own organic vegetables. You might be able to watch dolphins in the bay from your bedroom window if you're lucky, then pop over to a private cove for a swim.

Lisdonagh House

Caherlistrane, t (093) 31163, f (093) 31528, www.lisdonagh.com (*expensive*)

Near the Hill of Knockma, where Finvarra, King of the Faeries, holds court, you'll find this faeryland where dinners and breakfasts prepared from homegrown organic ingredients magically appear in your luxurious 18th-century room. Visitors can be accommodated in the grand house with its *trompe-l'oeil* mural of the Four Virtues, or in a Victorian gate lodge or French-style coach-house apartment. Just outside the main house there is also a 'honeymoon' pavilion suite with apyramid roof and Venetian window. Families are welcome to explore the grounds and fish or row out to the *crannóg* on Lough Hackett where St Patrick is said to have converted the King of Connacht to Christianity. Hosts are friendly but unobtrusive and let you get on with whatever you want to do in the grounds, offering helpful advice when requested. The quiet evenings and centuries-old charm of this estate allow you to truly relax.

Man of Aran Cottage

Inishmore, Aran Islands, t (099) 61301, f (099) 61324 (*moderate*)

Older children and teenagers with their parents are welcome here in high season, while families can rent the whole cottage Nov–Feb. During the main season, Man of Aran's delightful proprietors Joe and Maura Wolfe serve healthy breakfasts, teas and dinners. Joe, originally from Co. Kildare, moved to Inishmore after falling in love with the Arans, while Maura is an Irish-speaking Aran native. The cottage was built for the movie *Man of Aran* by Robert Flaherty, from which it acquired its name. Joe is an enthusiastic organic gardener and Maura prepares tasty drinks and freshly cooked dishes using the herbs and vegetables her husband grows. She can also tell you all about how people lived on Inishmore in her youth.

B&Bs and guesthouses

Ard Alainn

Inishmaan, Aran Islands, t (099) 99 73027 (*inexpensive*)

Near Ard Alainn B&B and Synge's Chair, this recently built 3-bedroom old-style Aran cottage has a lovely view of the ocean and free play-space for children.

Ben View House

Bridge St, Clifden, **t** (095) 21256, **f** (095) 21226 (*inexpensive*)

Truly traditional family-run B&B in the middle of Clifden, with TVs in en-suite rooms; fine breakfasts.

Camillaun

Eighterard, Oughterard, **t** (091) 552 678, **f** (091) 552 439, **www**.camillaun.com (*moderate*)

This comfortable, modern, wooden-floored home is perfect for visitors who, after an excellent breakfast, want to play tennis on hard courts or paddle down the River Owenriff, beside the garden. Environmentalist proprietor Greg Forde can arrange for a guide to take you to Lough Corrib in one of his boats, where you can fish or explore the ruins of two monasteries on Inchagoill Island. Families are welcome here, and he and his teacher wife Deirdre have a child of their own. Good home cooking is offered for breakfast and dinner in a friendly, home-like setting. The village of Oughterard is a short stroll away down a leafy lane.

Col-Mar House

Salahoona, Spiddal, **t** (091) 553247 (*inexpensive*)

This house is in a lovely setting and offers especially good breakfasts. The Keadys are very friendly owners, who prefer old-fashioned ways.

Hazel House Farmhouse

Mausrevagh, Headford, **t** (091) 791204 (*inexpensive*)

You'll get a traditional Irish welcome at this modern bungalow from Mrs Cunningham, who provides tea and scones when you arrive. Matt, the man of the house, plays the accordion, banjo and fiddle, and he is happy to play to his guests.

Killary Lodge

Derrynasliggaun, Leenane, **t** (095) 42276, **f** (095) 42314, **www**.killary.com (*moderate*)

Family rooms are available in this B&B on the shores of Killary Harbour. With advance notice they can cater for special diets and arrange guides for cycling, walking and other outdoor activities.

Norman Villa

86 Lower Salthill, Galway City, **t** (091) 521 131, **www**.normanvilla.com (*moderate*)

This city house has a country atmosphere, with elegance and lighthearted banter indoors and oak trees in the field behind. Children are welcome; two family rooms are available.

Self-catering

Lucy O'Toole

Annaghvane, Bealadangan, **t** (091) 572120 (*moderate*)

Two 200-year-old traditional reed-thatched cottages by the sea, with three bedrooms in each.

Renvyle Thatched Cottages

Renvyle, Tullycross, **t** (095) 43464, **f** (095) 43994, **www**.irishcottageholidays.com (*inexpensive*)

Nine modernized cottages of various sizes.

Hostels

Radharc Na Mara Hostel

West Village, Inisheer, Arans, **t** (099) 75024 (*inexpensive*)

Family and private rooms, and a camping site.

Camping and caravanning

Ballyloughane Caravan and Camping Park

Ballyloughane Beach, Renmore, **t** (091) 755 338/752 029, **f** (091) 753 098 (*inexpensive*)

Renvyle Beach Caravan and Camping Park

Renvyle, **t** (095) 43462, **f** (095) 43894 (Jul-Aug only), (*inexpensive*)

County Mayo

Hotels

Ashford Castle

Cong, **t** (092) 46003, **f** (092) 46260, **www**.ashford.ie (*luxury*)

Stunning grounds surround this opulent castle with very comfortable if rather impersonal rooms full of Victorian furniture. Guests can sail on Lough Corrib or use the onsite health club, while children enjoy Irish music in the Dungeon Bar or ride horses in the grounds of this impressive castle.

Downhill Hotel

Ballina, **t** (096) 21033, **f** (096) 73411 (*moderate*)

Family rooms are available in this hotel with a leisure centre that has an indoor toddler pool and swimming pool. A children's activity club runs in summer.

Westport Woods Hotel and Leisure Centre

Quay Road, Westport, **t** (098) 25811, **f** (098) 26212 (*expensive*)

With a backdrop of woods in Westport town, this lively modern hotel is notable for its 'Kiddies' Club' for 3–16 year olds in summer and at Christmas and Easter. Youngsters take part in everything from crazy golf and water-sports to treasure hunts and face-painting. Events such as Pyjama Breakfasts or Fancy Dress Dinners add to the fun. Family rooms (2 + 3), a children's play area and babysitting services are available all year. For adults, horse-riding and golf can be arranged, or they can relax in a jacuzzi, swim in the indoor pool or maybe take part in a murder mystery weekend or other events. Those who don't wish to join in organized activities may prefer the childrens' pool, fitness studios or health and beauty treatment rooms, which include facilities for the disabled.

Country houses

Newport House

Newport, **t** (098) 41222, **f** (098) 41613 (*moderate*)

Cots, high chairs, a babysitting service and early evening meals are available for children in this superb Georgian house hotel with old-fashioned service and its own home-smoked salmon. 18th-century antiques add to the elegance and beauty of the house, which overlooks a river.

B&Bs and guesthouses

Boheh Loughs

Liscarney, Westport, **t** (098) 21797 (*inexpensive*)

This house stands in 40 acres, with two lakes, at the foot of Croagh Patrick, beside Togher Patrick walk, where you'll find St Patrick's Chair. Non-smoking en-suite bedrooms are stocked with herbal toiletries, and children are welcome in this traditional cottage with organic and vegan/macrobiotic breakfasts and dinners. It's 5 miles (8km) from Westport, where many musicians and craftspeople live.

Rathoma House

Killala, **t** (096) 32035 (*inexpensive*)

Pleasant farmhouse in the depths of the country. Lots of activities, and Mrs Carey will arrange horse-riding for you.

Self-catering

Enniscoe House

Castlehill, near Crossmolina, Ballina, **t** (096) 31112, **f** (096) 31773 (*expensive*)

Families with teenagers might enjoy renting one of the cottages in the grounds of this Georgian house in parklands on the shores of Lough Conn more than a stay in the house itself.

Kiltartan House

Botharnasup, Ballina, **t** (096) 73301, **f** (096) 73299 (*inexpensive–moderate*)

A modern house with one-, two- and three-bedroom self-catering apartments in the town of Ballina. Your supremely helpful host will be delighted to introduce you to his home county of Mayo, should you request a tour. If you or your children are curious about Irish folklore, he can tell anecdotes of his own and put you in touch with locals who can tell you even more. For anglers, this is a great place, famous for its salmon fisheries, and you can even fish in the middle of the town.

Westport House Estate

Westport Estate, **t** (098) 25430 (*moderate*)

Renovated self-catering apartments and estate houses, sleeping 6–10, which have been modernized but retain period characters, within farm cottages and the Old Coach House. Occupants have access to the amenities of Westport Estate.

Hostels

Club Atlantic Holiday Hostel

Altamount Street, Westport, **t** (098) 26644, **f** (098) 26241 (*inexpensive*)

Just 5 mins' walk from Westport town centre, opposite the railway station, you'll find these non-smoking family/private rooms and dormitories. There's also a games room, children's playroom, cooking and laundry facilities.

Camping and caravanning

Parkland Caravan and Camping Park

Westport Country House, **t** (098) 27766, **f** (098) 25206, **www.westporthouse.ie** (*moderate*)

County Sligo

Hotels

Castle Arms Hotel

Enniscrone, t/f (096) 36156, www.castlearmshotel.com (*moderate*)

Two brothers run this two-star roadside hotel in a seaside town where everyone knows everyone else. Just ask and your hosts will send you to the fellow or lady down the road who'll be glad of a chat with you about this or that subject. From the hotel, you can walk to the seaweed bathhouse, Waterpoint leisure centre and 3 miles (5km) of sandy beach. In summer, there's entertainment nearby, as well as horse-riding and golf, pitch'n'putt for children, surfing, snooker, tennis and a playground. The restaurant has fresh, wholesome Irish cooking for breakfast, lunch and dinner.

Yeats Country Hotel and Leisure Club

Rosses Point, t (071) 9177211, f (071) 9177203, www.sligoaccommodation/yeats (*moderate*)

Special family activities are arranged by this large family-run hotel with indoor swimming and kids' pools, sauna, jacuzzi, gym, tennis, basketball and indoor bowling. Supervised crèche and indoor play areas are available on bank holiday weekends and in July–Aug. Facilities include kids' meals and price reductions, playroom and babysitting service.

Country houses

Coopershill House

Riverstown, t (071) 916 5108, f (071) 916 5466, www.coopershill.com (*expensive*)

Children are welcomed by friendly owners Brian and Wendy O'Hara, who maintain a clean, crisp feel in one of Ireland's finest Georgian mansions surrounded by woodland with roaming peacocks. Spacious rooms – some connecting – are filled with furniture and books, and warmed by log fires.

Markree Castle

Collooney, t (071) 916 7800, f (071) 916 7840, www.markreecastle.ie (*expensive*)

Bring your children here to give them a sense of what living in a real castle must have been like. Markree has a castellated façade looming up out of grounds where royalty once hunted and today visitors ride horses. Inside, three interconnecting reception rooms hold tall mirrors and fine plasterwork from 1845.Guestrooms have been restored in similar style, but with ample bathrooms. The views over the surrounding countryside are magical, and formal gardens lead down to the River Unsin.

Markree House

Coolooney, t (071) 9167800, f (071) 9167840, www.markreecastle.ie (*moderate*)

A family room is available in this house converted from the stables of Markree Castle. There's a garden, riding and fishing nearby, and children's meals and family discounts are available.

Ross House

Ross, Riverstown, t (071) 916 5787, t/f (071) 916 5140 (*moderate*)

There are three family rooms in this farmhouse, where children are surrounded by farm activity and animals. Nearby are Carrowkeel passage tombs.

Temple House

Ballymote, t (071) 918 3329, f (071) 918 3808, www.templehouse.ie (*moderate*)

Since 1665 the Perceval family have looked after some of the most beautiful land in Ireland here. Within the house, the faded grandeur of old Ireland's Anglo-Irish aristocracy remains, with canopied beds, ancient curtains, and family paintings. By the lake are the remains of a Knights Templar castle from 1200, and various other ruins are scattered around the grounds. Sandy and Deb Perceval use fresh organic garden produce in delicious breakfasts and dinners. Boats are available for fishing on Temple House Lake and they will cook your catch for you. Sandy Perceval is chemically sensitive, so guests should avoid all perfume, aftershave and aerosols; call for advice.

B&Bs and guesthouses

Ardtarmon House

Ballinfull, t/f (071) 916 3156, www.ardtarmon.com (*moderate*)

Families are welcome in this peaceful country house with a 19th-century ambience and a tree house perched inside a huge cedar in the grounds. Simple breakfasts are prepared by friendly owners Charles Henry and his German wife Christa. The house is a mix of Victorian styles, which grew up around the original thatched cottage, now used by self-catering guests. Interiors are a little austere, but there is a lovely easy walk to the sea, and the quiet atmosphere is something to remember.

Hostels

Eden Hill Holiday Hostel

Pearse Road, Sligo Town, **t/f** (071) 43204/44113 (*inexpensive*)

Family rooms and a wide range of other facilities.

Camping and caravanning

Greenlands Caravan and Camping Park

Rosses Point, **t** (071) 77113/45618 (*inexpensive*)

On sand dunes above two Blue Flag beaches.

Leitrim and Roscommon

Hotels

The Bush Hotel

Carrick-on-Shannon, Co. Leitrim, **t** (071) 9620014, **f** (071) 9621180 (*moderate*)

This small, friendly and central hotel offers sturdy Irish cooking, plus babysitting and children's meals.

Royal Hotel

Bridge Street, Boyle, Co. Roscommon, **t** (071) 9662016, **f** (071) 9664949 (*moderate*)

This town centre inn by the River Shannon has been in business for over 250 years. It has a Chinese restaurant and coffee shop on premises, riding and fishing nearby, plus price reductions for children.

The Abbey Hotel

Galway Road, Roscommon, **t** (090) 6626240, **f** (090) 6626021 (*expensive*)

An attractive Georgian building with 20 en-suite bedrooms. Children's meals and price reductions are available, and there's a babysitting service.

Country houses

Glebe House

Ballinamore Road, Mohill, Co. Leitrim, **t** (071) 9631086 (*moderate*)

Fishing and riding excursions can be arranged by the Maloney family at this old rectory (min. stay 2 nights), and there's a pony for children to ride.

Glencarne Country House

Ardcarne, near Carrick-on-Shannon, Co. Leitrim, **t/f** (071) 9667013 (*inexpensive*)

Children are welcome in this fine Georgian farmhouse near Lough Key Forest Park, with pleasant rooms, lovely old furniture and well-cooked meals.

Riversdale Farm Guesthouse

Ballinamore, Co. Leitrim, **t** (071) 964 4122, **f** (071) 964 4813 (*inexpensive–moderate*)

This Edwardian-era farmhouse has light, spacious rooms, indoor pool, squash court, sauna, good home-cooked food and delightful hosts, the Thomases, who run trips on the Shannon.

Riversdale House

Knockvicar, near Boyle, Co. Roscommon, **t** (071) 966 7012 (*inexpensive*)

Once the home of film star Maureen O'Sullivan, this spacious Georgian farmhouse has its own lake and river fishing. Families welcome.

B&Bs and guesthouses

Gleeson's Townhouse

Market Square, Roscommon, **t** (0906) 626954, **f** (0906) 627425 (*moderate*)

Centrally located, with well-appointed rooms and a restaurant. Babysitting available.

Self-catering

Abbey House

Boyle, Co. Roscommon, **t** (071) 966 2385 (*inexpensive-moderate*)

Lovely old houses available to rent in the grounds of Boyle Abbey; babysitting service available.

Clonalis House

Castlerea, Co. Roscommon **t/f** (094) 9620014 (*expensive*)

Victorian-Italianate house in a lovely wooded estate. Shooting and fishing can be arranged as can dinner, with notice. Several four-bedroom mews houses may be rented.

Primrose Cottage

Killukin, Carrick-on-Shannon, Co. Leitrim, **t** (071) 9621658 (*inexpensive*)

Nigel and Jacqui Laird rent out a two-bedroom cottage on their eco-friendly dairy farm.

Camping and caravanning

Lough Key Caravan Park

Rockingham, **t** (071) 9662212 (*inexpensive*)

Within Lough Key Forest Park, with a children's play area, café and shop.

ULSTER

County Antrim

Belfast

Hotels

The Culloden Hotel
142 Bangor Road, Craigavad, t/f (028) 9042 5223, f (028) 9042 6777 (*luxury*)

This is one of Belfast's nicest hotels, on the north-east of Belfast Lough. Very plush, with lovely grounds, an indoor swimming pool, fitness centre and luxurious old-style furnishings.

McCausland
34–38 Victoria Street, t (028) 9022 0200, www.mccauslandhotel.com (*expensive*)

Classical Italianate architecture, but the rooms are rather small. Children's meals, price reductions and babysitting are available.

The Wellington Park Hotel
21 Malone Road, t (028) 9038 1111, f (028) 9066 5410 (*expensive*)

A modern and comfortable hotel, close to the Botanic Gardens, with secure car parking, children's meals, price reductions and babysitting.

B&Bs and guesthouses

Many of these are in the quiet, leafy streets of the university district. They are often busy in summer, so it's best to book ahead.

Ash-Rowan Townhouse
12 Windsor Avenue, t (028) 9066 1758, f (028) 9066 3227 (*moderate*)

Children are welcome in this non-smoking, cosy, attractive family home near Queen's University, 10 mins from Belfast city centre. The ex-restaurateur owners cater for special diets. It's popular with classical musicians.

Camera Guesthouse
44 Wellington Park, t (028) 9066 0026, f (028) 9066 7856 (*moderate*)

Comfortably elegant Edwardian terraced house whose friendly proprietress, Caroline Drumm, can advise you on things to do with children in Belfast. There are two family rooms, discounts for children, self-catering apartments and a wide selection of organic options and herbal teas for breakfast.

Greenwood Guesthouse
25 Park Road, t (028) 9020 2525, f (028) 9020 2530 (*moderate*)

This inviting Victorian house across from Ormeau Park, with its leafy paths, bandstand and children's play area, makes you comfortable the moment you arrive. Built in 1897, it has many original features – cast iron and slate fireplaces, fine plasterwork and maple floors – and contemporary-style bedrooms. Owners Jason and Mary Harris welcome children and adults equally hospitably, and cook a tasty range of vegetarian and organic food. Cots, babysitting, laundry service and a secure car park behind the house are available. The city centre, Waterfront Hall and Queen's University are all less than 10 mins away by car.

Ravenhill House
690 Ravenhill Road, t (028) 9020 7444, f (028) 9020 2590, www.ravenhillguesthouse.com (*moderate*)

This non-smoking Victorian home in the tree-lined university area is an ideal resting place from which to explore Belfast. One family room contains two beds and sleeps a maximum of three. Rooms are bright, spacious and furnished with locally made hardwood furniture. Breakfast incorporates seasonal organic produce, home-made bread and preserves. Cots, cribs, high chairs, babysitting, laundry services and free car park are available.

Around Co. Antrim

Hotels

Bushmills Inn
Main Street, Bushmills, t (028) 2073 2339, f (028) 2073 2048, www.bushmillsinn.com (*moderate–expensive*)

This attractive and charming inn offers turf fires, gaslights and intriguing rooms. Comfortable, good service, excellent food, children's meals, price reductions, gardens and a babysitting service all form part of the hotel.

Causeway Hotel

40 Causeway Road, Giant's Causeway, Bushmills, t (028) 2073 1226/2073 1210, f (028) 2073 2552, www.giants-causeway-hotel.com (*moderate–expensive*)

This delightful family-run hotel offers children's meals, price reductions, babysitting and gardens for kids to run around in.

Galgorm Manor Hotel

136 Fenaghy Road, Ballymena, t (028) 2588 1001, f (028) 2588 0080, www.galgorm.com (*luxury*)

A spectacular 17th-century castle with lovely lawns transformed into a plush hotel with river views. Children's meals, price reductions and babysitting provided; riding and fishing nearby.

Radisson Roe Park Hotel and Golf Resort

Limavady, t (028) 7772 2222, f (028) 7772 2313, www.radisson.com (*expensive*)

Grounds and hotel date from the 18th century. Facilities include an indoor pool, whirlpool, sauna and a health club with a steam room and fitness suite. Price reductions and upgrades, free breakfast for 4 and a 'Family Go Pack' are also offered.

Country houses

The Moat Inn

12 Donegore Hill, Templepatrick, t (028) 9443 3659, f (028) 9443 3726, www.themoatinn.com (*expensive*)

This former coaching inn (1740) has been redecorated in Victorian style with William Morris wallpaper and a library filled with old books, antiques and a grand piano. It is the home of Rachel and Robert Thompson, both accomplished pianists – all the breakable objects strewn about mean this may not be such a good place for toddlers or active school-age kids. But, this very comfortable country house has won awards for its candlelit dinners, luxurious bedrooms and fabulous breakfasts. All rooms are en-suite and family rooms are available.

Whitepark House

Whitepark Bay, Ballintoy, t (028) 2073 1482, www.whiteparkhouse.com (*inexpensive*)

This pretty 17th-century house on a hill overlooking the Atlantic, luxuriously furnished with mementoes from the owners' Asian travels, is better for families with teenagers than young children. It's a good stopping place for coastal walkers and not far from the Giant's Causeway by car. The friendly hosts make sure their guests are introduced and comfortable. In the morning, visitors will be pampered with one of the north's best full-Irish breakfasts, for meat-eaters and vegetarians. Three bedrooms share a large bathroom.

B&Bs and guesthouses

Ahimsa

243 Whitepark Road, near Ballintoy, Bushmills, t (028) 2073 1383 (*inexpensive*)

A traditional cottage with two rooms, and an organic garden and vegetarian meals. Yoga and reflexology available on request.

Maddybenny Farmhouse

18 Maddybenny Park, Loguestown Road, Portrush, nr. Coleraine, t/f (028) 7082 3394, www.maddybenny.freeserve.co.uk (*inexpensive*)

The riding centre is a great attraction for children here, not to mention the animals and space out in the fresh air. There's an easy-going atmosphere, and great breakfasts. The owners also have self-catering cottages for rent.

Margaret's House

10 Altmore Street, Glenarm, t (028) 2884 1307 (*inexpensive*)

Welcoming old house, close to hills and beach.

Rathlin Guesthouse

The Quay, Rathlin Island, t (028) 2076 3917 (*inexpensive*)

Very friendly base, run by Mr and Mrs McCurdy, from which you can explore the beautiful island.

Self-catering

North Irish Lodge Holiday Cottages

Islandmagee, t/f (028) 9338 2246 (*expensive*)

These multi-award-winning luxury Irish cottages, equipped for the disabled, are set in a Victorian farmyard in the centre of Islandmagee, 5 mins from three sandy beaches. A unique hotel service package is offered in which guests may choose from traditional Irish dishes delivered to their 3- or 4-star cottage. There is a play area for under-12's and you can take guided walks or ride horses. Diving and sea fishing boats can also be arranged.

O'Harabrook Old Dairy

Bann Road, Ballymoney, t/f (028) 2766 6273 (*moderate*)

On a farm, three large secluded apartments in stone-built outhouses ideal for families, which sleep six each. Communal facilities include a laundry and games room.

Hostels

Cushendall Youth Hostel

24 Layde Road, Cushendall, t (028) 2177 1344, f (028) 2177 2042 (*inexpensive*)

In the Glens of Antrim; some family rooms.

Sheep Island View Hostel

42a Main Street, Ballintoy, t (028) 2076 9391 (*inexpensive*)

In a handy position for exploring the Causeway coast is this comfortable new hostel with ocean views, and bikes for rent.

Waterside House

Oxford Island, Lurgan, Craigavon, t (028) 3832 7573 (*inexpensive*)

Hostel located in the conservation area by Lough Neagh; wide range of watersports and activities.

Whitepark Bay International Youth Hostel

157 Whitepark Road, Whitepark Bay, Ballintoy, t (028) 2073 1745, f (028) 2073 2034, (*inexpensive*)

Nice hostel on Whitepark Bay near the Giant's Causeway and other Antrim attractions. Excellent facilities, with sea views and some family rooms.

County Down

Hotels

Burrendale Hotel and Country Club

51 Castlewellan Road, Newcastle, t (028) 4372 2599, f (028) 4372 2328, www.burrendalehotel.com (*expensive*)

Hydrotherapy baths are available in the modern rooms here, along with tea/coffee-making facilities and TV, and cots are available on request. Its country club has the best golf centre in the area, and a leisure centre with an indoor pool, jacuzzi, sauna, steam baths and exercise equipment across from a beauty salon. Everything is clean, comfortable and quiet in this 1980s hotel, and there's a nice garden: children's meals, playroom and family rates are also offered.

Clandeboye Lodge Hotel

10 Estate Road, Clandeboye, Bangor, t (028) 9185 2500, f (028) 9184 9011 (*expensive*)

This hotel with rooms for families and non-smokers is sited in the Clandeboye Estate in extensive landscaped gardens. The hotel will arrange golf for residents.

Country houses

Edenvale House

130 Portaferry Road, Newtownards, t (028) 9181 4881, f (028) 9182 6192, www.edenvalehouse.com (*moderate*)

Diane and Gordon Whyte are delighted to welcome children, as they have five grandsons of their own and Mrs Whyte even helps to run a local toddlers' group. They keep cots, high chairs and toys inside their perfect Georgian home, a climbing frame and swing outdoors near the big flower garden, and ponies, a dog and two cats who are used to children. They don't provide dinner, but are happy to make snacks for children before parents go out to eat, and to arrange babysitting. All the comforts you could possibly need are in bathrooms and bedrooms. Breakfast is wonderful too, with an eye-grabbing array of choices. If you need touring advice, Mrs Whyte is most helpful too. A stay here provides a wonderful introduction to Co. Down.

B&Bs and guesthouses

Drumgooland House and Equestrian Centre

29 Dunnanew Road, Seaforde, near Downpatrick, t (028) 4481 1956 (*inexpensive*)

B&B is offered particularly to riders, including families (disabled riders welcome) in this fully modernized 100-year-old home.

Dufferin Coaching Inn

31 High St, Killyleagh, t (028) 4482 8229, f (028) 4482 8755, www.dufferincoachinginn.co.uk (*moderate*)

This B&B does not have family rooms but a discount is offered for children, depending on their age. In or near the small village of Killyleagh (close to Strangford Lough), there are also occasional outdoor events for children, such as sailing and horse-riding. The pub/restaurant next door is happy to serve families early in the evening.

Self-catering

Castle Espie Cottages

11 Ballyglighorn Road, Comber, t (028) 427 873 011, f (028) 427 820 946 (*moderate*)

Two cottages on a working farm, with a play garden for children; sleeps 4–6. Babysitting, cots and high chairs are available.

Camping and caravanning

Meelmore Lodge

52 Trassey Road, Bryansford, Newcastle, Co. Down, t (028) 4372 6657, www.meelmorelodge.co.uk (*inexpensive*)

This has a coffee shop, showers, and guides who offer guided walks in the Mourne mountains. Walkers are especially welcome.

Murlough Cottage Farm Caravan Park

180 Dundrum Road, Newcastle, t (028) 4372 3184/4372 2906 (*inexpensive*)

Open Mar–Oct for touring caravans only, adjacent to Murlough Bay National Nature Reserve and beach. Children like this spot with its sand dunes. It's a short walk into town for the supermarket.

Tollymore Forest Park

176 Tullybrannigan Road, Newcastle, t (028) 437 22428 (*inexpensive*)

Open all year; camping for families only.

County Armagh

Hotels

The Charlemont Arms Hotel

63 English Street, t (028) 3752 2028, f (028) 3752 6979 (*moderate*)

Recently refurbished family-run hotel with children's meals and price reductions.

B&Bs and guesthouses

Deans Hill

34 College HIll, Armagh, t (028) 3752 4923, f (028) 3752 2186 (*inexpensive*)

Pretty 18th-century house with lovely gardens, close to the Observatory. Two en-suite rooms, one with a four-poster,and also a self-contained, self-catering chalet with room for four.

De Averell Guesthouse

3 Seven Houses, English St, Armagh, t (028) 3751 1213, f (028) 3751 1221 (*moderate*)

Georgian town-house with a good restaurant.

Hillview Lodge

33 Newtownhamilton Road, Armagh, t (028) 3752 2000, f (028) 3752 8276, www.hillviewlodge.com (*inexpensive*)

Beside a floodlit golf driving range just outside Armagh City, friendly, helpful Alice and Dermot McBride run this purpose-built B&B that's a bit like a small hotel. Its rooms are well equipped with modern amenities, and family rooms are available.

Hostels

Armagh City International Youth Hostel

39 Abbey Street, Armagh, t (028) 3751 1800, f (028) 3751 1801, www.hini.org.uk (*inexpensive*)

New purpose-built and well-sited hostel with high security, en-suite two-, four- and six-bed rooms; the atmosphere is somewhat functional.

County Londonderry

Hotels

Beech Hill Country House Hotel

32 Ardmore Road, Derry City, t (028) 7134 9279, f (028) 7134 5366, www.beech-hill.com (*expensive*)

This hotel has lovely grounds and is renowned for its cuisine. Facilities include a sauna, steam room, jacuzzi, fitness suite, tennis courts and treatment programme including massage and Reiki. Plus children's meals, price reductions and babysitting.

Quality Hotel Da Vinci's

15 Culmore Road, Derry City, t (028) 7127 9111, f (028) 7127 9222, www.derryhotels.com (*moderate*)

Stylish 70-room hotel complex, 10 mins walk from the city with children's playroom, meals and price reductions and babysitting service.

B&Bs and guesthouses

Aberfoyle B&B

33 Aberfoyle Terrace, Strand Rd, Derry City, t (028) 7128 3333, f (028) 7128 8255 (*inexpensive*)

A 19th-century mid-terrace house 5 mins from Derry city centre, 10 mins from Donegal, 40 mins from Giants' Causeway. Late breakfasts available.

Brown Trout Golf and Country Inn

209 Agivey Road, Aghadowey, south of Coleraine, **t** (028) 7086 8209, **f** (028) 7086 8878, **www**.brountroutinn.com (*expensive*)

In pretty grounds near a river, with good food, kids' meals, family rates, gardens, play area, gym, babysitting; also riding, golf and fishing tuition.

Drumcovitt House

704 Feeny Road, Feeny, **t/f** (028) 7778 1224 **www**.drumcovitt.com (*moderate*)

Families and children are welcome at this lovely Georgian farmhouse in scenic countryside. They also have three self-catering cottages.

Elagh Hall

Buncrana Road, Derry City, **t** (028) 7126 3116 (*inexpensive*)

An 18th-century farmhouse, 2 miles (3.2km) from the city centre, overlooking the hills of Donegal.

Laurel Villa

60 Church Street, Magherafelt, **t** (028) 7963 2238 (*moderate*)

Run by Blue Badge guide Eugene Kielt and his wife Geraldine, this house was once the home of a Victorian doctor, and is full of antiques. The present owners' influence is felt in the framed and illustrated poems hanging on the walls. Eugene is an inspired student of Irish history, and can tell you all sorts of snippets about his country. If you take him as a guide, he will find the best places to go, according to your interests Families are welcome (the Kielts have two sons of their own), and the fresh breakfasts are good. Guided tours of South Derry, based on the works of Seamus Heaney, are your host's speciality.

Streeve Hill

25 Dowland Road, Drenagh, Limavady, **t** (028) 7776 6563, **f** (028) 7776 8285 (*moderate*)

Lovely 18th-century house with delicious food and nice walks in parkland and a 'moon garden'.

Self-catering

Lough Beg Coach Houses

Ballyscullion Park, Bellaghy, **t** (028) 7938 6235, **f** (028) 7938 6416 (*moderate–expensive*)

Six well-appointed cottages (each sleep 6) on a large estate bordering Lough Beg, with games room, horse-riding and lovely walks. Full Irish breakfast and dinner can be ordered.

Hostels

Downhill Hostel

12 Mussenden Road, Castlerock, **t** (028) 7084 9077 (*inexpensive*)

A sociable hostel on a stretch of beach west of Castlerock. It offers a kitchen, laundry room, dorms and family rooms.

Dungiven Castle

Main St, Dungiven, **t** (028) 7774 2428, **f** (028) 7774 1968, **www**.dungivencastle.com (*inexpensive*)

En suite and dorm rooms and a kitchen are available in this restored Gothic and Tudor-style castle in 22 acres of parkland. Walking, gliding, riding, cycling, fishing and birdwatching are all possible.

County Tyrone

Hotels

The Valley Hotel

60 Main St, Fivemiletown, **t** (028) 8952 1505 (*moderate*)

This 2-star 22-bedroom hotel is comfortable and cheerful and has family rooms and a restaurant.

Country houses

Charlemont House

4 The Square, Moy, Dungannon, **t** (028) 8778 4755 (*inexpensive*)

This Georgian town-house with period furnishings and lots of atmosphere has a lovely garden with a view of the Blackwater River at the back.

Grange Lodge

7 Grange Road, Dungannon, **t** (028) 8778 4212, **f** (028) 8778 4313 (*moderate*)

Children over age 12 are welcome at this comfortable Georgian house by the Blackwater River, with outstanding breakfasts. Non-smoking rooms.

B&Bs and guesthouses

Braeside House

23 Drumconvis Road, Coagh, Cookstown, **t** (028) 8673 7301 (*inexpensive*)

There's a family- and a double room in this old house with garden on a working farm, with fishing on the Ballinderry River and Lough Neagh.

Self-catering

Blessingbourne Luxury Flats

Near Fivemiletown, **t** (028) 8952 1221 (*expensive*)

You could imagine you are visiting this Victorian mansion in wooded grounds in the era of leisurely house parties. Three self-catering apartments with comfortable rooms that sleep 6–8.

Gortin Accommodation Suite and Activity Centre

62 Main St, Gortin, **t** (028) 8164 8346, **f** (028) 8164 8390, **www.gortin.net** (*moderate*)

Outdoors-oriented centre, with self-catering apartments sleeping 4 and 6 for families or a hostel for independent travellers, in a village from which you can explore the Sperrins on foot, by bike, or by canoe. Facilities include breakfast and TV.

Grange Court

21–27 Moyle Road, Newtownstewart, **t** (028) 8166 1877, **f** (028) 8166 1956, **www.grangecourt.co.uk** (*moderate*)

This 4-star self-catering apartment complex on the Mourne River is central for visiting the Sperrins. Facilities include a café, TV, laundry, garden, play area, barbecue, cots and high chairs.

County Fermanagh

Hotels

Killyhevlin Hotel

Dublin Road, Enniskillen, **t** (028) 6632 3481, **f** (028) 6632 4726, **www.killyhevlin.com** (*moderate*)

Comfortable, modern hotel overlooking Lough Erne that's good for outdoor activities and offers children's meals, family rates, play area and babysitting. The bar is a great chatting-place for fishermen and there's a good lunchtime carvery.

Country houses

Rosfad House

Killadeas, P.O. Ballinamallard, **t** (028) 6638 8505, **f** (028) 6638 8505 (*inexpensive*)

Children are welcome in this Georgian-Victorian house not far from Enniskillen where in summer you can swim in Lower Lough Erne – with parental supervision, of course. They can also play croquet or badminton in beautiful gardens.

Tempo Manor

Tempo, **t** (028) 8954 1450, **f** (028) 8954 1202, **www.tempomanor.com** (*expensive*)

This Victorian manor house overlooks gardens and lakes. Built in 1863, the house stands in 300 acres of grounds and guests are treated to home-cooked breakfasts, log fires and an informal atmosphere. There are three four-poster bedrooms and a twin, and children are very welcome.

B&Bs and guesthouses

Arch Tullyhona Farm House

Marble Arch Road, Florence Court, **t** (028) 6634 8452, **www.archhouse.com** (*inexpensive*)

This old-fashioned farmhouse in its own grounds beside Upper Lough Erne offers family rooms, a children's play area, a play house, and a baby-listening service. Award-winning home cooking, and children's menus and high chairs are available.

The Cedars

301 Kiladeas Road, Castle Archdale, Irvinestown, **t/f** (028) 6862 1493, **f** (028) 6862 8335, **www.cedarsguesthouse.com** (*moderate*)

This family-friendly guesthouse with antique furniture offers traditional fare made from fresh local produce for all meals, and a children's menu. There are good-value rates for families.

Drumrush Lodge

Boa Island Road, Kesh, **t** (028) 6863 1578, **f** (028) 6863 2084, **www.drumrush.co.uk** (*inexpensive*)

This family-run watersports centre with en-suite rooms and all mod cons is beside a lake and has a restaurant with home cooking, and a camping and caravan park on site overlooking Lough Erne marina. Lake swimming and tennis are available.

Self-catering

Belle Isle Estate Cottages

Lisbellaw; contact **t** (028) 6638 7231, **f** (028) 6638 7261, **www.belleisle-estate.com** (*luxury*)

This estate of traditional buildings converted into luxurious apartments and cottages with spacious, modern interiors is at the northern end of Upper Lough Erne. They sleep 4–6.

Corralea Activity Centre and Holiday Cottages

Corralea, Belcoo, Fermanagh, **t/f** (028) 6638 6668 (*moderate*)

Five self-catering cottages available at this outdoor activity centre for all ages on Lough MacNean; full board also possible; qualified instructors for caving, watersports, and more.

Hostels

Castle Archdale Youth Hostel

Lisnarick, Irvinestown, t/f (028) 6862 8118, (*inexpensive*)

Family rooms and group accommodation in a historic listed building.

Camping and caravanning

Lough Melvin Holiday Centre Caravan Park

Main St, Garrison, t (028) 6865 8142, f (028) 6865 8719, www.fermanagh-online.com (*inexpensive*)

An outdoor activity centre on Lough Melvin that is suitable for the disabled and has a restaurant and dormitory and bedroom accommodation.

Cavan and Monaghan

Hotels

Creighton Hotel

Fermanagh Street, Clones, Co. Monaghan, t (047) 51055, f (047) 51284 (*moderate*)

Family-run, traditional hotel on Clones' main thoroughfare with full menu and children's meals.

Hillgrove Hotel

Old Armagh Road, Monaghan, Co. Monaghan, t (047) 81288, f (047) 84951, www.quinnhotels.com (*moderate–expensive*)

Children's menus and babysitting services are available in this comfortable, welcoming hotel.

Country houses

Glynch House

Newbliss, Clones, Co. Monaghan, t (047) 54046, f (047) 54321, www.glynchfarmhouse.com (*moderate*)

Children are welcome in this Huguenot farm-house built in 1772, with comfortable rooms. Its owners are funny and friendly. Very recommended.

Lisnamandra Farmhouse

Crossdoney, just west of Cavan Town, Co. Cavan, t (049) 433 7196, f (049) 433 7111 (*inexpensive*)

Family rooms are available 10 mins' drive from Lough Oughter at this award-winning traditional-style farmhouse. It has a very restful atmosphere, with comfortable rooms and home cooking.

B&Bs and guesthouses

Bavaria House

Garrymore, Ballinagh, Co. Cavan, t (049) 433 7452 (*inexpensive*)

Children are welcome in this relaxing house close to local historic sites. Organic vegetables, fruits and herbs are used; vegan, macrobiotic and non-vegetarian food are available on request.

Fort Singleton

Emyvale, Co. Monaghan, t (047) 86054, f (047) 86120, www.fortsingleton.com (*moderate*)

Children love sleeping in this house's Victorian train carriage, Bedouin's tent, boat-shaped bunkbed or bishop's chamber rooms, while those seeking country-house style can move upstairs to discover rooms packed with antiques.

MacNean House

Blacklion, Co. Cavan, t (072) 53022, f (072) 53404 (*inexpensive*)

This 10-room en-suite, comfortably furnished B&B offers babysitting services and children's meals and can arrange horse-riding and trekking and angling. It has a high reputation for fine food.

Rockwood House

Cloverhill, Belturbet, Co. Cavan, t (047) 55351, f (047) 55373 (*moderate*)

A very clean, quiet B&B amid peaceful woodland. Good breakfasts are served in the conservatory-style room with garden views. A pleasant place to rest and regain your stamina.

Self-catering

Cabra Castle Hotel

Kingscourt, Co. Cavan, t (042) 966 7030, f (042) 976 7039, www.cabracastle.com (*luxury*)

You can choose to stay in this lavish 15th-century pile with landscaped gardens and a 9-hole golf course, or in one of its self-catering units in the grounds. Children's meals, family rates, babysitting service, plus riding and fishing are all available.

Killykeen Forest Chalets

Killykeen Forest Park, Co. Cavan, t (049) 433 2541, f (049) 436 1044, www.coillte.ie (*moderate*)

Wood chalets and cabins in Killykeen Forest Park.

County Donegal

Hotels

Rathmullan House Hotel

Rathmullan, t (074) 915 8188, f (074) 915 8200, www.rathmullanhouse.com (*luxury*)

Families and children are welcome in this 18th-century country house on the edge of Lough Swilly, offering children's meals, family rates and babysitting. Excellent food is served, and the hotel has a very cosy bar with a turf fire, an indoor pool and sports courts. Stroll from here along a sandy beach.

Country houses

Ardnamona House

Lough Eske, near Donegal Town, t (074) 972 2560, f (074) 972 2819 (*expensive*)

Magical views over landscaped gardens, with kind hospitality from storyteller Amabel and pianist Kieran Clark. Children may roam across the grounds to the lake, and meet grazing ponies and animals . Dinner and breakfast are genial, gourmet affairs. There is also a self-catering cottage.

Bruckless House

Bruckless, t (074) 973 7071, f (074) 973 7070, www.iol.ie/~bruc/bruckless.html (*expensive*)

A charming 18th-century house near Donegal Bay. Its owners will point you in the right direction, whether your interest is walking, prehistoric sites or just exploring. It's a good base for families who want to ride, as it's down the road from Deane's Equestrian Centre.

Frewin House

Ramelton, t (074) 915 1246 www.accommodationdonegal.net (*moderate–expensive*)

This 17th-century rectory in its own grounds is owned by farmer Thomas Gibson, a goldmine of local folklore and history, and his wife, Regina, who prepares excellent breakfasts with fresh ingredients, including unsweetened fruit and homemade bread. The house is more suited to children over 7, but a self-catering cottage is also available for 2 adults and one child. For a sense of the peace once enjoyed in Irish homes, you should visit the benign ghost who haunts this place.

B&Bs and guesthouses

The Green Gate

Ardvally, Ardara, t (074) 9541546 (*inexpensive*)

For families who want to experience what living in a Donegal stone cottage must have been like a century ago, this is the place. Welcomed by French proprietor Paul Chatenoud, people relax and really talk to each other here, breathing in the scent of a turf fire in winter, or over breakfast on a summer morning. Chatenoud is determined to give back to the Irish the magic they have given him and to convey it to the world, which, he says, visits him here so that he doesn't have to travel anywhere.

Self-catering

The Gate Lodge and Buncronan Cottage

Salthill House, Mountcharles, t (074) 9735014 (*moderate*)

A choice of two places to shed the cares of modern life, close to the lake near Mountcharles. Children can explore the beach and the woods, swim in the sea or explore the organic garden.

Tyrella Cottage

Cottian, Kilmacrennan, near Letterkenny, t (074) 913 9029 (*moderate*)

A traditional whitewashed cottage on the road towards Glenveagh National Park. It's set between three fields, one of which you cross to reach a lake. The house has two double and two single iron beds and a sensitively modernized interior with mildly eccentric decoration and modern conveniences.

Hostels

Cliff View Holiday Hostel

Coast Road (to Killybegs), Donegal Town, t (074) 972 1684, f (074) 972 2667 (*inexpensive*)

A purpose-built hostel, 2 mins from the town centre, in which all bedrooms have en-suite facilities. Full Irish breakfasts and children's meals are available, and laundry and babysitting services.

Malin Head Hostel

Malin, t (074) 937 0309 (*inexpensive*)

Clean and comfortable, with an organic garden and orchard available for visitor use.

Camping and caravanning

Lakeside Caravan and Camping

Belleek Rd., Ballyshannon, t (071) 985 2822, f (071) 985 2823, www.donegalbay.com (*inexpensive*)

Travel

09

GETTING THERE

All kinds of general information on travel to Ireland and on transport throughout the island can be obtained from **Tourism Ireland, t** UK 0800 039 7000, **t** US and Canada 1 800 223 6470, **www**.tourismireland.com.

This is now the sole international tourist information service for the whole 'island of Ireland', covering the Republic and Northern Ireland.

By Air

Flights

Since the low-cost revolution in European air travel it's easier – and cheaper – than ever before to fly to Ireland from Britain and many parts of Europe, and there's also a choice of flights from different departure points in North America.

From Britain

Thanks to the low-cost airline boom there are now direct flights to a variety of airports in Ireland from most parts of Britain, and fares can often be under £20 one-way. The occasional problems of no-frills airlines are well-known – long check-in times, delays – although the low-cost operators can claim that punctuality has improved significantly since 2002. An essential part of the low-cost package is that no food or drink is included with the ticket, and should you then buy any of the refreshments available on board they are notably expensive (so take at least some snacks, water and/or other drinks with you, especially for kids).

These problems aside, something else to be highlighted is that low-cost airlines are not always as cheap as their advertising can suggest (note, too, that to get significant extra savings you must book online rather than by phone). Fares for each airline vary greatly on the same route, according to when you travel and how far in advance you book; the real rock-bottom deals are often for seats at inconvenient times (very early-morning, early-in-the-week flights), and on popular routes prices leap up at busy times such as Friday evening (from around £10 to £90, Stansted–Dublin). Also, one benefit of the no-frills revolution that often goes unnoticed is in the concessions it has forced on the older mainstream carriers. Obliged to compete, they have responded with lower and lower fares – especially Aer Lingus, which now operates as a low-cost airline itself, with prices comparable to Ryanair's. Because of this changing price system, the rules to follow when booking flights are – **always check around all the airlines operating on the route you want**, and bear in mind that the **new-model no-frills airlines may not always be the cheapest**, especially on very popular routes at peak times.

Good to know...
Airfares for Children

The terms under which children fly vary from airline to airline. A few offer discounts of around 20%–30% from a full adult fare for children aged from 2–12, but on most airlines operating between Britain and Ireland (especially low-cost ones) any child occupying their own seat will simply be charged the full normal fare.

Children under 2 who do not have their own seat (i.e., who travel in an adult's lap) travel for free on several airlines, but others charge 10% of the adult fare, or a set fee, usually of around £5/€8.

On long-haul (i.e., transatlantic) flights the discounts available vary not only between airlines but also between flights of the same airline, so check carefully when booking. On most airlines children under 2 travel for 10% of the full fare if they share the adult's seat, but this can be an uncomfortable option on long flights.

Airlines Operating between Britain and Ireland

Since the airline market has become so changeable nowadays, routes change frequently, and new airlines are also still starting up, so always check current routes and future plans on websites and in the travel press.

Aer Arann
t UK 0800 587 2324, **t** IR 0818 210 210, **www.aerarann.ie**
Routes: to **Dublin** from Isle of Man; to **Cork** from Birmingham, Bristol, Edinburgh and Southampton; to **Galway** from Luton and Manchester; and to **Kerry** and **Waterford** from Luton.
Fares for children Discounts of around 33% are offered for children aged 2–12 on many flights; for children under 2 sharing a seat the charge is 10% of normal fare. No car seats allowed.

Good to know...
Flying with babies and toddlers

Sucking on a bottle or dummy (a soother) helps ease earache on take-off and landing; many chemists/pharmacists (especially at airports) stock 'earplanes', small plastic devices that fit in the ear and are quite effective if you or your child suffers from air pressure problems.

Insist that you take your buggy up to the door of the aircraft – it's more convenient and the buggy is less likely to get damaged. Inside, if you don't want to have your baby sit on your lap all through the flight it can be a good idea to book a separate seat and take a familiar car seat for the child to sit in comfortably. If you do, though, you will usually have to pay full fare for the seat, and if you want to do this, check carefully with your airline when booking: some airlines do not allow car seats inside the aircraft, or only allow specific types.

On long-haul (transatlantic) flights most airlines offer a range of facilities for small children – infant cots, child seats, on-board bottle-warming, baby-changing facilities, children's meals – on request, but they must be ordered in advance. Check what is available when booking, and be sure to make clear exactly what you need. Many airlines will also allow you to use your own child seats, cots and so on, but, again, check when booking to ensure that the type you have is one the airline allows on board.

Aer Lingus
t UK 0845 084 4444, **t** IR 0818 365 000,
www.aerlingus.com
Routes: to **Dublin** from Birmingham, Edinburgh, Glasgow, Jersey, Heathrow and Manchester; and to **Cork** and **Shannon** from Heathrow.
Fares for children Discounts of around 15% of the adult fare for children aged 2–11 on some flights, depending on the class, but on most UK–Ireland flights they must pay full fare. For children under 2 sharing a seat with an adult the fare is 10% of the normal fare.

Air Wales
t UK 0870 777 3431, **t** IR 1 800 654 193,
www.airwales.co.uk
Routes: to **Dublin** and **Cork** from Cardiff, Plymouth and Swansea; and to **Belfast City** from Cardiff.
Fares for children No discounts for children aged 2–12; for children under 2 sharing a seat the fare is £5/€8, for any flight. No car seats allowed.

Bmibaby
t UK 0870 264 2229, **t** IR 01 435 0011,
www.bmibaby.com.
Routes: to **Dublin** from East Midlands, to **Belfast International** from Cardiff, East Midlands and Teesside, and to **Cork** from Cardiff, East Midlands and Manchester.
Fares for children No discounts for 2–12s, but children under 2 sharing a seat travel for free.

British Airways
t UK 0870 850 9850, **t** IR 1 890 626 747,
www.britishairways.com
Routes: to **Dublin** from Bristol, Gatwick, Manchester and the Isle of Man; to **Belfast City** from Edinburgh, Glasgow and Manchester; to **Cork** from Glasgow and Manchester; to **Knock** from Manchester; to **Derry** from Glasgow and Manchester; and to **Shannon** from Manchester.
Fares for children No discounts for children aged 2–12 on European flights. Children under 2 sharing a seat are charged 10% of the adult fare.

British Midland (bmi)
t UK 0870 607 0555, **t** IR 01 332 854 854,
www.flybmi.com.
Routes: to **Dublin**, **Belfast City** and **Cork**, from Heathrow.
Fares for children No discounts for 2–12s; children under 2 sharing a seat pay 10% of full fare.

easyJet
t UK 0871 750 0100, **www.**easyjet.com
Routes: to **Belfast International** from Bristol, Edinburgh, Gatwick, Glasgow, Liverpool, Luton, Newcastle and Stansted.
Fares for children No discounts for children aged 2–14. Children under 2 sharing a seat travel for free.

Good to know...
Cheap flights online

With so many flights running between Ireland and Britain, it's usually pretty easy to get tickets directly from the airlines, but in case you get stuck, the services below are handy ports-of-call for finding a wide range of bargain flight options.

www.cheapflights.com
www.cheaptickets.com
www.dialaflight.com
www.farebase.net
www.flightline.co.uk
www.lastminute.com
www.travelocity.com

Flybe
t UK 0870 889 0908, **t** IR 1 890 925 532, **www.flybe.com**
Routes: to **Dublin** from Exeter, Jersey, Isle of Man and Southampton; to **Belfast City** from Birmingham, Bristol, Exeter, Gatwick, Isle of Man, Leeds-Bradford, London City, Newcastle and Southampton; and to **Cork** and **Shannon** from Birmingham.
Fares for children Variable discounts for children aged 2–12 on many flights; for children under 2 sharing a seat the fare is 10% of the adult fare.

Jet Magic
t UK 0870 1780 135, **t** IR 0818 200 135, **www.jetmagic.com**
Routes: to **Cork** from Edinburgh, Liverpool and London City.
Fares for children No discounts for 2–12s; for children under 2 sharing a seat, 10% of the adult fare.

Jet 2
t UK 0870 737 8282, **www.jet2.com.**
Routes: **Belfast International** from Leeds-Bradford.
Fares for children No discounts for 2–12s, but children under 2 sharing a seat travel for free.

MyTravelLite
t UK 0870 1564 564, **t** IR 0818 300 012, **www.mytravellite.com.**
Routes: to **Dublin**, **Belfast International** and **Knock** from Birmingham.
Fares for children No discounts for children aged 2–12. For children under 2 sharing a seat there is a fare of £5/€8, for any flight.

Ryanair
t UK 0871 246 0016, **t** IR 0818 30 30 50, **www.ryanair.com**
Routes: to **Dublin** from Aberdeen, Birmingham, Blackpool, Bournemouth, Bristol, Cardiff, Edinburgh, Gatwick, Glasgow (Prestwick), Leeds-Bradford, Liverpool, Luton, Manchester, Newcastle, Stansted and Teesside; and to **Cork**, **Kerry**, **Knock**, **Derry** and **Shannon** from Stansted.
Fares for children No discounts for children aged 2–12. For children under 2 sharing a seat there is a fare of £7/€10, for any flight. No car seats allowed.

From North America

Direct flights from North America to Ireland arrive in **Dublin** and **Shannon** airports – Aer Lingus offers the widest choice of departure airports around the US. Fares have been falling overall, and at many times of year it's possible to get return fares of around $200 or less. There are also many charter flights each year, especially during summer, and many more flight options, often with good fare deals, are also available with a change of flight in Britain or at another European airport. Flying indirect like this via Britain is the best way to get to Ireland from Canada.

Airlines with Direct Flights between the USA and Ireland

Aer Lingus
t US and Canada 1 800 IRISH AIR, **t** IR 0818 365 000, **www.aerlingus.com**
Flights to Dublin and Shannon from Baltimore, Boston, Chicago, Los Angeles and New York (JFK).

Delta Airlines
t US and Canada 1 800 241 4141, **t** IR 1 800 768 080, **www.delta-air.com**
Flies to Dublin and Shannon from Atlanta.

Continental Airlines
t US and Canada 1 800 231 0856, **t** IR 1 890 925 252, **www.flycontinental.com**
From Newark to Shannon and Dublin.

US Airways
t US and Canada 1 800 622 1015, **t** IR 1 890 925 065, **www.usairways.com**
A direct service from Philadelphia to Shannon and Dublin, May–October only.

Good to know...
Consolidators in North America

Tickets are often cheaper than usual when bought via consolidators, but be aware that their tickets are usually non-refundable or carry stiff cancellation penalties, often as high as 50% to 75% of the ticket price.

Air Brokers Travel, t 1 800 883 3273, **www.airbrokers.com**
TFI Tours International, t 1 800 745 8000
Travac Tours and Charters, t 1 800 872 8800, **www.travac.com**
Unitravel, t 1 800 325 2222, **www.unitravel.com**

Charter Operators in the USA and Canada

Air Transat Holidays, t 1 800 587 2672
Signature Vacations, t (US) 1 800 268 7522, **t** (Can) 1 800 268 7063
Sunquest Vacations, t 1 800 268 8899
World of Vacations, t 1 800 387 4860

Arriving in Ireland

Airports in the Irish Republic

The Republic's three main airports – Dublin, Cork and Shannon – are all run by the same national body, Aer Rianta. The other regional airports are run by local authorities.

As well as the bus services from the different airports to the nearest cities and towns, there are bus services between the airports and from towns further away to Dublin and Shannon airports, all run by the national bus company **Bus Eireann**. For contact details for timetable and fare information, *see* p.286.

Cork Airport

t 021 431 3131, **www**.aer-rianta.ie
Getting there 3 miles (5km) south of Cork City on the Kinsale road (N27).

There are around two buses each hour, 7.50am–8.45pm Mon–Fri, between the airport and Cork city, with a less frequent service at weekends. The trip takes about 25 mins. A taxi into Cork city will cost around €11.

Dublin Airport

Information **t** 01 814 1111, **www**.aer-rianta.ie
Getting there 6 miles (10km) north of Dublin near Swords, just west of the Dundalk road (M1).

The quickest and most convenient bus service between the airport and Dublin is the **Aircoach** (**t** 01 844 7118, **www**.aircoach.ie), which runs every 15 mins every day in each direction during the day, and every 30 mins about 12 midnight–4.30am, on a circular route from the airport, through the city centre and down to south Dublin, and then back again. There is a flat-fee fare of €6, one way, from any stop on the route, or €10 return. There are set stops on the route (which are not the same as city bus stops), which are well signposted.

Several city bus (**Dublin Bus, t** 01 872 0000, **www**.dublinbus.ie) routes also serve the airport. Routes **747** and **748** are the main **Airlink** buses that run between the airport and the city centre, stopping at the Central Bus Station (Busáras) and Connolly and Heuston rail stations; other routes run to different parts of Dublin. These buses are cheaper than the Aircoach; Airlink routes run approximately 6.40am–11pm, Mon–Sat, and less frequently on Sundays, but do not run at night.

A taxi from the airport into central Dublin will usually cost around €15–€20, depending very much on the traffic.

Galway Airport

Carnmore, **t** 091 755 569, **www**.galwayairport.com
Getting there 4 miles (6km) east of Galway City.

As well as having flights from Britain this is the airport for Aer Arann flights to the Arann Islands. There is only a very infrequent bus service; the airline often provides a shuttle bus into town, but otherwise the main way to get into Galway is by taxi; the fare should be around €10.

Kerry Airport

Farranfore, Co. Kerry, **t** 066 976 4644, **www**.kerryairport.ie
Getting there the airport is at Farranfore, 9 miles (14km) north of Killarney on the road to Tralee (N22).

A shuttle bus operates regularly to Killarney, stopping in Farranfore village, where passengers can also change onto buses for Dingle and the Ring of Kerry. Fares are €6 single to Killarney, €10 return, or €2 to Farranfore. A taxi from the airport to Killarney costs around €15.

Knock International Airport

Knock, near Charlestown, Co. Mayo, **t** 1 850 67 22 22, **www**.west-irl-holidays.com
Getting there Knock airport is next to the N17 Galway–Sligo road, 24 miles (38km) east of Castlebar.

There are no regular bus services from Knock airport, but taxis will take you to any of the towns in the region, at a set rate of €1.27 per mile. Note that all passengers departing from Knock (over the age of 12) must pay a special extra local airport charge of €10 per ticket.

Shannon Airport

Shannon, Co. Clare,
General information **t** 1 890 742 6666,
Flight information **t** 061 712 400,
www.aer-rianta.ie
Getting there 16 miles (26km) west of Limerick just off the Ennis road (N18).

Buses operate between the airport and Limerick city centre approximately 8am–midnight, daily. The journey time is about 40 mins. Bus Eireann also runs direct buses from Shannon to many towns in Ireland; check the company website for details (*see* p.286). A taxi to Limerick will cost around €15–€20.

Waterford Regional Airport

Killowen, Co. Waterford, t 051 875 589, www.flywaterford.com
Getting there **the airport is 8 miles (13km) south of Waterford town on the local road to Clohernagh.**

Taxis are the only means of transport between this small airport and Waterford town. The usual fare will be around €10 or less.

Airports in Northern Ireland

Belfast has two airports, one of them (Belfast International, once known as Aldergrove) much further from the city than the other. Make sure you know clearly which airport your airline is using.

Belfast City Airport

t 028 9093 9093, www.belfastcityairport.com
Getting there **the airport is only 4 miles (7km) from central Belfast, east of the city on the A2 Holywood–Bangor road.**

Airport buses run every 40 mins between the terminal and Europa Bus Terminal in Belfast, 6.25am–9.50pm daily; the fare is £2.50. Shuttle buses also run to Sydenham Halt rail station, from where there are two trains each hour to Belfast, 6am–6pm Mon–Fri, and one hourly Sat, Sun; and Citybus 21 runs from near the airport terminal to the city (and is cheaper than the airport bus).

Taxis into Belfast cost around £6.

Belfast International Airport

Aldergrove, Co. Antrim, t 028 9442 4610, www.belfastairport.com
Getting there **the airport is 18 miles (29km) northwest of Belfast, 6 miles (10km) west of the M2 motorway.**

Northern Ireland's largest airport. An **Airbus** service runs every 30 mins between the airport and Belfast city centre, 5.45am–11.30pm Mon–Sat, and every hour on Sundays. The fare is around £5.

A taxi to Belfast will cost around £20..

City of Derry Airport

Airport Road, Eglinton, Co. Derry, t 028 7181 0784, www.cityofderryairport.com
Getting there **7 miles (11km) northeast of Londonderry on the A2 Coleraine road.**

A variety of Ulsterbus services run from the airport to Londonderry city and Coleraine, and Bus Eireann buses run to several destinations in the Republic. The taxi fare to Derry City will be around £8.

By bus

Travelling to Ireland by coach with children in tow can seem an endurance test, with the ferry journey and plenty of stops en route. The plus is that you can travel direct from many departure points in Britain to a huge range of small towns and villages in Ireland, without the need to transfer from an airport or ferry port. And, since air fares have fallen so much, bus fares are even cheaper.

The international bus network **Eurolines**, which includes National Express in Britain and Bus Eireann and Ulsterbus in Ireland, offers many routes between Britain and Ireland, and has a central booking service. In London, coaches leave from Victoria Coach Station; a bus to Dublin costs from £29 return, and takes 11–12 hours (each way).

There are many more small companies that run buses to Ireland, often to provincial towns. A good way to find out about them is through ads in Irish newspapers such as the *Irish Post*.

Eurolines

In the UK t 08705 808080, www.eurolines.co.uk
In Irish Republic t 01 836 6111, www.eurolines.ie

By sea

Ferries across the Irish Sea run from a variety of British ports to **Dublin**, **Dun Laoghaire** (just outside Dublin), **Rosslare** (near Wexford) and **Cork** in the Republic, and **Belfast**, **Larne** and the little port of **Ballycastle** in Northern Ireland. There are also direct ferry services to Dublin, Rosslare and Cork from Cherbourg and Roscoff in France.

The great attraction of crossing by ferry is, of course, if you want to travel around with your own car, and all the many things you can pack into it. As with airlines, it's worth shopping around between the different companies. Comparing prices is sometimes complicated: fares on each route vary greatly by season and how long you intend to stay. Between Holyhead and Dublin a return ticket for a trip of over five days for a car, two adults and two under-15s costs from around £250, low season, to about £340 in midsummer. Also, most companies still base their fares on a simple return fare for a car and one driver, to which must be added extra charges for each additional person and any extras like cabins (which families with kids will almost certainly want, on the longer overnight crossings). This can make working out fares annoyingly difficult. The 'extra person' charge is generally lower for under-14s or under-15s, and under-4s usually travel free. It tends to be the smaller companies – Norse Merchant, Swansea–Cork – that have more generous (or at least simpler) fare structures, with which up to four people with car can cross, perhaps with cabin included, for around £300–£320 return. Virtually all the companies now offer cheaper rates if you book directly online, not through agents.

For foot passengers, fares are very low. From Dublin and Dun Laoghaire harbours there are frequent buses to central Dublin, and from Rosslare there is a direct rail link to Wexford and Dublin and many Bus Eireann services to these or other towns. From Larne harbour there is a rail link to Belfast.

Sailing times vary a lot between routes (*see below*). Ferries are comfortable and offer a range of family facilities, especially on longer crossings – kid-friendly restaurants, baby-changing rooms, play areas, video rooms. Take note, though, that the Irish Sea often gets rough, especially towards winter.

Ferry Companies between Britain and Ireland

Argyll & Antrim Steam Packet Co.

t UK 0870 552 3523, **t** IR 1 800 551 743

Ferries for cars and passengers between Campbeltown on the Mull of Kintyre, Scotland, and Ballycastle on the Antrim coast, May–Oct only.

Irish Ferries

t Britain 08705 171717, **t** IR 1 890 31 31 31, **t** Northern Ireland 0800 018 2211, **www.irishferries.com**

Several standard 'Cruise Ferries' and faster 'Swift Ferries' run daily Holyhead–Dublin and Pembroke–Rosslare. Swift Ferries are slightly more expensive.

Isle of Man Steam Packet Company

t UK 01624 661 661, **www.steam-packet.com**

Liverpool–Dublin, Feb–Nov only; also several routes to the Isle of Man.

Norse Merchant Ferries

t UK 0870 600 4321, **t** IR 01 819 2999, **www.norsemerchant.com**

Liverpool–Belfast: at least one ferry daily each way, all year round. Relatively little known, Norse Merchant often has some of the best fare offers.

P&O Irish Sea Ferries

t UK 0870 2424777, **t** IR 1 800 409 049, **www.poirishsea.com**

Routes served are Liverpool–Dublin, Mostyn (North Wales)–Dublin, Fleetwood–Larne, Cairnryan–Larne and Troon–Larne. On the Larne routes from April to October only there are both standard ferries and fast catamarans, for which fares are higher.

SeaCat

t 0870 523 523, **www.seacat.co.uk**

Fast catamarans between Troon and Belfast, still with space for cars and passengers.

Stena Line

t UK 08704 006 798, **t** IR 01 204 7777, **www7.stenaline.co.uk**

Sailings all year, Holyhead–Dublin, Holyhead–Dun Laoghaire, Fishguard–Rosslare, Stranraer–Belfast. Stena has some of the most modern Irish ferries, both conventional 'Superferries' and HSS Fastcraft giant catamarans, which offer the fastest crossings to the Republic. Fastcraft fares are predictably a bit higher.

Swansea–Cork Ferries

t UK 01792 456 116, **t** IR 021 427 1166, **www.swansea-cork.ie**

Overnight between Swansea and Cork. Fares are very competitive.

Good to know...

Average Crossing Times

Cairnryan–Larne 1hr 45mins
Campbeltown–Ballycastle 2hrs 45mins
Fishguard–Rosslare 1hr 40mins Fastcraft, 3hrs 30mins Superferry
Fleetwood–Larne 8hrs
Holyhead–Dublin 3hrs 15mins
Holyhead–Dun Laoghaire 1hr 39mins Fastcraft, 3hrs 15mins Superferry
Liverpool–Belfast 8hrs
Liverpool–Dublin 7hrs 30mins
Mostyn–Dublin 6hrs
Pembroke–Rosslare 3hrs 45mins
Stranraer–Belfast 1hr 45mins Fastcraft, 3hrs 15mins Superferry
Swansea–Cork 10hrs
Troon–Belfast 2hrs 30mins
Troon–Larne 2hrs

GETTING AROUND

Ferry Companies between France and Ireland

Brittany Ferries

t IR 021 427 7801, www.brittany-ferries.ie

Ferries once a week between Cork and Roscoff in Brittany, April–Sept only. Sailing time 11 hours.

Irish Ferries

t IR 1 890 31 31 31, www.irishferries.com

Ferries once a week from Rosslare to Cherbourg and Roscoff in France. Sailing time around 12 hours.

Border Formalities

UK citizens do not need a passport or visa to enter Ireland, but most airlines and ferry companies now require you to show some form of identification with a photograph when boarding, usually either a passport or driver's licence. Check with your airline, ferry or tour operator what form of identification is required before travelling. Other EU nationals and citizens of other countries must have a valid passport or national identity card to enter the Republic or Northern Ireland.

No visas are required for travel to the Republic or the UK by citizens of the USA, Canada, Australia, New Zealand or South Africa. Citizens of other countries should check with their nearest Irish and/or British Consulate before travelling. There are not usually any customs checks between the Irish Republic and the UK, but there are still limits on the amount of goods that can be brought in by travellers arriving from non-EU countries.

VAT Refund Scheme

Residents of non-EU countries are entitled to reclaim the VAT or Value-Added Tax (currently 20.6% in the Republic, and 17.5% in Northern Ireland) paid on some goods when they leave Ireland. They must spend more than €180, or £150, in any one shop, which must be part of the Retail Export Scheme (if so, it will have a sticker on the door). Show your passport to the shop staff and ask for a Tax-Free Shopping Form. Fill in the details, and present it to Customs when you finally leave the Irish Republic or the UK to go home, to reclaim the tax. You cannot reclaim VAT when travelling between Ireland and Britain or another EU country.

By air

Given the size of Ireland, few travellers are in such a hurry that they want to take internal flights, but there's a wide range of domestic services, mainly operated by **Aer Arann** and **Aer Lingus** (*see* pp.280–1), and to airports such as Sligo and Donegal as well as those listed on pp.283-4. One local air route that can be both handy and memorable is the light-plane service run by Aer Arann from Galway to the **Arann Islands** (*see* p.164).

By bus

Bus Eireann, in the Republic, and Ulsterbus in Northern Ireland are the two principal, interconnecting bus companies that, between them, cover the whole of Ireland. In addition, many towns have their own local transport authorities (notably Dublin Bus, and Citybus in Belfast), and there are many small regional and county-based companies. There are few places in rural Ireland that cannot be reached by bus in some way – so long as you're able and ready to take your time. Country buses can be infrequent and very slow. Local tourist offices are the best guides to the full choice of bus services in each area.

Bus Eireann

The Travel Centre, Busáras (Central Bus Station), Store Street, Dublin 1, t 01 836 6111, www.buseireann.ie

The Republic's national bus lines have routes to every part of the country from Dublin, and many others between regions. There are reduced fares for children under 16, and student discounts. Bus Eireann also offers several kinds of multi-journey tickets for discount travel, some allowing you to combine train and bus (*see* p.287 **Discount Tickets**).

Ulsterbus

Europa Bus Centre, Great Victoria Street, Belfast, t 028 9066 6630, www.ulsterbus.co.uk

Ulsterbus runs all buses in Northern Ireland except those in Belfast city. As well as sharing some multi-journey tickets with Bus Eireann tickets, Ulsterbus has its own **Freedom of Northern Ireland** unlimited travel tickets (*see* right, p.287).

Good to know...
Discount Tickets

There are reduced fares for children under 16 on all public transport in Ireland, North and South, and also significant discounts for students with a student card. Fares in general are reasonable, but change quite often, so check current rates when you travel. Ireland is also part of the Eurail Pass and Interail networks, which allow unlimited rail travel on European railways, including the Republic of Ireland but excluding the UK, and discount ferry crossings from France to Ireland. To obtain a Eurail Pass you must be resident of a non-European country and purchase it outside Europe. For details of these schemes check **www**.raileurope.com.

Ireland's bus and train companies also offer a range of multi-journey, unlimited travel tickets directed at foreign visitors, some of which can be used across different networks. These are:

Emerald Card Unlimited travel on buses and trains in the Republic and Northern Ireland (all Iarnród Eireann, Bus Eireann, Northern Ireland Railways and Ulsterbus services). Can be valid for 8 days (adult €180/£130, under-16s €90/£65) or 15 days (adult €310/£225, under-16s €155/£112).

Freedom of Northern Ireland Unlimited travel on Northern Ireland bus or trains for 1 day (£12), 3 days (£30) or 7 days (£45), with reductions for under-16s.

Irish Explorer Unlimited travel on buses and trains in the Republic (Iarnród Eireann and Bus Eireann). Valid for 8 days (adult €160, under-16s €80).

Irish Rambler Unlimited travel on all Bus Eireann buses in the Republic, for 3 days (adult €50, under-16s €30), 8 days (adult €110, under-16s €70) or 15 days (adult €160, under-16s, €100).

Irish Rover Unlimited travel on all Bus Eireann buses in the Republic and Ulsterbus services in Northern Ireland. Can be bought for 3 days (adult €65/£47, under-16s €36/£26), 8 days (adult €145/£105, under-16s €80/£58) or 15 days (Adult €215/£155, under-16s €118/£85).

By car

Taking a car around Ireland is a great option when you're travelling with a family. It gives you the freedom to pace your journey to suit yourself, and it makes it easier to travel around once you get where you're going. Remember too that large parts of Ireland, particularly in the west, are only accessible by car – unless you spend ages waiting for buses. However, it's equally worth considering that travelling by train and bus might be more fun and less stressful if your children are old enough to be mobile themselves. While we're not recommending it, it's worth taking note that the Irish travel writer Dervla Murphy rode all over India on a bike with her baby and then wrote a book about it called *Full Tilt*, not to mention Connacht's pirate queen Grace O'Malley who, just after childbirth, fought a battle on a ship, grumbling all the while because her male mariners were losing heart.

If you take your own car from Britain to Ireland, it is advisable to have breakdown coverage via the AA or RAC, your home insurance company, or another specialist breakdown service. Be sure to take your car registration and insurance papers as well.

Car hire

Valid UK, US or Canadian driver's licences are all accepted for hiring a car in the Irish Republic, but you will normally have to show another form of ID as well (a passport). Hire-car companies in the Republic and Northern Ireland usually require that the hirer must have had a licence for at least one year, or in some cases may ask for an international driving licence issued in the home country.

The major international car hire chains such as Avis, Hertz, Europcar and so on are all present in Northern Ireland and the Republic. Car hire tends to work out cheaper if you rent a car in advance before you arrive in Ireland, especially if coming from North America. However, it's still best to contact different companies and compare prices. It will usually be cheaper to hire in a city rather than at an airport. Most hire cars have manual gearshifts, and automatics will cost more to rent.

If you hire a car in Northern Ireland, make sure that its insurance will cover you if you take the car to the Republic, and vice versa. Collision damage waiver and other insurance coverage may also vary, so check the details before you sign up.

Seatbelts and child seats

It is mandatory to use seatbelts for all car drivers and front seat passengers in Ireland, and motorcyclists must wear crash helmets. In both the Republic and Northern Ireland the law requires all children travelling in cars to use an appropriate child restraint or adult seat belt. These must be in

Good to know...
Speed limits
Speed limits in Northern Ireland are the same as in Britain:
30mph/50kph in towns unless otherwise signposted
60mph/95kph on most highways
70mph/112kph on motorways and highways without any other speed restriction.
Speed limits in the Republic of Ireland are:
30–40mph/50–65kph in built-up areas
60mph/95kph on most roads
70mph/112kph on motorways and dual carriageways

place on infant carriers, baby or child car seats or booster cushions. Children normally cannot be carried in the front seat of a car unless they are either in a child restraint or are using a seat belt, but please check current laws. If a child under 18 years of age is sitting in the front passenger seat of a car, make sure the airbag on that side has been removed. It is the driver's responsibility to ensure that children under age 14 are using an appropriate child restraint or an adult seat belt. For information on seat types, try **www.childcarseats.org.uk**.

If you are hiring a car, make sure that you order a child's seat in advance. Baby or child car seats can be hired from most car hire companies for around €6/£4 per day or €34/£24 per week.

Some rules of the road

Vital note for visitors from North America and most of Europe: drive on the left and overtake on the right. Cars already on a roundabout (traffic circle), circulating clockwise, have right of way over those entering the roundabout – so look to your right carefully before going ahead. Distances on road signs can be confusing: in Northern Ireland, they're all in miles, but in the Republic they may be in miles (on older signs) or kilometres.

Never park in restricted areas or your car will be towed away. In the Republic and the North, a single yellow line parallel to the kerb indicates restricted parking (with a sign usually nearby indicating the times when parking is banned), and double yellow lines indicate that you cannot park there at any time. Do not park in a clearway or bus lane between designated times; if it is towed away it may cost €100 to get it back. Always lock your car and do not leave tempting items exposed to view.

By train

Ireland's railways are centred on its main cities, Dublin and Belfast, and there are not many local lines, except for suburban networks around the two capitals. Trains, though, can be very useful and enjoyable for getting from the cities to smaller towns. Also, as well as the multi-journey tickets most useful for people doing a lot of touring (*see* p.287 **Discount Tickets**), the rail networks offer very attractive **low fares** for anyone travelling with children, such as the 'Family Fares' on Iarnród Eireann (for two adults and up to four children) and the 'Kids Go Free' scheme on some Enterprise trains (no charge for up to four children travelling with two adults). It's always worth checking on current family train fares when planning a trip.

Enterprise Trains

t UK 028 9066 6630, t IR 01 703 4070, www.translink.co.uk, www.irishrail.ie

Run jointly by Irish Rail and Northern Ireland Railways, this special Dublin–Belfast express service has eight trains daily in each direction Mon–Sat, and five Sun. It also stops in Drogheda, Dundalk, Newry and Portadown. A single ticket costs around €31/£22, and there are very good 'Kids Go Free' offers for adults travelling with children.

Iarnród Eireann (Irish Rail)

Information t 1 850 366 222, Reservations t 01 703 4070, www.irishrail.ie

Irish Rail's lines run out from one of Dublin's two main stations: from Dublin Heuston there are trains to the west and southwest (Ballina, Westport, Galway, Ennis, Limerick, Tralee, Cork, Kilkenny and Waterford, and stops en route), and from Dublin Connolly lines run along the east coast and to Northern Ireland (Wexford, Leitrim, Sligo, Belfast, Derry). There are two classes on most trains. For details of **DART** suburban trains in the Dublin area, also run by Iarnród Eireann, *see* p.47.

Northern Ireland Railways

Central Station, Belfast, t 028 9066 6630, www.translink.co.uk

NIR has trains from Belfast to Coleraine, Portrush and Derry, local lines around Belfast to Bangor, Larne harbour and Portadown, and runs the Belfast–Dublin line (via Newry) with Irish Rail. It's administered by the same Translink authority as **Ulsterbus** (*see* p.286), and many services connect.

Practical A–Z

10

Babysitters

Many hotels in Ireland will provide babysitters on request, usually for an extra charge, but check the details of the services available when you book. B&Bs and guesthouses can normally arrange babysitting so long as you inform them of what you need well enough in advance.

Beaches

Many Irish beaches have now been awarded Blue Flag status, under a Europe-wide quality-control scheme. When a beach carries the Blue Flag this means that local authorities (such as county councils) have committed themselves to maintaining certain standards during each summer season. In brief, Blue Flag status means that beaches are kept tidy and clean; that they have toilets, showers and other sanitary facilities that are well maintained; that camping, driving motor vehicles and dumping on the beach are prohibited; and that dogs, horses and other pets are not normally allowed in bathing areas. Lifeguards should be on duty throughout the summer season and there should be adequate lifesaving equipment. Look out for the Blue Flag (or just the Blue Flag symbol) on signs by any beach you think of using.

The local authorities are also committed to passing on any complaints they receive about the state of their beaches to the Foundation for Environmental Education in Europe.

Climate and when to go

Ireland's weather is notoriously changeable, and in a single day you can experience 'a fine mist' (as the Irish call it) under a cloud-heavy sky, then strong winds, and end up with bright sunshine. You can also suffer a whole month of rain and storms in midsummer, or be lucky enough to come across two weeks of warm, balmy sunshine in the months of autumn.

The weather in April, May and September is sometimes better than that from June to August, which can be especially variable. From late November to February you can usually expect dull cloudy weather that makes you want to sleep a lot and dream, with the occasional very cold snap. In March it's usually still a bit cool for spring clothes, but you will probably experience the odd beautiful day, as you will in October, when in addition the leaves are changing colour and the days turn brisk.

Good to know...

Average Daily Temperatures

Jan/Feb	3–7° C (37–44° F)
Mar/Apr	4–10° C (39–51° F)
May/Jun	8–16° C (46–61° F)
Jul/Aug	10–18° C (51–65° F)
Sept/Oct	8–15° C (46–59° F)
Nov/Dec	3–8° C (37–46° F)

The sunniest months are usually May and June (though September can be bright); average annual rainfall is 43 inches. Temperatures in Ireland have scarcely ever fallen below freezing (0°C, 32° F) in winter, or topped 32°C (90°F) in summer.

For more information, you can consult:

Met Eireann, t IR 01 806 4200, **www.weather.ie**

The Irish Republic's national weather service.

Met Office, t UK 0845 300 0300, **www.metoffice.co.uk**

The official British government weather centre.

Clothing

It's best to be frank: the best thing to do is expect the worst and hope for the best, making sure that you and your children have clothing you can add or remove as required. At some point during any stay in Ireland, it will rain. It's especially important to have with you some good, comfortable and rain-secure walking shoes, warm sweaters or fleeces, tights or socks, rainwear, a cap (you can buy lovely woollen ones in Ireland) and/or a scarf and gloves, even in summer. Wearing layers of clothes is the safest thing to do in Ireland, with plenty of items you can remove and carry easily, like a cagoule or sweatshirt, with a T-shirt underneath in case it suddenly gets hot, just as unpredictably as when it decides to rain.

For a winter stay, of course, you will need a bigger supply of warmer clothes. However, you can always buy sweaters, scarves and other items that are perfect for the climate right in Ireland if you find you haven't brought what you need. Plan for them in your budget for the trip, as you may be unable to resist the amazing Aran knits, even though you probably won't need the heavier versions in the summer. Lightweight, loose windbreakers with hoods and pockets are good to have at any time of year, and perfect for walks beside the seashore on a brisk sunny day. Good pockets are important for collecting seashells and rocks or carrying sandwiches, fruit and bottles of water.

Electricity

The standard electricity supply in the Republic and in Northern Ireland is 220–240 volts AC, and both systems use the same 3-pin plugs. Visitors with equipment with either North American- or European-style 2-pin plugs will need plug adaptors to use them in Ireland, and anyone with North American 110-volt appliances will also need a current transformer.

Embassies and consulates

For Ireland and Britain, with Northern Ireland:

Canada

Canadian Embassy 65–68 St Stephen's Green, Dublin 2, **t** 01 478 1988

Canadian High Commission Canada House, Trafalgar Square, London W1, **t** 020 7258 6600

British Embassy in the Irish Republic

31–33 Merrion Road, Dublin 4, **t** 01 269 5211

USA

US Embassy 42 Elgin Road, Dublin 4, **t** 01 668 8777

US Consulate 14 Queen's Street, Belfast, **t** 028 9032 8239

US Embassy 24 Grosvenor Square, London W1, **t** 020 7499 9000

Environmental matters

Children need to know that the land is the home of animals as well as humans, not to mention unseen beings. Irish country people used to throw their washing water outdoors, and every time they did so they'd cry out 'feet water', just in case a passing invisible person was about; they believed that if they didn't do that a faery might play a trick on them. So please don't pick wildflowers, light fires outdoors (especially in forests), disturb wildlife or leave behind food, pets' waste or rubbish you bring to picnic and tourist sites (there can be on-the-spot fines for doing all these things).

Horse-riding, walking, camping, swimming and so on may not be allowed everywhere, so check for regulations or ask local people about restrictions and permitted places to go. If you want to see a site that's marked as being on private land (even when it's an official heritage spot), people expect you to knock on the door of the nearest farmhouse and ask whether permission is required to walk on it, especially in the light of the recent Foot and Mouth disease outbreak.

Emergency Numbers

Republic of Ireland

112 or **999**

Call either one of these freephone numbers for **fire, police** or **ambulance** services. They must only be used in cases of genuine emergency.

Crime victims can also call **t** 01 478 5295

In case of a vehicle breakdown:

Automobile Association (AA), **t** 1800 667 788

RAC, t 1800 535 005

Northern Ireland

999

Call this freephone number for **fire, police** or **ambulance** services. It must only be used in cases of genuine emergency.

Crime victims can also call **t** 028 9065 0222

In case of a vehicle breakdown:

Automobile Association (AA), **t** 0800 887 766

RAC, t 0800 828 282

Some Irish environmental organisations are:

Irish Wildlife Trust, 107 Lower Baggot Street, Dublin 2, **t** 01 676 8588

The Woodland Trust in Northern Ireland, 1 Dufferin Court, Dufferin Avenue, Bangor, Co. Down, **t** 028 9127 5787

Food and Eating Out

Many Irish restaurants offer children's portions from their main menus, while others offer special menus for children. It's a good idea to check with the restaurant beforehand, and also whether any special rules or limited hours apply to children. It is usual for families with small children to book an early meal at restaurants. Many have 'early bird menus' (normally available 5–7pm) especially for children. Restaurants and other establishments in Northern Ireland with licences to sell alcohol must, by law, ensure that children are not on their premises after 9.30pm.

Restaurant price categories

Restaurants listed in this guide are categorised in the price bands shown here, based on the cost of a three-course meal for an adult, without drinks.

Luxury	Cost no object
Expensive	Over €65/£40
Moderate	€32–65/£20–40
Inexpensive	under €32/£20)

Pub rules

Ireland's pubs, naturally, are a near-unmissable alternative to restaurants as such for refreshments, socialising and, increasingly, eating, and adults with children will very likely want to visit a few too. Pubs in the country generally have more relaxed rules when it comes to admitting families than those in cities, as in Ireland the local village pub quite often doubles as a community centre. However, it is the law in both Northern Ireland and the Republic that children are not allowed to remain in places with licenses to sell alcohol past 9.30pm, and landlords in cities would certainly not expect to cater for families after this time. Still, in more remote areas, you may well find that such rules tend to slip by the wayside. Just ask and people will tell you whatever the policy is.

Kids can have soft drinks and snacks in pubs, but otherwise there's not much for them to do unless the pub has an outdoor play area. If restaurant-style meals are not offered, you can often get a sandwich, tea, coffee or even soup, but do not expect their quality to be very high. Most country pubs are quite basic. Live music does not usually start in pubs until 9–10pm, especially during the summer months. You're more likely to see musicians playing in pubs during the daytime during town festivals. However, pubs can get pretty smoky, which isn't very healthy for youngsters.

Good to know...

Country Markets

The markets listed here are among the best places to find and buy Irish farm produce, organic and traditional foods, direct from producers.

Co. Cork

Bantry Market. **Open** Fri am, plus a fair in the market square on the first Fri of each month.

Castletownbere, Beara Peninsula. **Open** first Thurs of each month.

Cork: Cornmarket, Cornmarket St. **Open** Sat.

Macroom Market. **Open** Tues am.

Skibbereen Market **Open** Fri 12 noon–2pm.

Dublin City

Cow's Lane Market, Meetinghouse Square, Temple Bar, Dublin 2. **Open** Sat 9–6. Organic fruit, fish, cheeses, breads, preserves.

Moore Street Market, behind O'Connell Street, Dublin 2. **Open** Sat am.

Dublin's oldest open-air market.

Co. Galway Galway City Saturday Market, outside St Nicholas church. **Open** Sat am.

Co. Kerry Kenmare Farmers' Market, Casey's Car Park, Sneem Road, Kenmare. **Open** Wed am.

Milltown Organic Farmers' Market. **Open** Sat.

Co. Kildare Friday Country Market, Town Hall, Naas. **Open** Fri 10.45–12 noon.

Co. Mayo Westport Thursday Market, Town Hall, Westport. **Open** Thurs 10–5.

Co. Wexford Country Market, The Bull Ring, Wexford. **Open** Fri from 9am.

Co. Wicklow Brook Lodge Inn Sunday Market, Macreddin Village, **t** 0402 36444. **Open** Sun am.

Roundwood Market, Roundwood. **Open** Sun.

Northern Ireland St. George's Indoor Market, near Waterfront Hall, Belfast. **Open** Sat am.

Shopping for food

Traditional Irish foods like salmon, barmbrack (*see* p.103), soda bread, organic cheeses and medieval mead are available from many specialist local producers. For gluten-free, vegetarian, or wholefood products, you can find health shops and delicatessens in most large towns.

Around Ireland there are fine weekly country markets where local growers sell their produce. For information contact the **Irish Country Markets Association**, Swanbrook House, Morehampton Road, Dublin 4, **t** 01 668 0560; for places where organic growers sell their products contact the **Organic Trust**, **t** 01 853 0271, or the **Irish Organic Farmers & Growers Association**, **t** 0506 32563. Selected local markets are listed on the left.

Insurance

It's essential to take out travel insurance before your trip. The policy should cover cancellation due to illness, delays, accidents, lost luggage, loss of passports or other belongings, theft, personal liability, legal expenses, emergency flights and medical cover. A wide range of travel insurance policies is available, so it's worth shopping around.

Most insurance companies offer free insurance to children under the age of 2, as part of their parents' policy. When travelling, keep the insurance company's 24-hour emergency number close to hand, and, if you have a mobile phone, store it in the memory. Report stolen or lost items to the police, however trivial, so that you can make a claim when you get back home.

In the UK

Association of British Insurers, t 020 7600 3333
Insurance Ombudsman Bureau, t 0845 600 6666
These government-appointed regulators of the insurance industry can help with complaints.
ABC Holiday Extras Travel Insurance, t 0800 171 000
Columbus Travel Insurance, t 020 7375 0011
Endsleigh Insurance, t 020 7436 4451
Medicover, t 0870 735 3600
World Cover Direct, t 0800 365 121

In North America

Access America, t US 1 800 284 8300, **t** Canada 1 800 654 1908
Travel Assistance International, t US and Canada 1 800 921 2828
MEDEX Assistance Corporation, t US 410 453 6300

Lost property

If you lose important documents like a passport, contact your consulate or embassy. For insurance purposes you must also report the loss to the local police, who also might be able to find it for you.

Medical matters

In a medical emergency, the best thing to do is to call an ambulance, by phoning **112** or **999** in the Irish Republic or **999** only in Northern Ireland (*see* p.291). Don't try to drive a sick child to hospital if you don't know a city; it could waste valuable time. If you are staying in self-catering accommodation, make sure that you have either a landline or a working mobile phone. Be sure too to ask the house owners or keyholders about local doctors and taxis, which sometimes double up as ambulance services in very rural areas, and on what to do in the case of a medical emergency.

Medical insurance

British visitors to Northern Ireland receive treatment as they would in Britain. In the Republic British visitors are covered under an agreement with the Irish Department of Health, but you need to show form of identification or a validated E111 form (*see* below). Visitors from all other EU countries travelling to Ireland should obtain a validated E111 form prior to departure.

The Irish National Health Plan does not cover either US or Canadian visitors. Check the details of your insurance policy before travelling to ensure that you have full health cover in Ireland.

First aid kit

Be sure to have with you a basic first-aid kit, for dealing with children's minor ailments. Always keep it out of reach of small children.

- Antiseptic cream, spray and wipes
- Calamine lotion and aloe vera gel (for soothing bites, burns and stings)
- Calpol or equivalent for lowering high temperatures
- Cotton wool, bandages and plasters (Band Aids) – both fabric and waterproof
- Decongestant and children's aspirin
- Earplanes (plastic devices that fit in the ear and help prevent air pressure problems on flights)
- Scissors and tweezers
- Strip or digital thermometer
- High-factor sun protection cream
- Chewable vitamins and/or drinks
- Travel sickness preparations
- Vaseline or similar nappy/diaper cream

For all visitors from non-EU countries to Ireland, private medical insurance is pretty much essential, especially if you are travelling with children. If you are from the US or Canada your existing insurance plans may provide you with sufficient medical cover while abroad, so, again, check your policy details thoroughly before taking out additional travel insurance coverage.

The E111

The E111 is the form with which EU citizens can make free use of the health services in any other EU country. In the UK they are available free from health centres and main post offices, but you must have them stamped and validated by the issuing centre before you can use them. Many travellers, though, prefer to take out private travel insurance with full medical cover rather than handle the bureaucracy sometimes involved in using different national healthcare systems.

Visiting a doctor

For non-emergencies, ask hotel staff or the owners of your accommodation to help you contact a doctor. The local police will always have the number of a local doctor on duty, and during office hours tourist offices should be able to help.

If a medical problem seems more serious or urgent, especially if you're in a town, make your way to the Casualty (Emergency) department of a local hospital. EU visitors may go into any hospital to find a doctor, so long as they have a validated E111 form; non-EU visitors should follow the instructions of their insurance carrier.

In order to get prescriptions for drugs renewed in Ireland, it's advisable to visit an Irish general practitioner (local doctor), explain your situation and get an Irish prescription, which you can then use in any local pharmacy. Hospital admissions, where necessary, are also usually arranged by a doctor. E111 forms should be presented to the doctor or hospital, along with identification, if and when required. In emergencies initial hospital services will be provided free of charge for all visitors, but you and/or your family should be able to present some identification.

If British or EU citizens think they are entitled to cash benefits while in the Republic, they should apply within three days of becoming ill to:
Department of Social Welfare EU Records, Floor 1, O'Connell Bridge House, Dublin 2.

Medication

If you or any of your children has a pre-existing medical problem, you will need a letter from your doctor describing the illness and any prescription medications, including the generic name of the drugs, to obtain further supplies in Ireland. Bring your own pre-packed sterile needles and syringes as required.

Good to know...
Natural Remedies for Children

Aloe vera: skin injuries or irritations (check if a product should be used internally or externally)
Arnica cream: bruises
Calamine lotion: heat rash, skin irritations and sunburn
Calendula cream: skin rashes and abrasions
Calendula liquid: use on scalp to deter or get rid of nits
Lavender oil: use diluted on young skins (never get it near the eyes, and wash them out immediately with warm water if any oil gets in them) as an insect repellant, against burns and sunburn, and for a bedtime bath (for soporific qualities).
Lemons: fresh juice repels insects
Neem cream: soothes skin irritations
Rosemary oil: mild stimulant, soothes headache when sniffed on cotton wool or a pad
Tea Tree oil: deters bugs and nits, and an antiseptic

Good to know...
Travelling with Children – First-Aid Tips

Countering in-flight air pressure: breastfeed or give a bottle to your baby; give toddlers something to swallow or suck (i.e., by drinking juice with a straw); give older children something soft to chew or get them to yawn or blow their noses.
Eye protection: UVA/UVB sunglasses.
Minor cuts on skin (for external use, to avoid infections): iodine, diluted hydrogen peroxide, Bach's Rescue Remedy.
Skin irritations or rashes: aloe vera, Calamine, calendula, neem or zinc creams or gels; diluted hydrogen peroxide.
Sleeplessness and anxiety: herbal sleeping remedies are available, but ordinary foods like bananas, milk and lettuce are soporific also; sweet things tend to stimulate children, so honey is a better option before bedtime than sweets or biscuits; milk helps to counteract sugar's speedy effects.
Stomach aches: camomile or peppermint.
Sunburn: waterproof UVA/UVB sun cream with a factor of 15+ or more, and Calamine lotion; infants should not be exposed to direct sunlight.
Travel sickness: get some fresh air or nibble a dry cracker or biscuit; avoid big meals, greasy foods, and lots of fluid before travelling.

Money and banks

The Republic of Ireland is one of the 12 European Union countries that now uses the European single currency the **Euro**, the symbol for which is €. Each euro is divided, like the US Dollar, into 100 cents.. There are eight euro coins, for 1, 2, 5, 10, 20 and 50 cents and 1 and 2 euros, and seven notes, for 5, 10, 20, 50, 100, 200 and 500 euros. The notes are entirely the same throughout the EU, but euro coins have a common design on one side, with the amount, and a design specific to each country on the other. However, all euro coins can be used equally in any of the eurozone countries.

In Northern Ireland the currency is still the British **Pound** (£), each one of which divides into 100 pence (referred to for short just as the letter *p*, so you have 10p, 20p and so on). There are eight coins (1p, 2p, 5p, 10p, 20p, 50p, and £1 and £2), and four denominations of notes, for £5, £10, £20 and £50.

Many businesses in border areas, especially in towns like Dundalk on the Republic side and Newry in the North, will accept both Euros and Pounds, and so do many places all across Northern Ireland. Otherwise, though, you'll need to change money if you go between the Republic and Northern Ireland.

Exchange rates vary, but in late 2003 the average Pound/Euro rate was **£1 = €1.40**, and average rates against the US Dollar were around **€1 = $1.15**, and **£1 = $1.70**. You can check current rates on Internet currency converters, such as **www**.xe.com/ucc/.

Money can be exchanged in banks and at private bureaux de change, or obtained direct from bank ATMs (cashpoints). All small towns have at least one bank; otherwise, though, exchange offices can be scarce in the south and west of Ireland, so make sure you have enough cash with you. Be careful when carrying money around with you. Ireland is safer than most European countries regarding pickpockets, but they may operate in the shopping areas of big towns and at tourist attractions.

Bank opening hours

Banks are generally open Mon–Fri 9.30–4.30, with some branches open until 5pm on Thurs. In Northern Ireland, banks are usually open Mon-Fri 9.30–4.30. Some banks, usually those in shopping centres, are open late on Thursday and all day Saturday. All banks are closed on public holidays.

Credit cards

Many shops and restaurants in the Republic and Northern Ireland accept all the big-name credit and debit cards – Visa, Delta, Mastercard, American Express, Cirrus – but in country areas many places are cash-only. Nearly all Irish cash dispensers (ATMs) dispense money on foreign credit or bank cards linked to the international Cirrus or Maestro networks. There will be a handling fee for each withdrawal, which can vary between banks; your own bank will be able to advise you on different rates. Diners Club cards are less widely accepted.

In Northern Ireland, most ATMs accept Visa, Cirrus and Mastercard, but if in doubt check with your home bank before travelling. AmEx and Diners Club are not widely accepted in Northern Ireland.

Traveller's cheques

Traveller's cheques in US Dollars, British Pounds and Euros are readily cashed at any bank, for a commission. Most banks also cash traveller's cheques in other major currencies, such as the Japanese Yen. Hotels will usually cash traveller's cheques, but charge a big transaction fee. The main airports all have banks with exchange windows.

Opening hours

In the Republic of Ireland opening hours vary according to the habits of the local population, although, as a rule, Sundays are still usually quiet on the commercial front – both the Republic and Northern Ireland still consider Sunday to be a day of rest. On the other hand, you will often find shops open in the evenings, especially in the Republic, until 10pm or even later, according to their location.

In general, though, most shops in the Republic and the North are open Monday to Saturday, 10am to 5–7pm (in Northern Ireland shops tend to open earlier, at 9pm). Some close for lunch, usually for one hour 12 noon–2, and in main towns many stores have a weekly late-opening day, usually Thursday, when they stay open till 8–9pm. In cities large department stores and shopping centres also open on Sundays, from 12 noon to 5–6pm. Many country towns, in contrast, still have an 'early closing day' once a week (usually Wednesday or Thursday) when all shops are closed after 1–2pm.

Tourist attractions are generally open Mon–Sat, 9–10am till 5–6pm or dusk, or sometimes earlier. Museums often open on Sundays but close on Mondays; theatres are closed on Mondays and Tuesdays as well as Sundays.

All tourist attractions are open in the June–Aug high season, but in May and September they may close earlier or not open at all on some days. Variations also occur due to public holidays; some places, for example, open for Easter then close again till summer. It's always a good idea to ring before you drive a long way to see a tourist site, as you will find that time is a little bit more malleable in Ireland than in some countries of the world.

Post and post offices

Post offices, north and south, are usually open Mon–Fri 9–5.30, and Sat 9–1 and 2.15–5. In main towns there's always one prominently placed in the middle of town, but in villages they may be hidden away in shops or even pubs. There is usually one closing day or afternoon each week, but it varies from place to place. You can buy telephone top-up cards for mobile/cell phones in post offices as well as stamps and stationery. Postal charges to the UK are the same as those within Ireland.

To mail a letter or postcard, in the Republic you need to look out for green letterboxes, while in Northern Ireland, as in Britain, they are red.

Public holidays

All shops, banks and visitor attractions close on St Patrick's Day, Christmas Day and usually Boxing Day. However, many open on other public holidays.

In The Republic of Ireland
New Year's Day 1 January
St Patrick's Day 17 March
Easter Monday March/April – date varies
May Bank Holiday 1st Monday in May
June Bank Holiday 1st Monday in June
August Bank Holiday 1st Monday in August
October Bank Holiday last Monday in October
Christmas Day 25 December
St Stephen's Day/Boxing Day 26 December

In Northern Ireland
New Year's Day 1 January
St Patrick's Day 17 March
March/April Good Friday is widely observed as a holiday, but is not official
Easter Monday March/April – date varies
Spring/May Bank Holiday end May
The Twelfth 12 July (Battle of the Boyne)
Summer/August Bank Holiday late August
Christmas Day 25 December
Boxing Day 26 December

Safety

Lost children

It's easy to get separated from children in busy airports, railway and bus stations and markets. Make sure toddlers know their full names and that, if they are lost, they should go into a shop and ask a female assistant for help. Generally people in Ireland will be only too happy to assist. Teenagers also can easily stray. Make sure they know where to go to make a public announcement at a station or airport, and fix a place to meet if you are separated.

Road safety and awareness

Make sure your children are fully aware that the Irish drive on the left side of the road, and that they know where to look for oncoming traffic. The dangers are the same in Ireland as they are at home. In cities, be as vigilant and as cautious, if not more so, as you would normally be at home.

Teen issues

Mobile phone theft is a problem everywhere. Make sure your children are careful where they use their phones, and are aware that it's not worth a fight if someone tries to steal it.

The drug scene in Ireland is similar to that of the rest of Western Europe. Soft and hard drugs are available. It's illegal to be in possession of drugs and even a small amount of marijuana could land you in jail. In the UK, look for the leaflet *Drugs Abroad*. For more information, in the UK call the National Drugs Helpline, **t** 0800 776 600.

Shopping for children

Gifts of quality for children can be found all over Ireland. Apart from leprechaun figurines, souvenirs that might interest them are the St Bridget's Cross, Crolly dolls, toy soldiers and child-sized *bodhrán* drums or tin whistles, if not a real Irish harp made by an Irish instrument maker. Irish bookshops often have good stocks of mythology and fairytales, and towns tend to promote famous authors associated with them. As a special gift you could buy children's stories by Oscar Wilde or Jonathan Swift in Dublin, the Narnia tales of CS Lewis in a Belfast store or poems by WB Yeats at Thoor Ballylee. Music is in the blood in this part of the world, and as well as the most popular Irish acts like Enya or Westlife you could consider Gael-Linn's excellent recordings of traditional artists singing in Irish, available in traditional music shops. Recordings of Irish storytellers are riveting also (*see* p.26).

Irish crafts, from pottery to bogwood sculptures and Irish lace, linen, crochet, tweed and knitwear will interest old and young. For hardy woollen goods that are warm as well as beautifully coloured, visit shops like Magee's in Donegal and Avoca in Wicklow, or skilled independent knitters who sell intricately handwoven Aran sweaters in the Arans and Connemara. Among many other things, you will also see fine crystal in Galway, Tyrone and Waterford, Parian china in Belleek (Fermanagh), ceramics, blackthorn walking sticks, compressed peat ornaments, and jewellery produced by excellent craftspeople on this island.

Smoking

Pubs in Ireland can be unbearable due to their lack of ventilation and the number of smokers puffing away. However, the Irish are growing more sensitive to this issue, and some restaurants are now beginning to institute non-smoking areas. If you require smoking or non-smoking rooms, check with hotel staff or B&B owners if this is available when you book.

Special interest and activity holidays

For more on family holiday possibilities, *see* pp.246–8 and pp.298–9. More locally-based agencies offering tours, walks and so on are listed in the province chapters of this book.

Find Tour Operators

www.find-tour-operators.com/ireland

A website with information about special interest tours all over the world, including Ireland.

In Britain

Angler's World Holidays, 46 Knifesmithgate, Chesterfield, Derbyshire, S40 1RQ, **t** (01246) 221 717, **www**.anglers-world.co.uk

Can arrange for families to holiday in Ireland and try a spot of game fishing for salmon and sea-trout, and coarse fishing in Irish rivers and lakes.

Back-Roads Touring Company, 14a New Broadway, London W5 2XA, **t** 020 8566 5312, **www**.backroadstouring.co.uk

Off-the-beaten-track tours of Dublin, Killarney, Galway, Sligo and Donegal.

Enjoy Ireland, **t** (01254) 692 899, **www**.enjoyireland.net

Golfing, riding, angling and walking holidays.

HF Holidays, Imperial House, Edgware Road, London, NW9 5AL, **t** 020 8905 9556, **www**.hfholidays.co.uk

Dingle Way and West of Ireland guided walking holidays, or stays in Killarney National Park.

In Ireland

Ardress Craft Centre, Kesh, Co. Fermanagh, **t** 028 6863 1267

Arts and crafts courses.

Association of Irish Riding Establishments (AIRE), 11 Moore Park, Newbridge, Co. Kildare, **t** 045 431 1584

Horse-riding and pony-trekking information.

British Horse Society, House of Sport, Upper Malone Road, Belfast, **t** 028 9038 1222

Horse-riding information for Northern Ireland.

Colclough Tours, 71 Waterloo Road, Dublin 4, **t** 01 668 0109, **www**.tourismresources.ie

Informative tours anywhere in Ireland: tailor-made itineraries, car with driver-guide and accommodation from farmhouses to castles. Tours can take in gardens, genealogy, ghosts, gourmet meals, and sites of historical importance.

Equestrian Holidays Ireland, 1 Sandyford Office Park, Foxrock, Dublin 18, **t** 01 295 8928

Horse-riding holidays.

Go Ireland, Killorglin, Co. Kerry, **t** 066 976 2094, **www**.goireland.fexco.ie

Guided or independent walking, golf, cycling and cultural holidays, with tours of Connemara, the Burren, the Aran Islands or the Dingle peninsula.

Irish Country Holidays, The Discovery Centre, Rearcross, Co. Tipperary, **t** 062 79330, **www**.country-holidays.ie

Gives you an opportunity to live as part of a small, rural community in self-catering properties or B&B-style accommodation.

Irish Cycling Safaris, Belfield Bike Shop, University College, Belfield House, Dublin 4, **t** 01 260 0749, **www**.cyclingsafaris.com

A family-run business that offers leisurely one-week cycling holidays, with bikes supplied and luggage transported for you, in many parts of Ireland, and especially Cork, Kerry and Connemara.

Kerry Holidays, Kerry Airport, Farranfore, Co. Kerry, **t** 066 976 322, **t** UK 0800 039 0088, **www**.kerryholidays.com

Fly-drive, B&B, city breaks, self-catering and golf.

In the US and Canada

Ireland Travel Specialists may be found through the Shamrock Club, **www**.shamrockclub.net

Backroads, 801 Cedar St, Berkeley, CA 94710-1800, **t** 1 800 GO-ACTIVE, **www**.backroads.com

Multi-sport: golf, walking and biking, with packages in Counties Kerry, Cork and Galway.

CIE Tours International Inc, 100 Hanover Ave, PO Box 501, Cedar Knolls, NJ 07927-0501, **t** 1 800 CIE-TOUR, **www**.cietours.com

Escorted coach, self-drive or independent holidays, including theme tours.

Classic Adventures, **t** 1 800 777 8090, **www**.classicadventures.com

Guided biking holidays in southwest Ireland.

Green Earth Travel, 7 Froude Circle, Cabin John, MD 20818, **t** 1 888 246 8343, **www**.vegtravel.com

Vegetarian and ecologically-oriented families are catered for by these specialists.

Irish Folklore Tours, Hemisphere Travel Service, Inc., Biddeford, ME 04005, **t** 1 800 848-4364, **www**.irishfolkloretours.com

This group arranges tours for families who want to explore aspects of Irish culture, including music, mythology, archaeology and the landscape.

Special needs

Access facilities for wheelchair users and other disabled people are more common in Ireland than they used to be, but it is still a good idea to check beforehand any time you wish to visit a tourist attraction, hotel or guesthouse that facilities are available or that there are rooms at ground level. Where possible, information on access has been listed for attractions and accommodation in this guide. In general you will find the Irish helpful to anyone with special needs. There are often facilities to accommodate wheelchairs on boats and coaches, and many restaurants have suitably large toilets, so don't hesitate to ask.

For Northern Ireland, a guide called *Accessible Accommodation 2002* is available from any tourist office in the province or via the tourist board website, **www**.discovernorthernireland.com. Additional information is available from **Disability Action, t** 028 9029 7880, **www**.disabilityaction.org. For the Republic, contact the **National Disability Authority, t** 01 608 0400, **www**.nda.ie.

Useful addresses

In the UK

Council for Disabled Children, t 020 7843 6000
Information on travel health and resources.

Holiday Care Service, 2nd Floor, Imperial Building, Victoria Road, Horley, Surrey RH6 9HW, **t** (01293) 774 535
Provides information sheets for families with disabilities. All sites have been visited and assessed by Holiday Care representatives.

RADAR, Unit 12, City Forum, 250 City Road, London EC1V 8AF, **t** 020 7250 3222
Provides specialist advice on travelling with mobility problems, and publishes a guide to facilities at airports called *Getting There*.

Royal National Institute for the Blind, 224 Great Portland Street, London W15 5TB, **t** 020 7388 1266
Advises blind people on travel matters.

In the US

American Foundation for the Blind, 15 West 16th Street, New York, NY 10011, **t** 1 800 232 5463

Mobility International, PO Box 3551, Eugene, OR 97403, **t** 541 343 1284

SATH (Society for the Advancement of Travel for the Handicapped), 347 Fifth Avenue, Suite 610, New York 10016, **t** 212 447 7284

Sports for the disabled

Irish Wheelchair Association, Aras Chuchulain, Blackheath Drive, Clontarf, Dublin 3, **t** 01 833 8241

Share Centre, Smith's Strand, Lisnaskea, Co. Fermanagh, **t** 028 6772 2122
Activity holidays for families with special needs.

Sports

Canoeing

White-water racing and slalom can be tried on the rivers Liffey, Barrow and Nore in the east of Ireland. For sea canoeing, try activity and leisure centres in Cos. Clare, Cork and Galway. The Barrow in Wicklow is probably the best river for canoeing, but canoeing centres can also be found on the Boyne, the Nore (Co. Kilkenny) and the Suir (Co. Waterford) and on the Lee, Blackwater and Shannon (best for lake canoeing). All along the western seaboard from Donegal to Cork there are good sites for sea canoeing and canoe surfers.

Diving

Underwater swimming and diving are superb in the Gulf Stream surrounding Ireland. Noted diving centres are in Dublin, Waterford and Wexford, and other popular ones can be found on the Atlantic coast in Cos. Donegal, Mayo and Galway, although Cork and Kerry also have wonderful conditions.

Fishing

Central Fisheries Board, t 01 837 9206
The board will tell you to how to get a fishing licence for the area where you wish to fish, and has information on fishing in Ireland with kids.

Fermanagh Lakeland Visitors' Centre, Enniskillen, Co. Fermanagh, **t** 028 23110

Foyle Fisheries Commission, 8 Victoria Road, Derry City, Co. Londonderry, **t** 028 7134 2100
For game-rod licences in Northern Ireland.

Sailing

There are sailing schools all round Ireland's coasts; many are residential, and provide other outdoor sports as well. Tuition standards are high. In the southwest, in Co. Cork, excellent courses are given at Baltimore, Bere Island in Bantry Bay and Cobh. In the west there are fine facilities at Renvyle in Connemara and Clew Bay, Co. Mayo. More sheltered lakeland sailing schools are on Lough Derg, Co. Tipperary, and the Blessington Lakes in Wicklow. Sailing holidays can be enjoyed north of Dublin in Malahide, and just to the south in Dun Laoghaire.

Surfing

Great surfing conditions can be found on Ireland's west and south coasts. Ireland's largest surf club is in Rossnowlagh, Co. Donegal. Not far away in Co. Sligo there are renowned surf beaches at Easkey, Enniscrone and Strandhill. Farther south in Cos. Clare (Doolin Point) and Kerry (Inch) there are more excellent places to surf. Small, medium and even high levels of surf can be found from southern Kerry through Cork and Waterford to Wexford. There are occasional rideable waves, particularly in winter, along the east coast. Make sure children surf with a qualified instructor.

Walking and mountaineering

For contact details for the Republic and Northern Ireland's Youth Hostel Associations, *see* p.248.

The House of Sport, Upper Malone Road, Belfast, **t** 028 9038 1222

For details on climbing in the Mournes; also handles grants and serves as an advice centre.

Irish Ways, Ballycanew, Gorey, Co. Wexford, **t** 055 27479

Courses and holidays.

National Mountain and White Water Centre, Tiglin, Ashford, Co. Wicklow, **t** 0404 40169, www.tiglin.com

Details of training courses in mountaineering.

Tullymore Mountain Centre, Bryansford, nr Newcastle, Co. Down, **t** 028 4372 2158

For climbing in the Mourne Mountains.

Ulster Federation of Rambling Clubs, 128 Breda House, Drumart Drive, Belfast, **t** 028 9064 8041

Water-skiing

There are several well-equipped water-ski centres in the Republic that also offer training. Favourites are in Macroom, Farran Forest Park and on the River Lee (an official site for the disabled) – all in Co. Cork; Parknasilla on the Ring of Kerry; Ballymore Eustace and Blessington on the Blessington Lakes in Co. Wicklow; and Lough Muckno in Co. Monaghan.

Windsurfing

Conditions are delightful for windsurfing in Ireland. Along the west coast there are excellent locations at Cobh, Oysterhaven and Schull in Co. Cork, and Glenans Sailing Club for Clew Bay in Co. Mayo. On the east coast, Carlingford in Co. Lough, Malahide, the Grand Canal Dock in Dublin, and Rosslare in Co. Wexford are good places also. A good inland spot is Lough Allen in Co. Leitrim.

Telephones

Eircom was once the Republic's sole national phone company, but today other companies can provide public phones. Similarly in Northern Ireland, as in the rest of the UK, while British Telecom (**BT**) is still predominant there are also pay phones of other companies. However, non-Eircom payphones in the Republic are expensive.

Both Eircom and BT provide coin and card phones in their territories, some with (overpriced) e-mail devices. It's much better to use phonecards (of the right company) than coins, as they give substantial discounts. They can be bought in newsagents, train stations, post offices and many other shops.

Mobile/cell phones are hugely popular in Ireland. Most UK mobiles will work in Ireland, but check charges with your phone provider; US cell phones will only work in Europe if they have a triband facility. In mountainous or distant places a mobile telephone may not work, but it's a good idea to keep one with you if you're travelling around by car.

During 2003 changes were introduced in area codes in the Republic, especially those beginning 04, 05, 07 and 09. If you ring a number that has been changed, you should get a message with the new number, or you can check the website: www.eircom.ie or phone (in the Republic) **t** 1901.

To call Northern Ireland from the rest of the UK, the prefix for the whole province is **028**, but within Northern Ireland you need only dial the remaining 8-digit number, without 028. To call Northern Ireland from the Republic, simply replace the 028 with **048**. Calling the Republic from Northern Ireland still counts as an international call (but at cheaper rates): dial the international access code (**00**), followed by the code for the Republic (**353**) and the number, **omitting** the initial zero.

To phone the Republic from mainland Britain or any other country the process is the same (the international access code, **00** in the UK, then **353** and then the number, omitting the first 0). To call Northern Ireland from outside Ireland or Britain dial the international access code, the UK code (**44**) and the number, **omitting** the 0 before the 28.

The way to make an international call **from** Ireland is the same north and south: **00** followed by the country code (UK, from the Republic, **44**; US and Canada **1**; Australia **61**; France **33**; New Zealand **64**), then the area code (minus the 0 in UK numbers) and the number.

Time

The saying 'When God made time, He made plenty of it' is no longer heard quite so often in Ireland, but there is still a sense of it, mainly in country towns and villages. Ireland and the UK are in the same time zone. Therefore, they are 5hrs ahead of US Eastern Standard Time and 8hrs ahead of Pacific Standard Time. Each country moves to Summer Time (daylight saving) roughly at the same time, so these differences are maintained. By mid-December, it can be dark in Ireland by 4pm, but during summer it may stay light until 11pm.

Tipping

Some people claim that tipping is not expected in Ireland, as it hasn't always been the custom, but leaving something behind discreetly is appreciated. In hotels and restaurants, when a service charge is not included, 10-15% of the bill is appropriate. Taxi drivers are usually tipped 10% of the fare, and porters about 75 cents per bag. In pubs, tipping is unusual but at the customer's discretion.

Toilets

In just about every public place you go, there are toilets in Ireland. The better tourist attractions usually have excellent clean ones, often with baby-changing areas where new mothers can breastfeed if they need to. Many museums, restaurants, hotels and tourist attractions now have wheelchair or disabled access toilets also. If you stay near tourist attractions, it is unlikely you will find yourself anywhere without easy access to clean public toilets. Even in remote places, there will probably be pubs and hotels not far away that will have places you can stop off at.

Useful Websites

www.tourismireland.com	Tourist info
www.heritageireland.ie	Irish heritage sites
www.irelandonthenet.ie	General info
www.ireland.travel.ie	Planning your trip
www.shamrock.org	Info on Ireland
www.irelandtravel.co.uk	Info from UK
www.irelandvacations.com	Info North America
www.goireland.com	Info on food, etc.,
www.nci.ie	Irish Yellow Pages
www.local.ie	Regional info
www.wildireland.com	Nature in Ireland

Good to know...
Sightseeing discounts

The card schemes below can give big savings if you expect to visit a range of heritage sites.

Dúchas Heritage Card
t 1 850 600 601, **www.heritageireland.ie**
Annual card prices Adult €20, over-65s €15, child (5–16) €7.50, family ticket (for 4) €50

This well-priced card gives unlimited admission to some 65 sites, buildings and monuments run by the Republic's National Heritage department. They can be bought in advance or at any of the sites; a full list is on the website.

National Trust Northern Ireland
t 028 9751 0721, **www.ntni.org.uk**

The National Trust administers some 50 properties (historic houses, monuments, places of natural beauty) in Northern Ireland. At most sites family tickets are available; annual membership charges are complicated, with several options, but all give unlimited admission to Trust sites. National Trust members from Britain can use their cards equally in Northern Ireland. Many family and children's events are held at Trust sites in school holidays.

Tourist information

Since the 1998 peace agreement in Northern Ireland there is a single information and international promotion service for the whole of Ireland, **Tourism Ireland**, combining the work of the Republic's Irish Tourist Board and the Northern Ireland Tourist Board. Each still runs information offices in its own territory. Irish tourist offices, north and south, are plentiful and extremely helpful; as well as providing all sorts of advice, leaflets, maps and information they have local accommodation booking services. For addresses, *see* under individual destinations in this guide.

Tourism Ireland offices outside Ireland

Freephones UK **t** 0800 039 7000
US and Canada **t** 1 800 223 6470
www.tourismireland.com.
Main Office in Britain All Ireland Desk, British Visitors Centre, 1 Regent Street, London SW1Y 4XT, **t** 020 7518 0800
Canada 2 Bloor St. West, Suite 1501, Toronto, Ontario M4W 3E2, **t** (416) 929 2777
USA 345 Park Avenue, New York, NY 10017, **t** (212) 418 0800

Index

Main page references are in **bold**.
Page references to maps are in *italics*.